THE NEW YORK TIMES ENCYCLOPEDIA OF SPORTS **Volume 3**

BASKETBALL

THE NEW YORK TIMES ENCYCLOPEDIA OF SPORTS

THE NEW YORK TIMES
ENCYCLOPEDIA OF SPORTS

VOLUME 3

BASKETBALL

EDITED BY
GENE BROWN
INTRODUCTION BY
FRANK LITSKY

ARNO PRESS
A NEW YORK TIMES COMPANY
NEW YORK 1979

GROLIER EDUCATIONAL CORPORATION
SHERMAN TURNPIKE, DANBURY, CT. 06816

Library of Congress Cataloging in Publication Data

Main entry under title:

Basketball.

(The New York times encyclopedia of sports; v. 3) Collection of articles reprinted from the New York times.
Bibliography.
Includes index.
SUMMARY: Traces the history of basketball as presented in articles appearing in the "New York Times."
1. Basketball. [1. Basketball] I. Brown, Gene. II. New York times. III. Series: New York times encyclopedia of sports; v. 3.
GV565.N48 vol. 3 [GV885] 796s [796.32'3] 79-19939
ISBN 0-405-12629-8

Manufactured in the United States of America

Appendix © 1979, *The Encyclopedia Americana*.

The editors express special thanks to The Associated Press, United Press International, and Reuters for permission to include a number of dispatches originally distributed by those news services.

The New York Times Encyclopedia of Sports

Founding Editors: Herbert J. Cohen and Richard W. Lawall
Project Editors: Arleen Keylin and Suri Boiangiu
Editorial Assistant: Jonathan Cohen

CONTENTS

Basketball is truly an American game, invented in that most American of institutions, the YMCA. It is extremely popular in the United States in high school and colleges, and professional basketball ranks with baseball and football as a major American professional sport. Internationally, it has become an increasingly important and popular sport, especially in the Olympic Games.

Basketball is relatively young, going back only to 1891. By 1980, college teams attracted 30 million spectators a season and the National Basketball Association, the major professional league, drew 10 million annually. High school attendance more than matched the colleges and professionals combined, making basketball probably the most popular spectator sport in the United States.

Basketball was invented in 1891 at the International YMCA Training School in Springfield, Mass., now known as Springfield College. The school trained men and women to work at YMCA's throughout the country, and all students had to take physical education courses.

Dr. Luther S. Gulick, head of the physical education department, had a problem, and he asked Dr. James A. Naismith to solve it. Naismith was 30 years old, a Canadian-born physical education instructor.

In the fall, the students played football outdoors. In the spring, they played baseball outdoors. In the winter, they needed a sport that would not bore the students. They already had calisthenics, chinning on a bar, lifting weights and swinging Indian clubs, but the students rejected those as dull and noncompetitive.

In addition, Gulick feared that the YMCA's would lose members unless they came up with an exciting indoor game. It had to be appropriate for evenings indoors and in winter. It had to offer recreation, not physical development.

Naismith tried first to modify existing games, but that did not work. He then decided that a ball was needed, but a ball large enough so that it would not have to be hit. He did not want the running with the ball that had made football so rough. He thought the ball should enter a goal. If the goal were elevated, the ball would have to be thrown in an arc and thus not with force. And if the goals were high enough, the defense could not congregate around the goal. If the ball were handled with the hands only, there would be less chance for roughness.

From that base, Naismith used a soccer ball and invented basketball. For goals, he wanted to suspend boxes from opposite ends of the gymnasium balcony, but the janitor could not find boxes. He did find peach baskets, so they became the goals. They were hung 10 feet from the floor, not because of careful, scientific planning but because the balcony happened to be 10 feet high.

Metal baskets soon replaced the peach baskets and in 1906 the bottoms of the baskets were opened. Backboards were later introduced to prevent spectators from interfering with the ball. The backboards were mesh, then wood. Now they are often glass so that spectators can see through them.

Naismith wrote 13 rules, 12 of which are still in use. But the popularity of his game grew so quickly that baskets were erected in gymnasiums and games played without anyone having the rules. At one point, the YMCA's, Amateur Athletic Union, National Collegiate Athletic Association and high schools played under separate rules. And women played under still another set of rules.

Basketball was played in YMCA leagues all over the country. Colleges started playing it in 1895, and games became rough. In 1915, the AAU and the NCAA formed the joint Basketball Rules Committee, standardized the rules and discouraged roughness.

The game was still essentially slow and low scoring. Two major rule changes reversed that. In 1935, a new rule eliminated basket hanging—the practice of an offensive player stationing himself under his home basket—by limiting the time allowed his stay in the free-throw lane near the baskets to three seconds, with or without the ball. In 1937, the center jump after each field goal was eliminated.

Since then, players have become more skilled, but the game is essentially the same. The idea is to shoot the ball into the basket. A player in possession of the ball may not carry it but may advance it by dribbling (bouncing it while he is moving) or by passing the ball to a team mate.

There are five players on the court for each team. One is a center, two are forwards and two are guards. In professional basketball, the positions have become known as center, power forward, small forward, point (playmaking) guard and off (primarily shooting) guard.

The position names are deceptive. The "small forward" in professional basketball may be 6′ 9″ tall and is never shorter than 6′ 4″. "Big men" are often 7 feet or taller. "Small men" are often 6′ 4″ or 6′ 5″. Basket ball has become a big man's game, and players less than six feet tall are unusual in colleges and rare among professionals.

The game is usually played indoors. The rectangular court can vary in size from 74 by 42 feet to 94 by 50 feet. The ball is larger than the original soccer ball; about 30 inches in circumference and covered with leather.

College games consist of 20-minute halves. Professionals play 12-minute quarters. College teams use man-to-man and zone defenses, and there is no requirement to shoot the ball within a given period. To keep the game moving and prevent stalling and low scores, professionals have banned the zone defense and require a team to shoot within 24 seconds of gaining possession. International amateur rules require a team to shoot within 30 seconds after gaining possession.

For many years, women's rules required six players on a team rather than five. Three women played forward and three played guard, and each group could not cross the midcourt line. Most women, including those in international competition, now play men's rules, though a few states still use the old rules for high school games.

College basketball received great impetus because Ned Irish, a New York sportswriter was covering a game at Manhattan College in New York City, and the gymnasium was so cramped that he had to get in through a window.

Irish was convinced that college basketball in New York City needed a better and larger home. Coincidentally, in 1931, during the depression, Mayor James J. Walker asked Irish and other sportswriters to raise money for the many unemployed. They did it by staging a successful college basketball tripleheader at Madison Square Garden involving six New York City teams.

In 1934, Irish, at age 29, quit his job and became a full-time college basketball promoter. He rented Madison Square Garden for six college doubleheaders. The public responded so well that he staged eight doubleheaders in the 1934-35 season and averaged 12,000 attendance.

College basketball has never been the same. Intersectional competition was stimulated, and soon the best teams in the country played in New York. Madison Square Garden became the Mecca of college basketball.

In 1936, Stanford University of California traveled cross-country to play Long Island University at the Garden. LIU had won 43 consecutive games, but it lost to Stanford, 45-31. Stanford's star, Angelo (Hank) Luisetti, astounded Eastern spectators with his one-handed shots, and in time, the two-handed shot disappeared. "We had no idea that we would bring on a revolution," said Luisetti.

In 1938, Madison Square Garden staged the first postseason competition, the National Invitation Tournament. In 1939, the NCAA held its first postseason championship tournament. For years, the two tournaments competed for the best teams, a battle the NCAA inevitably won because it controlled the college sport.

In 1951 and 1952, college basketball suffered a stunning blow. Law-enforcement officials reported that from 1947 to 1950, at least 86 games had been fixed. They were played in 23 cities in 17 states, and the scandals involved 32 players from seven colleges.

Ater the 1949-50 season, City College of New York had won both the NCAA and NIT titles, beating Bradley University of Peoria, Ill., in each final. All five starters from CCNY were arrested in the scandals. So were three Bradley players. As were Ralph Beard and Alex Groza, All-American players from the University of Kentucky.

There were later scandals, too. In 1961, 37 players from 22 colleges were cited. In 1965, two players from Seattle University were involved.

The players were not asked to lose the games intentionally. Instead, they were asked to control the final score. Bookmakers, finding that bettors shunned games in which one team was a strong favorite, tried to make the teams equal by adding a given number of points to the poorer teams' score. This so-called point spread stimulated betting. The gamblers who fixed games generally asked the players they controlled to win by fewer points than the point spread.

The colleges in the first scandals included four from New York City—City College, Long Island University, New York University and Manhattan College. People in other sections of the country blamed Madison Square Garden and its frequent capacity crowds of 18,000, many of them bettors, for the scandals. The NCAA urged a boycott of the Garden, and many colleges complied. College basketball in Madison Square Garden has never been the same.

College basketball regained prestige nationally with the help of such superstars as Wilt Chamberlain of Kansas, Bill Russell of San Francisco, Oscar Robertson of Cincinnati, Jerry West of West Virginia and Lew Alcindor (later known as Kareem Abdul-Jabbar) and Bill Walton of the University of California, Los Angeles. Alcindor and Walton were part of the UCLA dynasty under coach John Wooden. From 1964 to 1975, UCLA won the NCAA championship 10 times in 12 years and had winning streaks of 47 and 88 games, the 88-game streak being the longest in college history.

Professional basketball, like the college game, struggled for years before achieving wide success. The National Basketball League was organized in 1898 with teams representing Philadelphia, Southern New Jersey, New York City and Brooklyn. It survived two years. The New England League also was formed in 1898 and paid its players $150 to $225 per month. Its life was short, too.

The American Basketball League started play in 1925 with nine teams. The season lasted six months, and the top players received $1,500 per month. Interest waned after six seasons.

The ABL is best remembered for its outstanding team, the original Celtics. The Celtics started in 1915 as a semi-pro team and disbanded in 1928. The ABL threw them out of the league because they were too good. They played home games in New York and they seldom lost. From 1920 to 1928, they won 720 of 795 games.

Their stars were Nat Holman, Joe Lapchick, Pete Barry, Johnny Beckman and Dutch Dehnert. Holman, who started playing for $5 per game, improvised moves that became the foundation of the slick style known as New York basketball. Lapchick, at 6 feet 5 inches—a giant in his day— was a mobile and innovative center. He and Holman became celebrated college coaches.

A new National Basketball League started in 1937 and the Basketball Association of America began in 1946. In 1949, they merged into the National Basketball Association, which is still the major professional league.

The NBA had 17 teams in its first season, 11 teams in its second, eight teams in the 1957-58 season. It played the 1979-80 season with 22 teams, a national television contract and incredibly high salaries.

The average salary was more than $100,00 per year. David Thompson of the Denver Nuggets was the highest-salaried player at $800,000 per year until Bill Walton, a 6-foot-11-inch center, signed with the San Diego Clippers in 1979 as a free agent for $1 million annually.

The most coveted collegians entering the NBA in the 1979-80 season were Larry Bird of Indiana State, the college player of the year the previous season, and Earvin (Magic) Johnson, the star of Michigan State's NCAA champions. Both signed long-term professional contracts, Bird with the Boston Celtics for $650,000 per year and Johnson with the Los Angeles Lakers for $600,000 per year.

The most recent threat to the NBA came when the American Basketball Association started in the 1967-68 season with 11 teams. To stimulate interest, it adopted a three point field goal for shots outside a 25-foot circle; a red, white and blue basketball and a no-foul-out rule.

In nine years, the ABA went through 22 franchises, seven commissioners, many antitrust suits against the

NBA and $40 million in losses. In 1976, four of the six remaining ABA teams merged with the 18 NBA teams, each newcomer paying a $3.2 million admisson fee.

The outstanding professional player in the post-World War II era was George Mikan of the Minneapolis Lakers. He was 6 feet 10 inches and bulky, but he was a deadly shot close to the basket. To limit his effectiveness, the NBA doubled the width of the free-throw lane to 12 feet, forcing him to operate farther from the basket. It did not stop him. He was so good that once the marquee at Madison Square Garden read: "Tonight George Mikan vs. Knicks."

From the 1956-57 season to 1965-66, the Boston Celtics won nine of 10 titles (eight consecutively) under their colorful coach, Arnold (Red)Auerbach. The Celtic heroes included Bob Cousy, Bill Sharman, Bill Russell, Tom Heinsohn, K.C. and Sam Jones and John Havlicek.

Cousy's sleight of hand became legendary, and he was all pro 10 straight seasons. The 6' 9½" Russell was so awesome a defensive center that he revolutionized the game. At age 32, still a player, he succeeded Auerbach as coach, becoming the first black man to coach a major-league team in a major sport.

Russell's great rival was 7' 2" Wilt Chamberlin, the greatest offensive player in pro history and the NBA's all-time scoring leader. "I think my impact on basketball is going to be everlasting," said Chamberlain, and it was, but he played on a champion team only twice in 14 years.

Modern major-league baseball had its first black player (Jackie Robinson) in 1947, pro football its first (Tank Younger) in 1949. The NBA's first black was Chuck Cooper, signed by the Celtics in 1950. Thirty years later, two-thirds of the NBA players, including most of the stars and most of the highest paid, were black. Several teams had black coaches.

Internationally, the best-known basketball team is the Harlem Globetrotters, who have played in more than 90 nations since they began in 1927. The players are black and most can play high-level basketball, but they are famous for their clowning routines. They are so popular that they sometimes have three teams in different cities at the same time, all using the same routines. Frank Deford called them "part show biz, part sporting event and part Jack Benny."

Women's basketball, which for years barely existed beyond the highschool level, grew in the 1970's. One reason was the formation of the Association for Intercollegiate Athletics for Women to govern all college sports for women. Another was the Title IX regulations that forbid colleges to discriminate against women's athletics if the colleges received any federal funds.

— Frank Litsky

CHAPTER 1

COLLEGE BASKETBALL

L.S.U.'s "Pistol" Pete Maravich—the greatest
scorer in college basketball history.

BASKET BALL AND ITS SUCCESS.

A Game that Has Become Popular in Girls' Colleges—How It Is Played.

The game of basket ball, although comparatively new, has within two years acquired a popularity which places it on a par with the oldest and best known indoor sports. The devotees are numbered by the thousand, and they are as loud in its praise as an energetic bowler can be over his favorite pastime.

Basket ball is a modified kind of football with every element of roughness eliminated. It is particularly adapted for indoor practice, and may be played on any gymnasium floor or other suitable place. When it is known that the game is played in hundreds of gymnasiums from New-York to San Francisco, has recently been introduced into Japan, is a popular sport with young athletes in Australia, and is played by scores of handsome athletic young ladies in Wellesley and Smith Colleges, it will be seen that it possesses more than ordinary elements of interest.

The great stronghold of the game lies at present in the gymnasiums of the various Young Men's Christian Associations, but it is rapidly being taken up by colleges, seminaries, and similar organizations. The game is simple, easily learned, and not incumbered with a list of difficult rules. It is played with a regulation association football and two baskets, which are fastened to the walls, if played indoors, opposite each other, and about ten feet from the floor. As in football there are two teams, but the number on a side is smaller, generally varying from five to nine men, although if the playing space is large enough the teams may be considerably larger. Nine, however, makes a good, perfect team.

Many of the football terms are retained, although the pastime lacks such incidental features of the genuine game as sprained ankles, dislocated shoulders, broken noses, and other casualties to which spectators of a contest between brawny college teams are frequently witnesses.

The baskets are the goals, and the aim of the teams is to throw the ball into the opponents' goal. At first thought this may appear as a comparatively simple thing to do, but five minutes' play by a novice would convince him of the truth of the adage that "appearances are deceptive," and he would begin to realize that a considerable amount of skill and practice are necessary to make a goal.

The ball can only be struck by the open hand, no kicking or hitting it with the fists is allowed, nor can a player be struck or seized in an attempt to wrest the ball from him. Tackling, of course, is out of the question, although a player may run with the ball, if possible, to an advantageous position from which to throw a goal. It is perfectly proper to knock the ball from the hands of another player, provided it is done by simply slapping the ball with the open hand. A failure to conform to the rules counts a foul, and the penalty for this is one point for the opposing team. The baskets are about 15 inches in diameter at the top and of the same depth. The regulation baskets consist of strong iron hoops with braided cord netting, which are securely fastened to the wall. Any ordinary basket large enough for the ball to enter will answer the purpose. In the Young Mens' Christian Association building on Twenty-third Street, where there are eight or nine teams playing the game during the Winter, the net work has been taken off from the iron hoop. This saves the trouble of getting a long pole to boost the ball out of the basket when it is thrown in. The ball falls through the iron hoop to the floor, and is immediately put in play again by the referee without any loss of time.

The ground or floor is divided into three equal sections crosswise, and in a team of nine, three are stationed in each section. A man called the goalkeeper stands in front of this goal, in which the opposing team endeavors to throw the ball, and the goalkeeper's duty is to keep the ball away from that part of the floor. This sometimes calls for remarkably lively work, and the keeper has as assistants two men at the ends on either side of him called the right back and the left back. The men in the middle section are the centres, the man in the middle being called the centre, and those on the sides the left and right centres. The man in front of the opponents' goal in the last section is the home man. The two men assisting him are the left and right forwards. When the ball gets into this territory the home man tries to throw it into the basket, or if the forwards have a good opportunity they also try for a goal.

Most of the goal throwing is done by the home man and the forwards. Occasionally a trial may be made by the centres, but a player must have a very steady aim to throw from the centre of the field. The opposing team occupies similar positions, only the men are reversed—that is, in front of the home man will be the goalkeeper, and the left forward will be opposed by a right forward. The skill lies in passing the ball quickly from one to another, so as to get it down to the opponents' goal. If a player is at all slow, it will be snatched away in a twinkling by one of the other side. The ball is continually passing from one team to the other. In may change back and forth as many as fifty times in five minutes.

The game is started by the referee, who places the ball in the middle of the floor. A goal counts three points, and after each goal the ball is again put in play by the referee. Two halves of twenty minutes each are usually played. The better the teams the less points will be made, as it will be more difficult to get the ball into the baskets. Six points is a good score in a well-played game, but poorer teams may roll up twenty or more.

The game of basket ball was the invention, if such it can be called, of James Naismith, one of the instructors in the Young Men's Christian Association training school for General Secretaries and athletic directors at Springfield, Mass. Mr. Naismith is a graduate of the McGill University, in Canada, and, after taking a course at Springfield, was retained as one of its teachers. He has always taken a pronounced interest in athletics.

The game was first played at Springfield in 1891. Dr. McCurdy, physical director at the Central Twenty-third Street Building, was in Springfield at the time the game was launched before the public, and when he returned to this city he was the first to introduce it among the Twenty-third Street members. The boys took to it from the start, and last year, besides the regular association team, there were eight or nine others, each having its particular day and hour for practice. There will be fully as many teams this year, and practice is just beginning. The association team will be picked in about a month, and the star players are working hard for positions. Among the best basket-ball men at the Twenty-third Street building are W. H. Rose, G. B. Mathewson, H. S. Thompson, William Baumgard, Benjamin Ettlinger, Alfred T. Ford, and F. Rubins.

There were also teams last year in the Eighty-sixth Street, Harlem, and Washington Heights branches, and the game will be vigorously revived in those places this season. It is proposed to have a series of interassociation match games this Winter. This will be a new departure and will add additional interest to the game. The basket-ball team of the Central Young Men's Christian Association in Brooklyn is now hard at work and is composed of Edward Williamson, L. Beatty, A. Rieffenstahl, Isaac Rieffenstahl, H. Jarrison, F. Hillman, and A. Cameron.

The game has found favor at Oxford and Cambridge in England. It was taken to Australia a few months ago by A. P. Stockwell, the General Secretary at Melbourne, Victoria. He learned the game while in the Springfield training school, as did many others who have since carried the sport to their respective headquarters. A Japanese student took it to his native country. Stagg, the famous Yale baseball player, was the first to teach the game to the athletic young men of Chicago. Amherst College and the Leland Stanford University are among the colleges having basket-ball teams, while in the girls' colleges it has found high favor at Wellesley, Smith, and Mount Holyoke,

November 12, 1893

Dr. James Naismith recycled some old peach baskets one winter—and the game of basketball was born.

YALE WINS AT BASKETBALL.

The University of Pennsylvania Team Defeated with Ease.

NEW HAVEN, Conn., March 20.—Yale defeated the University of Pennsylvania here this evening at basket ball by the score of 32 to 10. Yale's players took the lead at the start, and maintained their advantage until the close of the contest. The team play of the visitors was inferior, although several fine individual plays were made. The summary:

Yale.	Position.	Pennsylvania.
Clark	Right forward	Milligan, Capt.
Beard	Left forward	De Loffre
Sharp	Centre	Hedges, Schrack
Peck, Capt.	Left guard	Stewart
Rockwell	Right guard	Margraff

Goals—Milligan, (2,) De Loffre, Schrack and Stewart, Beard, (3,) Clark, Sharp, (6,) Peck, (3,) Rockwell, (2.) Goals thrown from foul—Beard and Sharp. Referee—Louis A. Leyerzapf, New Haven. Umpires—Messrs. Mannager and Abbott of Pennsylvania, and George A. May of the Yale Gymnasium.

March 21, 1897

Changes in Basket Ball Rules.

At a meeting of the Basket Ball Committee of the Amateur Athletic Union held at 16 Park Place yesterday afternoon, a number of changes were made in the rules for playing the game. The following statement has been added to Rule 11, Section 1: "The ball must enter and remain in the basket until after the referee's decision of said goal." This, of course, means that the official goal must be used in match games and that the bottom of the basket is not to be cut out. Discussion has arisen in a number of clubs as to whether a throw resulted in a goal or not, because the ball passed so rapidly through the basket that it left the spectators in doubt as to whether a goal was made or not. This will be avoided if the bottom is left in the basket, as it was intended, but was not specifically stated in last year's rules.

Rule 11, Section 18, has been changed slightly, as follows: "The man who dribbles the ball with both hands cannot again touch it with both hands until the ball has been played by some one else." Last year's rules permitted this if the ball was touched by some one else. Further, the player who dribbles the ball cannot throw for goal until the ball has been played by another player. That player may throw for goal or return it to the man who dribbled it, who may then, if he desires, throw for goal.

Rule 11, Section 27, has been changed as follows: "After an attempt for goal from outside the boundary line the ball, whether the goal is made or not, must be thrown up in the centre of the field, and the goal if made does not count." An addition to Rule 12, Section 4, provides that a protest must be presented in writing within forty-eight hours.

October 10, 1900

YALE CHAMPION AT BASKET BALL

The Blue Team Finishes Season by Defeating the Harvard Five Easily.

COLUMBIA IN SECOND PLACE

Cambridge Players Failed to Score a Field Goal During the Entire Game.

Special to The New York Times.

NEW HAVEN, Conn., March 9.—Harvard made a new low record in intercollegiate basket ball to-night, failing to lift a single basket from the floor during her annual game with Yale.

The Crimson landed 6 points, all on fouls. In the first half she scored but 1, and that was made after Yale had made 14. Yale closed the first half with a lead of 17 to 1.

In the second half Harvard held Yale down well till the last five minutes of play, netting 5 points on fouls and making the final score 27 to 6. The victory to-night gives Yale the intercollegiate championship, with Columbia second.

Van Vleck and Capt. Noyes were the heroes of the game. Noyes boosted 9 fouls into the cage, although he missed 11, and Van Vleck threw 4 of Yale's 9 baskets from the floor. Each side made 20 fouls, 15 of Harvard's being called on Capt. Burnham. Amberg was able to throw only 6 of the 20 called on Yale.

Harvard made an effort to smooth out the fuss caused in the football season in picking officials for the annual football game. She requested Al Sharpe, a former Yale basket-ball Captain, to officiate as referee to-night, and he consented.

Line-up:

Yale, 27.	Positions.	Harvard, 6.
Cushman	Right forward	Currie
Clifford	Left guard	Allen,
		Downey
Van Vleck	Centre	Amberg,
		Miles
Noyes	Right guard	Brooks
J. Murphy, Wrenn.	Left guard	Burnham

Goals from floor—Murphy, (2,) Clifford, (3,) Van Vleck, (4,) Goals from foul—Noyes, (9,) Amberg, (6.) Referee—Dr. Al. Sharpe.

By her victory over Harvard last night Yale won the intercollegiate championship in basket ball. Columbia gets second place, with Pennsylvania third. The record of the teams and the results of the games follow:

	W.	L.	P.C.		W.	L.	P.C.
Yale	9	1	.900	Harvard	4	6	.400
Columbia	8	2	.800	Princeton	2	8	.200
Pennsylvania	6	4	.600	Cornell	1	9	.100

Results of games—Columbia, 27; Cornell, 13. Columbia, 20; Princeton, 14. Columbia, 16; Princeton, 15. Harvard, 30; Cornell, 11. Harvard, 17; Princeton, 12. Yale, 29; Princeton, 20. Pennsylvania, 24; Princeton, 18. Pennsylvania, 33; Princeton, 15. Yale, 19; Pennsylvania, 16. Yale, 26; Cornell, 21. Yale, 14; Harvard, 13. Columbia, 23; Cornell, 16. Yale, 11; Columbia, 0. Pennsylvania, 30; Cornell, 26. Cornell, 22; Princeton, 17. Yale, 41; Cornell, 9. Columbia, 18; Harvard, 6. Princeton, 32; Harvard, 20. Pennsylvania, 29; Cornell, 18. Harvard, 53; Cornell, 13. Yale, 30; Princeton, 16. Columbia, 22; Pennsylvania, 18. Columbia, 10; Yale, 8. Yale, 20; Pennsylvania, 17. Columbia, 17; Harvard, 10. Princeton, 31; Cornell, 18. Pennsylvania, 20; Columbia, 16. Yale, 17; Harvard. Pennsylvania and Harvard each forfeited to the other.

March 10, 1907

NO BASKET BALL CODE.

Colleges and A. A. U. to Continue to Play Under Separate Rules.

There will be no unification of the basket ball codes about which so much has been said recently. The Amateur Athletic Union and the intercollegiate authorities in conference have decided that the best interests of the sport will be conserved by two separate codes. The reason assigned is that the game which the collegians play is too strenuous to be adapted for the use of men in athletic clubs and Y. M. C. A.'s who are not in constant training, and the college men do not want a less vigorous game. In consequence both authorities have agreed to continue the present disparity of rule and to discourage games between colleges and athletic clubs. If possible there will be no such games hereafter.

The college basket ball authorities met in conference to discuss the basket ball situation at the Hotel Imperial on Friday and completed their labors at an early hour yesterday morning. Plans were formulated to change the rules materially for the elimination and punishment of rough play and to control the basket ball situation effectively. There were present at that conference representatives of twelve different colleges, and what is done will be binding upon the whole collegiate body. The rules are to be recodified in exactly the same way as was done in football.

A committee was appointed to do this work. They were instructed to make such changes as would secure the better enforcement of rules rather than the extensive alteration of the code. However, there were changes made, adding certain restrictions against rough play, compelling disqualification for obvious offenses, and plans made to so define all fouls that there can be no mistaking them.

The most important thing, however, was the starting of a movement to obtain efficient officials. In precisely the same way as the Intercollegiate Football Rules Committee has assumed the supervision of the appointment of football officials so the authorities are to take up the basket ball official situation. Lists of competent basket ball officials are to be prepared, men are to be systematically coached in the interpretation and enforcement of rules, and there are to be conferences of officials until the strict enforcement of rules is assured.

It is believed that by this means the main evils in basket ball will be eliminated

in the colleges. Then by strictly prohibiting collegians from playing on outside teams, by discouraging competition between colleges and athletic clubs, and long barnstorming trips about the country it is expected that the whole situation will be cleared up.

The colleges did more than take up the basket ball situation. They continued their work for the correction of the Summer baseball evil. The committee of the Intercollegiate Association of the United States, which has this in charge, is now obtaining elaborate data on the Summer baseball question. The most stringent regulations will be presented to the next conference of the association. There will be no temporizing with the situation, but Summer baseball will be rooted out completely. It is regarded by the authorities as the most prolific source of evil now extant, and will be cut out determinedly.

The habit of track athletes competing for both athletic clubs and colleges is also likely to receive attention. Both the Amateur Athletic Union and the colleges will take this matter up, and it will be prevented, the half-way measures taken last year proving ineffective.

Important accessions have recently been made to the membership of the Intercollegiate Association. President Palmer E. Pierce of West Point is very hopeful of enlisting all but two of the big institutions before the end of another year. Forty colleges have joined the association since the last meeting, and the membership now includes Chicago, Minnesota, Nebraska, and Pennsylvania. Yale, Harvard, Cornell, and other institutions may be enrolled shortly.

The Executive Committee of the association has formulated its football plans in conformance with the resolution of the last conference, when it was resolved to make such change in the method of selecting the Rules Committee as would satisfy the large colleges and cause them to enlist in the new association. The rule now prepared was determined upon after conference with the larger institutions, and it is believed to be satisfactory to them. It will not be adopted, however, until the next conference.

June 30, 1907

A.A.U. CONTROLS BASKET BALL

Metropolitan Association Clubs Can Play Registered Organizations Only.

The basket ball situation has cleared, and the Amateur Athletic Union will control all games played by athletic clubs, colleges, Young Men's Christian Associations, and educational institutions. The colleges, in nearly every instance, have decided to play educational institutions, and if they play outside games they will meet only Amateur Athletic Union and Young Men's Christian Association teams. Nearly all of the college schedules have been published. The only college schedule that contains a date with a professional team is that of the University of Pennsylvania, and the officials of the Metropolitan Association have called the attention of George W. Orton, President of the Middle Atlantic Association, to this game, and it will probably be canceled. If it is not canceled, the University of Pennsylvania basket ball team will disqualify itself.

Stringent measures will now be taken to insist that all club members of the Metropolitan Association shall play only registered teams. The officials will insist that Amateur Athletic Union members of the association shall play amateur basket ball, and amateur basket ball only.

The Metropolitan Association has been greatly strengthened this year by the addition to its membership of the Public Schools Athletic League, which means that all the public schools and high schools will play registered ball only. Settlements, the Catholic Athletic League, the Military Athletic League, and others can play only registered Amateur Athletic Union basket ball teams.

The following law will be strictly enforced: "General Rules, Rule III.—Any club a member of any association of the Amateur Athletic Union of the United States which sanctions the competition of any member, or any team, under its club name or its club emblem, in unregistered sport or professional contest, or which persists in playing disqualified athletes, or which permits professionals to compete under its auspices in any competition in a sport over which the Amateur Athletic Union assumes jurisdiction, where such competition is announced as a competition between amateurs, shall be liable to forfeit its membership in the association."

November 13, 1907

BASKET BALL COMMITTEE.

New Intercollegiate Legislative Body Created to Control Game.

Through the agitation started by the Intercollegiate Athletic Association of the United States, there has been formed a Collegiate Basket Ball Rules Committee, which will have jurisdiction over the game for terms of three years, to effect any changes necessary in the code from time to time.

This committee will include most of the men who formerly had the framing of the rules. It will be headed by R. B. Hyatt of Yale, Chairman; Randall Morgan of Pennsylvania, Secretary; O. De G. Vanderbilt of Princeton, Harry A. Fisher of Columbia, Walter Randall of Harvard, Lieut. Joseph W. Stillwell of West Point, George C. Appel of Williams, E. D. Angell of Wisconsin, James E. Raycroft of Chicago, and Isadore Anderson of Missouri.

...e committee will not only make rules, but will follow the lead of the Football Rules Committee and organize a competent staff of umpires and officials, who shall serve in the games between the various college teams on appointment from a central board.

December 24, 1907

NEW BASKET BALL RULES.

Collegiate Committee Makes Changes to Eliminate Rough Play.

The Collegiate Basket Ball Rules Committee held its annual meeting at the Hotel Imperial yesterday and made several important changes in the playing rules for next season.

With the design of eliminating rough play, two officials, a referee and an umpire, were determined upon. Heretofore a single official, the referee, was in control of the play. The dribble was defined as a continuous passage of the ball, and it was decided that the ball must not remain motionless in the hands of a player after he has started his dribble. It was further decided that a player can shoot for a basket after a dribble. This is a sweeping change, and one calculated to make the game more popular. Further, as a penalty for rough playing a rule was passed disqualifying any player having five fouls called upon him.

Roswell B. Hyatt of Yale University was re-elected Chairman of the committee; Ralph Morgan, University of Pennsylvania, Secretary-Treasurer, and Harry A. Fisher, Columbia University, editor of the Rule Book. A central committee on officials was appointed: R. Morgan, University of Pennsylvania, Chairman; George C. Appell of Williams College, representing the East; Dr. Joseph E. Raycroft, University of Chicago, representing the Western conference; Isadore Anderson of the University of Missouri, representing the Southern conference, and Dr. E. D. Angell of Oregon State Agricultural College, the Northwest.

June 29, 1908

CHANGE BASKETBALL RULES.

Penalty for Coaching During Game— Foul Rule Modified.

Two important changes in the basketball rules were made yesterday by the Intercollegiate Basketball Rules Committee at the annual meeting held at the Cumberland Hotel. The first had to do with coaching, a rule being promulgated to obviate the members of any team being helped by one of their number on the side lines, and the second change took up the question of fouls and the ruling out of a player for committing such. Last year a man came under the ban after committing five fouls, and was forced out of the

3

game. The rule this season is something of a modification, it being held that the old rule worked an injustice. Under the present rule a player committing four " personal fouls " is ruled from the game, but the term " personal fouls " is defined to mean the more flagrant violations, and not the mere technical ones, such as running with the ball.

The rule first mentioned reads: " There shall be no coaching during the progress of the game by anybody connected with either of the teams." For the violation of this the offending side shall be warned once by the referee, and if the offense is repeated the offended side shall be given a free throw for the basket. The rule in relation to fouls reads: " A player making four 'personal fouls' shall be disqualified for the remainder of the game." "Personal fouls " are distinguished as holding, blocking, pushing, tripping, running into, or charging an opponent, and unnecessary roughness. It is thought that this rule in particular will work to good advantage. It will have the effect of eliminating the roughness the same as was intended by the old rule, and at the same time not force a penalty on a player where there was no intent to violate in a manner which would call forth condemnation.

The committee took up each rule in detail, but there were no other important changes. The reports from the members in the various sections of the country who were present showed that the rules in the entirety had met with general approval, and in the West it was stated that the intercollegiate rules were supplanting the rules of the Amateur Athletic Union in schools and athletic clubs.

The officers for the ensuing year were elected as follows: President—Dr. J. E. Raycroft of the University of Chicago; Secretary and Treasurer—Ralph Morgan of Pennsylvania; Editor of the Guide—Harry A. Fisher of Columbia.

June 6, 1910

BASKET BALL RULES AID OPEN GAME

Officials and Coaches Reach Uniform Interpretation of Code.

At a conference of basket ball coaches and officials, held at the Hotel Astor yesterday, the intercollegiate basket ball rules were discussed and the meaning of many of the rules, on which a difference of opinion existed, was made clear. Dr. Joseph E. Raycroft of Princeton, Chairman of the Rules Committee, presided at the conference. Ralph Morgan of the University of Pennsylvania, Secretary-Treasurer of the committee; Lory Prentiss of Lawrenceville, and Oswald Tower of Phillips Andover, members of the committee, were present. Prominent basket ball coaches from East and West were present and they desired a uniform interpretation of the rules. The officials present wanted to get the consensus of opinion of the conference so that in officiating at games a uniform system of calling fouls could be used.

The most important matter discussed was the latitude allowed a man dribbling the ball. Complaint was made that officials varied considerably on this point and, after an exhaustive study of the subject, it was decided that the spirit of the rules meant that in case a man dribbling the ball runs into or fails to avoid a guard standing to block his progress, a foul is committed by the dribbler. The members of the Rules Committee stated that their idea was to encourage the passing game in place of dribbling, and for the past three or four years they had this object in view in framing the rules. It was decided that a guard in order to be the aggressor in a case of dribbling would have to charge into the dribbler.

Another important question brought up was the system of timing the game. Frequent disagreements over watches were recited and the conference decided that the best practical way of avoiding trouble in this phase of the game was to have one watch with two timers and in case of a difference between

the two, the referee's ruling was to be supreme.

Harry Fisher, of Columbia, brought up a question of always calling a foul on the guard attempting to cover the ball when it is in the possession of an opposing player. He said that never in his experience had he seen a case where a foul was called on the man having possession of the ball when another man was covering. Mr. Fisher claimed that frequently the man with the ball was to blame and committed the foul. After a long discussion it was decided that when a player purposely held the ball or it was so situated that it could not be put in play, the referee would declare the ball held and it would be tossed up. The conference sanctioned the use of one straight arm in playing the ball when the man who has possession of the ball is bending and has the ball on the floor. The referee is vested with the authority to call a foul on the guard whenever he thinks that the arm is being used to hold or push the opposing player.

While these matters were being discussed, Billy Lush stated that he thought that the inability of the officials to enforce the rules was more to blame than their knowledge of the rules. He stated that he thought all points brought out during the discussion were fully covered in the rules and the officials would strictly enforce them if not intimidated or criticised. Mr. Fisher replied that he thought that any difference in calling fouls was due to the lack of uniform understanding. An interesting point which was placed before the rules committee for its consideration was the suggestion of a change in the rules so that it would be possible for a player after having left the game to return.

At present when a player leaves the game he is not permitted to return, and it was asserted that this was a decided advantage to the home team, as it would be impossible for a visiting team to take more than eight players on its trips without incurring excessive expense. Dr. Raycroft stated that the committee would give serious consideration to the suggestion when the meeting to frame next year's rules was held. He thought the idea a good one and said it was used successfully in football and thought it could be satisfactorily adopted for basket ball.

When a centre persists in hitting the ball, on the toss-up, before it has reached its highest point, the referee will call a foul on the offender for delaying the game. The note to Rule 11, Section 1, was changed so that if a player takes "another" position after the start of the game and interferes with an opponent's progress a foul will be committed. At present the note states "if a player takes a position," and there were several versions of its meaning.

November 28, 1914

COLLEGE BASKET BALL.

Encouraging Growth of Winter Sport with Bright Future.
By Harry Fisher.
Graduate Manager Columbia University Athletics.

The year of 1915, with its bright prospects, marks the tenth anniversary of collegiate basket ball played under collegiate rules. True, basket ball was played by colleges as early as 1894, when Yale first organized a team, but from the introduction of the game in New Haven until April of 1905 the game was played under the Amateur Athletic Union rules.

The game received its greatest impetus as a collegiate sport when delegates from a dozen or more colleges met in the Spring of 1906 to draft rules that were more adaptable to college men. The game has grown rapidly in popularity throughout the country in both colleges and schools, with the result that it deservedly is entitled to its position as the king of indoor Winter sports.

Practically every college in the United States is represented by a team, and the number that are without the circle are growing fewer every year. As a spectacular game there is none that can be compared with it. Passing, dodging, dribbling, shooting, and clever team work make it an ideal game for player and spectator alike.

Prospects for the coming year are all that the well-wishers of the game could hope for. Collegiate basket ball should have its banner year in 1915. The Eastern Collegiate League, with Columbia, Cornell, Dartmouth, Pennsylvania, Princeton, and Yale is marking time for the beginning of the league series early in January.

Those who have given our best endeavors to place basket ball on a plane with other collegiate sports feel that the game has taken the place that it justly deserves, and the coming year of 1915 holds out bright prospects for continued success and popularity.

December 20, 1914

SPORTING NEWS

DRIBBLE RULE UNIFORM.

A. A. U. and College Basket Ball Rules Alike Now.

For the first time in the history of basket ball the amateur and collegiate rules for the game will be similar this year. During the Winter the A. A. U. officials held conferences and obtained a consensus of opinion from the different amateur basket ball authorities as to their attitude toward uniform rules for collegians and the amateur fives. Since that time George T. Hepburn has discussed the matter with collegiate authorities, with the result that the basket ball rules, when issued next month, will be alike for A. A. U. teams and for the college fives.

There were a number of different points on which the two sets of rules differed, but the most important and troublesome was the dribbling question. There did not seem to be any common ground on which the two bodies could agree for this system of play, but after the conferences of the A. A. U. men had taken place Mr. Hepburn went over the matter with the Collegiate Committee. When Mr. Hepburn and the college men had reached an agreement, a mail vote on the matter was taken among the A. A. U. men, and it was decided to have a uniform rule.

The new uniform dribble rule in substance follows: Dribbling will be permitted, and at the end of the dribble a player will be allowed to throw for

goal, and if he makes the goal it will count. Heretofore the amateur rules did not permit of the scoring of a goal after a dribble, but the amateur authorities have conceded this point to the college men, and in the future amateur teams will permit this style of play.

George T. Hepburn, Dr. C. Ward Crampton, Secretary of the Public Schools Athletic League, and H. D Henschel of the Young Men's Hebrew Association were appointed a committee by Frederick Rubien, Secretary-Treasurer of the Amateur Athletic Union, to conduct a study of the basket ball question, and, if possible, reach an agreement with the college committee as to the uniformity of rules. This committee held open meetings during the Winter and obtained the opinions of different amateur and Y. M. C. A. authorities on the game. At these conferences the amateur men suggested many changes which brought the amateur rules to practically the same working basis as the college rules.

But it was on the dribbling question that the men disagreed, and it was the opinion of the amateur officials that the dribbling rule made for an individual style of play rather than for team work, and, further, that it tended to make the game rougher than it would be without allowing the dribble. The meetings ended with the body of amateur authorities deadlocked on the question. Later Mr. Hepburn was able to bring about an understanding on the matter, and the rules which will be tried out this year have the indorsement of both college and A. A. U. experts.

It was the collegiate committee, which was appointed some years ago to make an exhaustive study of college sports, with a view of bettering the game, that took up this basket ball matter and reached an agreement in the rules.

August 31, 1915

BASKET BALL IN FAR EAST.

Game Popular Among Chinese and Filipinos—Japanese to Play.

The progress of American sports in Far Eastern countries and South America is well shown by the growth of basket ball. Reports in Spalding's official guide book show that in South America, Hawaii, China, Porto Rico, and the Philippines the Winter sport is becoming as popular as baseball.

B. E. Wiggins, Supervisor of Athletics and Playgrounds, writes this about the sport in the Porto Rico public schools: "Prior to the Winter of 1913 basket ball was practically unknown here. It is true that there had been some activity in the girls' style of game at the Normal School and at Ponce, but the game as a sport remained quiescent because of the misconception that it was fit for girls only, and because there had been no organized efforts or capable instruction to develop its possibilities. Climatic conditions and the temperamental reluctance to engage in so strenuous a sport were also marked handicaps. The game's development since 1913 has been rapid. At the present time it is played in fifty of the school centres. It is played on clay courts in the open, because there are no covered courts. The game is improving the general type of physique, and is developing co-ordination and alertness and self-mastery."

Chinamen Play It, Too.

This report was made by J. H. Crocker, Secretary of the National Y. M. C. A. of China: "Basket ball was first introduced in China by Robert R. Galley of Princeton, at Tientsin in 1904. In 1908 the first basket ball league was formed. Basket ball was never popular until 1913, when Dr. C. A. Siler organized a league. The same year A. N. Hoagland of Princeton came to Peking as physical instructor for the Y. M. C. A., and in 1914 Dr. D. W. Walker arrived to teach in the Government schools at Tientsin. These men boosted basket ball until North China teams were superior to all others. The team representing China in the Far Eastern championships was selected entirely in the north.

"Basket ball is a strenuous game for the Orient, where the climate is hot and the humidity intense. Japan has not begun to play basket ball, but since she will hold the third Far Eastern championship games at Tokio in 1917, it is certain that the Empire will have a team in the next championship."

In the Philippine Islands are hundreds of teams. The Fillipinos won the Far Eastern championship this year, and were far superior to all their rivals. The United States soldiers in the Philippines have done much to promote interest in the sport.

Of the game in South America, Jess T. Hopkins, Technical Director of the National Committee of Physical Education in Uruguay, writes that the most important event last year was the adoption of a uniform code of rules by delegates from the Y. M. C. A. in Argentina, Brazil, Chile, and Uruguay. The Y. M. C. A. is co-operating with the Basket Ball Union in furnishing coaches for teams. The game was a welcome addition to the recreation of a people whose most lively athletic game was soccer football, Mr. Hopkins says.

October 31, 1915

NEW COACHES FOR C. C. N. Y.

Basket Ball and Swimming Teams Get More Instructors.

Nathaniel Holman, a professional basketball player, has been appointed an instructer of hygiene at the College of the City of New York. His brother, "Mussy" Holman, is a star guard on the C. C. N. Y. basketball five. Holman has starred in many branches of athletics, chiefly in basketball and soccer, and he will assist Coach Joe Deering in coaching the freshman basketball team. He will also train the new soccer representation.

To fill another vacancy due to former instructors' assignments to war duties, "Manny" Gerstenfeld, captain of the water polo team, has been made a swimming and polo coach. Eli Simon, 1917, formerly on the basketball team, has also been appointed to the gymnasium staff.

October 21, 1917

Sports

Third Crown for Quaker Five.

A long and extraordinarily successful run of college basket ball comes to an end this month. The University of Pennsylvania, although having two games still to play, clinched this season's intercollegiate championship by trouncing Cornell at Ithaca last Friday night. This is Penn's third title, and carries permanent possession of the Heppe trophy, the prize all six member colleges have had as their goal for years.

For the last five seasons the Quaker quintets of Lon Jourdet have dominated the league, just as Harry Fisher's invincible Columbia teams held sway from 1909 to 1914. Penn won legs on the trophy in 1916 and 1918. A victory last year, the third, was disallowed because Dartmouth did not have a wartime team and because Princeton, Yale and Cornell did not play a full schedule of games. No championship was awarded, and Pennsylvania was forced to wait still another year for the crowning honor which seemed inevitably hers. With the championship and trophy assured, Penn now seeks to establish a record, namely, a league season without defeats. In 1910, with only four teams in the league, Columbia performed the extraordinary feat of winning all games. This year Penn has won every league contest played so far, and has only two more to wage. Moreover, the Quakers have announced they would challenge the University of Chicago, champions of the Western Conference, for the national collegiate title. It is to be regretted, however, that Penn has refused to meet New York University, by long odds the strongest team in the East outside the league.

For the last few years the league has provided sport of the highest type. Questions of amateurism and eligibility are never raised. The teams have steadfastly refrained from playing freshmen and graduates. The league had its inception in 1901. Harvard was a member until 1907 and Dartmouth joined in 1911. In 1908 and 1909 there was no organized league, but the group reformed in 1910, and a little later the Heppe trophy was offered for competition. Columbia leads with seven championships, including a tie with Cornell in 1914. Yale has won five titles and Penn six, including a tie with Princeton, which was the Tigers' only finish at the top. Cornell has won twice, including the 1914 tie, but neither Dartmouth nor Harvard ever finished in the lead. Harry Fisher, one-time Columbia star and later coach, holds the individual record of an average of seven baskets a game, made in 1904.

It is to be hoped that another trophy will be forthcoming immediately, without the lapse of a season.

March 8, 1920

MAKE CHANGES IN BASKETBALL RULES

Intercollegiate League Alters Code Governing Substitution of Players.

Important rule changes made by the Intercollegiate Basketball League for the coming year were announced yesterday by officials of the league through Robert W. Watt, Graduate Manager of Athletics at Columbia University. The changes, which are two in number, were made at a meeting of the league at C. C. N. Y. some weeks ago, announcement of the action taken having been withheld until yesterday.

The most radical of the alterations to the rules will permit a player who has been taken from the game at any time to be sent back in the contest later, provided he has not committed four personal fouls, an offense which automatically results in his disqualification for the entire game. Coach Joe Deering of Columbia explained yesterday that the new ruling will allow a coach to withdraw a player who has become exhausted and later return him to the line-up after he has been rested. The ruling will allow substitution similar to that in football, although there will be no restrictions as to periods, as in the grid-iron sport. The new regulation, however, will not affect the rule that calls for the banishment of a player exceeding the allowance for personal fouls.

The second change provides that after a held ball beneath the basket, the ball will be brought out to the 15-foot line, where it will be tossed up. This new practice was tried out in the latter part of the last season, and, having proved practicable, was officially adopted by the league this Fall.

November 24, 1920

GIRLS HAVE SPECIAL BASKETBALL RULES

Intersettlement League Finds They Haven't Enough Sportsmanship to Play as Boys.

"When is a professional not a professional?" This question arose in organizing the Intersettlement Girls' Basketball League when some settlement teams refused to play others because they considered them professionals.

Not finding rulings sufficiently clear on the subject, the "League" has drawn up a set of rules defining an amateur sportswoman to its own satisfaction and limiting the conditions under which she may play. Under these rules, which are based on those of the Amateur Athletic Union, any girl in any settlement who wishes to join in athletic contests of any sort registers with the Athletic Committee of the Intersettlement Senior Girls' Association, and automatically becomes an amateur. If she breaks the rules by unsportsmanlike conduct, or by receiving money for playing or for coaching, she ceases to be an amateur thenceforth and forever.

The Intersettlement Senior Girls' Association, which includes all the older girls in settlement houses throughout the city, is trying hard to get all the teams playing according to girls' rules—or as they say "playing girls' rules" instead of "boys' rules," as most of them are now doing. The association finds this a hard problem to handle, however, as boys' rules, the girls claim, are so much more fun. When one has had the freedom of the whole field, it is mighty hard to be confined to a small space, and not to be able to lay violent hands on anything but the ball.

Not Fitted to Play Boys' Rules.

In the opinion of Miss Edna Blue of Hudson Guild, Chairman of the Athletic Committee, the change must come about. She says:

"Girls are not fitted to play boys' rules. It is impossible for them. The intense exertion necessary when they play all over the field is too much of a strain on the heart. These girls are not in training. Many of them are only in the gymnasium once a week when they practice basketball. And this over-exertion when they are not in condition tells on them severely in the long run.

"Girls are not up to playing boys' rules in a clean sportsmanlike way. This sounds harsh, and I hate to say it, but it's true. Boys play a clean game and play the ball, when girls play boys' rules they don't play a clean game. Girls are not such good sports, and I think it is because they have lacked training in sport for generations and generations. The whole idea of sport is brand new to their psychology, and they don't know how to live up to it. There is no tradition bred in them to be a dead game sport, as there is in a man. We used to give girls dolls to play with, and now when we give them a basketball instead, and talk to them about team play, it's going to take them some little while to get on to the game.

"Of course there are glorious exceptions, but the majority of the girls don't know how to work for the good of the team. They take everything too personally. For instance, when one boy is replaced by another in the second half of a game, the first boy cheers his successor, even though his heart be heavy. But what happens when you try to shift a girl? It almost splits the team in two. Just the other day I tried it. A girl wasn't going to play in the match the following week, and I thought it would be a good time for her substitute to get some practice in the last quarter of the game. Foolishly, at the end of the first half I told the first girl my plans.

Whole Team Nearly Explodes.

"Up she went like a rocket, and then off to put on her shoes and stockings, declaring that she wouldn't play another minute if she was going to be put out like that. Then her 'girl friend' joined her in a sympathy strike. The whole team was near the exploding point, and little Molly, the substitute, was the loudest of all, declaring that she wasn't going to play and then have every one saying she put the other girl out.

"Now, what are you going to do with a team spirit like that? And yet it's a good team when it plays well. It isn't that it lacks team spirit, but it's got the wrong kind, maybe too much of the 'spirit' and not enough of the 'team' in its work. The only thing to do is just to keep working away at the problem, and sometimes results are shown which give great hope for the future, as when recently after a good, stiff game the best players of each team of their own accord met in a handshake after the game was over. That is a matter of course with men, but it's something that has to be developed in these girls.

"The girls are all in every settlement tremendously interested in athletics. That subject at a meeting always brings up the hottest discussion and the greatest enthusiasm, and it is our purpose to try to use this enthusiasm and turn it in the right direction away from a tendency to professionalism toward a real conception of sport for sport's sake.

Trying to Standardize Athletics.

"We are trying to standardize athletics for girls and also to get more girls interested in sport. As yet none of the settlements are able to set aside sufficient time in their gymnasiums for the girls. The gymnasiums are really organized for the boys, and the girls usually are given off periods, maybe only once or twice a week. The constant plea of the settlements is that the space must be used by the greatest number possible, and that not enough girls come out to make the giving of more time to them advisable. This has always been a sore point with the girls, and last Summer at the Senior Girls' Conference at Bound Brook, N. J., where there were many representatives from all settlements, this desire for more gymnasium accommodations was given first consideration."

Later the Intersettlement Senior Girls' Association was formed, with an Athletic Committee. A Girls' Basketball League was organized among fifteen different settlements, and a series of matches is now being played off. The series will be finished about April 1, and a banner awarded the winning team. Already a much friendlier spirit among the various settlement teams is noticeable, and the girls are learning to enjoy the game even if they are beaten.

March 20, 1921

C.C.N.Y. players lift coach Nat Holman to their shoulders after becoming the first and only team to win both the N.I.T. and N.C.A.A. tournaments in the same year. The game-fixing scandals that followed dampened Holman's joy.

NEW RULES LIVEN BASKETBALL GAMES

Fewer and Shorter Halts Now Experienced—Wachter Is Enthusiastic.

As a result of observations made thus far in the realm of basketball, the new rules, put into effect this year for the first time, have served to speed up the game considerably. Followers of the sport are enthusiastic over the prospects of the floor game and think it may soon become one of the major sports in intercollegiate athletics. Many coaches and officials who have attended games this year have noticed an increased interest. Coach Ed Wachter, in charge of the Harvard basketball team, reports that interpretation meetings have aroused interest and have been featured by lively discussion of the new rules.

One reason for the increased popularity in the sport is seen in the introduction of the new rules formulated by the rule-makers. Games played thus far have demonstrated that the list of technical fouls in which free throws are allowed has been decreased. Illegal dribbling, illegal jumping, traveling with the ball and striking the ball with the fist are now termed violations rather than technical fouls. The offender now loses the ball to the rival who throws it in from out of bounds, thereby necessitating fewer halts in the play. Another measure serving to clarify the rules gives the attacking team two free throws when a personal foul is committed by a defender within the end zone, which is distinguished by a line drawn across the court at the foul mark, fifteen feet from the end boundary.

Coach Wachter's plan for this year, as shown in the opening games of the season, has been to send a four-man attack against opponents, including a running back, the centre and both forwards. The system has worked well in the two games played thus far. By shifting McLeish, last year's captain and offensive star, to a guard position, equipped with plays which enable him to run the floor, Wachter has laid the foundation for an attack which is likely to puzzle formidable opponents.

December 24, 1922

adept at the practice. The old rules did not specify who should make the free throws. As a consequence each team had its one or two, perhaps three star shooters from the foul line who alone devoted their time to practicing for the throws and exclusively received the attention of the coach in this department of the game.

The new rule, which declares that the person against whom the foul is made must make the throw, will make it necessary for every member of the team to be adept at the art. It will make for a full-rounded, well-balanced team and will do away with the premium that has been placed in the past upon the ability of one or two members of the five, just as the try for point after touchdown in football partly does away with the premium set upon the kicking ability of a single member of the eleven under the old rule of goal-after-touchdown.

Technical Fouls Unchanged.

The new rule applies only in the case of personal fouls committed. When a technical violation has been declared the team fouled may select whomever it chooses to make the throw. However, the ratio of technical fouls to personal is so small that the new rule, for practical purposes, may be regarded as sweeping. It was figured that during the past year of play there had been only three technical fouls on the average to a game.

The other changes and additions made to the rules were as follows: The awarding of two free throws to a player fouled in his own goal zone only when he has possession of the ball or when he is in the act of throwing the ball outside his zone; the awarding of one free throw to each team when a double personal foul occurs in a goal zone; the taking of time out when two or more free throws are awarded to one team; the awarding of the ball to the team that put the ball out of bounds when the opponent does not put it into play at the point indicated by the referee; the calling of a technical foul when a team captain calls for time out without being entitled to it; the permitting of a captain to call time out when his team is in possession of the ball and the ball is dead.

April 11, 1923

BASKETBALL FOUL RULE IS CHANGED

Intercollegiate Body Makes Drastic Alteration in Playing Code.

ONE-MAN TEAMS ARE HIT

Player Against Whom Personal Foul Is Committed Must Make Try for Point Hereafter.

The eighth meeting of the joint rules committee of the Intercollegiate Basketball League at the University of Pennsylvania Club, 35-37 East Fiftieth Street, yesterday, marked the passing of the star foul-goal tosser from basketball. Among the several additions and changes made to the rules of the game at the meeting, which began Monday afternoon and continued Monday evening and yesterday afternoon until 7 o'clock, the outstanding one was the favorable action taken by the committee on the proposal to make the man fouled make the subsequent try for goal.

Henceforth, coaches will cease to devote their time to teaching one or two individuals to make the free throws. Every man on the team will have to be

BASKETBALL HEADS CURB THE DRIBBLE

New Rules Penalize Man With Ball With a Foul When He Charges Opponent.

AIM TO CHECK PLAY'S USE

Dribble Causes Too Many Fouls, Officials Contend—"Guarding From Rear" Also Penalized.

Although not going so far as to restrict the dribble to a single bounce, an action which was taken last year and then rescinded after a storm of controversy, the new basketball rules announced yesterday for 1928-29 have considerable to say about regulating this spectacular feature of the game, according to The Associated Press.

A new clause is added (Rule 15, Section 9, under the head of personal fouls), which reads:

"A player shall not hold, trip, charge or push an opponent whether or not either player has possession of the ball. If a dribbler charges into an opponent or makes personal contact with an opponent, without an apparent effort to avoid such contact, a personal foul shall be called

on the dribbler.

Intended to Check Fouls.

"If, despite the dribbler's effort to avoid contact, personal contact ensues, either player, or both, may be guilty; but the greater responsibility is on the dribbler if he tries to dribble by an opponent who is in his path."

This is designed to "emphasize the responsibility of the dribbler in connection with the fouls resulting from the dribble," said Oswald Tower, Andover, Mass., official interpreter of the rules.

"Most of those who advocate restriction of the dribble," he added, "think that the dribble is used too much or that it is impossible to check satisfactorily the many fouls resulting from its use. The former is a matter of coaching; the latter is a problem for the rules and officials to solve.

Dribbler Must Pass.

"If the dribbler's path is blocked, he is expected to pass or shoot. This is, he ought not to try to dribble by an opponent unless there is a reasonable chance of getting by without contact, but more attention than hitherto is to be directed to the dribbler's responsibility."

Among other changes are provisions designed to penalize "guarding from the rear" by a personal foul, making it illegal for a player to capitalize his height by tapping the ball and then catching it on two successive jump balls, and stating that "an unguarded player may hold the ball indefinitely in the court, but as soon as an opponent takes a position close by (say within a yard of) the player with the ball, the latter must get the ball into play."

The new code also makes it clear that a ball striking an official does not become a dead ball.

October 9, 1928

Big Ten to Curb Jeering At Basketball Officials

CHICAGO, Dec. 5 (AP).—The right of basketball fans to razz the officials is slated for discard in the Western Conference. Big Ten athletic directors and coaches have decided that booing and hissing must go and are ready to take drastic steps, if necessary, to stop jeering. Education will be tried first, and if that fails the crowds are to be policed. Booing and hissing of officials by spectators last year reached the stage where athletic directors expressed fear for the existence of basketball as a Big Ten sport. George Huff, director of athletics at Illinois, sent letters to all Illinois students asking their cooperation in abolishing razzing at the Illini school. A mass meeting of students will be held tomorrow to draw up a sportsmanship code. Other Big Ten schools are expected to adopt similar programs before the opening of the season Jan. 5.

December 6, 1928

BASKETBALL IS KING OF INDIANA SPORTS

State Abandons Even Politics While High School Tournaments Are Being Played.

800 TEAMS IN COMPETITION

Association Rules With Iron Hand Game That Has Become Builder of Community Spirit.

By HAROLD C. FEIGHTNER.

Editorial Correspondence, THE NEW YORK TIMES.

INDIANAPOLIS, March 24.—High school basketball isn't a sport in Indiana; it is a mania which has transcended all other community ventures. Nothing has tended to weave Hoosierdom so closely as has the annual competition in which one school team out of 800 is crowned champion of the State. At present Indiana is sinking back to prosaic discussions of politics, glum reflections on the depression and other colorless topics after having collectively indulged in a Winter-long spree during which squads of youngsters, typifying not only school spirit but community enterprise, battled for the title that symbolizes achievement.

As a stimulus toward scholastic attainment, as an incentive to neighborhood building, as a promoter of good sportsmanship and as a solvent for the blues, the Indiana High School Athletic Association is of incalculable value. The peculiar thing about the association is that, while it has no legal standing, being purely voluntary, it has grown so strong that it can successfully defy politicians who have sought to get their fingers on its comfortable financial reserves.

To gain a picture of an institution that literally stands an entire State on edge, an understanding of the unique machinery is necessary. No doubt the tendency of Hoosiers to enter whole-heartedly into anything that strikes their fancy explains to a large extent the success of the undertaking, but the credit for stimulating that interest goes to the organization.

Thousands Turned Away.

A few days ago 14,000 Hoosiers, old and young, sat in the field house at Butler University here and watched sixteen high school teams battle for two days until a champion emerged. Thousands more vainly sought tickets and almost the entire population clustered around radios and bulletin boards vicariously participating. Arthur L. Trester, secretary of the athletic association, estimates that between three and four times as many people would attend these matches if the seating capacity were available.

There are 800 high schools in the association, or every one in the State except those whose enrolment is not large enough to permit the formation of two basketball squads. Early in the Winter 767 schools with 9,204 boys declared scholastically and physically eligible began the march toward the championship. That meant 767 communities intensely interested.

Sectional tournaments composed of from eight to sixteen schools reduced the number of participants to sixty-four and a week later the regional contests cut the competing teams to sixteen. These were brought to Indianapolis for the finals.

Of the 800 school members of the association 750 have adequate gymnasiums which in a few instances been built without the help of the taxpayers' dollars. Basketball has paid for these centres which not only permit athletic contests but encourage other civic ventures as well. These gymnasiums have taken the place of the old town halls and are literally the rallying points for intensified community spirit.

That the competitive spirit has caused communities to vie with each other in the construction of gymnasiums is beyond question. Educators will say that it has stimulated school attendance. It would seem that something other than the normal population increase has been responsible for the rise in high school enrolment from 78,516 in 1920 to 142,200 in 1930.

Association Is Wealthy.

In a financial way, too, the association has been successful. It has $140,000 invested in Liberty bonds, and a few years ago when Butler was trying to build its field house, the association signed a ten-year lease for the building at $10,000 annual rental and advanced $40,000 for construction. The total receipts of the last State tournament were approximately $40,000 and that figure, of course, does not take into account the income from the various games throughout the Winter.

The athletic association is managed by a council of twenty-five principals or faculty members from five districts, but the actual control is vested in a board of five, which in turn employs a permanent secretary. That official, backed by his board, rules with an iron hand, and frequently the supreme penalty is invoked—banishment from the association for infractions of the rules. That is the way professionalism has been kept out and clean competition assured.

The association has no standing in law, but its rules are more stringent than those set by the State Board of Education. All coaches must be qualified teachers, all players must meet high scholastic standards and each must pass rigid health examinations.

Of course, other sports are encouraged and regulated, but basketball is king in Indiana.

March 27, 1932

CURB ON STALLING IS ADDED TO CODE

Provision Requires Quintets to Advance Ball in 10 Seconds or Lose Possession.

PIVOT BLOCK IS CHANGED

Joint Committee at Annual Meeting Follows Coaches in Giving Approval to Proposals.

Already one of the fastest of all games, basketball will be speeded still further as a result of action taken by the joint basketball committee at its annual meeting at the Hotel McAlpin yesterday.

This body, the final authority when it comes to matters pertaining to the game, made two important changes in the playing code, both designed to put a stop to stalling.

The first, known as the "ten second rule against stalling," makes it necessary for a team in possession of the ball to advance it beyond mid-field before ten seconds have elapsed; the second is aimed at the post or pivot block play.

Wording of New Rule.

The wording of the new ten-second rule, which met with unanimous approval at the recent meeting of the National Basketball Coaches' Association in Chicago and passed yesterday, is as follows:

"A two-inch line known as the centre line shall be drawn laterally across the court, bisecting the centre circle; when a team obtains possession or control of the ball in its own back court it must advance the ball over the centre line within a period of ten seconds, unless the ball has been touched by an opponent, in which case a new play results and timing begins again when possession and control is regained in the back court; when the ball has been advanced over the centre line it must not be returned back over the centre line until a try for goal has been made or possession of the ball has been lost.

"When the offensive team obtains possession and control of the ball in its offensive half of the court or if the offensive team shoots for the basket and recovers the ball it may pass the ball back over the centre line but once.

"The penalty for failure to comply with the foregoing sections constitutes a violation and the ball goes to opponents out of bounds at the nearest side line.

"Rulings on touching the centre line shall be made in accordance with the present practice in regard to out-of-bounds decisions.

"Touching the centre line shall be construed as over."

Rule on Free Throws.

The other rule relating to the free-throw lane and circle is worded as follows:

"When a player gains possession of the ball in the free-throw lane with his back to the basket he must throw or dribble the ball out or try for a basket within three seconds."

While those were the two major changes made there were several clarifications made. "Blocking" was defined as being personal contact which impedes the progress of an opponent not in possession of the ball.

The words "personal contact" were inserted into the code. This change does away with a cause of confusion by legalizing screening, which was defined as "cutting off an opponent's approach without personal contact."

"Face guarding," which was defined as "taking place when a player disregards the ball and faces an opponent, thus interfering with the latter's progress," will hereafter be ruled foul.

Of the fifty or more attending the meeting, including leading coaches, Dr. W. E. Meanwell of Wisconsin, Harold Olson of Ohio State University, Gus Tebell of Virginia and F. C. Allen of Kansas, opinion seemed to be unanimous that the rule would be a great help to the game and give it increasing popularity. For one thing, it was pointed out, it will prevent teams in the lead from refusing to enter opponents' territory and thus stall for time.

Election of Officers Held.

Before adjourning the committee re-elected its officials for 1932-33 with L. W. St. John of Ohio State as chairman; William McK. Barber of New York, vice chairman; George T. Hepbron of New York, secretary; A. E. Metzdorf of Rochester, treasurer, and Oswald Tower of New York, editor of the rules. E. M. Kelleher of Boston, representative of the National Charter Boards of Officials, was added to the executive committee, on which the other officials were John Brown Jr., Floyd A. Rowe, Paul Menton and J. H. Crocker.

The body will meet in New York again next year at the McAlpin on April 8, 9 and 10.

April 10, 1932

TAP-OFF IS BARRED IN TRIAL CONTEST

Holman Presents Demonstration Basketball Game at 92d Street Y. M. H. A.

MANY OFFICIALS PRESENT

Play Proves Speedier Under New Plan—Home Team Beats C. C. N. Y. and St. John's Stars, 28-25.

Nat Holman's plan for the elimination of the customary centre tap-off was put into effect in an experimental basketball game last night at the Ninety-second Street Y. M. H. A. A capacity crowd, including numerous coaches and officials, which taxed every available seat in the small gymnasium, saw the Ninety-second Street Y. M. H. A. quintet defeat a team composed of C. C. N. Y. and St. John's College stars, 28 to 25.

Holman, coach of the C. C. N. Y. varsity, explained in detail his plan. The game started with the tap-off at centre, but instead of returning to this after each score, the teams alternated at taking possession of the ball out of bounds on the centre line. The game was played in quarters and only at the start of each period was the tap-off used.

Referees Are Non-Committal.

While the majority of the Eastern intercollegiate basketball referees were non-committal, Holman stated that he was satisfied with the result and he would propose that his plan be incorporated into the rules of the National Coaches' Association when that body convenes next Saturday.

The effect on the game of basketball noticeable in last night's contest was that it was speeded up considerably with the elimination of the tap-off. The players had more opportunities to handle the ball. Handicapped by the smallness of the court, the men were unable to work many plays from the starting point, but this could have been made possible by a larger court.

The general opinion of the officials present seemed to be one of skepticism, but they were willing to be shown. Holman's objection to the tap-off is that it gives the team with the taller centre too much of an advantage.

Murray Among Onlookers.

Among the officials present were Jack Murray, Ed Shaw, John Norton, Arthur McNulty, Charles Brumbaugh, Ben Silverman, Frank Brennan, Arthur Carroll, Dave Walsh, Orson Kinney, Dick Meehan, William Greive, Buck Freeman, Neil Cohalan, Irving Dickstein, Max Pincus, Jim Jordan and John McCormack.

The line-up:

92D ST. Y.M.H.A. (28)	G.	F.	P.	College Stars (25)	G.	F.	P.
Greenberg, lf.	3	2	8	Trupin, lf.	0	3	3
Fraiman	0	1	1	Winograd, rf.	2	0	4
Weisbrodt, rf.	1	0	2	Kaufman, c.	1	1	3
Kornblum	1	0	2	McGuiness, lg.	3	1	7
Mandel, c.	0	0	0	Solomon	0	2	2
Lambert	1	0	2	Berenson, rg.	2	2	6
Trokie, lg.	3	3	9	Siegel	0	0	0
Helfand	0	0	0				
Jackowitz, rg.	1	0	2				
Heft	2	0	4				
Total	11	6	28	Total	8	9	25

Referee—Dave Tobey. Time of quarters—10 minutes.

April 3, 1933

BASKETBALL BODY AVERTS A BREAK

Rules Group Reorganized to Give Colleges and Schools More Representation.

ACTION ON CODE TODAY

Coaches Urge Zone for Courts Under Eighty Feet and Change in Out-of-Bounds Play.

By ARTHUR J. DALEY.

With its membership ratio completely altered, the Joint Rules Committee will continue to legislate for basketball for another year at least, it was announced yesterday by L. W. St. John of Ohio State, the chairman.

A break between the National Collegiate A. A. and the high school federations on the one hand and the Amateur Athletic Union and the Y. M. C. A. on the other, was narrowly averted as an agreement was reached for a complete reorganization of the committee.

Founded by the A. A. U. nineteen years ago, this joint committee has functioned with the N. C. A. A., the A. A. U. and the Y. M. C. A. on a par as to representation. But the new committee will find the college group the dominating body, with the scholastic federation granted increased strength and the A. A. U. and Y. M. C. A. sitting in on a reduced basis.

April 9, 1933

N. Y. U. FIVE STAGES LATE SPURT TO HALT CITY COLLEGE, 24-18

Becomes First Metropolitan Team in 25 Years to End Campaign Unbeaten.

5,000 WATCH STRUGGLE

Excited Crowd Sees Lavender String Broken After 14 Victories in Row.

RUBENSTEIN LEADS DRIVE

Sets Scoring Pace for Winner With 11 Points—Anderson Also Stars.

By ARTHUR J. DALEY.

Playing with fiery aggressiveness and forcing the pace in relentless fashion, the New York University quintet became the first unbeaten team that the metropolis has produced in a quarter of a century by toppling undefeated City College, 24 to 18, last night.

Before a wildly excited gathering of 5,000 that packed every nook and corner in the 102d Engineers Armory, the Violet snapped the Lavender winning streak at fourteen victories in registering its own sixteenth triumph of the campaign.

Coach Howard Cann's veteran troupe, hustling every second of the way, wrested the lead from the Lavender combination in the first period and held it to the end.

In a nip-and-tuck initial half the lead changed hands four times, the score was tied twice and then just before the gun the University Heights contingent broke away to a 13-to-12 advantage.

Starts Scoring Barrage.

City was never close after that. Famed for its whirlwind second-period finishes, N. Y. U. unleashed a streak of scoring that left Nat Holman's youngsters far behind. The Violet registered eight points to one for the Lavender during that spurt and the game was settled then and there.

There could be no doubt as to which was the better team last night. N. Y. U. outclassed the Lavender in every department of play. It rarely made a mistake and capitalized on the many errors that City made. Its shot-making was well-nigh flawless.

Willie Rubenstein set the tempo for the fast traveling Violets by sinking five field goals and one foul for 11 points. Most of them were long shots and all came at critical times.

But close behind him was Hagan Anderson, the blond-haired sensation, who more and more gives the appearance of the perfect basketball player.

Despite the superb guarding of Pete Berenson, who covered him diligently, Anderson came through with eight points, was the key man in the Violet passing and a stalwart figure on the defense.

But to single out any individuals on that inspired N. Y. U. team would be unfair to the rest of them. They all played excellently—better, perhaps, than they ever have before.

Joe Lefft held Captain Moe Goldman of City scoreless from the floor. Sid Gross was a capable forward and Phil Rosen, substituting for Captain Jim Lancaster, was outstanding in keeping the tricky Sam Winograd under control.

Not once did C. C. N. Y. resemble the team that had won its previous twenty games in two seasons of play. The principal reason was N. Y. U.'s great work. The Lavender wilted in the face of the continual pressure that the Violet applied.

Violet Players Tireless.

Only in the first period, when they were fresh, did the City players stay in the ball game. The Violet, in sharp contrast, was tireless and its drive was terrific.

Two men stood out on the C. C. N. Y. team. One was Berenson, who had his hands so full in trying to hold down the irrepressible Anderson that he could do little scoring. The other was Abe Weisbrodt, benched for the greater part of the season, who came through with nine points, half the City College total.

The City College passing was erratic. Instead of the short, crisp tosses that Nat Holman teaches so well, the Lavender was attempting long heaves that generally were intercepted by Rubenstein, Anderson and the others.

Although it was hard, rugged basketball, with plenty of bodily contact, Jack Murray and Dave Tobey always had the battle under control.

The foul tries were about even, 14 to 13.

Only in the first half did the C. C. N. Y. rooters have any chance to cheer.

Takes Lead at 8—3.

In its opening drive City piled up an 8-to-3 lead. New York University tied the count at 8-all, went to the fore and was tied at 12-all a minute before the gun.

The C. C. N. Y. supporters were a silent gathering in the second session. It was then New York's turn to cheer. And as the N. Y. U. total mounted, the City College play became more and more disorganized.

As the game sped along toward its close the Violet made no concerted attempt to freeze the ball. It just became more cautious.

Hardly a shot was attempted in the last five minutes. The white-jersied New York combination moved the ball around near the centre line, passing slowly and deliberately. If a man cut he received a pass, but there were no long tosses at the hoop.

In fact, N. Y. U. made only one field goal in the last eleven minutes when Anderson dribbled under and pitched in a one-hander.

Starts Stealing Tap.

The story of this tense struggle really is compressed in the first nine minutes of the second half. Hardly had the period begun when N. Y. U. started stealing the tap, a move it was to continue making successfully for the rest of the game.

City College was getting the jump, but was unable to capitalize on it. The Violet started this period with a none too secure lead of one point. Rubenstein picked the ball off the backboard and twisted in a pretty follow shot. Anderson sent a long

one swishing through the nets and the margin was boosted to five.

Goldman cut into this with a foul, but the Violet resumed its scoring streak shortly afterward. Gross dribbled down the side lines and sent a sensational overhead shot whirling through. Rubenstein, measuring the distance carefully, flicked in a long one.

The count at this stage was 21 to 13 and the game was as good as over. City rallied a bit to revive some hopes on a foul by Kaufman and a mid-court toss by Weisbrodt, but then Anderson came through with his field goal that settled the issue.

Use Man-to-Man Defenses.

Neither team attempted anything fancy. Both used man-to-man defenses and City did not dare attempt the zone alignment it occasionally employs. The Violet always played carefully, used not a single scoring play under the basket and seemed to know just what it was doing every instant.

Of the nine New York field goals only two were made right under the basket. City had two close ones and four long ones.

With this victory N. Y. U. ties C. C. N. Y. in the series standing with ten triumphs each in twenty games. It was the second time that N. Y. U. ruined an unbeaten season for the Lavender.

In the preliminary game the C. C. N. Y. junior varsity vanquished the N. Y. U. freshmen, 28 to 21.

The line-ups:

VARSITY GAME.						
N. Y. U. (24)			CITY COLL'GE (18)			
	G.F.P.			G.F.P.		
Gross, lf	1 0 2		Berenson, lf	1 0 2		
Rubenstein, rf	.5 1 11		Winograd, rf	1 0 2		
Klein, c	0 0 0		Goldman, c	0 3 3		
Lefft	0 0 0		Weisbrodt, lg	4 1 9		
Rosen, lg	1 1 3		Pincus, rg	0 0 0		
Anderson, rg	.2 4 8		Kaufman	0 2 2		
Total	9 6 24		Total	6 6 18		

Referee—Murray, E. I. A. Umpire-Tobey, E. I. A. Time of halves—20 minutes.

PRELIMINARY GAME.						
C.C. N.Y. J.V. (28)			N. Y. U. FR. (21)			
	G.F.P.			G.F.P.		
Demarest, lf	.3 1 7		Brown, lf	0 1 1		
Sidrer, rf	1 0 2		Dubby	0 0 0		
Stitch	1 1 3		O'Neill, rf	2 1 5		
Sherrer, c	0 0 0		Urben	0 0 0		
Yaeger	.2 1 5		Terjessen, c	2 1 5		
Weiss, lg	1 3 5		Greenberg, lg	4 1 9		
Schacter	0 0 0		Trachtenberg	0 1 1		
Singer, rg	1 4 6		Handweiler, rg	0 0 0		
Abramovitz	.0 0 0		Shulman	0 0 0		
Total	9 10 28		Total	8 5 21		

Referee—Spunnberg. Time of quarters—8 minutes.

March 4, 1934

Hank Luisetti, Stanford University star of the mid-1930's, was one of the first big stars of the college game.

N. Y. U. FIVE NOT TO PLAY.

Athletic Board Refuses to Sanction Notre Dame Game.

New York University's board of athletic control announced yesterday that it would not sanction a post-season game for its undefeated basketball team. Graduate Manager Albert B. Nixon, speaking for the committee, said that N. Y. U. is not interested in any post-season contest.

It is expected that this will put a halt to any further talk concerning a meeting in this city between the Violet and Notre Dame quintets, which had been proposed for either March 20 or 21.

March 6, 1934

Basketball on Program For 1936 Olympic Meet

LAWRENCE, Kan., Nov. 9 (AP).—Dr. F. C. Allen, athletic director of the University of Kansas, was advised in a cablegram today from the secretary of the Olympic committee in Berlin that basketball had been admitted as a contesting sport in the 1936 Olympics.

Dr. Allen is chairman of the committee of the National Association of Basketball Coaches.

Allen said he expected eighteen or twenty countries to have basketball teams in the competition.

November 10, 1934

COLLEGE QUINTETS TO PLAY IN GARDEN

Basketball Will Be Conducted on Major Scale, With Six Double-Headers Carded.

College basketball on a major scale will be played in Madison Square Garden this Winter. Six double-headers, bringing together leading metropolitan teams and prominent out-of-town quintets, have been scheduled.

This announcement was made at a meeting of metropolitan basketball coaches and writers at the White Horse Tavern yesterday.

Five out-of-town teams. Notre Dame, Westminster, Kentucky, Duquesne and Purdue, will play here.

Chief interest will attach to the Notre Dame-New York University clash on Dec. 29. On that same night Westminster will face St. John's. Another intersectional contest will be between N. Y. U. and Kentucky on Jan. 5. Duquesne faces Manhattan on Jan. 30 and Purdue opposes Fordham on Feb. 9.

Intracity games on the program include City College-St. John's, St. John's-Long Island U., Manhattan-City College, Fordham-N. Y. U., St. John's-Manhattan. N. Y. U.-City College and Manhattan-Fordham.

A special portable floor is to be built for the Garden. It is likely that the seating arrangement will be the same as that used for hockey.

The metropolitan coaches who attended the meeting yesterday were Nat Holman, City College; Howard Cann, N. Y. U.; James (Buck) Freeman, St. John's; Neil Cohalan, Manhattan, and Vincent Cavanagh, Fordham.

The complete schedule of games at the Garden:

Dec. 29. New York University vs. Notre Dame: St. John's vs. Westminster. Jan. 5. City College vs. St. John's: New York University vs. Kentucky: 30. St. John's vs. Long Island University; Manhattan vs. Duquesne. Feb. 9. Fordham vs. Purdue; Manhattan vs. City College: 20. Fordham vs. New York University: St. John's vs. Manhattan: 27. New York University vs. City College; Manhattan vs. Fordham.

December 5, 1934

CHECK IS PLACED ON THE PIVOT PLAY

Action of Basketball Body Virtually Eliminates the Disputed Manoeuvre.

CENTRE JUMP IS AFFECTED

Will Not Be Used After a Successful Foul Shot—Wider Power for Referee.

By ARTHUR J. DALEY.

Three drastic changes in the playing code were made by the National Basketball Committee of the United States and Canada yesterday as it concluded its deliberations at the Hotel McAlpin. Two other alterations of less importance and numerous minor changes and clarifications were completed before the two-day session came to an end.

Most important of the changes, which are among the most sweeping in the history of the sport, is the new rule that so hamstrings the pivot play as to legislate it practically out of existence. By permitting offensive players to remain within the free throw lane for no more than three seconds with or without the ball (the "without" is new) the teeth have been taken right out of the annoying bucket play as a scoring weapon. Its effectiveness is gone.

Almost on a par with this in rank are two other changes. One is a capitulation to the growing movement for the elimination of the centre tap. This provides that the team scored against by the foul route shall take the ball out of bounds and put it in play from there. The other is one giving the referee discretionary power to permit the counting of a field goal that is made after the shooter has been fouled and the whistle blown.

Text of the Changes.

Pending rephrasing by Oswald Tower, editor of the rule book, here are the five more important changes as formally announced by the committee:

1—On jump balls it is illegal for a player to step on or across the diameter of the jumping circle after the ball is tossed and before

it is tapped. Penalty violation—Outside ball; if done repeatedly, a technical foul.

2—After a successful free throw, instead of a jump ball at centre, the team scored upon shall put the ball in play out of bounds at the end of the court where the goal was made. This does not apply to technical fouls or double fouls.

3—A player may not remain in his own free throw lane with or without the ball for more than three seconds, except while trying for a loose ball. Corollary of Rule 3—Whenever a jump ball takes place at the free throw line, all players except the jumpers must remain outside the free throw circle, the present arc to be extended by a broken arc into a complete circle. Penalty violation—Outside ball.

4—The intermission between halves shall be fifteen minutes but may be ten by mutual agreement. This does not apply to games played in eight-minute quarters.

Answers to Objections.

5—An attempt is to be made to provide that a goal thrown by a player immediately after he is fouled shall count even though the whistle may have blown before the ball left his hands, provided the whistle did not affect the defensive side's play. Corollary of Rule 5—A provision is to be made that an official must disqualify players for flagrantly unsportsmanlike violation of the personal contact rule.

The two corollaries were answers to objections that committeemen made themselves when they studied the new rules. Tests have shown that there are more jump balls at either foul line than at any place in the court except the centre circle.

Hence, they said, a player standing in the free-throw lane while awaiting a ball on a jump would technically be violating the code that forbids any one to stand there for more than three seconds. To obviate that difficulty, the entire lane will be cleared of offensive players during the jump.

The other trouble arose when it was suggested that a defensive player who was ready to foul a man shooting might conceivably give him a bit more energetic push while he was at it in order to prevent a field goal under any circumstances. The corollary takes care of that contingency. Such a foul will merit disqualification.

Effective at the Garden.

The curbing of the pivot play virtually removes from the game a style of offense that caused more criticism and adverse comment than any other factor in the sport. It radically changed both offense and defense and gave basketball a play that cannot be halted except through a foul.

Three years ago the rules committee attempted to put the brakes

on it by permitting a player to hold the ball in the free-throw lane for no more than three seconds. Now he cannot even stand in position three seconds. Ned Irish experimented with the rule as it now stands during one of the court double-headers at the Garden last Winter and it entirely eliminated roughing, tugging, fouling and all the other evils the play has caused.

Basketball players, officials and coaches last night hailed the new moves as among the most notable advances taken in years, comparable to the ten-second rule that was inserted in the code three years ago.

April 9, 1935

L. I. U. QUINTET SETS FAST SCORING PACE

Has Made 451 Points in Winning 9 Games—Bender, With 91 Markers, Shows Way.

Long Island University's undefeated basketball team is maintaining its average of 50 points per game, having scored 451 counters in nine contests this season. The Blackbirds set a record for L. I. U. teams last season with 1,411 markers for twenty-six clashes.

Jules Bender, leading scorer in the East last year, is leading the Long Islanders with 91 points made on thirty-nine field goals and thirteen free throws. The surprise of the quintet's campaign has been the work of Arthur Hillhouse. Called upon to fill the place of former captain Archie Kameros at center, he has proved a sensation and holds second place in scoring with 83 counters.

Another player who has pleased Coach Clair F. Bee is Leo Merson who occupies the guard post formerly held by Phil Rabinowitz. Merson has accounted for 69 points. Captain Ben Kramer, leading scorer in the East during the 1933-34 season, is next with 66. Marius Russo has 54, while Willie Schwartz has made 49.

The high scoring of the L. I. U. quintets dates back to the 1933-34 campaign when 1,265 points were made in twenty-seven contests. Kramer was high that year with 263 points, the top place being won by Bender last season with 258. In the sixty-two games since the start of the 1933-34 season, the Blackbirds have lost only three games. They have not been defeated since early in 1935, having captured their last sixteen contests in a row.

December 25, 1935

BASKETBALL TIE CONCEDED

Northwestern Officials Admit Error Beat Notre Dame.

EVANSTON, Ill., Jan. 1 (P).—Northwestern athletic officials today conceded that last night's basketball game against Notre Dame ended in a 20-all tie.

A mistake by the two undergraduate scorers, representing both universities, resulted in the strange and controversial finish. Overlooking a free throw made by Meyer, Notre Dame forward, the scorers ruled that Northwestern had won, 20 to 19.

The rival coaches and players accepted the score and walked from the floor, while spectators and newspaper men vainly awaited an overtime period. When the error became known to the players it was too late to do much about it.

Kenneth (Tug) Wilson, Northwestern athletic director, today said he was satisfied the game ended in a tie. The game cannot be replayed.

January 2, 1936

M'PHERSON OILERS CONQUER ALL-STARS

Spirited Rally in Last Half Turns Back Collegians, 45-43, at Garden.

BROOKLYN COLLEGE WINS

Subdues Crescents, 24-19, in Final for Metropolitan A. A. U. Honors.

By ARTHUR J. DALEY

The famed Oilers of McPherson, Kan., came on with a surging rush in the homestretch to nip the Metropolitan College All-Stars right at the tape last night, defeating the collegians, 45 to 43, in the most brilliantly played and spectacular basketball game Madison Square Garden ever has seen.

In a preliminary contest, Brooklyn College subdued the Crescent Athletic-Hamilton Club, 24 to 19, to capture the Metropolitan A. A. U. title. The victors held a 14-10 lead at the half.

Behind for the first thirty-six minutes—on occasions as much as fourteen points—the Oilers, Missouri Valley A. A. U. champions, rallied magnificently in the final four minutes to capture a game that seemed irretrievably lost.

By an odd quirk of luck the smallest Garden crowd of the year, a mere 6,000, saw one of the finest displays of the dribble diversion that ever has been witnessed anywhere. First it was the superb set-shooting of the collegians that captivated the spectators and then it was the machine-like perfection of

the furious Oiler closing drive.

The battle itself was waged at breathless pace, which was a suitable tempo for it, for it left the onlookers breathless, too. In the end the No. 1 candidates for the American Olympic team berth were still moving at the same terrific pitch as when they started. And at the finish few in the crowd were willing to dispute the flamboyant Oiler description as the world's best basketball team.

Losers Set Pace at 24—10

The shot-making of the local youngsters in the beginning was positively uncanny. Three of the first five hit the cords and of thirty-two tries in the initial half the extraordinary total of twelve swished through the nets. Midway in this period the college players had a big advantage at 24—10 and at the intermission the count had been pared down to 27—21.

Still the lads from the Corn Belt had never held the lead for as much as a single second. Eight minutes from the finish they were ten points behind at 40—30. Still they pressed onward, intercepting passes with that crazily unorthodox zone defense of theirs and setting up the plays.

For vocal enthusiasm the crowd was more spirited than during any game this year. Four minutes from the finish the collegians held a picayune one-point margin at 42—41. Then and not until then did the McPherson quintet forge ahead.

Big Joe Fortenberry raised himself to his full height of 6 feet 8 inches, palmed the ball in one huge hand, and pitched it up. It grazed the front of the hoop and rolled in. The Kansans had the lead.

Rubenstein Ties the Score

But they could not hold it long because the All-Stars were playing harder than they ever had for their own colleges during the course of the season and were battling for every point. Willie Rubenstein of N. Y. U. stepped up to the foul line at this juncture and flicked in the ball to tie the score.

A minute from the end Francis Johnson did likewise and snapped the deadlock. The crucial play

came a mere forty-one seconds from the finish when Ruby missed the tying foul, but just before this Fortenberry had batted away Ben Kramer's dead-set shot from the corner, reaching up in the front of the basket to do it. And Fortenberry's foul just before the close concluded the scoring, an anticlimax as it proved to be.

The collegians were hampered by the fact that Coach Clair Bee had fifteen men to work with. He made substitutions right and left, forcibly benching men who were playing beautiful ball. Tony DePhillips of Fordham, Rip Kaplinsky of St. John's, Art Hillhouse, Kramer and Leo Merson of Long Island University and Rubenstein played superbly. Ruby was high scorer with seven points.

There was no picking a star for the Oilers. Johnson was the best amateur forward ever seen in New York and he was high gun with fourteen tallies. Jack Ragland and Bill Wheatley were magnificent guards, Fortenberry a grand center and Vernon Vaughn a splendid forward.

The line-ups:

BROOKLYN (24).				CRESCENTS (19).			
	G.	F.	P.		G.	F.	P.
Perkel, lf.	1	1	3	Meinhold, lf.	1	3	5
Gimplowitz	2	0	4	Condict, rf.	0	0	0
Geller	0	0	0	Shea	0	0	0
Ratzan, rf.	3	0	6	Mooney	0	0	0
Dass	0	0	0	Heck, c.	2	0	4
Seeger	0	0	0	Leuschner	0	0	0
Weissman	2	2	6	McGu'ness, lg.	2	3	7
McGuire	0	0	0	Christie, rg.	1	1	3
Rosenblum, lg.	2	0	4	Travers	0	0	0
Persky	0	0	0	Walters	0	0	0
Lubar, rg.	0	0	0				
Glickman	0	1	1	Total	6	7	19
Total	4	4	24				

Officials—Frank Brennan, E. I. A., and Lew Peltz, American Basketball League. Time of halves—20 minutes.

OILERS (45)				ALL-STARS (43)			
	G.	F.	P.		G.	F.	P.
Schmidt, lf.	0	0	0	Russo, lf.	0	0	0
Vaughn	2	1	5	Kaplinsky	2	0	4
Gibbons	0	0	0	Maidman	1	1	3
Johnson, rf.	6	2	14	Rubenst'n, rf.	3	1	7
Fortenberry, c.	3	2	8	Kramer	1	0	2
Wheatley, lg.	3	2	8	Klein	1	0	2
Bailey	0	0	0	Hillhouse, c.	1	3	5
Ragland, rg.	4	1	9	Levine	0	0	0
				Merson, lg.	2	1	5
				Bender	2	0	4
				Lynch	0	0	0
				Schwartz	0	0	0
				Norton, rg.	0	0	0
				DePhillips	3	0	6
				Kopilko	2	1	5
Total	16	13	45	Total	17	9	43

Officials—Jack Murray, E. I. A. and Pete Sinnott, American Basketball League. Time of halves—20 minutes.

March 12, 1936

U. S. FIVE ANNEXES FINAL BATTLE, 19-8

Takes First Olympic Crown, Routing Canada in Rain and a Sea of Mud.

SPORT NOW WORLD GAME

But American Supremacy Stays Unchallenged—Mexico Takes 3d—Philippines Win.

BERLIN, Aug. 14.—The Olympic basketball tournament ended tonight with an American victory over Canada by 19–8. As a result the United State became the gold medalist and Canada automatically the silver medalist. Mexico took the bronze from Poland in a 26-12 triumph in a match played just before the final.

Basketball is one sport in these Olympics for which the prophecies of those "in the know" were right all the way through. The tournament proved two things. First, it is now clear that basketball is no longer is merely an American game, but a genuine world game.

Oriental Teams Fast

The tournament proved, in the second place, however, that North America still is unthreatened in its basketball supremacy.

More remarkable than he guaranteed American victory, however, was the generally high level of play shown by teams from all parts of the world. The mere fact that the three final games today were played by nations so far apart geographically and historically as the United States and Canada on the one hand and Poland and Mexico and the Philippines and Uruguay on the other is evidence enough of the place that the "Y. M. C. A. game" has taken in the world.

Americans Take Early Lead
By The Associated Press.

BERLIN, Aug. 14.—The United States basketball team won the first Olympic championship today on a court swept by wind and rain and deep in mud.

America's five roared away to a 15-4 lead in the first half, but had neither the strength nor the need to do much thereafter. The Canadians' center, Art Chapman, scored the only field goal of the half for his side.

Joe Fortenberry, rangy American center from McPherson, Kan., who was the game's high scorer with eight points, contributed some good work on the defense, twice leaping up and catching balls headed for the net.

The Canadians relied on a zone defense to check their taller opponents and succeeded well, considering the fact that their players were obviously inferior.

Art Chapman did particularly well in guarding Fortenberry, who usually is up around twenty points per game.

The line-up:

U. S. (19)				CANADA (8)			
	G.	F.	P.		G.	F.	P.
Johnson, lf.	1	0	2	Stewart, lf.	0	0	0
Knowles, lf.	1	0	2	Allison	2	0	4
Bishop	0	0	0	Peden, rf.	0	0	0
Fortenberry, c.	3	2	8	Atchison	0	0	0
Ragland, lg.	1	0	2	A. Chapman, c.	1	0	2
Wheatley, rg.	2	1	5	Wiseman, lg.	0	1	1
Shy	0	0	0	C. Ch'pman, rg.	0	0	0
Total	8	3	19	Total	3	2	8

Personal fouls—United States: Johnson 2, Knowles, Fortenberry 2, Wheatley, Canada—Allison, Atchison, A. Chapman 3, Wiseman 2, C. Chapman.

August 15, 1936

HEIGHT IN BASKETBALL

Baskets Should Be at Different Levels for Tall and Short Teams.

To Sports Editor of The New York Times:

While I admit that the passing of any "height" law probably would be unfair to those basketball players of unquestioned ability who happen to be above the average height, you undoubtedly agree that there is some merit in the complaint of the Japanese that they were at a decided disadvantage when playing against our six-and-a-half footers.

Because of the nature of the game and the evident advantage a taller player has over a shorter one, I would like to make the following suggestion, not alone in the interest of the Japanese players, but in the interest of the game itself whenever and wherever played:

Would it not be possible to have all baskets and their backboards placed on a sliding rail and the height of each basket set according to the average height of the team playing for that particular basket, so that a team whose average height is only 5 feet 8 inches would be shooting at a basket approximately eight feet high, while a team with an average height of 6 feet 1 inch playing against a shorter quintet would have to shoot at a basket eight feet five inches high? The height of the baskets, of course, would be changed as the teams shifted from one side of the court to the other.

Although I admit that the passing advantage of the taller team would not be curtailed, its players at least would not be able to drop the ball into the basket.

J. M. COLE.
New York, Aug. 26, 1936.

Editorial Note: Officials agree that the height of the basket would have to be uniform at both ends of the court. Otherwise a team of low average height might put in one tall player to do all the shooting for his side. Raising the basket has been considered, but as yet it has not found favor with the rulemakers.

August 29, 1936

Basketball Inventor Played It Only Twice; He Used Peach Baskets as Goal Targets

Dr. James A. Naismith, 74-year-old Professor of Physical Education at the University of Kansas, who invented the game of basketball in 1891, when it was played 7ith peach baskets for goal targets, has played the game only twice in his life.

He had so much to do with other athletic activities that he "just didn't get around to playing," he said yesterday while being interviewed atop the Woolworth Building during a visit here. His first game, he said, was in 1892. The second in 1898. He used a soccer ball the first time.

It was while a member of the staff of the Springfield (Mass.) Y. M. C. A. training school, where he taught psychology, Bible study and boxing that he invented basketball, a sport now played, it is said, by 18,000,000 persons each year in many countries.

A class composed of eighteen secretaries at the Y. M. C. A. school wanted a change—something new in the line of sport. Dr. Naismith, remembering his boyhood

game of "duck on the rock," in which a rock is tossed at a "duck," got busy.

Two peach baskets, a soccer ball and a smooth floor were provided and basketball was born. To guard against tackling which might cause injury, he thought of passing the ball. That went into the game, too. Soon the Y. M. C. A. took over the game, he said, and promulgated its rules.

In 1905 Dr. Naismith became associated with the Y. M. C. A. in Denver, Col., teaching physical training and studying medicine on the side at the Gross Medical School, now affiliated with the University of Colorado. In 1907 he became physician at the University of Kansas, a post he held for seven years.

He is still with the University of Kansas, having worked there in the physical training department since 1914. He is married, has three daughters and two sons. They are not basketball enthusiasts, he said.

April 3, 1936

STANFORD CRUSHES L. I. U. FIVE BY 45-31

Luisetti's 15 Points Help Bring About First Defeat for Rival Since 1935.

GEORGETOWN TOPS N. Y. U.

Wins by 46-40 to Take Violet From Unbeaten Ranks in Garden Twin Bill.

By FRANCIS J. O'RILEY

Stanford University's fine basketball team finally put an end to Long Island University's long string of victories last night with a 45-to-31 triumph in the second game of the double-header at Madison Square Garden. In the opening contest Georgetown made it a clean sweep for the visiting teams by scoring over New York University, 46 to 40.

A record crowd for the season in New York, 17,623, attended the twin bill, and it could not be estimated how many were unable to gain admittance.

New York spectators, who had heard, with considerable skepticism, of the prowess of the Indians after their fine performance against Temple on Monday night, were unanimous in their opinion that, if anything, the visitors were underestimated. They combined shooting which was as good as any ever seen in New York with a defense so effective that the vaunted power of the Blackbirds, who had been averaging better than a point a minute for the last two seasons, was not in evidence at any time.

Last Defeat in 1935

The defeat was the first in forty-four starts for Long Island and marked the termination of the longest winning streak in the country for a major team. The Blackbirds had not been upset since the game with Duquesne on the Garden court in 1935.

It was the sixth victory in a row for Stanford this season and was in the nature of a personal triumph for Hank Luisetti, who has been hailed as one of the best players ever to perform in the East.

The Coast sensation surpassed everything that had been said about him. In addition to showing the way to the scorers of both teams with 15 points, he was the best play-maker of the night.

It seemed that Luisetti could do nothing wrong. Some of his shots would have been deemed foolhardy if attempted by any other player, but with Luisetti doing the heaving, these were accepted by the crowd as a matter of course. He took the ball on almost every out-of-bound play.

Others Share in Credit

However, brilliant as Luisetti was, the Stanford victory could not be construed as a one-man triumph

Times Wide World Photo.

WHEN STANFORD ENDED L. I. U.'S STRING OF VICTORIES
Hank Luisetti, high scorer for the winners, leaping for ball in Garden feature

by any means. He received fine cooperation from his teammates, especially Howie Turner, set-shot artist, and Art Stoefen, towering center.

And Captain Dinty Moore and John Calderwood also did their share. In fact, it was a genuine team triumph.

The Coast outfit did not seem to have any set style of offense or defense. Its plays were set up on the spur of the moment. Long Island, in reaching the end of its string, fought hard, but was powerless against the team from the Pacific Coast, which gave one of the finest demonstrations seen in this section in many years, comparable to that of Duquesne, which was the last team previously to stop L. I. U., two seasons ago.

Jules Bender made a valiant effort to stem the tide of Cardinal points, but even though he tossed in 14 points, six of them on three shots from almost half the court, he could not avert his team's defeat.

Hillhouse Starts Scoring

After the first ten minutes of the opening half the result was never much in doubt. L. I. U. took the lead at the outset on a basket by Art Hillhouse and, after Turner had tied it up for Stanford, went ahead on a foul by the tall center. Stoefen put Stanford in front, never to be headed, on a left-handed shot under the basket, and the best

L. I. U. Record

1934-35 SEASON
43—Catholic U.	29	47—John Marshall	30
73—Lowell Textile	32	56—Wagner	24
51—Ithaca	20	56—Brooklyn Phar.	19
74—Seton Hall	30		

1935-36 SEASON
56—Cooper Union	13	48—Niagara	25
46—Alumni	23	49—La Salle	9
49—Savage	33	51—St. John's U.	20
60—Dickinson	25	50—Northeastern	27
42—Springfield	32	69—E. Stroudsb'g.	35
47—Wash. Coll.	22	57—Catholic U.	33
63—W. Va. State	18	33—Brooklyn Coll.	21
35—St. Joseph's	30	46—Canisius	31
44—Geneva	17	45—St. Thomas	36
73—Oglethorpe	33	45—Rice Institute	29
36—Duquesne	34	43—Geo. Wash.	31
56—Alfred	20	46—Gallaudet	21

1936-37 SEASON
61—Princeton Sem.	27	63—Hampden Syd.	41
56—Newark U.	13	41—Marshall Coll.	33
73—Montclair Tea.	35	62—Seton Hall	27
40—Alumni	14	41—Ill. Wesleyan	29
63—Panzer	29	31—Stanford	45
49—Clarkson Tech	24		

Note—L. I. U. lost to Duquesne, 30—25, on Feb. 15, 1935, at Madison Square Garden.

the Brooklyn outfit could do from then on was to tie the contest midway in the opening half.

At the end of the half Stanford led, 22—14.

The opening encounter was a rough and tumble affair which marked the first defeat of the season for N. Y. U. after four straight conquests. The Violet was no match for its rival. A ten-point scoring splurge by Georgetown near the end of the first half in which Ed Kurtyka, who entered the game

as a substitute for Petroskey, was the chief point-maker, gave the Washington outfit an advantage which the Violets could not overcome.

Kurtyka tied with Joe Murphy, sophomore sensation, for high scoring honors at 11 points, while Bernie Carnevale and Captain Milt Schulman led N. Y. U. with one point less.

It was the third victory in a row for Georgetown and kept its record unblemished for the season.

The line-ups:

STANFORD (45)	G.	F.	P.		L. I. U. (31)	G.	F.	P.
Turner, lf.	5	1	11		Kramer, lf.	3	1	7
Robertson	0	0	0		Norton	0	2	2
Luisetti, rf.	5	5	15		Torgoff, rf.	0	0	0
Suде	0	0	0		Sewitch	0	0	0
Stoefen, c.	2	3	7		Hillhouse, c.	3	2	8
P. Zonne	2	0	4		Merson, lg.	0	0	0
Calderw'd, lg.	1	0	2		Bender, rg.	4	6	14
R. Zonne	0	2	2					
Moore, rg.	2	0	4		Total	10	11	31
Lee	0	0	0					

Total......17 11 45

Officials—Pat Kennedy and Dave Tobey. Time of halves—20 minutes.

GEORGETOWN (46)	G.	F.	P.		N. Y. U. (40)	G.	F.	P.
Bassin, lf.	0	2	2		Carnevale, lf.	5	0	10
Kurtyka	5	1	11		Boardman, rf.	3	1	7
Murphy, rf.	5	1	11		Terjesen, c.	2	3	7
Petroskey, c.	3	1	7		Brown	0	1	1
Bertran'	2	0	4		Schulman, lg.	4	2	10
Nolan, lg.	1	1	3		Ceffen	0	0	0
Shore	0	0	0		Tarlow, rg.	2	1	5
Gibeau	0	0	0					
Zola	0	0	0		Total	16	8	40

Total......19 8 46

Officials—Dave Tobey and Frank Brennan. Time of halves—20 minutes.

December 31, 1936

CENTER JUMP ELIMINATED

The elimination of the center jump after each basket as recommended by the Rules Committee last Spring was the major change adopted by the National Basketball Committee of the United States and Canada, according to the 1937-38 rules contained in Spalding's Official Basketball Guide, which was released yesterday. Oswald Tower, editor of the Guide, is a member of the committee.

The new rules provide that the ball be put in play by the team scored upon, out-of-bounds under its opponent's basket, the same as was the case when a successful foul was made last season.

Several minor changes were also made. The definition of face-guarding has been taken out and under the new regulations a personal foul can occur only when there is contact.

Various sections were revised for greater clarity and new interpretations have been inserted in the code in order to make the rules clearer to the players and officials.

October 21, 1937

Best U. S. College Quintets to Be Matched In Writers' Garden Tournament in March

Plans for a nation-wide intercollegiate invitation tournament to be held in this city in March were discussed at the Metropolitan Basketball Writers Association luncheon at the Hotel Lincoln yesterday. It was decided to stage the tourney, which will be promoted by the association, at Madison Square Garden on March 9, 14 and 16. Teams from all sections of the country will be considered before the final selections are made.

On the opening night the two leading metropolitan fives will be pitted against two outstanding quintets from other sections of the East. The two survivors will qualify for the next round of the tournament and will meet two teams selected from among the leaders of the Pacific Coast, the Rocky Mountains, the Midwest or any other section of the country that produces a standout aggregation.

On the final night the two winners of the games on the 14th will oppose each other for the tournament honors. The preliminary game will be between the two losing teams of the 14th.

Feelers have already been sent out to some of the colleges, and their coaches have received the idea with enthusiasm.

Cy Young, coach of the Washington and Lee team, was one of the speakers at the luncheon. He thought the tournament idea a splendid one. He cited the annual Southern Conference tournament as an example. "In my opinion," he said, "this tournament does more to help basketball in the South than all the other games combined. It attracts wide interest and serves as a meeting place where basketball enthusiasts renew contacts. It is really a spectacle."

February 2, 1938

TEMPLE CRUSHES COLORADO, 60-36

14,497 See Owls Triumph in National Tournament After Leading at Half, 33 to 18

OKLAHOMANS ROUT N. Y. U.

Fine Ball-Handling by Aggies Marks 37-to-24 Victory in Third-Place Play-Off

By ARTHUR J. DALEY

Mighty Temple, flashing a brand of basketball that never has been surpassed in Madison Square Garden, routed Colorado in the final of the national invitation college tournament last night, 60 to 36.

A crowd of 14,497 that came to watch a close battle between two high-scoring teams remained to marvel at the overpowering magnificence of the towering Owls. The Buffaloes were game and ever-trying, but they could not halt a super-team, riding the very peak of its effectiveness.

Midway in the second half Whizzer White turned to a Colorado mate and remarked, "How do you like this part of the country, my friend?" It was as bad as all that.

The champions from the Rocky Mountains had not a ghost of a chance from the opening whistle. They trailed at 10—1 in the first five minutes and 33—18 at the half. Then Jimmy Usilton, the Owl coach and apparently a merciful citizen, began withdrawing his var-

Times Wide World

TEMPLE STAR MAKING RECOVERY OFF THE BACKBOARD
Shields taking ball after a Colorado player missed basket in last night's game at Garden

sity after six minutes of the second session, but still the points rolled in.

Stage Scoring Outburst

Not since the McPherson Oilers displayed their collective skill in the Olympic tryout tournament two years ago has there ever been anything that could quite compare with the giants in Temple's red. It is doubtful that Stanford or any college team could have stemmed the furious scoring outburst of the Owls.

Temple was so red hot it was afire. The crowd just sat there and gasped in astonishment. It never had seen such shot making. Not only was it the point-getting that impressed but the way the Eastern Conference champions made the nets dance.

They pegged bullet passes so high in the air that none but their own giants could catch them. And they shook loose men in easy lay-ups, pegged long range baskets from all sections of the floor and curled in dazzling hook shots that were slightly more impossible to stop than they were to make.

Colorado was helpless. The nice looking youngsters from the Rockies never quit for an instant, a tribute to their courage and spirit, but such intangibles as that were of no avail. Just to make things slightly worse, the Temple zone defense was as rugged as a rock barrier.

Bat Away Buff Shots

Mike Bloom and Don Henderson, two midgets of 6 feet 6 inches each, were the "goal-tenders" who batted away nearly everything in sight and clamped down on the Buff shooters like a net.

Don Shields was the outstanding figure of the game—and the tournament, too, for that matter. The angular senior in his last college game (Bloom is the only other senior on the team) was a wraith in his cuts for the basket. Not only was he high scorer with sixteen points, but he fed half of the other baskets to his mates in a dazzling all-around display.

Howie Black and Ed Boyle were not far behind Shields with fourteen apiece, a three-man total that would have beaten the Buffs without any outside assistance. Jack Harvey, a great player last night on offense and defense, was high gun for Colorado with eleven, and right in back of him came the one and only White with ten.

Gives Superb Exhibition

Oklahoma A. and M. gave a superb ball-handling exhibition in the third-place play-off as the Cowboys administered to N. Y. U. the most decisive beating the Violet has received all year, a 37-24 walloping. New York, wearied from two magnificent exhibitions in the preliminary stages of the tournament, could not get going at all. The law of averages had caught up with it at last.

In forty minutes N. Y. U. could make only seven field goals, a new low for the campaign. The Missouri Valley champions were simply greedy in the way they hogged the ball. They passed with deft perfection and refused to shoot until the Violet was wide open.

The Cowboys had such speed that they could have rolled up any number of points had they continued their drive right through in metropolitan style. As it was, they gave so magnificent an exhibition of well-coached team play that N. Y. U. was simply helpless, especially since no one had his shooting eye.

The top scorers were Dick Krueger of Oklahoma, 13, and Si Boardman of N. Y. U., 10.

In a between-halves engagement, the Avenue A Boys Club defeated the lower West Side team of the Children's Aid Society in a 100-pound fray for the city championship, 9 to 7.

The line-ups of the college games:

TEMPLE (60)			COLORADO (36)		
	G.	F.	P.		G.	F.	P.
Shields, lf	8	0	16	Schwartz, lf	1	5	7
Usilton	1	0	2	Grove	0	0	0
Alfano	0	0	0	Hendrick, rf	2	1	5
Black, rf	7	0	14	Sidwell	0	0	0
Freiberg	1	0	2	Thurman	0	0	0
Bloom, c	2	2	6	Harvey, c	3	5	11
McDermott	1	0	2	Willcoxon, lg	1	1	3
Henderson, lg	0	1	1	White, rg	5	0	10
Nicol	1	1	3				
Boyle, rg	7	0	14	Total	12	12	36
Busha	0	0	0				
Total	28	4	60				

Officials—Pat Kennedy and Pete Sinnott. Time of halves—20 minutes.

OKLA. A. & M. (37)			N. Y. U. (24)		
	G.	F.	P.		G.	F.	P.
Krueger, lf	6	1	13	Carnevale, lf	0	0	0
Friels	0	0	0	Watson	1	1	3
Smelser, rf	1	2	4	Boardman, rf	3	4	10
Kalsu, c	0	2	2	Barbarito	0	0	0
Barringer	1	1	3	Witty, c	0	3	3
Scheffler, lg	2	2	6	Schilling	0	1	1
Slade	2	0	4	Loewits	0	0	0
Doyle, rg	2	1	5	Dowd, lg	1	0	2
				Tarlow	1	1	3
Total	14	9	37	Lewis, rg	1	0	2
				Total	7	10	24

Officials—Frank Brennan and Chuck Solodare. Time of halves—20 minutes.

March 17, 1938

Added Speed Given to Game —Temple, Stanford Had Best Records in Nation

Operating for the first time under a new and radically revised code, basketball was stepped up on the court and in regard of its vast army of followers last season to reach new heights of popularity. The jump ball at center was eliminated and the game seemed to be all the faster and all the better for it.

It was with considerable reluctance and misgivings that Easterners accepted the abolishment of the center tap, a move fostered mainly by John Bunn of Stanford and his Pacific Coast colleagues. But the East and the country at large seized this change once they saw it in operation.

The fans also received it with enthusiasm and the capital of the basketball world, Madison Square Garden, attracted more persons than ever before, regular and post-season double-headers drawing approximately 200,000 to the arena in a three-month span.

Temple Won Tournament

The post-season part of the program was something new. The Metropolitan Basketball Writers Association hit upon the idea of sponsoring a national invitation tournament. It was a signal success.

A great Temple University quintet emerged the winner and took rank with Stanford, Notre Dame and Purdue as America's standout teams for the 1937-38 campaign. These four were the best in the land, with Temple and Stanford perhaps a shade superior to the other two.

In the metropolitan area there was a clear-cut champion for the first time in several years. New York University was the winner, going unbeaten against regularly scheduled local foes and then toppling Long Island University in the invitation tournament to settle the issue.

Local teams had a none too good season of it, all things considered. Neither City College nor St. John's made good on early promises, fading badly toward the end. L. I. U. also sagged, but N. Y. U., uncertain of itself in the beginning and never too polished at any time, managed to win when the stakes were highest. Manhattan had a young team that Neil Cohalan brought along well for perhaps the year's best coaching job. Fordham had its worst season in a long while.

Luisetti the No. 1 Star

From start to finish it was a campaign of upsets and not a single team of any consequence was undefeated. Temple was inexplicably overturned by both Georgetown and Villanova, two teams not in its class. Stanford ran into occasional trouble (including a setback by the Owls) but held up well throughout a long and arduous schedule.

Where the Californians had it on all other teams was that they had Hank Luisetti in their line-up. He was the greatest player of the year and one of the greatest of all time.

He set an all-time collegiate scoring record of 1,550 points (exclusive of the Pacific Coast Conference play-offs). He also set a new one-game mark of 50 points against Duquesne.

In this contest the Stanford players plotted beforehand to make Luisetti score. He personally preferred to "feed" his team-mates. The Stanford ace, incidentally, was supreme when the going was most severe.

The new rules without the center jump made scoring uniformly high, with practically every conference record of the past shattered. Among the more important conference winners were Dartmouth in the Eastern League, Temple in the Eastern Conference, Duke in the Southern Conference, Georgia Tech in the Southeastern, Arkansas in the Southwest Conference, Purdue in the Big Ten, Colorado and Utah in the Big Seven, Kansas and Oklahoma in the Big Six, Oklahoma Aggies in the Missouri Valley and Stanford in the Pacific Coast.

The national A. A. U. crown went to the Kansas City Healeys, a quintet that upset the Denver Safeways, defending champions, in the final.

December 25, 1938

Dr. Naismith Deplores 'Rougher' Basketball as Result of Some Modern Trends

ZONE DEFENSE HIT AS STALLING DEVICE

By ARTHUR J. DALEY

The zone defense is a violation of the fundamental principles of basketball, it was charged yesterday by Dr. James Naismith, venerable inventor of the sport, in a denunciation of some modern trends of the game before the Metropolitan Basketball Writers Association at the Hotel Lincoln.

The mild voice of this 77-year-old athletic figure could not disguise the bitterness of his words as he lashed out at the zone with such feeling that he remarked: "I feel, at times, I'd rather not see basketball."

Present-day misuse of the dribble, improper officiating and elimination of the center jump also stirred the ire of the director-emeritus of physical education at the University of Kansas. Yet, for all of that, he still loves the game that he has watched grow by leaps and bounds for the last forty-eight years.

His first target yesterday was the dribble. "When the original thirteen rules were drawn up," he said, "the dribble was put in there to be an intrinsically defensive action. Its purpose was to enable the man who was cornered to get away from close guarding. The old dribble was waist-high and the guard had a chance to snatch the ball away.

Wrong Man Penalized

"But nowadays the dribbling is so close to the ground that it becomes an offensive action, and time and time again I have seen dribblers deliberately crash into a defensive man. The whistle blows and the officials penalize the defense instead of the dribbler who brought about the contact. The guard has the first right to his position on the floor and this improper interpretation of the rules by officials is hurting the sport. It has grown too rough.

"As for the zone defense, I have

no sympathy with it. The defensive team is stalling which lays back and waits for the offense to come to it. If a soccer team hung back and grouped itself in front of the goal, what could the other team do? The zone is much like that.

"In one game in the national A. A. U. championship tournament one year I counted the number of times one team passed the ball around, trying to entice a zone defense out. It was, incredible as it seems, 345 times. I counted it myself. Officials should penalize a defensive team like that for stalling. The rules committee, unfortunately, puts the responsibility on the wrong team. Roughness is the result. A zone defense has no part in basketball. It is a violation of the fundamental principles of the game.

Ban on Tap Slows Play

"I don't care too much for the elimination of the center jump. I'm not wedded to the jump, mind you, but I think that it has slowed the sport up instead of made it faster. In the old days it took the referee four seconds to throw up the ball at center after a score. Now the team scored against can take fifteen seconds to bring it beyond the center line. I also think the new style is monotonous.

"Yet for all of this, any game that can draw 18,000 to the Garden here in New York and have thousands turned away in other parts of the country because the crowds cannot be handled must have something fine about it. I think that Ned Irish has done a wonderful thing for the game. He has made it national instead of sectional."

Dr. Naismith digressed a bit to admit that he had played basketball only twice in his life. And then he committed foul after foul. "I guess my early training in wrestling, boxing and football was too much for me," said the doctor sheepishly. "My reflexes made me hold my opponents. Once I even used a grapevine wrestling clamp on a man who was too big for me to handle. So I have sympathy for boys who make inadvertent fouls, but I cannot stand deliberate ones."

Will See Games Tomorrow

Dr. Naismith is in New York for a radio broadcast on the "We, the People" hour over WABC tonight. He will remain over for the doubleheader in Madison Square Garden tomorrow to see N. Y. U. play St. John's and Manhattan tackle Syracuse. The doctor has not seen any Garden basketball since the Olympic tryouts in 1936.

Other speakers at the luncheon were Paul F. Cieurzo of Rhode Island State and Jim Decker of Syracuse. The Rhode Islander discussed in particular his team, unbeaten in eleven games, and in general basketball in New England.

The Rams have averaged 73.6 points a game this season, a total that astounded the scribes, to a 43-point average for opponents. Chief marksman has been Chet Jawroski, who has scored 268, or 24.4 per game. Cieurzo said that he was closer to the great Hank Luisetti than any player he ever saw.

Decker spoke of the Syracuse chances of toppling Manhattan and told in detail of the Orange court background up to the present.

January 31, 1939

Letters to the Sports Editor

BALM FOR DR. NAISMITH

Former C.C.N.Y. Captain Views Zone Defense as Aid to Game

To Sports Editor of The New York Times:

I read with interest the recent speech of Dr. James Naismith wherein he deplored the development of the zone defense in basketball and urged that it be ruled out. As C. C. N. Y. basketball captain of 1919-20, may I refer Dr. Naismith to some basketball history?

I would like to remind the father of basketball that zone defenses are as old as the game itself. Joe Deering, my first coach at C. C. N. Y., taught only the zone defense.

For several years under Deering, C. C. N. Y. held its opponents to an average of 15 points a game by using a zone. It was only when Nat Holman became coach in 1919 that we took up the man-to-man defense.

On the other hand, under both Deering and Holman, C. C. N. Y. repeatedly demonstrated its ability to penetrate a zone defense when it had the ball. It is merely a question of developing a sound offensive system.

The fact that college teams today have difficulty in breaking through the zone defense should not be counted against that alignment but rather against the skill of the players and perhaps also the skill of the coaches.

Don't be alarmed, Dr. Naismith. Basketball is still in the ascendancy and the zone defense will be broken through by good players and good coaches just as it has been broken through in the past.

The offense is too strong and there is too much scoring in basketball, anyway. The defense should be strengthened to equalize the game. The use of the zone strengthens the defense and also develops better basketball players in the interest of better basketball.

Hy FLIEGEL.
New York, Feb. 1, 1939.

February 4, 1939

Jaworski Breaks Court Record

KINGSTON, R. I., March 7 (P).— Chet Jaworski, star center of the Rhode Island State basketball team, broke the one-year scoring record established by Hank Luisetti while at Stanford University when he caged 14 points tonight as the Rams bowed to Worcester Tech, 64 to 61. His evening's work lifted Jaworski's total to 477. Luisetti's record was 465.

March 8, 1939

18,033 See Unbeaten L. I. U. Five Win National Tourney With 24th Triumph

L. I. U. STOPS LOYOLA AT GARDEN, 44 TO 32

Close Guarding That Shackles Novak Halts Chicago Quintet at 21 Straight Victories

TORGOFF MAKES 12 POINTS

By ARTHUR J. DALEY

A team that never made a mistake, Long Island University snapped Loyola's twenty-one-game winning streak and extended its own to twenty-four by scoring a smashing victory over the Chicagoans in the final of the national invitation basketball tournament at Madison Square Garden last night, 44 to 32.

The Blackbirds were strategically perfect and just as flawless in their shooting. The ball whisked through the nets as if pulled by a string and the feared Rambler attack faded to only a faint whisper of the original as the unbeaten Busy Bees clamped down on the scorers of hitherto undefeated Loyola.

A crowd of 18,033 that had come to see a tight battle with thrill piling upon thrill remained instead to marvel at the wonder team from Brooklyn. Long Island had been expected to wear down the invaders from the Midwest with reserve strength, but except for the last three minutes, when Coach Clair Bee cleaned his bench, there were only eight Blackbirds in the fray. This was not just brute strength grinding down lesser manpower. It was a great team operating at the height of its efficiency.

Tourney Attendance 50,682

The huge crowd that brought the three-day tournament total to 50,682 did not see such breath-taking struggles as had made Monday's semi-finals a matchless card. But the fans did see basketball at its most proficient stage.

What made it so easy for Long Island was the shrewd way Mike Novak, the 6-foot 9-inch center, was guarded. The Busy Bees swarmed over him with never less than two men harrassing him. The result was that Big Mike was held to the grandiose total of 1 point.

That might not have been so bad in itself, but the hampering business also hindered his effectiveness as a feeder. From the beginning Loyola seemed lost, basketball's "headless horsemen" with no sense of direction. The criss-cross attack generating around the pivot never showed itself and the Rambler offense was merely a succession of long shots that found every man on the team wild and inaccurate.

In sharp contrast, the Long Islanders were deadly. They even changed their style of shooting from straight for the hoop to carom shots off the backboard. This was to evade the "goal tending" activities of Novak. Against St. John's the giant had deflected nine perfect shots. Against L. I. U. he never touched one.

The Blackbirds were firing away in back of his outstretched hand and in a short while Novak made the discovery that he was wasting both his time and his energy. So he stopped it. Then the Long Islanders went back to their natural style and still the ball poured through the hoop.

No L. I. U. Standout

Perhaps the strangest part of the fray was that there was not a standout L. I. U. player. This was strictly a team victory with Irv Torgoff (high man with 12 points), Captain-elect Ossie Schechtman, Joe Shelly, John Bromberg, Danny Kaplowitz and the rest hustling every minute, never ceasing their pace and splitting Loyola wide open all night.

Prior to the big show the two teams that had been eliminated in the semi-final round met in a playoff for third place. The game furnished something of a surprise as Bradley Tech toppled a St. John's quintet that would have been about an even choice against L. I. U. had it reached the final.

The score was 40 to 35 and what won for the Braves was a 14-point outburst in the second half. The Redmen, uncertain of themselves in the beginning, finally got organized enough to take the lead. Hardly were they in front, however, when Bradley fired its terrific blast that lifted the count to 36—21.

But St. John's came bouncing back with 8 points in succession to tighten things, only to have the Braves hold fast to the remnants of their advantage.

The Peoria quintet was infinitely better than it had been against L. I. U., and St. John's much worse than against Loyola. There was no incentive left for the Brooklynites and they played spiritless ball.

Furthermore the law of averages finally caught up with Bill Lloyd, who had totaled 90 points in his last four games. Big Bill netted precisely 2 counters and even had trouble in hitting the backboard, much less finding the hoop.

Dar Hutchins, the highly touted Bradley center who had been below par on Monday, showed his worth by scoring 13 points. Ted Panish had 11, but the entire team deserved a share in the plaudits.

After the game Haggerty and Bill McKeever were appointed St. John's co-captains for 1939-40.

The line-ups:

BRADLEY (40)	G.	F.	P.	ST. JOHN'S (35)	G.	F.	P.
Schunk, lf.	3	1	7	Dolgoff, lf.	4	1	9
Orsborn, rf.	1	1	3	Lloyd, rf.	0	2	2
Hutchins, c.	6	1	13	Palmer, c.	0	0	0
Panish, lg.	4	3	11	McKeever	4	1	9
Olson, rg.	2	2	6	Garfinkel, lg.	2	1	5
Bortel	0	0	0	Haggerty	2	2	6
				Vocke, rg.	2	0	4
Total	16	8	40	Total	14	7	35

Officials—Pete Sinnott and Ed Kearney.
Time of halves—20 minutes.

L. I. U. (44)	G.	F.	P.	LOYOLA (32)	G.	F.	P.
Torgoff, lf.	5	2	12	Hogan, lf.	2	0	4
King	0	0	0	Schell	1	0	2
Kaplowitz, rf.	4	1	9	O'Brien, rf.	4	1	9
Schwartz	0	2	2	Graham	1	0	2
Scharf	0	0	0	Novak, c.	0	1	1
Sewitch, c.	0	1	1	Kautz, lg.	3	0	6
Lobello	0	0	0	Driscoll	0	0	0
Newman	1	1	3	Wenskus, rg.	4	0	8
Shelly	1	0	2				
Bromberg, rg.	2	1	5				
Schechtman	1	4	9				
Zeitlin	0	1	1				
Total	17	10	44	Total	15	2	32

Officials—Pat Kennedy and Dave Walsh.
Time of halves—20 minutes.

March 23, 1939

OREGON FIVE HALTS OHIO STATE IN FINAL

Coast Champions Top Big Ten Titleholders, 46-33, for N. C. A. A. Laurels

EVANSTON, Ill., March 27 (Æ).—The University of Oregon, displaying superior ball handling and shooting ability, defeated Ohio State tonight, 46 to 33, on the Northwestern court in the final for the basketball championship of the National Collegiate Athletic Association.

The Webfeet connected for 6 points before the Buckeyes found the range and the Pacific Coast five was never headed. The Bucks were unable to overcome the height of Oregon and the fancy floor work of their foes.

5,000 Attend Contest

The Webfeet delighted the 5,000 spectators with their splendid handling of the ball. On defense they were just as alert, seldom giving Ohio State more than one shot at the basket before regaining possession.

The Pacific Coast Conference champions, victors in the N. C. A. A. Western regional meet, built up a 21-to-13 lead shortly before the intermission, but the ever-battling Bucks cut this to 21 to 16 with a field goal by Captain Jimmy Hull and a free throw by Bill Sattler shortly before the gun.

Ohio State remained in the running until ten minutes from the end, when the Webfeet had a 34-to-25 lead. Thereafter Oregon stalled, precluding any sustained rally by the Western Conference champions.

Dick Scores 13 Points

Scoring honors for the winners were well divided. John Dick made 13 points, Captain Bob Anet and Lauren Gale 10 each and Wally Johansen 9.

Hull, leading scorer of the Big Ten, played brilliant ball, but on offense was held to 12 points, five under his average this season. Bob Lynch and Sattler were next for the Ohioans with 7 each.

The line-up:

OREGON (46)	G.	F.	P.	OHIO STATE (33)	G.	F.	P.
Gale, lf.	3	4	10	Hull, lf.	5	2	12
Dick, rf.	4	5	13	Baker, rf.	0	0	0
Wintermute, c.	2	0	4	Stafford	0	0	0
Anet, lg.	4	2	10	Shick, c.	1	0	2
Johansen, rg.	4	1	9	Sattler	3	1	7
Pavalunas	0	0	0	Lynch, lg.	3	1	7
Mullen	0	0	0	Boughner	1	0	2
				Dawson, rg.	1	0	2
Total	17	12	46	Mickelson	0	0	0
				Maag	0	0	0
				Scott	0	1	1
				Total	14	5	33

March 28, 1939

Colorado Downs Duquesne in National Basketball Tourney Final at Garden

TEAM FROM ROCKIES TRIUMPHS BY 51-40

15,201 See Colorado Quintet Draw Away After Duquesne Rallies to Tie at 29-29

15 POINTS FOR BOB DOLL

Sophomore Is Most Valuable Player—Oklahoma Aggies Defeat De Paul, 23-22

By ARTHUR J. DALEY

Two magnificent teams, playing a superb brand of basketball to the very hilt, staged a spectacular show before 15,201 enraptured fans in Madison Square Garden last night in the final of the national invitation tournament. Colorado, a mite better than Duquesne in this battle of court titans, marched off with top honors, 51 to 40.

This was a gorgeous display that saw the lead change hands five times before the Golden Buffaloes from the Rocky Mountains put on the pressure with a relentless drive in the last ten minutes. They made no mistakes from that point on and scored a merited triumph.

Colorado entered this fray with a record of sixteen victories in eighteen games, eleven of these triumphs in a row. The Iron Dukes had won nineteen of twenty, sixteen in succession. So the talent was there on the sleek hardwood surface in a game that thrilled the crowd.

Elements for Thriller

The shot-making was gorgeous, the passing breath-taking in its

WINNER OF THE MOST-VALUABLE-PLAYER TROPHY AT GARDEN
Bob Doll raised aloft by his Colorado team-mates after he received prize last night. The sophomore scored fifteen points to help the Golden Buffaloes beat Duquesne in the final. *Times Wide World*

deftness and the team play marvelous to see. And this was no gentle engagement, either. It was rough and hearty all the way.

The Buffs set the pace all through the first half and had a 22-18 advantage at the intermission. But Duquesne kept hammering away until it had pulled up at 27—all. Then it was 29—all. Back and forth the lead passed, then Colorado surged ahead at 33—32.

The Rocky Mountain champions were never headed again. In fact they seemed to get better as they moved along, poured in seven successive baskets to break the game apart and then, smoother than ever, really turned on the heat.

For the Dukes this was a heartbreaker. They had beaten Colorado earlier this season in a 47-45 overtime game and really did a grand job. Their defense, especially in the early stages, was airtight and their shot-making grand. Coach Chick Davies had to send into action Moe Becker, who was injured on Wednesday, but Becker held up well and scored 8 points.

Sophomore Wins First Time

The two lads who were terrific for Colorado were Sophomore Bob Doll and Captain Jack Harvey. They captured the rebounds and did tremendous damage under the basket. Doll was high scorer with 15 points, to 14 for Harvey, and was the deserving recipient of the most valuable player trophy. It was the first time a sophomore ever won it.

But they did not deserve all the credit. Don Thurman, Don Hendricks and George Hamburg—all five starters played practically without relief—turned in a great job.

Now Coach Frosty Cox sets his sights for other, but not bigger game, in the National Collegiate A. A. championships. The Buffs may win this, too, because on what they showed in their two nights in New York they are a mighty combination.

They had speed and drive and shooting skill. All of them could pass and all could score. Some of the multiple flips underneath and the twisting baskets had to be seen to be believed. And yet the Dukes, with Ed Milkovich, Bill Lacey and Paul Widowitz in particular, were able to hold them off for the major part of the fray. It was a great victory by a great team over a great team.

Opening Period Slow

There has not been a more peculiar game at the Garden all year than the third-place play-off between the Oklahoma Aggies and De Paul. Both teams were so tense in the first half that each gave a poor exhibition, but once they relaxed they staged a thriller. The Aggies triumphed, 23 to 22.

It took the Demons almost twelve minutes to score their first field goal, seven more for their second, and their point total at the intermission was a miserly 7 points to 12 for the Aggies. Nothing worked.

But in the second half the Chicagoans made this game with a 9-point rally that lifted them to an 18-18 tie. They tied again at 21-all with less than three minutes left to go. Then a pretty field goal by Jess Renick, the Choctaw Indian, decided things a minute from the end.

Renick and Harvey Slade were the Aggie floor men, with Stan Szukala the star performer for the Chicagoans. The Oklahomans flew back to Oklahoma City last night for a game in the N. C. A. A. championship tournament. Their season's record now is twenty-six victories and two defeats.

The line-ups:

COLORADO (51)				DUQUESNE (40)			
	G.	F.	P.		G.	F.	P.
Hendricks, lf.	3	0	6	Kasperik, lf.	3	0	6
Doll, rf.	6	3	15	Becker	3	2	8
Harvey, c.	4	6	14	Milkovich, rf.	0	2	2
McCloud	1	0	2	Reiber	1	0	2
Hamburg, lg.	1	2	4	Lacey, c.	2	3	7
Thurman, rg.	4	2	10	Widowitz, lg.	7	0	14
				Debnar, rg.	0	1	1
Total	19	13	51				
				Total	16	8	40

Officials—Pat Kennedy and Pete Sinnott. Time of halves—20 minutes.

OKLA. A. & M. (23)				DE PAUL (22)			
	G.	F.	P.		G.	F.	P.
Johnson, lf.	0	0	0	Possner, lf.	2	1	5
Smelser	1	0	2	Norris, rf.	0	1	1
Eggleston, rf.	3	0	6	Weisler	0	0	0
Slade	2	0	4	Gainer, c.	1	1	3
Schwertfeger,c.	0	0	0	Wozny	1	1	3
Frances	0	0	0	Szukala, lg.	3	1	7
Doyle, lg.	1	0	2	Sachs, lg.	1	0	2
Hopkins	0	0	0	Skrodzki	0	1	1
Renick, rg.	1	1	3				
Total	11	1	23	Total	8	6	22

Officials—John Norton and Joe Byrnes.
March 16, 1940

N. C. A. A. LAURELS GO TO INDIANA'S QUINTET

Hoosiers Rout Kansas, 60 to 42, for Title—McCreary Star

KANSAS CITY, March 30 (AP)— Jay McCreary poured in 12 points tonight as Indiana University defeated the University of Kansas, 60 to 42, for the basketball title of the National Collegiate Athletic Association.

McCreary did not start for the Hoosiers but once he got onto the floor he made Coach Branch McCracken realize the oversight. He registered five times from the field in the final 20 minutes.

The Hoosiers, only second in the Big Ten Conference but winners of the recent Eastern N. C. A. A. play-offs, replace the University of Oregon at the top of the collegiate cage heap. Kansas, representing the area west of the Mississippi, shared the Big Six Conference championship with Missouri and Oklahoma.

It took Indiana eight minutes to get its first goal, but it learned the trick well and after that there was no stopping the victors. By intermission time they were out in front, 32 to 19.

After the rest and with victory apparent they turned loose a spectacular passing attack which hypnotized the 10,000 fans and almost lulled the Kansas athletes to sleep.

The line-up:

INDIANA (60)				KANSAS (42)			
	G.	F.	P.		G.	F.	P.
Schaefer, f.	4	1	9	Ebling, f.	1	2	4
McCreary	6	0	12	Hunter	0	1	1
Armstrong	4	2	10	Engleman	5	2	12
Gridley	0	0	0	Hogben	2	0	4
Bill Menke, c.	2	1	5	Allen, c.	5	3	13
Bob Menke	0	0	0	Kline, c.	0	0	0
Huffman, g.	2	5	12	Miller, g.	0	2	2
Zimmer	2	1	5	Voran	0	1	1
Dro	3	1	7	Harp	2	1	5
Dorsey	0	0	0	Sands	0	0	0
Francis	0	0	0	Johnson	0	0	0
Total	26	8	60	Total	15	12	42

Officials—Ted O'Sullivan and Gill McDonald, Missouri.
March 31, 1940

QUINTET RAN 24.01 MILES

Middlebury Pedometer Check-Up in Recent Game Revealed

How many miles does a very active basketball player cover during a game? On the assumption that somebody wants to know, Ben Beck, coach of the Middlebury College quintet, has supplied the answer by attaching pedometers to his players.

Beck's figures, released yesterday, reveal that his entire squad covered a distance of 24.01 miles during a recent game with Vermont, the guards topping all others with a total of 5.32 miles for four men who shared those positions.

The player who covered the most ground was Fred Lapham, right forward, who raced up and down the court for 5.31 miles, 2.30 in the first half and 3.01 in the second half.

Tom Neidhart, left forward, covered 5.14 miles, 2.74 in the first half and 2.40 in the second, and Bob Adsit, center, traversed 4.25 miles, 2.02 in the first half and 2.23 in the second.

As for the guards, Will Ouimette, left guard, who was replaced by Earl Bishop, led in mileage for his position with 1.98 in the first half and 1.76 in the second.

Beck's squad covered 11.97 miles in the first half and 12.04 miles in the second.

January 24, 1941

L. I. U. Halts Ohio U. Five in Garden Final Before 18,377

BLACKBIRDS RALLY FOR 56-42 TRIUMPH

Behind at Half, 25-21, L. I. U. Routs Ohio to Win National Invitation Basketball

19 POINTS FOR BAUMHOLTZ

By ARTHUR DALEY

A fierce second-half drive lifted Long Island University to a victory over Ohio University in the final of the national invitation basketball tournament at Madison Square Garden last night before a gathering of 18,377, the third successive record crowd of a dramatic tourney.

The Blackbirds rallied with a ruthless spurt that bowled over the brilliant Buckeye Bobcats in a spectacular game, 56 to 42. The spectators enjoyed it to the full as Ohio scored with unerring accuracy in the first half, only to fall before the automatic precision of the Busy Bees in that final session.

The crowd topped Saturday's record by twenty persons to bring the total for the four nights to an astounding 70,826. The fans certainly received their money's worth, even in the preliminary third-place play-off, in which City College beat Seton Hall, 42 to 27.

Ohio was the "people's choice" from the opening whistle. From the noise made at every Bobcat point, it almost seemed as if the Midwesterners were the home team and Long Island an outlander.

Five Shots in Row Succeed

The lads from Little Athens, Ohio, missed their first ten shots and then made the next five in a row, a furious scoring streak that might have broken the game wide open had they been facing any quintet except Long Island. But these Blackbirds did not even know the word quit.

They pecked away cautiously after they had been held scoreless from the floor for ten minutes, an incredible thing for a team with the scoring skill of the Blackbirds, but they pulled up slowly until they were behind by only 25 to 21 at the half. It was nip and tuck for a stretch then until Long Island took the lead at 32-30. The Busy Bees never were headed again, as their margin widened right down to the end.

The man who kept Ohio in the battle was a fleet little blond wonder-worker, Frank Baumholtz. He scored 19 points with one amazing shot after another, and it was easy to guess who would be the choice of a committee of coaches in the selection of the outstanding player of the tournament.

Yet the crowd was not too certain.

As Neil Cohalan of Manhattan walked to the center of the court to make the presentation, the spectators began to chant "Baumholtz," and Baumholtz it was. He left behind him new records for total points and total fouls. The presentation of the team prize was made by Professor Walter Williamson of City College.

Baumholtz Starts Fast

Baumholtz had 15 points in the first half, sufficient to lift Ohio into the thick of the fight. But he did not have so much luck in the second session and his team did not give him the help it had in the earlier stages.

This game was beautifully played all the way, clean and comparatively free of fouls. Furthermore it was well officiated and the score was a pretty good indication of the relative strength of the two teams.

Long Island was not hitting the net in the first half, but it was right on top of it in the second. Butch Schwartz was particularly deadly and his 19 points matched the

TRIUMPHANT L. I. U. SQUAD AFTER GAME IN THE GARDEN

Coach Clair Bee and Si Lobello holding trophy following the Blackbirds' victory over Ohio

Times Wide World

L. I. U. (56)				OHIO U. (42)			
	G.	F.	P.		G.	F.	P.
Lobello, lf......	5	1	11	Baumholtz, lf..	8	3	19
Cohen, rf.....	1	1	3	Snyder, rf.....	2	0	4
Schneider	0	1	1	Deinzer	0	0	0
Beenders, c....	2	4	8	Blickensderfer	0	0	0
Holub	1	0	2	Lalich, c.....	1	2	4
Shechtman, lg.5	5	2	12	Miller	1	0	2
Schwartz, rg..	7	5	19	McSherry, lg..2	2	2	6
				Wren	0	0	0
Total.....	21	14	56	Ott, rg......	2	3	7
				Total......	16	10	42

Officials—Pat Kennedy and Pete Sinnott.
Time of halves—20 minutes.

March 25, 1941

WISCONSIN QUINTET WINS N.C.A.A. TITLE

Beats Washington State by 39-34 Despite 21 Points for Gebert of Cougars

KANSAS CITY, March 29 (Æ)— Wisconsin pulled the Washington State defense out tonight, then sneaked behind it for a 39-to-34 victory to keep the National Collegiate A. A. basketball title in the Big Ten Conference.

The Badgers stopped all the Far Westerners except Kirk Gebert, junior guard, who scored 21 points in the vain effort to bring to the Pacific Coast the crown won last year by Indiana University.

Wisconsin, with little Johnny Kotz and Gene Englund snaring the rebounds off both boards, built a 21-to-17 advantage at the half.

So effective was the Big Ten team's defense that the Cougars were held without a single point for nine minutes in the first half and struck another scoring drought of more than five minutes in the period after the rest.

March 30, 1941

Baumholtz total. He and Ossie Schechtman, the latter the runner-up for the outstanding player trophy, were the stars of a brilliant team.

Hank Beenders played well underneath the basket and the entire team did just what it was supposed to do. The Blackbirds moved the ball in superb fashion, cut skillfully against the strong Ohio defense and handled themselves like the great team they are.

The third-place play-off was a tense struggle in its early stages, but Seton Hall could not withstand the terrific City College pressure and collapsed completely. Both teams finished with second and third stringers on the floor, a sour

ending for a game that had held such rich promise.

The Pirates presented a pretty smooth front for a while, holding City without a field goal for five minutes, but then went five minutes itself before they could count again. After that the teams were tied at 18-all and rushed down to the intermission with the Beavers in front, 22 to 19.

The sophomore redheads, Red Holzman and Red Phillips, were the Beaver scoring aces with 11 points apiece. Phillips played his best game in a month, while Holzman, still on the rough side but bearing a charmed life in avoiding personal fouls, was a marvel in directing play.

Bob Davies made 11 Seton Hall points off the Holzman guarding. No mean feat in itself.

The line-ups:

C. C. N. Y. (42)				SETON HALL (27)			
	G.	F.	P.		G.	F.	P.
Holzman, lf...5	5	1	11	Davies, lf.....	4	3	11
Judenfriend ...0	0	0	0	Behan	0	0	0
Edwin	0	0	0	Poettler	0	0	0
Phillips, rf...4	4	3	11	Fisher, rf.....	1	0	2
Deitchman ...0	0	0	0	Delaney	1	1	3
Caprero	0	0	0	King	0	0	0
Gerson, c.....	4	0	8	K. Pine, c....	0	2	2
Lozman	0	1	1	Negratta	0	0	0
Peck	0	0	0	Michaels	0	0	0
Winograd, lg.2	1	5		Holm, lg.....	1	1	3
Monitto	0	0	0	Ryan	2	0	4
Scheinkman ..0	0	0	0	R. Pine	0	3	3
Hertzberg, rg..1	0	2		Rutheno'g, rg.0	2	2	
Goldstein 1	2	4		Studwell	0	0	0
Miller	0	0		Total......	9	9	27
Total......17		8	42				

Officials—Chuck Solodare and Sam Schoenfeld. Time of halves—20 minutes.

West Virginia Halts Western Kentucky in National Invitation Basketball Final

MOUNTAINEERS WIN AT GARDEN, 47 TO 45

West Virginia Rallies to Top Western Kentucky in Final Minute Before 18,251

BARIC SCORES 17 POINTS

By ARTHUR DALEY

Roger Hicks, a slim little youngster with tousled blond hair, stepped to the foul line with the

score tied and twenty seconds left in the national invitation basketball final at Madison Square Garden last night and, as the tumultuous cheers of the season's record crowd of 18,251 rang in his ears, sank the shot that won the tournament for West Virginia.

A split second before the horn sounded the tourney's end, Scotty Hamilton was fouled. He dropped in an anti-climactic extra point for a smashing 47-to-45 victory over Western Kentucky State.

Thus was the last crushing blow delivered to the selection committee that had seeded the eight combatants. For it was West Virginia, the last-ranking quintet, that came through to a triumph over the seventh-seeded contestant in the final.

It was a rousing finish to a sensational tournament. That Creigh-

ton upset higher-ranked Toledo, 48 to 46, in the third-place play-off was a perfect touch to the crazy-quilt pattern this affair followed right from the start.

Even West Virginia's victories over top-seeded Long Island University and Toledo in previous games could not match the smooth performance the Mountaineers gave against the equally smooth Bluegrass entrants.

A less determined team might have folded before the amazing shot-making of Western Kentucky in the first half. The Hilltoppers sank fourteen of their thirty-one pitches, one of the most accurate exhibitions ever given in the midtown arena, but even so Coach Dyke Raese's Mountaineers took the lead once before they left the

floor at the intermission trailing by 32 to 24.

It was a different story in the second half. The Hilltoppers lost the range and missed eight shots before they made one after five full minutes. Before that toss swished through the net, West Virginia had boxted into a 33-32 lead. They regained it at 35-34 and were overhauled at 37-37. Then it was ding-dong right down to the wire.

Western Kentucky lost some of that smoothness when the pressure was on, got it back and lost it again. Throughout, however, gold-jerseyed West Virginia was as steady as the Blue Ridge Mountains.

They took care of the rebounds, snatching them away from the big Hilltoppers, and Rudy Baric, a tremendous man under the basket throughout the tournament, was rewarded by being named the most valuable player. A committee of coaches selected him.

Hamilton a Fine Player

Baric was ably abetted by Scotty Hamilton, Dick Kesling, Lou Kalmar and Hicks, all eminently sound players who could shoot, pass and dribble and do all well. Baric was the high gun with 17 points, while Kesling had 14.

The line-ups:

W. VIRGINIA (47)	G.	F.	P.	W. KENTUCKY (45)	G.	F.	P.
Hicks, lf	3	3	9	Day, lf	0	0	0
Rollins	0	0	0	Blevins	4	1	9
Hamilton, rf	2	1	5	Shelton, rf	2	1	5
Raese	0	0	0	D. Downing	0	0	0
Kesling, c	5	4	14	McKinney, c	4	1	9
Baric, lg	7	3	17	Ray	2	0	4
Kalmar, rg	1	0	2	Sydnor, rg	4	1	9
Total	18	11	47	Total	20	5	45

Officials—Pat Kennedy and John Nucatola. Time of halves—20 minutes.

March 26, 1942

Stanford Victor Over Dartmouth, 53-38, In Final of N. C. A. A. Basketball Tourney

By The Associated Press.

KANSAS CITY, March 28—Hitting their stride in the last ten minutes, the Stanford Indians slipped into a three-point-a-minute pace against Dartmouth tonight to transform a tight game into a 53-38 rout and win the N. C. A. A. basketball championship before 6,000 spectators.

Inaccurate passing nearly cost the big Californians the game, but they pulled themselves together just in time to dissolve Dartmouth leads and finally wound up in a flurry of field goals.

Jim Pollard, the sensational sophomore, did not play for Stanford because of a sinus infection which put him in bed yesterday with a high temperature. He was on the sidelines tonight without a fever, but Coach Everett Dean preferred to keep him out of action.

The Pacific Coast team started as if it sorely missed Pollard and trailed by six points at one time in the first half as Dartmouth poured through spectacular one-handed shots. But sophomore Howard Dallmar came to the rescue with 11 points to tie the count before the half-time gun. Then Jack Dana took a long pass and plunked the strings to give Stanford a 24-22 lead.

In the first five minutes of the final period, Dartmouth had knotted the score twice, then pulled ahead, 27—26, on George Munroe's foul-line shot. It was the last point the Hanover Indians got for five minutes.

During that time, Dallmar, voted the game's most valuable player, poked in a one-hander and fast Fred Linari dribbled furiously down the floor to add another basket. That gave Stanford a three-point advantage which rapidly mounted.

In 90 seconds, Dalimar, Dana, Ed Voss and Bill Cowden burned the nets for seven points as Stanford went into a 37-29 lead and Dartmouth collapsed.

In the closing ten-minute surge

Voss, Dana and Linari collaborated for 15 points. The nearest Dartmouth came to closing the gap was by nine points as Stubby Pearson, Munroe and Big Jim Olsen shoved in far-spaced baskets.

Points shuttled back and forth at the rate of four a minute in the free-scoring first half. Midway in the period, Munroe and Myers gave Dartmouth a 12-6 margin with a remarkable demonstration of one-handed shooting from the corners.

Leading scorers for Stanford were Dallmar with 15 points, Dana with 14 and Voss with 13. Myers and Olsen each contributed eight for the losers and fast-breaking Munroe came through with 12.

The silky smoothness of the teams was shown in the first half—no foul was called for eight minutes as they felt each other out like a couple of boxers.

The line-up:

STANFORD (53)	G.	F.	P.	DARTMOUTH (38)	G.	F.	P.
Dana, lf	7	0	14	Meyers, lf	4	1	8
Fikelman	0	0	0	Parmer	1	0	2
Burness	0	0	0	Munroe, rf	5	1	12
Linari, rf	3	0	6	Shaw	0	0	0
Voss, c	6	1	13	Pogue	0	0	0
Madden	0	0	0	Olsen, c	4	0	8
Cowden, lg	2	3	5	Pearson, lg	2	3	6
McCaffrey	0	0	0	McKernan	0	0	0
Dallmar, rg	6	0	15	Skaug, rg	1	2	2
Oliver	0	0	0	Briggs	0	0	0
Total	24	5	53	Total	17	7	38

Officials—Curtis, Fort Worth, and Adams, Columbus, Ind.

March 29, 1942

Wyoming Downs Georgetown to Capture N. C. A. A. Basketball Title

COWBOYS WIN, 46-34, IN EAST-WEST FINAL

Wyoming's Late Surge Against Georgetown Quintet Decides N. C. A. A. Title at Garden

SAILORS MAKES 16 POINTS

By LOUIS EFFRAT

Crushing the opposition with a spectacular offensive in the final two minutes, the University of Wyoming captured the National Collegiate A. A. basketball championship by downing Georgetown before 13,206 spectators at Madison Square Garden last night. The final score was 46—34, although it had been tied at 31-all four and a half minutes before the end.

Seldom has there been so devastating a finish to a basketball contest as the Cowboys staged. They got 9 points in a row in those last two minutes and the weary Hoyas, crumbling after a magnificent

stand, were unable to stem the attack. The better team won, but the margin of victory does not tell the true tale of this spirited playoff between the Eastern and Western division champions.

With a mere six minutes to play, Georgetown, alert to seize every opening, held a 31-26 edge. Then the Cowboys found the range with their eye-opening one-hand shots and soon brought about the tenth deadlock of the contest.

Komenich Breaks Tie

Milo Komenich, powerfully proportioned Cowboy center, sank a foul to snap the tie. Then, in quick order, Substitute Jim Collins batted in two straight rebounds, Komenich added a foul and Wyoming soared to a 37-31 lead.

But the Hoyas would not give up. Bill Feeney converted a pass from the brilliant Danny Kraus and Lloyd Potolicchio dropped in a foul. Now two minutes remained and the difference was only three points.

It was then that the Cowboys, with the dynamic Ken Sailors sparking them, launched their 9-point scoring spree to clinch the title, as well as a shot in tomorrow night's Red Cross benefit classic at St. John's, the national invitation tournament survivor.

Sailors was the key man. His

ability to dribble through and around any type of defense was uncanny, just as was his electrifying one-handed shot.

The little fellow among so many huge athletes caged 16 points to pace the scorers, but even if he hadn't tallied a point he would have been worth his weight in ration coupons for his all-around value to his team.

The selection committee recognized Sailors, too. Immediately after the buzzer ended activities, it was announced that Sailors had been voted the game's outstanding player.

Height Proves Big Factor

Wyoming had a tremendous height advantage. Whereas the Hoyas could depend only on John Mahnken, so far as size was concerned, the Western champions had Komenich, Jim Weir and Floyd Volker to hog the rebounds.

Another important factor was that Kraus was charged with three fouls early and had to be overcareful. The Georgetown guard was relieved two minutes before the opening half ended with Wyoming ahead, 18—16, and remained out until nine minutes of the game remained.

Both teams stressed possession, the Hoyas making doubly certain to retain the ball as long as possible. This strategy held up for the longest while.

However, Komenich hit his

stride and with Sailors just about wrecking the Hoyas with his dribbling and shooting Georgetown's fate was sealed. That this did not happen until the closing minutes was, indeed, a tribute to Elmer Ripley's aggregation.

The line-ups:

WYOMING (46)	G.	F.	P.	GEORGETOWN (34)	G.	F.	P.
Sailors, lf	6	4	16	Reilly, lf	1	0	2
Collins	4	0	8	Potolicchio	1	2	4
Weir, rf	2	1	5	Gabbianelli, rf	1	2	4
Waite	0	0	0	Hyde	0	0	0
Komenich, c	4	1	9	Mahnken, c	2	2	6
Volker, lg	2	1	5	Hassett, lg	3	0	6
Roney, rg	0	0	0	Finnerty	0	0	0
Reese	1	0	2	Kraus, rg	2	0	4
		—	—	Feeney	4	0	8
Total	19	8	46	Duffey	0	0	0
				Total	14	6	34

Officials—Pat Kennedy and Matty Begovich.

March 31, 1943

18,374 See St. John's Win Invitation Basketball Final Second Year in Row

REDMEN VANQUISH DE PAUL, 47 TO 39

St. John's Conquers Favored Five Before the Season's Record Garden Crowd

By LOUIS EFFRAT

A St. John's aggregation that never for an instant doubted itself or its right to its rule in the national invitation college basketball tournament conquered the favored Blue Demons of De Paul, 47—39, in the final at Madison Square Garden last night.

And every cheer, every bit of praise and admiration that the season's record crowd of 18,374 sent the way of Coach Joe Lapchick and his gallant lads was merited, to say the least.

For less than two weeks ago the war-riddled Brooklyn squad was virtually ignored, its chances to survive the first round considered negligible.

A Gallant Performance

However, none can deny that the defending Redmen, performing gallantly against all odds and types of opposition, proved themselves real champions as in succession they overcame Bowling Green, Kentucky and last night De Paul, winding up in the proverbial blaze of glory, completely forgetting the precedent that no team ever had won the national invitation, symbolic of the nation's crown, two years in a row in the history of the post-season competition.

Few, if any, were the mistakes that could be charged to St. John's in this struggle. The victors kept pace with the speedy, fast-breaking Blue Demons, did a wonderful task in bottling up George Mikan, Dick Triptow and Jack Dean, as dangerous a trio as every stepped on a hardwood floor.

Bill Kotsores, voted the most valuable man in the tourney—an excellent choice—Hy Gotkin, Wade Duym, Ray Wertis and Ivy Summer all carried out their assignments and the outcome proved it.

St. John's went to town. De Paul went to pieces. In a flash, this sums up last night's final. The Blue Demons, trailing by 26 to 24 at the half, following a closing spurt, were definitely in this exciting encounter until Mikan, their tallest operator, was banished after having committed his fourth personal foul.

Mikan Lost to De Paul

Right then and there the handwriting was on the wall, because without Mikan, who scored 13 points and was high man for the

ST. JOHN'S DEFENSE BALKS A DE PAUL SCORING THRUST

Dick Triptow of the Chicagoans is attempting to pass to Gene Stump (extreme left). However, Ivy Summer (11) intercepted and recovered the ball for the Redmen. Other players are George Mikan (second from right) of De Paul and Captain Hy Gotkin (on right) of the winners. *The New York Times*

game, De Paul was stripped of its most potent weapon.

Little less than six minutes had elapsed in the half when De Paul lost Mikan, at a stage when the St. John's lead was only 35—31. A foul shot by Kotsores preceded a pivot shot two-pointer by Dean, but immediately after the Redmen put on the pressure, counted nine points in a row to gain a 45-35 advantage that cracked the ball game wide open and determined the issue.

It wasn't so much that St. John's did anything vastly different upon Mikan's departure. The Redmen merely continued to play their own brilliant game, stepping up only their fast breaks. Rather, it was the De Paul team that fell apart. Mikan's replacement, Jack Phelan, lasted less than seven minutes before going out via personals and, generally, things went from bad

to worse for the well-beaten losers.

Last night's crowd, which might have been an all-time record if the sale of standing room had not been stopped early in the evening, boosted the tournament total to 71,197, a new mark for the three-night carnival.

The line-ups:

ST. JOHN'S (47)				DE PAUL (39)			
	G.	F.	P.		G.	F.	P.
Kotsores, lf	3	4	10	Triptow, lf	4	2	10
Larkin	0	0	0	Dean, rf	4	0	8
Wertis, rf	6	0	12	Condon	0	0	0
Summer, c	4	1	9	Allen	1	0	2
Webr	1	1	3	Mikan, c	4	5	13
Gotkin, lg	2	0	4	Phelan	0	0	0
Duym, rg	3	3	9	Stump, lg	1	0	2
	—	—	—	Riordan	0	0	0
Total	19	9	47	Cumerford	1	0	2
				Kachan, rg	1	0	2
				Di Benedetto	0	0	0
					—	—	—
				Total	16	7	39

Officials—Pat Kennedy and Joe Burns.

March 27, 1944

Utah Upsets Dartmouth in Extra Period to Take N. C. A. A. Basketball Title

WILKINSON'S GOAL TOPS INDIANS, 42-40

Utah Set Shot With 3 Seconds Left in Overtime Defeats Dartmouth at Garden

14,990 FANS SEE THRILLER

Desperate McGuire Toss Ties Regulation Score at 36-36 —Mitchel Field Victor

By LOUIS EFFRAT

Three seconds before time ran out in the second half, Dick McGuire's desperate angle set shot hit the target and lifted Dartmouth into a 36-36 tie with Utah in the East-West play-off for the National Collegiate A. A. basketball championship at Madison Square Garden last night.

Then followed a tense five-minute overtime period that thrilled a crowd of 14,990 and just when it seemed another extra session would be required to decide this struggle Herb Wilkinson did it for Utah.

Wilkinson followed the precedent set by McGuire, because with three seconds left in overtime the sandy-haired, baby-faced Ute let go with a set effort that paid off. It wasn't a perfect shot. The ball hung for a fraction of a second on the back of the rim and then fell through the hoop for a 42-40 upset triumph for the Western regional champions.

Floor work, ball-handling and finesse were lacking on both sides and both were guilty of numerous miscues. The shooting was faulty, too, but the game did have more than its share of excitement and the tournament could not have had any better conclusion.

Red Cross Game Tomorrow

With Dartmouth not available for tomorrow night's Red Cross game because of a Navy ruling against extended leaves for the Indians' trainees, Utah was set to meet St. John's, national invitation ruler, regardless of last night's outcome. Now, the Utes will go into the benefit contest as champions and it should be a fine game.

At no stage did either team gain a lead of more than four points. For the greater part Utah was on top. The youthful Utes, who had been eliminated in the first round of the national invitation and who had replaced Arkansas in the

UTAH FORWARD TAKING REBOUND IN TITLE GAME AT GARDEN

Smuin has recovered the ball following an unsuccessful Dartmouth attempt for a field goal. Other players are Brindley (3) and Gale (4) of the losers, and Ferrin (22) and Sheffield (29) of the champions.
The New York Times

Western N. C. A. A. Regionals to win that title, took advantage of many Dartmouth lapses and just lasted to scalp the Hanover Indians.

Utah was sparked by Arnold Ferrin, who threw in 22 points. Little Walter Misaka's speed bothered the Indians and Bob Lewis also did his share for the Utes, but for all their good work the triumph almost eluded them.

Certainly, after McGuire had made good on a three-man break to force overtime—it was 18—17 in Dartmouth's favor at the half—the outlook was none too bright for Utah. Experience was on the side of the Big Green and Utah did not seem in as good shape as the Hanoverians.

Walter Mercer, a Dartmouth substitute, dropped in a foul, but Ferrin sank a pair of free throws and now Utah was in the van. Aft-

er 2:22, Aud Brindley caged a foul and it was deadlocked again.

To spoil what looked like a perfect shot, Mercer fouled Ferrin at 3:32 and the Ute made both tries good, but Brindley, converting a pass from McGuire, succeeded from the pivot a few seconds later and it was 40-all, 1 minute 40 seconds from the buzzer.

Only twenty seconds remained when the Utes received the ball out-of-bounds with the score still deadlocked. Moving rapidly down the court, they sought an opening which the close-guarding Indians refused to allow. Then Wilkinson, planted several feet beyond the circle, took aim and let go. It was this heave, three seconds from the finish, that won the game.

Four times during the final two minutes of regulation play Utah waived foul shots. This strategy was questionable, especially since

the Utes held a 4-point lead when three of these penalties were called.

Dartmouth performed in disappointing fashion. The Indians failed to match the drive and alertness of Utah and bogged down underneath the baskets. Brindley, who had made 28 points against Ohio State in the Eastern final on Saturday night, was limited to 11.

The line-ups:

UTAH (42)	G.	F.	P.	DARTMOUTH (40)	G.	F.	P.
Ferrin, lf	8	6	22	Brindley, lf	5	1	11
Smuin, rf	0	0	0	Leggat, rf	4	0	8
Sheffield, c	1	0	2	Nordstrom	0	0	0
Misaka	2	0	4	Gale, c	5	0	10
Wilkinson, lg	3	1	7	Mercer	0	1	1
Lewis, rg	2	3	7	McGuire, lg	3	0	6
				Murphy	0	0	0
Total	16	10	42	Vancisin, rg	2	0	4
				Goering	0	0	0
				Total	19	2	40

Officials—Osborne and Menton.

New Basketball Rule Penalizes 'Goalie'; Limit of Five Personal Fouls Is Voted

Four major rule changes were enacted by the National Basketball Committee of the United States and Canada, better known as the joint rules committee, yesterday at the Hotel Biltmore.

On the recommendation of the coaches the joint rules committee voted that a defensive player would be forbidden to touch the ball on its downward flight on a try for a field goal. When the shot is obviously short the rule will not apply.

This rule, together with the current restriction which stops a defender from touching the ball within the circumference of the rim, will eliminate "goal-tending" by tall players, the committee is hopeful. Penalty for infraction is award of a field goal to the shot-maker.

Next in importance was the increase from four to five personal fouls per game. It was pointed out that since the elimination of the center jump, approximately eight minutes of playing time had been added to a game, but no provisions had been made for fouling.

Another rule revision will permit unlimited substitution next winter. This season players were disqualified after having been in the game three times. This move will prevent happenings like that in the Oklahoma Aggies-De Paul game in the Madison Square Garden tourney, when the Aggies finished with four men, because of their nine-man squad two were out on personal fouls, one with an injury and two had enjoyed the limited entries.

The fourth change will permit referees to call time for an injured player, regardless of which team is in possession of the ball. In the past the official could blow his whistle for such a cause only when the stricken player's team was in possession.

March 29, 1944

2 Collegians Bribed by Gamblers to Throw Tourney Basketball Games, Allen Charges

LAWRENCE, Kan., Oct. 20 (AP) —Professional gamblers already have caused two boys to throw basketball games in Eastern intercollegiate tournaments, Dr. Forrest C. Allen, Kansas basketball coach, charged today in predicting the betting fraternity would create a "scandal that will stink to high heaven" unless college presidents intercede to save the game.

"There hasn't been enough publicity given known cases where bribes were taken," Allen asserted.

He said Vadal Peterson, Utah coach, had knocked down a gambler who went to his room and asked, "How much would it cost to have Utah lose to Dartmouth?" in the National Collegiate A. A. final in New York's Madison Square Garden, last spring. "What Peterson told the gambler is unprintable but that doesn't mean that they won't eventually get to boys on the teams," Allen said.

A spectator ran out on the floor and kissed a Utah player who had made a last-minute goal against Kentucky in the National Invitation tournament last year because the goal had saved the man $15,000, the contentious doctor related. "The betting boys had laid 10 points on Kentucky and that last-minute score gave the Kentuckians only an 8-point margin," Allen explained.

"More money is bet on collegiate football and basketball than on horse racing," the outspoken basketball tutor declared, "but all the trouble it causes could be eliminated if college presidents would get together and appoint an absolute czar over all college sports. If they don't some of these college boys who have never seen big money are going to sell out and it will cause a scandal that will stink to high heaven. It could ruin intercollegiate sports.

"There was only one reason why no eyebrows were raised over the Browns' four straight victories over the Yanks at the end of the American League baseball season," Allen concluded. "The reason was Judge Landis. We need the same kind of czar in intercollegiate sports. If the college presidents don't provide one, it will be just too bad."

October 21, 1944

3 Named as Gambling Overlords At Sports Events by Valentine

Police Commissioner Lewis J. Valentine told Kings County Judge Samuel S. Leibowitz in Brooklyn yesterday that even if college basketball games went back to their campus gymnasiums gambling could not be stopped. The jurist, sitting as a committing magistrate, was told that such a move, however, might aid in the drive to end corruption.

Mr. Valentine named Frank Costello, alleged slot-machine czar; Frank Erickson, race-track gambler, and Joe Adonis, alleged Brooklyn underground boss, as those who controlled big-time gambling in New York City. He characterized them as "those with the big money."

It was the third of a series of hearings before Judge Leibowitz as a result of the confession of five Brooklyn College basketball players that they had taken money to "throw" a game scheduled with Akron University in Boston. The game was called off.

Questioning by Assistant District Attorney Charles N. Cohen brought out that Mr. Valentine had conferred with Ned Irish, acting president of the Madison Square Garden Corporation, in the hope the gambling evil could be curbed, especially at intercollegiate basketball games. The Commissioner said Mr. Irish had been cooperative.

Mr. Valentine made public the names of about fifty individuals who were on the Garden "blacklist." Among them was Martin Krompier, who was alleged to have been a member of the Arthur (Dutch Schultz) Flegenheimer gang.

Before the hearing was adjourned until next Tuesday, two other police officials told of the vigilance maintained at Madison Square Garden to clean up the gambling situation. Even a six-point program was drawn up to bar all known gamblers from the Garden.

"Commissioner, do you feel that amateur basketball would be safer if confined to the gymnasiums of the colleges?", Mr. Cohen asked.

"Unquestionably," the Commissioner answered. "If confined to the campus, it would reduce and maybe entirely do away with any possible corruption, but it would not prevent gambling. At present there are two sheets published, one in Philadelphia and one in Indianapolis, that give the names of the players of all the colleges and their past scores. That information is used by gamblers."

"If it is established that professional gambling is brazen at Madison Square Garden with no attempt to cover up, and the gamblers operate in the aisles, in the lobby and in certain sections of the Garden, would you not say then that there is something 'rotten in Denmark'?" Judge Leibowitz inquired.

"If that is so, yes," Mr. Valentine said. "But I can't assume that is true. We have been making arrests of these damnable pests. They operate in the arcade and even in the men's room, but it is difficult to get legal evidence. No money passes. The pay-off comes later on."

"Supposing the condition does exist, where would you look for the cause of this condition?" Judge Leibowitz asked.

"It would be a serious reflection on the Police Department and it would show something was wrong on the part of the management of Madison Square Garden," the Commissioner said. "I do not mean Mr. Irish. It is a personal loss to him to have these gamblers in or around the Garden, just as it is a very important matter to me in official capacity as Police Commissioner."

Mr. Valentine explained that big-time gamblers do not operate in the Garden. He said the Garden gamblers were only agents for the higher-ups.

"I believe that Frank Erickson controls a large part of the gambling in New York City," he said. "Of course, he doesn't work at it. The gambling is also controlled by Joe Adonis and Frank Costello. They are big shots who have the money. If games were fixed, it is not the runner who does the fixing but the one with the financial interest. The man behind the fix would be the man with the big money."

"What in your opinion, Commissioner, ought to be done to prevent and to punish those who tamper with college boys?" Judge Leibowitz asked.

"Well, I might say here, I was shocked to hear about the situation among certain basketball players at Brooklyn College," the Commissioner answered. "I felt and do feel very sorry for the boys. I have given much thought to the problem. We can't condemn the game. It is a fine sport and excellent recreation. We should arrest everyone who seeks to corrupt these boys. We should have the cooperation of the magistrates in our efforts against the gamblers. Imposing fines or short sentences does no good. It is hard to get evidence on the really guilty ones.

Deputy Chief Inspector John J. O'Sullivan of the Third District Uniformed Force told of a conference with Mr. Irish. Other police officials were present. It was agreed, he said, that all known gamblers would be barred from the Garden and a six-point program was drawn up.

The next witness, Lieut. Thomas Corcoran, told of having eighteen plainclothes men assigned under him for events at the Garden. He said the Garden authorities had ejected nine undesirable patrons since last November.

For the next hearing, Judge Leibowitz ordered Lieutenant Corcoran to bring in every plainclothes man assigned to the Garden since last November.

February 24, 1945

N. Y. U. RALLY BEATS OHIO STATE QUINTET IN OVERTIME, 70-65

10 Points in Last 2 Minutes of Final Half Tie N. C. A. A. Eastern Basketball Final

RISEN WASTES 26 TALLIES

Buckeyes Fade When He Goes Out on Personals—Kentucky Conquers Tufts, 66-56

By LOUIS EFFRAT

Ten points behind Ohio State, two minutes before time ran out in the second half, its hopes low, but with spirit flaring, the New York University basketball team defied every rule of logic that told the Violets they couldn't do it and proceeded to achieve what appeared far beyond their reach.

For, in the presence of a gasping gathering of 18,161 at Madison Square Garden last night, Howard Cann's lads struggled desperately until they gained a 62-62 tie in the closing seconds and then spurted away from the Buckeyes in the five-minute overtime period to record a 70-65 victory, the details of which will be told and retold for a long while.

To capture this Eastern regional National Collegiate Athletic Association final and thus earn a berth in Tuesday night's East-West engagement against Oklahoma A. and M., the Violets were, indeed, lucky. Not in their shots or floor work, but in that Ohio State, definitely a smart, alert aggregation, suddenly went into a mental lapse that cost heavily.

Risen Out on Personals

With Arnold Risen, their ace, out of the game on personal fouls, the Buckeyes still had a 4-point spread, 62—58, 1 minute 14 seconds from home. At that instant a foul was awarded to them, but instead of doing the rational thing—taking possession out of bounds—the Ohioans elected to try for the point. They missed the free throw, but N. Y. U. did not capitalize—not right then.

Exactly 1 minute 1 second remained when Ohio State received another foul. One would think that the Buckeyes had learned a lesson, but they had not. Again they sought a 1-pointer and again they failed.

This time N. Y. U. captured the ball and a few second later Adolph Schayes rapped in a rebound that cut the deficit to two points. Still, with the seconds ticking away, and the score favoring them by two points, the decision appeared to belong to the Buckeyes.

In any league, they say, three strikes are out, so when, with 36 seconds left, the Ohioans refused to waive a third foul—and missed—the handwriting was on the wall or, better yet, on the ball. Twenty-six seconds remained when little Don Forman poised just outside the foul circles and threw in a set shot that sent the teams into an extra session.

Realizing that Risen, their most persistent tormentor, who had scored 26 points to lead all the others, no longer was on the floor, the Violets started the overtime, brimming with confidence.

Schayes Hits Target

Moving out of the pivot, Schayes, the promising freshman, hit the target in 10 seconds with a one-hander on a pass from Forman. Before the first minute had elapsed, Rodney Caudill dribbled all the way down court and curled in the lay-up that produced the seventh tie of this exciting, rough contest. The next rally came just before the 4-minute mark, when Don Grate dropped in a foul for Ohio State.

Short-lived, indeed, was that slim advantage, because, in the next 37 seconds, the red-hot Violets counted three field goals. Al Grenert clicked with a corner toss, Forman converted Marty Goldstein's backhand pass and Schayes, taking an out-of-bounds flip from Sid Tanenbaum, hooked in a 2-pointer.

There were flashes of topnotch basketball from both sides, but the officials were kept busy throughout, calling a record high of fifty-one fouls.

Without Risen, the Buckeyes suffered. He dominated the rebounds underneath both backboards and the 26 points he tallie almost ruined the Violets. Warren Amling, too, was a standout for the losers.

Among the Violets, who trailed at the intermission, 36—34, after having a 17-10 lead, credit for this conquest was shared by all Schayes, Frank Mangiapane, who scored 17 points, Tanenbaum, Grenert and Forman matched Ohio State's bulk and drive with speed and precision and a pat on the

An N. Y. U. Player Gets Clear for a Field Goal at the Garden

Mangiapane about to shoot a two-pointer against Ohio State. Others are Huston (3), Dugger (12) and Sims (7) of the Buckeyes

back is due big Herb Walsh, whose play in spelling Schayes was by far his best of the campaign.

Kentucky, conquered by Ohio State in the semi-finals, gained third place in the competition by virtue of a 66-56 victory over Tufts, victim of N. Y. U. on Thursday night. The heavily favored Wildcats, holding a 24-23 edge at half-time, performed apparently without spirit, but still had enough power to prevail.

Throughout the first half, the Kentucky players suffered in comparison with the drive and dash of the Jumbos from Medford, Mass., who played as if the championship were at stake. Little Jim Cumiskey, formerly of Columbia, and Bob Skarda, tallying 20 points, sparked the losers. Individual high, however, was Kentucky's Wilbur Schu, who notched 21 points.

In the second period, Kentucky switched tactics, driving in more often to set up plays at close range. It was in this half that Adolph Rupp's Wildcats sewed up the decision.

The Oklahoma Aggies, N. Y. U.'s opponents for the N. C. A. A. title, beat Arkansas, 68 to 41, at Kansas City, Mo., last night in the Western Regional final.

The line-ups:

KENTUCKY (66)				TUFTS (56)			
	G.	F.	P.		G.	F.	P.
Parker, lf.	6	2	14	Moran, lf.	4	1	9
Tingle	0	0	0	Johnson	0	1	1
Schu, rf.	10	1	21	Giordano	0	0	0
Campbell, c.	3	1	7	Skarda, rf.	8	4	20
Vulich	4	5	13	Andreason	0	0	0
Parkinson, lg.	4	1	9	Burgbacher, c.	4	2	10
Stough, rg.	0	1	1	Walz	0	1	1
Sturgill	0	0	1	Matthews	0	0	0
Durham	0	0	0	Comiskey, lg.	3	2	8
				Walker	0	0	0
Total	27	12	66	Cooney, rg.	1	5	7
				Beers	0	0	0
				Dougherty	0	0	0
				Total	20	16	56

Officials—Tut Melman and Glenn Adams.

N. Y. U. (70)				OHIO STATE (65)			
	G.	F.	P.		G.	F.	P.
Grenert, lf.	2	2	6	Grate, lf.	2	2	6
Benanti	0	0	0	Sims	2	3	7
Forman, rf.	4	2	10	Dugger, rf.	1	2	4
Most	1	0	2	Caudill	3	1	7
Schayes, c.	5	4	11	Risen, c.	8	10	26
Walsh	2	2	6	Huston, c.	2	1	5
Tanenbaum, lg.	5	3	13	Amling, rg.	5	0	10
Mangiapane, rg.	7	3	17				
Goldstein	1	0	2				
Total	27	16	70	Total	23	19	65

Officials—Edward J. Boyle and James Beiersdorfer.

March 25, 1945

DE PAUL QUINTET TRIUMPHS BY 71-54

Tops Bowling Green to Take Invitation Laurels, Overcoming 11-0 Deficit

MIKAN SCORES 34 POINTS

By LOUIS EFFRAT

Breaking from the barrier with an 11-point scoring splurge, Bowling Green of Ohio appeared to have George Mikan handcuffed and De Paul stopped in the final of the eighth annual national invitation college basketball tournament at Madison Square Garden last night. But such calculations were wrong

and the final buzzer found the Blue Demons on top, 71—54, a margin that was convincing to a crowd of 18,166 persons.

For a team that had fallen behind, 11—0, De Paul remained remarkably cool. Undaunted by this sudden reversal in form, the Chicagoans never lost hope or poise. They seemed to know that it would be merely a matter of time before they would begin to click. And click they did, with Mikan sparking the attack in the fashion which has characterized the team throughout the campaign.

That it was principally Mikan's work that turned the tide was obvious. This 6 foot 9 inch bespectacled all-America player, frustrated at the outset by Don Otten's defensive tactics, lived up to his reputation in every sense.

120 Points in 3 Games

When, with one minute of the game remaining and the decision neatly clinched, Coach Ray Meyer removed Mikan, he had to his credit 34 points. This meant that the big fellow had amassed 120 in his three tournament games, a 40-point average that may never be matched.

To list the number of records smashed by Mikan and De Paul would be gilding the lily. The principal marks for Mikan were his 53 points against Rhode Island State, his aggregate of 120 against West Virginia, Rhode Island and Bowling Green; his total of 49 field goals and 22 fouls. In all, some fifteen team and individual standards were wrecked by Mikan and his team.

Of course, for his part, Mikan was named the outstanding player in the tourney, the understatement of the season.

For more than five minutes, this final belonged to Bowling Green. With Otten doing a fine job guarding Mikan and Wyndol Gray and Payak pacing the outfit, the Falcons took the advantage at the start. Exactly 5 minutes and 38 seconds passed before Mikan caged a foul for the initial De Paul point, but, at least, the Blue Demons were on their way.

Ahead at Half by 30—22

The first field goal was accounted for by Mikan, who pivoted neatly at 8:35. Immediately, the Chicagoans caught fire, pressing their rivals all over the court, setting up

their scoring plays brilliantly and generally outsmarting and outmaneuvering the opposition.

At the 15-minute mark they pulled even at 20—20 and then Mikan rapped in the rebound that sent his team ahead for the first time. At the half it was 30—22.

Bowling Green never quite caught up with the Blue Demons, although there was a time late in the second period when only 4 points separated the clubs.

Otten, for the first eight minutes, turned in a whale of a defensive job for Bowling Green. Immediately after, though, the 6-foot 11½-inch center showed definite signs of fading.

With Otten weakening, there remained little question concerning the outcome. Mikan was the head man, an inspiration to his mates and a hero to the crowd that boosted the four-night total attendance to 72,622, a tournament record.

Rhode Island Finds Range

Incredible, indeed, was the third-place play-off preliminary encounter, in which St. John's defeated Rhode Island State, 64—57. The visiting Rams, ineffectual and in-

A BATTLE OF THE GIANTS IN NATIONAL FINAL

Don Otten (white jersey), 6-foot 11½-inch Bowling Green center, and George Mikan, 6-foot 9-inch De Paul ace, leaping for the ball after a shot by one of the winners bounced off the rim of the basket.

The New York Times

ept throughout the first half, fell behind at 42—27 at the intermission. Nothing Rhode Island attempted was right as compared to the smoothness and teamwork of St. John's.

After the intermission, however, it was a different story. The Rams, with Ernie Calverley sinking 10 straight points, began to find the range and at the half-way mark in the period had completely erased that early 24-point deficit as they gained a 50-49 edge. Then the Redmen regained their poise and 8 consecutive points pulled the game out of the fire.

Calverley was high scorer, with 25 points, 4 more than Ray Wertis, who was outstanding for the victors.

The line-ups:

DE PAUL (71)	G.	F.	P.	BOWLI'G GREEN (54)	G.	F.	P.
Stump, lf	.6	3	15	Gray, lf	.4	1	9
Phelan	.0	0	0	Whitehead, rf	.7	3	17
DiBenedetto, rf	.1	2	4	Inman	.0	1	1
Comerford	.0	0	0	Otten, c	.3	1	7
G. Mikan, c	.15	4	34	Rosendale	.0	0	0
E. Mikan	.0	0	0	Knierim, lg	.1	0	2
Allen, lg	.2	1	5	Kubiak	.1	2	4
La Rochelle	.0	0	0	Piel	.1	0	2
Furman	.0	0	0	Payak, rg	.5	2	12
Kachan, rg	.6	1	13	Gantt	.0	0	0
Niemiera	.0	0	0				
Halloran	.0	0	0	Total	.22	10	54
Total	.30	11	71				

Officials—Pat Kennedy and Joe Burns.

ST. JOHN'S (64)	G.	F.	P.	R. ISLAND STATE (57)	G.	F.	P.
Kotsores, lf	.1	3	5	Santoro, lf	.4	1	9
Barreras	.1	0	2	Coy	.2	0	4
Larkin	.0	0	0	Hole, rf	.5	2	12
Hurley	.0	0	0	Calverley, c	.12	1	25
Wertis, rf	.9	3	21	Shea, lg	.2	1	5
Summer, c	.8	1	17	Nichols, rg	.2	2	6
Fressman	.0	0	0	Smith	.0	0	0
Gotkin, lg	.5	0	10				
Robinson, rg	.3	1	7	Total	.24	9	57
Total	.29	6	64				

Officials—Dave Tobey and James Osborne

March 27, 1945

OKLAHOMA AGGIES DOWN N. Y. U., 49-45

Westerners Win Play-Off for N. C. A. A. Basketball Crown Before 18,034 at Garden

KURLAND GETS 22 POINTS

7-Footer Also Defensive Star —Coast Guard Trips Valley Forge in Overtime, 60-55

By LOUIS EFFRAT

Oklahoma A. and M., its entire offense revolving around 7-foot Bob Kurland, who planted himself in the bucket and from that position controlled the ball, defeated New York University, 49—45, in the East-West final for the National Collegiate Athletic Association basketball championship at Madison Square Garden last night.

It was Kurland who made the difference and earned for his team the right to oppose De Paul's national invitation tourney victors in tomorrow night's Red Cross benefit at the Garden.

Even taller than De Paul's George Mikan and Bowling Green's Don Otten, Kurland accounted for 22 points. On the attack and on defense, the lanky lad they call Foothills was the outstanding individual on the floor.

For his efforts Kurland was voted the most valuable player in the tourney by the basketball writers. He was, too, and merited the gold medal presented to him by Tug Wilson, Big Ten athletic commissioner.

A crowd of 18,034 voiced approval and recognition of Kurland's domination of the entire scene. When he was not scoring, he was setting up the scoring plays for the other Oklahomans.

Great Duel in Prospect

Nor did Kurland confine his activities to a spot underneath one basket. With remarkable agility he sped back on defense and wrecked the home team's opportunities to capture rebounds. His prospective duel with Mikan tomorrow night had the fans talking in circles as they departed.

Oklahoma, which had gained a 44-41 decision over the Violets early in the campaign, again was smart, alert and deliberate. The Aggies waited for Kurland to assume his position and rarely wasted a pass. The Violets, on the other hand, devoted so much attention to Kurland that they neglected to switch when opposing players cut in at close range. It was this failure to pick up the man in possession that pointed to an N. Y. U. defeat, even before half-time, at which stage the Aggies held a 26-21 advantage.

Despite Kurland's domination, N. Y. U., on two occasions, forged into a moderate lead. Once it was 5 points and once 6, thanks to the offensive efforts of Don Forman and Al Grenert. However, Howard Cann's men could not hold their margins, playing as they were in spurts.

The Aggies, midway through the second period, soared to an 11-point pull. When the Western champions did fly to a 39-28 lead at the 10-minute mark, N. Y. U. looked like a badly beaten outfit, but the Violets, pressing their rivals in the backcourt, outfought them and subsequently found themselves back in the thick of some rough going.

Fouls Frequent at Close

The finishing stretch made it appear as if the officials had lost control and fouls were plentiful. Having drawn Kurland out of the pivot zone, the Violets fared better. With less than four minutes remaining, only four points separated the teams. The same was true with less than one minute left, but the Eastern titleholders could not quite close the gap entirely.

That the superior team prevailed could not be questioned. N. Y. U. flubbed too many shots at short range to help its cause.

For the losers, Grenert, with 12 points, and Forman, with 11, were high. Cecil Hankins, who counted 15 points, 10 in the second half, was runner-up to Kurland.

In the preliminary the New York District Coast Guard rallied to pull even at 50—50 in the second half and then beat Valley Forge General Hospital, 60—55, in the five-minute overtime. This was the third and rubber meeting between the teams.

Bill Davis of Valley Forge, who used to play at Notre Dame,

counted 22 points. Bobby Dorn, ex-Temple ace, paced the winning team with 19.

The line-ups:

OKLA. AGGIES (49)	G.	F.	P.	N. Y. U. (45)	G.	F.	P.
Hankins, lf	.5	3	15	Grenert, lf	.5	2	12
Parks	.0	0	0	Forman, rf	.5	1	11
Kern, rf	.1	0	3	Goldstein	.0	2	2
Wylie	.0	0	0	Schayes, c	.2	2	6
Kurland, c	.10	2	22	Walsh	.0	0	0
Williams, lg	.2	0	4	Tanenbaum, lg	.2	0	4
Parrack, rg	.2	0	4	Mangiapane, rg	.2	2	6
				Most	.1	2	4
Total	.22	5	49	Total	.17	11	45

Officials—Ab Curtis and Glenn Adams.

DISTRICT C. G. (60)	G.	F.	P.	VALLEY FORGE (55)	G.	F.	P.
Frey, lf	.5	3	13	Niemiera, lf	.5	6	16
Goebel, rf	.0	0	0	Craddock, rf	.1	0	2
Pajak	.5	2	12	Tanitsky	.1	0	2
Dorn, c	.5	9	19	Davis, c	.10	2	22
Levane, lg	.2	1	5	Graf, lg	.0	0	0
Bloom	.0	0	0	Metzen	.0	0	0
Krygier, rg	.4	3	11	Szukala, rg	.6	1	13
Gerhardt	.0	0	0	Caruso	.0	0	0
Balser	.0	0	0				
Total	.21	18	60	Total	.23	9	55

Officials—Hagan Andersen and Ed Russell.

March 28, 1945

OKLAHOMA AGGIES TOP DE PAUL, 52-44

N.C.A.A. Champions Take Red Cross Game for U. S. Title Before 18,158 at Garden

MIKAN EXIT TURNING POINT

Demons Lead, 21-14, When Ace Fouls Out in 14 Minutes— N. Y. U. Five Wins, 63-61

By LOUIS EFFRAT

To Oklahoma A. and M., a 7-point underdog, went the national basketball championship last night at Madison Square Garden, where the Aggies upset De Paul University, 52—44. The Blue Demons, who lost the services of their ace, George Mikan, less than fourteen minutes after the start, made a valiant effort, pulling up within 3 points in the closing stages, but in the end the Aggies had what they needed.

That Coach Hank Iba's boys from Stillwater would win was sensed by the crowd of 18,158 the instant Mikan committed his fifth personal foul and was ruled off the floor. At the time, De Paul held a 21-14 advantage, but the Chicagoans were to miss the 6-foot, 9-inch center, who had scored 53 points in a national invitation tourney game and had achieved a 40-point average in that competition.

Mikan's enforced idleness, without detracting from the victorious Aggies, who made the most of their opportunities, cost De Paul heavily. Without him, Oklahoma's Bob Kurland, a seven-foot sparkplug, was left to control the rebounds and seal De Paul's fate. Before the final buzzer, four of the five starters for the losers had been banished on fouls.

At the intermission in this con-

test, played for the benefit of the American Red Cross, which profited to the extent of more than $50,000—the ball was auctioned for $8,000—De Paul clung to a 26-21 edge. However, there were few who could not foresee a radical change. The Aggies were alert and very much in the ball game.

Aggies Get 9 Points in Row

Came the start of the second half and the Aggies counted 9 straight points, 7 by Cecil Hankins, the top scorer in the engagement. De Paul, floundering about the court, spent the first five minutes without a tally.

Mikan's replacements, John Phelan and Gene Larochelle, proved inadequate, certainly not of the height or caliber to cope with Kurland. This was the beginning of the end for the Blue Demons.

In victory, Kurland and Hankins were outstanding. The latter, a dribble artist with a remarkable one-handed shot from any angle, collected 20 points. Boyle Parrack and Weldon Kern also handled their assignments well for the National Collegiate Athletic Association champions, as did Blake Williams before he, too, went out on fouls.

Kurland, of course, outscored Mikan. Big George, before he departed, clicked for 9 points and was ahead of his rival center, but the latter finished with 14. What might have happened if Mikan had lasted longer is a matter of opinion, but there was little doubt among the experts that the decision would have gone the other way.

For about three minutes, late in the second period, De Paul followers nursed a hope that things would turn out all right. That was when the Blue Demons rallied to cut the deficit to 47—44 less than four minutes before time ran out.

Kurland Sets Up Basket

With 2 minutes 20 seconds remaining, though, the big break of the game saw Kurland take a rebound underneath the De Paul backboard and rifle a long lead pass to Kern, who missed. However, Hankins retrieved the rebound and, before a De Paul man could molest him, sent the ball into the net for the back-breaking field goal.

After Mikan's dismissal, De Paul's attack sputtered and did not approach the fast break which had carried the Blue Demons to the top of the national invitation tourney. The Aggies, more deliberate and artful, clicked when they needed to and that told the story.

In the consolation game between beaten finalists in the two tourneys, New York University's N. C. A. A. Eastern regional champions eked out a 63-61 victory over Bowling Green of Ohio, but this does not begin to tell the tale of one of the wildest finishes in Garden history.

Seven times in the last 3 minutes the lead changed hands until Sid Tanenbaum clinched the verdict for the Violets. Of the 25 points Tanenbaum netted, the last three were most important.

After N. Y. U. had blown a 47-27 lead and the crowd had become hysterical because of the amazing closing spurt by the Falcons, the clock showed 48 seconds to play and Bowling Green on top, 61—60. However, Tanenbaum scored with his own rebound for the Violets. Then, with 27 seconds remaining, the same player caged a foul, waived a second penalty shot in order to take the ball out of bounds and that was that.

The line-ups:

OKLA. A & M (52)	G.	F.	P.	DE PAUL (44)	G.	F.	P.
Hankins, lf	8	4	20	Stump, lf	5	2	12
Kern, rf	0	5	5	Comerford	0	0	0
Kurland, c	4	6	14	DiBendetto, rf	5	2	12
Halbert	0	0	0	Furman	1	1	3
Williams, lg	0	1	1	Mikan, c	2	5	9
Parrack, rg	3	0	6	Phelan	1	0	2
Parks	3	0	6	Allen, lg	0	1	1
				Niemeyera	0	0	0
Total	18	16	52	Kochan, rg	2	0	4
				Larochelle	0	1	1
				Halloran	0	0	0
				Total	16	12	44

Officials—Hagan Andersen and Pat Kennedy.

N. Y. U. (63)	G.	F.	P.	BOWLING GREEN (61)	G.	F.	P.
Grenert, lf	3	0	6	Gray, lf	3	4	10
Benanti	0	0	0	Inman	4	0	8
Forman, rf	2	0	4	Whitehead, rf	1	2	5
Most	0	0	0	Gantt	0	0	0
Schayes, c	4	0	8	Otten, c	5	1	11
Walsh	0	0	0	Knierim, lg	1	1	3
Tanenbaum, lg	10	5	25	Payak, rg	3	1	7
Mangiapane, rg	4	2	10	Kubiak	8	1	17
Goldstein	5	0	10	Total	25	11	61
Total	28	7	63				

Officials—Chuck Solodare and Matty Begovich.

March 30, 1945

KENTUCKY DEFEATS RHODE ISLAND, 46-45

Beard's Last-Minute Foul for His 13th Point Wins Final of Invitation Basketball

RAMS LEAD AT HALF, 27-26

By LOUIS EFFRAT

To the Wildcats of Kentucky went top honors in the ninth annual national invitation college basketball tournament, but the hearts of 18,475 fans, thrilled by the gallantry of courageous underdogs who refused to concede an inch, belonged to the Rams of Rhode Island State.

Battling to the end, Rhode Island finally succumbed, 46—45, to the experienced, taller Southerners in a nerve-tingling finale that left the experts in a state of bewilderment last night at Madison Square Garden.

If the experts were in such a condition, one is privileged to guess how Kentucky's players felt, struggling to convince the Rams that they just were not supposed to make it that close. For here was a heavy favorite, rated superior by 11½ points, barely pulling the title out of the fire.

Kentucky was behind, 27—26, at the half, and two minutes before the finish the Wildcats still found themselves a point in the red, 45—44.

This was not according to script. Rhode Island, under the tutelage of Frank Keaney, was not supposed to be equipped with the defense necessary to stop so smooth an aggregation as Kentucky. The helter-skelter, hipper-dipper New England attack, with its electrifying one-handers, had been subjected to ridicule and certainly did not compare with Kentucky's orthodox offense, revolving around the pivot man in the key hole.

Rupp Receives Kelleher Trophy

In fact, everything pointed to a comfortable victory for Kentucky. However, it was the Wildcat coach, Adolph Rupp, who summed it all up in a nutshell a few minutes after he had accepted the Edward A. Kelleher Trophy from Mrs. Kelleher.

"Who," Rupp asked, "said Rhode Island State had no defense?"

"Who," he continued, "said Rhode Island State had no offense?"

The Rams had both. They had, also, Ernie Calverley, who, though held to a mere 8 points by Freshman Ralph Beard, Kentucky's standout offensively and defensively, clinched the most valuable player award in the tournament with another sparkling all-around exhibition. Calverley, feeding his mates, intercepting passes and setting up numerous scoring plays, unquestionably merited the honor.

Still fortune frowned on the slim, 145-pound New Englander, who had amazed the basketball world with a 55-foot shot in the first round. Perhaps it was a miscarriage of justice that he was the cause of Kentucky's winning point, which came exactly 40 seconds before the final buzzer and sent Ernie out on personals.

Perhaps it was, but none in the crowd, which helped set a tournament attendance record of 73,894 for four nights of competition, put the blame on the youngster. It was a heart-breaking windup for so outstanding an individual.

Campbell's Foul Ties Score

The clock showed forty seconds to play when Calverley fouled Beard. As Ernie walked to the bench, Beard calmly caged the free throw that snapped the twelfth tie of the game. Going back a bit farther, it was a foul by Calverley that sent Kenton Campbell to the 15-foot line for a successful penalty toss that enabled Kentucky to tie it at 45—all.

Even after Beard's 1-pointer, the Rams had a chance in the form of a free throw by Dick Hole. Twenty-three seconds remained when Hole flubbed the shot. Between then and the finish, Rhode Island players got their hands on the ball a half a dozen different times, but never got off a shot clearly.

If sloppy at times, this was a feverishly waged contest, in which the lead changed hands eleven times. The Rams, never stopping their running tactics, fell seven points behind, 23—16, but a tremendous surge gave them a 27—26 edge at the intermission.

Thereafter neither side boasted a lead of more than 3 points. There was enough good, spectacular basketball to offset the faulty plays. Kentucky tried to play its own game, but too often was lured into wildness.

For Kentucky, Beard, with his excellent job of defending against Calverley and the 13 points he tallied to be individual high, was the big man. Besides Caverley, playing in his last college game, Jack Allen, a substitute Ram, turned in a surprisingly good effort.

In the third-place preliminary, favored West Virginia conquered Muhlenberg, 65—40, after soaring to a 33—18 advantage at the half. Leland Byrd, with 18 points, topped the scorers.

The line-ups:

WEST VIRGINIA (65)	G.	F.	P.	MUHLENBERG (40)	G.	F.	P.
Carroll, lf	6	2	14	Baldwin, lf	1	0	2
Shreve	1	0	2	Staudinger	1	0	2
Beverly, rf	1	3	5	Combs, rf	6	1	13
Laverte	6	0	12	Podany	1	0	2
Wilson, c	3	0	6	Hale	0	2	2
Fox	0	0	0	Doran, c	0	1	1
Byrd, lg	7	4	18	Rubbert	0	1	1
Miller	2	0	4	Martini	1	0	2
Green, rg	1	0	2	H. Donovan, lg	3	2	8
Chaff	1	0	2	E. Donovan, rg	2	1	5
				Borrell	1	0	2
Total	28	9	65	Total	16	8	40

Officials—Chuck Solodare and Joe Burns.

KENTUCKY (46)	G.	F.	P.	RHODE ISLAND (45)	G.	F.	P.
Tingle, lf	2	1	5	Hole, lf	5	2	12
Holland	1	0	2	Nichols, rf	5	1	11
Schu, rf	3	3	9	Palmieri	0	0	0
Jones, c	3	4	10	Calverley, c	2	4	8
Campbell	0	2	2	Shea, lg	1	2	4
Parkinson, lg	1	0	2	Allen, rg	3	4	10
Beard, rg	5	3	13	Sclafani	0	0	0
Parker	1	1	3	Total	16	13	45
Total	16	14	46				

Officials—Pat Kennedy and Matty Begovich.

March 21, 1946

Campbell of Kentucky blocking the underhand try by Shea on the Garden court

The New York Times

OKLA. AGGIES HALT NO. CAROLINA, 43-40

Western Five Withstands Late Rally in Play-Off at Garden to Keep N. C. A. A. Title

---

KURLAND SINKS 23 POINTS

Dillon Makes 16 for Tarheels —18,479 Watch Ohio State Rout California, 63-45

By LOUIS EFFRAT

North Carolina's best efforts fell short of stopping Bob (foothills) Kurland, so the National Collegiate A. A. basketball championship, which virtually everyone had conceded to the Oklahoma A. and M., went, for the second straight year, to Coach Henry Iba's team. When a closing rally by the Tarheels missed the mark, the Aggies gained a 43-40 decision that could not be questioned by any one of the 18,479 fans at Madison Square Garden last night.

True, there might have been considerable speculation concerning their success had the Aggies been without the services of Kurland. The fact, however, remains that the seven-foot redhead has been a regular for four years, and he had every right in the world to be on the floor. That he was made the big difference in the ball game.

Kurland scored 23 points, his greatest output at the Garden in ten appearances. Horace (Bones) McKinney, the darling of the gallery, was assigned to defend against the tallest man in the court sport, but did not fare too well.

McKinney, at 6 feet 6 inches, is no midget, but the six inches that Kurland towered over him made the Tarheel appear like a pygmy. There just was nothing he, Bob Paxton or Jim Jordan, who took over the unenviable task after McKinney had fouled out after six minutes of the second half, could do to stop Foothills.

No Romp for Westerners

The score in this well-played, if not too exciting, final between the Eastern and Western regional survivors is evidence that the Aggies did not enjoy a romp. Lieut. Bernie Carnevale's Tarheels did not give up when, after five minutes of the second half, they fell 13 points behind. Rather, with an admirable display of hustle, they fought their way into the thick of things as John Dillon's hook shots sparked his mates until only three points separated the teams at 36—33.

That was shortly before the ten-minute mark, but North Carolina was at a distinct disadvantage, for when McKinney was banished on personals the Tarheels had to go along without their best man. Kurland accounted for the last nine Oklahoma points then to provide the cushion that enabled the Aggies to withstand North Carolina's bel... .. oid for an upset.

The Southerners did ge a gallant uphill struggle even then, moving from a 43-34 deficit to within three points before time ran out. North Carolina, an 8½-point underdog, went as far as it could against so great an obstacle as Kurland presented.

Expertly drilled in maintaining possession, the Aggies placed a premium on that phase and a hardship on the Tarheels. There rarely was a false or waste move on the part of the Aggies, who, at the half, enjoyed a 23-17 lead, gained chiefly in the last two minutes of the period.

Kurland Gets Nine Baskets

Everything revolved around Kurland. The big fellow planted himself in the bucket, from where he ran in nine field goals and set up three others. Since the Aggies totaled sixteen baskets, Kurland's worth to his team is obvious.

A committee of five basketball writers unanimously voted Kurland the game's outstanding individual. He was, with plenty to spare, but little Weldon Kern's all-around play for Oklahoma could not be ignored entirely.

For North Carolina, McKinney was an inspiring, tireless worker, but he did not last long enough. Dillon counted 16 points and led his team's offense and the others tried their utmost, but whenever the Tarheels showed signs of threatening they inevitably ran into Kurland.

Time was too short and Kurland too tall. Half a minute remained when Foothills was banished on fouls, but by then North Carolina's cause was hopeless.

It's a pity that the N. C. A. A. winner and Kentucky will not get together for the Red Cross. Someone, somewhere, missed the boat on that one and now the Oklahoma Aggies and the National Invitation ruler have to share the national championship.

It did not appear that way at half-time, when Ohio State held a mere 22-21 lead, but the Big Ten champions were far superior to California in the preliminary game for third place in the N. C. A. A., and beat the Golden Bears, 63—45.

The Buckeyes, with Jack Underman controlling the rebounds, stressed possession and were too fast for the Californians, whose scoring ace was Merv LaFaille, with 22 points. Underman, with 19, was high for Ohio. The line-ups:

OKLA. A. & M. (43)	G.	F.	P.	NO. CAROLINA (40)	G.	F.	P.
Aubrey, lf.	.5	0	1	Dillon, lf.	.6	4	16
Bennett, rf.	.3	0	6	Anderson	.3	3	8
Kern	.3	1	7	Paxton, rf.	.2	0	4
Kurland, c.	.9	5	23	McKinney, c.	.2	1	5
Williams, lg.	.0	0	2	White, lg.	.0	1	1
Bell	.0	1	1	Thorne	.1	0	2
Parks, rg.	.0	0	0	Jordan, rg.	.0	4	4
Bradley	.1	1	3				
Total	16	11	43	Total	13	14	40

Officials—Pat Kennedy and Jocko Collins.

OHIO STATE (63)	G.	F.	P.	CALIFORNIA (45)	G.	F.	P.
Bowen, lf.	.6	4	16	La Faille, lf.	.9	4	22
Wells	.0	0	0	Riemke	.4	0	8
Snyder, rf.	.3	4	10	Wolfe, rf.	.3	0	6
Lovett	.0	0	0	Anderson	.0	0	0
Underman, c.	.6	7	19	Smith, c.	.2	0	4
Elliott	.1	1	3	Walker	.1	2	4
Huston, lg.	.2	1	5	Holcombe	.0	1	1
Johnson	.0	0	0	Wray, lg.	.0	1	1
Amling, rg.	.5	0	10	Mower	.0	1	1
Kuhn	.0	0	0	Hogeboom, rg.	.2	2	6
				Dean	.0	0	0
				Larner	.0	0	0
Total	23	17	63	Total	17	11	45

Officials—William Orwig and John Nucatola.

March 27, 1946

Boykoff's 54 Points for Garden Record Feature Victory of St. John's Five

ST. FRANCIS BEATEN BY REDMEN, 71 TO 52

Boykoff of St. John's, With 54 Points, Tops Mikan Record by One Before 18,452

CITY COLLEGE WINS, 91-60

Beavers, Off to Speedy Start, Achieve Highest Total Ever Scored Against N. Y. U.

By LOUIS EFFRAT

When Gladys Gooding, the organist, played "I'm Just Wild About Harry" at the conclusion of the St. John's-St. Francis game last night, she expressed the sentiment of 18,452 persons, or every man, woman and child who had witnessed the greatest one-man basketball act ever presented on the Madison Square Garden floor.

The Harry concerned was Harry Boykoff, six-foot-nine-inch center for St. John's, who enjoyed the most sensational night of his college career, which will end with graduation in June. Big Harry accumulated 54 points, personally accounting for more than the entire opposing team as St. John's routed St. Francis, 71—52.

With this electrifying performance Boykoff established an all-time Garden scoring record. First, he erased from the books the regular season high of 45 which Boykoff himself had achieved against St. Joseph's in 1943. Not content with that and with his mates feeding him continually, he also surpassed the 53-point production by De Paul's George Mikan versus Rhode Island State in the 1945 National Invitation tournament.

Nor was that all Boykoff did. He did so many things that the feature contest that followed, in which C. C. N. Y. routed New York University, 91—60, became virtually lost in the shuffle. On any other night, Nat Holman's Beavers would have hogged the headlines for running away from the Violets.

Redmen End Regular Season

Credited to Boykoff were the records for most points and most four goals, 54 and 12. In sinking twenty-one field goals, Harry tied Mikan's mark, also made in the 1945 post-season game. Although the Brooklyn Redmen ended their regular season, Boykoff will have further opportunity to add to his laurels, since St. John's is in the national invitation tournament, starting Saturday night.

Boykoff started to score when the contest was just 15 seconds old and he didn't stop until only 38 seconds remained. It was then that he set the record, with everyone in the arena realizing that Harry needed one point to tie and two to snap Mikan's mark.

There was a heated scrimmage and John Zeitler of St. Francis was charged with a foul. Zeitler was tugging away at Harry's arms, so Referee Johnny Nucatola did not hesitate to award two shots. When both swished through the net the fans went wild.

Not alone was Harry hitting with his shots, but this was his best all-around performance. The big fellow was defending brilliantly, intercepting passes and capturing rebounds. In the end there was nothing left for the scribes to do except vote him the outstanding player, for which he received the Catholic Youth Organization Trophy, presented annually in this series between Brooklyn rivals.

Beavers Seize Early Lead

City College, hopeful of being asked to play in the Eastern regionals of the National Collegiate Athletic Association, which will get under way on the night of March 20, outsped and outshot N. Y. U. The Beavers hopped off to an early 15-point lead and though the Violets rallied momentarily to cut that deficit to 5 points, half-time found C. C. N. Y. on top, 43—26.

Everything the Lavender attempted was right, while almost every move made by the Violets was wrong, and the result was the worst beating ever handed to N. Y. U. by City College. It was the highest total ever scored against the Violets and ranked as one of the heaviest setbacks in all

N. Y. U. history.

Sparked by Lionel Malamed and Mason Benson, who netted 15 and 14 points, respectively, the Beavers put on the pressure and never relaxed it. Where C. C. N. Y. was consistent, the Violets showed to advantage only when they put together ten straight points in the opening period.

Thus the regular court campaign closed with City College annexing its sixteenth victory in the traditional series. N. Y. U., which had won seventeen, ended a disappointing season. The Violets, regarded as best in the city at the start of the season, ended with twelve games won and nine lost, including five straight defeats.

The line-ups:

ST. JOHN'S (71)	G.	F.	P.	ST. FRANCIS (52)	G.	F.	P.
Redding, lf	0	0	0	Mele, lf	6	2	14
Doctor	3	2	8	Aggolia, rf	3	1	7
Jacobson	8	0	0	Zeitler	2	0	4
Dalton, rf	1	0	2	Morgan	0	0	0
Frascella	2	0	4	Sabello	0	0	0
Boykoff, c	21	12	54	McNiff	0	0	0
Oldham	0	0	0	Dolan, c	3	1	7
McGuire, lg	0	1	1	Grady, lg	1	1	3
Tolan, rg	0	0	0	Labanowski	0	0	0
Buckley	0	0	0	Gumbrecht	1	0	2
Plantamura	1	0	2	Lindeman	0	2	2
				Gallagher, rg	4	3	11
				Ferraro	0	0	0
				Cammeyer	1	0	2
Total	28	15	71	Total	21	10	52

Officials—Hagan Andersen and Lou Eisenstein.

C.C.N.Y. (91)	G.	F.	P.	N.Y.U. (60)	G.	F.	P.
Benson, lf	7	0	14	Forman, lf	1	2	4
Brenberg	0	1	1	Dolhon	4	4	12
Farbman	1	2	4	Maher	0	1	1
P. Malamed	3	0	6	Kelley, rf	1	2	4
Trubowitz, rf	4	1	9	DeBonis	0	0	0
Schmones	0	0	0	Goldstein	0	0	0
Brickman	0	0	0	Roth	0	0	0
Dambrot, c	6	1	13	Schayes, c	8	3	13
Jameson	3	1	7	Wells	0	0	0
Shapiro, lg	1	3	5	Lexsat	1	0	2
Ernestone	3	4	10	Regen	0	0	0
Millman	1	1	3	Tanenbaum, lg	4	3	11
Malamed, rg	5	5	15	Derderian	1	0	2
Finger	2	0	4	Lumpp, rg	0	0	0
Dubow	0	0	0	Kaufman	2	5	9
				Benanti	0	0	0
Total	36	19	91	Total	20	20	60

Officials—Matty Begovich and John Nucatola.

March 12, 1947

Schayes (23), Lumpp, both of N. Y. U., and Benson (12) of C. C. N. Y. attempting to recover a rebound in the first period. Following the play is Shapiro (7) of City College.

The New York Times

Utah Five in Startling Upset Over Kentucky in National Invitation Final

WILDCATS TOPPLED BY THE UTES, 49-45

Utah Confounds Experts by Dethroning Kentucky in National Invitation

LOSER TOP-HEAVY CHOICE

By LOUIS EFFRAT

Midnight still was an hour away, but the clock was wrong—as wrong as all the experts who predicted that Utah didn't have a chance against mighty Kentucky in the final of the tenth annual National Invitation college basketball tournament at Madison Square Garden last night.

For at 11 o'clock last night, the Utes, who back in 1944 were called the "Cinderella team," completed their upset victory over the Wildcats, 49—45.

With this unexpected conquest of an all-powerful court aggregation that had won thirty-four of thirty-six games, Utah's undermanned and certainly underestimated squad sealed for all time its right to exclusive ownership of the "Cinderella" tag.

The Utes came from nowhere to win in 1944, and some may have felt they were lucky to have reached last night's final. But some sixty minutes before the legendary hour of midnight, they didn't ask the Cinderella team to try a golden slipper for size. It was a crown and it fitted perfectly.

Over-All Margin of 7 Points

Utah, it will be recalled, survived the first round by virtue of a 45-44 triumph over Duquesne. Against West Virginia in the semi-finals, the Utes prevailed, 64—62. Last night, four points divided the finalists, so that an over-all margin of 7 points brought to Utah its second national invitation championship.

There was little of the sensational connected with the final, but Utah's performance against a heavily favored, high-scoring group that looked like a cinch to annex its second successive invitation diadem, won the admiration of 18,467 fans.

Undoubtedly, Coach Vadal Peterson had instructed his men to slow down the pace and stress possession at all time. The Utah plan of battle never deviated although the Wildcats tried to force the Utes into faster action. The Utes knew what they wanted to do and did it—handsomely.

Vern Gardner, the blond bombshell who was named the most valuable player in the tournament, did an excellent job for the winning team. He captured most of the rebounds, fed his mates and still found time to share, with Arnold Ferrin, individual scoring honors. Each made 15 points.

All Come In For Applause

Little Wat Misaka, American-born of Japanese descent, was a "cute" fellow intercepting passes and making the night miserable for Kentucky. Leon Watson and Fred Weidner, the other two starters, and Lyman Clark, lone substitute, who did everything asked of him, also came in for applause.

And what of Kentucky? The Wildcats did not play poorly, but they did not match Utah's all-around superiority. Trailing at the half, 27—21, Adolph Rupp's lads three times were confronted with 7-point deficits. They rallied to within one point of the leaders, 45—44, with little more than three minutes remaining. If Utah was destined to crack, this was the spot.

But Ferrin caged a twisting, underhand lay-up. Wah-Wah Jones caged a Kentucky foul that brought the Wildcats a point closer, but not close enough. The Utes held the ball as the precious seconds ticked away.

Obviously, the 2-point lead was

sufficient, but five seconds before the end, Ferrin spied Gardner underneath and alone, so he fired the pass that produced the cushion.

Beard Held to a Point

Alex Groza and Jim Line, the freshmen with the southpaw one-handed shot, counted 12 points each for Kentucky, but Ralph Beard was held to a mere point by Misaka. They say Kentucky goes as Beard goes. Last night he just didn't go.

For an appetizer, the fans were treated to a preliminary encounter, which proved to be neither an appetizer nor a treat, as North Carolina State routed West Virginia, 64—52, in a ragged contest for third place. Whatever incentive there was in this exhibition, the Wolfpack had most of it.

At half-time, when North Carolina State had a 36-20 advantage, the crowd voiced its disapproval with the loudest series of boos heard at the Garden all season.

Bob Negley, who notched 22 points for North Carolina State,

was much more effective. Dick Dickey, aside from the 16 points he scored, also did a fine job for the victors.

The line-ups:

UTAH (49)	G.	F.	P.	KENTUCKY (45)	G.	F.	P.
Watson, lf	3	7	13	Holland, lf	1	0	2
Misaka, rf	0	2	2	Jones, rf	4	0	8
Gardner, c	5	5	15	Groza, c	5	2	12
Ferrin, lg	6	3	15	Tingle	0	0	0
Weidner, rg	1	2	4	Barker	0	0	0
Clark	0	0	0	Rollins, lg	3	0	6
				Line	6	0	12
Total	15	19	49	Beard, rg	0	1	1
				Jordan	1	2	4
				Total	18	9	45

Officials—Matty Begovich and John Nucatola.

N. C. STATE (64)	G.	F.	P.	WEST VA. (52)	G.	F.	P.
Cartier, lf	2	2	6	Schaus, lf	4	2	10
Stine	0	1	1	Repass	0	0	0
Negley, rf	8	6	22	Duff, rf	4	1	9
McComas	0			Zirkel	2	2	6
Bartels, c	3	3		Beach, c	3	5	11
Sloan	1	1	3	Carroll	0	0	0
Hahn	0	0	0	Laverte	0	0	0
Dickey, lg	7	2	16	Byrd, lg	3	4	10
Katkavek, rg	2	3	7	Kraus	0	0	0
Snow	0	0	0	Walthall, rg	3	0	6
				Jackson	0	0	0
Total	23	18	64	Green	0	0	0
				Total	19	14	52

Officials—Jocko Collins and Sam Schoenfeld.

COLLEGE BASEBALL

Duke 13 .... Davidson 7

March 25, 1947

Holy Cross Downs Oklahoma Quintet for N.C.A.A. Title at Garden

CRUSADERS ANNEX 23D IN ROW, 58-47

Holy Cross Defeats Oklahoma in East-West Play-Off After Trailing at Half, 31-28

SCORE IS TIED 11 TIMES

Texas Halts C. C. N. Y., 54-50, for 3d Place in N. C. A. A. Tourney Before 18,445

By LOUIS EFFRAT

To Holy Cross went the National Collegiate Athletic Association basketball championship last night at Madison Square Garden, as the smartly drilled Crusaders from Worcester, Mass., running away from the opposition in the last three minutes, fashioned a 58-47 victory over the University of Oklahoma in the East-West play-off before 18,445 persons.

That eleven-point margin at the finish belied the closeness of one of the keenest struggles of the season. This was a battle between beautifully coached quintets that played top-flight basketball all the way. Eleven times the score was tied and eleven times the lead changed hands, as both sides made the most of their opportunities.

SNARING A REBOUND IN N. C. A. A. FINAL LAST NIGHT

Paine, Oklahoma, getting ball after shot by Kaftan (12), Holy Cross. The others are Tucker (33), Courty (46) and Reich (36) of the Sooners and Oftring (20) and O'Connell (14) of the Crusaders.

The New York Times

Perhaps Holy Cross is not 11 points better than Oklahoma's Sooners. Perhaps Bruce Drake's men were unlucky with some of their shots. Perhaps another meeting might produce a different outcome. But there were no maybes connected with this twenty-third straight triumph by the Crusaders. They never forfeited their poise, not even when they dropped five points behind late in the opening period.

Crusaders Change Tactics

Coach Doggy Julian instructed his lads to switch tactics following the intermission. No longer deliberate on attack, the men from Worcester, most of whom learned their early basketball in metropolitan New York high schools, stepped up the pace to employ a faster break.

When the clock showed less than three minutes to go with Holy Cross clinging to a 48-45 edge, it still was anyone's game. Those closing minutes showed the Crusaders at their best as they tallied 10 points to a pair of fouls for the Oklahomans.

Burly George Kaftan, a product of Manhattan's Xavier High School; Frank Oftring of Brooklyn Tech, Bob Curran, Dermott O'Connell, Bob McMullen, Ken Haggerty and all the other Crusaders played their parts masterfully, particularly the first three. Kaftan, who paced his team with 18 points and again was a standout underneath the backboards, was voted the most valuable player in the contest.

It was figured that Holy Cross would have to stop Oklahoma's all-American, Gerald Tucker, to win. The Crusaders didn't even slow him down and his 22 points made hime high man, but they did shackle the other Sooners.

Holy Cross became the first Eastern team to win the East-West final in the five years it has been staged on the Garden floor. The Crusaders had hoped to play Utah for the mythical national championship tomorrow night, but plans for such a meeting were dropped at dawn yesterday when the national invitation winners, who had upset Kentucky in the final Monday night, boarded a plane for home.

Vadal Peterson, Utah coach, who stayed on for last night's game, said that his players had to go back because registration would begin at the university Friday morning.

Third place in the N. C. A. A. competition went to University of Texas via a 54-50 victory over C. C. N. Y. in an exciting preliminary. The Beavers fell into an early 16-point deficit, but after a long uphill struggle they moved within two points of the Longhorns, who were protecting a 51-49 lead with only two minutes of the game remaining.

Just when it appeared that the Lavender might save the night, Roy Cox of Texas, a standout, flipped a pass to John Hargis, who curled in a lay-up at 18:40. A half minute later Al Madsen caged a foul that Phil Farbman matched for City College, but the Longhorns were home by then.

C. C. N. Y. suffered because of repeated misses at close range. The speedy Texans, featuring one-handed shots, outran the Beavers, but almost ran themselves out of the ball game.

In the end, Coach Jack Gray's lads prevailed, thanks to their early advantage. Texas, which enjoyed a 27-11 margin at the eleventh-minute mark, had to be content with a 32-28 edge at the intermission.

Hargis, notching 17 points, was high man. Slater Martin, his teammate, and Everett Finestone of City shared runner-up honors with 14 each.

The line-ups:

HOLY CROSS (58)				OKLAHOMA (47)			
	G.	F.	P.		G.	F.	P.
Ka'tan, lf	7	4	18	Reich, lf	3	2	8
Laska	0	0	0	Waters	0	0	0
O'Connell, rf	7	2	16	Courty, rf	3	2	8
Curran	0	0	0	Pryor	1	1	
Oftring, c	6	2	14	Tucker, c	10	2	22
Riley	0	0	0	Paine, lg	2	2	6
Bollinger	0	0	0	Landon, rg	1	0	2
Mullaney, lg	0	0	0	Merchant	0	0	0
McMullen	2	4	8	Day	0	0	0
Haggerty, rg	0	0	0				
Cousy	0	2	2	Total	15	17	47
Graver	0	0	0				
Total	22	14	58				

Officials—Pat Kennedy and Hagan Andersen.

TEXAS (54)				C. C. N. Y. (50)			
	G.	F.	P.		G.	F.	P.
Hargis, lf	7	3	17	Jameson, lf	4	2	10
Hamilton	0	0	0	Schmones	1	0	2
Martin, rf	7	0	14	Dambrot, rf	5	3	13
Langdon, c	4	1	9	Galiber, c	0	1	1
Madsen, lg	2	2	8	Farbman	0	0	0
Cox, rg	2	4	8	Finestone, lg	6	2	14
Wagner	0	0	0	Shapiro	1	0	2
				Malamed, rg	3	0	6
Total	22	10	54	Trubowitz	0	0	0
				Total	21	8	50

Officials—William Haarlow and William Orwig.

March 26, 1947

Notre Dame Defeats N. Y. U., Ending Violets' Streak at 19

SOUTH BEND FIVE TRIUMPHS, 64 TO 59

Notre Dame Topples N. Y. U. From Ranks of Unbeaten in Upset at Garden

IRISH COME FROM BEHIND

O'Shea Sparks Uprising That Erases First-Half Deficit —Lumpp Paces Violets

By LOUIS EFFRAT

True to the spirit of the Fighting Irish, the Notre Dame basketball team erased an early 9-point deficit and came roaring down the stretch to conquer New York University, 64—59, in their fifteenth annual court clash last night at Madison Square Garden.

So near to a perfect season, and yet so far, the Violets saw their 19-game winning streak snapped in the campaign's roughest, toughest and most exciting court clash of the year.

Rough and tough it was and, for a crowd of 18,435, its sentiments divided, this was the vehicle for a continuous series of thrills, unsurpassed throughout the campaign. Tempers raged among the athletes—the spectators, too—and if there were no actual punches tossed, the threat of a brawl was ever prevalent, averted only by quick intervention by the officials on several occasions.

Have Height Advantage

The nation's last unbeaten major college quintet, N. Y. U., fell before an outfit that had known defeat seven times. The Violets, because of the height advantage afforded by Adolph Schayes and because they were playing on their home court were favored to annex their twentieth straight victory.

Nor can it be reported that N. Y. U. did not come close to taking the measure of its traditional rival from South Bend. Right up to the final five seconds, when Schayes, driving in for a lay-up and a most vital, potential 3-point play, flubbed his shot—he was trying to draw a foul simultaneously—the issue was in doubt.

N. Y. U. was trailing by 3 points at the time and success by Schayes might have sent the fray into overtime. But the usually dependable Schayes missed and a superfluous, sleeper basket by Jim O'Halloran put the Irish on easy street.

There was, too, one stage in the opening half when N. Y. U., having clicked for ten straight points, enjoyed a 32-23 margin. Right then and there, followers of the Violets were all for chalking up victory No. 20. However, the visitors proved their mettle when, sparked by the brilliant Kevin O'Shea, fought back into contention. Their half-time deficit was a mere 3 points, 35—32.

Lead Changes Often

Before this heart-stopping encounter finished, there were nine ties and seventeen changes of leads. First one team gained an edge, only to forfeit it, as O'Shea, Leo Barnhorst and company matched strides with Ray Lumpp, Don Forman and the other Violets.

Each team lost the services of two players because of five personal fouls. It was that type of a struggle, with the rivals, obviously tense and overanxious, resorting to football tactics from time to time. Fifty fouls were called, twenty-six against Notre Dame.

But it was the ball game that most concerned the fans. Notre Dame, which had beaten N. Y. U. eleven times previously, took advantage of New York's early lethargy to notch an 11-5 spread before the 5-minute mark. O'Shea and Barnhorst were the big guns then. However, the Violets, with Lumpp finding the range with his favorite southpaw one-handers, regained their poise and soon gained an 11-11 tie.

Thereafter, until Forman got hot and paced that spectacular spurt, it was give-and-go. From a 23-22 trailer to a 32-23 leader was N. Y. U.'s superb exhibition in less than four minutes. Then O'Shea took over and a Notre Dame team that appeared on the way out suddenly was back in the fight. Following the intermission, neither quintet held a lead long enough to enjoy it.

Both Sides Waive Fouls

At 15:25, O'Shea, playing with a taped leg, tapped in a rebound that gave the South Benders a 56-55 edge. Foley then hit with a one-hander and added a foul, as did O'Shea. Now the visitors had a 60-55 pull and the seconds were ticking away. At 18:02 the margin was 62-56, but Joel Kaufman's corner set and one of two free throws by the same man brought the Violets to within three points of the leaders.

Notre Dame waived two fouls and N. Y. U. one in the final half-minute. This was sound strategy on both sides. Notre Dame did not need any more points and N. Y. U. needed more than one. The problem of the Violets was how to fashion three points for a tie. They elected to drive in for a field goal and hope for a foul at the same time.

This, then was the situation as the ball was passed in to Schayes, who had planted himself in the bucket. Pivoting, Schayes drove toward the backboard and he did have a chance to get off the shot —but missed.

So far as individual scoring honors were concerned, it was a stand-off. Lumpp and O'Shea each netted 18 points. Mainly, though, the victory of Notre Dame was a team proposition.

The line-up:

NOTRE DAME (64)				N. Y. U. (59)			
	G.	F.	P.		G.	F.	P.
Barnhorst, lf	3	3	9	Lumpp, lf	5	8	18
O'Halloran, rf	3	2	8	Kelly, rf	0	0	0
Riller	3	0	6	Kaufman	4	2	10
Kluck	0	0	0	Schayes, c	2	5	9
Foley, c	3	1	7	Dolhon, lg	1	4	6
Brennan	3	1	7	De Bonis	0	1	1
O'Shea, lg	7	4	18	Derderian	0	0	0
Gordon, rg	2	4	8	Forman, rg	7	1	15
Goeuen	0	0	0				
Total	24	16	64	Total	19	21	59

Officials—Matty Eggovich and Joe Burns.

March 2, 1948

St. Louis Conquers N. Y. U. in National Invitation Basketball Final at Garden

FLASHY BILLIKENS TRIUMPH BY 65-52

18,491 See St. Louis Trounce N. Y. U. in College Final to Attain Olympic Tryouts

MACAULEY GETS 24 POINTS

Schayes (4) of N. Y. U. and Wilcutt and Macauley (50) of St. Louis jumping for ball under the Violets' basket. Following action are Lumpp (8), Dolhon (5) and Kelly (7), all of the New York squad, and Cary (left, background) of the Billikens.

The New York Times

By LOUIS EFFRAT

To the Billikens of St. Louis, most talented college basketball team seen here in many a season, went top honors in the eleventh annual national invitation tournament last night at Madison Square Garden. Before 18,491 fans the Missouri Valley Conference rulers passed the Violets of New York University dizzy and registered a 65-52 victory that was even more conclusive than the score.

The St. Louis players, knowing the value of sound, fundamental basketball that played a premium on possession, capitalized on every opening, and long before halftime, when the Billikens enjoyed a 25-18 margin, had the situation well under control. Only merciful Coach Ed Hickey, who had his third-stringers on the floor during most of the last five minutes, saved the once haughty Violets from an utter rout.

Control was the most deadly weapon employed by the visitors. They tried at all times to maintain possession, rarely attempting a shot longer than fifteen feet. With easy Ed Macauley working out of the key hole and passing perfectly to his mates, the formula was as successful as it was sound.

Macauley netted 24 points, easily the game's individual high and just as easily the outstanding performance of the tournament. Official recognition as such was accorded to the lanky junior by the vote of a special committee.

Billikens Earn Points

N. Y. U., seeded second, two notches above St. Louis at the outset, was outclassed. The Violets were taken into camp, just as Bowling Green (69—53) and Western Kentucky (60—53) had been, by a combination that followed a pre-meditated plan of attack with every step a measured one. Seldom, indeed, has a quintet earned so many points as St. Louis.

Only once did N. Y. U. hold a lead. At the two-minute mark, Ray Lumpp caged a foul for a 1-0 advantage. Bob Schmidt tied the score a minute later and at 4:15, D. C. Wilcutt captured a loose ball and curled in a St. Louis lay-up. The Billikens, though they controlled the ball, did not take a shot for four minutes.

Joe Dolhon, driving in to tally from close range, lifted N. Y. U. even at 4:35. Thereafter it was all St. Louis, passing deftly.

Setting-up scoring plays beautifully, the Billikens clicked with twenty-five of their sixty shots from the floor. Macauley made eleven of his twenty-three and Wilcutt seven of his twelve.

True, Macauley led the scorers and was a tremendous inspiration, but this was far from a personal triumph for the 6-foot-8-inch stylist. Prior to the contest, billed as a duel between the St. Louis center and Adolph Schayes of N. Y. U., easy Ed expressed this sentiment: "So far as I'm concerned, it's St. Louis against N. Y. U., not Macauley against Schayes."

Thereupon, Macauley proceeded to outplay the Violet ace by the widest of margins. Macauley left the floor to a thunderous acclaim, five minutes before the finish.

Schayes was battling, like all the other Violets, for a hopeless cause. He scored eight points, six fewer than Lumpp and Joel Kaufman of N. Y. U. and half as many as Wilcutt.

When Macauley, Wilcutt, Schmidt, Dan Miller and Marvin Schatzman were removed for the last time, St. Louis had a 19-point spread. Against the Billiken reserves, N. Y. U. made progress, but not nearly enough.

While the Billikens were displaying their expert ball-handling and maneuvering the locals were forced into continual errors. The team that earlier had fashioned a nineteen-game winning streak and impressed as one of the nation's best quintets did not perform up to its capabilities, but the Mound City squad had more than a little to do with upsetting the smoothness of Howard Cann's charges.

St. Louis earned a berth in the forthcoming Olympic trials at the Garden, but there is no certainty that the Billikens, who will head for home tomorrow will return for the trials. Hickey said studies might keep the lads in school. A definite decision is to be made later

Third place in the competition was won by Western Kentucky, which outlasted De Paul of Chicago, 61—59, in the overtime preliminary. Ahead, 30—21, at halftime, the Kentucky Hilltoppers soared to a 14-point spread, but the Blue Demons drew even at 53-53, as regulation time ended.

The line-ups:

ST. LOUIS (65)	G.	F.	P.	N. Y. U. (52)	G.	F.	P.
Wilcutt, lf	7	2	16	Kelly, lf	0	1	1
Cordia	1	0	2	Kaufman	6	2	14
Ossola, rf	1	3	5	Lumpp, rf	5	4	14
Schatzmann	1	1	3	Barry	1	1	3
Wrape	0	0	0	Dolhon, lg	3	1	7
J. Schmidt	1	1	3	Schayes, c	4	0	8
Macauley, c	11	2	24	De Bonis	1	0	2
B. Schmidt, lg	1	4	6	Benanti	1	0	2
Lehman	0	2	2	Derderian, rg	0	0	0
Cary	0	0	0	Kor	0	0	0
Miller, rg	2	0	4	Quilty	0	1	1
Raymonds	0	0	0				
Totals	25	15	65	Total	21	10	52

Officials—Matty Begovich and John Nucatola

WESTERN KY. (61)	G.	F.	P.	DE PAUL (59)	G.	F.	P.
Spears, lf	1	2	4	Allen, lf	4	0	8
Parsley	0	0	0	Leddy	1	1	3
Ray, rf	8	3	19	Gillespie, rf	0	1	1
Mann	0	1	1	Federinko	1	0	2
McKinney, c	4	2	10	Mikan, c	7	7	21
Oldham, lg	7	2	16	Kachan, lg	3	1	7
Bohannon	0	0	0	Vukovich	2	0	4
Gibson, rg	2	2	6	Coorlas, rg	3	3	9
Givens	2	1	5				
Total	24	13	61	Total	21	17	59

Officials—Jocko Collins and James Osborne.

March 18, 1948

Kentucky Defeats Baylor in N.C.A.A. Basketball Final at Garden

WILDCATS TRIUMPH OVER TEXANS, 58-42

Kentucky Annexes National Honors, Beating Baylor Quintet Before 16,174

GROZA LEADING SCORER

By LOUIS EFFRAT

Kentucky's Wildcats, at no time in jeopardy, easily conquered Baylor, 58—42, last night at Madison Square Garden and romped to their first N. C. A. A. basketball championship. Off to an early 17-point lead, Adolph Rupp's powerhouse completely outclassed the Bears from Waco, Tex.

The second smallest turnout of the season, 16,174, witnessed this one-sided East-West final, in which Baylor's strategy—slowdown and stress possession—succeeded only in holding down the score. Baylor, lightly regarded at the outset of the Western regionals, qualified for the title clash with a pair of upset victories over Washington and Kansas State, but last night ran out of surprises.

Perhaps the best way to describe Kentucky's thirty-fourth and certainly most important triumph of the campaign is to report that form held up. Nearly every pregame prediction pointed to the size, speed and depth of the Wildcats from Lexington and figured that these would determine the outcome. They did, too, even if Coach Rupp, who wanted to win this one above all others, saw little need to turn to his bench. He did not substitute until 6:30 of the second half, by which time the decision was just about clinched.

Big Center Is Honored

Alex Groza, the tallest man on the floor, was the high scorer for Kentucky and the game. His 14 points were two more than Ralph Beard tallied and four more than Bill Johnson made for Baylor. The latter was unable to handle Groza's height and most of the rebounds were dominated by the 6-foot 7-inch center, who was voted the outstanding player of the tournament.

But Groza was far from being the only Wildcat in a starring role. Beard, an irrepressible digger; Ken Rollins, an all-around ace; Wallace (Wah Wah) Jones, a dependable workhorse, along with the steady Cliff Barker—all contributed handsomely toward a victorious cause.

That Baylor, because of Kentucky's height advantage, would resort to a deliberate style of at-

Alex Groza, 6-foot 7-inch center of Kentucky

tack, was anticipated. The Bears, reluctant to risk forfeiting possession, attempted to make certain that every shot be a clear one and from close range. As a result they had taken only one chance in the first four minutes and six in the first seven and a half, not one finding the target.

Gain 12-Point Advantage

Thus Kentucky enjoyed a 13-1 spread—Jim Owen caged a foul at 5:25—and Baylor followers foresaw a rout.

Finally, when the clock showed 7 minutes and 35 seconds gone, Don Heathington dribbled in with a lay-up and the Texans, on their seventh attempt from the floor, achieved their initial basket.

However, this was not repeated often enough to lighten Baylor's burden and at 12:35 Kentucky's lead was 17 points at 24—7. This shrunk slightly to 29—16 at the intermission and later the Bears rallied to cut the deficit to 9 points, but the Wildcats packed too many weapons and triumphed going away.

Kentucky, obviously superior in all departments, was most impressive during the early stages. One 2-minute spurt netted 7 points, as Jones, Rollins and Groza excelled. The Wildcats were driving hard and harassing the Bears at every turn. Thereafter they performed commendably enough, but their rallies were intermittent and the Kentuckians did not again look that superb.

Probably the reason for this let-up was lack of incentive. They were en route to victory and knew it and no end of grimaces from Rupp on the bench sufficed to re-awaken them. Baylor, on the other hand, did not have the power to take full advantage and suffered its sixth setback of the year.

Clicks on 23 Shots

In victory, Kentucky attempted a total of 83 shots, clicking with 23, as compared to 15 out of 64 for the losers. Both teams automatically qualified for the Olympic trials which get underway Saturday afternoon at the Garden.

Third place in the competition went to Holy Cross, the Crusaders, despite an early 16-point lead, staggering to a 60-54 victory over Kansas State in the preliminary encounter. At half-time, Holy Cross was on top, 36—24, but midway through the second period the battling Kansans drew even at 40—40.

The victors used their first-stringers sparingly during the opening half, but operated with virtually all the regulars thereafter. Howard Shannon of Kansas State was high scorer with 17 points

Between halves of the opener, Dr. H. C. Carlson, Pittsburgh coach, was honored as the one who had done the most for basketball over a period of years. The award, made annually by the Metropolitan Intercollegiate Basketball Association, was presented to Dr. Carlson by Howard Hobson of Yale, outgoing president of the National Association of College Basketball Coaches.

The Line-Ups

KENTUCKY (58)	G.	F.	P.	BAYLOR (42)	G.	F.	P.
Jones, lf	4	1	9	Owen, lf	2	1	5
Line	3	1	7	Pulley	0	0	0
Barker, rf	2	1	5	Dewitt, rf	3	2	8
Groza, c	6	2	14	Hickman	1	0	2
Holland	1	0	2	Heathington, c	3	2	8
Beard, lg	4	4	12	Preston	0	0	0
Rollins, rg	3	3	9	Johnson, lg	1	3	4 10
Barnstable	0	0	0	Srack	0	0	0
				Robinson, rg	3	2	8
Total	23	12	58	Total	15	12	42

Officials—William Haarlow and Gil MacDonald.

HOLY CROSS (60)	G.	F.	P.	KANSAS STATE (54)	G.	F.	P.
Cousy, lf	2	1	5	Harman, lf	3	3	9
Laska	2	0	4	Catherby	0	0	0
Oftring, rf	4	3	11	Lahnerty	0	0	0
Kaftan, c	4	3	11	Howey, rf	4	2	10
Bollinger	1	0	2	Stranium, c	1	2	4
Forman	0	0	0	Clark	0	0	0
Curran, lg	2	1	5	Dean, lg	5	2	12
McMullan	3	0	6	Langston	0	0	0
Mullaney, rg	3	0	6	Kron	1	2	4
O'Connell	5	0	10	Shannon, rg	6	5	17
Dolan	0	0	0	Thornton	0	0	0
Total	26	8	60	Total	20	14	54

Officials—Matty Begovich and James Osborne.

March 24, 1948

BASKETBALL HEADS VOTE FOUR CHANGES

Rule Revisions Recommended by Coaches Win Favor of National Committee

The National Collegiate Basketball Committee voted favorably yesterday on four rules changes recommended by coaches and agreed to give several others further consideration.

These rules and others which the committee may adopt today will become part of the rule book next season, Committee Secretary H. V. Porter announced. The changes are:

1. A coach be permitted to talk to his team at his bench on charged timeouts or during intermission. It was felt this would eliminate illegal sideline coaching.

2. Substitutes be permitted to enter a game merely by reporting to the scorekeeper instead of both to this official and the referees on the court. He cannot enter the game, however, until the referee beckons him.

3. A player who has committed a foul must raise his hand so he can easily be recognized by the crowd.

4. All jump balls be made at the nearest of three six-foot circles. The committee felt this would eliminate scrambling and pushing for positions around the sidelines and bring the play nearer to the center of the court.

In answer to a request for clarification by the coaches, the committee pointed out that a technical foul may be shot by any player on the team and not necessarily by the fouled player.

The question of what constitutes "continuous motion" on a foul committed while a player is attempting a field goal was given considerable study. There was a tendency among the twenty-member committee to be more liberal with the shooter.

The committee also discussed at length an idea to place a six-foot circle inside the foul line territory in an effort to keep players farther away from the backboard.

"This would be a sort of modified free-throw line," Porter said. "It would put more stress on the three-second rule and it would make it more difficult for the taller player to tip in those unsightly rebounds. These big boys, instead of being stationary, as they are now, would be forced to move around more."

In its closing session tomorrow, the committee will discuss an official backboard, the clarification of the three-minute rule and numerous other recommendations for rule changes offered by various groups.

March 26, 1948

U. S. Basketball Squad Scores Easy Victory Over France for Olympic Title

AMERICAN QUINTET TRIUMPHS BY 65-21

Entire Oiler-Kentucky Team Sees Action—French Trail at Half-Time by 28-9

By BENJAMIN WELLES
Special to THE NEW YORK TIMES.

LONDON, Aug. 13—America's highly-touted basketball team swamped a hard-fighting French quintet in Harringay Arena tonight by a score of 65 to 21 to capture the Olympic laurel wreath in token of the world championship.

By crushing the French team the United States not only retained the title gained at Berlin in the 1936 games, but re-emphasized American world superiority in this particular brand of athletics.

Unprecedented in a championship match was the International Federation's permission for both teams to use their entire contingent as substitutes. The Federation waived the normal ruling limiting the teams to five playing members and five substitutes.

The American team took the lead at the start and quickly began to outmaneuver, outdribble and outshoot the French players, many of whom had learned the fine points of the game from Americans stationed in France during the war.

Crowd of 6,000 Watches

The crowd, estimated at 6,000, was one of the largest ever to view a basketball contest in Britain.

Brazil beat Mexico, 52 to 47, in an exciting match for third and fourth places. The Brazilians, who were behind, 17 to 25, at the half, came back in brilliant style and at the end Brazilian rooters and

FINALISTS IN ACTION AS OUR PLAYERS WIN IN LONDON

Bob Kurland (90) taking a rebound off backboard in the game played yesterday with the French team, which was defeated by 65 to 21. Other players identified are Gordon Carpenter (66) and Lew Beck (11), both Americans.

Associated Press Radiophoto

officials raced onto the court, hugging and kissing the players.

A Slick Combination

LONDON, Aug. 13 (AP)—The slickest basketball team ever seen in England, possibly anywhere, bewildered France's cinderella kids tonight to win the Olympic cage title for the United States.

Everyone of the fourteen United States players got into the game and thirteen of them scored. Only Cliff Barker of University of Kentucky failed to get a point.

The Americans could do nothing wrong tonight and the French, surprise finalists, were too nervous to offer opposition. On offense they stumbled, lost the ball and lacked team coordination.

When on defense, they simply were bewildered by the United States passing attack.

So certain were the Olympic officials that the United States, where the game was born, would triumph that they brought only one flag to the arena for the postgame ceremonies.

It was the Stars and Stripes and after the gong sounded to end the massacre, the rival teams lined up facing each other as the flag was unfurled and the band played the Star Spangled Banner.

After that the United States players rushed forward and carried Jesse Renick, a player today but who will coach the Phillips Oilers next year, off the floor on their shoulders.

It wasn't a contest after the first two minutes. Lew Beck of the Oilers, whose first five men started the game, sank a field goal to open the scoring. France retaliated. Gordon Carpenter, also of the Oilers, then got two free throws and again the French tied it up. But it was their dying gasp —and still 38 minutes to play. At the half the Americans led, 28 to 9.

Bob Kurland, seven-foot center, got his usual round of boos, but he wasn't bothered.

"I don't care," he said after the game, "I've been booed by Americans, and they really know how to boo."

The line-up:

UNITED STATES (65)				FRANCE (21)			
	G.	F.	P.		G.	F.	P.
Beck, lf	2	2	6	Guillon, lf	0	1	1
Pitts	3	1	7	Pierrier	2	1	5
Boryla, rf	1	1	3	Even, rf	0	0	0
Robinson	1	0	2	Quenin	0	0	0
Beard	1	2	4	Girardot	0	0	0
Lumpp	5	0	10	Desaymonnet	0	0	0
Kurland, c	2	0	4	Derency, c	0	1	1
Barksdale	2	8		Thiolin	1	1	3
Groza	5	1	11	Buffiere, lg	0	0	0
Carpenter, lg	0	2	2	Chochet	3	2	8
Renick	1	0	2	Offner, rg	0	2	2
Rollins, rg	1	0	2	Rebuffic	0	1	1
Jones	1	2	4	Barrais	0	0	0
Barker	0	0	0				
Total	26	13	65	Total	7	7	21

Score at half—U. S. A. 28, France 9.
Free throws missed—Barksdale, Lumpp, Barker 2, Pierrier, Girardot, Buffiere, Thiolin 3.
Officials—Ugolini (Italy) and Ashri (Egypt).

August 14, 1948

Arizin Gets 85 Points, Villanova Wins, 117-25

By The Associated Press.

VILLANOVA, Pa., Feb. 12— Paul Arizin set what is believed to be an all-time individual college scoring record of 85 points tonight in leading the Villanova Wildcats to a 117-25 victory over the Philadelphia Naval Air Material Command Center's quintet.

The team scoring also set a new mark for the Villanova field house, which was jammed with 2,000 fans.

The former Villanova team mark of 99 points was registered last year against the Fort Dix, N. J., team.

The game was distinctly a one-man show, with Arizin's teammates feeding him continually. Many of his shots, however, were made strictly on his own after he had feinted the sailors into defensive errors.

February 13, 1949

Lavelli Lifts Total to Record 1,891 Points as Yale Downs Harvard Quintet

ELI CAPTAIN GETS 21 IN 77-TO-58 VICTORY

Lavelli's 1,891 Points in Four Years Top Mikan's Modern College Mark of 1,870

YALE KEEPS LEAGUE LEAD

Late Surge Pins 10th Circuit Defeat on Harvard Despite Rockwell's 23 Counters

One contest each with Columbia and Harvard remain for the Elis, who hold a one-game edge over runner-up Princeton. It was also the twenty-first triumph of the season against five setbacks for the representatives of District I in the National Collegiate Athletic Association tourney.

The Elis were hard pressed throughout by a stubborn Harvard five. The Crimson, which now has dropped all ten of its league games, led by 55—54 before a spirited Eli surge in the last seven minutes clinched the verdict.

John Rockwell of the Contabs was high man. He collected 23 points, two more than Lavelli.

Art Fitzgerald shot the Elis to the front immediately with a one-handed push from the left side. After Bill Prior had matched those points for Harvard, Dick Joyce moved Yale into a 4-2 lead as Lavelli fed him a lay-up.

Tom Gannon tied the score with a long set before Lavelli missed a brace of four tries at 1:06. Then the Cantabs, paced by Rockwell, Dick Covey and Gannon, swept into a 10-4 advantage before Joyce hooked in a basket to leave Yale trailing, 10—6, after five minutes.

Shortly thereafter, Lavelli sank the foul which surpassed Mikan's record and after Covey had hit from the left side he added a brace of fouls to narrow the gap at 12—9. The Bulldogs continued to trail until Ted Anderson's push shot from eight feet out provided

a 32-31 lead three minutes before half-time.

Coach Howard Hobson's Elis led at the intermission, 37—36, but fell in arrears again early in the second session and had to fight an uphill battle.

The line-up:

YALE (77)				HARVARD (58)			
	G.	F.	P.		G.	F.	P.
Lavelli, lf	6	9	21	Bramhall, lf	0	0	0
Osbourn	1	0	2	McCuidy	4	0	8
Anderson, rf	1	0	2	Davis	0	1	1
Aberg	1	0	2	Rockwell, rf	9	5	23
Joyce, c	5	1	11	Prior, c	2	3	7
Johnson	0	0	0	Smith	3	1	7
Decoursey	0	0	0	Crosby	0	0	0
Fitzgerald, lg	5	2	14	Covey, lg	1	2	4
Jackson	0	1		Gannon, rg	3	2	8
Nadherny, rg	2	1	5	Petrillo	0	0	0
Upjohn	3	1	7				
Breen	0	0	0	Total	22	14	58
Total	31	15	77				

Officials—Matthew W. Begovich and J. Dallas Shirley.

March 6, 1949

Special to THE NEW YORK TIMES.

NEW HEAVEN, March 5—Capt. Tony Lavelli of Yale tallied 21 points tonight to establish a modern scoring record for a major college player as the Elis rallied in the late stages of an Eastern Intercollegiate Basketball League contest to overpower Harvard, 77-58. Lavelli now has 1,891 points for his four-year total. He had tied George Mikan's old mark of 1,870 in the Elis' victory over Connecticut on Wednesday night.

It was the ninety-third college game for Lavelli, who has played eight fewer than the former De Paul center did in manufacturing his record. The Bulldogs retained first place in the league by triumphing before a prom crowd of 3,000 which jammed Payne Whitney Gymnasium.

Yale now has a league record of eight victories and two defeats.

Wildcats' Star Honored After Contributing 25 Points to 46-36 Victory Over Oklahoma Aggies in the National Final at Seattle

SEATTLE, March 27 (AP)—Back to the blue grass state goes the national collegiate basketball championship — won by a great University of Kentucky team that broke the heart of the fighting Oklahoma Aggies last night, 46-36.

A big, hulking bear of a man who moves with deceptive grace was the key to the Wildcats' victory.

When 6-foot 7-inch Alex Groza fouled out five minutes before the end of the game he had poured in 25 points and literally carried Kentucky to its triumph on his burly shoulders.

There was no doubt in the minds of sports writers who had watched the All-America senior center in action. They unanimously voted him the most valuable player award for the second straight National Collegiate Athletic Association tournament.

Big Nine Team Victor

Before the title game, watched by a turn-away crowd of 12,500 at the University of Washington pavilion, the Big Nine champions from Illinois had taken third place by defeating the Pacific Coast Conference winners from Oregon State, 57—53.

The jubilant Kentuckians, heading back by chartered plane today to Lexington, took with them half of basketball's double diadem for which they had been aiming.

They lost their chance at a twin sweep in the national invitation tournament at New York where they were rudely dumped on their press clippings by unawed Loyola of Chicago.

But in the roaring finish that carried them through the Eastern N.C.A.A. finals and the championship here, the Wildcats proved their No. 1 rating in the eyes of the fans.

A Bad Night, Says Iba

After it was all over, beaming Coach Adolph Rupp said:

"It was a tough game all the way. We had to play this one the hard way, almost to the finish. We beat a good team and we're mighty happy about it."

The Aggies' coach, Hank Iba, shrugged off defeat with "We just had a bad night; we were away off on our shots."

But hitting or not, Oklahoma would have still had that Groza edge to overcome. Fouls cost big Alex his chance to crack the all-time N.C.A.A. single game scoring record of 31 set in 1941 by George Glamack of North Carolina. With four personals against him, Groza was benched for eight minutes in the second half, then got back in just past the midway mark and finally went out via the foul route five minutes before the gun.

Oklahoma A. & M. stepped off to a 5-2 lead with its ball-control style of play. Then Groza started to roll. At the half it was 25—20 for Kentucky and the big guy had accounted for 15 points.

The Aggies' battle was lost when lanky Bob Harris, who matches Groza in height but is 28 pounds lighter at 198, was whistled to the sidelines with five personals early in the second half. Then near the end of the game Oklahoma's scrappy J. L. Parks went out on fouls and it was all over. Kentucky stalled to the finish.

Illinois had a different fight on its hands. Blowing a 28-19 half-time lead, the Illini were forced to come from behind in the last five minutes when Oregon State led, 45—41. Walt Osterkorn was the sparkplug of the Big Nine team's late rally and led his team with 17 points. Cliff Crandall, Oregon State's all-coast center, was high man with 18.

Kentucky's triumph, its second in a row, gave the East its fifth N.C.A.A. championship against six for the West. The Wildcats joined the Aggies as the only two-time winners since the tournaments started in 1939.

The Line-Up

KENTUCKY (46)				OKLAHOMA A. AND M. (36)			
	G.	F.	P.		G.	F.	P.
Jones, lf	1	1	3	Yates, lf	1	0	2
Hirsch	1	0	2	Jaquet	0	1	1
Line, rf	2	1	5	Shelton, rf	3	6	12
Groza, c	9	7	25	McArthur	0	2	2
Beard, lg	1	1	3	Harris, c	3	1	7
Barker, rg	1	3	5	Bradley, lg	0	3	3
Barnstable	1	1	3	Parks, rg	2	3	7
				Pilgrim	0	2	2
Total	16	14	46	Smith	0	0	0
				Total	9	18	36

March 28, 1949

18,000 SEE C. C. N. Y. TOP BRADLEY, 69-61, IN FINAL AT GARDEN

Beaver Quintet Wins National Invitation Though Trailing After 14 Minutes, 29-18

DAMBROT SINKS 23 POINTS

By LOUIS EFFRAT

Hats off to a real champion! The C. C. N. Y. basketball team,

Helping City College to Win National Invitation

Co-Captain Dambrot leaps high to sink a field goal against Bradley as Behnke attempts to defend. Following the play are Roman (left) of the Beavers, Unruh (15) and Grover (14) of the Braves.

The New York Times (by Neal Boenzl)

which thundered down the stretch like a thoroughbred, overcame top-seeded and favored Bradley and triumphed, going away, 69—61, in the final of the thirteenth annual national invitation tournament at Madison Square Garden last night. Not since 1944, when St. John's captured top honors, had a local quintet bagged the coveted prize.

For the overflow turnout of 18,000 it was, indeed, a popular victory for Nat Holman's Beavers. Overlooked completely when the seedings were made, they eliminated San Francisco, the 1949 winner; upset Kentucky, routed Duquesne and then scooped up all the marbles with their merited triumph over Forrest Anderson's talented Bradley quintet.

It was not easy. On the contrary, the Lavender had to shake free from seventeen minutes of woefully weak work.

Beavers Start Poorly

Guilty of faulty passing, sloppy shooting and a horrendous exhibition of foul shooting, the Beavers fell 11 points behind the fast-moving, hard-driving Braves from Peoria, Ill. When, at the 14-minute mark in the opening half, Bradley enjoyed a 29-18 spread, it looked

like the beginning of the end for C. C. N. Y.

With Gene Melchiorre, Paul Unruh and Bill Mann flashing spectacularly, the Braves were good, really good, on offense, but it cannot be said that City College was not presented with numerous openings. The Beavers, employing a fast break, had eight brilliant opportunities, accentuated by 2-on-1, 3-on-2 and 3-on-1 blasts, but none ended with success.

There was even one time when C. C. N. Y. got a 4-on-1 quick break, only to see Al Roth flub the easy hanger. This type of basketball was heart-breaking for the City College rooters and most discouraging to their coach, who had left a sick-bed (Holman's temperature was 103 and he had his personal doctor on the bench) to be with his charges.

The outlook was dark. Here was City College 11 points in the red and getting nowhere in an awful hurry. It behooved Holman to get an idea right then and there. He did.

Turning to the bench, the mentor hurriedly dispatched Norman Mager into action. Almost immediately, the change was noticeable. For City College, despite the

springiness in the legs of Ed Warner, Floyd Layne, Irwin Dambrot and Ed Roman, had been doing hardly any rebounding. Possession, it seemed, always fell to Bradley

Mager Captures Rebound

Then it was that Mager, a senior, who had been used rather sparingly throughout his career at St. Nicholas Heights, made his presence felt. Norm lost no time in capturing a rebound and his mates, catching on quickly, began to follow suit. Thereafter, it was a different City College crew, which more than held its own underneath both backboards.

The result was that Bradley, apparently headed for an easy victory and the N. I. T. title, suffered through the remaining minutes without a field goal. In fact, the Braves failed to tally from the floor in exactly seven minutes and when the half-time buzzer sounded, their margin had dwindled to a mere three points, 30—27.

Warner and Dambrot were the big offensive guns during this City College spurt, but it was Mager, the substitute, who had ignited the spark.

Six ties and seven lead-changes studded the second half before

C. C. N. Y., with Dambrot, Roman and Warner performing wonderfully, edged ahead, 57—56, at the fifteen-minute mark.

Never again did City College trail. Roman's set shot had given the Beavers the lead and a vital 3-point play by Dambrot widened the gap. Bradley, showing signs of physical exhaustion—the pace had been breath-taking—still had some life left.

Aaron Preece, replacement for the sensational Melchiorre, who had fouled out at 10:40 (an irreplaceable loss) converted a pass from Mann and only 2 points separated the teams.

Roman tapped in a rebound, but Mann, fed by Unruh, nullified that basket. Warner, with a driving lay-up, gave his team a 4-point bulge with two minutes remaining.

Elmer Behnke caged a Bradley foul, but Roman's tap-in, two fouls by Warner and one by Joe Galiber put the decision on ice for the Beavers. When possession was a "must" during the final two minutes, Mager did another fine job.

Speed Helps Bradley

Bradley, like C. C. N. Y., had speed to burn, and made the most of it in the opening half. The Beavers almost wrecked themselves because of bad foul shooting. missing their first seven attempts and ending the period with one out of eight, against eight out of nine for the Braves. Even at the finish, City College pointed to a sorry eleven out of twenty-eight, missing ten more than the Peoria men.

Roman, outstanding in the bucket, netted 19 and Warner 16, most in the second period. Behnke and Unruh produced 15 points each for the losers.

Warner, who had scored 26 points against San Francisco, same number against Kentucky and 19 at the expense of Duquesne, was voted the outstanding player in the tournament. Melchiorre was the runner-up, followed by Dambrot, who outplayed everyone in the final.

Warner, Roman and Dambrot, in particular, rallied after the intermission. Dambrot took scoring honors with 23 points.

The Braves fly today to Kansas City, where they will engage Kansas tomorrow night in a play-off for the District 5 berth in the National Collegiate Athletic Association tourney. Since City College will compete in the Eastern division as District 2 entrant, there is a possibility of a Bradley-City College rematch.

St. John's Victory a Thriller

If nothing else, the preliminary engagement blasted the general belief that consolation-round conflicts are humdrum. Certainly the 69-67 victory of St. John's over Duquesne, achieved in overtime, had the crowd cheering all the way, with never a dull moment.

Top-flight basketball was played by both sides, making for an exciting struggle that was tied eighteen times, including the 62-62 count at the end of regulation time. There were fifty-seven seconds of overtime remaining when a drive-in lay-up by Jack McMahon pulled the Redmen even at 67—67. McMahon missed a foul awarded on the play, but St. John's gained possession a few seconds later, and, following a time-out, it was obvious that the Redmen were maneuvering for one play.

Four seconds were left when that one play was executed perfectly. Zeke Zawoluk, taking a bounce pass into the bucket by McMahon, pivoted successfully and third place in the tourney belonged to Frank McGuire's Brooklynites, who were seeded fourth, one notch below the Dukes.

Gerry Calabrese of the victors and Ed Dahler of Duquesne shared scoring laurels at 21 points each.

The line-ups:

CITY COLLEGE (69)

	FG	ST	F	FT	Pts.	A	PF
Dambrot, lf	10	19	3	4	23	3	3
Warner, rf	6	23	4	9	16	3	3
Roman, c	9	17	1	2	19	3	5
Galiber	0	0	0	0	0	4	5
Roth, lg	0	4	0	5	0	4	1
Cohen	0	1	0	0	0	1	1
Mager	2	6	0	0	4	1	3
Layne, rg	2	6	2	4	6	1	0
Total	**29**	**76**	**11**	**28**	**69**	**16**	**16**

BRADLEY (61)

	FG	ST	F	FT	Pts.	A	PF
Grover, lf	3	16	0	2	6	4	4
Preece	2	7	0	1	4	2	3
Unruh, rf	7	12	1	2	15	5	5
Schlimman	1	4	0	0	2	0	1
Chianakas	0	1	0	0	0	0	1
Behnke, c	6	10	3	3	15	2	5
Kelly	0	3	1	3	1	0	0
Mann, lg	4	10	0	0	8	1	5
Melchiorre, rg	2	8	5	7	9	4	0
Total	**25**	**71**	**11**	**18**	**61**	**18**	**24**

Half-time score—Bradley 30, C.C.N.Y. 27.
Officials—John Nucatola and Hagan Andersen.

ST. JOHN'S (69)

	FG	ST	F	FT	Pts.	A	PF
Calabrese, lf	10	18	1	1	21	4	3
Noonan	0	0	0	0	0	0	0
Tully, rf	1	0	0	0	2	0	0
Dombrosky	3	4	6	0	8	0	2
Zawoluk, c	3	6	1	2	7	1	2
McMahon, lg	7	22	3	6	17	4	1
Mulzoff	0	1	1	1	1	3	2
McGuire, g	1	7	5	9	7	5	5
Dalton	2	3	0	0	4	0	1
Redding	0	1	0	0	0	1	1
Total	**29**	**85**	**11**	**21**	**69**	**20**	**18**

DUQUESNE (67)

	FG	ST	F	FT	Pts.	A	PF
Dahler, lf	8	14	5	7	21	2	4
Cerra	1	0	0	0	2	0	2
Farrell, rf	8	22	3	3	19	4	3
Pacacha	0	0	0	0	0	0	0
Cooper, c	5	19	1	2	11	2	4
Skendrovich, lg	2	2	3	4	7	7	3
Dougherty, rg	3	14	1	4	7	2	3
Manning	0	0	0	0	0	0	0
Total	**27**	**72**	**13**	**20**	**67**	**17**	**18**

Half-time score—St. John's 36. Duquesne 35.
Officials—Charles Eckman and Leonard Toff.
KEY: FG, field goals; ST, shots taken; F, fouls; FT, free throws; Pts., points; A, assists; PF, personal fouls.

March 19, 1950

City College Conquers Bradley for First Sweep of National Basketball Titles

BEAVERS TRIUMPH AT GARDEN, 71-68

C. C. N. Y., Invitation Victor, Becomes First Five to Win N. C. A. A. Title Also

LEADS AT HALF BY 39-32

Bradley's Late Drive Fails— North Carolina State Downs Baylor, 53-41, for 3d

By LOUIS EFFRAT

Running out of basketball worlds to conquer, Nat Holman's City College Beavers became—undisputedly—the nation's No. 1 college quintet by virtue of a breath-taking 71-68 victory over Bradley last night at Madison Square Garden.

The vehicle in which the Lavender players drove to unprecedented heights was the East-West final of the National Collegiate A. A. championship tournament. If it was a bumpy ride, endangered at the finish by a fast-draining gas-tank, it made this trip to the top all the more dramatic.

Pitfalls confronted C. C. N. Y. at every turn against so capable a club as Bradley, and it is to the credit of the conquerors that they reached their goal, as 18,000 fans looked on.

So well played and exciting was this contest that an unbiased rooter disliked to see either side lose. However, since a decision must be reached in every basketball game, the one that gave C. C. N. Y. the grand slam was just. That the better team won was generally acknowledged, statistics of the game stressing City College's superiority.

Battle Tensely Waged

The rematch of the year produced one of the most tensely waged court clashes of many a season. C. C. N. Y. downed Bradley, 69—61, in the final of the National Invitation tournament March 18. Then both teams moved into this competition, Bradley prevailing in the Western half at Kansas City and C. C. N. Y. finishing on top here.

Thus, City College was in position to become the first team in history ever to have won both the N. I. T. and N. C. A. A. crowns. At the same time, Bradley had the opportunity to avenge last week's setback by the Beavers.

Everything pointed to a thriller and that is precisely what developed. After six ties, C. C. N. Y., piercing the zone-defense thrown by the Braves, enjoyed a 39-32 spread at half-time.

After ten minutes had elapsed in the second period, the margin had soared to eleven points, 58—47. It looked like a romp, but the lads from Peoria—though six of them had to proceed cautiously because of four fouls against each—got their second wind, switched to a man-to-man defense, capitalized on an all-court press, picked misdirected passes out of the air and suddenly it was a contest, all over again.

Wearied by the tremendous early pace, the Beavers almost folded in the closing minute. They had gone into the two-minute book-rule, which dictates possession regardless of success or failure with a foul-try, with a 5-point lead. Ordinarily, a 66-61 advantage at this stage is monumental. But the Lavender was not up against an ordinary outfit, one that might succumb without a struggle, and what happened in the last minute almost defies description.

Mager Sinks Foul

Gene Melchiorre, the smallest man on the floor, intercepted a pass, dribbled half the length of the court and curled in a lay-up. Less than a minute remained when Norman Mager, whose contributions to City College's triumph were king-sized, caged a foul. Two seconds later, Irwin Dambrot, encircled by defenders, converted a pass from Floyd Layne and tallied. This made it 69—63, with only fifty-seven seconds to go.

So near and yet so far, City College might have felt that it was home-free. But desperately, the resurgent Braves fought back. Joe Stowell dropped in a foul, Melchiorre drove in with a lay-up and then, after intercepting a weak pass, dribbled in with another 2-pointer. In twenty seconds, Bradley counted five points and with forty seconds left, only one point, 69—68, separated the teams.

Ten seconds later a wild City College pass gave Bradley possession and Melchiorre, digging toward the basket, attempted to go all the way. However, as Gene tried to get his shot off from the key-hole, Dambrot made the game's most vital "save." Then, Dambrot, undaunted by a trio of converging Braves, spotted Mager alone on the opposite foul-line.

Dambrot Passes to Mager

Dambrot delivered a softly arched lead-pass to Mager, who scored unmolested. Since only ten seconds remained, Bradley was beaten, but hardly disgraced.

For his excellent work, Dambrot was voted the game's outstanding player, a selection that brought agreement from the fans. Irwin was that good, but Mager, Layne, Warner, Ed Roman, before he fouled out early in the second half, and Al Roth merited more than a few pats on the back.

Melchiorre, whose 16-point out-

BRADLEY PLAYER FOULED IN TITLE CONTEST AT GARDEN

Gene Melchiorre (23) being hacked by Al Roth (7) of City College in first half of last night's game. In on the play are Irwin Dambrot (5) of the Beavers, Elmer Behnke (32) of the Braves and Ed Roman and Floyd Layne of the Lavender team.

The New York Times

in The Associated Press poll during part of the season, first mentioned the bribe offer in a speech to a church dartball dinner in nearby Pekin, Ill., last night.

He said the man offered to pay $100 if Bradley won a game by six points and $500 if it won by two points in any tournament game.

Bradley beat Syracuse by 78—66 and St. John's by 83—72 in the N. I. T., before losing the title game to City College of New York, 69—61.

April 20, 1950

TWO EX-STARS HELD IN BASKETBALL 'FIX' AT $2,000 A GAME

Manhattan Co-captains of Last Year and 3 Others Accused of Bribery and Conspiracy

ONE ADMITS HE GOT CASH

Attempt to Induce Player to 'Throw' the DePaul Contest Leads to Call for Police

By MEYER BERGER

Henry E. Poppe and John A. Byrnes, co-captains and consistent scorers on Manhattan College's 1949-1950 basketball team, were held in bail yesterday on bribery and conspiracy charges growing out of alleged "fixing" of games for gamblers.

Three other men described by authorities as gamblers, two with long police records, were held on similar charges. They are alleged to have paid Poppe and Byrnes $5,000 each at the rate of $1,000 a game for "fixes" in the 1949-1950 season. The police said Poppe has made a "complete confession."

All five men are to have a hearing on the charges next Wednesday.

The five arrests grew out of alleged attempts by Poppe and the gamblers to persuade Junius Kellogg, center on the Manhattan College team, to "throw" the Manhattan College-DePaul University game played at Madison Square Garden on Tuesday night. Mr. Kellogg said $1,000 was offered to him.

Player Helps to Trap 5

Instead of taking the bribe, Mr. Kellogg pretended to be interested, informed Kenneth Norton, his coach, and helped trap Poppe, Byrnes and the three other men. Manhattan College won the Tuesday night game, 62 to 59. Several

---

put made him high-gun; George Chianakas, Aaron Preece, Elmer Behnke and Paul Unruh must be credited with a game, fine effort, made futile by the fact that C. C. N. Y. had five players in double-figures.

Mager and Preece were involved in a head-on collision just before the close of the first period.

looked bad when Norm, after capturing a rebound and whirling underneath the Eighth Avenue backboard, and Preece, in a defensive maneuver, rammed heads. Both went sprawling and were knocked unconscious, blood streaming from Mager's forehead.

After the stricken players were revived, they left the game. Preece was all right, but the 2-inch gash, high on Mager's forehead, required five stitches by Dr. Vincent Nardiello. Patched-up, Norm returned after the intermission and continued to play top-notch basketball, just as he had in all the post-season games.

Thus ended another collegiate campaign, leaving only the East-West Fresh Air Fund all-star game Saturday night. Holman, in his thirty-first year as coach at C. C. N. Y., was lionized by everyone. Elated, Nat, in the dressing room, said: "This is the greatest team I ever have coached in C. C. N. Y."

It is pertinent to note that City College will lose only Dambrot from the starting five. Warner, Layne, Roman nad Roth are sophomores, with two more years ahead

of them, a thought that should make rival coaches shudder.

Third place in the competition went to the Wolfpack of North Carolina State, via a convincing, if not too neat, 53-41 rout of Baylor. Held to a 21-20 half-time edge, the Wolfpack drew away as Sam Ranzino opened fire for the winners. Ranzino scored twenty-one points, all except one in the second half, and was the big difference in this yawn-provoking consolation game. The line-ups:

CITY COLLEGE (71)

	FG	ST	F	FT	Pts.	A	PF
Dambrot, lf	7	14	1	2	15	2	0
Roman, rf	6	17	0	2	12	1	5
Warner, c	4	9	6	14	14	3	2
Roth, lg	2	7	1	5	5	3	2
Mager	4	10	6	6	14	2	2
Galiber	0	0	0	0	0	0	1
Layne, rg	3	7	5	6	11	4	4
Nadell	0	0	0	0	0	1	1
Total	**26**	**64**	**19**	**35**	**71**	**16**	**17**

BRADLEY (68)

	FG	ST	F	FT	Pts.	A.	PF
Grover, lf	0	10	2	3	2	3	3
Schlictman	0	3	0	0	0	0	2
Unruh, rf	4	9	0	0	8	2	5
Behnke, c	3	10	3	3	9	2	4
Kelly	0	1	0	2	0	0	0
Mann, lg	2	7	5	5	9	1	5
Preece	6	11	0	0	12	1	5
D. Melchiorre	0	0	0	0	0	0	0
G. Melchiorre, rg	7	16	2	4	16	3	4
Chianakas	5	7	1	3	11	1	4
Stowell	0	0	1	1	1	0	0
Total	**27**	**74**	**14**	**21**	**68**	**14**	**32**

Half-time score—C. C. N. Y. 39, Bradley 32.
Officials—Lou Eisenstein and Ronald Gibbs.

NORTH CAROLINA STATE (53)

	FG	ST	F	FT	Pts.	A	PF
Ranzino, lf	5	25	11	15	21	0	2
Cartier	3	11	3	4	9	0	3
Dickey, rf	2	14	2	3	6	2	2
Horvath, c	2	8	1	3	5	0	2
Harand, lg	1	3	2	2	4	0	1
Terrill	1	9	0	2	2	2	1
Bubas, rg	1	7	4	6	6	5	4
Total	**15**	**77**	**23**	**35**	**53**	**9**	**15**

BAYLOR (41)

	FG	ST	F	FT	Pts.	A.	PF
Dewitt, lf	2	7	3	4	7	0	5
Cobb	1	1	1	2	3	0	5
Fleetwood	0	6	0	0	0	0	5
Srack, rf	5	17	1	3	11	0	5
Preston, c	1	7	3	5	5	3	2
Harris	0	0	0	0	0	1	0
Heathington, lg	3	14	1	5	7	2	5
Hickman, rg	4	14	0	0	8	1	0
Johnson	0	0	1	2	1	0	0
Hovbe	0	0	0	0	0	0	0
Carrington	0	0	0	0	0	1	0
Mullins	0	0	0	0	0	0	0
Total	**16**	**60**	**9**	**20**	**41**	**9**	**27**

Half-time score—N. C. State 21, Baylor 20.
Officials—Remy Meyer and John Morrow.
KEY: FG, field goals; ST, shots taken; F, fouls; FT, free throws; Pts., points; A., assists; PF, personal fouls.

March 29, 1950

BRIBE OFFER IS REPORTED

Unruh of Bradley Five Says He Turned Down Money Here

PEORIA, Ill., April 19 (AP)—Paul Unruh, All-America player on Bradley University's basketball team, said today he received a bribe offer in New York last month during the National Invitation Tournament.

He said an unidentified man asked him in front of a New York hotel if he would like to "make some easy money." He brushed off the fellow, went his way, and did not mention it to Bradley officials because he didn't think it was important, the player added.

Unruh, scoring ace on the Bradley team which was ranked No. 1

BARES SPORT BRIBE

Junius Kellogg at Manhattan College yesterday.
The New York Times

hours later the police closed in and made the arrests.

Coach Norton praised Mr. Kellogg for his integrity. So did Brother Bonaventure Thomas, Manhattan College president. Mr. Norton bitterly denounced the gamblers as "termites" and said that, if the fixers were putting money before his players' faces, men on other teams must have been similarly tempted.

"This racket is not purely local," he said, and indicated he thought that not only players and gamblers were involved, but possibly basketball court officials, too. He did not amplify this statement.

Edward F. Breslin, chief assistant District Attorney in the Bronx, who conducted the investigation, was up all through Tuesday night and until dawn yesterday questioning Poppe, Byrnes, the alleged gamblers and young Kellogg. Coach Norton sat in with him, obviously dismayed and completely unhappy.

Scandal Third of Kind Here

The scandal was the third of its kind in New York in the last five years. In the two previous cases the gamblers went to prison for their attempts to corrupt student basketball players.

Mr. Breslin said that Poppe confessed he figured in fixed games against three teams in the 1949-1950 season—on Dec. 3, 1949, when Manhattan College lost to Siena College of Loudonville, N. Y., 48—33; on Dec. 26, 1949, when his team lost to Santa Clara College of California, 73 to 64; and on Jan. 12, 1950, when Manhattan lost to

Bradley College of Peoria, Ill., 89 to 67.

Poppe is also alleged to have confessed that he and Byrnes agreed for a fee from the gamblers to do all they could to exceed the point spread in their team's victories over St. Francis College of Brooklyn and against New York University in the 1949-1950 season. Gamblers do all their betting on points in any given game, rather than on the over-all result. Players in their hire agree to "go under" a fixed score margin, or "go over."

January 18, 1951

Point System of Betting Began About 10 Years Ago

About ten years ago gamblers introduced the point betting system into college play.

Prior to that, bets were made on the straight odds system, as in almost any form of sport, including horse racing.

Under the point system in basketball, one team goes into the contest favored to win by a given number of points, figured from that team's past performance as against its opponent's play record.

A bookmaker will take bets from both sides. If a client wants to bet that his team will lose by less than the figured points, the bet is taken. If another bettor wants to bet that his team will win by more than the figured number of points, the bookie will take that, too. He takes his profit from commission.

Th crooked "fixer," certain of the outcome, makes killings under the point system because he knows beforehand, within a point or two, what the outcome will be.

January 18, 1951

3 CITY COLLEGE ACES AND GAMBLER HELD IN BASKETBALL 'FIX'

Hogan Says Players Admitted Taking Up to $1,500 Each for 'Throwing' 3 Games Here

By ALEXANDER FEINBERG

Three City College basketball players, members of the team that won two national championships last season, were arrested yesterday on bribery charges.

District Attorney Frank S. Hogan said they had admitted receiving sums up to $1,500 each for

"fixing" three Madison Square Garden contests in the current season. In each case they were supposed to lose or to keep the margin of victory below the point-spread that City College was favored by in advance betting. City lost all three games.

Taken into custody when they returned with Coach Nat Holman and the remainder of the squad from a record-setting victory over Temple University at Philadelphia on Saturday night, the three—Co-captains Ed Roman and Ed Warner, and Al Roth—were questioned all night. Confronted with incriminating testimony, they shamefacedly acknowledged a gambler's payoffs, Mr. Hogan said.

Four Others Arrested

Arrested with them were Salvatore Tarto Sollazzo, 45-year-old jewelry manufacturer and ex-convict described as a "sure-thing" gambler; Eddie Gard, a Long Island University senior named by Mr. Hogan as Sollazzo's intermediary, and Harvey (Connie) Schaff, a basketball player at New York University. Mr. Hogan said Schaff had attempted to line up a teammate at N. Y. U. for the gambler, but had been rebuffed.

Later, Robert Sabatini, 60, of 25 Central Park West, was held as a material witness. Mr. Hogan described Sabatini as "a person who had gambling contacts" with Sollazzo. The prosecutor said he had "no information" to the effect that Sollazzo's address, 115 Central Park West, was the same apartment building in which Frank Costello is a tenant.

The prosecutor, in disclosing the details of the latest college basketball scandal, the implications of which, because of the wholesale briberies, seemed to reach deeper than the earlier isolated cases, emphasized that no culpability attached either to the schools mentioned or to other players.

Arraigned last night before Chief Magistrate John M. Murtagh in Felony Court, Sollazzo was held without bail. He was excoriated by the Chief Magistrate as one who "appears to have corrupted these young men and brought disgrace on a great institution." Mr. Murtagh mentioned that he himself was an alumnus of City College. Bail of $15,000 each was set for the City College players despite pleas by attorneys for Roman and Roth for a lower figure. Bail for Schaff was fixed at $10,000. All four later posted bonds and were released. Gard, after giving his consent, was remanded to the custody of Acting Capt. William Grafnecker, head of the District Attorney's police squad.

Attendants relieved the three players of the zipper bags that held the basketball uniforms they had worn in the Temple contest, returning them after the arraignment.

The City College youths appeared abashed and nervous dur-

ing the proceedings, while Sollazzo seemed worried but slightly defiant. Sollazzo attempted to correct an entry in his criminal record, which was read in court, saying that a conviction for armed robbery should have read unarmed robbery, but Mr. Murtagh said he was not concerned with the "correction."

February 19, 1951

3 PLAYERS AT L.I.U. ADMIT COLLECTING $18,500 BRIBE CASH

Basketball Stars Confess to 'Fixing' 4 Games in This Season and 3 Last Year

By ALEXANDER FEINBERG

Three Long Island University basketball players, including the high scorer among the country's major teams, admitted yesterday that they had taken $18,500 in bribes to "fix" seven games, four this season and three last year.

After more than ten hours of questioning, District Attorney Frank S. Hogan announced the arrest in the early morning hours of Sherman White, probably the No. 1 collegiate player in the nation; Adolph (Al) Bigos, team captain, and Le Roy Smith, a high-scoring senior.

All finally admitted, the prosecutor said, that they had been paid by Salvatore T. Sollazzo, the ex-convict who bribed three City College stars, through Eddie Gard, L. I. U. senior. The latter, also named as Sollazzo's recruiting agent and intermediary in the case of the City College "fixes," was an outstanding player on the L. I. U. team in the 1949-50 season, when he used up his eligibility.

The board of trustees of Long Island University took quick action upon the disclosures. At a special meeting last night it voted to end all participation in intercollegiate sports. This includes cancellation of the university's four remaining basketball games, two in Madison Square Garden.

Despite rumors of still other "fix" disclosures, the District Attorney's office would not acknowledge that any were in the making. The reports, which mentioned school and players by name, became widespread after the L. I. U. arrests. Mr. Hogan said "as flatly as I can" that these rumors were "not true," but that "naturally the investigation is continuing."

February 21, 1951

Sports of The Times
By ARTHUR DALEY
Whole Hog or None

PHIL WRIGLEY of the Chicago Cubs once offered the sage observation: "Baseball is too much a sport to be a business and too much a business to be a sport." College athletic authorities would do well to ponder those words. Reluctant though they be to admit it, the description now applies unerringly to the entire intercollegiate athletic set-up.

In theory they cling to the ideal of amateurism. In practice they act contrary to what they preach. Even the Sanity Code was too restrictive for their tastes and was overthrown. Yet the imperfect Sanity Code actually failed to adhere to the highest tenets of pure amateurism, which frowns on any boy "capitalizing on his athletic fame." Acceptance of an athletic scholarship is capitalization.

Wesley Fesler resigned as football coach at Ohio State because the mania for all-winning football teams was more than he could bear. But then he unaccountably accepted a similar job at Minnesota, where that same kind of pressure had blown the revered Bernie Bierman out of what seemed to be a lifetime position.

Dick Larkins, the athletic director at Ohio State, lashed back bitterly at all Grandstand Quarterbacks with the charge that the gridiron game had become "a Frankenstein, a monster." He added, "Football is killing itself."

Indivisible Sum

The basketball scandal is merely an eruption of the same festering sore. It can't be separated as something apart from intercollegiate athletics as a whole. What is the answer? One radical solution has been offered to this department by Delbert Clark, who usually does his thinking on a more global basis from Berlin or Washington. He writes:

"Certainly it is no answer to remove basketball from Madison Square Garden any more than it would stop gambling on heavyweight prize fights if they were barred from the Garden. The answer is bigness and overcommercialization. Colleges have gone commercial first of all in order to satisfy the alumni demand for winning teams.

"Winning teams, plus lowered academic standards, plus the pathological belief that anyone without a college degree is somehow déclassé, has swollen college enrollment. Swollen enrollment has necessitated more 'plant,' which calls for money, and money can be obtained least painfully, the colleges have found, by putting on super-gladiatorial games. Round and round she goes and where she stops nobody knows, as the wheel-of-fortune man used to intone at county fairs.

Simple Solution

"But the answer, to my mind, is quite simple. The colleges have a bull by the tail, and they don't know how to let go. The answer is: Don't let go—climb aboard the bull and ride it. In plain words, let the colleges go frankly and completely commercial, so far as athletics are concerned. Let them drop all this nonsense about athletes attending classes and getting degrees.

"No one compelled Babe Ruth to study Latin or history as a condition of playing for the New York Yankees. Why should Josip Silovitzky have to meet such abnormal standards for the privilege of tossing a round ball into a basket or an elliptical one across a goal line?

"Once college sports are fully commercialized, a number of current problems, including moral problems, will fold their tents like the Arabs and silently steal away.

"I personally doubt that the young men who accepted bribes to throw basketball games are fundamentally vicious. They simply needed money or thought they did. One of them related in a penitent mood how he had been ashamed to ask his poor old father for pocket money, or indeed for pockets in which to put it. He shouldn't have to. He works, doesn't he? Okay, pay him!"

Medicine Man

That's a rather rugged cure that the Medicine Man has ordered. But a schoolboy athlete gets his first shock when colleges bid against each other for his services—self-righteous schools and out-and-out boiler factories. One by one his scruples go as hypocrisy and shady practices surround him. The what's-in-it-for-me attitude develops. He lives in a twilight zone between pure amateurism and out-and-out professionalism. And there is the fundamental flaw in intercollegiate athletics as it exists today. The structure is built on a foundation of sand.

One choice is open professionalism. The other choice is pure amateurism, the idea and the ideal that John Kieran used to advocate. Do away with gate receipts and you eliminate scandal or even a threat of scandal. Only Johns Hopkins has had the courage to try it, and it's worked beautifully—no gate receipts, no pressure to win, no guarantees given or taken, no subsidization. Sports merely is a healthy part of the over-all educational system.

Whole hog or none. Which is it to be?

February 22, 1951

CITY COLLEGE BANS GAMES AS 4TH STAR CONFESSES 3 'FIXES'

By ALEXANDER FEINBERG

Floyd G. Layne, 22-year-old basketball star at City College, was taken from the campus at 3 P. M. yesterday by detectives of District Attorney Frank S. Hogan's staff. Within an hour he admitted participation in the "point-fixing" of three games at Madison Square Garden this season.

Immediately before this admission, which the player made with an air of relief, Dr. Harry N. Wright, president of City College, announced suspension of the college's two remaining basketball games, both in the Garden. One was to have been played tomorrow night against Manhattan College, and the second next Tuesday against City College's traditional basketball rival, New York University.

Layne was booked at the Elizabeth Street station at 9:15 P. M. on a charge of accepting bribes. Hatless, he stood silent before the desk sergeant. He was to be held overnight until his arraignment today in Felony Court.

Layne's arrest on charges of accepting bribes was the fourth of a City College basketball star of the "Cinderella" team that last season swept to surprising triumphs in both the National Invitation Tournament and the National Collegiate Athletic Association postseason contests, symbolic of the national championship.

In disclosing Layne's admission of participation in "fixed" games, Mr. Hogan said the player received $1,500 for helping to shave the gambling point margin in the Missouri game on Dec. 9 last, and $1,000 for the Arizona game on Dec. 28. He was promised $1,500 for the Boston College game on Jan. 11 of this year, Mr. Hogan said, but never received the money.

In addition, Layne got "bonuses" of $250 each for the Washington State game on Dec. 14 and the St. John's game on Jan. 2. Mr. Hogan emphasized that neither of the last two games was "fixed" but that the payments were made, as had other previously brought to light, to induce the player to go along with the "sure-thing gamblers" on future contests.

In Layne's company, detectives last night visited his home, at 1091 Prospect Avenue, the Bronx, where they recovered $2,890 of the bribe money. He led them to a flower pot in the bedroom, where the money, rolled up in a handkerchief, was found embedded in the dirt. It consisted of twenty-three $100 bills, one $50 bill, fourteen $20 bills and twenty-five $10 bills and two $5 bills.

The Layne "fixes," like those of his teammates taken into custody a week ago—Al Roth, Ed Roman and Ed Warner—were engineered by Eddie Gard, former Long Island University basketball player who acted as intermediary for Salvatore T. Sollazzo, jeweler and former convict, Mr. Hogan said.

February 28, 1951

N.C.A.A. Urges Colleges to Keep Basketball Games Out of Garden

Council Hints Future Tournaments May Be Held Elsewhere—Cites Bribery Cases in Backing Campus Competition

CHICAGO, March 2 (UP)—The National Collegiate A. A. Council today recommended a boycott, by its members of Madison Square Garden basketball games and intimated that in the future none of its tourney games would be scheduled at the New York arena.

Though the Garden was not mentioned specifically in a prepared statement on "bribery revelations in connection with college basketball," it was obvious that the recommendation of the council, policy making committee of the N. C. A. A., had only one place in mind.

The recommendation, which was described as "not binding" on the membership, had six points. Four of these were pertinent. These were:

1. Member institutions should hold their athletic competition on campus fields and in campus buildings.

2. Where such campus facilities are not adequate, it is recommended that institutions play only on fields r in buildings of which the collegiate institution has effective control.

3. Because of previously committed contractual and lease arrangements, which it is deemed unwise and impracticable to void at this time, the N. C. A. A. will hold certain of its 1951 basketball tournaments in buildings not on college campuses. However the N. C. A. A. Council is convinced that college sports belong in campus locales and that concentration of them in any other areas contributes to the conditions which have been brought to light in recent weeks.

4. N. C. A. A. future policies shall be definitely guided by these principles.

Games in the 1951 N. C. A. A. tournament are scheduled for the Garden March 20, 22 and 24. These will not be moved, but it was clear that unless the N. C. A. A. obtains more effective control of future games in the Garden, that the site would not be selected for future tournament contests.

Asked whether the N. C. A. A. had "effective control" of games now being played in the Garden, Kenneth L. Wilson, executive secretary-treasurer, said "No." He explained that competing schools received only a certain proportion of tickets for games and that the Garden controlled other blocks.

The council also decided to move for the expulsion of any member which does not comply with the convention-approved one-year "moratorium" on live television of football games.

March 3, 1951

Illinois Tops Columbia, St. John's Wins

LION STRING ENDED AT 31 IN ROW, 79-71

Illinois Comes From Behind to Knock Columbia's Five From Regional Tests

ST. JOHN'S VICTOR, 63-52

Defeats a Game Connecticut Team After Rolling Up Big Early Lead at Garden

By LOUIS EFFRAT

Columbia's basketball team last night suffered its first defeat since Feb. 15, 1950, at Madison Square Garden. After thirty-one straight conquests, all except nine this season, Lu Rossini's Lions fell before an Illinois squad that had captured the Big Ten crown, and 17,107 observers will attest to the merit of the 79-71 victory of Harry Combes' Illini.

The occasion was the Eastern regionals of the thirteenth annual National Collegiate A. A. championship tournament, launched simultaneously at Raleigh, N. C., and here, where the curtain-raiser resulted in a 63-52 triumph for St. John's over Connecticut.

Because of last night's developments, the Garden program tomorrow night will send Illinois against North Carolina State and St. John's will engage Kentucky in the Eastern semi-finals. The final is set for here Saturday night, after which the surviving team will meet the Western regional winner at Minneapolis, March 27.

Illini Snag Rebounds

Oddly, the two local teams last night suffered second-half letdowns, but where St. John's managed to remain ahead, Columbia, after having gained a 45-38 spread at the intermission, missed out. Gone was the spring in the legs of the Lions, who forfeited possession because of their failure to cope with the Illinois rebounding. Gone was the magic of Jack Molinas, John Azary, Bob Reiss and Alan Stein, whose shooting accuracy vanished.

Gone too was the characteristic fast-breaking offense that had wrecked every opponent prior to last night. Error after error hurt the Lions, and, if these were not bad enough, at least a half-dozen field goals were of the in-and-out variety in the second half.

However, none can detract from the Illinois triumph. Ted Beach kept the Illini in the game with his remarkable one-handers—he clicked with seven straight in the initial period—and the clever Don Sunderlage sparked them home with his clever dribbling and feint-

THWARTING AN ATTEMPT TO SCORE BY LIONS AT GARDEN

Follmer (33) of Illinois steals ball from Molinas (4) of Columbia, who was about to make a lay-up shot during first half of N. C. A. A. play.

The New York Times

ing, finishing with 25 points, tops for the game. Molinas tallied 20 for Columbia, two fewer than Beach.

Lions Close Gap

Rarely getting the ball off the boards in the second half, Columbia, nevertheless, was decidedly in contention so late as 17:10. Less than three minutes earlier, Illinois had soared to a 70-61 bulge, but Reiss, Molinas and Azary quickly hit the target. A lay-up by Sunderlage and a foul by Beach then eased the situation for Illinois, but the Lions bounded back with one-handers by Azary and Lee Guittar.

It was 73—71 in favor of Illinois and the clock showed 2 minutes 10 seconds to go when the most damaging blow to Columbia was inflicted by Rod Fletcher. This was a spectacular drive-in, Fletcher feinting his guard out of position, curling in the lay-up, and, since he was hacked on the play, adding the foul. A 2-pointer by

Sunderlage and Beach's free toss were superfluous.

The Illinois total marked the highest number of points scored against any Columbia quintet.

Overmatched Connecticut, virtually certain to be eliminated, won the admiration of the spectators with its second-half comeback, which cut a 27-point (54—27) deficit to 11 at the final buzzer.

Vince (Yogi) Yokabaskas and Ed Gates inspired the Nutmeg squad, which, after falling behind by 34—19 at the intermission, discarded its zone-defense for man-to-man guarding and made the Redmen suffer.

St. John's, with Jack McMahon and Ronnie MacGilvray hobbling about, appeared to be overworked and tired, even while winning. None of the Redmen matched the drive and speed of Yokabaskas and Gates, even if Zeke Zawoluk's 18-point output was close to Yokabaskas' 22.

The line-ups:

ST. JOHN'S (63)

	FG	ST	F	FT	Pts.	A.	PF
Dombrosky, lf	6	13	5	5	17	2	0
O'Shea	0	0	0	1	0	1	2
McGuire, rf	0	0	0	0	0	1	2
McGilvray	2	8	1	5	5	1	3
McCuol	0	1	0	0	0	1	2
Zawoluk, c	7	18	4	5	18	2	3
Giancontieri	0	0	0	0	0	0	0
McMahon, lg	5	12	0	0	10	2	1
Noonan	0	0	0	0	0	0	0
Mulroff, rg	2	7	1	1	5	5	5
Dunn	2	4	0	0	4	1	2
McAndrews	0	0	0	0	0	0	0
Total	24	63	15	20	63	15	19

CONNECTICUT (52)

	FG	ST	F	FT	Pts.	A.	PF.
Yokabaskas, lf	7	15	8	11	22	3	2
Widholm, rf	2	5	3	7	3	5	3
Silverstein	0	1	0	0	0	0	1
Demir	0	0	0	0	0	0	1
Ebel, c	5	12	2	3	12	0	1
Fleischman	0	2	0	0	0	0	0
Kleckner	1	3	0	0	2	4	1
Clark, lg	1	6	0	1	2	2	3
Brouker	0	2	0	0	0	0	1
Gates, rg	3	17	1	3	7	3	2
Total	19	63	14	21	52	15	16

Half-time score—St. John's 34, Connecticut 19.

ILLINOIS (79)

	FG	ST	F	FT	Pts.	A.	PF
Follmer, lf	1	6	1	3	3	3	3
Beach	10	17	2	2	22	3	1
Bemoras, rf	2	4	5	8	4	2	2
Peterson, c	1	2	1	1	3	1	0
Baumgardner	1	4	1	3	3	1	0
Hagan	6	18	1	4	13	5	3
Fletcher, lg	1	1	1	1	3	3	3
Sund'lage, rg	9	19	7	10	25	4	1
Total	30	79	19	28	79	20	15

COLUMBIA (71)

	FG	ST	F	FT	Pts.	A.	PF
Azary, lf	5	14	3	3	13	6	2
Reiss, rf	4	9	1	2	9	2	3
Molinas, c	8	19	4	5	20	2	4
Powers, lg	1	9	3	3	5	5	5
Lewis	0	6	1	2	0	0	2
Brandt	0	4	1	2	0	0	2
Maratos	0	1	0	0	0	1	0
Stein, rf	4	31	1	1	9	4	4
Guittar	1	6	1	1	9	1	1
Rohan	0	1	0	0	0	1	1
Total	28	86	15	18	71	17	24

Half-time score—Columbia 45, Illinois 38.

KEY: FG, field goals; ST, shots taken; F, fouls; FT, free throws; Pts., points; A. assists; PF. personal fouls.

March 21, 1951

Kentucky Beats Kansas State Quintet in N.C.A.A. Final

SOUTHERN SQUAD WINNER BY 68-58

Kentucky Rallies in Second Half to Beat Kansas State —Illinois Victor, 61-46

MINNEAPOLIS, March 27 (AP)—Bill Spivey, a sleeping giant the first half, became a ball of fire after the rest period and led Kentucky to its third N. C. A. A. basketball title in four years tonight by crushing Kansas State, 68 to 58.

Soundly outplayed underneath the baskets during the first half, the seven-foot Spivey was a rebounding demon in the final session and dominated the play so thoroughly that many of the 15,-438 spectators started for home early.

Thus the nation's top basketball title returns to the Blue Grass country. Kentucky ruled the collegiate cage world in 1948 and again in 1949, but its reign was interrupted last spring by City College of New York.

Oklahoma Is Beaten

Before Spivey put on his amazing demonstration, Illinois had defeated Oklahoma A. & M., 61 to 46, for third-place honors. Both tonight's victors won the right to come here in Eastern N. C. A. A. playoffs at Raleigh, N. C., and New York City.

Lew Hitch, the 6-foot-7 center for Kansas State, gave the mighty Spivey a trying time during the first half and the Big Seven cham-

pions, playing for the first time in the national final, went off the floor with a two-point edge on baskets by Jack Stone and Bob Rousey.

Kentucky, which had trailed throughout the first half, finally had pulled even at 14:55 on Cliff Hagan's bucket.

Hagan, who missed the final practices because of the flu, did not start and came off the bench just seconds before tossing the equalizing basket.

But once the second half got under way there was no question which team was superior. With Hitch showing weariness from his rugged task of holding Spivey in check, the budding champions romped away.

Spivey Breaks Loose

After Shelby Linville had dropped a free throw to make the count 29 to 28, Spivey broke loose for the first of his six baskets in the first ten minutes of the second half.

That put the Kentuckians in front and they never trailed again. Three minutes later they were ahead only 39 to 36, but then the Kansas State offense slumbered for eight minutes without a basket. By that time it was 54 to 40, and they were beginning to dust the trophy case in Lexington.

Spivey, who collected 22 points, was the hero of the fray, but he received stellar aid from Hagan, the ailing forward, who tossed in ten points during his brief stay, and Bobby Watson, the ball-hawking guard who measures but 5 feet 10 inches.

Jack Stone was the best of the Kansas State point makers, hitting for three baskets and adding six more tallies from the free-throw line.

"Spivey just got over the idea of letting Hitch shoot in the second half," said Coach Adolph Rupp after receiving the first-place trophy. "And that Hagan played the best game of his career for us."

The Kentucky-Kansas State line-up:

KENTUCKY (68)					KANSAS ST. (58)				
	G.	F.	PF.	P.		G.	F.	PF.	P.
Whitaker, lf	4	1	2	9	Head, lf	3	2	2	8
Linville, rf	2	4	5	8	Stone, rf	3	6	2	12
Spivey, c	9	4	2	22	Hitch, c	6	1	3	13
Ramsey, lg	4	1	5	9	Barrett, lg	2	0	1	4
Watson, rg	3	2	3	8	Iverson, rg	3	1	3	7
Hagan	5	0	5	10	Rousey	2	0	3	4
T'sropoulous	1	0	1	2	Gibson	0	1	5	1
Newton	0	0	0	0	Upson	0	0	1	0
					Knostman	1	1	1	3
Total	28	12	23	68	Peck	2	0	0	4
					Schuyler	1	0	2	2
					Total	23	12	23	58

Half-time score—Kansas State 29, Kentucky 27.
Free throws missed—Stone 2, Barrett 2, Iverson, Knostman, Peck, Schuyler, Linville 4, Spivey 2, Ramsey 2, Watson 2, Hagan 2.

March 28, 1951

COLLEGES BLAMED IN 'FIX'

Greed Chief Cause of Gambling Scandals, Coaches Charge

MINNEAPOLIS, March 27 (UP) —A special committee of basketball coaches today blamed the greed of colleges for the gambling "fix" scandals.

The committee, set up by the National Association of Basketball Coaches to see if such scandals could be avoided, turned in a report that laid the blame at the doorstep of the colleges and the coaches themselves.

"We believe that the recent gambling expose has grown out of a laxity on the part of college administrators to actively uphold the standards which would discourage such practices," John Bunn, Springfield, Mass., coach who headed the special committee, said.

"Entirely too much emphasis has been placed by the schools and coaches on income and winning the game. We have found vicious and often illegal recruiting practices and over-emphasis on winning teams and the income therefrom."

The committee said that coaches "should check the background of players more so we could guide

them," adding that "in the desire to win games, we have let players in the game who aren't a credit to their school or to the sport."

Much of the report was directed at college presidents, alumni groups, and college administrators. School administrators were urged to "exercise a closer and more active supervision of all phases of our athletic program."

The only legislative correction suggested was a strengthening of anti-bribery laws and "strict enforcement."

Other members of the committee besides Mr. Bunn, the chairman, were: Everett Dean, Stanford; Clarence (Nibs) Price, California; Stan Watts, Brigham Young University; Jack Gray, Texas; Bill Henderson, Baylor; Al Duer, George Pepperdine; Bruce Drake, Oklahoma; Howard Hobson, Yale; Howard Cann, Yale; Cliff Wells, Tulane; Pete Newell, Michigan State, and Wilbur (Sparky) Stallcup, Missouri.

March 28, 1951

---

14 Players Admit Basketball Fix Plot

Fourteen former college basketball players pleaded guilty yesterday in General Sessions to conspiracy charges arising out of the fixing of games played at Madison Square Garden in recent seasons.

The majority of the defendants will be witnesses against Salvatore T. Sollazzo when he goes to trial July 16 on charges that he had paid players as high as $7,750 to control the point score of their team. Sollazzo, the alleged master fixer, has been indicted in a thirty-count true bill for conspiracy and bribery.

Judge Saul S. Streit fixed Oct. 2 for sentencing the players, whose bail was continued. By their change of plea they

41

escaped prosecution on more serious bribery charges pending against them. For conspiracy each may receive an indeterminate term up to a maximum of three years in the penitentiary.

The players, who had been star performers for City College, Long Island University and New York University, made frequent appearances before the grand jury, telling how they had been approached by at least five alleged fixers, including Sollazzo and his so-called intermediary, Edward Gard, a former L. I. U. player, on propositions to hold down the scores against out-of-town teams.

Gard, who starred at L. I. U. several years ago, has been scheduled to go on trial with Sollazzo before Judge Streit. However, Assistant District Attorney Vincent A. G. O'Connor, who gathered the evidence against the defendants, said he expected a disposition on this matter within a few days.

Among those who withdrew their original pleas and pleaded guilty yesterday were:

Edward Roman, 21 years old, of 1372 Teller Avenue, the Bronx; Alvin Roth, 21, of 480 Montgomery Avenue, Brooklyn; Edward Warner, 22, of 302 West 138th Street; Floyd Layne, 22, of 1091 Prospect Avenue, the Bronx; Norman Mager, 25, of 1633 East Fourth Street, Brooklyn; Herbert Cohen, 21, of 76 Clara Street, Brooklyn, and Irwin Dambrot, 23, of 110 Seaman Avenue. The seven had been outstanding members of a City College team which captured two national championships last year.

Six others, all former L.I.U. players, were Louis Lipman, 26, of 1834 Caton Avenue, Brooklyn; Richard Feurtado, 25, of 669 East Thirty-eighth Street, Brooklyn; Adolph Bigos, 26, of 651 Penn Street, Perth Amboy, N. J.; Nathan Miller, 25, of 159 Eastern Parkway, Brooklyn; Sherman White, 22, of 90 Forest Avenue, Englewood, N. J., and LeRoy Smith, 22, of 20 Fairview Avenue, Newark.

The final defendant to plead was Harvey (Connie) Schaff, 22, of 93 East Ninety-first Street, Brooklyn, a former N.Y.U. player.

In recommending that the court accept the new pleas, Mr. O'Connor mentioned the concurrence of District Attorney Frank S. Hogan and said:

"We do not believe the public interest requires that these young men receive felony convictions. In our view justice is adequately served by the acceptance of misdemeanor pleas from them."

Mr. O'Connor said that the trial of Sollazzo was "the major objective" in the inquiry into college basketball corruption.

The grand jury has handed up bribery indictments against Jack Goldsmith, 31-year-old former L. I. U. player; William Rivlin, a fugitive, and Eli Klukofsky, alias Eli Kaye.

Two of City College's former players, Roth and Roman, pleaded guilty to conspiracy counts in two separate indictments, one of which related to alleged bribes received from Sollazzo and the other concerned a bribe charged to Klukofsky.

Two of the sixteen games involved in the bribery allegations were played away from Madison Square Garden. One contest N. Y. U. played against St. Francis College at the former's gymnasium on its Bronx campus and the second game, also involving N.Y.U., was held at Durham, N. C., against North Carolina.

In another development in the pending trial of Sollazzo, Judge John A. Mullen granted a motion by Mr. O'Connor for a special panel of talesmen. It was granted over the opposition of William W. Kleinman, Sollazzo's attorney. The latter, who was defense counsel in the trial of four firemen convicted Tuesday on extortion charges, told the court he was tired and would seek to have the original trial date of July 12 adjourned. Later it was agreed to move it back to July 16.

July 6, 1951

8 BRADLEY PLAYERS INVOLVED IN FIXING BASKETBALL GAMES

Melchiorre, an All-American, Is Among Five Who Confess in Peoria to Accepting $6,700

HOGAN SPARKS THE INQUIRY

Two Brooklyn Brothers Seized as Fixers—Alarm Sent Out for Third Man Here

By ALFRED E. CLARK

The collegiate basketball scandal erupted anew yesterday involving eight former players of Bradley University of Peoria, Ill., one of the country's top-flight teams, on charges they had accepted $6,700 in bribes to fix games.

Five of the players, including Gene (Squeaky) Melchiorre, diminutive All-American guard who sparked the team to a leading position in college competition in the last four seasons, confessed in Peoria that they had taken money from sure-thing gamblers to hold down scores on two games.

Confirming revelations made by District Attorney Frank S. Hogan, whose investigation turned up this latest phase of the worst college sport scandal in history, were Melchiorre and four other stars, William Mann, captain of last year's team; Charles (Bud) Grover, Aaron Preece and James Kelly.

Late yesterday three other Bradley players, whose identities were not made known, were being questioned by Michael A. Shore, state attorney of Peoria County, and Assistant District Attorney Vincent A. G. O'Connor, whom Mr. Hogan sent to aid in the inquiry.

Other Teams Seen Involved

Mr. Shore said preliminary questioning indicated that "some other teams are involved." "Bradley isn't the only one," he said, adding that he understood Mr. Hogan was planning to report this morning evidences of still more sports corruption in at least one other out-of-town school.

July 25, 1951

3 BASKETBALL ACES ON KENTUCKY TEAM ADMIT '49 FIX HERE

Hogan Links Beard, Groza and Barnstable to $1,500 Bribe in Game at the Garden

TWO NOW PROFESSIONALS

But Are Suspended by League —Third, a Teacher, Comes Here Voluntarily for Inquiry

Three former University of Kentucky basketball players, two of them All-America stars, admitted yesterday they had accepted $1,500 in bribes to "throw" a National Invitation Tournament championship game at Madison Square Garden on March 14, 1949.

This disclosure, made by District Attorney Frank S. Hogan, was the most spectacular so far in the growing list of nation-wide college basketball scandals. The two All-America players, Ralph Beard and Alex Groza, were among the modern "greats" of the game. The third player, Dale Barnstable, was their mate and former captain of the team that won 130 games and numerous championships between 1946 and 1949.

The game the three admitted "throwing" was in the first round of the tournament; it was won by Loyola University of Chicago, 67—56, although Kentucky was the pre-game favorite.

7 Colleges Involved in Fixes

The involvement of the University of Kentucky brought to seven the number of leading colleges figuring in "fixed" games played at Madison Square Garden in the last several years. Twelve gamblers have been indicted for corrupting twenty-six players by bribing them either to "shave" points from the winning margin

Dale Barnstable, former captain of the famous Kentucky team, who came here voluntarily with a New York detective.
Associated Press Wirephoto

or deliberately to lose games.

Beard and Groza, who were members of the Indianapolis Olympian Club of the professional National Basketball Association, were arrested early yesterday in Chicago. Held as fugitives, they will be brought here tomorrow.

Barnstable, who, according to Mr. Hogan, made his confession in Louisville, where he is coach of the DuPont Manual High School team, voluntarily flew to New York yesterday afternoon in the company of Detective John F. Conway of the prosecutor's staff. He told reporters here. "I hope the public will be lenient in their opinion of the boys until after the trial."

Suspended by League

As a result of their arrest and admissions, both Beard and Groza were immediately suspended from professional basketball. But this appeared to be among the least of their troubles. In announcing their detention, Mr. Hogan indicated they would be questioned about additional games in which they participated.

Both men were taken into custody Friday night at Chicago Stadium where they were watching a game between the Rochester Royals, a professional team, and the College All-Stars, managed by Adolph Rupp, their coach at Kentucky when they lost to Loyola.

The two players told the Chicago police and Assistant District Attorney Vincent A. G. O'Connor of Mr. Hogan's staff that they were en route to Moline, Ill., where they were to play a professional game with the Milwaukee Hawks last night.

Clifford Barker and Joseph Holland, also former Kentucky players and now on the Indianapolis team, were questioned by the police but were released.

Beard and Groza at first denied taking bribes. Mr. Hogan's announcement said. but confessed after they had been confronted by Nicholas (The Greek) Englisis, free in bail here on charges of bribing collegiate basketball players, and Nat (Lovey) Brown, a material witness in Mr. Hogan's investigation.

Although Englisis and his brother, Anthony, who also is free in bail, had told Mr. Hogan they paid $1,000 to Groza to "shave" points in the Loyola game, and $500 each to Beard and Barnstable, Groza said yesterday he had received only $500, the prosecutor reported.

Mr. O'Connor told reporters in Chicago that "practically every game" played by Kentucky in the 1948-49 season was under investigation. He said Beard and Groza had admitted to accepting bribes of $200 each to reduce the winning margin on two Kentucky games played outside of New York. The point margin is used in gambling on basketball games.

There were repercussions of yesterday's disclosures in quarters where the accused athletes were known. Dr. H. L. Donovan, president of the University of Kentucky, said in Lexington that the three had been the "inexperienced victims of an unscrupulous syndicate."

Coach Cites Views

Coach Rupp, who had said in August that "gamblers couldn't reach my boys with a ten-foot pole," commented in Lexington that "the whole world has known for years how I feel about gambling on athletic contests."

Maurice Podoloff, president of the National Basketball Association, who flew to Chicago where he suspended Beard and Groza, said the association's directors would meet at 11 A. M. tomorrow in the Park Sheraton Hotel here for a "complete appraisal" of the situation. The two suspended players are

stockholders in the Indianapolis team.

Mr. Podoloff said he had met last month with Mr. O'Connor to discuss the basketball inquiry as it affected the professional league, and had told the assistant prosecutor "I was most anxious to clean house, if the house had to be cleaned."

After being in custody for fifteen hours Beard and Groza were released yesterday afternoon in $1,-000 bail posted by a professional bondsman.

The Kentucky team whose record was blackened by the bribe revelations was one of the great-

FORMER BASKETBALL PLAYERS WHO ADMIT FIX

Ralph Beard, seated left, and Alex Groza, seated right, being questioned in a Chicago police station early yesterday by Detective James Canavan, standing left, and Jack Doyle of the state attorney's office. They confessed to accepting bribes to shave points in important games. *Associated Press*

est in modern basketball. Beard was selected on The Associated Press All-America teams for 1948 and 1949 and Groza on the 1949 team. Other Kentucky players were chosen for sectional all-star teams. The Kentucky team represented the United States in the 1948 Olympic Games.

Beard, who is 23 years old, lives in Indianapolis. Groza, 25, is a resident of Martin's Ferry, Ohio. The 26-year-old Barnstable lives in Louisville.

In another development yesterday, Joseph Benintende, who was

held in $75,000 bail last Tuesday as an alleged member of the basketball-fixing ring, served Mr. Hogan with a habeas corpus order seeking reduction of his bail. The application is returnable tomorrow before Supreme Court Justice Edward Koch.

In addition to Kentucky, the other colleges involved in the New York basketball scandals are New York University, City College, Long Island University, Manhattan College, Bradley University of Peoria, Ill., and the University of Toledo in Ohio.

October 21, 1951

Kansas Quintet Routs St. John's in N.C.A.A. Championship Final

LOVELLETTE STARS IN 80-TO-63 VICTORY

Kansas Ace Tallies 33 Points Against St. John's in Final Before 11,700 at Seattle

SEATTLE, March 26 (AP)—Clyde Lovellette scored 33 points tonight and paced Kansas to a record-shattering 80—63 victory over St.

John's of Brooklyn in the National Collegiate Athletic Association basketball championship final before 11,700. Illinois edged Santa Clara for third place in the consolation game, 67—64.

The Kansans never let St. John's make a race of it, leading from the first point to the last. Lovellette, who set the N.C.A.A. tourney scoring mark last night, added 16 points to his three-game total of 108 in the first half tonight and 17 in the second.

The 80 points scored by the new champions was a new high for the title game, beating by 9 the total posted by City College of New York in 1950.

St. John's never quit trying in the fast, rough battle, but Lovel-

lette's power on the backboards was too much for the Redmen.

Zawoluk Scores 20 Points

Bob Zawoluk, ace center of the losers, counted only 6 points in the first half, but waged an even scoring battle with Lovellette in the last half until the Brooklyn star fouled out 3½ minutes before the final gun. Zawoluk scored 20 for the evening.

The game's first point was looped by Lovellette from the free throw line in the opening minute and St. John's never caught up. The Redmen stayed close to the Jay Hawks through the first quarter, trailing at its close. 18—13. They pressed desperately all over the court throughout the game. but the Kansans usually managed

to find their 6-foot-9 giant with a pass or carom the ball to him off the boards.

By half-time the count was up to 41—27 and Kansas had hit eighteen of its thirty-eight field goal tries for a .474 average. St. John's, not far back, averaged .407 while getting only twenty-seven shots and hitting eleven.

The losers surged for a time in the third stanza as Zawoluk hit 4 points and Forward Jack Mc-Mahon 2 to cut the margin at 48—36. From there on, Kansas built its lead steadily. disdaining to go into a stall against the Redmen.

Broncos' Rally Fails

John Kerr's 26-points paced Illinois to victory over Santa Clara.

The Illini dominated the game for three quarters only to have Santa Clara come roaring back to go ahead 56—55, after 3½ minutes of the final period. The Broncos had trailed twice by 8 points in the third stanza, 48—40 and 50—42.

Illinois got the lead back on free tosses by Max Hooper and Clive Follmer. Herb Schoenstein tide it at 58—all and the Broncos went into a stall with four minutes left.

Then Bob Peterson, who alternated with Kerr at center for Illinois, hit a rebound after Santa Clara lost the ball on a missed basket. The Illini broke into scoring territory and when Peterson was fouled on his shot, he hit from the charity line to make it 61—52 and Illinois stayed in front the rest of the way.

With consent of the two coaches, the consolation game was planned under suggested rule changes that:
1. Permitted no waiving of free throws.
2. Gave a second shot when the first was missed on any foul before the final three minutes, and after the three-minute mark considered all fouls intentional and worth two shots.

In either case, if the last toss was missed the ball remained in play; if converted the opposing teams took possession out of bounds.

The rules committee said the experiment was an attempt to correct the "freeze and foul-drawing type of play" in the final minutes. The line-ups:

KANSAS (80)					ST. JOHN'S (63)			
	G.	F.	PF.	P.		F.	F.	PF.	P.
Kenny, lf	.4	4	2	12	McMahon, lf	.6	1	4	13
Davenport	.0	0	1	0	Davis	.1	2	4	4
Keller, rf	.1	0	2	2	Walsh, rf	.1	3	0	3
Hoag	.2	5	5	9	Zawoluk, c	.7	6	5	20
Lovellette, c	.12	9	4	33	Peterson	.0	0	0	0
Born	.0	0	0	0	McGilvray, lg	.3	2	3	8
D. Kelley, lg	.2	3	5	7	Giancontieri	.0	0	0	0
Smith	.0	0	0	0	Duckett, rg	.2	2	4	6
Lienhard, rg	.5	2	4	12	Walker	.0	0	4	0
Hougland	.2	1	2	5	McMorrow	.1	0	3	2
Heitholt	.0	0	0	0	Sagona	.2	0	5	4
A. Kelley	.0	0	0	0					
Total	.28	24	25	80	Total	.25	13	35	63

Kansas ....18 23 19 20—80
St. John's ....13 14 14 22—63
Free throws missed—Kenny 2, D. Kelley 3, Lovellette 2, Hoag 2, Hougland 2, Davis, Zawoluk 5, Giancontieri 2, MacGilvray 3, McMahon 3.
Shots attempted—Kansas 63, St. John's 55.

ILLINOIS (67)					SANTA CLARA (64)			
	G.	F.	PF.	P.		G.	F.	PF.	P.
C. Follmer, lf	.6	5	1	17	Sears, lf	.4	2	4	10
Gerecke	.2	3	1	7	Gatzert	.1	2	4	4
Bemoras, rf	.1	3	0	3	Young, rf	.6	4	18
Peterson, c	.1	3	0	5	Schoenst'n, c	.2	4	3	8
Kerr	.10	6	3	26	Soares	.0	2	4
Fletcher, lg	.1	2	4	4	Peters, lg	.4	5	2	13
Hooper	.1	1	3	3	Benedetti, rg	.0	0	5	2
Bredar, rg	.1	0	5	2	Garibaldi	.0	0	0	0
Wright	.0	0	0	0	Brock	.2	1	2	5
Total	.22	23	17	67	Total	.22	20	21	64

Illinois ....12 20 20 15—67
Santa Clara ....14 14 17 19—64
Free throws missed—Peters 2, Bemoras, Kerr, Peterson 2, Gerecke, Fletcher 4.
Shots attempted—Illinois 57, Santa Clara 76.

March 27, 1952

Judge in Fix Case Condemns Kentucky Teams and Coach

By ALFRED E. CLARK

The basketball and football teams of the University of Kentucky were described yesterday as "the acme of commercialism and over-emphasis" by General Sessions Judge Saul S. Streit in a sixty-three page report that revealed several meetings between Adolph Rupp, the school's basketball coach, and Ed Curd, a bookmaker termed the "Frank Erickson of Kentucky."

The court loosed its third blast since November at intercollegiate sports practices as it suspended penitentiary sentences and placed on indefinite probation three former Kentucky court stars who had admitted accepting bribes to "shave points" in games played three years ago. The three accepted $3,500 for their parts in games against Loyola University of Chicago at Madison Square Garden in March, 1949, and the University of Tennessee in Lexington, Ky., the previous month.

Judge Streit warned that not many more storm flags would be hoisted to alert intercollegiate groups to rid themselves of the "disintegrating influence of money-mad athletics." He urged all colleges to adopt minimum standards that had been recommended by the executive committee of the American Council on Education for the elimination "of the vices and evils existing in intercollegiate sports."

Prior to yesterday's proceedings, Judge Streit had held a series of hearings in his chambers in which he obtained sworn testimony from the defendants, Alex Groza, Ralph Beard and Dale Barnstable, their former coach, Mr. Rupp, as well as university officials and representatives of various college groups.

In his report, which ran to almost 15,000 words and took one hour and fifteen minutes to read, the judge went into detail on testimony given early this month by Mr. Rupp.

He quoted Mr. Rupp, who was named in 1950 by the Metropolitan Basketball Writers Association, as the "Coach of the Year," as admitting he had known Curd, had visited him at his home on at least two occasions and had telephoned him once to learn what the "point spread" was on a game to be played by Kentucky against the University of Alabama.

Further testimony released by Judge Streit pictured "an after supper snack" that the coach had shared with Curd at the Copacabana, a night club at 10 East Sixtieth Street, after a game in which Kentucky had played at the Garden.

Another meeting in the same club occurred during the 1947-48 season, the report said. Mr. Rupp said that on that occasion he was present with A. B. (Happy) Chandler, then commissioner of baseball, and Bernie Shively, former Kentucky football coach and now athletic director.

"Happy Chandler, Mr. Shively and one or two others and I went to the Copacabana," Mr. Rupp testified. "Ed [Curd] came in and sat down with us.

"Did he take the check then?" the Judge asked. "I don't know who paid it, I didn't pay it," Mr. Rupp replied.

The coach, who last month completed his twenty-second season with the "Wildcats," admitted that Curd's reputation as a bookmaker in Lexington, was "general knowledge," but he denied that he received information from Curd on the margin of points by which Kentucky was favored in various games. The coach also denied betting on games.

Judge Streit said his inquiry showed that both Mr. Rupp and the university "must share the responsibility" for the plight of the three defendants, as well as two other former members of the Kentucky varsity who had admitted accepting bribes to limit their team's margin of victory.

In addition to Groza, Beard and Barnstable, other former undergraduates at the school who were entangled in the widespread scandal were James Line and Walter Hirsch, William (Bill) Spivey, who was indicted for perjury on Monday, and Nicholas Englisis, a onetime member of the football team and admitted briber of basketball players at Kentucky and Bradley University in Peoria, Ill. Line and Hirsch testified before a grand jury but were not indicted.

Assails School's Practices

Intercollegiate basketball and football at Kentucky "have become highly systematized, professionalized and commercialized enterprises," the judge charged. "I found covert subsidization of players, ruthless exploitation of athletes, cribbing at examinations, 'illegal' recruiting, a reckless disregard of their physical welfare, matriculation of unqualified students, demoralization of the athletes by the coach, alumni, and townspeople, and the most flagrant abuse of the 'athletic scholarship.'"

The court condemned the "athletic scholarship racket as the most fruitful device and scheme yet invented to destroy the amateur code." He charged it was the "darkest blot" on American college athletics and said that coaches, their assistants and the alumni go prospecting for athletic talent like miners searching for gold.

Noting that the present athletic scandal at the school and the defendants' plight can be traced directly to the "inordinate desire" by the school's trustees and alumni for prestige and profits from sports, Judge Streit declared that such methods "paid off" in large financial returns.

The report said that the gross income from basketball jumped from $42,454 in 1945 to $194,076 last year. The gross income from football, according to the report, "climbed from $16,985 in 1945 to the staggering sum of $662,021 in 1951."

The report said the costs of maintaining university teams "are

Associated Press
Coach Adolph Rupp

far in excess of the normal and average cost of the operation and maintenance of a first-rate professional football or basketball team."

Judge Streit backed this contention with statements on the expenses of the American and National Professional Football Leagues and financial records of the National Basketball Association.

113 Get Athletic Scholarships

Groza and Beard, who were All-America selections when they played at Kentucky and were instrumental in bringing the Olympic basketball title to this country in 1948, admitted they had attended the school on athletic scholarships. The report pointed out that the 113 members on the current football and basketball squads are on athletic scholarships.

Barnstable, the third defendant, Line, Hirsch and Englisis also testified they had received scholarships. The players told more or less the same story of receiving from $10 to $50 from either Mr. Rupp or from "boosters" and alumni who were basketball fans.

Barnstable was quoted as saying that if the players had turned in a good winning game they each would receive a cash bonus of $10 to $20. "The amount depended upon the type of game and how well they had played," the athlete said.

When asked by Judge Streit if he ever received any additional money when a game was lost, Barnstable was quoted as replying:

"No, sir. You were lucky to get something to eat then."

Barnstable testified further that in the Sugar Bowl game at New Orleans against St. Louis University he had missed a shot. "Rupp came back and gave me the devil," the player added. "Said that the shot I missed just cost his friend, Burgess Carey, $500."

Mr. Rupp, who is paid an annual salary of $8,500 and has an expense account up to $1,500, conceded that Hirsch had received $50 after a game against the University of Kansas in December, 1950, but contended this was "money laying around that had not been spent" from a sum raised to send the Kentucky players to the Olympics two years previous.

The coach said that he understood that Groza received $50 a month from an alumnus named Owen Campbell. The latter, owner of a liquor-distributing company, was quoted by Groza as saying that the youth should come down to the warehouse "during the off season, one or two days a week, if he had some spare time."

Beard also testified, according to the report, that prior to a game here with St. John's University he was suffering from an injured ankle and at Mr. Rupp's suggestion had his ankle injected with novocaine to deaden the pain.

As a result, Beard said, the injury took a month to heal and he was incapacitated. Mr. Rupp declared the first he knew of such an incident was recently when "my freshman coach" said it was "one of those things you were not supposed to know."

The coach admitted that his attitude has changed as to the "immorality of shaving points," saying that he previously he "didn't think it was as serious as going out and deliberately throwing a ball game."

"But now then, since it hit into our family, I think it is a bad thing," he added. When word of the basketball scandal elsewhere broke, Mr. Rupp was quoted in the press as saying fixers could not touch his players with a ten-foot pole.

Judge Streit, commenting on Mr. Rupps' testimony, asserted:

"It is unnecessary at this time to decide the issues raised by the coach. The undisputed facts are that he aided and abetted in the immoral subsidization of the players."

Judge Backs Council's Plan

Judge Streit said he was in accord with the committee of the American Council on Education, which called for normal academic procedures for athletes and urged that athletic scholarships be abolished; recruiting of athletes prohibited; post-season games eliminated and the freshmen be barred from playing on varsity teams.

BASKETBALL PLAYERS AND COACH BLASTED BY COURT

Former Kentucky University stars, who pleaded guilty to conspiring to shave points in a National Invitation tournament game in 1949, as they arrived at Criminal Courts Building yesterday, where General Sessions Judge Saul S. Streit suspended sentences. They are, left to right, Dale Barnstable, Ralph Beard and Alex Groza.

He recommended that the National Collegiate Athletic Association adopt the committee's proposals, and that regional athletic conferences appoint a committee with power to police and impose sanctions in connection with the athletic activities of any of its members.

Both Assistant District Attorney Vincent A. G. O'Connor and Harold O. N. Frankel, counsel for the defendants, urged the court to grant clemency to the former players. Mr. O'Connor pointed out that they had cooperated since their arrests and would be willing witnesses against several fixers now awaiting trial. Mr. Frankel declared his clients had been the victims of a vicious system.

After sentences were suspended the defendants reported to the probation department and then left for their homes. Barnstable, who is 27 years old, married and the father of twins, lives in Louisville; Beard, 24, is married, has one child and is a resident of Louisville. Groza, 26, is single and lives at Martin's Ferry, Ohio.

Mr. Rupp could not be reached for a statement at his home in Lexington. Jack Wild, the university's director of public relations, said no comment would be made until Judge Streit's statement had been received.

April 30, 1952

U. S. CLINCHES OLYMPIC GAMES UNOFFICIAL TEAM TITLE

RUSSIA OVERTAKEN

By ALLISON DANZIG

Special to The New York Times.

HELSINKI, Finland, Aug. 2—Once again the United States is the champion nation in the Olympic Games.

In a tremendous sweep of honors on the last full day of competition in the games of the Fifteenth Olympiad, the Americans collected a total of 111 points to 30 for Russia, which had led by 24½ this morning. The Soviet Union now trails by 610 to 553½ in the unofficial scoring system.

With the Prix des Nations jumping event the only remaining competition on tomorrow's closing program, the Americans have completely killed off the challenge of the Soviet Republic, a participant in the games for the first time, to maintain their traditional supremacy. Four years ago at London they finished with a total of 662 points to 353 for Sweden, the second highest nation.

Victorious over Russia, 36—25, in basketball after a bad scare, and scoring heavily in the water as Fred Konno won the 1,500-meter free-style and its women platform divers swept three medals, the United States also gained its greatest triumph in boxing in Olympic history.

Five American fighters went into the ring in the finals tonight and all five of them won gold medals. Floyd Patterson, 18-year-old New York high school student, knocked out his opponent in 20 seconds of the first round in the middleweight division.

Two Russian Boxers Lose

The United States collected 50 points in boxing to 24 for Russia both of whose finalists were beaten tonight. The Americans earned 34 points today in swimming and diving, 26 of them in the women's division. They picked up 10 in basketball, 4 in equestrian competition and 3 in water polo, in which the

45

United States team made its best showing ever in taking fourth place.

Russia, aside from boxing, added only 5 points today as runner-up in basketball and 1 for a sixth placing in the women's platform diving. During the past two days the Soviet had failed to gain a single point.

No fewer than 188 of Russia's total points were won in men's and women's gymnastics. The United States far outscored its chief rival in track and field, 224-57, in the men's division. In weight-lifting it was a stand-off between them and Russia had a small advantage in free-style wrestling.

The United States excelled in rowing, yachting and basketball as well as track and field, swimming and boxing.

Ten World Records Set

Early in today's competition, Russia threatened to furnish one of the most shocking reversals of the games, which provided so much excitement in track and field as Olympic marks were broken the fantastic number of 151 times and ten new world marks were established.

With the United States heavily favored after its 86-58 victory in the previous meeting of the teams, the Soviet five took its opponent by surprise with its tactics. The Russians slowed play almost to a standstill and had the Americans on edge until the last few minutes of one of the lowest scoring games in Olympic annals.

The crowd that paced every inch of standing room watched in awe as only 6 points were scored in the first ten minutes of play. It remained mystified throughout the first half, which ended with the United States leading by 17—15 on a field goal almost at the bell. There was genuine concern in the American camp with the tally standing at 29—25 in the United States favor fewer than five minutes before the end.

Not until the last minute of play, which found the Americans holding the ball in a deep freeze, emulating the tactics the Russians had pursued from start almost to finish, were the favorites' adherents able to draw an easy breath.

American Attack Checked

The Russians went into the game committed to a policy of freezing the ball and breaking up the attack pattern of their opponents with a defense so strong that seldom were the Americans able to score from the inside until late in the game. The Reds started their five fastest men instead of their five best. They sent out Iljmar Kullam, who had seen action for only a few minutes previously in the tournament and he proved to be not only speedy but clever in handling the ball and in footwork.

The Soviet team was not interested in scoring, it appeared. All it wanted to do was to keep the ball out of American hands and rattle its rivals.

A number of times the Russians worked the ball down into shooting position but refrained from

Basketball
CHAMPIONSHIP GAME

UNITED STATES (36)	G.F.PF.P	RUSSIA (25)	G.F.PF.P
Hoag. lf	1 0 1 2	Butautas. lf	2 2 3 6
Hougland. rf	3 0 2 6	Dzh dzhikija	0 1 1 1
Kelley	0 0 1 0	Konev, rf	0 0 0 0
Kenney	2 2 3 6	Korkilia, c	2 4 4 8
Lovellette, c	3 3 3 9	Kullam, lg	3 0 2 6
Frieberger	0 0 2 0	Ozerov, rg	0 0 3 0
Pippin, lg	0 1 2 1	Moiseev	1 2 0 4
Williams. rg	2 0 4 4	Kruus	0 0 2 0
Bontemps	0 0 0 0		
Kurland	2 4 1 8	Total	8 9 15 25

Total 13 10 19 36
Half-time score—United States 17. Russia 15. Free throws missed—United States: Hougland. Lovellette 2. Pippin. Kurland. Russia: Butautas 2. Dchordzhikija 2. Konev, Korkilia 2. Kullam 3. Ozerov. Kruus 2. Officials—Wahby, Egypt, and Vanderperren, Belgium.

Fifth-Place Play-Off
Chile 58, Brazil 49.

trying for the basket until the crowd shouted its impatience and dislike for the tactics. Otar Korilia star play-maker of the team, did not make a single shot from the floor until more than ten minutes had passed.

At times the lack of action was so boring that the game took on the character of a truce meeting in Korea. That was how much progress was being made on the scoreboard.

After the United States had led by 4—2, the Russians went ahead 7—5, as Korilia counted on a free throw and a pivot in the bucket. The Americans got going briefly as Howard Williams hit with a long set shot, Clyde Lovellette scored from the foul line and Bill Hougland threw in another long one.

Hougland tallied twice more in the half on spectacular set shots, the last one scoring almost at the bell after Lovellette had counted on one of his few tip-ins of the game. Lovellette had ruined the Russians in the first meeting of the teams but did not have nearly so big a day this time, though he was the high scorer.

The Americans were off in their shooting throughout, and only occasionally were able to score from the inside. The Russians, too, missed plenty and their lack of accuracy on free throws hurt them after Korilia went out of the game on personal fouls near the middle of the second half.

The Americans tallied only seven times from the floor on thirty-two attempts in the first half and thirteen of sixty-five for the game. The Russians hit six of twenty-two in the first half and two of twenty-two in the second.

Many Fouls Called

It was expected that the United States would find itself in the second half and break the game open but instead, after Lovellette had counted on a free throw and from the bucket for a 20-17 lead, Russia went ahead by 21—20. Fouls were called repeatedly and rather technically it seemed, on the Americans and Korilia, completely uncovered, dropped the ball in on a lay-up.

The score went to 22—all and then the Americans became aroused and went ahead, 28—22.

Fouls then were called on Russia and the Americans made the most of them. The tension mounted again as the Reds pulled up to 29—25. Lovellette came back in the game for Kurland and scored from the bucket and then the United States began to freeze the ball. The Russians were so stymied

by this dose of their own medicine that one of them sat down on the floor.

Lovellette scored on a free throw, Bob Kennedy on a lay-up and Kurlund on a tip-in. The score was now 36—25 with less than a minute left to play and the Americans retained possession of the ball.

It was a dearly won victory for the United States and a remarkable showing for Russia. The American coach said that the Soviet team compared with some of the best in the United States and the belief was expressed that from now on Russia will be very much of a factor in basketball.

August 3, 1952

WILDCATS CHARGED WITH 2 VIOLATIONS

Kentucky Goes on Probation for Year After Council's Finding on Infractions

BRADLEY ALSO PENALIZED

Both Schools Figured in 'Fix' Scandals—N. C. A. A. Group Reprimands Midwestern

KANSAS CITY, Nov. 3 (AP) — The National Collegiate Athletic Association today doled out punishment to a couple of its better-known basketball playing members—Kentucky and Bradley—for rules violations.

The N. C. A. A. council announced it was recommending to the association at its annual convention in Washington next January that Kentucky be put on probation for all sports during the 1952-53 academic year for infractions during 1947-48-49-50.

Bradley of Peoria, Ill., would not be permitted to participate in the N. C. A. A. basketball tournament next March, according to the recommendations.

Both schools announced acceptance of the council's recommendations. Kentucky complied by advising President H. C. Willett of the N. C. A. A. that it had canceled all of its intercollegiate basketball games for the 1952-53 season.

No Mention of Scandals

Both Kentucky and Bradley figured prominently in the basketball "fixes" although no mention of the scandals was made in the council's report.

A third N. C. A. A. member, Midwestern University of Wichita Falls, Tex., was reprimanded for giving a high school basketball player a "tryout."

The names of the players in-

volved were not disclosed.

Kentucky's football team will not be affected since final action on the recommendations cannot be taken before the January convention.

Kentucky was found guilty on the following counts:

"1. Athletes received pay for participation in athletics in violation of a constitutional principle (Article 111 of the Constitution, Section 1).

"2. Athletes were certified as eligible for N. C. A. A. events when ineligible and the coaches involved had knowledge of the facts which made them ineligible, in violation of a by-law (Article 4 of the By-Laws)."

Four Incidents Cited

The council said it had found four incidents in which outstanding members of Kentucky basketball teams received $50 payments from sports enthusiasts.

The council said Bradley was guilty on the same counts as Kentucky, but it did not charge Bradley coaches with knowledge of the facts regarding its ineligible athletes.

The council also noted that Bradley officials had "taken immediate and effective action in correcting and improving athletic practices at their institutions * * *."

In a lengthy statement at Peoria, Bradley officials accepted the penalty, but urged a more far-reaching investigation into the recruiting practices of other schools.

"Bradley University gives its complete support to the efforts of the N. C. A. A. to insure the amateur character of intercollegiate athletics," the statement continued.

At Lexington, Ky., Senator Thomas R. Underwood declared he would inquire into the Kentucky case with the possibility of asking a Senate investigation.

Underwood said a Senate committee "could very probably inquire to see whether discrimination is being practiced."

November 4, 1952

Kentucky to Keep Coach Rupp Despite Basketball Disclosures

But University Aide Has 'No Comment' on Whether Mentor Will Be Disciplined for Use of Ineligible Players

LEXINGTON, Ky., Nov. 4 (AP)— The University of Kentucky has no intention of firing Coach Adolph Rupp over disclosures that he knowingly used ineligible players.

Dr. Leo M. Chamberlain, vice president of the university, said that flatly today and replied, "no comment," when asked if the institution planned any other disciplinary action against the coach.

The N. C. A. A. Council put Kentucky on a one-year basketball probation yesterday for having violated subsidization and eligibility rules. The school announced it would cancel its 1952-53 basketball schedule as a result of the council's recommendation that other N. C. A. A. schools should refuse to play Kentucky.

One university official, who declined to be quoted by name, said Rupp had protested to the donors when he learned they were making cash gifts to players. He added:

"Rupp was wrong in not telling the administration that some of his players were accepting extra cash. But what would any other coach have done when he had a championship team?"

The school estimated that the probation would cost $125,000 to $150,000, meaning that $80,000 for payments on mortgages on Memorial Coliseum would have to be raised from sources other than gate receipts.

Rupp's salary, officials said, will be paid from available athletic funds.

Other sources, meanwhile, blasted away at the N. C. A. A. ruling.

William H. Townsend, president of the Alumni Association, said: "We contend that no man or set of men, reeking with athletic halitosis, has any right to point an accusing finger at a speck on Kentucky's vest."

"It is simply not true," he added, "and ought never to be true, that the sins of Kentucky's executioners have no relation to Kentucky's guilt."

This was pointed directly at both the N. C. A. A. Council and the Southeastern Conference, which beat the N. C. A. A. to the punch in handing Kentucky a one-year basketball suspension.

A stepped-up intramural program was mapped today for the institution's mammoth colliseum to help make up for the loss of intercollegiate basketball.

November 5, 1952

Sports of The Times

By ARTHUR DALEY

Caesar Was Ambitious

THERE are tragic overtones to the downfall of Nat Holman. Here was a man who had won the respect and admiration of all. He had become Mr. Basketball. Once regarded generally as the game's greatest player, he had gained similar acclaim as a coach. But now the slimy fingers of the fixing scandal have reached out and brushed against him.

The Board of Higher Education, forthrightly and persistently investigating the scandals as they involved City College players, has accused Holman of "conduct unbecoming a teacher, neglect of duty and disobedience of a direction of the board and this committee." There is no charge that Nat had anything to do with the briberies per se. But he is blamed for complicity in the smuggling of unqualified athletes into school and then keeping them there by the tampering with scholastic records.

Nat had always seemed to be a dedicated man. He had appeared to be much along the same lines of Bill Klem, that paragon of umpires, who once roared, "Baseball is more than a game to me. It's a religion." Basketball was a religion to Holman. He worshipped at its shrine. Perfection was a minor diety and his overambitious striving for the kind of players who could give him that perfection brought him low.

Et Tu, Brute?

William Shakespeare once wrote a great tragedy, Julius Caesar. It persists in coming back to mind, almost as if it illustrates in part the unhappy Holman situation. There is a famous scene, just before the glowing Marc Antony oration, where Brutus explains to the populace in the Forum why he killed his beloved friend, Caesar. Substitute for the part of Brutus the personification of Basketball. Substitute for Caesar the name of Holman. Then listen. This is Brutus (Basketball) speaking: .

"As Caesar loved me, I weep for him; as he was fortunate, I rejoice at it; 'as he was valiant, I honor him; but, as he was ambitious, I slew him."

Holman was a proud man and a vain man. His position at the top of his profession was secure. Yet he wasn't satisfied. Even the winning of both major intercollegiate championships for a never-before-achieved Grand Slam by his City College quintet wasn't enough. This merely was an upward step in the road. The supreme goal was to lead these same boys to the 1952 Olympic basketball championship as a glorious climax to a glorious career.

The Dagger Is Poised

Because Nat was coaching at City College, far higher honors accrued to him than he would have gained anywhere else. The oldest—and weakest—joke in the sportswriting business was that City College was one of the few completely amateur colleges in the country, largely because entrance requirements were so high.

Holman had no Hessians. He didn't go out and grab schoolboy stars the way Clair Bee did at L. I. U. or Adolph Rupp did at Kentucky. He had no money for subsidizing them or joke courses to offer. He not only had to use students but brilliant students. Yet for most of his thirty-three years on the job he did extraordinarily well, though few athletes successfully combine brains and brawn.

Then someone hit on the unfortunate device of cutting corners. High school records were tampered with and marks raised so that otherwise unqualified schoolboy wonders could matriculate at City. There later was similar connivance to keep them there. Professionalism during the summer on the Borscht Circuit was blinked at. Athletes became privileged persons.

The Dagger Plunges

The investigators have not accused Holman of actual guilt in any of those practices. But they saddled him with one of those damned-if-you-do-and-damned-if-you don't dilemmas. He either is grossly culpable of guilty knowledge and therefore unfit to continue as coach or else he is far too naive to be trusted again as coach.

If Holman were a person like Rupp, no one could feel sorry for him. But he never was and that's why this blow hurts so much. He always seemed to be a man of high principle, lofty ideals and exemplary character. Sure, he was vain. So what? It merely was that he was good and knew it.

Since chicanery brought so many of his otherwise unqualified stars to City and since chicanery kept them there, there had to be a cynicism created among the boys. This was to lead to some of them accepting bribes. Because the whole basketball structure had been built on sand, it crumpled at the first touch.

The relentless and unsparing way the City College authorities pursued their investigation must evoke admiration. There was no attempt at a white-wash, such as Kentucky produced. Holman, the most sacred cow of all, was punished because it was felt that he could not avoid some responsibility for the mess. His ambition had been his undoing. It's a pity.

Once again we can listen to Brutus (Basketball) as he says of the prostrate Caesar:

"There is tears for his love; joy for his fortune; honor for his valor, and death for his ambition."

November 20, 1952

O'Brien Passes 3,000 Points

SPOKANE, Wash., Feb. 15 (AP)— Seattle's Johnny O'Brien had his greatest night with 51 points tonight and became the first college basketball player in history to score 3,000 as his Chieftains overwhelmed Gonzaga, 109—68. O'Brien, who now has 3,032 points, had scored 47 against Gonzaga in another season for his previous high. He got his 3,000th point in the opening moments of the second quarter on a free throw and Gonzaga's officials gave him the ball for his trophy case in a half-time ceremony.

February 16, 1953

SETON HALL TAKES 27TH GAME IN ROW

Sets Major College Season Court Record, Defeating Baldwin-Wallace, 83-75

Special to The New York Times.

SOUTH ORANGE, N. J., Feb. 27—Seton Hall University established a national major college basketball record for successive victories in one season, beating Baldwin-Wallace College of Berea, Ohio, 83—75, before 3,600 tonight at the Seton Hall gymnasium. It was Seton Hall's twenty-seventh straight victory, breaking the mark held jointly by L. I. U. and Holy Cross.

Walter Dukes and Richie Regan, both seniors playing their last game at the Seton Hall court, led the unbeaten Pirates. Dukes scored 21 points and Regan had 18.

Trailing through most of the game after Seton Hall took a 21-16 lead at the end of the first quarter, Baldwin-Wallace rallied against the Pirate reserves and narrowed the score to 80—74 with less than two minutes to play.

Honey Russell waved back his first-stringers at that point and Ronnie Nathanic sank three straight points to pull the Pirates out of danger.

February 28, 1953

Seton Hall, Upset by Dayton's Quintet, Suffers First Setback of the Season

PIRATES BOW, 71-65, ON OHIOANS' COURT

Dayton's Paxson Tallies 23 Points While Dukes of Seton Hall Scores 19

FIRST LOSS IN 28 GAMES

Jersey Five's Failure on Foul Shots Costly—Rivals Make Good With 23 of 28

DAYTON, Ohio, March 1 (Æ)—A University of Dayton team that has been beaten thirteen times in twenty-seven games knocked Seton Hall, the nation's top-ranked collegiate basketball team, out of the unbeaten ranks, 71—65, tonight in one of the biggest upsets of the season.

The Dayton starting five, going all the way, held Walter Dukes, the country's third-ranked scorer, to 19 points. This was his fourth lowest total of the season. With Dukes bottled up, Seton Hall never had a chance. Dayton was never behind and led most of the way.

Forward Jim Paxson was the key man for Dayton as the Pirates suffered their first setback in twenty-eight games. He tallied 23 points.

Reverses Early Game

The Flyers thus reversed the pattern of an early season defeat by Seton Hall on the Pirates' floor. Then Dayton outscored them from the field but lost at the foul line. Tonight Dayton was topped by four points from the field but made 23 of 28 free throws while Seton Hall connected on only 13 of 21.

A crowd of 6,054, largest ever to witness a basketball game in the Dayton fieldhouse, saw the Flyers confuse the great Dukes, who committed two fouls in the opening period and played with some caution thereafter. Seton Hall lost Richie Regan on fouls late in the fourth period, but not before he had matched Dukes' point total.

Dukes, second best rebounder in the country, never was able to capitalize on his board talents as Paxson and John Horan stole the show from him.

The Decisive Break

The decisive break in the contest came with one minute and 30 seconds left in the last quarter. Dukes, fouled, missed the second of two free throws and the Flyers' Jack Sallee grabbed the ball and whisked it down to Don Donaher, who flipped in the two points that gave Dayton a 70-65 lead. The Flyers then played control ball until Chris Harris netted a free throw in the final seconds and it was all over.

Horan, who played for Dayton's national invitation tournament finalists last year, made things miserable for Dukes. He pulled the big center out of position repeatedly and kept him from coming too close to the boards.

Dukes, who has been almost all of the Pirate attack this season, was not up to par from the field. He has been held to 16 points by Scranton, 17 by Xavier of Cincinnati and 15 by Loyola of Chicago. His performance in general tonight was in keeping with those battles rather than with some of the brilliant efforts that brought him acclaim.

The line-up:

DAYTON (71)	G.F.PF.P.	SETON HALL (65)	G.F.PF.P.
Paxson, lf	7 9 2 23	Nathanic, lf	2 1 1 5
Donoher, rf	6 2 3 14	Regan, rf	8 3 5 19
Horan, c	7 6 3 20	Dukes, c	8 3 3 19
Sallee, lg	4 2 3 10	Brooks, lg	5 2 2 12
Harris, rg	0 4 2 4	Cooper, rg	2 2 4 6
		Hannon	1 1 2 3
		Ring	0 1 3 1
Total	24 23 13 71		
		Total	26 13 20 65

Dayton ....24 19 11 17—71
Seton Hall ....18 17 11 17—65
Free throws missed—Paxson, Donoher 3, Harris, Nathanic, Dukes 3, Brooks, Hannon, Cooper, Ring.

March 2, 1953

Indiana Trips Kansas for N.C.A.A. Court Title

HOOSIER FIVE TOPS JAYHAWKS BY 69-68

Indiana Gains N.C.A.A. Title on Leonard's Free Throw With 27 Seconds to Go

10 TIES IN THRILLING DUEL

Schlundt Registers 30 Points as Tempers Flare in Final —Washington Is Third

KANSAS CITY, March 18 (Æ)—A free throw by Bob Leonard with 27 seconds to go gave Indiana a thrilling 69-to-68 victory over Kansas tonight for the National Collegiate A. A. basketball championship.

It was a tingling contest, tied ten times, which went down the stretch with the teams never more than 3 points apart in the final period.

Washington won the third-place consolation prize by downing Louisiana State, 86—69, with Bob Houbregs scoring 42 points.

The championship game was exciting all the way.

After Leonard, fouled by Dean Kelley of Kansas, had made good on the second of two free throws, having missed the first, Coach Forrest (Phog) Allen called his Jayhawks to the bench for what he hoped would be the final winning strategy.

The Hawks took the ball out and passed to the forecourt, watching the clock with every move. Jerry Alberts, a substitute who came in when the star center, B. H. Born, went out on personal fouls, tried a one-handed push shot from the side as the clock registered six seconds to go.

Last Kansas Chance Fails

The ball never had a chance. It slammed against the rim as the partisan crowd of 10,500 groaned.

It was Don Schlundt of Indiana who shattered Kansas' almost fanatical pressing defense and brought the Hoosiers their second N.C.A.A. championship. Indiana won in 1940 when it defeated Kansas here, 60—42.

Schlundt, a 6-foot-2 210-pounder, poured in 30 points to win an individual scoring duel with Born, who had 26 when he went to the sidelines with 5:36 left in the last period.

A few moments earlier Born had been the center of a controversy that saw tempers flare and charges hurled by the rival coaches.

When Born banged into Indiana's Charlie Kraak, with the score 53—52 in favor of Kansas and a minute to play in the third period, the official scorer blew his whistle and called Born out of the game on five fouls.

The Kansas bench and Coach Allen vigorously protested and, after a check, the scorer changed his decision and said Born could play.

Indiana Coach Protests

This brought Branch McCracken, Indiana coach, storming to the table.

There was a mild flurry. The decision appeared to be reversed and then reversed again as the crowd yelled::: "No. four, four."

"Your book shows five personals," shouted McCracken. "Born should be out. We're your guest and you're robbing us."

This was just one incident in the game between the hard-running, sharpshooting teams, never more than 6 points apart in the bitterly fought contest.

Schlundt and Leonard both drew technical fouls for making offensive remarks to the officials and in the riotous last period Kraak was charged with a technical when he rammed an elbow into the ribs of Kansas' Harold Patterson.

The game came to a dramatic climax when Dean Kelley drove under Indiana's basket and sank a lay-up to tie the score, 68—68, with a minute and five seconds to go.

The role quickly shifted from hero to goat for the hard-playing little Kansas captain who was charged with fouling Leonard in the mad flurry under the Kansas basket.

Leonard, closely guarded by Dean Kelley throughout the game, nervously took the free throw line for two shots. The score was tied. There were 27 seconds to play.

His first attempt was wide and the crowd yelled. Then he arched another at the hoop. This one was true, and Indiana was champion of the college basketball world.

Indiana, Big Ten champion and No. 1 in The Associated Press poll, led, 20—19, at the end of the first quarter. The score was tied, 41—41, at the half, and it was Indiana by 59—58, at the end of the third period. The Indiana-Kansas line-up:

INDIANA (69)	G.F.PF.P.	KANSAS (68)	G.F.PF.P.
Kraak, lf	5 7 5 17	Patterson, lf	1 1 7 3
Deakyne	0 0 1 0	A. Kelley, rf	7 6 3 20
Farley, rf	1 0 5 2	Davenport	0 0 0 0
Schlundt, c	11 8 3 30	Born, c	8 10 5 26
White	1 0 2 2	Smith	0 1 1 1
Leonard, lg	5 2 2 12	Albert	0 0 1 0
Poff	0 0 0 0	D. Kelley, lg	3 2 2 8
Scott, rg	2 2 3 6	Reich, rg	2 0 2 4
Byers	0 0 0 0		
Total	25 19 21 69	Total	21 25 17 68

Indiana ....21 20 18 10—69
Kansas ....19 22 17 10—68
Free throws missed—Kraak 3, Schlundt 3, Leonard 2, Scott, Patterson, A. Kelley 2, Born 2, D. Kelley 2.

March 19, 1953

Francis Gets 113 Points For Rio Grande Quintet

JACKSON, Ohio, Feb. 2 (AP)—Bevo Francis scored 113 points tonight as his Rio Grande College basketball team walloped Hillsdale, Mich., 134—91.

The feat set a record for individual scoring for a small-college player. Francis held the previous record with eighty-four points two weeks ago against Alliance College.

In nineteen games this season against four-year schools, the 20-year-old sophomore has tallied 929 points, for an average of nearly forty-nine per game.

Francis—with three tall men guarding him—had forty-three points at the half tonight. After three quarters he had poured in seventy-four points as he hit on about 75 per cent of his shots.

In a game last season against Ashland (Ky.) Junior College, Francis scored 116 points. But the National Collegiate Athletic Association refused to recognize that feat and also discounted Bevo's season total of 1,954 points because many of its opponents had been junior colleges, service teams and the like.

February 3, 1954

Selvy's 100 Points Clip 2 Major College Marks

GREENVILLE, S. C., Feb. 13 (AP)—Frank Selvy of Furman rewrote the major college basketball scoring record book again tonight with a tremendous 100-point spree as Furman defeated Newberry, 149—95.

Selvy's phenomenal performance broke the single-game record of 73, set by Bill Mlkvy of Temple in 1951 against Wilkes, and gave him a career record, in less than three seasons, of 2,197—43 more than the previous four-year career total, set by Jim Lacy of Baltimore Loyola in 1948-49.

February 14, 1954

Another Selvy Record: 1,000 Points in Season

COLUMBIA, S.C., Feb. 20 (AP)—Furman University's Franklin Delano Selvy tonight became the first player in major college basketball history to make 1,000 points in one season.

The 6-3 guard from Corbin, Ky., hit his final four points on free throws in the last minute of a 68-50 triumph over South Carolina. Selvy got 30 in all.

The 1,000th point came with 12 seconds left as the overflow crowd, estimated at 4,500, cheered.

Selvy holds 21 national individual scoring records, and has a 41.6 point average in 24 games this season.

Selvy's scoring was on 8 field goals and 14 free throws.

February 21, 1954

KENTUCKY WINS NO. 24

Ends Campaign Undefeated by Whipping Alabama, 68-43

TUSCALOOSA, Ala., March 1 (UP)—Kentucky's Wildcats tonight became the first major college basketball team since 1939 to roll to an undefeated season of twenty or more games. They routed an outclassed Alabama five, 68 to 43, for their twenty-fourth victory.

Slowed down by Alabama's "wait-for-the-breaks" style of play, Kentucky was held to its lowest point total of the season.

The Wildcats' stars were the three players who will be ineligible for the national collegiate tournament—Cliff Hagan, Frank Ramsey and Lou Tsioropoulos.

Hagan was the game's high scorer with 24 points while Ramsey, with 12, and Tsioropoulos, with 11, were outstanding.

Kentucky, by winning, at least clinched a tie for the Southeastern championship. L. S. U., which beat Mississippi, 56—53, tonight can share the crown and force a play-off with Kentucky by beating Tulane Saturday night.

March 2, 1954

LA SALLE DEFEATS BRADLEY FOR TITLE

Third-Period Spurt, Sparked by Gola, Gains N. C. A. A. Crown by 92 to 76

KANSAS CITY, March 20 (AP)—La Salle's Explorers burst the Bradley bubble tonight with a brilliant third-quarter spurt that carried them to a record-shattering 92-76 triumph and the National Collegiate basketball championship before a crowd of about 10,500.

Penn State defeated Southern California, 70 to 61, in the consolation game for third place.

Bradley, which had parlayed borrowed luck into a winning streak that carried it almost all the way, faded before the effective zone defense and powerful thrusts of the Explorers in the third quarter.

Bradley had dominated the first 20 minutes and led by 7 points early in the second quarter, but its one-point half-time lead vanished as All-America Tom Gola, with brilliant help from two fine sophomores, Charles Singley and Frank Blatcher, tore open the contest between the third and eighth minutes of the third quarter.

The 92-point total broke the previous high in a championship game by a dozen points and equalled the record for an N. C. A. A. contest, set last year by the University of Washington.

Kansas scored 80 points in beating St. John's of Brooklyn in the 1952 classic.

The total of 168 points also broke the record, 165, set in two different regional games a year ago.

Gola scored 19 points before he fouled out. His tip-in with 4:28 left broke the previous 80-point game record.

Singley kept La Salle in the running the first half with perfect set shooting, and although he drew his fourth foul when the third quarter was only three minutes old and scored 23 points.

Blatcher was the game's high man from the floor, collecting eleven goals and a total of 23 points to share high honors with Singley.

Blatcher Gets 23 Points

Bradley, which had lost twelve of twenty-seven games before being picked as a desperation choice to fill out the Western regional bracket, kept its faint hopes alive with an excellent free-throwing performance. The Braves scored 32 points from the foul line, equaling the tournament mark. They had forty-four chances.

From the field it was no contest. The Explorers tried ninety-one times and connected on thir-

ty-seven for an average of 30.7 per cent. Bradley hit 36.6 per cent in the first half when La Salle was playing a man-for-man defense. But when the Explorers shifted into their zone the Braves started missing and ended with 27.5 per cent on eighty shots.

La Salle in Five Games

La Salle had not previously tried its luck in the N.C.A.A. tournament and it had to play five tough games to win the silver cup taken by Indiana a year ago.

In the first round La Salle tripped Fordham in overtime. They came victories over North Carolina State and Navy in the Philadelphia regional. Last night the Explorers outclassed Penn State for the Eastern honors.

The line-ups:

CHAMPIONSHIP GAME

LA SALLE (92)	G.	F.	PF.	P.	BRADLEY (76)	G.	F.	PF.	P.
Singley, lf	8	7	4	23	Petersen, lf	4	2	2	10
Gr'nberg, rf	2	1	1	5	Babetch, rf	0	0	0	0
Maples	2	0	4	4	King	3	6	4	12
Blatcher	11	1	4	23	Gower	0	1	1	1
Gola, c	7	5	5	19	Estergard, c	3	11	1	17
O'Malley, lg	5	1	4	11	Carney, lg	3	11	4	17
Yods'kis, rg	0	0	5	0	Utt, rg	0	0	1	0
O'Hara	2	3	1	7	Kent	0	8	2	16
					Riley	1	1	1	3
Total	37	18	28	92	Total	22	32	16	76

La Salle .... 19 23 30 20—92
Bradley .... 22 21 14 19—76

Free Throws Missed—King, Gower, Estergard, Carney 6, Kent 2, Riley, Singleyn 3, Greenberg, Blatcher, O'Hara.

March 21, 1954

Holman Is Reinstated To City College Staff

Associated Press
Nat Holman

Special to The New York Times.

ALBANY, Aug. 27 — The State Education Commissioner today ordered Nat Holman, former basketball coach at City College in New York, reinstated to his faculty post with full back pay. Dr. Lewis A. Wilson reversed a decision made by the New York City Board of Higher Education last March 3, in which the twenty-one-member body had found Mr. Holman guilty of neglect of duty and conduct unbecoming a teacher.

The case had revolved on the coach's conduct with regard to two incidents involving City College basketball stars: an apparent attempt to pay one man for an off-season tour in 1950 and a reported fix attempt of two players in 1945.

"While I fully understand the Board of Higher Education's desire to insure the highest standards at its institution," Dr. Wilson declared, "in my opinion the record in this case * * * upon all the facts is insufficient to warrant his [Holman's] dismissal."

The Commissioner ordered that Mr. Holman be restored to his post as associate professor of hygiene with back pay, less any money he may have earned during his twenty-one-month suspension. The former coach could therefore receive $15,750, based on his annual salary of $9,000.

While ordering Mr. Holman's reinstatement, Dr. Wilson expressed sharp criticism of the way in which basketball had been conducted at City College.

The record of the case indicated, he declared, that Mr. Holman and others in charge of athletics at the municipal college were "subject to censure" for the degree of professionalism that dominated the sport.

More than 3,500 pages of testimony, Dr. Wilson said, presented "a sordid tale of the extreme efforts made by those in charge to insure the success of the athletic team."

"Players were quite evidently permitted to continue on in college irrespective of academic achievement," the commissioner said. "Indeed, in certain instances the fact that they were ever admitted upon their pre-college record is astounding. Various inducements were utilized in obtaining the attendance of good athletes at the institution.

"Certainly, if the testimony and record are to be believed, those in charge of this program, including appellant herein, are subject to censure."

In reversing the Board of Higher Education, the Commissioner sustained an earlier report by a trial committee appointed by the board. The trial committee had recommended the dismissal of the charges against Mr. Holman after 125 hours of hearings between May 4 and Dec. 1, 1953.

Rulings by the State Education Commissioner in cases of this type are normally not appealable in the courts, unless it is contended that they are unreasonable, arbitrary and capricious or have violated constitutional rights in some manner.

Coach's Charge Given Weight

In opposing Mr. Holman's appeal for reinstatement before the State Education Department, the board had maintained that the coach had "concealed by silence" both an apparent offer to pay Ed Warner, a 1950 star, for a South American tour that summer and an alleged "fix" attempt in a

1945 City College-Holy Cross game.

With regard to these charges, Dr. Wilson concluded that:

"In the exercise of good judgment it would have been better" if Mr. Holman had reported the "offer" to Warner to President Harry N. Wright, but that the coach's contention that his superiors, who also knew of it, were responsible for such a report "is also entitled to some weight."

Mr. Holman's failure to bring up again during the 1952 basketball investigation a seven-year-old bribe incident already known to several college officials including his superior was "not altogether unreasonable."

"The trial committee conducted a very long and careful hearing," Dr. Wilson said. "It had seen the witnesses and heard their testimony.

"Its conclusion apparently was that, while this appellant undoubtedly should have presented all the facts to the president in connection with both incidents, pursuant to the president's directive, and while appellant in not doing so had exercised bad judgment, in their opinion such failure on his part was insufficient to warrant a dismissal from his position."

Hails 'Greatest Victory'

Mr. Holman, who first as a basketball player and then as a coach became one of the game's greatest stars, heard the news of his reinstatement here yesterday only an hour after he and his wife returned with 300 boys and girls from the summer camp they operate at Elizaville, N. Y. His first words were: "Thank God, there's justice in America."

"I thought the biggest thrill of my life was winning the double championship in 1950," he went on, "but it isn't any more. Today's vindication is my greatest victory."

August 28, 1954

LOYOLA ENDS BIAS BARS

Basketball Games With Mixed Teams Are Set in New Orleans

NEW ORLEANS, Nov. 25 (AP) —Loyola University of the South dropped today all segregation barriers — among both players and spectators — at its basketball games.

The Jesuit institution has scheduled three home contests with teams listing Negroes on their rosters, La Salle College, Philadelphia, the University of Illinois and Keesler Air Force Base, Biloxi, Miss.

The La Salle game Dec. 5 will mark the dedication of the new 6,500-capacity Loyola field house and will be the first New Orleans collegiate basketball game participated in by both Negroes and whites.

While school officials made no official announcement, it is known that there will be no special section set aside for Negroes in the field house. All seating and other facilities will be on the same basis.

November 26, 1954

Furman Wins, 154-67, For Basketball Record

GREENVILLE, S. C., Jan. 8 (UP)—Furman University set a national basketball scoring record for major colleges tonight by walloping The Citadel, 154 to 67.

Furman scored eighty-four points in the first half to lead the dazed cadets, 84—35. Despite the fact that Furman Coach Lyle Alley played a sophomore team nearly the entire second half, the Purple Hurricanes went on to break the old team scoring mark.

Darrell Floyd, who succeeded record-breaking Frank Selvy as the Furman scoring ace, led the Hurricanes with a 50-point production.

January 9, 1955

National Scoring Mark Set

GREENVILLE, S. C., Jan. 22 (AP) — Morehead State Teachers College of Kentucky defeated Furman, 130—117, tonight despite a 67-point scoring spree by Darrell Floyd, the nation's leading point-maker. The 247 points set a national scoring record for a major college game. The previous high was 242, set by Furman and Newberry last February.

January 23, 1955

DUQUESNE DOWNS DAYTON, 70 TO 58, IN GARDEN FINAL

Green Gets 33, Dick Ricketts 23 Points—Tourney Trophy to Stokes of St. Francis

By JOSEPH M. SHEEHAN

On the tremendous play of Si Green and Dick Ricketts, Duquesne defeated Dayton, 70—58, last night to win the eighteenth annual National Invitation Tournament. The finale of the local college basketball season attracted a capacity crowd of 18,496 spectators to Madison Square Garden.

Cincinnati outscrambled St. Francis of Loretto, Pa., 96—91, in a five-minute overtime period and took third place in the tournament. Jack Twyman tallied 7 points in the extra session to give the Bearcats the decision. The teams had reached the end of regulation playing time in an 83-all tie.

Maurice Stokes, the 6-foot-6-inch, 235-pound center of St. Francis, scored 31 points for a four-game total of 124. He was named the outstanding player of the tournament.

In command from the late stages of the first half, Duquesne breezed to its victory in the final. Coach Dudey Moore's Iron Dukes from Pittsburgh, sharp and sure in their ball-handling, firmly closed the door on Dayton once they gained the edge.

Close-to-Vest Play

Playing it close to the vest all the way, Duquesne concentrated on feeding Green and Ricketts underneath. Green, unstoppable on driving thrusts, poured in 33 points. Ricketts, equally effective on hooks out of the pivot post, tallied 23.

Between them, the Duke aces scored all their team's points in a half that ended with Duquesne in front, 35—30. No other Duquesne player made a point until Mickey Winograd sank two fouls at 7:30 of the second half and no other Duquesne player made a basket until Jim Fallon pumped in a one-hander three minutes later.

It was not a case of Green and Ricketts hogging the ball. This was purposeful strategy that paid off handsomely. While Duquesne's back-court men— Winograd, Fallon, Dave Ricketts and Lou Severine—did not figure prominently in the box score, they contributed their full share to the victory by keeping the ball moving and getting it to the scorers.

Dayton Ahead at 27-25

Bill Uhl, 7-foot center, and Johnny Horan, 6-foot 8-inch forward, were effective workmen for Dayton. Uhl, on target with soft hook shots, scored 25 points, and Horan contributed 20. But they were no match for Duquesne's big guns.

Dayton was ahead only once in the contest, by 27—25 at 13:00 of the first half. The Flyers clung close for the first ten minutes of the second period, but each time they threatened, Duquesne would shake Green or Ricketts loose.

In desperation, Coach Tom Blackburn ordered Dayton to use a zone defense midway in the second half. The Dukes responded with a dazzling display of ball-handling that evoked an appreciative uproar from the crowd and the Flyers had to abandon the tactic.

The victory marked Duquesne's first N. I. T. success in eight tries. The Dukes twice before had reached the final. Dayton, a four-time competitor in the tournament, was turned back in the final round for the third time.

The Dukes completed their season with a 22-4 won-lost record. Dayton finished the campaign with a 25-4 mark. The Flyers had beaten the Dukes twice in three previous games this season. But this time they were conclusively outclassed.

Cincinnati and St. Francis played as furiously as though the tournament title, instead of the consolation prize, was at stake.

The Frankies forced the pace most of the way but their distressing habit of missing key shots kept them from breaking away to a commanding lead.

The Bearcats, trailing 42—40, at half-time, hit a hot streak late in the second half and built a nine-point advantage.

They were in front, 80—71, with only one minute and forty-five seconds to play and seemed to have the situation well in hand.

But St. Francis, with its swarming defense and relentless fast-breaking, closed in with tigerish ferocity.

In a twinkling, the Frankies were only two points down. And two seconds under the buzzer, the brilliant Stokes drove under for a basket to tie the score.

A rebound goal by Bill Saller sent St. Francis off on top in the extra period. But Frank Nimmo hit twice in rapid succession for Cincinnati. A foul and a basket by Stokes and a bucket by Saller, who was fed by Stokes, returned the edge to the Frankies.

Then Twyman went to work. The Bearcat sharpshooter recaptured the lead for his team with a jump shot and added another basket and a foul before the end. Nimmo also tallied for the Ohioans, as St. Francis had to be content with a foul by Saller.

George Smith's Bearcats completed their season with a 21-8 record.

Besides his scoring, Stokes grabbed twenty-four rebounds and was credited with ten assists on passes that led to St. Francis tallies.

The line-ups:

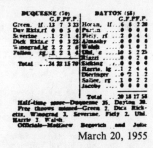

DUQUESNE (70)				DAYTON (58)			
	G.	F.	PF.	P.		G.	F.	PF.	P.
Green, lf	13	7	3	33	Horan, lf	6	2	2	14
Dav Rickart	0	0	5	0	Paxson	0	0	2	0
Severine	1	2	1	4	Fiely, rf	0	0	0	0
Dick Ricks, rf	7	9	3	23	Almasby	0	0	4	0
S. inegrad, lg	1	2	2	4	Walsh	0	0	1	0
Fullen, rg	2	1	1	5	Uhl, c	9	5	2	23
					Blazzi	0	0	0	0
Total	24	22	15	70	Sicking	0	0	0	0
					Harris, lg	1	2	4	4
					Dietringer	0	7	1	7
					Sallee, rg	1	1	1	0
					Jacoby	0	0	0	0
					Total	20	18	17	58

Half-time score—Duquesne 35, Dayton 30.
Free throws missed—Green 2, Dick Rickers, Winegrad 3, Severine, Fiely 2, Uhl, Harris 3, Walsh.
Officials—Mathews Begovich and John

March 20, 1955

N.C.A.A. TITLE WON BY SAN FRANCISCO

La Salle Five Bows, 77-63, as Russell Stars for Dons —Colorado Halts Iowa

By The United Press.

KANSAS CITY, March 19— San Francisco's Dons lived up to their No. 1 national ranking tonight. They administered a decisive defeat to La Salle's defenders and won the National Collegiate basketball championship. The score was 77—63.

Bill Russell, 6-foot 10-inch All America center of the Dons, electrified a sell-out crowd of more than 10,000. He gave an amazing display of all-around court skill. He poured in 23 points to spark the twenty-sixth consecutive San Francisco victory. That brought the first national championship to the West Coast school.

Colorado, the Big Seven champion, defeated Iowa, 75—54, in the consolation game. The Big Ten champion had been an 8-point favorite.

Billed as a "Battle of All-Americas," the N. C. A. A. final began as that. But ultimately La Salle's Tom Gola was forced to concede the honors to his taller rival.

The lean San Francisco Negro star coupled his size with unbelievable jumping ability to thrust an arm above the basket and guide many shots through. Several of those counters were credited by the official scorer to team-mates of Russell.

Any time the ball neared the Don goal Russell was there to (1) assist the ball through the meshes, (2) grab the rebound and score or (3) pass to a team-mate.

But it wasn't a one-man San Francisco triumph by any means. K. C. Jones, the 6-foot 1-inch guard with two of the quickest hands in the collegiate sport, also performed brilliantly. He did a great job in guarding Gola. He tallied 24 points—18 in the final half.

It was Russell's 18-point first-half performance that enabled the West Coast five to lead by a 36-24 margin at the intermission.

Gola scored 16 points for the Explorers. But Charley Singley was the high scorer for the Philadelphia school with 20.

Gola Held to 9 Points

The 6-foot 10-inch Russell played phenomenally in the open half of the final. He sank seven field goals and four of five free throws. The Explorers' All-America player, Tom Gola, had 9 points at the intermission.

The lead changed hands three times before the Dons moved ahead, 20—18, at the ten-minute mark.

Russell's tremendous rebounding artistry amazed the capacity crowd of 10,500 in Municipal Stadium. It helped the Dons surge ahead, 30—20, about five minutes before the intermission.

San Francisco's cause appeared hurt when Forward Jerry Mullen apparently reinjured an ailing ankle. However, he continued in the game.

Phog Allen of the University of Kansas said at half-time that Russell's performance was the most exciting he had seen in his forty-five-year coaching career.

The line-ups:

SAN FRAN. (77)				LA SALLE (63)			
	G.	F.	PF.	P.		G.	F.	PF.	P.
Mullen, lf	4	2	5	10	O'Malley, lf	4	7	1	15
Kirby	0	0	1	0	Maples	0	0	0	0
Buch'nan, rf	3	2	1	8	Singley, rf	8	4	1	20
Wirbuson	2	0	0	4	Blatcher	4	0	1	8
King	0	0	0	0	Gola, c	6	4	4	16
Russell, c	9	5	1	23	Fredericks	0	0	0	0
Lawless	1	0	0	2	Lewis, lg	1	4	1	6
Jones, lg	10	4	2	24	Greenberg, rg	1	1	4	3
Bush	0	0	0	0					
Perry, rg	1	2	4	4	Total	24	15	12	63
Zemmine	0	0	0	0					
Baxter	0	0	0	0					
Total	31	15	14	77					

Half-time score—San Francisco 36, La Salle 24.
Free throws missed—Mullen 3, Russell 2, O'Malley, Gola, Lewis 2, Greenberg.

March 20, 1955

San Francisco Gains 40th in Row, 33 to 24

By The United Press.

BERKELEY, Calif., Jan. 28 —The University of San Francisco set a major college mark of forty consecutive victories tonight by defeating California, 33—24, in a "freak" defensive ball game.

A capacity crowd of more than 7,200 crammed every corner of the California gymnasium and the local partisans had the thrill of seeing their ball club lead the nation's No. 1 team for the first seventeen minutes.

Coach Pete Newell pulled all defensive stops in an attempt to upset San Francisco. California employed three tactics throughout:

¶The stall—in the second half a substitute center, Joe Hagler, held the ball for eight minutes without passing or dribbling.

¶Sought to draw All-America Bill Russell into the forecourt, the principal reason for Hagler's eight-minute stall.

¶Used a squirrel-cage, revolving offense when not stalling, seeking to mix up the San Francisco man-to-man defense—the best in the country.

But California's freak tactics began to crumble with thirteen minutes gone in the first half when the Dons' coach, Phil Woolpert, used a full-court press.

In the last seven minutes of the first half the Dons outscored California, 17—3, with Capt. K. C. Jones accounting for 8 of these points. Jones was the game's high scorer with 15, including 13 free throws.

The Dons surpassed a major college mark held jointly by Long Island University and Seton Hall. However, they are still well short of the all-college record of fifty-five, set over a five-year span from 1921-26 by Peru (Neb.) State Teachers.

Russell was held to two baskets and five free throws for 9 points. California used only five men for the first twenty-three minutes of the game. San Francisco used only seven men, but Woolpert constantly rotated the two substitutes, with only Russell and Carl Boldt going the route.

SAN FRAN. (33)				CALIFORNIA (24)			
	G.	F.	PF.	P.		G.	F.	PF.	P.
Farmer, lf	0	0	3	0	Friend, lf	0	4	0	4
Boldt, rf	1	0	0	2	Blake, rf	0	0	2	0
Preaseau	1	0	0	2	Asplund, c	2	1	5	5
Russell, c	2	5	2	9	Hagler	0	0	1	0
Jones, lg	1	13	3	15	Washington	0	0	1	0
Perry, rg	1	0	2	2	Robinson, lg	1	4	2	6
Erown	0	3	0	3	Simpson, rg	2	3	4	7
					Diaz	0	2	2	2
Total	6	21	10	33	Total	5	14	17	24

Half-time score—San Francisco 20, California 16.

January 29, 1956

Frank Selvy went on a scoring rampage in 1954, averaging over 38 points per game.

San Francisco Quintet Tops Iowa for N.C.A.A. Crown, Extends Skein to 55

DONS KEEP CROWN IN 83-71 TRIUMPH

Russell Notches 26 Points as San Francisco Nips Iowa in Final at Evanston

EVANSTON, ILL., March 23 (P)—Accurate shooting and all-America Bill Russell's tremendous individual play swept San Francisco's Dons to their second straight national collegiate basketball title with a 83-71 victory over Iowa tonight.

It was the 55th consecutive triumph in two years for the Dons who became the first team in N. C. A. A. history to win the crown in capping an unbeaten season. The Dons have not been beaten since a 47-40 loss to U. C. L. A. on Dec. 3, 1954.

San Francisco's twenty-ninth victory of the campaign, led by Russell's 26-point shooting, came after the Big Ten champion, Iowa, had grabbed an early 11-point lead at 15—4.

In the consolation opener Temple defeated Southern Methodist, 90—81, as Hal (King) Lear scored 48 points and established three tournament records before a capacity 10,653 at McGaw Memorial Hall.

Although leading at half-time by only five points, 38—33, San Francisco surged to a 13-point lead at 50—37 before the second half was five minutes old.

Iowa Skein Ends at 17

After that the Dons toyed with the Hawkeyes, who had won seventeen in a row, although the Iowans gave their followers cause to whoop it up when the gap closed to seven points at 76—69 with 2:06 left in the game.

But Warren Baxter came through with a lay-up, Russell dropped in a pair of free throws and followed with a lay-up to put the game on ice at 82—69.

San Francisco became the third team to win the N. C. A.

title two successive years. Oklahoma A. & M. did it in 1945-46, and Kentucky in 1948-49.

San Francisco's field goal percentage was .402 with Russell scoring eleven of twenty-four shots. The Dons hit on thirteen of sixteen free throws for .813. Iowa had a field goal mark of .325.

Iowa got some consolation by setting two records for a four-game N. C. A. A. series. The Hawkeyes' 71 points tonight gave them a total of 340 for the tournament, breaking the mark of 310 by Indiana in 1953.

The Dons also topped the record with 333 points.

Field Goal Mark Set

Iowa's 119 field goals for the four games, including triumphs over Morehead, Kentucky and Temple, broke the mark of 118 set by Washington in 1953.

The 48 points by Temple's Lear set a single-game mark, beating the 45 by Bob Haubregs of Washington in 1953.

Lear, who entered the contest with 112 points for four previous games, thus finished with a five-game mark of 160 points. This smashed the former

series record of 141, set by Clyde Lovellette of Kansas in four games in 1952.

The previous five-game series mark of 118 points was set last year by Russell of San Francisco.

Lear scored 19 points in the of sixty-three also bettered the old record of fifty-seven credited to Houbregs in 1953.

SAN FRANCISCO (83)				IOWA (71)			
	G.	F.	PF.	P.		G.	F.	PF.	P.
Boldt. lf	7	2	4	16	Cain. lf	7	3	1	17
Farmer	0	0	2	0	Schoof. rf	5	4	3	14
Preseau, rf	3	1	3	7	Sebolt	0	0	0	0
Russell. c	11	4	2	26	Logan. c	5	2	3	12
Nelson	0	0	0	0	George	0	0	0	0
Perry. lg	6	2	2	14	Sch'rman. lg	4	3	2	11
Brown. rg	5	4	4	16	Seaberg. rg	5	1	1	17
Baxter	2	0	4	Martel	0	0	0	0
Bush	0	0	0	McConnell	0	0	0	0
Payne	0	0	0	Hawthorne	0	0	0	0
Total	35	13	13	83	Total	26	19	10	71

Half-time score—San Francisco 38, Iowa 33.

Free throws missed—Preseau, Russell. Cain. Scheuerman, Seaberg 3.

TEMPLE (90)				S. M. U. (81)			
	G.	F.	PF.	P.		G.	F.	PF.	P.
Norman. lf	8	1	3	17	Krog. lf	4	0	1	8
Reinfeld	3	8	2	12	Showalter	0	0	2	8
Fleming. rf	2	1	5	Herrscher,rf	2	1	0	5
Cohen. c	0	0	1	Krebs. c	9	11	1	29
Van Patton	2	4	6	Miller	0	0	1	0
Rodgers. lg	6	2	4	14	Morris. lg	2	8	4	12
Lear. rg	17	14	4	48	Mills. rg	6	7	4	19
Total	35	20	17	90	Total	27	27	13	81

Half-time score—Temple 41, Southern Methodist 38.

Free throws missed—Norman. Fleming. Lear 3. Herrscher 2. Krebs. Mills 2.

March 24, 1956

U. S. 'STUFF SHOT' IS CALLED LEGAL

Russell's Dunking Technique Not Official's Cup of Tea, but Aids American Five

MELBOURNE, Australia, Wednesday, Nov. 28 (UP)—The all-victorious United States basketball team, which hasn't neede any help, gained a new lift today on an official ruling that the "stuff shot" of Bill Russell was perfectly legal.

The Yankee quintet breezed to an 85-44 victory over Bulgaria last night in a semi-final game marked by a controversy over the 6-foot 10-inch Russell's dunking technique.

The United States is in a semi-finals double-elimination bracket with Bulgaria, Russia, and Brazil.

Whether Russell would take advantage of the rules clarification that makes his "stuff shot" permissible was not certain, because after Referee Charley Sien of Singapore disallowed one of his tap-ins last night, he stayed away from the goal most of the time.

The incident occurred in the first half. It was on a maneuver Russell had executed successfully on numerous occasions with the San Francisco University

team, which he led to a national championship.

As a team-mate shot, Russell timed a leap which put his hands above the goal and enabled him to guide the ball into the basket. Sien ruled that Russell was not permitted to touch the ball while it was on the rim of the basket.

The United States coach, Gerald Tucker, protested and asked for a conference at the half of the game. Apparently he convinced the Olympic basketball officials that Russell times his maneuver so perfectly he contacts the ball while it still is above the rim and releases con-

tact before it touches the hoop.

The line-up (UP):

U. S. (85)				BULGARIA (44)			
	G.	F.	PF.	P.		G.	F.	PF.	P.
Houghland	3	3	2	8	Atanassov	2	4	4
Jones	3	8	2	12	Mirtchev	2	4	5	7
Russell	5	3	2	12	Radev	6	3	1	15
Walsh	1	1	3	Kanev	0	1	1	6
Haldorson	3	4	2	9	Mantchenko	0	2	0	1
Tomsic	3	2	1	8	Totev	3	1	3	6
Boushka	1	1	2	Savov	1	2	3
Ford	3	0	0	6	Panov	0	3	1	2
Jeangerard	7	5	0	19				
Darling	1	1	0	3	Total	17	18	18	44
Evans	0	3	0	3				
Total	30	31	12	85				

Half-time score—United States 48. Bulgaria 19.

Free throws missed—Houghland. Jones 2. Russell. Haldorson. Boushka. Atanassov 2. Mirtchev, Kanev Mantchenko. Totev, Savov. Panov.

November 28, 1956

U. S. Quintet Routs Russia In Melbourne Final, 89-55

By The United Press.

MELBOURNE, Australia, Sunday, Dec. 2—America's all-victorious basketball heroes, reaching Olympian heights with one of the finest team efforts ever displayed in the games, drew a citation from their coach, Gerald Tucker, today as "the best in the world."

"This team is as good as any ever assembled," said the former University of Oklahoma All-America player, after his stars swept past Russia, 89—55, last night to gain a gold medal.

Bill Russell, the 6-foot 10-inch player from San Francisco University, who paced the gold-medal effort, declared this is "my proudest moment" and

hastened to dispel any suggestions that he might now turn professional.

"I have no plans at this time for a professional career," said Russell. "All I can think about right now is that we won."

The tall star, filled with emotion, was near tears as fellow Americans descended to congratulate him and his team-mates.

"You coached a mighty good team," Russell said to Tucker, grasping his coach with both hands.

Russell, who has been drafted by the Boston Celtics of the National Basketball Association, and who also has been scouted by the Harlem Globetrotters, said he was getting married in California on Dec. 9 and "I haven't got time to go thinking about anything else."

Tucker indicated he was a little disturbed over the tendency to demean the efforts of the Americans because they had not faced top-flight competition in the Olympics.

"Everybody down there has tried to figure out that these kids are not as good as they really are," he said. "But what more do they have to prove. They would be equal to any team in any league anywhere."

As good as the United States professional teams perhaps?

Tucker smiled and brushed off the question.

"I don't want to get involved in anything controversial," he said. "But they are the best amateur team—the best ever." '

He said the Russians were "good" and that they could play in American collegiate competition respectably. But that they would lose a lot of games.

"They would have to learn to play our game," he said. "American basketball differs considerably from that played in Europe. The Russians handle the ball well, though, and are well coached."

Jones Gets 15 Points

The repeat meeting of the finalists of the 1952 tournament was "no contest." Paced by Russell and his San Francisco teammate, K. C. Jones, who scored 15 points, the Americans completely dominated the play. Russell directed the ball-control strategy with his rebounds and brilliant all-around play.

The sluggish Soviet team was not even helped by Jan Kruminsh, their 7-foot 4-inch Goliath, who was cut down by the American "Davids."

Despite his overwhelming height, he was outmaneuvered for rebounds and consistently was left at the far end of the court when the Americans employed their fast break. He scored only four free throws and got no field goals.

Meanwhile Russell, with his whirling arms and his remarkable jumping ability, made it almost impossible for the Russians to drive in for close-range shots. As a result, the Soviet players were forced into a weaving pattern which sought to set up goals from outside.

The Russian shooters were only fair, and although most of their goals were scored on outside shots they never hit often enough to harass the victors.

In the final half, while trailing by 41 points, the Russians worked such a long-weaving pattern that it looked almost like

a stall, and the standing-room-only crowd of nearly 4,000 clapped impatiently for action.

U. S. Leads at Half, 56—27

The Americans broke up the game in the first half, and when they left the floor at the intermission they had a 56-27 lead.

During that period they connected on twenty of thirty-nine field goal attempts and sixteen of twenty-two free throws. Russia made good on ten of twenty-one field goal attempts—an indication of how few shots it had—and seven of twelve from the free-throw line.

The Russian "slowdown" in the second half prevented the Americans from going over the 100-point mark for the fifth time in their eight victories in the tournament. Even so, the Americans amassed a total of 793 points in maintaining the United States record of never having lost a game in an Olympic tournament.

Russell scored 13 points giving him a total of 113 for the tournament.

Bob Jeangerard, a former Colorado star, contributed 16 points and Jim Walsh, who played at Stanford, 14.

Uruguay took third place in the tournament with a 71-62 victory over France; Bulgaria defeated Brazil, 64—52, to clinch fifth place; and the Philippines earned seventh place by beating Chile, 75—68.

U. S. (89)	G	F	PF	P	RUSSIA (55)	G	F	PF	P
Cain	0	1	0	1	Valdman	1	2	5	4
Houghland	1	0	1	2	Torban	1	2	4
Jones	5	5	1	15	Petkar'ous	0	3	0	3
Russell	3	7	3	13	Botcharev	2	4	2	8
Walsh	4	6	3	14	Kruminsh	0	4	2	4
Evans	0	1	1	1	Semenov	7	1	4	15
Haldorson	4	1	4	9	Laouritenas	2	0	1	4
Tomsic	1	2	3	4	Ozerov	1	2	4	4
Boushka	3	3	1	9	Zoubkov	1	2	4	4
Ford	2	1	0	5	Stoudenet'l	2	1	2	5
Jeangerard	8	0	1	16					
Total	31	27	18	89	Total	17	21	26	55

Half-time score—United States 56, Russia 27.

Free throws missed—United States 5, Russia 5.

Referees—Blanthard, France, and Strath, Australia.

December 2, 1956

Stilt Thrives in Tall Corn Country

Chamberlain Super-Star in First Year on Kansas Five

By WILLIAM R. CONKLIN

No basketball player has a better chance for All-America honors this year than Wilt (The Stilt) Chamberlain, the 20-year-old Mount Everest of the courts.

The University of Kansas sophomore leads the nation's scorers this season. Seven feet tall, Wilt is one of the four major college players who have scored more than 50 points in a game this season. How does he do it?

His height is part of the answer, but only part. In addition to his rate-of-climb capabilities, Wilt has an unusual wingspread of 7 feet 2 inches. From a flat-footed stance, his reach takes him within four inches of the basket's rim. With running momentum he ascends to 12 feet 6 inches—two and one-half feet above the basket.

In his Philadelphia high school days Chamberlain was clocked in 49 seconds for the quarter-mile and 1:55.3 for the half. He had a 22-foot broad jump mark and a 6-foot-6-inch high jump clearance. A feat that might be included in the shooting department was his 48-foot toss of the 16-pound shot as a college freshman last year.

On the court Wilt is coached by Dick Harp, the successor to Phog Allen. Early in January Wilt led the nation's scorers with 32.9 points per game. His average of shots made from rebounds was .264, a mark that also led the country.

Praise From an Expert

Bud Palmer, one-time captain of the New York Knickerbockers,

thinks Wilt plays professional-type basketball. After playing against him in practice, Palmer said in an article in Sport magazine:

"This kid showed me something. He had the height, an incredible variety of shots and remarkable rebounding skill, but he had much more, too. His coordination and speed are unusual for a boy his size, and he moved me around the court with the shrewdness of a veteran pro."

College competitors comment in similar vein. Says Joe Ruklich, a fine sophomore center at Northwestern:

"I've seen guys who move better. I've seen guys who could do other things better. But that Chamberlain—he made me feel like a 6-year-old."

Aside from basketball, Wilt likes automobiles and the speed they produce, and modern jazz. His musical favorites are the Teen-Agers and Sarah Vaughn. Records by these performers abound in the 100-platter Chamberlain collection. His room in the Carruth-O'Leary dormitory on the Jayhawker campus is easily identified by the music that comes out of it.

"I've been interested in cars since I learned to drive at fourteen," Wilt says.

Last summer Wilt forsook his Philadelphia home to work in Kansas City. With his love of cars, it was natural that he approached automobiles from the ground up, as a tire salesman. He drove his own 1953 car from Philadelphia to Lawrence, the college town atop Mount Oread, forty-five miles west of Kansas City.

Time Out to Tinker

On a recent freezing midnight, bursts of automobile exhaust filled the air around Kansas City Municipal Auditorium. Inside, a tall figure clad in crimson Kansas warm-up gear worked the accelerator.

"What are you doing in there?" a sportscaster asked.

"Just warming up these pipes," replied Wilt. The player was still perspiring from the game he had

Wilt Chamberlain puts one in from above in Missouri contest

just finished. Before showering and changing clothes he thought he'd better look after the car, which had stood outside all day in the cold.

The public sometimes becomes confused over the 7-foot Wilt and the 6-foot 10-inch Bill Russell. On a Western swing, an occasional fan would point to Wilt and say:

"There's Bill Russell."

In Russell's home town of San Francisco, Wilt batted about .500 on being named correctly. A year ago Russell, then with San Francisco and now with the Celtics, visited the Chamberlain stamping grounds in Kansas City.

"I'd sure like to meet that Chamberlain," Bill said. "People have been calling me Wilt the Stilt ever since I got here."

"Can I ask you a question?" a 5-foot tall waiter once inquired of the Kansas star. Without breaking stride Wilt replied:

"Yup—seven feet tall."

Asked what he wants out of life right now, basketball's antenna says:

"I like being around friends who like me for something more than what I can produce for them."

His hope for his scoring average this season:

"High enough for us to win every game."

Wilt need have no worry on the score of his score. Barring injury he seems certain to top Clyde Lovellette's sophomore Kansas record of 545 points. On defense he has blocked seventy-nine enemy shots in ten games, a point potential of 158. Wilt is the sixth child in a family of nine brothers and sisters. He is studying business with his eye on a law degree after graduation.

January 14, 1957

BRADLEY QUINTET IS VICTOR, 84 TO 83

Sets Back Memphis State in Tourney Final at Garden on McMillon's Score

---

By WILLIAM J. BRIORDY

Bradley University's basketball team made its sixth National Invitation Tournament showing a victorious one yesterday afternoon. In one of the most thrilling finals in the history of the competition, the big Braves from Peoria, Ill., checked Memphis State's gamesters, 84 to 83, at Madison Square Garden.

A crowd of 11,327 saw Shellie McMillon, the Bradley center, crush the hopes of the hustling Tigers from Tennessee by com-

pleting a 3-point play with thirty seconds remaining.

Coach Bob Vanatta of the Tigers, who formerly coached Bradley, saw Memphis State move ahead with 1:06 of the rugged game remaining when Jack Butcher hit on a driving lay-up. That shot appeared to place Vanatta's lads in command.

Braves Capitalize on Height

But the Braves, using their greater height and rebounding strength to the fullest, stormed back to draw even as McMillon tallied on a rebound. When Shellie was fouled by Bob Swander, the Bradley center converted to sew it up.

After Butcher's shot, there ensued a session of wild and wooly play as each team pressed mightily. It was after Memphis State's Orby Arnold lost the ball at mid-court that Bradley hustled for the winning points. The play was so feverish that both outfits took

turns losing the ball in the final fifty-four seconds.

When Swander missed a long one-hander with five seconds left, Coach Chuck Orsborn's Braves had the victory and their first N. I. T. title.

The setback was a bitter one for the Tigers, who made their debut in the N. I. T. this year. They trailed by 51—43 at the intermission before setting the taller Braves on their heels with a 15-point spree as the second half opened. Win Wilfong, a jump-shot specialist who headed the scorers with 31 points; Swander, Butcher and Arnold figured in that spurt.

When Arnold converted twice from the foul line and then Butcher got two 1-pointers at 6:00, Memphis State had a 10-point bulge. But the hustling Tigers, essentially a six-man squad, fought their hearts out only to run out of gas against depth-laden Bradley.

Bradley, with Bobby Joe Mason and the 6-foot 7-inch Barney Cable supplying the spark, quickly put a halter on the Tigers' ambitions. Cable pegged three straight one-handers. Bobby Joe got a free throw and then tossed a one-hander from the side for a 74—73 lead at 12:15.

But the gamesters from Tennessee were not through by any means. Wilfong hooked one at 12:25 to return the lead to Memphis State. Then McMillon clicked with a hook shot. Wilfong drove for a lay-up at 13:35, but McMillon tied the score at 77-all with a free throw.

Bradley's Dick Dhabalt put the Indians ahead again with 4:50 remaining on a one-hander. Then Wilfong charged Dhabalt and the Bradley player converted two free throws. That was Wilfong's fifth personal, putting him out of the game with 3:55 to go.

Then the plucky Butcher hit with a one-hander and fed to Ragan underneath to tie it at 81-all with 3:20 left. When Butcher drove in for his lay-up with 1:06 to go, the Memphis State supporters went wild. Then

IT NETTED HIM NOTHING: Win Wilfong, right, of Memphis State trying for a basket yesterday at the Garden. Blocking him is Dick Dhabalt of victorious Bradley quintet.

Associated Press

MOST VALUABLE PLAYER of the National Invitation Tournament was Win Wilfong of Memphis State, who holds his trophy after completion of the game. A jump-shot specialist, he scored 89 points in four games. Tournament cup, right, a permanent display piece, will bear his name.

followed the feverish action and McMillon's 3-pointer.

Bobby Joe Mason paced the Braves with 22 points. McMillon had 18 markers, 1 more than Cable. Butcher hit for 21 points. McMillon topped the rebounders with twelve. The last time Bradley appeared in the N. I. T. was in 1950, when the Braves bowed to City College.

Wilfong received a trophy as the most valuable player of the twentieth annual tournament.

Orsborn received the Edward A. Kelleher Memorial Trophy from Walter T. McLaughlin of St. John's, the president of the Metropolitan Intercollegiate Basketball Association, at the end of the game. The M. I. B. A. is the sponsor of the N. I. T. The team members of the finalists also received awards from McLaughlin.

Temple's team gained third place in the tournament when it defeated St. Bonaventure, 67 to 50, in the consolation play-off.

The final, which was played first, was nationally televised by the Columbia Broadcasting System.

BRADLEY (84)					MEMPHIS ST. (83)				
	G.	F.	P.	P.		G.	F.	P.	P.
Cable, lf	5	1	4	17	Wilfong lf	10	11	5	31
McDade	3	3	5	Ragan rf	3	4	3	10
B. Mason, rf	5	12	2	22	Hockaday	0	2	1	2
Johnson	0	0	2	Arnold, c	5	4	4	14
McMillon, c	8	2	4	18	Butcher, lg	7	7	4	21
Emerson	0	1	1	Swander, rg	2	1	4	5
Sedgwick, lg	6	0	2	0	Hays	0	0	1	0
Myers	1	2	4						
Morse, rg	1	0	9	Total	27	29	22	83
Dhabalt	3	2	8						

Total ... 30 24 34 84
Half-time score—Bradley 31, Memphis State 43
Free throws missed—Cable 3, B. Mason 2, McMillon 2, Sedgwick, Morse, Dhabalt, McDade, Meyers, Emerson, Filfong, Ragan, Arnold 3, Butcher 3, Swander 2, Hays 2, Hockaday.
Officials—John Nucatola and John Stevens.

March 24, 1957

NO. CAROLINA FIVE NIPS KANSAS, 54-53, IN THIRD OVERTIME

Undefeated Tar Heels Extend Streak to 32 in Final of National College Play

QUIGG'S 2 FOULS DECIDE

Winning Tallies Made With Six Seconds Remaining— San Francisco Victor

By The United Press

KANSAS CITY, March 23 -- North Carolina defeated Kansas, 54-53, in three overtime periods tonight to win the National Collegiate basketball tournament. Joe Quigg won the game for the unbeaten Tar Heels with two foul shots in the final six seconds and then blocked a pass to Wilt Chamberlain to foil a Jayhawk scoring bid.

Quigg's jumping one-hand block kept Chamberlain from attempting one desperate shot in the last five seconds of the third extra period.

It was the first time a national championship game went into overtime. The Tar Heels' victory extended their unbeaten streak to thirty-two games.

The final, frantic fifteen minutes of play produced two heated incidents on the court. In the first one Pete Brennan of North Carolina clamped his arms around Chamberlain's waist and began to wrestle. The second occurred when Tommy Kearns of North Carolina swung aside Gene Elstun of Kansas.

It was North Carolina by 29-22 at the half. The score was 46—46 at the end of regulation play.

The two teams scored only 2 points each in the first overtime. Chamberlain hit for Kansas and Bob Young, a substitute, tallied for North Carolina. The second overtime was scoreless.

Chamberlain was the top scorer with 23 points. North Carolina's All-America, Lennie Rosenbluth, had 20. Rosenbluth fouled out with 1:45 remaining in standard playing time and did not play in the extra periods, which were mostly displays of stalling and ball control.

Kearns and Quigg won the game for North Carolina, hitting for all the Tar Heels' points in the third extra session. Kearns had a field goal and two free throws to match Chamberlain's overtime production.

Kansas Takes Time Out

Gene Elstun added another free throw to send Kansas ahead, 53—52, with twenty seconds left. Chamberlain blocked Kearns' shot, but fouled Quigg and Quigg hit for the 2 winning points.

Kansas took time out with five seconds left and tried to feed the ball to Chamberlain, but Quigg made the game-saving block.

North Carolina led the entire first half and Kansas did not catch up until it took the lead at 36—35 with 16:40 left.

Kansas was on top, 40-37, with ten minutes left. The score was twice tied and the lead changed twice before the 46-46 deadlock.

The pattern of stalling began as soon as Kansas got its 3-point lead. North Carolina started slowing it down and Kansas followed suit.

From ten minutes left to five minutes, not a shot was fired. Both teams continued the stalling in the first two overtimes.

In the first overtime, Young broke through for a lay-up for North Carolina. During the stall, which succeeded in pulling the Kansans out of position, Chamberlain retaliated with a two-handed push off the post to tie it at 48—48.

M'GUIRE SAYS HE GOT HIT

North Carolina Five's Coach Accuses Kansas Assistant

KANSAS CITY, March 23 (AP) -- Coach Frank McGuire of North Carolina said that Kansas' coach, Dick Harp, told him to "shut up" and that an assistant Kansas coach punched him in the stomach during a 'rhubarb' at the National Collegiate championship basketball game tonight.

"I moved up to see what was happening on the floor," McGuire said. "Then I heard Harp yell at me to shut up. I told Dick I hadn't said anything. Then a big fellow on the Kansas bench— I don't know his name —hit me in the stomach.

"Then everything calmed down. I have no argument with Harp but that big fellow on his bench had no right to punch me in the stomach."

Jack Eskridge, a 6-footer, who is Harp's assistant, said McGuire went over to the Kansas bench, but "nothing happened."

N.C.A.A. Line-Ups

N. CAROLINA (54)					KANSAS (53)				
	G.	F.	P.	P.		G.	F.	P.	P.
R'bluth, lf	8	4	5	20	Elstun lf	4	3	2	11
Lotz	0	0	0	Loneski, rf	0	2	2	2
Brennan, rf	3	3	11	L. Johnson	0	2	1	2
Young	0	1	0	2	Ch'berlain, c	6	11	3	23
Quigg, c	4	2	4	10	King, lg	3	5	4	11
Cunningham, lg	0	0	0	Parker, rg	1	2	4	4
Kearns, rg	4	3	4	11	Billings	0	0	2	0

Total ... 21 12 21 54   Total ... 15 23 14 53
Half-time score—North Carolina 29, Kansas 22. Regulation-time score—North Carolina 46, Kansas 46. First overtime score—North Carolina 48, Kansas 48. Second overtime score—North Carolina 48, Kansas 48.
Free throws missed—Brennan 4, Quigg, Cunningham, Kearns 4, Elstun 3, Loneski, Chamberlain 5, King.

S. FRANCISCO (67)					MICHIGAN ST. (60)				
	G.	F.	P.	P.		G.	F.	P.	P.
Day, lf	6	0	3	12	Lux, lf	2	1	2	5
Lillevand	0	0	0	Scott	2	0	1	4
J. King	0	0	2	0	Green, rf	1	5	5	9
Dunbar, rf	4	1	4	9	Quiggle	2	2	1	6
Brown, c	8	6	3	22	Ferguson, c	4	6	2	14
Farmer, lg	4	8	1	16	Hedden, lg	4	1	5	9
Presseau, rg	2	4	4	8	Bencie	0	0	0	0
Mallen	0	0	0	Wilson, rg	3	0	1	6
					Anderegg	2	3	5	7

Total ... 24 19 17 67   Total ... 23 14 23 60
Half-time score—San Francisco 33, Michigan State 30.
Free throws missed—Day 3, Dunbar 3, Brown 5, Farmer, Scott, Ferguson 3, Hedden, Wilson, Anderegg.

March 24, 1957

ROBERTSON NAMED PLAYER OF YEAR

Cincinnati Basketball Star Beats Seattle's Baylor in United Press Poll

Oscar Robertson, Cincinnati's outstanding 19-year-old basketball forward, today was named player of the year in the annual United Press poll.

Robertson, the first sophomore ever to win the honor, received 123 votes in nationwide balloting by 251 sports writers and broadcasters. Elgin Baylor of Seattle was the runner-up with fifty-five votes, and Dave Gambee of Oregon State was third with twelve.

Guy Rodgers of Temple was fourth with ten and Don Hennon of Pittsburgh was fifth with eight. Bailey Howell of Mississippi State followed with five, and Wilt Chamberlain of Kansas and Pete Brennan of North Carolina were next with four each.

Many observers rated Robertson's performances as the most polished ever produced by a sophomore. He averaged more than 35 points a game, and led his team in rebounds and assists. The 6-foot 5-inch star also was the top rebounder as well as scorer in the rugged Missouri Valley Conference.

His regular-season total of 898 points was the most ever scored by a sophomore in major college competition.

March 19, 1958

Rally by Kentucky Trips Seattle, 84-72

By The Associated Press.

LOUISVILLE, March 22—Kentucky battled to its fourth National collegiate basketball championship tonight, rallying to whip Seattle, 84—72.

A record National Collegiate Athletic Association crowd of 18,803—99 per cent supporters of Coach Adolph Rupp and his scrappy kids—roared as Vern Hatton and Johnny Cox combined for 35 points which paced a brilliant second-half rally that led the Southeastern Conference champions to a spectacular victory.

Hatton, whose driving lay-ups with twelve seconds left, snapped Temple's twenty-five-game winning streak last night, fired in 30 points, 17 of them in the second half. Cox, a deadly one-handed shooter from thirty feet away, scored 18 points after the intermission and closed with 24 for the night. The Seattle Chieftains, attempting to become the first independent team to bag the national title since 1950, suffered a blow when Elgin Baylor drew his fourth personal foul with sixteen and a half minutes remaining. Coach John Castellani switched to a zone defense in an attempt to minimize his star's chances of fouling out. Although Baylor lasted out the game, the Chieftains weren't the same team after that.

Cox eight times fired his one-hander over the zone while Hatton, taking advantage of Baylor's absence from the middle, fired in for one close-up shot after another.

When Baylor picked up his fourth foul, Seattle held a 44-38 lead. Within seven minutes, the Wildcats had pulled even for the first time since the fifth minute of play.

Seattle battled back to lead again at 60—58 but Don Mills scored 3 points, the last two on a hook over the timid Baylor, to put Kentucky in front to stay at 61—60.

Then Cox and Hatton took up the scoring burden. With Cox scoring 4 points and Hatton 6, the new champions dashed into a 72-63 advantage.

The closest the Chieftains could get after that was 5 points at 74—69 with about two and a half minutes left.

Until fouls hampered his play, Baylor was spectacular, despite painful rib bruises. Coach Castellani said the 6-foot 6-inch ace suffered the injuries against Kansas State last night.

Baylor scored 25 points for 135 in five tournament games. He also was brilliant in his playmaking and rebounding, regularly setting up Jerry Frizzell and Charley Brown, Seattle's other steady scorers. He grabbed nineteen rebounds, nearly half of his team's total.

Beck Draws 4 Personals

Seattle's handicap was partly balanced by Kentucky's having to do without Ed Beck, its top rebounder, for much of the second half. Beck drew his fourth foul with seventeen and one-half minutes remaining and sat out most of the rest of the game.

Mills, a 6-foot 7-inch sophomore, filled in nicely after Beck went to the sidelines. Mills scored 9 points and picked off five key rebounds in his limited appearance.

Kentucky's fourth championship is an extension of the Wildcats' own N. C. A. A. record. No other school has won more than two. The Wildcats, back to the top level of national powers, also hold N. C. A. A. records for appearances with ten, for games won with twenty, and consecutive victories in tournament play with twelve.

This one, however, was Kentucky's first crown since 1951. Rupp and his team previously won in 1948 and 1949. This was the fourth time a Wildcat team had reached the final and Wildcat teams have won every final in which they have participated.

Temple, paced by Guy Rodgers and Bill Kennedy, rallied in the second half to down Kansas State, 67—57, for third place.

Kansas State, the tournament favorite until crushed by Seattle last night, blew an 11-point half-time lead in losing to Temple. The Jayhawks got only one field goal in the first thirteen and a half minutes of the second half.

Temple simply ran away as the Big Eight champions went flat again—just as flat as against Seattle.

Bob Boozer of Kansas State hit with a jump shot with forty-five seconds gone in the second half. By the time K State got another field goal, there were 6½ minutes left in the game and Temple had breezed to a 53-47 lead.

Boozer got the second field goal on a tip-in, cutting the Owls' lead to 4 points, but that was as close as the big men from the Midwest got. Rodgers and Kennedy promptly went back to work and Temple quickly opened up a commanding lead.

Kennedy, who suffered a broken bone in his nose last night as Kentucky snapped Temple's twenty-five-game winning streak, led the scorers with 23 points. Rodgers had 17 points and did an excellent job of directing the victors.

It was the second time in three years the Owls, representing the Middle Atlantic Conference, had finished third. They seemed to need the first twenty minutes to shake off the disappointment of last night's heartbreaking 61-60 loss to Kentucky. After hitting on only 25 per cent of their shots in the first half, the Owls bagged thirteen of twenty-six after the intermission and wound up with a 34.8 percentage.

Boozer, with 19 points, led K-State, which hit on only five of thirty-three attempts after the intermission and wound up with 28.3 for the game.

CHAMPIONSHIP GAME

KENTUCKY (84)	G.	F.	P.	F.P.	SEATTLE (72)	G.	F.	P.F.	P.
Cox	10	4	3	24	Frizzell	4	8	3	16
Crigler	5	4	4	14	Ogorek	4	2	5	10
Beck	0	0	4	0	Baylor	9	7	4	25
Mills	4	1	3	9	Brown	6	5	5	17
Smith	2	3	4	7	Harney	2	0	1	4
Hatton	9	12	3	30	Saunders	0	0	3	0
					Piasecki	0	0	0	0
Total	30	24	21	84	Total	25	22	21	72

Half-time score—Seattle 39, Kentucky 36. Free throws missed—Crigler, Beck, Mills 3, Smith 2, Hatton 3, Frizzell 3, Baylor 2, Brown 2, Harney.

THIRD-PLACE GAME

TEMPLE (67)	G.	F.	P.F.	P.	KAN. STATE (57)	G.	F.	P.F.	P.
Norman	1	5	3	7	Boozer	6	7	4	19
Brodsky	4	2	3	10	Frank	3	2	2	8
Van Patton	1	1	5	3	Parr	1	5	2	7
Kennedy	8	7	0	23	Matuszak	1	1	4	3
Rodgers	7	3	2	17	De Witz	3	0	1	6
Fleming	2	3	4	7	Holwerda	0	0	2	0
					Abbott	6	2	3	14
Total	23	21	17	67	Ballard	0	0	1	0
					Douglas	0	0	3	0
					Total	20	17	22	57

Half-time score—Kansas State 39, Temple 28.
Free throws missed—Norman 3, Brodsky 3, Van Patton 2, Kennedy 2, Boozer 2, Frank, Parr 3, Matuszak 2, De Witz.

March 23, 1958

Russia Halts U. S. to Stay Unbeaten in World Basketball Tourney

SOVIET FIVE WINS IN CHILE, 62 TO 37

By JUAN de ONIS
Special to The New York Times.

SANTIAGO, Chile, Jan. 28—Russia defeated the United States at basketball tonight for the first time in international competition. The score of 62 to 37 in favor of the Soviet team was a faithful reflection of the difference between the two teams.

The victory kept the Soviet side undefeated in the final round of the third world amateur basketball championship. The United States, represented by the United States Air Force team, suffered its first defeat.

The Soviet victory was the result of superiority in every facet of a game in which the United States has been the world leader. The scarlet-shirted Russians outclassed the United States in shooting, rebounding, ball control, defense and poise.

After taking the first-half lead, 25 to 14, the Russians turned the game into a rout in the second half. They ran up a lead of 26 points with five minutes to play.

The United States did not have a player taller than 6 feet 5 inches on its squad of eleven lieutenants and one airman second class. Before the game the Americans were rated an even match to beat Russia.

That was based mostly on the United States' reputation and not on the material here. The deficiency had been evident in earlier squeakers. The United States had won by one point from Puerto Rico and by 63 to 58 against Bulgaria.

George Vayda led the United States scoring with 12 points before he fouled out in the second half.

Valdiz Muzhniecs, a lithe, blonde Russian forward, broke the game wide open in the second half, during which he scored 12 of the Russian's 37 points.

When the game ended the Russians wildly hugged each other and tossed their coach, Stepan Spandarian, into the air three times. They left the court with the crowd cheering. The United States players trailed off to their dressing room without congratulating the victor.

Brazil Beats Puerto Rico

In the preliminary game, Brazil defeated Puerto Rico, 99 to 71, before a crowd of 20,000 at the open-air National Stadium.

The referees for the United States-Russia game were Robert Blanchard of France and Jorge Righetto of Brazil.

The United States starters were Ron Olsen and James Coshow, forwards; Robert Hodges, center, and Jerome Vayda and Richard Walsh, guards. Their opponents were Maigoinis Valdamanis and Gerard Menashvili, forwards; Viktor Zhukov, center, and Mikhail Semionev and Juri Kroenev, in the backcourt.

The United States team, in white uniforms, opened with a zone defense against the scarlet-shirted Russians. Both teams were nervous and unable to solve each other's defenses at the start. After five minutes of play the score was tied, 4—4.

Taking advantage of fouls and hitting outside shots, Russia forged into a 20-5 lead after ten minutes.

One United States substitute, Bob Jeangerard, a former University of Colorado all-America star, played with his broken left hand in a cast and could not give the needed spark to his team.

Krumins Aids Russians

The Russians, taking advantage of United States defensive mistakes and controlling the backboards, pulled steadily ahead. With eight minutes left in the first half, Russia's 7-foot 1-inch center, Yan Krumins, a Latvian woodchopper, entered the game. He contributed 5 points of the Soviet team's 11-point lead at the half.

Vayda scored 7 of the United States points in the first half.

RUSSIA (62)				U. S. (37)			
	G.	F.	PF.P.		G.	F.	PF.P.
Muzhniecs	4	5	2 13	Hodges	0	0	5 0
Valdmanis	4	6	1 14	Miller	1	0	5 2
Torban	2	4	3 8	Olsen	0	0	2 0
Menashvili	2	0	3 4	Riley	0	3	2 3
Zhukov	2	2	2 6	Coshow	1	0	5 2
Bockkariev	2	0	5 4	McDonald	0	1	4 1
Krumins	2	3	5 7	Jeangerard	0	0	1 0
Seminov	2	0	4 4	Antonio	2	0	1 4
Kroneev	0	2	2 2	Vayda	4	4	5 12
Kutusov	0	0	0 0	Walsh	3	3	5 9
				Backer	2	0	1 4
Total	20	22	27 62	Total	13	11	36 37

Half-time score—Russia 25, United States 14.

Free throws missed—Valdmanis 4, Torban 2, Zhukov 2, Bockkariev, Hodges 2, Riley 2, Jeangerard, Antonio, Vayda 2, Walsh. Officials—Blanchard and Righetto.

SANTIAGO, Chile, Jan. 28 (UPI)—The United States has two games left to play in the world basketball tournament, one against Chile tomorrow night and another against Brazil on Friday night.

Russia has only one more game left—with Nationalist China on Friday night. But Soviet officials insist they will not play the game inasmuch as the U. S. S. R. does not recognize the Formosa government.

Tournament officials were still looking for "an amicable solution" although previously they had hinted that the game might be forfeited to Nationalist China. If it is, Russia will wind up the tourney with a 5-1 record, while the best the United States could hope for would be a similar 5-1 record.

January 29, 1959

ST. JOHN'S DOWNS BRADLEY IN OVERTIME FINAL, 76 TO 71, AND GAINS THIRD N.I.T. TITLE

JACKSON HONORED

Redmen's Ace Is Most Valuable in Tourney —N. Y. U. Victor

By LOUIS EFFRAT

A toss-up, the experts said in advance of the final of the National Invitation Tournament at Madison Square Garden yesterday. A toss-up, the odds-makers agreed. And a toss-up it was as the St. John's and Bradley basketball teams battled through forty minutes of regulation time and five minutes of overtime before St. John's scored a 76-71 triumph for the championship.

New York University beat Providence, 71—57, for third place.

The final, seen by a matinee turnout of 14,376, went down to the wire. St. John's, down twice by 8 points during the early going and never in front until less than four minutes remained, outsteadied the visiting Braves from Peoria, Ill., in the last three minutes of overtime.

The New York Times

TRIUMPH: Tony Jackson of St. John's, with most-valuable-player award, is happily hugged by Joe Lapchick, his coach, who holds tournament trophy awarded the team.

From the instant Bradley's Al Saunders had brought the Braves to a 63—63 deadlock at 19:21 of the second half until the clock ran out in the overtime period, hardly a person remained seated in the garden.

N. I. T. to win the title three times.

The Redmen, also under the tutelage of Lapchick, turned the trick in 1943 and 1944. Earlier this season, these Redmen, short on depth but long on skill, spirit and stamina, won the Holiday Festival at the Garden.

Jackson Gets 27 Rebounds

Tony Jackson, the sophomore with the remarkable spring in his legs; Alan Seiden, the senior without whose shooting, driving, feeding and steadying influence the Redmen would have been in trouble; Lou Roethel, Gus Alfieri and Dick Engert proved their right to the championship.

Jackson, who scored 21 points and captured twenty-seven rebounds in the game, was named the most valuable player in the tournament.

There were times when top-seeded Bradley appeared to be too strong for the Redmen. Bobby Joe Mason, alert, aggressive and a dangerous shot-maker at all times; Joe Billy McDade and Mike Owens forced St. John's into numerous errors. The surprise at the half, when Bradley held a 33-30 edge, was that the Redmen were so close.

Too many wild passes and too many gift baskets to the opposition hurt the Redmen. However, Lapchick reorganized his forces and once they cut down on mistakes they were in the ball game.

At that, St. John's might have ended it in regulation time, were it not for one of several steals by the Braves. Coach Chuck Orsborn's men had harassed St. John's with numerous interceptions, this the more important.

St. John's never trailed in overtime. One of Jackson's characteristic jump shots put

As the action became rougher, the Redmen became steadier. Mainly because Coach Joe Lapchick's quintet was able to maintain its poise, St. John's became the first team in the twenty-two year history of the

BREAKING THROUGH: Gene Morse of Bradley leaps to shoot for basket despite Dick Engert's defensive efforts.

sons. his Redmen have posted a 52-23 record, including yesterday's victory.

Lapchick was an all-round athlete. When he chose pro basketball as a career, he turned down opportunities to sign with the Dodgers as a right-handed pitcher and with Al Watrous as an assistant golf pro.

He is easy-going and amiable. But when his team is playing. he becomes highly nervous and suffers from contraction of the stomach muscles. In a previous N. I. T. he fainted on the bench while his team was rallying en route to a victory in the final.

Height Aids Violets

Coach Lou Rossini's N. Y. U. squad. which came within a basket of forcing Bradley into overtime in the semi-finals, had too much height and agility for Providence in the consolation contest.

Before the game was thirteen minutes old, Cal Ramsey. Tom Sanders. Russ Cunningham and company had sprinted to a 29-13 lead which was increased to 40-22 at half time. That was it. despite a strong late rally by the losers.

As is generally the case in these consolation rounds, both sides were relaxed. When a team like the stylish. fast-moving Violets is free-wheeling. it is hard to stop. Cunningham was especially brilliant with his ball-handling and feeding.

March 22, 1959

California Halts West Va. For N.C.A.A. Title, 71-70

By JOSEPH M. SHEEHAN
Special to The New York Times.

LOUISVILLE, March 21—The National Collegiate basketball title went to a Pacific Coast Conference team tonight for the first time since 1942. Fighting off a spine-tingling late challenge, California defeated West Virginia, 71-70, in a down-to-the-wire final witnessed by a capacity crowd of 18,498 in Freedom Hall at the Kentucky Fair and Exposition Center.

In the play-off for third place between the beaten semi-finalists, Cincinnati, led by Oscar Robertson's 39 points, downed Louisville, 98—85.

California and West Virginia squeezed the last drop of drama out of their contest. Seldom has a game had more sweeping changes of fortune.

In the early going, the high-scoring Mountaineers performed with such devastating effect that they piled up a 10-point lead in the first nine minutes.

Then California had its innings. Forcing West Virginia into costly mistakes with their vigilant, pressing defense and cashing in on almost every opportunity they developed with their beautifully - disciplined ball-control attack, the Golden Bears caught up at the thirteen-minute mark and went on to a 39-33 half-time lead.

Continuing its ascendancy in the early minutes of the second half, California built its margin to 13 points. With ten minutes to play, the Golden Bears still were 12 points in front.

Then West Virginia, noted for its whirlwind finishes, started its drive. Swarming all over California on defense, the Mountaineers destroyed the smooth, even tempo of t he California attack.

Under heavy pressure. the harried Golden Bears started throwing away passes, walking with the ball and committing other costly errors. West Virginia cashed in on most of them.

With Jerry West, who outshone Robertson in this tournament. leading the way. the Mountaineers started to close in.

The score went to 59 -53 on a jump short by West at 11:11. to 63 59 on a set shot by Jim Ritchie at 12:57 and to 69 68 at 19:04 when West was credited with a goal on the game's third goal-tending call against Darrall Imhoff, California's fine center.

With nearly a minute left. it still was either team's game. But after successfully controlling the ball for forty seconds. California shook Imhoff loose underneath. The 6-foot 10-inch pivot, shooting from point blank range missed. He immediately jumped high again and tapped in the rebound with a sweeping slap of his long left arm.

That put California 3 points ahead with seventeen seconds remaining. West Virginia tallied seve nseconds before the final buzzer on a basket by Willie Akers but that was the last chance for the Mountaineers.

California's well-balanced team had outstanding performers in Denny Fitzpatrick. who tallied 20 points: Bob Dalton. who scored 15, and Jack Grout and Imhoff. who made 10 each.

For West Virginia, West made 28 points. which gave him 66 for the two games here: Akers and Bob Clousson had 10 apiece.

St. John's in front. but two free throws by McDade tied the score at 65—65.

Alfieri made two free throws when fouled by Owens. and Jackson did the same when Saunders fouled him. Halfway through the overtime. St. John's had a 69-65 advantage.

But it was not yet over. With 1:28 left. Saunders intercepted and passed to Mason. who scored. Then came the key to the game. the tournament and the entire year for St. John's.

Alfieri Makes 3-Point Play

With thirty seconds to go. Alfieri drove in with a dynamic 3-point play. Hacked by Bradley's Gene Morse as the ball dropped through the net. Alfieri added the free throw and the Redmen had a 5-point lead. That did the trick.

The game's high scorer was Seiden with 22 points. Jackson had 21 and Alfieri 15. Mason led Bradley with 18 points.

At the buzzer. the St. John's players were mobbed by jubilant followers. The heaviest pummeling was reserved for Lapchick. who was lifted high on strange shoulders. He wept.

ST. JOHN'S (76)				BRADLEY (71)			
	G.F.PF.P.				G.F.PF.P.		
Engert. lf	2 0 2 4			Smith. lf	4 0 2 8		
Jackson. rf	9 3 1 21			Morse. rf	6 4 2 16		
Roethel. c	3 3 4 12			McDade. c	6 4 3 18		
Ryan	1 0 0 2			Mason. lg	7 4 4 18		
Seiden. lg	7 8 4 22			Saunders	1 1 3 3		
Pedone	0 0 0 0			Voegele	0 0 0 0		
Alfieri. rg	5 5 3 15			Owens. rg	4 2 4 10		
				Hewitt	0 0 0 0		
Total	29 19 14 76						
				Total	28 15 18 71		

Half-time score—Bradley 33. St. John's 30. Score at end of regulation time—Bradley 63. St. John's 63.
Free throws missed—Engert 2, Jackson. Seiden 2. Ryan. Morse. McDade 2. Mason 2. Saunders.
Officials—John Nucatola and Charles Eckman

unashamedly.

The victory marked another bright chapter in the career of Lapchick. a Yonkers native and resident who will be 59 next month. He earned his first basketball fame as a member of the Original Celtics. perhaps the greatest professional team in the annals of the sport.

In his first tenure as St. John's coach — from 1936 through 1947—his teams played seven times in the N. I. T. and had a 181-53 over-all record. The 6-foot 5-inch Lapchick then coached the professional New York Knickerbockers for nine seasons. returning to St. John's in 1956. In the last three seasons.

The Line-Ups

CHAMPIONSHIP GAME

CALIFORNIA (71)	G.	F.	PF.	P.	WEST VA. (70)	G.	F.	PF.	P.
Dalton, lf	6	3	4	15	West, lf	10	8	4	28
McClintk, rf	4	0	1	8	Clousson, rf	4	2	4	10
Imhoff, c	4	2	3	10	Akers, c	5	0	0	10
Buch, lg	0	2	3	2	Bolvard, lg	1	4	4	6
F'patr'k, rg	8	4	1	20	Smith, rg	2	1	3	5
Grout	4	2	1	10	Retton	0	2	0	2
Simpson	0	0	2	0	Ritchie	1	2	0	4
Doughty	3	0	3	6	Patrone	2	1	1	5
Total	29	13	18	71	Total	25	20	16	70

Half-time score—California 39, West Virginia 33.

Free throws missed—Dalton, McClintock, Fitzpatrick 3, West 4, Akers, Clousson, Patrone.

Officials—Red Mihalich and Tommy Bell.

CONSOLATION GAME

CINCINNATI (98)	G.	F.	PF.	P.	LOUISVILLE (85)	G.	F.	PF.	P.
Rob's'n, lf	12	15	3	39	Golds'tn, lf	8	5	4	21
W'hahn, rf	4	4	3	12	Turner, rf	4	1	4	9
Tenwick, c	2	2	2	6	Sawyer, c	0	5	4	5
Davis, lg	11	2	3	24	Andrews, lg	6	6	3	18
W'taker, rg	6	3	2	15	Tiem'n, rg	10	3	3	23
Landfried	1	0	2	2	Leathers	2	2	4	6
Nail	0	0	1	0	Kitchen	1	0	2	2
Willey	0	0	1	0	Stacey	0	0	0	0
Cetrone	0	0	1	0	Geiling	0	1	0	1
Bouldin	0	0	0	0	Mantel	0	0	0	0
					Watkins	0	0	0	0
Total	36	26	18	98	Total	31	23	24	85

Half-time score—Louisville 53, Cincinnati 49.

Free throws missed—Robertson 4, Wiesenhahn, Tenwick 2, Davis, Whitaker, Landfried, Goldstein, Turner, Tieman.

Officials—Al Lightner, Pacific Coast Conference, and Floyd Magnuson, Big Eight.

California Defense Tight

It was as even a game as anyone could have hoped for. California made 44 per cent of its shots as against West Virginia's 45.4 per cent. It is significant, however, that the Mountaineers, who had the nation's second highest scoring average, were not able to get off many shots against a California defense that has the best statistical rating in the country.

California, for all its ball control play, took more shots, letting fly sixty-six times to West Virginia's fifty-five.

It was a rugged game for both coaches, as well as for the players. With both sides pressing aggressively on defense, there were many controversial officiating calls. Pete Newell of California and Fred Schaus of West Virginia rate commendation for their restraint. The excited crowd was less orderly.

Cincinnati Rallies In Opener

Louisville, playing much better than it had against West Virginia the night before, led Cincinnati at half-time, 53—49, and was in front as late as five minutes after the intermission.

However, under Robertson's leadership, the Bearcats initiated a drive that regained the lead. They piled up a 10-point advantage, weathered a Louisville rally that closed the gap to 4 points with five minutes to go and finished with another scorching burst that carried them out of danger.

Robertson scored 39 points. This gave to the Cincinnati star a National Collegiate record for most points in two varsity seasons. His two-year total of 1,962 points topped the former mark of 1,947 set by Frank Selvy of Furman in 1953-54.

Experimental Rules Used

The consolation game was played under experimental rules that stopped the clock for all violations called by th e officials. This gave the teams increased freedom to make substitutions and had the effect of adding

about three minutes of playing time.

Such a change is under consideration for next season and the rules committee, which will meet here starting Sunday, requested the trial. Coach Peck Hickman of Louisville and Coach George Smith of Cincinnati consented.

The last Pacific Coast conference team to win the NCAA title was Stanford in 1942. California is the first PCC team since to get as far as the championship round. West Virginia was the first representative of the Southern Conference, as presently constituted, to play for the title.

March 22, 1959

Robertson Betters Record for Scoring

By The Associated Press.

CINCINNATI, Feb. 6.—Oscar Robertson of the University of Cincinnati tonight broke the major college career basketball scoring record. He set the mark on a field goal in the early minutes of the second half against Houston and the shot lifted his total to 2,589.

Robertson, a senior from Indianapolis, scored his record-breaking total in a little less than three seasons of college competition and in his seventy-sixth game.

The former record of 2,587, set by Rudy Dickie Hemric of Wake Forrest in 1955, was for four years of competition and covered 104 games.

In tonight's game, Robertson ended the first half with 16 points. He needed only 1 to

break the record. Early in the second half he dunked in a lay-up field goal.

Oscar finished with 29 points in the game and paced the Bearcats to a 67-55 victory.

Robertson's total for seventy-six games was 2,600 points.

It was only in the last three or four minutes that the Bearcats were able to pull away for their seventeenth victory in eighteen games.

Dick Molchany had been the guard on Robertson until Molchany fouled out late in the last half.

The New York Times
Oscar Robertson

CINCINNATI (67)	G.	F.	PF.	P.	HOUSTON (55)	G.	F.	PF.	P.
Robertson	9	11	4	29	Thompson	2	3	3	7
Willey	3	3	3	9	Molchany	2	0	5	4
Hogue	5	4	4	14	Luckenbill	7	7	4	21
Davis	4	0	4	8	Phillips	2	6	3	10
Bouldin	1	0	3	2	Tuffli	2	3	3	7
Wiesenha'n	2	1	2	5	Hathaway	2	0	1	4
					Markle	0	2	1	2
Total	24	19	20	67	Total	17	21	19	55

Half-time score—Cincinnati 34, Houston 33. Free throws missed—Robertson 3, Hogue 2, Davis, Boulden, Wiesenhahn, Thompson, Molchany, Luckenbill 4, Phillips 4.

February 7, 1960

CINCINNATI DOWNS WICHITA BY 97-76

Robertson Paces Bearcats With 37 Points and Breaks Career Field-Goal Mark

CINCINNATI, Feb. 27 (AP) —Oscar Robertson scored 37 points and picked up another record tonight as Cincinnati trounced Wichita, 97—76.

The Bearcats had a 10-point half-time lead, stretched it to 20 points early in the second half and coasted to victory in the Missouri Valley Conference basketball game.

Robertson's first field goal of the night—ninety seconds after the game started—broke Elgin Baylor's major-college mark of 956 field goals.

Robertson then added twelve more field goals, twenty-five rebounds and eight assists.

Ron Heller, a 6-foot 6-inch sharpshooter from Wichita, helped keep the score close in the first half and wound up with 28 points.

Cincinnati broke free from a 7-7 tie early in the first half with a 7-point spurt and stayed in front. The victory was the Bearcats' twenty-second in twenty-three games. The Shockers are now 13-11 for the season and 5-7 in the league.

CINCINNATI (97)	G.	F.	PF.	P.	WICHITA (76)	G.	F.	PF.	P.
Robertson	13	11	2	37	Tate	0	1	0	1
Willey	2	0	3	4	Heller	10	8	5	28
Hogue	9	2	3	20	Willey	4	3	4	11
Davis	6	3	0	15	Van Eman	1	0	3	2
W'senhahn	1	0	2	2	Brady	2	1	3	5
Sizer	1	0	0	2	Gales	4	3	5	11
Pomerantz	1	6	3	8	Allen	2	2	2	6
Calhoun	0	0	0	0	Durham	1	0	0	2
Bryant	0	0	0	0	Urban	0	0	1	0
					Mallot	0	0	0	0
					Cleveland	1	0	0	2
Total	37	23	16	97	Total	28	20	22	76

Half-time score—Cincinnati 43, Wichita 33. Free throws missed—Heller, Brady, Gales. Robertson 3, Hogue 2, Davis, Sizer, Pomerantz 2, Calhoun.

February 28, 1960

BRADLEY RALLY TOPS PROVIDENCE IN GARDEN INVITATION FINAL, 88-72

HERNDON EXCELS

Scores 26 Points for Bradley—Utah St. Five Wins, 99-83

By MICHAEL STRAUSS

In a tremendous comeback in the closing minutes that caught a crowd of 16,421 by surprise,

Bradley University won the twenty-third annual National Invitation Basketball Tournament yesterday.

The victim of the Braves' late surge was a determined, hard-fighting Providence College five. The Friars, who had dominated the contest for thirty minutes, fell apart before Bradley's finishing rush and bowed, 88—72.

Few who saw the final at Madison Square Garden could have predicted the finish. With ten minutes remaining, Providence led, 60—50. The Friars had played at a brisk pace and

turned in a smart effort. Bradley, on the other hand, had been guilty of repeated slovenly play.

But then the theme changed slowly. The Westerners began to hit from underneath and from outside. The Friars began to get rattled but still managed to keep the lead, helped by some fine shooting by Len Wilkens.

Bradley Takes 71-70 Lead

Finally, Bradley caught up and took a 71-70 lead when Al Saunders scored twice from the free-throw line. With 4:15 remaining, Bradley had the lead for the first time.

The New York Times (by John Orris)

THE HEIGHT OF ACTION: Dan Smith of Bradley snags rebound against Providence College in first period at Garden. Bradley won National Invitation basketball tourney.

the contest, cut Bradley's deficit to 66—65.

Saunders' two free throws forty-five seconds later put the Braves in front, and the game changed from a close duel to a rout. Billy Roecker, Saunders and Ed Wodka tore in for field goals before Wilkens stopped the spree with a jump shot.

Mike Owens hit from underneath for Bradley. Joe Mullaney, the Providence coach, asked for a time out with 1:32 remaining. Bradley used the rest period to excellent advantage. It scored 9 consecutive points, ending the game.

Although St. Bonaventure kept Utah State on close terms during most of the preliminary, the game lacked the fire seen in many of the earlier-round contests. Detracting from the performance was a tendency by some members of both squads to get a bit too fancy.

With fifteen minutes of the second half remaining, the Aggies led, 58—55, but seemed unable to gain a commanding lead. Then Jerry Schofield scored from underneath, Cornell Green connected on two free throws and Joe Worthen registered on a driven-in effort.

Despite the 6-point splurge, the Bonnies still refused to be outdistanced. They clung tenaciously, but the best they could do was narrow the gap four times to 5 points.

CHAMPIONSHIP GAME

BRADLEY (88)					PROVIDENCE (72)				
	G.	F.	PF.	P.			G.	F.	PF.	P.
Smith	6	3	2	15	Whelan	3	0	2	6
Herndon	11	4	4	26	Leonard	3	1	4	7
Walker	4	1	0	9	Hadnot	5	0	5	10
Saunders	1	9	2	11	Egan	5	10	2	20
Owens	5	3	1	13	Wilkens	10	5	5	25
Wodka	3	1	5	7	Moynahan	2	0	2	4
Tiemann	1	0	1	2	Guimares	0	0	0	0
Edwards	1	1	0	3	Folliard	0	0	0	0
Roecker	1	0	2	2	Gibson	0	0	0	0
Granby	0	0	0	0					
Kissock	0	0	0	0	Total	23	16	20	72
Sash	0	0	0	0					
Total	33	22	17	88					

Half-time score—Providence 37, Bradley 29.

Free throws missed—Herndon, Saunders 2, Owens, Tiemann 3, Leonard, Hadnot 6, Egan.

March 20, 1960

Then Bradley, the tournament's top-seeded team, proved the reason for its high estate among the nation's quintets. It scored 17 points while holding Providence to 2.

The consolation game, which preceded the final, also was highlighted by a closing drive. At the throttle of this one was alert Utah State, which turned back St. Bonaventure, 99—83.

Although beaten in the feature, Providence emerged with a small share of the spoils when Wilkens was voted the tournament's most valuable player. Fans from the New England city—more than 7,000 were on hand—whooped it up when the announcement was made.

Wilkens All-Round Star

Wilkens, as the Friars' playmaker and sparkplug, did a fine all-round job. He continually broke through to score and helped keep his team in the lead through most of the game. When it was all over, the tricky ball-handler from Brooklyn had 25 points and led his mates in scoring.

Only Mack Herndon, Bradley's 6-foot 5-inch star, surpassed Wilkens in the point-making department. He scored 26 points. Herndon, a sophomore from Chicago, was the Braves' bread-and-butter player. He kept them in the game during the earlier stages.

Herndon also provided the impetus for Bradley's second-half drive. He scored a dozen points early in the half when the Braves were finding it difficult to hit the mark.

The game's most surprising aspect was Providence's collapse in the closing stages. While it is true that Bradley played well, the Friars became completely inept. They couldn't pass, couldn't shoot and failed dismally in rebounding.

This performance provided a sharp contrast to the contest's earlier happenings. Providence, led by Wilkens and John Egan, another fine backcourt man, started with a rush and heaps of confidence. It caged nine of its first fourteen field-goal tries.

In the face of this, it was small wonder that Bradley found it difficult to keep pace.

Bradley trailed, 21—16, after 8:28 and seemed unable to cope with the Friars. At half-time, Bradley was behind, 37—29.

Although its all-court press had failed to bring results in the first half, Bradley continued these tactics after the intermission. Providence became rattled momentarily and two field goals apiece by Dan Smith and Herndon tied it at 37-all after only two and a half minutes.

But did this sudden onslaught daunt the Friars? Not in the least. With Egan—he scored 20 points—and Wilkens setting the pace, Providence soon was back in command and thriving. With eleven minutes to play, it enjoyed a 62-50 advantage.

No One Ready to Leave

One spectator in the front line of seats was heard to ask a neighbor whether he had seen enough and wanted to leave. The neighbor said no. He would leave at the five-minute mark.

But with five minutes to play, nobody was ready to leave. With Mike Owens, an artist in the dribbling department, and Herndon proving constant thorns to the Friars, Bradley had roared back into the game.

At exactly the five-minute mark, a 3-point play by Chet Walker, who has just re-entered

California Quintet Beaten By Buckeyes' Team, 75-55

By JOSEPH M. SHEEHAN
Special to The New York Times.

SAN FRANCISCO, Calif., March 19—Ohio State dethroned California as National Collegiate Athletic Association basketball champion tonight before 14,500 stunned spectators at the Cow Palace.

The capacity crowd had expected a good game but, along with most of the experts, had the Golden Bears tabbed as an almost certain winner. It was a shock to everyone when the Buckeyes not only won but also made a 75-55 runaway of the contest.

Prior to the championship game, Cincinnati overwhelmed New York University, 95—71, in the play-off for third place.

Ohio State's Big Ten champions proved altogether too big, too strong and too fast for California, which did not come close to matching the form it displayed in eliminating Cincinnati in last night's semi-finals.

The Buckeyes took command at the outset and, with a deadly hail of shots from long and short range that hit the mark on sixteen of nineteen attempts, roared to a half-time lead of 37—19.

California fought back after the intermission and Ohio State cooled a bit. But the Golden Bears' cause was irretrievable and they never drew closer than 12 points.

Ohio State, ranked third nationally in the news service polls, in which California and Cincinnati shared top honors, was the Big Ten's first N. C. A. A. winner since Indiana, the Western Conference's only other national court champion, scored the second of its two victories in 1953.

It was not unexpected that the Buckeyes should perform brilliantly on attack. Their 91.6-point scoring average was the nation's highest. The shocker was that they outdid the Golden Bears, the nation's stingiest point-givers, on defense.

For long stretches, California was smothered and on few occasions did the defending champions get rolling in their precision patterns.

Lucas Outplays Imhoff

A big part of the story was the tremendous edge as an all-round performer Jerry Lucas, Ohio State's 6-foot 8-inch sophomore center, had over Darrall Imhoff, California's all-America pivotman, who was listed as being 2 inches taller.

Not a showy type, but tremendously effective in his quiet way, Lucas just about took Imhoff out of the game. The big Californian, who had tallied 25 points and dominated the play under both boards

against Cincinnati in the semifinal last night, was held to 8 points and grabbed only five rebounds. Lucas' equivalent figures were 16 points and ten rebounds.

But Ohio State was far from a one-man team. All five Buckeye starters scored in double figures, Mel Nowell being second high man with 15. Dick Doughty led California with 11.

It was a tremendous triumph for Coach Fred Taylor's young Buckeye quintet, which included three sophomores and a junior. The triumph snapped a nineteen-game California winning streak.

Ohio State had a fantastic shooting average of 67.4 per cent, caging thirty-one of forty-one attempts from the floor. California made only twenty of fifty-nine shots for 33.9 per cent.

Violets Wilt in Pace

N. Y. U. kept on even terms with Cincinnati for ten minutes, trailing at the end of that time by only 20—19. Then the Violets wilted trying to keep pace with the bigger, faster Ohioans.

By half-time, Cincinnati was in front by 39—25 and N. Y. U. was not able to draw closer than 15 points of the lead after the intermission.

Tom (Satch) Sanders, N. Y. U.'s 6-foot 6-inch center, again won plaudits from the crowd for his fancy ball-handling, stalwart rebounding and brilliant shooting. He led the Violet scorers with 27 points.

But the chief luminary of the contest was Oscar Robertson. Cincinnati's three-time national scoring champion, limited to the modest total of 18 points against California last night, cut loose with 32 points tonight.

He had able assistance from Paul Hogue, Carl Boulden, Larry Willey and Carl Wiesenbahn, who also scored in double figures.

Cincinnati, which had been ranked first nationally in The Associated Press poll entering this tournament, closed its campaign with a 28-2 won-lost record. N. Y. U., ranked twelfth in the national standings, finished with a mark of 22—5.

Cincinnati's Robertson, three times a unanimous all-American choice, cemented his hold on three N. C. A. A. scoring records in closing his varsity career.

Big O, as Oscar is popularly known, tallied 2,973 points in eighty-eight games for Cincinnati, as against the former mark of 2,587 by Dicky Hemric of Wake Forest. Robertson's average of 33.8 points bettered the record of 32.5 set by Frank Selvy of Furman. Finally, Oscar finished with 1,052 field goals, as against Hemric's 956.

March 20, 1960

CHAMPIONSHIP GAME

OHIO STATE (75)	G.	F.	PF.	P.	CALIFORNIA (55)	G.	F.	PF.	P.
Havlicek	4	4	2	12	Gillis	4	0	1	8
Roberts	5	0	1	10	McClint'k	4	2	3	10
Lucas	7	2	2	16	Imhoff	3	2	2	8
Nowell	6	3	2	15	Wendell	0	4	2	4
Siegfried	5	3	2	13	Shultz	2	2	4	6
Furry	2	0	1	4	Mann	3	1	0	7
Nourse	2	0	1	4	Stafford	0	1	1	1
Gearhart	0	0	0	0	Doughty	4	3	1	11
Knight	0	0	1	0	Pearson	0	0	0	0
Hoyt	0	0	0	0	Morrison	0	0	1	0
Cedargren	0	1	1	1	Alexander	0	0	0	0
Barker	0	0	0	0	Averbuck	0	0	0	0
Total	31	13	13	75	Total	20	15	15	55

Half-time score—Ohio State 37, California 19.
Free throws missed—Havlicek, Roberts, Siegfried 3, Cedargren, McClintock, Stafford, Averbuck.

CONSOLATION GAME

CINCINNATI (95)	G.	F.	PF.	P.	N. Y. U. (71)	G.	F.	PF.	P.
Robertson	12	8	4	32	Barden	3	1	4	7
Willey	5	0	4	10	Filardi	1	1	0	3
Hogue	7	1	2	15	Sanders	11	5	4	27
Davis	3	3	0	9	Paprocky	6	3	3	15
Bouldin	7	0	2	14	Cun'gham	4	2	2	10
Sizer	0	1	2	1	Murphy	0	0	0	0
W'senhahn	4	2	1	10	Loche	1	2	0	4
Bryant	1	0	0	2	Reiss	2	1	3	5
Pomerantz	1	0	0	2					
Dierking	0	0	0	0	Total	28	15	16	71
Reis	0	0	0	0					
Total	40	15	15	95					

Half-time score—Cincinnati 39, N. Y. U. 25.
Free throws missed—Robertson 3, Hogue 4, Bouldin, Sizer, Barden, Sanders, Paprocky, Cunningham, Reiss.

MATH HITS GOAL ON BASKETBALLS

By GENE SMITH

Chances are that none of the famous Harlem Globetrotters, or any other basketball player for that matter, has ever heard of the Icosahedron mathematical principle. But they are experts at handling its product.

The Voit Rubber Corporation, a subsidiary of the American Machine and Foundry Company, has adopted the 2,500-year-old principle in order to build better basketballs.

Basically, an icosahedron is a symmetrical polyhedron of twenty faces and twelve equidistant points. As used in making basketballs it is the absolute maximum number of equidistant points that can be placed on a sphere. Voit adapted this idea to winding nylon over the bladder of the basketball, thus building a carcass in that form. The company reports that this provides the strongest, best balanced winding pattern that can be devised.

Years of Research

Years of research went into this process. Voit engineers called on several theoretical mathematicians from the California Institute of Technology to work it out. They also enlisted the aid of electronic calculators to prove the formulae.

The need for better basketballs evolved over the years. The first basketballs were made like baseballs or soccer balls: pieces of leather were sewed together and an inflatable rubber bladder was then inserted. This was the common ball until

about a generation ago when Voit perfected a molded rubber ball that provided longer life and much better wearing qualities than leather types.

It was found, however, that the molded ball needed better reinforcement in order to retain its shape for continual play. A method of cord-winding was the next step, but this also proved impractical since random coverage of threads sometimes loosened and slipped, creating uneven wear, lumps and soft spots.

Next came a fabric lining over the bladder and under the cover of the ball, but since the carcass had to be made by hand, there was still the element of human error to create problems.

Adapted for Machines

Eventually someone remembered the Icosahedron theory. Company technicians agreed that if uniform winding in a predetermined pattern could be perfected, the perfect basketball would result. The next problem was to adapt the theory to the development of complicated machines that could be fully automated and capable of exact performance.

The search led to guided missiles and a tool used by the experts in that field—the digital computer. They worked out an electronic guidance system to monitor the actual carcass winding machines and control each and every operation during the fabrication process.

In operation, the core is a butyl rubber bladder. Yard after yard of nylon is then spun onto this carcass until about two miles of filament completes the predetermined pattern. The starting point is a given set of poles. The machine winds the nylon strands on great circles equally spaced around the ball.

The electronically controlled machines make predetermined shifts to a new set of poles and the process is repeated. This continues through six shifts, winding from the twelve points (six sets of poles), which are the points of an icosahedron.

After dozens of repetitions of the basic pattern, each starting from a different set of poles, the bladder is completely and uniformly, covered. This takes some twenty minutes on the automated machines.

The nylon strands are then sealed with a substance that locks them in place and the carcass is cured in a smooth mold that fuses the nylon into a unitized carcass, said to be uniformly strong over every square inch. A thermoplastic cover is then molded over the carcass with machines that are also electronically controlled.

So successful has been this method of production that Voit has adopted it for all round inflated balls used in athletics. Company technicians are also trying to figure out an adaptation that would permit similar construction of footballs.

Basketball officials reportedly are pleased with the exactness of the icosahedron ball. Its control is so exact that there is less than one-quarter of an ounce variance in weight.

April 17, 1960

United States' Unbeaten Basketball Squad Routs Brazil in Olympic Final

AMERICANS CRUSH BRAZILIANS, 90-63

Capture Olympic Basketball Title—Lucas Paces U.S. Team With 23 Points

By ROBERT DALEY
Special to The New York Times.

ROME, Sept. 10—The United States crushed Brazil tonight in the final game of the Olympic basketball tournament, winning by 90 to 63, and making one final joke of the competition.

The United States has won every Olympic basketball tournament since the sport was installed in 1936. This time the Soviet Union finished second, having been beaten only by the Americans. Brazil was third and Italy fourth.

The United States' twelve-man all-star squad included three Amateur Athletic Union players and nine collegians. It led from the opening seconds after Jerry Lucas had slapped in a rebound.

Lucas played only about twenty-five minutes in all, but scored 23 points. He was the star of a show that had only one unpleasant note for the United States, a technical foul charged against Oscar Robertson of Cincinnati for slamming the ball down on the court. Robertson wanted to show his displeasure with an official decision. The United States was leading, 64 to 35, at the time.

The score at half-time was 50 to 24.

In addition to Lucas, the top American scorers were Robertson with 12 points, and Adrian Smith of Kentucky and Terry Dischinger Purdue, each with 11.

Every American played, and all but Walt Bellamy of Indiana scored.

Brazil's best man was 6-foot-1-inch Walmir Marques, who tallied 19 points.

Lucas Paces Attack

The Americans blew the game open in the first few minutes as Ohio State's 6-foot-8-inch Lucas sank 12 straight points on tips. He got another tip later, shot only twice all told and scored 18 points in the first half.

At the ten-minute mark, America led by 33 to 11, and one of the oddest incidents of this or any other tournament took place.

Leaping for a rebound under the Brazil basket, the 6-foot-11-inch Bellamy collided with Edson Bispo of Brazil. Bispo went down clutching his midsection, and Referee E. Alvarez Frausto began leaping about the court making digging motions with his elbow.

He charged Bellamy with deliberately injuring Bispo, and threw Bellamy out of the game. No foul was charged, however. The official simply lined the teams up for a jump ball.

Bellamy had attempted to plead his case, and there seemed to be tears in his eyes. But he was unable to change the verdict of Frausto, a Mexican. Bellamy finally left the court.

Many Tall Teams

The American triumph should not have been so easy in these Olympics, because eighty-six other countries play basketball now, nearly all have teams as tall, and some play the game very well indeed.

The United States owes its victory to the class of its players and to the coaching of California's Pete Newell. Newell built his reputation on ball control and a deliberate style. But faced with too little time to prepare his all-star team for the games, he changed his style. The Americans played fast-break, free-lance basketball throughout, scored more than 100 points in every game but two, and were "pressed" only by the Soviet Union (81—57).

Italy Suffers Setback

In the first game of the evening, the Soviet Union defeated Italy, 78 to 70, thereby consigning Italy to last place in the four-team final round. It was not known until the Americanot known until the Americathe Soviet team ranked.

This was the game the enormous crowd had come to see. The crowd wanted to wave Italian flags and chant "Italia, Italia" at the top of its lungs. In its way, it was as ugly a crowd as the one at Monday's boxing finals, which drowned out the Star Spangled Banner, punched at the American Flag and whistled so long and loud against an American boxer, Ed Crook, that the victory ceremony could not take place.

This crowd threw various objects down on the court every time an official called a foul against Italy. It hooted and whistled at every Soviet player who stepped to the foul line, attempting to distract the player.

This crowd roared "Italia, Italia" every time the home team climbed within 5 points of the Soviet quintet. But as soon as the visitors would get 7 or 8 points ahead, the crowd would lapse into silence.

Once a Soviet player and an Italian wrestled for possession of the ball. As they went to the floor, objects rained down on the referee (who had called only a jump ball) and on the Russian. The derisive whistling lasted ten minutes. Hundreds of fans stood to shake their fists at the officials and the visiting team.

Player Throws a Punch

The Italian who had wrestled for the ball took a punch at his opponent.

The Italian bench leaped up ready for a fight. The Soviet players all withdrew into a group, neither provoking trouble nor running from it. The incident blew over.

In fact, Soviet athletes usually don't argue decisions or complain.

The evening's basketball was preceded by a colossal traffic jam that probably hasn't been unraveled yet. It may have seemed a fine thing to the or-ganizers to send the marathon run down the Via Cristoforo Columbo and onto the old Appian Way. But somebody forgot to reopen the road afterwards.

The marathon ended at 8 P. M., the basketball began at 9, and the only main road out to the Sports Palace was closed. The back streets, by which motorists hoped to bypass the road-blocks, were clogged by cars four abreast, and more cars driving down the sidewalks.

The ten-mile drive from the center of the city took 1 hour 15 minutes for those who left early. Late starters may not have got here at all.

United States (90)					BRAZIL (63)				
	G.	F.	PF.	P.		G.	F.	PF.	P.
West	2	2	3	6	Pasos	6	5	1	17
Dischinger	4	3	2	11	Marques	7	4	1	18
Lane	3	3	2	9	Bispo	1	0	5	2
Lucas	11	1	2	23	Salvador	5	3	3	13
Robertson	4	4	4	12	Blatk'sks	0	0	5	0
Bellamy	0	0	1	0	De Azevedo	1	0	4	2
Boozer	1	4	4	6	Blas	0	0	3	0
Haldosen	0	1	1	1	Dominzos	3	2	2	8
Imhoff	2	0	2	4	De Souza	0	1	5	1
Keller	2	0	5	4	Schali	0	0	5	0
Smith	3	5	2	11	Geraldo	1	0	1	2
Arnette	0	1	2	1					
Total	33	24	30	90	Total	21	15	35	63

Half-time score—United States 50, Brazil 24.

Free throws missed—Dischinger 2, Lane, Robertson 5, Boozer, Smith, Arnette, Pasos 5, Bispo, Salvador 3, Domingos, Schall, Marques.

September 11, 1960

Jerry Lucas helped lead Ohio State to the pinnacle of college basketball in 1960. The rest of the Buckeye's starting lineup wasn't bad either—it included John Havlicek and Harry Siegfried, two star players.

2 Seized in College Basketball Bribery; Nation-Wide Fixing of Games Indicated

Players May Be Witnesses in Basketball Scandal

Associated Press

Art Hicks of Seton Hall is from Chicago   Henry Gunter, team-mate from the Bronx

By JACK ROTH

A new college basketball scandal was disclosed here yesterday. District Attorney Frank S. Hogan's office said that it might spread from coast to coast and dwarf the 1951 scandal.

Two gamblers were arrested on charges of bribing players of the University of Connecticut and Seton Hall University to hold down the scores of their own teams.

Three New York college teams were reported involved in the scandal, and the number of colleges implicated across the country may be as high as fifteen or twenty.

One of the defendants arrested yesterday, Aaron Wagman, was accused of paying $1,500 to a Connecticut player to keep his team's score down in a game against Colgate University on March 1. He is also accused of attempting to bribe a detective in Mr. Hogan's office to keep him informed on the investigation.

Wagman had been free on bail pending an appeal from a conviction for bribing a University of Florida football player to control the score of a football game.

The other defendant, Joseph Hacken, was charged with bribing two Seton Hall basketball players with $1,000 each to shave points and thereby keep down the score of their team in a game against Dayton University in Madison Square Garden on Feb. 9. He has a record of gambling arrests, most of them in the Bronx.

Gamblers and bookmakers bet according to advance reports showing one team a favorite by a certain number of points over another. If a bettor bets on the favorite team, the team must win by at least the number of points indicated for him to collect. If he bets on the underdog he can collect if his team's score plus the indicated points total more than the other team's actual score.

In the past, the usual attempt at a "fix" was to have the favored team win by a margin smaller than expected. However, in the new case the pattern appeared to be to have the underdog team lose by a greater margin than expected.

March 18, 1961

CINCINNATI FIVE TOPS OHIO STATE FOR N.C.A.A. TITLE

SCORE IS 70 TO 65

Ohio State's 32-Game Victory Streak Ends in Overtime Contest

By HOWARD M. TUCKNER

Special to The New York Times.

KANSAS CITY, March 25— At exactly 11:39 o'clock tonight, the basketball empire of Ohio State crumbled on the hardwood of the Municipal Auditorium. Another king, Cincinnati, emerged.

In as thrilling a game as any one would want to see, the Bearcats of Coach Ed Jucker upset the Buckeyes, 70—65, in the final of the National Collegiate championship.

But the old rulers, the defending champions in this competition and winners of their last thirty-two games, did not succumb without a fierce struggle. It took an overtime period to nail them down.

When the buzzer sounded, a second after Tom Thacker of Cincinnati had flipped in a one-hander from the corner, hundreds of Bearcat supporters in the overflow crowd of 10,700 dashed onto the court. They pummeled their heroes, who, by then, had bruised faces and bodies from the contact under the baskets.

St. Joseph's Wins

The game was the second cliff-hanger of the evenings. Earlier, St. Joseph's had to play four overtime periods before beating Utah, 127—120, for third place in the tourney. John Egan of St. Joseph's scored 42 points in that game.

The final marked the first time in the twenty-three-year history of this competition that two teams from the same state had fought for the title. Ohio State and Cincinnati, whose campuses are only 100 miles apart, had not faced each other on a basketball court since 1922. The victory was the twenty-second in a row for Cincinnati, which now owns the longest winning streak in major-college basketball.

Few thought the final would be as exciting as it was. The tension, at a high pitch from the start, mounted with 1 minute

41 seconds letf in regulation time.

Cincinnati, displaying a tight defense and paced by Bob Wiesenhahn, Thacker and Carl Boulding, led 61—59. Then Bob Knight drove in for a lay-up and the score was tied.

Bearcats Gain Possession

With fifty-six seconds left, the Bearcats gained possession and kept it until five seconds remained. Then Thacker, the dead-eye, shot from in close. He was short. Jerry Lucas, 6 feet 9 inches of basketball perfection, grabbed the rebound for Ohio State. He did not take a step.

Ohio State called time out. It put the ball in play and tossed it from one end of the court to the other. That took one seind. Another time out was caled. State wanted the last shot. On the sideline, Coach Fred Taylor called the play.

When play resumed, John Havlicek, the big f orward, tossed a high pass toward the bucket. Lucas, in what is called an Alley-Oop Special, was ready to leap and tap it in. But the ball was deflected and the game went into overtime.

Throughout the game Ohio State had been outrebounded by Paul Hogue, 6 feet 9 inches of strength and speed, and his team-mates—Weisenhahn and Thacker especially. Cincinnati, with its tenacious defense, had stopped State's famed fast break.

The Buckeyes were scoring, all right, but not off their usual patterns. Two points came hard—on twisting drives and long one-handers—for Ohio State tonight.

Now time was in again. Ohio State's two years of brilliant play rested on the outcome of the next five minutes.

And at that point, Ohio State fell apart.

Hogue Surprises Experts

On the opening scrimmage, Hogue was fouled by Lucas. It was Jerry's fourth foul of the night. One more and out. It was supposed to be the other way around. Knowing basketball coaches had said, Lucas would drive Hogue to distraction and foul him out in the first half.

Then Hogue came up with another surprise. Throughout the tourney he had found it difficult to make his free throws. Tonight, for example, he made only three of six. He picked this moment to make two of them.

So, it was 63—61. Then, after Havlicek had converted a free throw, Weisenhahn shoved the cadeful Lucas out of the way and tapped the ball in. The score 65—62. Bedlam replaced uproar at Municipal Auditorium.

But Lucas, a brilliant competitor, kept Ohio state alive on a short jumper. They were Jerry's 26th and 27th points of the night. And his last.

There was 1 minutes 6 seconds left when Tony Yates hit on a free throw for Cincinnati.

With the score 66—61, there was plenty of time left for Ohio State, the poised bunch from Columbus. The Buckeyes had beaten Louisville earlier in the tourney after being 3 points behind at the same stage.

But fate was not wearing a red-and-gray uniform tonight. The Ohio State players proved they were human, after all. Larry Siegfried, a superb player all season long, missed one of two free throws. Two for two would have tied it.

28 Seconds Left

There were twenty-eight seconds left. The Bearcats went into a freeze, never allowing the ball to touch the floor. The Ohio State players, the anguish of certain defeat on their wet faces, fouled Yates. He made both shots.

It was 68—65 and fifteen seconds left. There was still a chance for Ohio State.

They worked the ball into the forecourt. Their only hope was to feed Lucas, hoping that he could lure his opponent into a 3-point play. Lucas, who rarely loses his composure on or off the court, panicked. He shot wildly. The ball hit nothing but the end line.

Cincinnati danced down the court. The auditorium was chaotic. Fred Taylor wiped his glasses. Jerry Lucas bit his lower lip. Then Thackery rubbed it in with a final basket at the buzzer.

There were no special heroes for Cincnnati.

Wiesenhahn scored 17 points. Thacker got 15, Yates 13, Boulding 16 and Hogue 9.

No more than 5 points separated the teams during the game. One point—in favor of Ohio State—separated them at the half, 39—38. The Ohio State kingdom was not captured by a bunch of lucky stiffs.

As Juncker said in the dressing room after the game:

"We did nothing special. All we did was a job. Each person did a job."

Each did, indeed.

Utah, trailing by 13 points early in the game and by 48—41 at the half, made a great comeback to catch St. Joseph's in the last twenty minutes. With sixteen seconds left in regulation time, Joe Morton of Utah tied the score at 89—all by converting one of two free throws.

At the start of the first overtime, the tap was batted into the hands of Bill Hoy. St. Joseph's superb sophomore guard. Hoy, to the amazement of his team-mates, streaked the wrong way and dropped the ball into the Utah basket.

Hoy made amends for his unfortunate lapse later, however. He was a key player for the Hawks in the second and third overtime periods.

CHAMPIONSHIP GAME

CINCINNATI (70)				OHIO STATE (65)			
	G.	F.	PF.	P.		G.	F.	PF.	P.
Wies'nhhn	8	1	3	17	Havlicek	1	2	2	4
Thacker	7	1	0	15	Hoyt	3	1	3	7
Hogue	3	3	3	9	Lucas	10	7	4	27
Yates	4	5	3	13	Nowell	3	3	1	9
Bouldin	7	2	4	16	Siegfried	6	2	2	14
Fizer	0	0	0	0	Knight	1	0	1	2
Heidtotting	0	0	0	0	Gearhart	1	0	1	2

Total .. 29 12 13 70   Total .. 25 15 14 65
Half-time score—Ohio State 39. Cincinnati 38.
Free throws missed—Thacker 3. Hogue 3. Bouldin. Siegfried.
Attendance—10.700.

March 26, 1961

8 MORE PLAYERS NAMED IN FIXING

5 Colleges Are Also Added to Basketball Inquiry

By JACK ROTH

The college basketball scandal spread yesterday to five more colleges and universities. District Attorney Frank S. Hogan reported that eight more players had taken or had agreed to take bribes in the last two seasons to keep scores down.

The colleges mentioned for the first time yesterday were St. Joseph's College and LaSalle College in Philadelphia, the University of Tennessee, Mississippi State University and the University of North Carolina.

Three of the players were from St. Joseph's; two from the University of Tennessee; one from LaSalle; one from Mississippi State; and two from the University of Connecticut.

A Connecticut piayer had been mentioned as involved in the case last March 17, when disclosures first were made, but he was not identified at that time. Two Seton Hall University players had been previously identified.

Eight of the players named yesterday have been dismissed from their schools. The ninth has been suspended pending further investigation of his case by a disciplinary committee.

Mr. Hogan said a basketball player at the University of North Carolina, two former players at Alabama and a football player at Connecticut had served as "go-betweens" for a gambler, who was indicted yesterday for the second time.

He is Aaron Wagman, 27 years old, of 2260 University Avenue, the Bronx. He was arrested last month along with another gambler, Joseph Hacken, 41, of 142 West Eighty-third Street. Wagman had already been indicted for attempting to bribe a detective.

The prosecutor said the players had taken bribes that ranged from $750 to $1.500 in their "corrupt arrangements" and that the "usual going rate" was $1,000.

"The players were required to shave points so that if their team was favored it would either lose or win by a lesser margin than was anticipated," Mr. Hogan said.

He said that in some cases bribe offers were rejected because the players were facing

traditional rivals, or their teams were playing in sectional tournaments.

In other cases, he went on, the players did "their dishonest best" to please the gamblers but failed to meet the requirements established and had to turn back their bribes.

He pointed out that all of the players had received immunity from prosecution from the grand jury and were witnesses for the state. The go-betweens were named as co-conspirators in the indictment and no action has been taken yet against them.

12 'Completed Contracts'

The true bill contains thirty-seven counts. This, it was explained, referred to thirty-seven separate negotiations to fix games. Twelve contests, it was said, ended in "completed contracts" with the scores satisfactory to Wagman and his associates.

Mr. Hogan said he was "gratified" that one player, Lowery Kirk of Hornsby, Tenn., a senior at Memphis State University, had rejected a $1,000 bribe offer and had reported the bribe attempt to the college authorities.

"His name should be honored," Mr. Hogan said. "He acted as all the others should have after the illumination of this business during the last college basketball scandal of ten years ago."

He identified the players who had taken or had agreed to take bribes as these:

St. Joseph's College — John Egan, the team captain; Frank Majewski and Vincent Kempton. University of Connecticut — Peter Kelly, the team captain, and Glenn Cross. University of Tennessee—Richard Fisher and Edward Test. LaSalle—Edward Bowler. Mississippi State—Jerry Graves, the team captain.

The Very Rev. J. Joseph Bluett, president of St. Joseph's, announced that the three athletes involved there had been expelled. Andrew D. Holt, president of the University of Tennessee, said neither Fisher nor Test would be allowed to re-enter school without special permission, that they had been dropped from the student rolls. At LaSalle, Bowler was suspended "pending further investigation of his case." The president of the University of Connecticut, Albert N. Jorgensen, announced that Kelly and Cross and a football player named as a co-conspirator had been dismissed from school. Mississippi State's president, D. W. Colvard, said Graves was no longer in the school.

Those named as co-conspirators were Jerry Vogel, 24, of 1920 Osborne Place, the Bronx; Daniel Quindazzi, 24, of 85 Hart Avenue, Yonkers; William Minnerly, 24, of 39 Manitou Trail, White Plains; Lou Brown, 22, of 63½ Lafayette Street, Jersey City, and Joseph Green, 31, whose whereabouts are unknown but who formerly lived.

Local Players Involved in New Basketball Scandal

at 2307 Tiebout Avenue, the Bronx.

The Contact Man

Mr. Hogan said that Vogel, a graduate of the University of Alabama, had played basketball there between 1956 and 1959 and now was studying law at the Brooklyn Law School. Vogel, he said, "made contacts at the University of Connecticut which led to contacts at other schools."

The prosecutor said Quindazzi, a salesman, was also a graduate of the University of Alabama and had played basketball there between 1957 and 1960. He was said to have joined Vogel in lining up Connecticut players.

Minnerly, Mr. Hogan said, was a senior at Connecticut and captain of that team's football team last season. It was he, Mr. Hogan said, who "reached" the players on the basketball team.

Brown was described as a student at the University of North Carolina who played basketball there. He was said to have met his "greatest success at lining up players at St. Joseph's and LaSalle." Green's part was not detailed.

The bribing conspiracy charges are all felonies punishable on conviction by up to ten years in prison and $10,000 fines.

Another name mentioned by Mr. Hogan was that of Douglas Moe of Brooklyn, an all-American basketball player at the University of North Carolina. He said that Wagman had given Moe $75 as a "softening up gift" last year and that Moe had never reported this. The meeting between Wagman and Moe, he said, was arranged by Brown.

April 28, 1961

5 MORE COLLEGES, 6 PLAYERS NAMED IN BASKETBALL FIX

Brooklyn, St. John's, N.Y.U. Men Are Implicated in Scandal Investigation

By JACK ROTH

The basketball scandal spread yesterday to five more universities and colleges, including three in New York City.

The three here were St. John's University, New York University and Brooklyn College. Rumors had circulated since the scandal broke on March 17 that players or former players on local teams were involved.

Michael Parenti
St. John's

William J. Chrystal
St. John's

Henry Gunter
Seton Hall

Raymond Paprocky
N. Y. U.

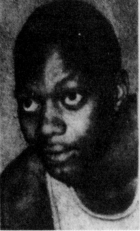

Arthur Hicks
Seton Hall

David Budin
Brooklyn College graduate

In all, seventeen players from eleven colleges and universities have now been accused of having taken bribes.

In announcing the return of an eighteen-count indictment against Joseph Hacken, a 41-year-old gambler of 142 West Eighty-third Street, District Attorney Frank S. Hogan said a graduate and former captain of the Brooklyn team was involved, as were a junior on the N. Y. U. squad and two former St. John's players who since have graduated.

'Hacken's Partner'

He identified the Brooklyn College man as David Budin, 28, of 2363 East Sixty-fourth Street, Brooklyn, who was named a co-conspirator in the true bill.

Budin, the District Attorney said, played with the Brooklyn team from 1956 to 1959 and

was captain of the team in the 1958-59 season. He was said to have served primarily as a recruiter of college players to be bribed and was identified as "Hacken's partner."

He taught physical education at a junior high school in Brooklyn until last fall, when he was arrested on a charge of attempting to fix a football game between Michigan and Oregon, Mr. Hogan said.

2 Given $4,450 Each

The two former St. John's players are Michael Parenti, 25, of 1684 Eighty-second Street, Brooklyn, and William J. Chrystal, 26, of 3420 Clarendon Road, Brooklyn.

The prosecutor said they had played for St. John's for three years, ending in the 1957 season. He said they had received a total of $4,450 each from Hacken for keeping their team's scores down in five games.

Mr. Hogan named Ray Paprocky, 23, of 19-23 Harman Street, Ridgewood, Queens, a junior at N. Y. U. who played guard on the team, as having been bribed to shave points in four games.

Two Seton Hall players, mentioned when the scandal first broke and suspended from the school, were said by Mr. Hogan to have received bribes for shaving points in six games. They are Henry Gunter, 22, of 1231 Fulton Avenue, the Bronx, and Arthur Hicks, also 22, of Chicago.

Thus far in the District Attorney's investigation, it has been found that current or former players from four institutions had served as go-betweens for the gamblers. The institutions are the University of North Carolina, Alabama University, the University of Connecticut and Brooklyn.

The indictment against Hackman disclosed that a number of players had rejected bribes but had failed to report that

65

they were approached. Among these were Tony Jackson of St. John's and Fred Crawford of St. Bonaventure.

Other players who did not accept bribes but failed to report them were Maurice Gilmore of Colorado University; Sylvester Blye, who played briefly at Seattle University; Salvatore Vergopia, formerly of Niagara University; and James Robinson, of Bradley University.

The Softening-Up

Assistant District Attorneys Alfred J. Scotti and Peter D. Andreoli said part of the conspiracy involved giving the players spending money, providing them with dates and telling them they would not be letting their school down if all they did was to shave points.

Mr. Hogan said Hacken had a "farm system" in which he had paid a total of $460 to players on two freshman teams, expecting that they might be ready for varsity play in coming seasons. In addition, he used them as "intermediaries," Mr. Hogan said.

The two mentioned were Roger Brown, 18, of 1353 Prospect Place, Brooklyn, a student at the University of Dayton, and Cornelius Hawkins, 19, of 86 Lexington Avenue, Brooklyn, a student at the University of Iowa. Hacken, the prosecutor said, paid Brown $250 for his "good offices," and Hawkins $210.

Mr. Hogan said another player, Alfred Saunders, 24, a senior at Bradley University, had accepted $200 in "spending money" from Hacken.

The usual bribes, Mr. Hogan explained, ran between $500 and $1,000, and in one contest in which the two former St. John's players managed to have their team lose, bonuses of $200 each were paid.

In some cases, Mr. Hogan observed, bribed players failed to keep their teams' scores low enough, although they tried, and in these instances Hacken either withheld payments or permitted the players to keep only a share of what they had already received. In other cases, the prosecutor said, Hacken failed to make payments.

The games in which Gunter and Hicks were involved while playing for Seton Hall were against Holy Cross, Niagara, Cincinnati, two with Dayton and Duke. Paprocky was paid to keep N. Y. U.'s score down in games against Utah State, West Virginia, Wake Forest and St. John's.

Cites Coach's Warning

"I knew what I was doing was wrong," Paprocky said last night, "and I know it even more now."

He said his coach, Lou Rossini, had warned the team many times about associating with gamblers.

"I was in debt and my wife was expecting a baby," he said. "If I had been single or if my wife hadn't been expecting, nobody could have bought me."

The management student completed his final examinations this month, but did not know

whether he would be able to return to school in the fall.

Paprocky, who is working in a grocery, said he had cooperated fully with the District Attorney. "Even so, the future looks jet black," he said.

Parenti and Chrystal received bribes in games going back to 1956 against the University of Utah, Bradley, George Washington, St. Joseph's and N. Y. U., Mr. Hogan said.

The players who testified before the grand jury were all granted immunity from prosecution. Hacken was arraigned in General Sessions Court and was continued free in $25,000 bail. The case was adjourned to next Thursday.

Another defendant being held on bribery charges is Aaron Wagman, 27, of 2260 University Avenue, the Bronx. He is being held in $60,000 bail. The investi-

gation by Mr. Hogan's office is continuing.

Bribing a player is punishable, on conviction, by up to ten years in prison and a $10,000 fine.

May 25, 1961

Seton Hall Quitting Big-Time Basketball

By The Associated Press.
SOUTH ORANGE, N. J., Sept. 9—Seton Hall University announced today it was through with tournament basketball competition.

The new policy, instituted six months after two Seton Hall players were accused in a point-fixing scandal, was outlined by Monsignor John J. Dougherty, the president of the university.

Monsignor Dougherty said the school would honor all existing contractual obligations and then abide by these points:

¶"The University will restrict its competition in basketball to schools in the New England and Middle Atlantic States areas.

¶"The University will not participate in any basketball tournaments, either during or after the regular season.

¶"All home basketball games will be played in the University gymnasium and not in any public arena."

September 10, 1961

DAYTON FIVE TOPS ST. JOHN'S, 73-67

FLYERS END JINX

Dayton at Last Wins N.I.T. Prize, Paced by Chmielewski

By GORDON S. WHITE Jr.
A long string of frustrations for the Dayton basketball team ended yesterday when the Flyers from Ohio gained a 73-67 triumph over St. John's in the final of the twenty-fifth annual National Invitation Tournament at Madison Square Garden.

Nine times Coach Tom Blackburn had brought a Dayton team to the N. I. T. and gone away a loser. This unhappy record included five runner-up finishes. But the Flyers weren't having any of that second-or-worse business this time.

Dayton erased a St. John's lead early in the game and moved on to the screaming delight of its many followers among the 16,037 spectators. At the final buzzer, there was no holding the Flyer fans. They made a charge for their heroes after the biggest victory in Dayton basketball history.

The Gang's All There

This dramatic conclusion to the tournament came after Loyola of Chicago had earned

third place by beating Duquesne, 95—84, in the consolation game.

In the rejoicing by Dayton supporters following the championship game, four or five persons were knocked down by rooters eager to touch or get near the men of Blackburn.

Two women and a man were bowled over. The man's glasses were crushed. No one was hurt, however, and finally order was restored.

But there was another wild surge when it was announced that big Bill Chmielewski of Dayton had been named as the most valuable player in the tournament. Again, no one appeared hurt, though the 6-foot-10-inch sophomore was bounced around and

slapped hard enough to knock the wind out of him.

Chmielewski earned the trophy with a concluding performance that gave him a big edge over Leroy Ellis, the St. John's star who also stands 6 feet 10 inches.

Though only in his first varsity year, Chmielewski outdid his senior rival, particularly in the first half when Dayton rallied from an 18-11 deficit. The Flyers led at intermission, 35-29, with Chmielewski contributing 15 points. He finished with 24 for the game.

In the battle under the boards, Chmielewski kept Ellis so busy that the Redman ace couldn't connect regularly on his fine hook shot. Ellis did manage a game total of 22 points, but the St.

After Dayton's victory over St. John's, Dayton supporters rush to the floor and become Chmielewski supporters.

John's leader was Kevin Loughery with 26.

It was when Harold Schoen tapped in a rebound that Dayton took the lead for the first time, at 27-25. Never again did St. John's even tie, let alone pass, the high-flying Flyers.

But the contest was fast and exciting enough to keep the fans yelling their loudest of the season. Dayton wasn't safely in until about two and a half minutes from the end. By this time the Dayton fans were yelling. "We want the N. I. T. We want the N. I. T." They got it.

In the closing stages, St. John's went more than three minutes without a point while Dayton built a 5-point lead into one of ten points.

To reach the final, Dayton had whipped Wichita, Houston and Loyola. St. John's had turned back Holy Cross and Duquesne.

The Flyers weren't seeded in the starting field of twelve teams, whereas St. John's, this year's leading metropolitan quintet, was. Thus the Redmen gained a first-round bye and played only three games to Dayton's four.

St. John's knows what it is to be an N. I. T. winner. Three St. John's teams under Coach Joe Lapchick have won the annual Garden tourney. Now Blackburn joins Lapchick in the sweet realm of N. I. T. success.

The Dayton triumph assured Ohio of having the two major post-season college basketball titles this season. For Cincinnati and Ohio State were the finalists in the National Collegiate tournament at Louisville

last night.

The flyers and the Redmen had entered the final with winning streaks of ten games. The outcome left Dayton with a season won-lost mark of 23—6. St. John's finished with 21—5.

Chmielewski totaled 107 points in his four games for tournament honors in that department.

FIRST PLACE

DAYTON (73)				ST. JOHN'S (67)			
	G	F	PF	P		G	F	PF	P
Reginold	3	2	3	8	Hall	2	0	1	4
Schoen	5	2	5	12	Loughery, rf	10	6	3	26
Gienzer	0	0	1	0	Ellis, c	5	12	3	22
Chmielew.	11	2	4	24	Kovac, lg	2	1	3	5
G. Hatton	3	0	3	6	Burns, rg	3	2	4	8
T. Hatton	4	3	3	11	O'Hara	0	0	1	0
					O'Sullivan	1	0	3	2
Total	29	15	19	73	Total	23	21	18	67

Half-time score—Dayton 35, St. John's 29
Free throws missed—Hall, Ellis, Kovac, Burns 2, G. Hatton 4, T. Hatton.
Officials—Lou Eisenstein and Steve Honzo.

March 25, 1962

CINCINNATI WINS

United Press International Telephoto

BATTLE OF THE LEADERS: Paul Hogue, right, Cincinnati stalwart, pursues Jerry Lucas, Ohio State star, in the final game of the N. C. A. A. tourney in Louisville, Ky. In the background is George Wilson of the Bearcats. Cincinnati retained the championship.

OHIO STATE BOWS

Bearcats Win, 71-59, for 2d N.C.A.A. Title —Hogue Is Star

By JOSEPH M. SHEEHAN
Special to The New York Times.

LOUISVILLE, Ky., March 24 —Cincinnati belayed all doubts as to its right to be called the nation's No. 1 college basketball power tonight by overwhelming Ohio State, 71—59, in the final of the twenty-fourth annual National Collegiate championship.

It had been considered an upset when the Bearcats beat the Buckeyes, 70—65, in overtime at Kansas City in the 1961 N. C. A. A. final. And, over the heated protests of Cincinnati adherents, Ohio State again had been ranked No. 1, over Cincinnati, in this season's polls.

So a lot of pride, as well as a lot of prestige, went into this all-Ohio final, contested before a noisy capacity crowd of 18,469 at Freedom Hall. Out of it, Cincinnati emerged with all the glory, and deservedly so.

In the third-place play-off that preceded the title match, Wake Forest downed the University of California at Los Angeles, 82—80.

After the first ten minutes of the championship final, Ohio State was out of the fight. With the score tied at 21—all, Cincinnati took charge, built a halftime lead of 37—29 and completely dominated the second half. At two stages of the final period, the Bearcats were in front by 18 points.

Paul Hogue was a dominating figure in Cincinnati's victory.

He outscored Ohio State's heralded Jerry Lucas, 22 points to 11. It was, however, essentially a team triumph for the Bearcats, whose starters played without relief until there was only a minute and a half to go.

Coach Ed Jucker's young Cincinnati quintet, on which Hogue is the only senior, played marvelously disciplined offensive basketball and, as long as it mattered, smothered Ohio State's high-scoring attack with vigilant guarding and powerful rebounding.

Ohio State threw every defense in the book at Cincinnati. Alternating between a man-to-man and various zone alignments in the first half, it went into a half-court and finally a full-court press in the last ten minutes. But the poised, polished Bearcats solved every problem the Buckeyes posed.

Injury Hobbles Lucas

The 6-foot-9-inch, 235-pound Hogue operated with equal effect from an inside station and from a high-post spot in the keyhole. Although the brilliant Lucas made many fine blocks of shots by Hogue, he couldn't withstand the bigger Cincinnati center's driving thrusts from the side and indefatigable tap-shooting.

In justice to Lucas, the Ohio State bellwether had wrenched his left knee in last night's victory over Wake Forest. However, with the aid of a supporting bandage, Jerry gallantly played the entire game. While he wasn't at his best, he seemed to have full mobility.

Up front, Hogue had strong corner support from the sopho-mores, Ron Bonham and George Wilson. The 6-foot 5-inch Bonham scored 10 points and the 6-foot 8-inch Wilson, while he made only 6 points, was a devastating rebounder.

Completing a beautifully-integrated Cincinnati unit were Tom Thacker and Tony Yates. These fast, clever, hard-driving guards did as fine a job of play-making as the N. C. A. A. tournament has seen in many a moon.

They did more than a fair share of Cincinnati's scoring, too. Thacker made 21 points, Yates 12. Time and again, they broke loose on change-of-direction thrusts off the posts set up by Hogue and Wilson. When they were picked up, they seldom failed to clear the ball to the team-mate left open by the defensive switch.

Buckeyes Effective Early

Ohio State did some effective work in the early stages, getting the ball into Lucas for close-range shots and shaking John Havlicek and Dick Reasbeck loose on driving forays from the side.

However, Cincinnati's stronger rebounding and tenacious ball-hawking kept the Buckeyes from working the fast break that had been one of their most effective weapons all season.

Under the increasing defensive pressure of the Bearcats, Coach Fred Taylor's Big Ten champions ultimately lost much of their usual poise and turned quite ragged.

Gary Bradds, held out of action in the first half, was Ohio State's high scorer with 15 points. Havlicek matched Lucas' total of 11.

Only three other colleges have won the N. C. A. A. title in successive years. They were Oklahoma A. and M. in 1945 and 1946, Kentucky in 1948 and 1949, and San Francisco in 1955 and 1956.

Shooters Solve Zone

Wake Forest's deadly outside shooters had no difficulty in solving the tightly-compressed 2-3 zone defense that U. C. L. A. had used so effectively against Cincinnati the night before.

The Atlantic Coast Conference champions, led by big Len Chappell and little Billy Packer hit on thirty-two of sixty-one shots from the floor. Chappell scored 26 points for a two-game total of 53. Packer scored 22 tonight.

For all its shooting success, Wake Forest had no breeze. Every time the Deacons opened a consequential lead, U. C. L. A. would rally furiously. Down by 8 points after fifteen minutes of play, the Bruins closed to 38—36 at half-time.

Eight points behind again with only four minutes to play, U. C. L. A. nearly pulled the game out of the fire. Gary Cunningham and Frank Slaughter each scored 17 points for the Big Five titleholders.

CINCINNATI (71)				OHIO STATE (59)			
	G.	F.	PF. P.		G.	F.	PF. P.
Bonham	3	4	3 10	Nowell	4	1	2 9
Wilson	1	4	2 6	Havlicek	5	1	1 11
Hogue	11	0	2 22	Reasbeck	4	0	4 8
Thacker	6	9	2 21	Lucas	5	1	3 11
Yates	4	4	1 12	McDonald	0	3	2 3
Sizer	0	0	0 0	Doughty	0	0	2 0
				Gearhart	1	0	3 2
Total	25	21	10 71	Bradds	5	5	7 15
				Total	24	11	19 59

Half-time score—Cincinnati 37, Ohio State 29.

Free throws missed—Havlicek, Lucas, Bradds, Hogue 2, Thacker 2, Yates 3.

WAKE FOREST (82)				U. C. L. A. (80)			
	G.	F.	PF. P.		G.	F.	PF. P.
Chappell	9	8	5 26	Cunningham	5	7	5 17
Christie	1	0	3 2	Blackman	4	3	2 11
Woollard	4	1	3 9	Slaughter	8	1	1 17
Packer	10	2	1 22	Green	3	1	5 7
Wiedeman	7	4	4 18	Hazzard	5	5	3 15
McCoy	0	3	3 3	Waxman	1	5	0 7
Hull	0	0	1 0	Hicks	2	0	1 4
Brooks	0	0	0 0	Stewart	1	0	2 2
Hassell	1	0	0 2	Milhern	0	0	0 0
Total	32	18	20 82	Total	29	22	19 80

Half-time score—Wake Front 38, U. C. L. A. 36.

Free throws missed—Chappell 2, Woollard 2, Wiedeman 2, Hull, Cunningham, Blackman, Green 2, Waxman, Hicks.

Attendance—18,469.

March 25, 1962

Special to The New York Times.

NEW YORK.
College basketball hailed a new champion today. It was Loyola University of Chicago, previously a stranger to such fame.

The Ramblers, unsung at the season's start, surged from 15 points behind to dethrone Cincinnati, 60-58, in overtime at Louisville on Saturday night in the finals of the National Collegiate tournament.

A tip-in basket by Vic Rouse in the final seconds won. Jerry Harkness, shackled for most of the game, gave the Ramblers their big chance by sinking a jump shot that tied the score 54-all just before regulation time ran out.

College basketball's other major post-season test saw Providence College's cool and clever Friars handily defeat Canisius, 81-66, in the finals of the National Invitation tournament at New York's Madison Square Garden.

In Denver, the Phillips 66 Oilers of Bartlesville, Okla., won the Amateur Athletic Union's national title for the twelfth time by routing the Denver-Chicago Truckers, 100-70.

Although Loyola had indicated its formidability by downing Duke, the nation's second-ranking team, 94-75, in Friday night's semi-finals there were few in the sell-out crowd of 19,153 who gave Coach George Ireland's Ramblers much of a chance against mighty Cincinnati.

In the national junior college championship final at Hutchinson, Kan., Independence of Kansas beat Moberly of Missouri, 73-68.

March 25, 1963

U. C. L. A. TOPS DUKE FOR TITLE

BRUINS WIN, 98-83

30th Victory in Row Gains N.C.A.A. Title —Hazzard Is Star

By GORDON S. WHITE Jr.
Special to The New York Times

KANSAS CITY, March 21—The undefeated University of California at Los Angeles basketball team proved to one and all, including some late-season skeptics, that it was the na-tion's top college quintet by charging to a 98-83 victory over Duke tonight to win the National Collegiate championship.

U.C.L.A. scored its 30th consecutive triumph of the year in the final of the National Collegiate Athletic Association's 26th tournament, played before 10,684 fans in Municipal Auditorium.

Michigan, without the services of the injured Cazzie Russell, defeated Kansas State, 100—90, in the consolation game for third place.

Only two other teams have gone through a season undefeated and continued on to the national championship. These teams were San Francisco in 1956 and North Carolina in 1957.

In a game that was exciting mostly because of its pace and fine ball handling by U.C.L.A, the Bruins and Blue Devils established scoring records for the final. U.C.L.A.'s 98 points surpassed the mark of 92 set by La Salle in 1954. The 181-point output by the two teams bettered the total of 168 in that 1954 championship.

Hazzard Leads Attack

Leading this scoring effort by the Bruins were Gail Goodrich and Ken Washington with 27 and 26 points, respectively. Jeff Mullins had 22 points for the Blue Devils.

But leading the over-all attack of the Bruins again was the fancy Walt Hazzard. The senior from Philadelphia set up scoring plays, stole the ball and generally interfered with Duke's offense. He consistently set up Goodrich and Keith Erickson.

It was a streak of 16 straight points that gave U.C.L.A. the advantage near the close of the first half.

The action was hard and fast from the start, as expected, and the score was tied eight times.

during the first 12 minutes. Then Jay Buckley, the hero of Duke's victory over Michigan in last night's semi-final, scored on three foul shots to put the North Carolinians ahead, 30—27.

But suddenly Duke began missing, while U.C.L.A. remained on target. With Hazzard doing most of the feeding and Goodrich and Washington most of the scoring, U.C.L.A. ran up its string of 16 for a 43-30 lead with 4½ minutes left in the half.

That was the end of Duke's championship hopes.

Duke Height No Advantage

The Bruins consistently out-played Duke's two 6-foot-10-inch players—Hack Tison and Buckley—whose height had been a factor in Duke being named a slight favorite before the game started.

The Bruins don't have a starter standing over 6-5 and their tallest player is Vaughn Hoffman, a rarely used fellow who stands 6-7.

Hazzard fouled out with 6:14 remaining, but U.C.L.A. held an 86-70 lead and the Bruin followers were no longer worried about the outcome. It was the first time this season Hazzard had fouled out of a game.

Within 30 seconds of Hazzard's departure, Mullins also fouled out. He had scored 73 points in the first two N.C.A.A. tourney games in Raleigh, N.C., to get Duke to the semi-finals.

It was the first championship for each of the four teams here. In fact, neither U.C.L.A. nor Duke had ever finished higher than third in this tournament.

In the opening game, Michigan did a fine job despite the absence of Russell, who aggravated an ankle injury in the semi-final with Duke last night.

Russell and three other Michigan starters will be back next year.

Bill Buntin, who with Russell forms a strong combination under the boards, made 33 points against Kansas State tonight.

Six of the members of the U.C.L.A. team automatically qualified for the United States Olympic basketball team trials set for St. John's April 2 through 4. Coach John Wooden will name the six later this month.

U.C.L.A. (98)	G.	F.	P.	Duke (83)	G.	F.	P.
Goodrich	9	9-9	27	Ferguson	2	0-1	4
Slaughter	0	0-0	0	Buckley	5	8-12	18
Hazzard	4	3-5	11	Tison	3	1-1	7
Erickson	2	4-4	8	Harrison	1	0-0	2
Hirsch	5	3-5	13	Mullins	9	4-4	22
McIntosh	4	0-0	8	Marin	8	0-1	16
Wash'gton	11	4-4	26	Vacendak	2	3-3	7
Darrow	0	3-4	3	Herbster	1	0-0	2
Stewart	0	0-0	0	Kitching	1	0-0	2
Huggins	0	0-1	0	Mann	0	3-4	3
Hoffman	1	0-0	2	Harscher	0	0-0	0
Levin	0	0-0	0	Cox	0	0-0	0
Total	36	26-32	98	Total	32	19-28	83

Half-time score—U.C.L.A. 50, Duke 38.
Fouled out—Hazzard, Erickson, Mullins.
Attendance—10,864.

March 22, 1964

Americans Keep Title by Downing Soviet Quintet, 73-59

U.S. SQUAD RETAINS UNBEATEN RECORD

Americans Lead by 8 Points at Half—Jackson Scores 17 and Caldwell 14

By EMERSON CHAPIN
Special to The New York Times

TOKYO, Oct. 23—The United States basketball team won the Olympic championship tonight by soundly defeating a hard-fighting Soviet team, 73 to 59. The victory extended the United States winning streak in Olympic competition to 47 games and brought the sixth consecutive basketball gold medal to the United States.

The American team, coached by Hank Iba of Oklahoma State, started slowly but opened a sizable lead with a 10-point streak midway in the first half. The score at the intermission was 39 to 31, and the United States team, with occasional dazzling displays of ball-handling and shooting, was in control the rest of the way.

Lucius Jackson of San Marcos, Tex., the Americans' 6-foot-9-inch center, led the scorers with 17 points and did a fine job of rebounding. Joe Caldwell of Texas City, Tex., had 14 points, 6 in the important first-half spurt that pulled the Americans ahead. Bill Bradley, a Princeton senior, and Jerry Shipp of the Phillips 66ers had 10 each.

Iba said his team "played 35 minutes of real fine ball," once it got started. He said the Russians displayed good basketball and played hard and warned that "Americans had better get serious about this because these foreign countries are playing better basketball all the time."

6,000 Fill Arena

Tonight's game, an eagerly awaited climax to almost two weeks of competition, attracted a capacity crowd of more than 6,000 to the National Gymnasium Annex. The Americans and Russians had won seven games each in preliminary round-robin competitions and then advanced to the last round with semi-final victories Wednesday night.

Fears had been expressed that United States basketball dominance was at an end when the American team had to rally to beat Puerto Rico, 62—42, after trailing by 24—23 at the half. The Russians, meanwhile, scraped past Brazil, 53—47, displaying a methodical style that some thought could cause the Americans real trouble.

In the first game of the final night's program, Brazil scored handily over the Puerto Rico team coached by Lou Rossini of New York University to capture the bronze medal. The score was 76 to 60, with the Brazilians showing superiority in shooting, rebounding and ball-handling.

In the final, the United States players occasionally showed flashes of brilliance, riddling the Soviet defense with sharp, accurate passes and sparkling plays to work a man free under the basket. But they also had occasional lapses, and much of the time were content to play slower-paced ball that kept them well ahead.

For a team composed mainly of men who star on offense, the Americans showed a surprisingly tight defense that forced the Russians to shoot from the outside most of the time.

Jan Kruminsh, the 7-foot-2-inch Soviet center, played less than half the game but scored 11 points. His bulk and height made him useful under the basket, but the speedier Americans ran all around him. Aleksandr Travin, a 6-foot-1-inch forward, led the Soviet attack with 12 points.

Iba said following the game that "the Russians showed us very early what they had, and that made it easier for us." But at the beginning the American play was unimpressive, and the pro-Russian minority of the spectators shouted joyfully as its team went ahead, 8—4, after four minutes. The Americans were off in their shooting and could not work the ball in close.

Not until the game was seven minutes old did the United States team go ahead for the first time, 11—10. The Russians countered with a 6-point splurge and led, 16—13, when the American plays started to click. Jackson, Bradley, Caldwell and Larry Brown of the Goodyear Wingfoots all scored as the Americans moved in front, 31—20.

By half-time, the Americans had gained confidence and loosened up. Halfway through the second half they had built up a 16-point lead and Iba began to substitute freely. Every member of the 12-man squad saw action and only two failed to score.

The Russians' tenacious defense was weakened when tall Gennady Volnov fouled out with the second half eight minutes old. Tempers flared in rough action soon afterward, and Yuri Korneev exchanged a few hot words with Bradley and other American players before being taken out of the game by his coach.

Aggressive play on both sides led to 28 fouls against the Russians and 22 against the Americans. The United States team had a 45 per cent shooting average to 36 per cent for the losers.

The audience was more partisan than at most of the Olympic competition, and raucous shouts and boos at key moments made the bright, new basketball arena resemble an American college gymnasium.

Prince and Princess Watch

But the spectators also included Japan's royal newlyweds—Prince Hitachi and Princess Hanako—and many notables and diplomats, including United States Ambassador Edwin O. Reischauer, who sat a few seats from the Prince.

The American players leaped in joy as the final gun sounded. Medals were conferred immediately, with the players of the first three teams mingling amicably as they awaited the ceremony.

Iba says his charges had never discussed the possibility of losing, despite the dire predictions by some commentators here. But he acknowledged that they had "played scared," with full awareness that they faced tough opposition.

The coach, hoarse-voiced from yelling instructions from the bench, said "certainly" he had had doubts about the game's outcome, but was fully confident of winning after the first half. The Americans probably could have run up a higher score, he said, but "this team has to play as a team—to play its own game the best way it can."

UNITED STATES (73)	G.	F.	P.	SOVIET UNION (59)	G.	F.	P.
Barnes	0	0	0	Muizhniex	0	0	0
Bradley	2	6-10		Bagiev	2	0	4
Brown	3	0	6	Alachachian	3	0	6
Caldwell	7	0	14	Travin	6	0	12
Counts	2	0		Khrynin	0	2	2
Davies	2	0	4	Kruminsh	3	5	11
Hazzard	1	0	2	Moseshvili	0	0	0
Jackson	6	5	17	Korneev	2	4	8
McCaffrey	2	0	4	Petrov	3	0	6
Mullins	0	0	0	Volnov	1	0	2
Shipp	5	0	10	Lipso	0	0	0
Wilson	1	0	2	Kaininsh	1	2	4
Total	31	11	73	Total	23	13	59

Half-time score—United States 39, Soviet Union 31.
Fouled out—Volnov.
Referee—Renato Righetto, Brazil. Umpire—Takeshi Matsuo, Japan.

October 24, 1964

Michigan Tops Princeton, 80 to 78, and Joins St. John's in Festival Final

RUSSELL SCORES IN LAST 3 SECONDS

Wolverine's Goal Decides— Bradley Gets 41 Points to 27 for Michigan Star

By LEONARD KOPPETT

Bill Bradley of Princeton won the individual honors but Cazzie Russell's jump shot won the ball game for Michigan at Madison Square Garden last night, as the 13th Eastern College Athletic Conference Holiday Festival experienced the wildest evening in its history with a capacity crowd of 18,499 screamed itself hoarse.

Bradley, after scoring 41 points and playing a commanding role in every other phase of the game, got a minute-long standing ovation when he fouled out. There were 4 minutes 37 seconds to play and Princeton led, 76—63. With 3:33 to go, the Tiger lead stood at 77—63.

Then Michigan, ranked as the No. 1 team in the nation and a prohibitive favorite in this game, finally exploded with a 16-1 closing burst. In just 65 seconds it wiped out a 78-68 deficit and with 36 seconds to go regained possession with the score tied. It waited for the last shot and gave it to Russell.

He took it from the left side, about 15 feet out, and made it with just three seconds remaining. It gave Michigan an 80-78 victory and a place in Saturday night's final against St. John's.

Cincinnati Loses, 66—64

For its part, Coach Joe Lapchick's team reached the final in just as dramatic a fashion. Two free throws by Jerry Houston with only two seconds to go gave the Redmen a 66-64 victory over Cincinnati in a bitter battle from start to finish.

In consolation games in the afternoon, La Salle defeated Temple, 83—70, and Syracuse crushed Manhattan, 87—64.

Bradley's performance in some ways surpassed his 36-point effort against Syracuse in the first round. It certainly met with more approval from a crowd heavily partisan for Princeton. In addition to making his fabulous assortment of shots (13 of 25 from the floor, 15 of 20 free throws), he defended well, picked off passes,

There have been many highlights in Bill Bradley's career. During his years at Princeton he established himself as the greatest player to come out of the Ivy league. He became a Rhodes Scholar and later was a valuable player on the N.Y. Knick's championship teams. He is now a United States Senator from New Jersey.

fed teammates for four baskets, took down nine rebounds and dominated whoever played him one-on-one.

In the second half as Princeton's lead grew, Michigan started to use a pressing defense and it was Bradley who kept bringing the ball up the court for Princeton. As it turned out, this is what Princeton missed most when he went out rather than his scoring.

Michigan Takes Charge

As soon as Bradley was out, Michigan started swarming all over the smaller, more tired, less agile Princeton players. The real panic started with 1:56 to play when Russell took a rebound and drove in for a lay-up which made the score 78-70. Within a minute, the score was tied and before three of the next four baskets Princeton never got the ball to the center line.

Larry Tregoning, John Thompson and Russell scored in that order, on a lay-up, a short spinner and a short hook. When Pomey stole the ball

from Chris Chimera, he gave it to Thompson for another lay-up and it was 78-78 with 51 seconds left.

Russell's final basket gave him 27 points, and he had nine rebounds and four assists. But during the first half he was held to 8 points by Don Rodenbach and the whole Michigan team seemed to lose its poise when Bradley prevented Princeton from rolling over dead.

Chimera, who alternated at quarterback with Gary Walters; Rodenbach and Bob Haarlow all produced a fine effort for Princeton, as did Robby Brown, the tall, skinny center, who fouled out two minutes before Bradley did. Bill Buntin and Oliver Darden of Michigan also fouled out.

Princeton Stymies Michigan

Essentially, Princeton prevented the two things that Michigan figured to do at will: Running and board control. Hustle and getting back quickly prevented fast breaks; good marksmanship and some shifty work by Brown and Bradley prevented the rebounding from

getting out of control. Once challenged, the Wolverines showed no pattern to offense, no accuracy in shooting and careless defense.

Once Bradley was gone, though, Princeton could stop nothing—except the crowd of interviewers who sought to reach Bradley after the game. By keeping the clubhouse door firmly locked, Coach Bill van Breda Kolff indicated that the young men brave enough to face Michigan's burley team were too tender-minded to be exposed to the press in a public building. It seems the Ivy League concept of sportsmanship remains limited in certain directions.

The St. John's game ended with referee Steve Honzo in the spotlight. The foul situation had become important early in the second half. St. John's, playing a fine defense but sputtering on offense, led, 35—32, at intermission. Roland West, a jump shooter with long range, had been Cincinnati's best weapon with 12 points.

In the second minute of the second half, West committed his fourth foul and went to the bench. His substitute, Jerry Couzins, provided a lift instead of a sag, however, and Cincinnati forged ahead, 56—51. St. John's rallied and took a 57-56 lead with 7:37 to play. But in the process Sonny Dove, its only reliable big man, picked up his fourth foul and sat down.

Dove Fouls Out

The score was 62-62 with 3:34 left when Dove returned—and fouled out 10 seconds later. Don Rolfes made two free throws on this play. When Cincinnati got the ball back, it played for one shot. With 2:51 left West came back in—and twice missed

Garden Line-ups

SEMI-FINAL ROUND

ST. JOHN'S (66)	G.	F.	P.	CINCINNATI (64)	G.	F.	P.
B.M'Int're	8	8-11	24	Smith	3	2-3	8
Duerr	3	0-0	6	Rolfes	3	6-8	12
Dove	4	5-7	13	Krick	6	2-2	14
K.M'Int're	3	7-7	13	West	6	0-3	12
Houston	2	4-4	8	Meyer	2	0-1	4
Swartz	0	0-0	0	Calloway	2	0-0	4
Jones	0	0-0	0	C'ngham	2	0-0	4
Wirell		0-1	2	Couzins	3	0-1	6
Cluess	0	0-0	0				
Hill	0	0-0	0				

Totals 21 24-30 66 | Totals 27 10-18 64
Half-time score—St. John's 35, Cincinnati 32.
Fouled out—Dove, West.

MICHIGAN (80)	G.	F.	P.	PRINCETON (78)	G.	F.	P.
Tregoning	6	0-0	12	Bradley	13	15-20	41
Darden	0	1-5	1	Haarlow	4	1-3	9
Buntin	7	10-10	24	R. Brown	4	0-0	8
Thompson	4	0-0	8	Rodenbach	3	0-0	6
Russell	8	11-14	27	Walters	2	1-2	5
Myers	2	0-1	4	Hummer	0	3-3	3
Pomey	2	0-0	4	Chimera	2	2-4	6
Clawson	0	0-0	0	Adler	0	0-0	0
Dill	0	0-0	0	Koch	0	0-0	0

Totals 29 22-30 80 | Totals 28 22-32 78
Half-time score—Princeton 39, Michigan 37.
Fouled out—Darden, Buntin, Bradley, R. Brown, Rodenbach.
Officials—Vic Di Gravio and Jimmy Lennon.
Attendance—18,499.

the first shot of a one-and-one foul.

Finally, with a minute to go, Bob McIntyre (who was high man with 24 points) put in a rebound on the third try and it was 64—64. Stalling for the final shot after a time out, Cincinnati started to move with 7 seconds left — and West was called for charging as he put his left shoulder down and turned into Houston.

Houston now drove for the basket and was tripped by Ken Cunningham. He sank both free throws with two seconds left and St. John's had its victory. A final fuss resulted when Honzo ruled that Cincinnati took longer than five seconds to put the ball back to play so the visitors never got even a desperate final shot.

December 31, 1964

U.C.L.A. REPEATS; GOODRICH EXCELS

Princeton Crushes Wichita for Third Place, 118-82, as Bradley Scores 58

By BILL BECKER
Special to The New York Times

PORTLAND. Ore., March 20 —The hustling, sleight-of-hand Bruins from the University of California, Los Angeles, repeated as National Collegiate basketball champions tonight with a surprisingly easy 91-80 victory over Michigan.

A singular magician masquerading as a guard, albeit an all-American, proved the hulking Wolverines' undoing. He was

Gail Goodrich, who scored 42 points and forced three Michigan starters to foul out with an amazing display of dribbling in the closing minutes.

His inspirational play raised the Bruins to such a pitch that they managed to wrest control of the backboards—hence the game—from the taller men of Michigan.

Bruins Lead at Half

"It was a supreme team effort," said Coach John Wooden, beaming with pride. His Bruins thus became the fifth university to repeat in N.C.A.A. tournament play.

Michigan has been ranked No. 1 nationally most of the season. The Bruins wound up No. 2, but except for a brief time in the first half when the Wolverines led, 20-13, there was little doubt about which was the quicker, more skillful team this night.

The Bruins, scoring in bursts as is their custom, pulled even at 24-all halfway through the half and led at intermission, 47-34.. Their cakewalk had to share top billing, however, with big Bill Bradley.

The nonpareil forward with the feathery touch set an individual scoring record of 58 points in leading Princeton to a 118-82 rout of Wichita in the consolation game for third place.

Bradley's amazing performance exceeded Oscar Robertson's 58 points for Cincinnati in 1958. The Missouri-bred marksman made three-fourths of his shots from the field, bagging 22 baskets and 14 free throws. His showing spurred the Tigers to a tourney team record.

The 13.204 spectators in Portland Memorial Coliseum rose in tribute when he left the game after sinking the 58th point.

Another all-American, Cazzie Russell of Michigan, also ex-

celled, leading his team's losing cause with 28 points. He also managed to escape fouling out.

Not so lucky were Bill Buntin, Larry Tregoning and Oliver Darden, all of whom incurred their fifth violation in trying frantically to stop the gay deceiver, Goodrich. Each time he drew two free throws. Each time he sank 2 points.

Goodrich wound up making 18 of 20 free throws. From the floor he sank 12 of 22.

As a team, the Bruins were superb, outhustling Michigan and taking 34 rebounds to 33 for the Wolverines. Especially outstanding were Freddie Goss, Edgar Lacey and Kenny Washington.

Washington, perhaps the best substitute in the nation, came in for ailing Keith Erickson and delivered in every respect. He sank 17 points and nabbed five rebounds, second only to Lacey's seven.

Buntin and Darden were second high in scoring for Michigan with 14 each, but this was not one of their better efforts.

Bruins Fifth to Repeat

Preceding U.C.L.A. as consecutive champions were Oklahoma State, 1945-46; Kentucky, 1948-49; San Francisco, 1955-56, and Cincinnati, 1961-62.

Goodrich was lauded by Wooden as "as fine a ball player as I've ever coached—he has so much poise, quickness and speed." At 6 feet 1 inch and only 170 pounds, Gail looked like a pygmy.

The Bruins completed their season with a record of 28 victories and two defeats. Last year's team went undefeated in 30 games, so the two-year mark is 58-2.

The Bruins finished 1965 by winning their last 15 games and setting a new team record of 400 points in their four tournament games. They previously eliminated Brigham Young, 100-76; San Francisco, 101-93, and Wichita, 108-89.

The previous high was U.C.L.A.s 359 last year. The Bruins, in fact, weren't far behind the five-game record of

427 set by West Virginia in 1959.

Michigan's coach, Dave Strack, credited U.C.L.A. with "a fine job" but declined to find fault with his men. His team just went cold when he expected a hot streak in the second half, he said.

U.C.L.A. hit .569 of its shots from the field and Michigan .516. But for real hot shooting, Princeton and Bradley were the prize winners tonight.

It was a fitting finale for Bradley, one of the greatest basketball players ever developed in the Ivy League. Bradley now can go off to his Rhodes studies at Oxford with a major consolation, if no gold basketball indicative of a national title.

His own previous best was 51 points against Harvard in 1964.

The unbelievable part about his performance tonight was that he could have reached 70 points quite easily. In the first half, he deliberately set up teammates for close shots instead of taking his chances from 20 feet. He is deadly from that range. At least half of his shots were 15 or 20 foot jumpers from outside the key. Several traveled 25 or 30 feet.

Bradley made 22 of 29 from the field, hit 14 of 15 free throws, captured 17 rebounds, and was credited with four assists. There were a half-dozen other scoring plays that he started.

Another mark set by the Princeton nonpareil was 177 points in five N.C.A.A. tournament games. This exceeded the 160 made in 1956 by Hal Lear of Temple and tied by Jerry West of West Virginia in 1959.

U.C.L.A. (91)	G	F	P		MICHIGAN (80)	G	F	P
Lacey	5	1-2	11		Russell	10	8-10	28
Erickson	1	1-2	3		Buntin	6	2-4	14
McIntosh	1	1-2	3		Tregoning	2	1-5	5
Goodrich	12	18-20	42		Pomey	2	0-0	4
Goss	4	0-0	8		Darden	8	1-1	17
Washington	7	3-4	17		Thompson	0	0-0	0
Lynn					Ludwig	1	0-0	2
Chambers	0	0-0	0		Clawson	3	0-0	6
Lyons	0	0-0	0		Dill	1	2-2	4
Levin	0	0-0	0		Myers	0	0-0	0
Galbraith	0	0-0	0					
Hoffman	1	0-1	2		Totals	33	14-18	80
Totals	33	25-33	91					

Half-time score—U.C.L.A 47, Michigan 34.
Fouled out—Buntin, Tregoning, Darden.
Attendance—13,204.

March 21, 1965

TEXAS WESTERN UPSETS KENTUCKY FOR N.C.A.A. TITLE

MINERS WIN, 72-65

By GORDON S. WHITE Jr.
Special to The New York Times

COLLEGE PARK, Md., March 19—Texas Western, overlooked in preseason ratings last December, became the collegiate basketball champion for the first time by whipping longtime powerful Kentucky, 72-65,

tonight in the final of the National Collegiate Athletic Association tournament.

The Miners never lost their poise in the face of a strong comeback attempt by the team rated No. 1 in the nation. Their rebounding strength and fine shooting kept them ahead from after 9 minutes 40 seconds of the first half until the end of the game.

It was a glorious moment for

the flashy players of Coach Don Haskins. The El Paso college got its first taste of the glory that Kentucky had fed upon four times in the past. The Wildcats have won more National Collegiate basketball championships than any other team.

Kentucky never before went as far as the final of this tournament without winning. But, before 14,253 fans at the University of Maryland's Cole

Field House, Coach Adolph Rupp's little men, who had done so well against taller teams all season, failed in their biggest game.

Duke defeated Utah, 79-77, in the game for third place.

Shed Makes Free Throw

Nevil Shed, a New York boy, sank the free throw that put Texas Western into the lead it never relinquished. Few in the capacity crowd believed that this was the beginning of the end for the Wildcats.

But the Texans, rated No. 3, believed in themselves and kept a tight grip on the situation. Kentucky, usually a fine shooting team, was off its usual marksmanship.

Dave Lattin, a strong 240-pounder from Houston, had too much power under the boards for Kentucky to cope with. Though in foul trouble in the late stages of the game, Lattin managed to keep off the Wildcats' big man, Thad Jaracz.

Yet it was a little man who filled the hero's assignment for Texas Western. He was Bobby Joe Hill, who used his cut-and-go skills to run around and through Kentucky. The 5-foot-10-inch junior from Detroit dropped in some of the fanciest shots of the tourney and scored 20 points. He also was a demon on defense, often taking the ball away from Kentucky players.

The championship quality of the Texans appeared in full in the second half. When Lattin sank a pair of fouls with four minutes to go in the first half, the Miners had an 8-point lead. Then the Kentuckians came charging back.

Point by point, the Wildcats moved closer to the Texans. All season long Kentucky had

managed to overtake team after team that dared to gain a lead against the squad backed by the aura of a great basketball tradition.

But the Texans didn't panic. After their lead was cut to a single point with 3½ minutes gone in the second half, the Miners rallied themselves. Orsten Artis and Hill combined for 6 straight points.

The lead was increased to 9 points and remained safe enough for the fancy ball-handlers to slow the game during the last three minutes.

Dampier Paces Kentucky

Louie Dampier and Pat Riley, two of Kentucky's short but excellent players, scored 19 points each. Dampier, only 6 feet tall, led the Wildcats in rebounds, with nine.

But all of Kentucky's efforts, so good for a small squad all season, were to no avail against a squad that measured 6-7 and 6-8 in a couple of spots. However, Hill and 5-6 Willie Worsley, another of the three New Yorkers on the Texas team, were the shortest men to reach the semi-finals of this tournament.

Both Kentucky and Texas Western reached the final after much of the same type of season. Each squad ran up undefeated strings of 23 games before suffering their first loss. Each lost two weeks ago tonight, just before the start of the N.C.A.A. tournament.

Texas Western then got into action in the first round of the

tournament and progressed to the semi-finals, where the Miners beat Utah. Kentucky, with a bye in the first round, went through the second and third rounds to the semi-finals, where the Wildcats defeated Duke in a game between the No. 1 and No. 2 teams in the nation.

As the Texans seemed sure of victory in the last minute, their fans began chanting, "We're No. 1." And as they left the arena, many were yelling, "We won this one for L.B.J."

Rupp gave Hill credit for the inevitable "turning point of the game." The Baron referred to Hill's stealing the ball twice within 10 seconds for layups just after Shed sank the foul shot to give the Miners the lead they never lost.

Duke Finishes 3d

The consolation game, usually a listless affair, turned into an exciting match between the Atlantic Coast Conference champion Blue Devils and the Western Athletic Conference champion Redskins. It was the second time in four years that Duke has finished third in the tourney. Coach Vic Bubas's Duke team finished second two years ago.

Jerry Chambers of Utah set a record of 143 points for four games in the N.C.A.A. tournament with 32 against Duke. This broke the mark of 141 set by Clyde Lovellette of Kansas in 1952.

The Line-ups

TEX. WESTERN (72)	G.	F.	P.	KENTUCKY (65)	G.	F.	P.
Hill	7	6-9	20	Dampier	7	5-5	19
Artis	5	5-5	15	Kron	3	0-0	6
Shed	1	1-1	3	Conley	4	2-2	10
Lattin	5	6-6	16	Riley	8	3-4	19
Worsley	2	4-6	8	Jaracz	3	1-2	7
Flourney	1	0-0	2	Berger	2	0-0	4
Cager	1	6-7	8				
Totals	22	28-34	72	Totals	27	11-13	65

Half-time score—Texas Western 34, Kentucky 31.
Fouled out—Conley, Jaracz.
Attendance—14,253.

DUKE (79)	G.	F.	P.	UTAH (77)	G.	F.	P.
Verga	7	1-1	15	Tate	1	2-5	4
Riedy	2	0-0	4	Jackson	6	2-2	14
Marin	9	5-5	23	MacKay	4	5-6	13
Vacendak	5	1-4	11	Ockei	5	0-0	10
Lewis	5	4-5	14	Chambers	11	10-12	32
Wendelin	2	0-2	4	Black	2	0-1	4
Kennedy	0	0-0	0	Day	0	0-0	0
Barone	1	0-0	2				
Chapman	2	0-1	4	Totals	29	19-26	77
Kolodziej	1	0-0	2				
Liccardo	0	0-2	0				
Totals	34	11-20	79				

Half-time score—Duke 41, Utah 37.
Fouled out—Riedy.

Duke led by 9 points midway through the second half when Mike Lewis, the Blue Devils' center, fell and sprained his left ankle. After he left the game, Utah moved within striking range.

But, with 7 seconds remaining and Utah behind by a point, Leonard Black of the Redskins went to the free-throw line with a one-and-one situation. Bubas then called time twice in a row, obviously to make Black aware of the situation. Finally given the chance to shoot, Black missed and Duke got another point to win the third-place spot.

Utah won the 1944 championship and finished fourth on 1961.

March 20, 1966

Alcindor Is Eager to Start Varsity Career

He Cites Pressure of Expectations, Prefers to Play

By BILL BECKER
Special to The New York Times

LOS ANGELES, Oct. 14—Ferdinand Lewis Alcindor, a basketball player of renown before he has played his first minute on the varsity, made his formal debut today before newsmen at the University of California, Los Angeles.

Lew was an unqualified success in his forensic bow. He fielded questions with the same aplomb and nonchalance with which he dunks the ball through the hoop.

The sophomore from New York City, who was shielded from reporters throughout his freshman year at U.C.L.A., said he was ready for the 24-game season.

"We've been getting a whole lot of pressure because of what we're expected to do," he said. "I'll be glad when we start playing games and let our playing speak for itself."

The first thing Lew did at the press conference was settle the question of his height. Seven feet 1⅜ inches, he said. Seven-1, this year's roster said.

Seven-1½, according to last year's roster. Take your pick.

At any rate, one of the lighter moments came when Lew took the microphone from his coach John Wooden, and raised it nearly a foot and a half. Wooden, 5-10, had introduced all of his players for questioning and saved the biggest attraction, Alcindor, for the last.

Alcindor said he planned to build his present weight of 230 pounds up to about 245 with a supplemental program of weight-lifting during the season.

"You can only develop your skills according to your physiological make-up," said Lew. "I have to build up my upper torso. I'm too skinny, and more bulk will help my rebounding work on the boards."

Attired in a natty blue blazer and dark gray slacks, Lew impressed the writers generally with quick, full answers. He is virtually a straight B student, now majoring in history for no special reason. "I'm just interested in it," he said.

During the summer he worked in Manhattan in Columbia Pictures' music publishing and recording division. A jazz fan, Lew enjoyed some things about the job. But he said he didn't think he would continue in it next year.

Why not? "Too blood-thirsty," he replied.

Lew Alcindor says he is ready for U.C.L.A. varsity career

This gangling lad has, despite all the acclaim foisted on him, a certain sensitivity and introspection not common in athletes. He said stamina may be another problem he will have as a varsity player.

"My stamina holds up when I put my mind to it," he explained. "But I'm inclined to get lazy and that defeats the purpose."

The purpose, of course, is to win. Last year, he led the U.C.L.A. freshmen to 21 straight victories, averaging 33.1 points a game. At Power Memorial High he set a scoring record of 2,067 points in leading his team to 95 victories and six defeats in three years.

He received scholarship offers from more than 100 colleges. He chose U.C.L.A. because of "Coach Wooden and the great teams he had." Lew acknowledged he had started becoming interested in U.C.L.A. in his sophomore year in high school.

Wooden said he planned to use Alcinder at a low post position just inside the opponents' free-throw line to get the maximum from Lew's scoring potential. "We don't want him to do too much running to start

with," the coach explained.

On defense, the lanky center probably will play the No. 1 position in the Bruins' celebrated zone press.

Following the news conference, the Bruins slipped into uniform and began practice. Starting Dec. 3, U.C.L.A hopes to regain the touch that brought it national championships in 1964 and 1965 The team is not scheduled to play in New York during the 1966-67 season.

Probable starters with Alcindor include another fine sophomore, Lucius Allen, at guard,

along with a junior returnee, Mike Warren. The likely forwards will be Edgar Lacey and Mike Lynn, seniors.

Wooden likes to play seven or eight men more or less as regulars. Two other sophs, Lynn Shackelford, a forward, and Kenny Heitz, guard, rate high.

But highest of all, of course, is Alcindor.

"I won't compare him with Bill Russell or Wilt Chamberlain," said Wooden. "That would be unfair. I just want him to be Lew Alcindor." And that, most observers here feel, may be plenty good enough.

October 15, 1966

SOUTHERN ILLINOIS FIVE CAPTURES N.I.T. FINAL, 71-56

SALUKIS IN RALLY

Win After Marquette Leads at the Half— Rutgers Victor

By LEONARD KOPPETT

Southern Illinois, roaring back with a strong counterattack after sputtering on offense for 27 minutes, defeated Marquette, 71-56, for the championship of the 30th annual National Invitation Basketball Tournament at Madison Square Garden yesterday.

Walt Frazier, who won the tournament's most valuable player award, and his Illinois teammates thus completed a campaign that is likely to change the basketball status of their school. They won 24 of 26 games, the last 19 in succession, and added a major tournament title to their No. 1 "small-college" ranking.

Only a shortage of "major" opponents has kept Southern Illinois, which has more than 18,000 students on its Carbondale campus, in the "small-college" classification. The prestige gained in this tournament will make the Salukis more acceptable gate attractions—and therefore social equals—in the future.

Scarlet Gains Prestige

In the consolation game, for third place, Rutgers also raised its basketball prestige by beating Marshall, 93-76, with Bob Lloyd scoring 44 points and set-

ting an N.I.T. scoring record. Lloyd's four-game total of 129 points erased the mark of 124 set by Maurice Stokes of St. Francis of Loretto in 1955.

All this was witnessed by another capacity crowd of 18,499, which brought the tournament total to 108,279, the second highest on record. The 1965 tourney, won by St. John's in Joe Lapchick's last year as coach, drew 114,714.

Once again, television timeouts for commercials marred the continuity of play, and the crowd booed lustily when four "officials' time-outs" were called in the first half, and two more in the second. In addition, Coach Al McGuire of Marquette protested vehemently to the referees after the fourth one.

"What's with these time-outs, it's killing our momentum," yelled McGuire, when for the second time a commercial message interrupted play just when Marquette was in the process of pulling away, with leads of 14-9 and 24-17.

As it turned out, this didn't prove decisive because Southern Illinois took such complete command after the intermission (which was 25 minutes long instead of 15, as the rule book states, again for the benefit of the home audience). But if the score had been close in the closing moments, another half-dozen time-outs could have been called by the coaches.

Even Jack Hartman, in the moment of his greatest triumph as a coach, conceded that the time-out situation "deserves more thought." But the result was so clear-cut that no controversy arose.

Frazier, who emerged as high scorer with 21 points, earned

the most valuable player award as much for his floor play, feeding and opportunism as for his scoring. He is a junior, although he sat out one year and will be eligible for pro offers this spring. From what the full quota pro scouts saw of him this week, he'll get some good ones.

In four games, he scored 88 points, took down 52 rebounds (although he plays guard and stands 6 feet 3 inches) and had 19 assists. In Southern Illinois' well-integrated patterns, he often isn't as eye-catching as players who form the hub of their teams' attack. In the showdown, though, he made the most important steals, passes and baskets.

Southern Illinois got into trouble during the last seven minutes of the first half. Outscored, 16-6, in that stretch, the Salukis went to the dressing room trailing by 11 points, 34-23.

In the second half, Coach Hartman switched to another style of attack, designed to produce more movement. Did it have a special name?

"We call it, 'our other offense'," he replied. "Essentially it's one high post instead of a high-low post."

It worked, but the Saluki defense worked even more. The offense chopped the margin to 39-34, while Marquette almost stopped scoring because of Saluki steals and interceptions.

With the score 42-34 and 13 minutes to play, Roger Bechtold replaced Ed Zastrow in backcourt for Southern Illinois, and the team really started to roll. Frazier, Dick Garret, Clarence Smith, Bechtold and Ralph Johnson formed the unit that did the damage, more by forcing turnovers and getting fast breaks and rebounds than by any set offense.

With 4:13 to go, it was 59-46. A brief flurry cut the score to 59-49 a minute later, but then the Salukis pulled away again.

Bob Wolf was high man for Marquette with 17 points, while

CHAMPIONSHIP GAME

SO. ILLINOIS (71)	G.	F.	P.	MARQUETTE (56)	G.	F.	P.
Garrett	5	2-3	12	Thompson	4	4-8	12
C. Smith	3	7-9	13	Brunkhorst	2	1-2	5
Johnson	3	1-3	7	P. Smith	1	2-2	4
Frazier	8	5-8	21	Burke	6	3-3	15
Zastrow	2	0-0	4	Wolf	7	3-5	17
Bechtold	3	4-4	10	Anderson	1	0-0	2
Griffin	0	0-0	0	Simmons	0	0-0	0
Westcott	0	0-0	0	Luchini	0	1-2	1
Whitaker	0	0-0	0	Curran	0	0-0	0
Taylor	0	0-0	0	Langenk'p	0	0-1	0
Benson	2	0-0	4				
Totals	26	19-27	71	Totals	21	14-23	56

Half-time score—Marquette 34, So. Illinois 23.
Officials—Lou Eisenstein and Steve Honzo.
Attendance—18,499.

CONSOLATION GAME

RUTGERS (93)	G.	F.	P.	MARSHALL (76)	G.	F.	P.
Milankow	1	0-1	2	Stone	9	8-12	26
Clark	5	3-7	13	Redd	6	2-7	14
Greacen	5	0-0	10	Allen	5	1-1	11
Lloyd	17	10-11	44	Davidson	5	1-1	11
Valvano	8	3-4	19	D'Antoni	4	2-5	16
Stewart	0	1-2	1	D.Bl'kens'p	1	0-0	2
Harley	0	0-1	0	Stepp	0	0-0	0
Britelle	0	0-0	0				
Smith	1	0-0	2	Totals	30	16-29	76
Penhall	1	0-0	2				
Goetz	0	0-0	0				
Pudesa	0	0-0	0				
Totals	38	17-26	93				

Half-time score—Rutgers 43, Marshall 41.
Fouled out—Redd, Allen, Greacen.
Officials—Jim Herniak and Hal Grossman.

Jim Burke had 15 and 10 assists. But the Marquette front court, including George Thompson, was pretty well blanketed. Nevertheless, Marquette completed the best season it has ever had with a 21-9 won-lost record.

Few teams have to come to the Garden in recent years and so thoroughly reflected credit on themselves as Rutgers did. In terms of raw material, Coach Bill Foster's squad certainly did not belong in the top half of the 14-team field, but such an evaluation should not imply condescension to its basketball ability. Rutgers won three of its four games because it played better than its opponents— offensively and defensively.

And it wasn't just Loyd, as brilliant as he was. Jim Valvano, his partner in backcourt, meant just as much to the success of the team—and, for that matter, of Lloyd. The front court, meanwhile, distinguished itself by making quickness and alertness, along with determination, make up for any deficiency in

The New York Times

THE OBJECT OF THEIR AFFECTION: Ralph Johnson, left, and Walt Frazier raise trophy won by Southern Illinois, victor of National Invitation Basketball Tournament here. Frazier was the tourney's most valuable player.

size and strength.

Bob Greacen, the 6-foot-6-inch sophomore, did the most in this respect, but Rick Harley, Dick Stewart and Barry Milankow outdid themselves too. Foster, who went to Rutgers three years ago, can take pride in having launched a winning basketball tradition that Rutgers seldom enjoyed in the past.

It all rested, of course, on Lloyd's remarkable shooting ability and the cohesive use of

it by the rest of the team. He finished his career with 2,045 points, and only 19 players ever scored more in major-college competition. This season he scored 810, an average of 27.9 a game. He made 92 per cent of his free throws and 47 per cent of his shots from the floor.

Yesterday, he scored 18 in the first half, which ended with Rutgers leading, 43-41, after 16 changes of lead. Early in the second half, Rutgers increased

its lead to 54-48, and then Lloyd hit his full stride.

By then, Marshall was a beaten team. Bob Redd, who had been doing an outstanding job of rebounding, fouled out with 8:09 to go and the score 71-58. Bob Allen, the Marshall big man, fouled out at 4:12 (shortly after Greacen), and the Rutgers lead went as high as 19 points — at 89-70.

Thus Rutgers finished its season with a 22-7 won-lost record

(Marshall wound up 20-8), and a final word should be said about the Rutgers fans, undergraduates and alumni who made up so large a portion of the crowds all week. Given the emotional circumstances and high hopes generated by the team, the followers of Rutgers were one of the best behaved (while enthusiastic) large groups ever to visit the Garden.

March 19, 1967

U.C.L.A. CRUSHES DAYTON IN N.C.A.A. FINAL, 79-64

ALCINDOR GETS 20

Bruins Control Game From Start to Win 3d Title in 4 Years

By GORDON S. WHITE Jr.
Special to The New York Times

LOUISVILLE, Ky., March 25 —Two years ago it was predicted that the University of

California, Los Angeles, would win the 1967 National Collegiate basketball championship. That was when Lew Alcindor, a 7-foot youngster playing high school ball in New York City, selected U.C.L.A. as his college.

Now 7 feet 1⅜ inches tall, mobile for his size and still learning the game as a sophomore, Alcindor carried the prediction to the point of reality tonight as he led the undefeated Bruins to their third national title in four years. Lew

and his teammates made it look easy as they defeated Dayton, 79-64, in the final of the 29th annual National Collegiate Athletic Association tournament before 18,892 at Freedom Hall.

It might have been even worse for Dayton except that Coach John Wooden took Alcindor and the best of his supporting cast out with 5 minutes to go and the Bruins ahead by 24 points.

Alcindor was just too much

for the Flyers, who surprised most persons by getting this far in the tourney. The losers simply did not have the height to compete with Lew.

Though Alcindor scored only 20 points, more than 9 below his season average, he was again dominant, controlling the boards and passing off for easy drives as he took two or three men out of the lane under the basket.

In the consolation game for third place, Houston defeated

North Carolina, 84-62, as Ken Spain scored 24 points and Elvin Hayes 23 for the Cougars. Houston, with three tall men, was the semi-final victim of U.C.L.A. last night in the game that most agreed was the only one in the tournament in which a team had a chance to beat U.C.L.A.

4th Unbeaten Champion

The Bruins, strong and frightening with Alcindor, are a well-coached team. The four other players know their assignments and take full advantage of opportunities presented when too many opponents hang around Alcindor. Lucius Allen and Mike Warren, in particular, scooted through the lane to get passes from Lew when he couldn't get a shot off from inside the crowd. Allen made 19 points and Warren 17.

U.C.L.A. became the fourth team in the history of the N.C.A.A. basketball championships to gain the title while going through a season unbeaten. The last to turn this trick was U.C.L.A.'s 1964 squad. Before that San Francisco in 1956 and North Carolina in 1957 were undefeated champions.

U.C.L.A., which also took the crown in 1965, became the second team to win the title three times in four years. Kentucky did it in 1948, 1949 and 1951. The Bruins' next goal will be Kentucky's record of four N.C.A.A. basketball championships.

Dayton had little to be ashamed of. Don May, a spectacular 6-4 player who stood 10 feet tall in the Flyers' victory over North Carolina in the semi-finals, was just outmanned. Each of U.C.L.A.'s 30 victims this season can claim that.

May Is High Scorer

May, who didn't score until well into the first half, finished with 21 points. With his 34 points against North Carolina, May was the high scorer of the semi-finals and final with 55 points. Alcindor had 39, with 19 in the semi-final.

U.C.L.A. opened a 6-0 lead before Dayton managed its first basket. Dayton was trying to run with the Bruins, who have speed in addition to height. There had been some who thought Coach Don Donoher of Dayton might select a stalling offense.

But the Flyers' plans were apparent from the outset. They were willing to trade speed for speed and hope that May might get enough points to overcome the problems. But May had difficulties at the start.

Dayton tried a man-to-man defense at the beginning. This didn't work. Late in the first half, Donoher called for a zone defense. It didn't work, either. Even if Dayton had stalled, the chances are that U.C.L.A. would have won. The Bruins

faced such tactics three times this season and pulled each game out. Now U.C.L.A. is riding a 34-game winning streak over two seasons, including four at the end of the 1965-66 campaign. In addition to shooting for the next couple of national titles, the Bruins may start thinking of San Francisco's record of 60 straight victories from 1954 to 1956.

Game Record in Jeopardy

The U.C.L.A. first-stringers took leads of more than 20 points many times before they were removed. Had they remained in the game, U.C.L.A. would doubtless have broken the record of 20 points as a margin of victory in a N.C.A.A. title game.

The Bruins beat all of their 26 regular-season opponents, winning the Pacific Eight crown to earn the tournament berth, and then they defeated Wyoming, the University of Pacific, Houston and, finally, Dayton. U.C.L.A. was ranked first in th nation throughout the season.

Houston had no more trouble in the consolation game than U.C.L.A. had in the final. The strong and big Cougars, led by Hayes, took off and left the Tar Heels far behind at an early point.

Last year another Texas team —Texas Western—became the first team from the state to win the N.C.A.A. championship. This year Texas Western was put out in the second round by Pacific.

TITLE GAME

U.C.L.A. (79)				DAYTON (64)			
	G.	F.	P.		G.	F.	P.
Heitz	2	0-0	4	Klaus	4	0-0	8
Alcindor	8	4-11	20	May	9	3-4	21
Allen	7	5-8	19	Obrivic	0	0-0	0
Warren	8	1-1	17	Sandler	2	1-2	5
Shackelford	5	0-2	10	Hooper	2	2-4	6
Nielsin	0	0-1	0	Torain	3	0-0	6
Wseck	1	0-0	2	Wiriman	4	2-2	10
Saffer	2	0-0	4	Shripint	2	4-5	8
Sanar	1	0-0	2	Indirian	0	0-0	0
Chirmin	0	1-2	1	Heckman	0	0-0	0
Lynn	0	0-0	0	Sminick	0	0-0	0

CONSOLATION GAME

HOUSTON (84)				NO. CAROLINA (62)			
	G.	F.	P.		G.	F.	P.
Grider	2	2-4	6	Grubar	1	0-0	2
Kruse	2	0-0	4	Lewis	9	5-6	23
Chaney	6	7-9	19	Bunting	1	2-6	4
Hayes	10	3-5	23	Clark	3	3-4	9
Bell	0	0-2	0	Miller	5	2-4	12
Lentz	3	0-1	6	Moe	0	0-0	0
Spain	9	6-9	24	Gauntlett	2	2-3	6
Lewis	0	0-0	0	Brown	0	0-1	0
Lee	0	0-1	0	Tuttle	1	0-0	2
Hamond	1	0-0	2	Fletcher	1	0-0	2
Benson	0	0-0	0	Fryer	0	0-0	0
McVey	0	0-0	0	Bostick	1	0-0	2

March 26, 1967

United Press International

GOING UP FROM DOWN UNDER: Elvin Hayes easing in a basket from underneath the hoop in the first quarter.

HOUSTON BREAKS 47-GAME STREAK OF U.C.L.A., 71-69

Hayes, With 39 Points, Gets Final Two Free Throws— Alcindor Is Held to 15

By The Associated Press

HOUSTON, Jan. 20 — Houston's inspired Cougars, led by Elvin Hayes, toppled the University of California, Los Angeles, 71-69, tonight and ended the Bruins' myth of invincibility in college basketball.

A howling, happy crowd of 52,693 in the Astrodome—a record for a basketball game—saw Hayes, Houston's all-American, toss in 39 points and help put the defensive clamp on Lew Alcindor.

Appropriately enough, it was Hayes's two free throws with 28 seconds remaining that broke a 69-69 tie—and U.C.L.A.'s 47-

game winning streak, second longest in history.

The Cougars, ranked No. 2 in the nation with a 16-0 won-lost mark going into their showdown with the top-ranked Bruins, turned U.C.L.A.'s own weapons on them—an outstanding performance by a superstar and a tenacious defense.

Cougars Lead by 3 at Half

Houston, sparked by Hayes' 29 points, established a 46-43 margin at intermission and spent the second half fighting off challenge after challenge by the cold-shooting Bruins.

When it was over, the delirious Houston fans and cheerleaders stormed onto the court, hoisted their heroes to their shoulders and began a rhythmic chant, "We're No. 1, we're No. 1."

If they are, they can thank their poise, which never broke in the face of the famous U.C.L.A. press defense.

Houston moved into a 13-12 lead with 13:45 to go in the first half on a basket by George Reynolds. The Cougars didn't trail again, although the game was tied three times.

The last deadlock occurred when Lucious Allen, the high scorer for the Bruins with 25 points, dropped in two free throws with 44 seconds to go. The Cougars then brought the ball down court, and when Hayes was fouled by Jim Nielson they went ahead to stay.

U.C.L.A. had one more chance, but blew it on an uncharacteristic mixup in signals on which Mike Warren of the Bruins tipped the ball out of bounds. Houston took over with 12 seconds left and ran out the clock.

"Isn't that Hayes great?" exulted the Houston coach, Guy Lewis. "Almost every game he plays is great."

"Houston played a tremendous game," said John Wooden, coach of U.C.L.A. "We'll just have to start over again."

It was a sweet revenge for Houston, whose last loss was to U.C.L.A. in the semi-finals of the national championship in Louisville, Ky., last March, 73-58.

If the Bruins had an excuse, it was poor shooting and a subpar Alcindor. The giant center missed the Bruins' last two games with an eye injury and was obviously off form. He finished with 15 points, but had only four field goals in 18 attempts.

Hayes and the 6-foot-9-inch Cougar center, Ken Spain, took turns giving big Lew the miseries. Hayes blocked three of Alcindor's shots, stole the ball from him twice and Spain teased him into an unusual and unnecessary foul.

Hayes Plays Outstanding Game

Hayes was magnificent. He finished with 17 field goals in 25 attemptts, grabbed 15 rebounds and blocked four shots, although playing the last 11 minutes with four fouls.

Alcindor had 12 rebounds in the nationally televised game.

Reynolds, a tricky backcourt man and suddenly a tough defender, finished with 13 points for Houston and Don Chaney had 11. Warren had 13 and Lynn Shackelford 10 for U.C.L.A.

The Bruins hit on only 26 of 77 field-goal attempts, a 33.6 percentage as compared with its season average of 50 per cent. Houston was 30 for 66 and 45.6 per cent.

U.C.L.A.'s winning streak fell 13 short of the record of 60 set by the University of San Francisco 12 years ago.

The game started in characteristic fashion for the Bruins. They spotted Houston a 5-1 lead and then appeared as if they were going to run off and hide. They forced Houston into four consecutive backcourt errors and established an 8-5 lead.

Houston Battles Back

But the Cougars refused to wilt, however, and, trailing 12-11, put on a 16-6 scoring burst for a 27-18 lead and never trailed again.

Reynolds scored 6 of those points and Hayes the rest, the last two on a long jumper over the reaching hand of Alcindor.

U.C.L.A. finally caught up at 54-54, but Reynolds broke the tie with a free throw. The Bruins tied it again at 65-65, but Hayes snapped it with a jumper.

U.C.L.A. (69)				HOUSTON (71)			
	G.	F.	P.		G.	F.	P.
Allen	10	5-9	25	Hayes	17	5-7	39
Warren	6	1-2	13	Spain	1	0-1	2
Alcindor	4	7-8	15	Lee	1	2-3	4
Lacey	0	0-0	0	Chaney	5	1-3	11
Shackelford	4	2-2	10	Reynolds	5	3-3	13
Lynn	2	0-0	4	Gribben	1	0-0	2
Nielsen	1	0-0	2	Lewis	0	0-0	0
Totals	26	17-22	69	Totals	30	11-18	71

Half-time score—Houston 46, U.C.L.A. 43. Attendance—52,693.

January 21, 1968

U.C.L.A. Routs Houston, 101-69, to Gain N.C.A.A. Final; No. Carolina Wins

COUGARS' STREAK IS SNAPPED AT 32

U.C.L.A. Dominant From the Start — Hayes Is Checked —Ohio St. Bows, 80-66

By GORDON S. WHITE Jr.
Special to The New York Times

LOS ANGELES, March 22—The big rematch in college basketball that fans were looking forward to became the most astonishing mismatch in the history of the National Collegiate Athletic Association championships as the University of California, Los Angeles, overwhelmed Houston, 101-69, tonight in an N.C.A.A. semi-final contest.

Now the Bruins will face North Carolina in the final of the tournament with what appears an easy chance to gain their second straight N.C.A.A. title and fourth in the last five years.

North Carolina gained the dubious distinction of being the Bruins' opponent by beating Ohio State, 80-66, in the first semi-final before 15,742 persons at the Los Angeles Sports Arena.

Cincinnati was the only team to win a semi-final game by more points than the Bruins did when it whipped Oregon State by 34 points in the next-to-last round in 1963. But tonight's game was supposed to have been a tight test, one between the team rated No. 1, Houston, and the No. 2 team, U.C.L.A.

In a Class by Themselves

There was little doubt in the minds of the fans present and those who watched the national telecast that the polls have made a mistake this time. U.C.L.A. was in a class by itself tonight.

From the outset the Bruins had the game completely under control and Houston completely bottled up. Each of the Bruins did an outstanding job. No one man stood alone in the hero role. Defense, as well as offense, was well executed by Coach John Wooden's crew of Lew Alcindor, Lucius Allen, Mike Warren, Mike Lynn and Lynn Shackleford.

The match within the match —Alcindor vs. Elvin Hayes— was no more a contest than the game itself was. Hayes was handcuffed by a tenacious defense that didn't permit him to get his hands on the ball very often. The "player of the year" scored only 10 points after averaging 37.7 a game in leading Houston through an undefeated regular season.

The loss was the first for the Cougars in 33 games. They hadn't been beaten since U.C.L.A. stopped them, 73-58, in last year's semi-final. Houston handed the Bruin's their only loss this season, 71-69, last January in Houston.

But then U.C.L.A. wasn't completely healthy. Operating on all cylinders tonight, however, the Bruins laid claim to being the best team in the land, even if they won't get a No. 1 rating since polls are finished for the year.

Alcindor, with his hook shots and easy underneath tosses, scored 19 points as did Lynn, primarily on sets, and Allen, mainly on driving layups when Alcindor, the 7-foot-1½-inch star, cleared the lane for him.

Regulars Take a Rest

U.C.L.A. could easily have rolled up the biggest margin of victory in a semi-final N.C.A.A. test. But Wooden and his team proved their point as they gained a 44-point lead toward the end of the game. Wooden then took his stars out one by one and Houston cut the margin from very embarrassing to just embarrassing.

As Alcindor left the game with 2:04 to go, he raised his long right arm with the index finger extended to indicate No. 1. No one could argue with him and the U.C.L.A. fans.

When Jim Nielsen drove in for a layup to give U.C.L.A. its 100th and 101st points, the fans loved it. The U.C.L.A. team that won the title in 1965 is the only other team to score 100 or more points in a semi-final game. The 1965 Bruins beat Wichita State, 108-89, in the semi-finals. No team has scored 100 points in an N.C.A.A. final.

Coach Guy Lewis of Houston said, "That was the greatest exhibition of basketball I've ever seen in my life. They could have beaten anybody—I mean anybody."

Defense and some good breakaways when the opportunity arose were the keys to North Carolina's success that carried the Tar Heels to the National final for the first time since they won the title in 1957.

OHIO STATE (66)				NO. CAROLINA (80)			
	G.	F.	P.		G.	F.	P.
Howell	6	1-2	13	Miller	10	0-1	20
Hosket	4	6-9	14	Bunting	4	9-10	17
Sorenson	5	1-3	11	Clark	7	1-1	15
Schnabel	0	0-0	0	Scott	6	1-4	13
Meadors	3	2-2	8	Grubar	1	1-2	3
Finney	8	0-2	16	Fogler	1	0-0	2
Smith	2	0-0	4	Braun	0	0-0	0
Barclay	0	0-0	0	Tuttle	1	0-1	2
Geddes	0	0-0	0				
Totals	28	10-18	66	Totals	33	14-20	80

Half-time score—North Carolina 34, Ohio State 27. Fouled out—Hosket.

U.C.L.A. (101)				HOUSTON (69)			
	G.	F.	P.		G.	F.	P.
Shackelford	6	5-5	17	Lee	3	0-0	6
Lynn	8	3-3	19	Hayes	3	4-7	10
Alcindor	7	5-6	19	Spain	4	7-10	15
Warren	7	0-0	14	Chaney	7	1-1	15
Allen	9	1-2	19	Lewis	1	2-2	4
Nielsen	2	0-0	4	Hamood	3	4-6	10
Heitz	3	1-1	7	Gribben	0	0-1	0
Saner	0	0-0	0	Bell	3	3-4	9
Sutherland	0	0-0	0				
Sweek	1	0-1	2				
Total	43	15-18	101	Total	22	25-37	69

Half-time score—U.C.L.A. 53, Houston 31. Attendance—15,742.

March 23, 1968

U.C.L.A. WINS BY 78-55

N. CAROLINA BOWS IN N.C.A.A. FINAL

By GORDON S. WHITE Jr.
Special to The New York Times

LOS ANGELES, March 23—The University of California, Los Angeles, remained on top of the basketball world tonight as the National Collegiate champion, in a class by itself because of perfectly balanced team power that carried it to the title for the second straight year.

The mighty Bruins produced just the game they had to play to whip North Carolina, 78-55, in the final of the 30th annual N.C.A.A. championship event before 14,438 in the Los Angeles Sports Arena.

This title victory did not compare with the way U.C.L.A. humiliated Houston in the semi-finals last night. The U.C.L.A. players seemed to perform with the assurance gained from the fact that they knew they were the best. It was a confident bunch that overcame an early Tar Heel slowdown and, after a few mistakes, took complete control to achieve U.C.L.A.'s fourth N.C.A.A. title in five years.

U.C.L.A. became the first institution to win the N.C.A.A. basketball title twice in successive years. Coach John Wooden's Bruins had been successful in 1964 and 1965.

U.C.L.A. finished its season as expected after Ohio State upset Houston, 89-85, for third place. Houston, undefeated until the Bruins trounced the Cougars, 101-69, last night, was not up to coming back in a consolation game, a contest few players care for.

Again it was Lew Alcindor who posed too much of a problem for U.C.L.A.'s opponent of the night. The 7-foot-1½-inch player from New York City was in fine form and proved he could handle the task of playing against a man 7 feet tall. In his battle with Rusty Clark of North Carolina, Alcindor forced Clark to retreat at times, took high passes by outreaching the Tar Heel center and finished with 34 points.

U.C.L.A. attacked North Carolina through Alcindor, whereas against Houston, the Bruins attacked from all angles. To get the ball to Alcindor, the Bruins showed their skills of ball-handling and maneuverability that have made them much too good for their opponents.

Thus the Bruins finished as champions with a record of 29 victories and one loss. A year ago U.C.L.A. was undefeated in winning the crown. But the one loss of this season seems to have been relegated to the list of sports mistakes. It was Houston that beat U.C.L.A. by 2 points last January when Alcindor and Lucius Allen were ailing.

Last night's semi-final triumph of power avenged that loss.

At the start, North Carolina chose to slow the pace. It had been done before against the current Bruin team but not with success in the last two seasons. Tonight's slowdown was no exception, though it was about all the Tar Heels could do.

They had sat through the first half of the semi-final mismatch between Houston and U.C.L.A. and had seen what happened when you tried to run with the quick, skillful Bruins. So, probably thinking you're "damned if you do and damned if you don't," Coach Dean Smith said, "slow down and let's see."

He saw, as did everyone else viewing the game, that U.C.L.A. can handle anything. Mike Warren and Allen stole the ball time and again as North Carolina tried to pass and keep control of the ball for a minute at a time. Lynn Shackelford did some stealing and even Alcindor got into the theft act.

Mike Lynn, the fifth starter for the Bruins, did his share to bother the worried Tar Heels. But Lynn fell into early foul trouble and Ken Heitz went in. Heitz was just another gadfly to North Carolina.

There was little hope for the Atlantic Coast Conference champions, who went further in this N.C.A.A. tourney than any other North Carolina team had since 1957, when it won the crown.

North Carolina's players couldn't do much on offense. They had to try scoring from outside and give up moving in close. In the first few minutes Alcindor slapped a half-dozen shots right back at Charlie Scott, a 6-5 driving guard; Clark, the 7-footer, and Bill Bunting, a 6-9 forward.

Larry Miller, the North Carolina forward with a good one-hand shot, hit on five field goals but had 13 attempts. He finished with 14 points, the most for any of the Tar Heels. It was a frustrating night for the Southerners.

North Carolina led for 59 seconds when the score was 5-3, then 5-4. But Shackelford, following a steal, scored to put U.C.L.A. ahead where it obviously belonged and knew it.

Spurts of 9, 8 and 7 points gave the Bruins a 32-22 lead.

In the second half North Carolina abandoned hope of stalling the issue. The Tar Heels were too far behind.

The title belonged to U.C.L.A. and it probably belonged to U.C.L.A. when the season opened. The team came just as far as everyone expected—all the way.

Houston's season came to a sad end after the Cougars had won their first 31 games, including three in the N.C.A.A. tournament. But Ohio State, the surprise team to reach the semi-finals where it lost to North Carolina, was able to bounce back more quickly than the Cougars.

Elvin Hayes scored 34 points and Theodis Lee got 27 for Houston but to no avail. However, Hayes finished his varsity career with a couple of record. He scored 1,214 points this season, a record for a major college player. He broke the 1953-54 mark of Furman's Frank Selvy by 5 points.

Also, Hayes made 70 field goals in this year's five N.C.A.A. tournament games, breaking the mark of 65 set by Bill Bradley of Princeton in 1965. However, Hayes fell 10 points short of Bradley's record total of 177 points for five N.C.A.A. games in 1965.

Hayes would have broken that record if U.C.L.A. hadn't done such a good job against him. The Bruins held Elvin to 10 points, the lowest total of his varsity career.

U.C.L.A. (78)	G.	F.	P.
Shackelford	3	0-1	6
Lynn	1	5-7	7
Alcindor	15	4-4	34
Warren	3	1-1	7
Allen	3	5-7	11
Nielson	1	0-0	2
Heitz	3	1-1	7
Sutherland	1	0-0	2
Sweek	0	0-0	0
Saner	1	0-0	2
Total	31	16-21	78

N. CAROLINA (55)	G.	F.	P.
Miller	5	4-6	14
Bunting	1	1-2	3
Clark	4	1-3	9
Scott	6	0-1	12
Grubar	2	1-2	5
Fogler	1	2-2	4
Brown	2	2-2	6
Tuttle	0	0-0	0
Frye	1	0-1	2
Whitehead	0	0-0	0
Delany	0	0-0	0
Fletcher	0	0-0	0
Total	22	11-19	55

Half-time score—U.C.L.A. 32, North Carolina 22.
Fouled out—Bunting.

HOUSTON (85)	G.	F.	P.
Lee	13	1-2	27
Hayes	14	6-8	34
Spain	4	2-4	10
Lewis	3	0-1	6
Chaney	4	0-1	8
Bell	0	0-0	0
Hamood	0	0-0	0
Total	38	9-16	85

OHIO STATE (89)	G.	F.	P.
Howell	5	2-2	26
Hosket	5	9-11	19
Sorenson	8	3-4	19
Meadors	3	3-4	9
Swain	1	0-0	2
Finney	5	3-3	13
Smith	0	1-2	1
Total	34	21-26	89

Half-time score—Ohio State 46, Houston 42.
Fouled out—Chaney. Attendance—14,438.

March 24, 1968

MARAVICH OF L.S.U. SET SCORING MARK

Elvin Hayes of Houston averaged 36.8 points a game during the 1967-68 college basketball season and was named player of the year. But his scoring output was good enough only for third place behind a pair of sophomores, according to the final official statistics issued yesterday.

The winner was Pete Maravich, of Louisiana State University, who averaged a record 43.8 Calvin Murphy of Niagara, with 38.2, was second.

THE LEADERS

SCORING

	FG.	FT.	Pts.	Avg.
Maravich, L.S.U.	432	274	1,138	43.8
Murphy, Niagara	337	242	916	38.2
Hayes, Houston	519	176	1,214	36.8
Travis, Okla. City	324	160	808	29.9
Portman, Creighton	303	132	738	29.5
Mount, Purdue	259	165	683	28.5
Hill, West Texas St.	227	99	573	27.3
Hallmon, Utah St.	256	159	671	26.8
Foster, Miami (Ohio)	230	157	617	26.8
Walk, Florida	259	185	663	26.5

FIELD-GOAL PERCENTAGE

	FG	FGA	Pct.
Allen, Bradley	258	394	.655
Hunt, Army	154	248	.621
Alcindor, U.C.L.A.	294	480	.613
Unseld, Louisville	234	382	.613
Sorenson, Ohio State	196	329	.596

FREE-THROW PERCENTAGE

	FT	FTA	Pct.
Heiser, Princeton	117	130	.900
Ward, Centenary	94	106	.887
Carpenter, Pacific	96	109	.881
Luchini, Marquette	107	124	.863
Williams, Rice	113	131	.863

REBOUNDING

	No.	Avg.
Walk, Florida	494	19.8
Smith, Eastn. Ky.	472	19.7
Hayes, Houston	624	18.9
Unseld, Louisville	513	18.3
Cunningham, Murray St.	410	17.8

April 4, 1968

PHILLIPS OILERS DROP BASKETBALL

BARTLESVILLE, Okla., April 9 (UPI)—The Phillips 66ers, kingpins of amateur basketball for decades, bowed out of the sport they helped to build to national prominence today after 11 national Amateur Athletic Union titles and two Olympic playoff championships.

"The growth of professional basketball to major, virtually nationwide status has made it difficult to attract outstanding graduating college players in order to field a first-class amateur basketball team," a spokesman for the Phillips Petroleum Company of Bartlesville said.

"Professional basketball, with its large, well-filled playing facilities in most cities and its attraction to television audiences has brought glamour and offers of initial salary income with which sponsors in amateur leagues cannot compete," the company spokesman said.

Although the action did not come as a great surprise, it was still a blow to long-time fans.

"I'm feeling pretty blue today," Elmer Sark, a retired Phillips employe said. "I'm really hurt. I hated to see it happen."

"It would be easier to count the games I didn't see, "said the 83-year-old fan who followed the team from its beginning and is currently writing the 66ers' history.

The 66ers rosters included such A.A.U. all-Americans as Hank Luisetti, the originator of the one-hand shot; Bob Kurland, the sport's first seven-footer; Jay Wallenstrom; Don Lockard; Shorty Carpenter; Jess (Cab) Renick; James McNatt; Chuck Darling; Arnold Short and many others.

The team was founded in the fall of 1920 by K. S. (Boots) Adams, a former Kansas University basketball player who decided to set up a team of some of his fellow workers at the small Bartlesville Oil Company.

April 10, 1968

Alcindor Clarifies TV Remark, Criticizes Racial Bias in U.S.

By SAM GOLDAPER

In what he thought was a guest appearance on television for the purpose of publicizing Mayor Lindsay's Operation Sports Rescue program, Lew Alcindor became involved last Friday in a discussion of why he did not try out for the United States Olympic basketball team.

Alcindor, the 7-foot-1⅜-inch center for the University of California, Los Angeles, team, wound up being cut off the air by an inflexible station break on the National Broadcasting Company's "Today" show, after this conversation with Joe Garagiola, one of the show's moderators:

"Yeah, I live here, but it's not really my country," Alcin-

dor said.

"Well, then there's only one solution," Garagiola said, "maybe you should move."

"Well, you see that would be fine with me, you know, that it all depends on where are we going to move," said Alcindor.

At this point an inflexible station break took place.

Discussion Is Resumed

When the program returned to the air the discussion was resumed briefly, but New York viewers did not see it because a local station break also took place.

After Alcindor had left the program because his time segment had run out, Garagiola and the show's other moderator, Edwin Newman, returned to the screen and said that

Alcindor had explained his statement further to them off the air.

Yesterday, in his home in Hollis, Queens, the Negro star explained what he was unable to say to the moderators on television.

"What I was trying to get across," Alcindor said, "was that until things are in an equitable basis [he repeated "equitable" several times] this is not my country.

"We have been a racist nation with first-class citizens and my decision not to go to the Olympics is my way of getting the message across.

"That's why I am working for Operation Sports Rescue," he continued. "It's a program where we go into the ghetto areas of South Jamaica, Bedford Stuyvesant, Harlem and the South Bronx and try to convince the junior high school and high school students to stay in school and go to college. If the Negro youngster is to qualify to take care of himself he must stay in school. If not, he is less equipped for the world of tomorrow."

Alcindor spoke after having returned from an Operation Sports Rescue clinic at the Richard S. Grossley Junior High School in South Jamica, Queens.

Disappointment Expressed

He declared he was disappointed that he didn't get a

chance to talk about Operation Sports Rescue on television. He went on:

"We have about 12 athletes in this program and kids like Gerry Davis, Marvin Roberts and Eddie Agard, whom I work with, don't live in Central Islip, L. I. They live in the ghettos. We find that we can get across to these kids where the parents and teachers have been shut out. They seem to identify themselves with us as athletes and that we live in their neighborhoods.

"It was gratifying talking to those 30 or so teen-agers," Alcindor said. "I felt as though I got the stay-in-school message across.

"I made my decision to stay out of the Olympics but it just wasn't because I was trying to get a message across. Sometimes what everyone seems to forget is that I would have lost a whole quarter (10 weeks in college) by going to the Olympics and that I would not have been able to graduate in June.

"I expected that I would be asked about the Olympics. I guess I knew. I don't really know what Garagiola meant when he said, 'Well, there is only one solution then, maybe you should move,' after I said it's not really my country. Where did he expect me to go to—Africa? A lot of people get discredited by occurrences like this. That's what happened to Muhammad Ali [Cassius Clay]."

July 23, 1968

United States Five Tops Yugoslavia, 65-50, For 7th Olympic Title in a Row

HAYWOOD EXCELS WITH 23 POINTS

White Gets 14 as Americans Break Open Tight Game With Second-Half Spurt

MEXICO CITY, Oct. 25 (AP) —Spencer Haywood and Jo Jo White exploded for 26 points in the space of 12 minutes at the start of the second half tonight to break open a hard-fought battle and give the United States its seventh straight Olympic basketball championship with a 65-50 victory over Yugoslavia.

In an earlier game, the towering Soviet Union, the pretournament favorite and upset by Yugoslavia in the semi-finals,

took the bronze medal by beating Brazil, 70-53.

The underdog Yugoslavs started the final game before an overflow crowd of 25,000 at the Sports Palace by grabbing an early lead over the Yanks. Leading through the early

Yugoslavia Stays Close

stages, at one time 7-4 and another 11-6, the Yugoslavs went off at half-time trailing only 32-29.

Then the 6-foot-8inch Haywood, a 19-yearold from Detroit, joined White, from St. Louis and Kansas University, in a wild and spirited scoring attack.

When the assault had ended with both Haywood and White leaving the game amid a standing ovation, the Yugoslavs were left dazed.

Haywood, starting slowly and going 12 minutes without a point, finished as the evening's top point-maker with 23 points. White had a total of 14.

During the Americans' powerful rush in the openings min-

UNITED STATES (65)				YUGOSLAVIA (50)			
	G.	F.	P.		G.	F.	P.
Clawson	0	0	0	Zorga	0	0	0
Spain	0	1	1	Korac	0	1	1
White	6	2	14	Karoevic	1	0	2
Barrett	3	0	6	Raikovic	2	09	4
Haywood	10	1	21	Cvetkovic	0	3	3
Sc...	2	1	5	Raznatovic	1	0	2
Hosket	1	1	3	Daneu	6	4	16
Fowler	2	0	4	Cosic	1	2	4
Silliman	3	0	6	Sciman	1	3	5
Saulters	2	0	4	Plecas	0	0	0
King	0	1	1	Cermak	4	0	8
Dee	0	0	0	Skansi	2	1	5
Total	**29**	**7**	**65**	**Total**	**18**	**14**	**50**

Half-time score—United States 32, Yugoslavia 29.

utes of the second half, the Yugoslavs had their scorers completely muffled by the aggressive United States defense. The game had gone 7:51 into the second half before the Yugoslavs were able to score from the floor.

Dragutin Cermak dropped in in a basket from the side to break the drought. Cermak, the best scorer for the East European team, was limited to five points wile being hounded by Haywood. Yugoslavia's top scorer was Ivo Daneu, who tallied 13.

In addition to his 23 points,

Haywood had 10 rebounds and blocked five shots.

His individual performance was one of the greatest ever seen in the Olympic Games.

White, who scored six points in the first half, added eight in the second half and played an outstanding all-round game.

The crowd in the domed stadium cheered wildly for the underdog Yugoslavs in the early stages of the game when they led 11-6, but the crowd suddenly shifted its allegiance when Haywood and White went on their rampage.

During this exciting spurt, many American flags appeared in the stands and there were numerous signs. One said "Go Get 'Em Yanks," another said "Yankee Gold Rush, 68."

The American defense was so effective that the Yugoslavs were able to make only seven of 30 shots in the second half. This was due largely to the work of Haywood and White, plus effective ball stealing by Mike Barrett and Charlie Scott.

October 26, 1968

U.C.L.A. DEFEATS PURDUE, 92-72, FOR N.C.A.A. TITLE

ALCINDOR EXCELS

Bruins Win Title 5th Time as Senior Star Gets 37 Points

By GORDON S. WHITE Jr.
Special to The New York Times

LOUISVILLE, Ky., March 22 —An era in collegiate basketball was concluded in the expected manner today when the University of California, Los Angeles, defeated Purdue, 92-72, to win the National Collegiate Athletic Association championship for a record third straight year.

Lew Alcindor, the 7-foot-2-inch New Yorker who created this era, completed his college career in the championship game at Freedom Hall and did so in championship fashion. He scored 37 points and completely dominated the boards.

In a consolation game for third place prior to the championship game, Drake defeated North Carolina, 104-84.

Ever since Alcindor began playing basketball at Power Memorial High School in New York he has been a dominating influence. There was no change from this pattern today before 18,669 persons, most of whom had been rooting for a major upset.

Rick Mount, the nation's No. 2 scorer, was the Boilermakers' chief threat. He had scored 36 points against the Tar Heels. But from the start it was clear the Mount-led Boilermakers were no match for U.C.L.A. and Alcindor. Although Lew's supporting cast was not considered as strong a unit as the players of 1967 and 1968, it complemented Alcindor's performance beyond reproach.

Alcindor Scores Quickly

Alcindor scored the first three U.C.L.A. baskets with those soft shots from close up. He either reaches up and drops the ball through or flips it lightly from inches away. His mates were doing well feeding him inside. Purdue couldn't block the passes in the early stages and Alcindor made 24 points in the first half.

United Press International
IN CONTROL: Lew Alcindor of U.C.L.A. grabbing the rebound from Jerry Johnson of Purdue in the National Collegiate Basketball Association championship at Louisville.

Mount, on the other hand, was stymied. He got only 8 points in the opening half during which U.C.L.A. built a 42-31 lead. The Purdue star managed to hit on only three of 18 field-goal attempts and Purdue had a poor 23.5 per cent in shooting.

Alcindor often moved from his defensive spot under the basket and lumbered toward Mount with a hand held high in an effort to block Mount's attempted shots.

Mount obviously was bothered by this maneuver. The other Bruins, Kenny Heitz in particular, did a fine job guarding against Mount. Mount managed to score 28 points in the game, but his 20 in the second-half came too late. Bill Keller, who scored 20 against North Caro-

lina, got only 11 for the Boilermakers.

It all added up to another record for U.C.L.A., which became the first team to win the N.C.A.A. basketball championship five times. Kentucky is the only other team to have won the title four times. The Bruins have won the five titles in the last six years.

Alcindor and his mates left no doubt that they are the top team in the nation. They displayed their superiority from the outset and Alcindor bowed out just the way he entered U.C.L.A.—a hero.

During Lew's career, the Bruins have won 88 games and lost only two. One defeat came two weeks ago in the regular-season finale when Southern California won and the other was at the hands of Houston in January, 1968.

This season, U.C.L.A. again had a 29-1 won-lost mark. In

his sophomore season, Alcindor's Bruins were undefeated in 30 games.

U.C.L.A. broke open the game after seven minutes of play when Curtis Rowe, Alcindor and Lynn Shackelford gave the Bruins 8 straight points for a 14-6 lead. Within the next four minutes the score rose to 26-10.

The lead increased in the second half and Coach John Wooden benched his starters briefly until Purdue began to hit consistently.

Alcindor and company returned and stemmed the abortive rally.

Lew was removed with one minute 19 seconds left. When the game ended Lew took a chair from the sidelines placed it under a basket and stepped on it so he could more easily cut off the net—the traditional championship trophy.

Alcindor is the first player in history to be named most valuable player in the N.C.A.A. championship tournament for three years in a row after leading the Bruins to their 20th consecutive N.C.A.A. tournament victory. These victories include early-round games.

The tall New Yorker, who took 20 rebounds today, has participated in 12 N.C.A.A. tourney games and has scored a total of 304 points, putting him third behind Elvin Hayes of Houston (358) and Oscar Robertson of Cincinnati (324).

While Lew was performing so expertly on the court, his father played the trombone, in the U.C.L.A. band that was seated directly behind the Bruins' bench.

Mike DiTomasso, an Eastern College Athletic Conference referee who was assigned to the title game, also officiated at Alcindor's final high school contest in 1965 when Power Memorial won the Catholic High Schools Athletic Association championship.

CHAMPIONSHIP GAME

U.C.L.A. (92)	G.	F.	P.	PURDUE (72)	G.	F.	P.
Shackelford	3	5-8	11	Gilliam	2	3-3	7
Rowe	4	4-4	12	Faerber	1	0-0	2
Alcindor	15	7-9	37	Johnson	4	3-4	11
Heitz	0	0-1	0	Mount	12	4-5	28
Vallely	4	7-10	15	Keller	4	3-4	11
Sweek	3	0-1	6	Kaufman	0	2-2	2
Wicks	0	3-6	3	Bedford	3	1-3	7
Schofield	1	0-0	2	Weatherford	1	2-2	4
Patterson	1	2-2	4	Reasoner	0	0-1	0
Farmer	0	0-0	0	Taylor	0	0-0	0
Ecker	1	0-0	2	Selbert	0	0-0	0
Totals	32	28-41	92	Totals	27	18-24	72

Half-time score—U.C.L.A. 42, Purdue 31.
Fouled out—Faerber, Kaufman.
Attendance—18,669.

March 23, 1969

MARAVICH SCORES 69 POINTS IN LOSS

Sets League Mark—L.S.U. Players Battle Fans After Alabama Wins, 106-104

By The Associated Press

TUSCALOOSA, Ala., Feb. 7— A rough, wide-open basketball game ended in a brawl between players and fans as Alabama beat Louisiana State, 106-104, today.

Pete Maravich of L.S.U., who played on sore legs, poured in 69 points for a Southeastern Conference record, getting 47 in the second half. He raised his career scoring record to 3,157 and broke his own conference-game mark of 61 set earlier this season against Vanderbilt.

Alabama scored a flurry of baskets with about eight minutes left in the game to take a 7-point lead and was never headed.

Maravich pursued a spectator when he left the floor at the end of the game, and several other L.S.U. players became involved in a fight with fans. The brawl was broken up quickly without any injuries.

The loss left L.S.U. with a 6-3 won-lost S.E.C. mark and 12-6 over all.

Alabama is 3-7 in the league and 6-12 for the season.

Alabama was led by Jimmy Hollon, who scored 30 points before fouling out in the final minutes.

Maravich sank 26 baskets and connected on 17 of 21 free throws to break his own record of 66 points for an S.E.C. player set against Tulane, a nonconference rival, last season.

He was charged with a technical foul in the first half, as was his father, Coach Press Maravich, late in the game. Danny Hester, L.S.U.'s second leading scorer, was thrown out of the game in the first half for striking an Alabama player.

Alabama overcame an early 21-16 deficit to take a 44-40 half-time lead. The lead changed hands several times in the second half before Hollon led the Crimson Tide's surge.

Coach Maravich would not let reporters talk to his son after the game, but said the younger Maravich had been hit on the back by the fan he was pursuing before being restrained.

February 8, 1970

U.C.L.A. TOPS JACKSONVILLE 80-69, FOR N.C.A.A. TITLE

4TH CROWN IN ROW

By GORDON S. WHITE Jr.
Special to The New York Times

COLLEGE PARK, Md., March 21—The day may come when a team other than the University of California, Los Angeles, wins the National Collegiate Athletic Association basketball championship. But that time seemed a long way off today as the Bruins utilized all their talent in defeating tall Jacksonville University, 80-69, to gain their fourth straight N.C.A.A. crown.

For three years, Coach John Wooden's Bruins easily moved to this championship as 7-foot-2-inch Lew Alcindor led the parade for titles. Following Alcindor's last N.C.A.A. championship game a year ago, many fans expected a new team to win the title this year.

What they overlooked was the fact that Wooden had a team that still could produce. He and U.C.L.A. adjusted to height problems and the Bruins gained their sixth basketball championship in seven years.

The victory was a tribute to U.C.L.A.'s starting five, who carried the Bruins from an early 9-point deficit to the triumph over the giants from Florida before 14,380 persons in the University of Maryland's Cole Field House. Curtis Rowe, Steve Patterson, Sidney Wicks, John Vallely and Henry Bibby started, adjusted, gained the lead and played 38 minutes before Wooden, satisfied that the title was in hand, took his heroes out.

Prior to this record performance by the Bruins, New Mexico State defeated St. Bonaventure, 79-73, in the consolation game for third place. Greg Gary of the Bonnies led the scoring with 22 points, but the Bonnies once again missed their big man, Bob Lanier, who was sidelined with a torn leg ligament.

Four of U.C.L.A.'s starters had 15 or more points and Bibby, who performs tricky maneuvers on the floor, scored 8 in the winning effort. But more than the scoring, the defense and surprising rebounding enabled U.C.L.A. to prevail.

Jacksonville, which assembled a strong team in a major recruiting campaign during the last two years, had Artis Gilmore, 7 feet 2 inches, and Rex Morgan, a 6-5 guard, who, with Gilmore, had been billed as Batman and Robin.

But all was sad in Gotham City tonight.

Jacksonville took an early lead of 12-4 before U.C.L.A. could get its defense organized. In addition the Bruins lacked ball control, turning over the ball about ten times in the first 10 minutes of play.

But U.C.L.A. settled down and then whittled away, cutting Jacksonville down to size.

Sidney Wicks, a 6-8 cornerman, was the key to the success. Assigned to defend against Gilmore, Wicks appeared headed for trouble when he drew two personal fouls within four minutes.

He played behind his taller opponent and was detected bumping when he went up with soft drop shots.

Wooden changed the alignment, stationing Wicks in front of Gilmore. Then Wicks no longer bumped Gilmore on the way up but he did manage to get more rebounds, many on missed shots by the big fellow. Wicks grabbed off 18 rebounds in the game, two more than Gilmore, who had averaged 23 rebounds a game during the season. Rarely has Gilmore been outrebounded as Jacksonville posted 27 victories against one loss prior to today.

Wicks, who was selected as the outstanding player of the tournament by the sports writers, drew only one more foul, while Gilmore was the first player to foul out when he received his fifth with 2 minutes to play. The next to foul out was the other half of dynamic duo—Morgan.

This was a game of turnaround. The Bruins, who trailed by 9 points with 9½ minutes to play in the first half, caught and passed the Dolphins with 1:20 left before intermission.

Bibby, the shortest of the Bruins, took a pass from Vallely on a fast break to make the score, 37-36, for U.C.L.A. Thereafter the West Coast champions never trailed.

U.C.L.A. then stepped up the tempo and Jacksonville was unable to keep up. Speed has always been a trademark of Wooden teams — speed with purpose and design on attack. This became evident during the second-half surge.

Rowe would run and connect from a corner. He scored 19 points to tie Gilmore for scoring honors. Patterson stayed at the line and hit with one-handed shots for 17 points, the same total that Wicks got shooting from inside, outside and from all angles. Vallely, the other guard with Bibby, shot from afar and tallied 15.

Defensively, the Bruins checked Morgan, who averaged 17.7 points this season, holding him to 10. Vallely defended expertly against Robin of Jacksonville.

Playing man-to-man at the guard positions and zone inside most of the time, U.C.L.A. did a fine restraining job against a team that scored more than 100 points in 18 games during the season and averaged well over 100 a game.

Thus U.C.L.A. retained its title. The Bruins have won a record 24 straight games in N.C.A.A. tournament play, winning four in each of its championship years—1964, 1965 and 1967 through 1970. U.C.L.A. did not win the Pacific Eight Conference title in 1966 so it did not play in the N.C.A.A. tournament that year.

There is good reason to expect a long reign by U.C.L.A. as four of its starters—Wicks, Rowe, Vallely and Bibby—are either juniors or sophomores.

CHAMPIONSHIP GAME

U.C.L.A. (80)	G.	F.	P.	JACKSONVILLE (69)	G.	F.	P.
Rowe	7	5-5	19	Wedeking	6	0-0	12
Patterson	8	1-4	17	Blevins	1	1-2	3
Wicks	5	7-10	17	Morgan	5	0-0	10
Vallely	5	5-7	15	Burrows	6	0-0	12
Bibby	2	4-4	8	Gilmore	9	1-1	19
Booker	0	2-3	2	Nelson	3	2-2	8
Seibert	0	0-1	0	Dublin	0	2-2	2
Ecker	1	0-0	2	Baldwin	0	0-0	0
Betchley	0	0-0	0	McIntyre	0	0-0	0
Chapman	0	0-0	0	Hawkins	0	1-1	1
Hill	0	0-1	0	Selke	0	0-0	0
Schofield	0	0-0	0				
Total	28	24-35	80	Total	31	7-8	69

Half-time score—U.C.L.A. 41, Jacksonville 36.
Fouled out—Gilmore, Morgan.
Attendance—14,380.

March 22, 1970

U.C.L.A. GAINS N.C.A.A. TITLE

VILLANOVA LOSES

Bruins Score, 68-62, and Capture Crown 5th Year in Row

By GORDON S. WHITE, Jr.
Special to The New York Times

HOUSTON, March 27—Villanova came closer to beating the University of California, Los Angeles in the final of the National Collegiate basketball tournament today than any of the Bruins' six previous opponents in N.C.A.A. title games.

But in the end it was the same old story as Coach John Wooden's Bruins forced Villanova to play their game and U.C.L.A. held firmly to win, 68-62, for its fifth straight N.C.A.A. championship and seventh in eight years.

Despite many boos from the crowd of 31,376 persons in the Astrodome, U.C.L.A. went into a stall late in the first half. The maneuver forced a change in Villanova's style and helped the Bruins add another notch to their record of most N.C.A.A. basketball titles by a single university.

Western Kentucky edged Kansas, 77-75, for third place. Jim McDaniels led the Hilltoppers with 36 points.

Villanova Gets Close

Villanova, the first Northeastern team in the final in 16 years, was within 3 points of U.C.L.A. with 1 minute 53 seconds to play. Coach Jack Kraft of Villanova said, "I thought we had an excellent shot at them. But that goal-tending call was a big play."

He referred to a play with 38 seconds remaining when Steve Patterson, U.C.L.A.'s tallest man, drove in for a shot and Villanova's Howard Porter, in desperation, slammed the ball against the backboard. The goal was awarded to Patterson, giving the Bruins a 66-60 lead.

The closest any team had come to beating U.C.L.A. in the Bruins' championship games was 11 points. Both Michigan in 1965 and Jacksonville last year lost to the Bruins by that margin.

Porter Voted Top Player

Some unexpected actions took place in today's game. One occurred when U.C.L.A. forced Villanova to switch from its outstanding zone defense to man-to-man defense. Another was Patterson's game high of 29 points. His career high had been 22 points, made this season.

Kraft said, "The game was played a bit differently than I expected. But I thought we did an excellent job in our man-to-man defense."

Porter had to play Sidney Wicks, one of the nation's best players, in that man-to-man setup. Porter did so well against Wicks that he was named the tournament's outstanding player.

Porter scored 25 points and took eight rebounds. Wicks had nine rebounds but scored only 7 points.

U.C.L.A. went into its slowdown late in the first half while leading by 11 points. It had a 45-37 lead at intermission and came right back with the slowdown at the start of the second half.

Five minutes later, U.C.L.A. got what it wanted. Villanova called time and switched to the man-to-man defense. U.C.L.A. continued its deliberate attack for most of the remaining time.

Siemiontkowski a Worry

Kraft said later that he wasn't too concerned about playing man-to-man defense per se. "But I was a little worried about Hank Siemiontkowski, who had three fouls on him when we went to man-to-man."

The slowdown early in the second half annoyed Clarence Smith, one of Villanova's tallest men. He said to U.C.L.A.'s Henry Bibby during the action, "Don't be pussy cats." A few seconds later, Smith said to Curtis Rowe of U.C.L.A., "You're national champions. Play ball."

The slowdown may have helped Villanova to stay close because U.C.L.A. wasn't shooting very often in that situation. An occasional steal by the Wildcats helped to cut the margin slightly.

U.C.L.A. was at its best on defense and Villanova was unable to use its running game and get the fast breaks it wanted. U.C.L.A. pressed full court most of the first half to prevent the Wildcats from running. Then the Bruins stopped the fast break most of the second half and Villanova was forced to go downcourt and work plays.

Jump Shot by Porter

When Porter hit a jump shot from the left corner, Villanova got to a 63-60 deficit and the fans were screaming for the

United Press International

GIVING THE HIGH SIGN: Sidney Wicks, all-America star for U.C.L.A., forming number one with three seconds to go in the Bruins' championship victory over Villanova.

big upset. But Bibby hit a free throw and Patterson got the goaltending 2 points for the assurance of victory.

The Bruins jumped to the early lead and were in front to stay after nine minutes. They got there largely by hitting from a distance, the usual way to upset a zone.

Yet Villanova would not move out of the tight zone just because the defending champions were bombing above their heads for 2 points regularly. It took the slowdown to change Villanova.

Patterson had an amazing game. He is a 6-foot-10-inch senior whom one expects to score from inside. But he hit from good range, as did Bibby, the little guard who made 17 points. It was a fine finish to Patterson's career. As the tall man on the team, he had a difficult act to follow when he became a starter for the Bruins last season. He succeeded Lew Alcindor, the 7-footer who took U.C.L.A. to three of the titles in a row.

Notre Dame Lone Conqueror

For U.C.L.A., it was almost routine. These Bruins are used to this road to victory and they made it as the N.C.A.A. championship team with a 1970-71 record of 29 victories and one loss—89-82 to Notre Dame in midseason.

Villanova made its best mark in history in its ninth N.C.A.A. tournament. Never before had the Wildcats gained the semifinals. And they reached the final after a thrilling double-overtime victory over Western Kentucky in that semifinal Thursday night.

Villanova finished with a 27-7 won-lost record. Siemiontkowski, who scored 31 points against Western Kentucky Thursday, and Porter were named to the tournament allstar team along with Patterson, Wicks and McDaniels.

The crowd today set a record for an N.C.A.A. final but it was the first non-sellout at a championship in 20 years. This arena holds 51,000 persons for basketball.

CHAMPIONSHIP GAME

U.C.L.A. (68)	G.	F.	P.	VILLANOVA (62)	G.	F.	P.
Rowe	2	4-5	8	Ingelsby	3	1-1	7
Wicks	3	1-1	7	Smntkwsk	9	1-2	19
Patterson	13	3-5	29	Ford	0	2-3	2
Bibby	6	5-5	17	Smith	4	1-1	9
Booker	0	0-0	0	Porter	10	5-6	25
Schofield	3	0-0	6	McDowell	0	0-0	0
Bechley	0	1-2	1	Fox	0	0-0	0
Total	27	14-18	68	Total	26	10-13	62

Half-time score—U.C.L.A. 45, Villanova 37. Attendance—31,765.

March 28, 1971

VILLANOVA OFFERS TO FORFEIT SLATE

Move Follows Disclosure of Porter's A.B.A. Agreement

PHILADELPHIA, June 17 (UPI) — Villanova University gave up its honors in the 1970-71 National Collegiate Athletic Association basketball season today because a previously denied professional agreement apparently made Howard Porter, its No. 1 player, ineligible.

The forfeit followed public disclosure in United States District Court in New York yesterday of documents signed by Porter, indicating that for an initial payment of $15,000 he agreed last Dec. 16 to play in the American Basketball Association. The agreement, initialed by Jack Dolph, A.B.A. commissioner, was turned over to the Pittsburgh Condors when they drafted Porter.

Porter, who eventually signed with the Chicago Bulls of the National Basketball Association for $1.5-million, repudiated the A.B.A. agreement and signed an affidavit for Villanova on Feb. 4 saying that he did nothing to violate N.C.A.A. rules and jeopardize the team's eligibility. A newspaper reporter in Charlotte, N. C., contended in January that he had seen Porter's name on an A.B.A. contract in Dolph's motel room.

School's Best Record

With the 6-foot-8-inch Porter gaining fame as the N.C.A.A. tournament's most valuable player, the Wildcats upset Pennsylvania and Western Kentucky before losing to University of California, Los Angeles in the championship game, 68-62, and finishing their best season with a 26-7 won-lost record.

After a conference of Villanova officials this morning, the Rev. Robert J. Welsh, university president, sent a letter to the N.C.A.A. forfeiting honors and "tournament receipts." Villanova received $66,000 for its second-place finish.

"In view of the evidence produced in the United States District Court in New York in the last few days, we must presume, unless Howard Porter can demonstrate otherwise, that Villanova was not eligible to compete in the National Collegiate basketball championship tournament this year," the letter read.

Villanova asked the N.C.A.A. for a hearing on the matter "in justice to Mr. Porter" and offered to "render any assistance it could" at the hearing.

"However, in the absence of any additional information, Villanova University will and should forfeit its record in the season and tournament and any receipts to which it would otherwise be entitled," the letter concluded.

Richard G. Phillips, a former Villanova football player who is Porter's attorney, said he was sure Porter had the option to decline a hearing, "but I doubt we would elect to choose that option." He said he would discuss the matter with both Porter and Villanova officials.

June 18, 1971

Why Villanova?

Basketball Fans Wonder When and If N.C.A.A. Will Quiz Other Schools

By SAM GOLDAPER

Why Villanova?

Why not dozens of other colleges?

That's what basketball followers were asking after Villanova forfeited its best season in history last Wednesday. Villanova's decision was based on documented evidence that its star, Howard Porter, had received $15,000 through an agent last Dec. 16 as part payment for signing an American Basketball Association document. The document later was turned over to the Pittsburgh Condors, the team that had drafted Porter first.

The move by Rev. Robert J. Welsh, president of Villanova, hardly closes the issue. If anything, it calls for a more intensive investigation by the National Collegiate Athletic Association or a restudy and a change in policy.

The N.C.A.A. has rules (O.I. 12 and 13) that prohibit players from having agents and prohibits players from signing pro contracts before the completion of their collegiate eligibility.

Yet, the N.C.A.A. has either looked the other way or found the rule unenforcable since player agents started running rampant three years ago.

The N.C.A.A. was unavailable for comment on whether it plans to investigate schools other than Villanova. But Richard G. Phillips, who has represented Porter since the

former Villanova star asked him to do so last March, said, "If the N.C.A.A. is going to investigate every college basketball team that played with at least one member having violated the N.C.A.A. eligibility rules, Tufts will wind up as the national champion."

Bulls' Coach Comments

Dick Motta, the coach of the Chicago Bulls of the National Basketball Association, may have put it best recently when he said, "The N.C.A.A. doesn't want to admit it's running a pro operation." Motta, not one who usually minces his words, has coached in the college and professional ranks. Three years ago when the big business of player agents started up with the player dollar war between the N.B.A. and the A.B.A., he was coaching at Weber State.

Early last basketball season, Don Kennedy, the St. Peter's coach, speaking to the Metropolitan Basketball Writers' Association, also warned of agent tampering and said some had approached his star, Rich Rinaldi.

Al McGuire, the Marquette coach, has taken a more realistic view of the talent war. Referring to his own star, Jim Chones, leaving college before the completion of his senior year to sign with the pros, he said, "I wouldn't blame him if he signed. I have looked in his refrigerator and in mine, and mine has meats, pastries and other goodies.

"His was empty, so why blame any kid who is tempted by $250,000 to sign. They can always finish college in summer school and be that much richer, too."

It's difficult to believe that Porter was the only one who wasn't telling the truth.

Not when player agents were introducing themselves at the Holiday Inn in Greensboro, N. C., the site of the A.B.A. draft, last January, revealing the names of players they represented.

Negotiations at N.I.T.

Also, the hectic negotiations took place last March among coaches, general managers, N.B.A. and A.B.A. officials and player agents during the National Invitation Tournament at Madison Square Garden. They were not there to see the games, but to talk dollars before the N.B.A. draft.

Wasn't it odd that players of the caliber of Porter, Artis Gilmore of Jacksonville and Jim McDaniels of Western Kentucky were not selected on the first round of the N.B.A. draft? Or that Sid Wicks of U.C.L.A. and Austin Carr of Notre Dame were not chosen on the first round of the A.B.A. draft? Ken Durrett of LaSalle, the Cincinnati Royals' No. 1 draft pick, had Pro Sports Inc. claiming to be his agent early in the season. But it was Tom Gola, his former coach, who got him the final legal advice.

The N.B.A. and A.B.A. selected players on the first round.

that they knew they could sign because negotiations had been going on long before their drafts. Many agents, too, are known to favor one league or the other, a determining factor in the negotiations.

At the Jan. 23 A.B.A. draft, Gilmore was not offered to the team with the worst record in the league, as is the usual practice, but to the team able to meet the agent's demands. A day after Jacksonville's elimination from the N.C.A.A. tournament, Gilmore's signing was announced by the Kentucky Colonels of the A.B.A.—hardly enough time to negotiate a million-dollar-plus contract.

Carl Scheer, who gained his experience negotiating and battling against the A.B.A. when he was administrative assistant to Walter Kennedy, the N.B.A. commissioner, took all that experience with him when he became president of the Carolina Cougars of the A.B.A. Wasn't it during the A.B.A. draft that a deal was made to sign McDaniels to a personal service contract with the Cougars, shutting out the Utah Stars, who had drafted him No. 1?

Heyday for Agents

Things have changed radically in college basketball in the four years since the emergence of the A.B.A. to challenge the supremacy of the N.B.A. and create the dollar war.

Agents, charging 5 and 10 per cent commissions on contracts, have sprung up everywhere. They are lawyers, like Norman Blass, Bob Wolff, Arthur Morse, Lou Schaffel and Jerry Davis. They are an owner of a dry-cleaning establishment, a scout for an N.B.A. team, a builder, a stockbroker and a trainer for a college team.

These agents have worked right under the view of college coaches and officials. Most of last year's top players were talked to as sophomores as agents battled between themselves for representation rights.

Some agents have paid players $300 a month during their remaining stay in college to get them under contract.

"What have we to lose?" said one agent. "It's a gamble. Like playing the stock market, shooting dice or playing poker for high stakes. We invest a couple of thousand dollars and get that back and a lot more as our commission when he signs a contract."

The 6-foot-8-inch Porter, the most valuable player in the N.C.A.A. tournament when his team was beaten by U.C.L.A. for the championship, later repudiated the A.B.A. agreement and signed with the Chicago Bulls.

Denial by Dolph

Yet, when a newspaper in Charlotte, N. C., contended in January that Porter's name had been seen on an A.B.A. contract in the motel room of Jack Dolph, the A.B.A. commissioner, Dolph denied the allegation.

Dolph, commenting on the Porter case, was quoted in the Jan. 26 issue of The New York Times:

"I deny the existence of any contract which binds a player on his part to play in the A.B.A. I have, and so has the N.B.A., and so have many individual teams, talked to persons claiming to represent college players. In those cases we have made offers to agents, which they can offer to specific players when it's appropriate. All of our dealings have been with agents and not players."

Dolph, reached at his home Friday night, refused to comment on the Porter issue at this time, but said, "Did you see where the Cincinnati Reds signed a 15-year-old kid pitcher the other day? Try that for morality."

And when Porter was asked if he had signed an A.B.A. contract, during an investigation by Villanova, he said, "Why should I? It would hurt my bargaining rights."

Yet the documented evidence that appeared in the Philadelphia Evening Bulletin showed contract correspondences between Dolph and Porter and the check for $15,000 given Porter was signed by Thurlo McCrady, the executive director of the A.B.A.

Again, why Villanova?

June 20, 1971

U.C.L.A. TAKES 6TH TITLE IN ROW

FLA. STATE LOSES

Bruins Take N.C.A.A. Final by 81-76 as Walton Tallies 24

By GORDON S. WHITE Jr.
Special to The New York Times

LOS ANGELES, March 25— There may come a day when the University of California, Los Angeles is no longer the National Collegiate basketball champion. But that time seemed far off today after the Bruins defeated Florida State, 81-76, to give U.C.L.A. its sixth consecutive national title and eighth in the last nine seasons.

This latest edition of Coach John Wooden's teams, with a starting cast of three sophomores and only one senior, Henry Bibby, did its usual thing by completing an unbeaten season with its 30th victory of 1971-72 and its 45th triumph in a row over two seasons.

There were some moments early in the final when U.C.L.A. was behind. But they were hardly cause for worry as the Bruins kept cool and came back as big Bill Walton began to score.

N. Carolina Takes 3d

However, following the game, Walton talked as if he had just lost. The sophomore, in a position to enjoy the first national championship of his life and selected as the outstanding player in the tournament, said:

"We didn't play well. There's no reason for elation. We don't like to back into things."

Someone said, "You sound like you lost."

"I feel like it," Walton said.

Nevertheless, it still remained an exciting event for the U.C.L.A. fans, who made up most of the crowd of 15,063 in the Los Angeles Sports Arena. They acted as if they can't get enough of national championships.

North Carolina defeated Louisville, 105-91, in the consolation game for third place.

Florida State opened in its race-horse fashion and managed to gain a lead as big as 7 points in the first 6½ minutes. The Seminoles accomplished this by virtue of hitting from outside rather consistently.

There were shots by Greg Samuel, Ron King, Rowland Garrett and Reggie Royals of Florida State that ranged from 10 to 21 feet while the South-

Associated Press

BIG MAN FOR U.C.L.A.: Bill Walton, a sophomore, towering over Florida State's Ron Harris (10), Roland Garrett (23) and Reggie Royals to score at Los Angeles.

erners were moving out front. Wooden sat calmly through this and, after the game said, "You can get behind because of excellent outside shooting but not beaten by outside shooting."

King Is High Scorer

In that early going, Walton didn't make a basket although he had a few of his inside shots and rebound attempts. The 6-foot-11-inch sophomore star finally got his first field goal on a six-foot bank shot that tied the count at 21-21.

From then on, he kept more to form, hitting well and going on to finish with 24 points. King was the game's high scorer with 27 for Florida State.

Walton did run into foul problem and Wooden sat him down for 6 minutes late in the game because the sophomore was carrying four personals. But U.C.L.A. was ahead, 67-56, when he went to the bench and still ahead, 77-68, when he returned to play out most of the remaining 5 minutes.

It had been the hope of the Seminoles to crack U.C.L.A.'s press defense with the fast-charging offense that broke open North Carolina's press defense in the semifinals Thursday night. There were moments early in the game as U.C.L.A. and Florida State both turned the ball over a few times and the Seminoles got away with some quick baskets.

But the Bruins played steadily and began to control their defense. When Tommy Curtis, a nonstarting sophomore, hit on a 12-foot baseline shot, U.C.L.A. took a 27-25 lead, never to fall behind or be tied again.

From this point on, U.C.L.A. got the ball in high to Walton's reaching hands over even the tall Seminoles, such as Royals (6-10) and Larry McCray (6-11). With the ball up there, Walton could turn and get his shots that gave him nine field goals in 17 tries.

Bibby, who appeared happier than Walton about the victory, registered 18 points in his last game for the Bruins. This fine guard from Franklinton, N.C., has never missed a start in three varsity seasons. That added up to 60 games, most of which were outstanding personal efforts.

As the point man in the attack, Bibby did another good job governing the attack against Florida State when it had to be deliberate.

Walton picked off 20 rebounds to lead U.C.L.A.'s domination of the backboards as the Bruins took 48 to 36 for the Seminoles.

The game was won inside because Walton dominated the play, moving extremely well for a man of his height. Not as physically strong as Lew

Alcindor was when he played at U.C.L.A., Walton, however, covers a wider range because of his mobility. He cuts off more shots and shoots from more spots than Alcindor did.

Alcindor (known now as Kareem Abdul-Jabbar) led the Bruins to the first three of their consecutive national championships, 1967-69. Walton is expected by many to lead U.C.L.A. to three titles in a row also. He got one leg on that today and will have another excellent supporting cast next season despite the loss of Bibby.

Thus U.C.L.A. added to its record of N.C.A.A. basketball achievements. Kentucky is the

closest to the Bruins with four national titles.

This marked the first season following a three-year probation period that Florida State was eligible for this tourney. The Seminoles entered the tourney with a 23-5 won-lost record and advanced by winning the Mideast regional and then its semi-final game with North Carolina.

U.C.L.A. (81)				FLORIDA ST. (76)			
	G.	F.	P.		G.	F.	P.
Wilkes	11	1-2	23	Garrett	1	1-1	3
Farmer	2	0-0	4	Royals	5	5-6	15
Walton	9	6-11	24	McCray	3	2-5	8
Bibby	8	2-3	18	King	12	3-3	27
Lee	1	0-0	0	Samuel	3	0-0	6
Holyfild	1	0-0	2	Harris	7	2-3	16
Curtis	4	0-1	8	Petty	0	1-1	1
Nater	1	0-1	2	Cole	0	0-0	0
Total	36	9-18	81	Total	31	14-19	76

Half-time score—U.C.L.A. 50, Florida ST. 39.
Fouled out—McCray.
Attendance—15,063.

NO. CAR. (105)				LOUISVILLE (91)			
	G.	F.	P.		G.	F.	P.
Chamb'lain	4	1-	9	Lawhon	4	5-6	13
Wuycik	8	11-16	27	Thomas	5	4-6	14
McAdoo	12	6-6	30	Vilcheck	3	2-3	8
Previs	2	3-5	7	Price	9	5-7	23
Karl	6	4-5	16	Bacon	3	6-8	12
Jones	4	3-4	11	Bunton	2	1-2	5
Johnston	0	0-0	0	Carter	1	0-0	2
Hite	0	1-3	1	Bradley	1	0-0	2
Chambers	0	4-4	4	Cooper	2	4-5	8
Corson	0	0-0	0	Meiman	0	0-0	0
Huband	0	0-0	0	Stallings	1	0-0	2
Eiston	0	0-0	0	Pry	1	0-0	2
Total	36	33-44	105	Total	32	27-37	91

Half-time score—North Carolina 51, Louisville 34.
Fouled out—Chamberlain, Karl, Jones, Price.
Attendance—13,362.

March 26, 1972

N.C.A.A. Expands Basketball Tourney

By SAM GOLDAPER

The National Collegiate Athletic Association will expand its championship basketball tournament to 28 teams in 1974. The additional three teams will come from new conference champions, still undecided, which will receive automatic bids. To make room for the new teams, first-round byes will be limited to one team in each of the four regions.

The byes each year will be decided on the winning percentages of the conference champions in N.C.A.A. play over a 10-year span.

The 1974 byes have been awarded to the Atlantic Coast Conference champion in the East; the Big Ten in the Mideast; Missouri Valley in the Midwest and the Pacific-8 Conference in the West.

The Southeastern, Big Eight and West Coast Athletic Conference champions; which had first-round byes in the last tournament, have lost them for 1974.

"We have had a big demand from the various new conferences for automatic bids," said Tom Scott, the athletic director at Davidson and chairman of the N.C.A.A. Basketball Conference, by telephone from North Carolina. "We have to open up automatic bids to new conference champions. We can't afford to cut down on any of our at-large teams."

Four Pressure Groups

Scott said much of the pressure for automatic conference bids has come from the Southland, Yankee, Midwestern and Eastern Athletic Conference.

The Yankee Conference used to have an automatic bid, but lost it when the quality of play among its teams deteriorated.

The Southland Conference championship was won by Southwestern Louisiana in its

first season of major-college competition. Southwestern Louisiana, which had the nation's leading major-college scorer in Dwight Lamar, played in last week's N.C.A.A. tournament, but was chosen as an at-large member.

Northern Illinois won the Midwestern Conference title, finished with a 19-4 won-lost record, but was snubbed by the N.C.A.A. and the National Invitation Tournament.

The Eastern Athletic Association, of which Howard is a member, is a seven-team conference composed of predominantly-black universities.

"We will make our decision when our committee meets on June 19 in Colorado Springs," said Scott. "We will then make our recommendations to the N.C.A.A. Executive Council."

What will the addition of three new teams do to the N.I.T., which had its lowest per game attendance since 1958?

"I don't think it will hurt the N.I.T. one bit," said Scott. "The college players and teams are getting better all the time and there will always be enough left over for the N.I.T."

March 28, 1972

SOVIET QUINTET WINS, 51-50, ENDING U.S. SUPREMACY
Disputed Basket Halts Streak

By NEIL AMDUR
Special to The New York Times

MUNICH, West Germany, Sunday, Sept. 10—In a chaotic finish unparalleled for the sport of basketball, the Soviet Union snapped the 63-game winning streak of the United States, 51-50, early this morning and won the Olympic gold medal.

The official result of the game, however, was delayed pending a protest made by Hank Iba, the American coach, and a hastily arranged meeting of a five-member jury of the International Amateur Basketball Federation (FIBA).

Ken Davis, the player representative for the American team, said the players would not accept a silver medal if the appeal was turned down. Davis said the vote had been unanimous.

A short while later, the F.I.B.A. jury said that it would announce its decision at 8 A.M. Sunday, New York time.

Iba's protest concerned the almost unbelievable events that occurred during the final few seconds of the game, after the United States took the lead for the first time on two foul shots by Doug Collins with three seconds left.

The Soviet Union took possession after the shots and put the ball in play from under its basket. The inbounds pass was deflected, however, and when time ran out, the American players began jumping up and down excitedly on the court believing they had won the game and the gold medal.

Their joy was short-lived. A ruling was issued at courtside by Robert Jones, secretary-general of FIBA.

The exact details of the ruling remain in conflict over whether Jones had decided that the Soviet Union had called time before putting the ball in play or whether the official clock was in error and showed only one second when the Soviet team took possession.

Either way, Jones informed the officials and the two coaches that the clock would be reset with three seconds left and

the Soviet team again would have one last play.

The 68-year-old Iba, who had coached American gold medal teams in 1964 and 1968, angrily stalked after the referees and the F.I.B.A. officials and had to be restrained by his players.

After order was restored at courtside, a Soviet player tried a desperation baseball pass that traveled the length of the court to Aleksander Belov, a muscular 6-foot-8-inch forward, who was being guarded under the American basket by Kevin Joyce and James Forbes.

All three players went up for the ball, but Joyce and Forbes were knocked to the floor in the battle for position.

Belov grabbed the ball at the full extension of his jump, brought it down and then went back up again for the layup that sealed the Soviet victory before a stunned and confused crowd.

Chaos ensued. Iba again rushed to the scorer's table, Forbes wept unabashedly, and photographers, newsmen and irate fans flooded onto the floor.

"I don't think it's possible to have made that play in three seconds," Iba shouted. "There's no damn way he can get that shot off in time."

Player Must Touch

Under international rules, the clock does not start on inbounds plays until the ball is touched.

"I've never seen anything like this in all my years of basket-

ball," Iba said later.

Both referees, a Bulgarian and Brazilian, signed the scoresheets after the game. Iba, however, refused and issued the formal protest that prompted the meeting of the F.I.B.A. jury.

The jury will have to consider several questions in what seems an endless number of disputes that have marred the two weeks of Olympic competition.

One question will be why a horn was sounded as Collins released the ball for his second foul shot?

Another is whether the Soviet team, in fact, called time after the first foul shot or whether they attempted a time-out after the second.

Delayed by Television

The game was unusual, in a sense, even before the first shot

United Press International

Alshan Sharmukhamedov of the Soviet Union shooting against Ed Ratleff of the U.S.

was taken. In deference to a request by the American Broadcasting Company two years ago, F.I.B.A. officials, along with the German organizing committee, agreed to schedule the final championship game for 11:30 last night here or 6:30 P.M. Saturday in New York.

The game would have been played Friday night, and thus in prime television time, but for the fact that all Olympic events were postponed a day because of the tragedies last Tuesday.

The final began at 11:45 last night, perhaps the first time that any basketball game was ever played at such a ridiculously late hour. It did not end until 1:14 this morning and as late as 3 A.M. (Munich time), players, fans and officials were lingering in the dressing rooms and tunnels waiting for a decision from the F.I.B.A. jury.

The Soviet five had led by as many as 10 points (38-28) with 10 minutes left and by 8 points with 6:07 left.

But the Americans changed defensive tactics and applied a full-court press in the last four minutes, and Joyce, the New Yorker who attends the University of South Carolina, hit a pair of baskets to close the deficit to 44-42.

Despite playing the last seven minutes without a field goal, before Belov's basket, the Russians managed to preserve their lead into the final minute.

But Collins picked up a loose ball at midcourt and drove for the basket with six seconds to play. He was fouled in the act of shooting and was knocked down, but still managed to convert both free throws, despite the horn sounding mysteriously as he was about to release the ball on his second shot.

The protest, signed by W. K. Summers, the United States basketball chairman, was delivered to the five-member jury at 2 A.M. The jury was composed of representatives from Italy, Puerto Rico, Cuba, Poland and Spain.

The United States had won every basketball game in the Olympics since the sport joined the Games in 1936. But the Soviet team had practiced together for almost a year, won eight of nine games during a tour in the United States last year and had a total of 739 international games among its starting five entering the Olympics, compared to only seven games for the American line-up, composed predominantly of collegians.

Neither team shot well. The Americans made only 19 of 57

The Box Score

SOVIET (51)	G	F	P	U.S. (50)	G	F	P
Polivoda	0	0-0	0	Davis	0	0-0	0
Paulauskas	0	3-4	3	Collins	1	6-6	8
Sxakndliidze	2	4-8	8	Henderson	4	1-2	9
Snrmkhmdv	1	2-4	4	Bantom	1	0-2	2
Boloshev	2	0-0	4	R. Jones	0	0-0	0
Edeshko	0	0-0	0	D. Jones	2	2-4	6
S. Belov	8	4-6	20	Forbes	1	0-0	2
Korkia	1	2-2	4	Brewer	3	3-4	9
Dvorni	0	0-0	0	Burleson	0	0-0	0
Volnov	0	0-0	0	McMillen	1	0-0	2
A. Belov	3	2-4	8	Joyce	3	0-0	6
Kovalenko	0	0-0	0	Ratleff	3	0-0	6
Total	17	17-28	51	Total	19	12-18	50

Half-Time score--Soviet 26, United States 21.
Fouled out--Bantom.
Attendance--6,500.

field-goal attempts, for 33 per cent, and not one player reached double figures. The Soviet team shot 36 per cent.

The main thrust of the protest concerned the extra three seconds granted the Soviet team. The Americans' contention was that, according to F.I.B.A. rules, the game was over.

"The U.S.A. was shooting the second of a two-shot foul," the protest read. "This free throw was made. At the point the free throw was made, there were three seconds remaining. At this point, according to F.I.B.A. rules . . . neither team can call a time-out."

The Americans also contended that the official scoresheet did not show a time-out in the last three seconds.

"The opponents played the

ball and ran off two seconds," the protest went on. According to F.I.B.A. rules, this was the only official way to continue the game. With one second remaining, spectators ran onto the playing court. The referees stopped the game at this time. At this point [one second remaining], according to F.I.B.A. rules, they acted correctly.

"When the spectators were removed, the game was started with one second to go. The one second was played and the horn sounded, officially ending the game. The official score, 50 United States, 49 Soviet Union.

"According to F.I.B.A. rules, the game is officially over."

In discussing the situation in a crowded news conference, Iba said, "We had already used one second when they put the ball in play the first time. But they put three seconds on the clock instead of putting up two."

Williams Wins Long Jump

The basketball finish capped another strange day for the United States. In track and field, the Americans also were frustrated despite a gold-medal performance by Randy Williams, a 19-year-old Californian, who won the long jump when his first attempt stood up.

September 10, 1972

U.C.L.A. BEATS NOTRE DAME FOR RECORD 61ST IN ROW

BRUINS WIN, 82-63

Surpass the Collegiate Mark Established by San Francisco

By GORDON S. WHITE Jr.
Special to The New York Times

SOUTH BEND, Ind. Jan. 27— The University of California, Los Angeles, gained its 61st straight basketball victory today for an intercollegiate record. The most surprising part of the record achievement was the ease with which U.C.L.A., the defending National Collegiate champion, whipped Notre Dame, 82-63, to break the standard of 60 games in a row set in 1956 by the University of San Francisco.

Nothing the Irish could do was going to stay these mighty

Bruins from another record achievement in the U.C.L.A. log that includes eight national championships, more than any other college, and the last six national championships, a record streak.

Coach Digger Phelps of Notre Dame even tried for help from the "sixth man" — the enthusiastic 12,000 fans who packed the Notre Dame Athletic and Convocation Center for the nationally televised game. A rally that had Notre Dame fans warmed up for the occasion was held an hour before the game.

Cool Record-Breakers

But the Walton Gang (so named because of its leader, Bill Walton) dominated play and Walton was again the individual star. He worked in excellent manner at both ends of the court, scored 16 points, took 15 rebounds, had four assists and blocked 10 shots.

When it was over and the

record was theirs, the U.C.L.A. players and coach reminded one of the old New York Yankees, who became so used to winning titles and setting records. There was calm joy without shouting in the dressing room and "happy" was about the strongest expression of feeling.

John Wooden, the 62-year-old native of Indiana, acted even more subdued than usual, probably because of his illness of last month, described as "a heart condition."

Wooden said, "Oh, I'm happy all right. But this does not compare to the first national championship."

His U.C.L.A. team won the college's first National Collegiate basketball title in 1964.

The U.C.L.A. coach reflected a bit and said, "You know, this is cease-fire day. We of U.C.L.A. are a lot happier about that than about any record 61 games."

This man, who coached at South Bend Central High School for 11 years before World War II, said, "This record was the combined work of three teams. Now the pressure is off on the streak and we can prepare for more conference play that we must win."

Walton, smiling, said, "The thing is that now that this 61st is over we still have to keep winning. We have to in order to get into the national championship, which is our main goal always. Though I like playing before a hostile crowd like this, I want to get back to Los Angeles. That's where we start winning more."

U.C.L.A. has 10 Pacific Eight Conference games remaining on its regular schedule, starting with Southern California next week in Los Angeles.

Greg Lee, a guard, acted more excited than any of the other Bruins. "We've got to break the record 14 more times," he said. He meant the 10 conference games left and

Keith Wilkes of U.C.L.A. grabbing the ball from Gary Brokaw as the Notre Damer went up to shoot at South Bend, Ind. Bill Walton is at the right.

United Press International

Bruins. U.C.L.A. suffered its last defeat in this same arena on Jan. 23, 1971, when Notre Dame beat the Bruins, 89-82.

Austin Carr scored 46 points for the Irish that day. Carr is now playing with the Cleveland Cavaliers and Notre Dame has no player who can score as Carr did.

Walton had 12 points and 10 rebounds in the first half. Larry Farmer, who also had a dozen points for U.C.L.A. in the first 20 minutes, finished with 16.

But Keith Wilkes, the outstanding forward who is sometimes overlooked because of Walton, scored 20 points for the Bruins.

Shumate was the game's high scorer with 21 points as Notre Dame suffered its second loss of the season to U.C.L.A. The Bruins gained the 50th victory in this string by beating the Irish, 82-56, in Pauley Pavilion, Los Angeles, last Dec. 23.

NOTRE DAME (63)

	fgm	fga	ftm	fta	reb	a	pf	pts
Shumate	8	20	5	5	12	6	3	21
Novak	0	4	0	0	1	1	1	0
Crotty	3	6	1	4	5	1	1	7
Brokaw	8	18	0	0	6	1	3	16
Clay	5	17	0	0	3	5	2	10
Silinski	2	3	1	1	0	0	0	5
W. Townsend	1	2	0	0	1	0	1	2
Stevens	0	2	0	0	0	0	1	0
Hansen	0	0	0	0	0	0	0	0
M. Townsend	0	0	0	0	1	0	0	0
Wolbeck	1	3	0	0	2	0	0	2
Total	28	75	7	10	31	14	13	63

U.C.L.A. (82)

	fgm	fga	ftm	fta	reb	a	pf	pts
Wilkes	10	16	0	0	9	0	1	20
Farmer	8	19	0	1	7	2	0	16
Walton	8	10	0	0	15	4	2	16
Lee	2	7	3	3	1	9	0	7
Hollyfield	4	10	0	0	4	3	2	8
Trovich	1	4	1	2	3	2	0	3
Meyers	3	3	0	0	3	0	2	6
Webb	0	1	0	0	0	0	0	0
Water	1	3	0	0	3	0	1	2
Carson	1	1	0	0	0	0	1	2
Franklin	0	2	2	2	0	0	0	2
Total	38	76	6	8	51	20	8	82

fgm-Field goals made. fga-Field goals attempted. fta-Free throws attempted. ftm-Free throws made. reb-Rebounds. a-Assists pf-Personal fouls. pts-Total points.

Notre Dame	25	38—63		
U.C.L.A.	38	44—82		

Referees—George Stranthere and Bob Brodbeck.
Attendance—11,343.

January 28, 1973

then the four games in the national tournament needed to win the title.

Wooden said, "My players seem to relish winning here where it's a big challenge before this crowd."

Who Needs Conversation?

The noise at the start was amazing. One could not hear words from the person sitting next to him. But that condition ended midway in the second half when U.C.L.A. had everything under control.

U.C.L.A. played a strong physical game and Notre Dame met the challenge of contact with gusto. The battle lines were drawn early for a rough struggle under the baskets.

Pete Crotty, one of Notre Dame's four starting sophomores, received a bloody nose in the first half in a match with Larry Hollyfield.

But Walton dominated the action and this junior, listed at 6 feet 11 inches though he looks to be over 7 feet, came out of all contact scraps on top. He

controlled the boards even though Phelps tried two men around him—Crotty and John Shumate, who are 6-8 and 6-9.

Lee got a number of high line-drive passes in to Walton early in the game and Walton just tipped them in for goals. U.C.L.A. broke an 8-8 deadlock and ran up an 8-point lead in seven minutes of action.

With U.C.L.A. leading, 38-25, at intermission, it seemed clear then that Notre Dame would not really have a chance as it had two years ago against the

Va. Tech Triumphs at Buzzer

Irish 92-91 N.I.T. Losers

By SAM GOLDAPER

Bobby Stevens, as unheralded as the Virginia Tech basketball team, dropped in a 20-foot jump shot at the buzzer yesterday to give his team a 92-91 overtime victory over Notre Dame in the final of the National Invitation Tourament before a Madison Square Garden crowd of 13,103.

Amazingly, a field goal by the Gobbler's Craig Lieder, also at the buzzer, had tied the game in regulation time.

The winning basket by Stevens, at 5 feet 10 inches the smallest player on the Gobbler roster, accounted for 2 of the 7 points he scored in the five-minute overtime period. Stevens, a junior college trans-

fer, scored the last three baskets in the final 1 minute 57 seconds of the game, and each brought his team back from what had appeared to have been almost certain defeat. He did it as follows:

¶At 1:57, Stevens hit on an arching one-hander from the left of the baseline to cut Notre Dame's margin to 87-85.

¶With 43 seconds left, Stevens scored on an off-balance one-hander and was fouled by Dwight Clay. The 3-point play made the score, 91-90, and set the stage for his game-winning basket.

¶With 12 seconds remaining, following a Virginia Tech time-out, Ed Frazier passed inbounds behind the center line to Stevens in backcourt. Stevens spun with Clay guarding him, took a shot from inside the foul circle and missed. But he grabbed the rebound, dribbled twice and shot from the right side of the lane as the buzzer sounded.

"I'm not noted as a rebounder," said Stevens, who switched from Ferrum (Va.) Junior College. "The play was to get the ball into Craig Lieder, but he was covered, so I soloed in on my own. When

I missed, I followed the ball because we were boxing out under the boards, and the ball came to me."

Lieder, who scored 26 points, 18 in the first half, was another strong factor in the Virginia Tech heroics. The 6-5 forward sent the game into overtime with a shot from the right of the key at the buzzer. It tied the game at 79-79, after Virginia Tech had trailed 70-58, with 6:13 to play.

Winning dramatically was nothing new for Virginia Tech in the tournament. The Gobblers' total margin of victory in the four games was 5 points.

The only easy victory for Virginia Tech, which was described as "too white, too small and too Virginian," was in the first round when it upset New Mexico, 65-63. The other triumphs, over Fairfield and Alabama, were by 1 point each.

While Allan Bristow and Lieder were walking away with the plaudits in the first three games, it was Stevens's free throws that were the margins of victory.

As the beaten Notre Dame players sat glumly on the bench awaiting the awards ceremony, they were consoled by the announcement that John Shumate, the 6-9 sophomore center, had been chosen most valuable player.

M.V.P. honors had been narrowed to Shumate, who is from Elizabeth, N. J., and the 6-7 Bristow, the Virginia Tech center. Each had entered the game with 67 points.

Shumate was such a dominant factor as Notre Dame, in the role of favorite for the first time in the tournament, seemingly had the victory clinched on several occasions. He scored 28 points, 18 in the second half while the Irish opened their 12-point lead with the help of a full-court press.

Shumate, who finished as the tournament's leading scorer with 95 points, turned in a spectacular field-goal percentage. He took a 28-for-32 shooting percentage into the game and shot 10 for 19 to finish with 38 for 51 or 75 per cent.

His defensive play was outstanding, too. He blocked numerous shots and intercepted three passes when the Irish press was bothering Virginia Tech.

"It's a perfect climax to a tremendous season," said Don DeVoe, the Virginia Tech coach, whose team scored its 22d vic-

tory against five defeats. "And it's fitting that none of our players got the most valuable player award. That proves that it's been a team effort all the way."

Shumate said: "I wasn't looking forward to being the M.V.P. I was only looking forward to wearing the watch that has champion engraved on it. Without that, the rest doesn't mean that much. It's a piece of silver and a name in a record."

It was hardly Shumate's fault that Notre Dame was not champion.

"I thought Virginia Tech did a tremendous job coming back," said Digger Phelps, the Notre Dame coach. "We had a couple of crucial turnovers and that made the difference. I didn't think any one play cost us the game. It's not the mistakes at the end that count; it's the ones you make all during the game."

One of those crucial errors was made by Pete Crotty, the sophomore from St. Agnes High School of Rockville Centre, L.I. With 32 seconds remaining in regulation time, and the Irish ahead by 78-77, Bristow fouled Gary Brokaw.

In a one-and-one situation, Brokaw made both free throws, but the second was nullified

because Crotty had stepped into the foul lane too soon. That gave Notre Dame a 79-77 lead. Had both free throws counted, the Irish would have had a 3-point edge, and Lieder's buzzer basket would not have tied the game.

Virginia Tech led, 44-40, at half-time, but Notre Dame opened the second half with a press that upset the Gobblers and led to a 14-4 scoring burst.

In the end, though, it was the Virginia Tech press that won it the title.

Final 12 seconds of the Notre Dame-Virginia Tech final, with winning score at buzzer

CHAMPIONSHIP GAME

VIRGINIA TECH (92)

	fgm	fga	ftm	fta	reb	a	pf	pts
Frazier	5	10	1	1	2	5	1	11
Lieder	12	20	2	7	3	1	1	26
Bristow	11	28	2	7	15	3	3	24
Stevens	3	11	1	1	4	4	4	17
Thomas	3	8	0	0	6	5	5	6
Wade	2	6	2	2	5	5	4	6
McKee	0	2	0	0	0	0	1	0
Sensibaugh	1	3	0	0	1	0	0	2
Total	42	88	8	13	42	22	22	92

NOTRE DAME (91)

	fgm	fga	ftm	fta	reb	a	pf	pts
Shumate	10	19	8	11	11	6	1	28
Novak	5	11	0	0	8	3	5	10
Crotty	4	8	0	4	9	2	4	8
Clay	8	17	2	2	3	7	2	18
Brokaw	10	22	3	5	5	4	6	23
W. Townsend	2	2	0	0	0	4	4	4
Total	39	79	13	22	41	20	17	91

fgm—Field goals made. fga—Field goals attempted. ftm—Free throws made. fta—Free throws attempted. reb—Rebounds. a—Assists. pf—Personal fouls. pts—Total points.
Half-time score—Virginia Tech 44, Notre Dame 40.
Regulation game score—Virginia Tech 79, Notre Dame 79.
Officials—Hal Grossman and Joe DeBonis.
Attendance—13,103.

DeVoe said the change in tactics late in the second half, had turned the game. He added:

"We applied full-court pressure with seven minutes to go and charged the tempo. We were down by 10 and had to make our move. As it turned out, their offense didn't set up as well as it had and they couldn't get the ball in to Shumate as easily as they had. They didn't make many mistakes, but just enough to get us going."

North Carolina took third-place honors by defeating Alabama, 88-69, in the consolation game. The Tar Heels, who had shooting problems in the semi-final round against Notre Dame, found the range and hit for 51 per cent.

Alabama, a near-50-per-cent-shooting team, fell to 33 per cent. The Crimson Tide dropped behind, 48-29, at half-time on 29 per cent shooting and never recovered. They had trouble penetrating the North Carolina zone.

George Karl led the North Carolina scorers with 23 points and Wendell Hudson and Leon Douglas scored 19 each for Alabama.

March 26, 1973

U.C.L.A. Wins 7th Title in Row; Walton Nets 44

By GORDON S. WHITE Jr.

Special to The New York Times

ST. LOUIS, March 26 — Bill Walton put on one of the greatest performances in college basketball tournament history tonight leading his University of California, Los Angeles team to its seventh straight National Collegiate Athletic Association championship.

Indiana defeated Providence, 97-79, in the consolation game.

His record 44 points was only part of his total effort as U.C.L.A. defeated an exciting Memphis State team, 87-66, for its 75th consecutive victory over 2½ seasons and its ninth N.C.A.A. title in the last ten years.

But Walton's amazing work was toned down when, with 2 minutes 51 seconds remaining, the 6-foot 11-inch red-

haired Bruin fell hard to the floor and hurt his left knee and ankle. He limped off the floor to an ovation from the 19,301 fans.

This most mobile of the present college basketball big men has always played with pain in his knees. He tapes them before every game.

Walton's outstanding effort, hitting on 21 of 22 field goal shots, taking 13 rebounds and controlling both boards, was even more noteworthy because he played with three personal fouls from the start of the second half and picked up his fourth after 10 minutes and 33 seconds more.

The fouls didn't hamper his motion in beating Memphis State's big men. He continued to play physically hard and in constant contact with the Ti-

gers who were trying their best to draw that fifth personal and send Walton to the bench.

When he was hurt, U.C.L.A. had finally taken command of the game and was leading, 75-62.

But earlier, when Walton drew his third personal with 4:14 to go in the first half and the U.C.L.A. lead at 37-31, Wooden benched him for the remainder of the first half. Memphis State suddenly was playing a normal team of mortals and gained a 39-39 tie at intermission.

Wooden, however, did not remove his big junior hero after he drew that fourth personal. The coach didn't dare do that. U.C.L.A. could easily have lost its slim lead — 61-55 — at the time. Without Walton, this U.C.L.A. team is just another good team — maybe not even

good enough to beat Memphis State.

Following the fourth foul, Walton scored 8 more points before falling while defending against Memphis State. Thus he broke the previous individual scoring mark of 42 points in an N.C.A.A. title game. Another U.C.L.A. player, Gail Goodrich, had set the record against Michigan in 1965.

Ronnie Robinson, Larry Kenon and Wes Westfall, Memphis State's tall men who worked on Walton in pairs and relays, drew a total of 12 personal fouls for their efforts. They scored 26 points together and managed to get a total of 15 rebounds—two more than Walton.

But Westfall eventually fouled out and Kenon, who started off matching Walton shot for shot, had to sit down early in the

Winning

With nice guys and a pyramid of principles

By Arnold Hano

United Press International

Bill Walton of U.C.L.A. shoots for the basket as Ronnie Robinson, left, and Larry Kenon of Memphis State defend during first-half action at St. Louis.

game with three personal fouls after 7 minutes.

They just couldn't handle the big fellow from La Mesa, Calif., who zipped back and forth across the lane at the low post as if he was under 6 feet tall. He took in high and low passes from Greg Lee, Keith Wilkes, Larry Hollyfield and others and scored by outreaching his defenders. He took rebounds jumping over the Tigers.

After the game, U.C.L.A. officials and Wooden explained that Walton's injury was to his left knee and ankle and was "not too serious." However, Walton, walking the dressing room, refused to talk to reporters, saying, "Excuse me, I want to go see my friends."

He was not limping then as he walked out of the arena with a big crowd of Bruin fans.

Although the final count was large, it was a 20-10 scoring advantage by U.C.L.A. during the first nine minutes of the second half that did the damage. Walton scored the first 6 points in that spurt and 14 of the important 20.

The biggest jump came on a 4-point scoring play by Walton that raised the lead from 51-47 to 55-47. Walton scored on an inside shot off a pass from Lee and was fouled in the process. The officials said it was an "under-cutting" foul which gave Walton two free throws, instead of one. He made both.

Walton was selected the outstanding player of the tournament for the second straight year as he led his team to victory for the 60th straight time. He has not suffered defeat as a varsity U.C.L.A. player and

has a personal winning streak of 129 games dating back to high school.

Larry Finch, Memphis State's star guard, scored 29 points in the losing effort. He did his best as the Tigers rallied for the half-time tie. But he seemed like a fly bothering a giant with his long shots down the stretch.

Gene Bartow, Memphis State coach, said, "Walton is about as physical a big man as I've ever seen. We didn't play him well. But he just dominates a game."

Walton's lone missed field goal was a tap rebound that bounced back from the board. He was charged with four offensive goaltending violations.

Championship

U.C.L.A. (87)								
	fgm	fga	ftm	fta	reb	pf	a	pts
Wilkes	8	14	0	0	7	2	1	16
Farmer	1	4	0	0	2	2	0	2
Walton	21	22	5	13	4	2	4	44
Lee	1	1	3	3	3	2	14	5
Hollyfield	4	7	0	0	3	4	9	8
Curtis	1	4	2	2	3	1	0	4
Meyers	2	7	0	0	3	1	0	4
Nater	1	1	0	0	3	2	0	2
Franklin	1	2	0	1	1	0	0	2
Carson	0	0	0	0	0	0	0	0
Webb	0	0	0	0	0	0	0	0
Total	40	62	7	11	38	18	26	87

MEMPHIS STATE (66)								
	fgm	fga	ftm	fta	reb	pf	a	pts
Buford	3	7	1	2	3	1	1	7
Kenon	8	16	4	4	8	3	3	20
Robinson	3	6	0	1	7	4	1	6
Laurie	0	1	0	0	0	0	2	0
Finch	9	21	11	13	1	2	2	29
Westfall	0	1	0	0	0	5	0	0
Cook	1	4	2	2	0	1	2	4
McKinney	0	0	0	0	0	0	0	0
Jones	0	0	0	0	0	0	0	0
Tetzlaff	0	0	0	2	0	0	0	0
Liss	0	1	0	0	0	0	0	0
Andrews	0	0	0	0	0	0	0	0
Total	24	57	16	24	19	17	11	66

min-Minutes played. fgm-Field goals made. fga-Field goals attempted. ftm-Free throws made. fta-Free throws attempted. reb-Rebounds. a-Assists. pf-Personal fouls. pts-Total points.
Half-time score: U.C.L.A. 39, Memphis State 39.
Attendance—19,301.

March 27, 1973

LOS ANGELES. In the summer of 1973, as he does every summer, John Wooden, head basketball coach at U.C.L.A. and the most successful coach in America, wrote a letter to his squad.

The letter of 1973 does not differ much from the letter of 1972, nor does that one differ from the one of the year before or the year before that.

Wooden does not pretend to be an innovative thinker. He likes to do things by rote; he says, "Repetition is the last law of learning," by which he means the final law, the ultimate law.

And so his players, all but the first-year men, know what to expect in their mailboxes. Wooden will exhort them to sacrifice individual exploits for team play. "There is much truth in Kipling's Law of the Jungle," Wooden wrote in his letter of July 28, 1971, "when he says, '. . . the strength of the Pack is the Wolf, but the strength of the Wolf is the Pack.'"

Team play is not the only theme head coach John Wooden plays over and over in his communications. Each letter asks his players to adhere to a code of personal appearance that seems a throwback in this era of the Rollie Fingers look.

Wooden writes each summer (and these words never vary), "Wear no mustache, beard or goatee; have sideburns no longer than the top of the lobes of your ears; have the hair of reasonable length with the coaches being the judge as to what is reasonable length."

That is the way his players show up for the first practice in October. With occasional exceptions. One recent season, a player appeared with overlong sideburns, another with mutton chops, and a third with a goatee. Said Wooden quietly: "You have 20 minutes to decide whether you're going to play basketball at U.C.L.A. this year or not. There are clippers and razors in the training room."

"You'll be crucified," one player said.

"That may well be, but you won't be around to see it," answered Wooden.

They went back and barbered.

Perhaps the most interesting aspect of this incident is the choice of words used by the player: "You'll be crucified." John Wooden comes as close to an embodiment of Jesus Christ as anyone on the current sporting scene. One rival coach once thought he had successfully recruited a young prep star to attend that coach's college. "We thought we had the kid sewed up," said the coach. "But then Jesus Christ walked in." Wooden, of course, was Jesus Christ. The youngster played at U.C.L.A.

John Wooden is a throwback. Nice guys finish first. Neatness counts. It isn't whether you win or lose, but how you play the game. When Wooden flew back East to meet the parents of Lew Alcindor (now Kareem Abdul-Jabbar) after having recruited Alcindor to play at U.C.L.A., Alcindor's mother said of Wooden, "He's more like a minister than a coach." "He is," wrote Herbert Warren Wind of Wooden several seasons ago, "an island of James Whitcomb Riley in a sea of Ken Kesey...."

Now, nobody believes — least of all John Wooden— that the length of a man's hair and his lack of a goatee are the reason for the most astonishing record in American sports. So maybe it is this stance of Wooden as a moral island in a sea of savage rip-off tides that plays a part. Something must. John Wooden's U.C.L.A. teams have become the winningest teams in college basketball history. They have won the last seven N.C.A.A. national titles, nine in the last 10 years. Going into the 1973-74 season, they had won 75 games in a row, breaking the old college mark of 60 set by Bill Russell's teams at the University of San Francisco in the mid-nineteen-fifties. You stretch for comparisons, but there are none in America's major sports.

The New York Giants, under John McGraw, once won 26 baseball games in a row, back in 1916. The Miami Dolphins last season won 17 straight, and then the first game of this season, before they finally lost, and the football world marveled at such a winning string. The Los Angeles Lakers won 33 basketball games in a row a few seasons back, a streak that lasted nearly two full months. At tip-off time in 1973, U.C.L.A.'s winning streak had lasted two and a half years.

Neither Knute Rockne, nor McGraw, nor Connie Mack, nor Casey Stengel, nor Vince Lombardi, nor any other coach or manager has compiled anything close to the record of Wooden's teams. Nor is this a sudden success, a one-time thing. Before the current string, Wooden's Bruins had won 41 straight, and before that 47 straight. In 25 years at U.C.L.A., Wooden has never had a losing season.

In two years at Indiana State Teachers College, before he joined U.C.L.A. in 1948, Wooden enjoyed big winning seasons. And Wooden's high-school won-lost mark is even better than his college coaching record. He is sport's most enduring, most successful winner.

Two questions intrigue the observer. Why such a phenomenal streak? And does it really matter?

JOHN WOODEN is 63 years old. His brown hair has turned gray, although his short sideburns remain surprisingly sandy. Wooden is clean as a hound's tooth, a deacon of the First Christian Church of Santa Monica, a man who neither drinks nor says anything stronger than "Goodness gracious sakes alive!" He used to smoke but gave it up several years ago.

While on the bench during a U.C.L.A. game he grips a rolled-up program in his right hand, while his left hand clutches a crucifix in his suit pocket. Wooden keeps a well-thumbed New Testament on his desk and, to visitors and players, he hands out Xeroxed copies of his "Pyramid of Success": a graphic representation, evolved over the years, of his philosophy of life in relation to the game of basketball. The cornerstones of Wooden's Pyramid of Success are Industriousness and Enthusiasm (the capitals are his); the peak of the pyramid is Success, and just beneath Success are the words Faith, with a brief subheading, "Through prayer," and Patience, "Good things take time."

Wooden carries in his wallet some words his father once penned for his son when John was an Indiana farmboy. "Be true to yourself. Make each day a masterpiece. Help others. Drink deeply from good books. Make friendship a fine art, and build a shelter against a rainy day." Joshua Wooden, John's father, needed some sort of shelter; he lost his farm and ended up a masseur in a sanitarium in Martinsville, Ind.

Farm life and bankruptcy have combined with a stern family upbringing to turn John Wooden into a man of

thrift, moral rectitude and austerity. He keeps farmer's hours today, except when his team plays at night. Otherwise he is up at 5:45 A.M., dresses quickly, and arrives before 7 at the U.C.L.A. campus, some 20 minutes from his Santa Monica apartment, where he next spends 70 to 75 minutes on the track, walking five miles. Doctors don't let him jog anymore, now that he has developed a mild heart condition. He and his wife Nell—whom he met in high school where she played the trumpet in the Martinsville High School band, when Johnny Wooden was the school's star basketeer — retire by 9 at night. A vacation is a stay of three or four days at Lawrence Welk's resort in Escondido, Calif., some 80 miles below Los Angeles; Wooden swims, plays golf, does crossword puzzles and catches up on his Zane Grey novels.

The Woodens spend their Sundays, after church, with their married son and daughter and the Woodens' seven grandchildren. When Dick Nixon phoned Wooden at home to congratulate U.C.L.A. for winning the 1970 national title, not only did Wooden speak with the President, but he managed to get three of his grandchildren on the phone.

Life is a family affair. Wooden is relatively underpaid, as big-time coaches go, receiving in the neighborhood of $40,000 a year. He knows he could do much better. Several times, in fact, Wooden has received lucrative offers to coach elsewhere, either in college or in the professional ranks. Each time, he has turned down the offer, but not before taking it up with his family and with God. Wooden is a man of rigid moral code, still staggered by the realization that some of his players, on occasion, have been known to take a drink or, goodness gracious sakes alive, try a marijuana joint.

In a book, "The Wizard of Westwood," written by a couple of Los Angeles sportswriters, Wooden was charged with once chastising his players between halves of a game as "women chasers and potheads." Wooden strongly denies he ever used such

language, but he truly loathes the notion that a player of his could turn on. He has also been known to discourage woman-chasing. When he coached in high school, he used to keep his players in the locker room for quite some time after a game's end. "That way their girl friends outside would get impatient and would leave instead with some other fellows. My players would likely get home earlier and get more rest."

None of which, obviously, has a clear bearing on Wooden's current, or even past, success. Just what bears on this success, nobody knows for sure. Rival coaches play with the question, without coming up with anything totally convincing. Guy Lewis, of Houston, thinks U.C.L.A. keeps winning because the team plays as a "complete unit." Jerry Tarkanian, who coaches the rising basketball power, Cal State at Long Beach, says of Wooden: "He's unique. His theories wouldn't work for everyone, but he does a tremendous job of organizing and getting teams ready to play. He makes very few adjustments during games, but maybe the major part of his success is that he's very, very basic." Another coach once said, "It doesn't pay to scout U.C.L.A. What they do is terribly predictable. The difficulty is, they do it so well."

Abe Lemons, Oklahoma City coach, sums up the attitude of most coaches when he suggests a way to beat Wooden: "Wait, and some night when the moon is full and the clock strikes midnight, drive a silver stake into his heart. He is unreal."

THE very real John Wooden, all 5 feet 10 inches, 183 pounds, can't tell you why his teams keep winning. In his office in the small Athletic Department building across from U.C.L.A.'s modern Pauley Pavilion, where the Bruins play, Wooden pondered the question of his team's success.

"It's the result of a lot of things, no one thing," he says. "First, there must be a fine university, to attract youngsters. U.C.L.A. is a great university. That's why a young

Bill Walton's intensity and concentration, combined with height and natural talent, helped him lead U.C.L.A. to several consecutive national titles. He has since had a checkered and controversial career as a pro.

North Carolina State's David Thompson (#44) goes up and over Wake Forest's Red Griffen to score in a 1975 game. Thompson's jumping ability made him a prodigious scorer.

person goes to college, to get an education. You get a great education here."

So the university and its strong academic reputation draw young people—as does the basketball program, says Wooden. "Our program has proved itself. We play in a modern facility. We travel each year to the Midwest and back East. We play a game the players enjoy to play and spectators enjoy to watch—a fast-moving game. If a player wants preparation for the pro game, that is the kind of game we play at U.C.L.A."

Another advantage, says Wooden, is the locale. "We have all-year basketball weather, great summer leagues, a huge population to draw from." Somehow it doesn't sound like enough. It doesn't sound like enough to Wooden. He also says, with an element of modesty, "I like to feel our coaching has had something to do with our success."

And that is that. Recruiting? "We don't recruit in numbers. I have never initiated contact with an out-of-state player. I don't go back East to watch high-school teams. Yet coaches from all parts of the country come out here, to scout our prep teams."

It is not quite as clear as all that, however. U.C.L.A. may not actively recruit out-of-state players, but it gets its share. Lew Alcindor, Walt Hazzard, Mike Warren, Lucius Allen and Henry Bibby all came from out of state. Interestingly, all are blacks. U.C.L.A. has never recruited a top-flight white prep star from out of state. The attraction California holds for America's blacks is a powerful one. When Lew Alcindor held his press conference back at Power Memorial Gym in Manhattan to announce which college he would attend in the fall of 1965, he said, "I have always been captivated by California."

THE Alcindor—Abdul-Jabbar—case is perhaps the most complex, and it is one that has made it appear that U.C.L.A. does indeed reach across the continent for talent. Wooden has said several times, "We did not contact

Wooden in the U.C.L.A. gym last month during Bruin practice. "I am a practice coach," he says.

Alcindor. Lewis contacted us."

In a sense he is correct. Alcindor's coach at Power Memorial, Jack Donohue, contacted Wooden after Alcindor's junior year and told Wooden that he—Donohue—would be attending a coaching clinic in Philadelphia, and could Wooden stop by. Wooden went, and Donohue told him that Alcindor had narrowed his choice of colleges to five—U.C.L.A., Michigan, St. John's, Boston College and N.Y.U. Said Donohue to Wooden: "Don't contact him. Lewis will be in touch with you." And Wooden said shrewdly, "The only thing I want is for him to see our campus last."

The last campus you see is the freshest in mind when you make that final decision. More important, U.C.L.A. was still building its new sports arena, Pauley Pavilion, modern and handsome, to seat 12,800 persons. The longer Alcindor stayed away, the more finished the building would be.

Alcindor visited U.C.L.A. in April of 1965. Wooden bought Alcindor a hamburger, and saw to it that he was driven around town, where the youngster attended a dance, a rock concert and a Catholic service; Wooden was ignorant of Alcindor's impending conversion to the Moslem faith. Alcindor saw the 411 acres of the sprawling Westwood campus. And of course he saw

Pauley Pavilion.

When he left, Alcindor said to Wooden: "I'll be back in September. This is my choice."

That is one side of the Alcindor recruitment story, but there is another side. U.C.L.A. did not actively recruit Alcindor, but former Bruin guard, Dr. Ralph Bunche, then with the United Nations, wrote Alcindor a letter, and sent a copy to Wooden, extolling the university and suggesting Alcindor attend. Willie Naulls, former U.C.L.A. basketball star who later played ball in the N.B.A., met privately with Alcindor several times and kept pressing the university on the boy. Other U.C.L.A. alumni contacted Alcindor.

But too much can be made of the Alcindor case. U.C.L.A won two national titles before Alcindor ever arrived on campus, and the current 75-game winning streak began after Alcindor had left U.C.L.A.

WHAT is it then? U.C.L.A. does not pay or pamper its athletes any more than any basketball-oriented school. Its scholarship players get room, board, books, tuition and fees, plus $15 a month for incidentals. Tutoring is arranged for athletes who need help. The athletic department helps uncover those courses which Wooden refers to as "Mickey-

Mouse" classes, to help a player through an otherwise difficult academic quarter.

But do not assume that the U.C.L.A. basketball squad packs its roster with dumdums. "I'm very proud of the academic accomplishments of our players. I bet we have as high a percentage of lettermen getting their degree as almost any college in the country. On this current team, Bill Walton and Keith Wilkes are brilliant students. This may be the best squad I have ever had academically."

Which leaves us where we began. Why this success? If there is a quick dull answer, Wooden is a better practice coach than most. He spends two to three hours planning each day's practice, though the practice itself may last less than two hours. Wooden is a nut on drill. He keeps notebooks that go back 25 years and tell him in a moment exactly what drills he put his players through on any day since he joined the university. He and his two full-time assistants, Frank Arnold and Gary Cunningham, break down the practice into a dozen or so brief modules of time—5 to 15 minutes each —so that no single drill becomes too monotonous. All drills have running as a byproduct. You shoot fouls, and then run a few laps. You pass the ball back and forth, always driving toward the basket. Movement plus fundamentals constitute the heart of each practice session, plus a segment of time set aside for game condition scrimmaging.

All this movement fits in with Wooden's offensive style. Wooden likes his teams to feature a fast break, with quick ballhandling, passing the ball forward (never backward) rather than dribbling, and aggressive rebounding. He does not much like the pro method of screening out opponents on rebounds; it's too negative for John Wooden. He wants his players to crash the boards.

Naturally he adapts his offense to his personnel. His first title teams, with small, quick guards, played a racehorse, fast-break game. Then when Alcindor came along, Wooden was obliged to slow the tempo to give Alcindor time to position himself under the basket, both on offense and defense. After Alcindor left, Wooden shifted the offense, because his new big man was Steve Patterson, whose most effective shooting came from just outside the foul circle. Now, with big Bill Walton, Wooden has gone back to the Alcindor-style offense, with Walton beneath the basket.

But always, the style is based on fundamentals. Wooden says, "I am not a strategy coach. I am a practice coach." What his players learn, they learn during drills, and they learn by doing, over and over, not by seeing it drawn for them on blackboards, though there is a blackboard in Wooden's office, and he surely knows as much strategy as the next coach. (Perhaps the most famous bit of Wooden strategy in recent seasons was U.C.L.A.'s defense against Elvin Hayes and his Houston teammates in the N.C.A.A. tournament of 1968. Earlier, Houston had beaten U.C.L.A. by two points at the Astrodome, when Alcindor played with a scratched eyeball and blurred vision. For the rematch, Wooden and his assistants instituted a diamond-and-one defense — the diamond placing Alcindor under the defensive basket, with two men at the wings, and a fourth Bruin to meet the Houston attack at midcourt. The "one" was Lynn Shackel-

ford, whose job all game was to dog Elvin Hayes no matter where Hayes went. The pattern destroyed Houston, and U.C.L.A. triumphed, 101-69. Guy Lewis, Houston coach, called U.C.L.A.'s effort "the greatest exhibition of basketball I have ever seen.")

So Wooden can get a bit exotic, when it is demanded. But few coaches — perhaps none — are so dedicated to drill by rote, the fundamentals of passing, dribbling, shooting and moving, dinned into the heads of the squad by constant repetition.

The result is not only a team superbly skilled in the fundamentals but a squad in equally superb physical condition. All the running pays off. Gail Goodrich, now with the Lakers, and a member of Wooden's first national title team in 1964, says, "Coach Wooden's words were always the same, 'Don't panic, keep your poise, the other guy will break.' They did, too. And, heck, how many games did we win on pure condition? No one was in better shape."

Wooden has another fetish on the court. He hates to call the first time-out in any game. To him it is a contest of endurance, between him and the rival coach, his players and their rivals, a test of strength determining who will find it necessary to ask for time out first.

Wooden employs a pressing defense, his players a clutch of octopi, all over their foes, sometimes covering their rivals the full length of the court, but usually picking them up at half-court. The pressing defense — which Wooden learned from his Purdue college coach, Ward (Piggy) Lambert—is designed not only to steal the ball or cause breakdowns in the pattern of play. Says Wooden: "We want to keep constant pressure until we get to the emotions of the other team." Condition and pressure, together, wreck their foes. Plus the odd bit about emotion. Other teams have emotions, which are like Achilles' heels, weak spots to be exploited. U.C.L.A. teams have no emotions, at least none that are visible. Wooden does not try to psych up his team, with pep talks before a game or

during halftime. "I try to prevent the team from getting too high or too low. I practice it myself. I don't permit myself to be elated or depressed. All I ask is that the players give their best effort, and win or lose, they hold their heads up after the game."

Sometimes this control of emotions results in negative feedback from a player or two. A couple of seasons ago, Vince Carson quit the squad, charging, among other things, that Wooden ran the team "like a machine."

"He was right," answers Wooden today. "I try to make it a well-oiled machine. I put each player into his niche. He loses individuality."

So there is that other fetish, team play. Wooden will not tolerate stars. He will not say it, but he was not happy during the Alcindor era. Not that he did not like Alcindor: "He was as easy to coach as any player I've ever had," Wooden says. "He never gave me one ounce of trouble. He was totally unselfish, a team player." But he adds: "Alcindor's being here brought problems that were not of his making." Fellow players resented the attention paid Alcindor, by autograph seekers, the press and fans. And Alcindor brought to the front the problems of black-white relations that have caused some dissension at U.C.L.A.

Once when U.C.L.A. was on the road, Wooden overheard a woman say of Alcindor: "Look at the big black freak." Wooden hastened to Alcindor's side: "I tried to explain that she didn't mean to be rude, that his size did startle

people, and that it had nothing to do with race. That the woman wasn't insulting him."

"Do you think, Coach," Alcindor asked, "if Mel Counts [a 7-foot professional basketball player] walked in she would have said, 'Look at the big white freak'?"

Wooden still does not believe the woman insulted Alcindor. Nor does he think he was wrong in advising Mike Warren, a black teammate of Alcindor's, not to date a white girl at U.C.L.A. Explains Wooden today: "I think mixed dating is unwise in our society. It can bring grief. I would advise against it, for the player's own sake. I'm not saying the situation is right, but that mixed dating presents too many problems."

Yet when a reporter once asked Curtis Rowe, another black who now plays in the N.B.A., whether Wooden was prejudiced against blacks, Rowe answered, "Coach Wooden doesn't see color. He sees players."

Perhaps what Wooden sees —and must avoid—is any friction that may erode his squad's ability. There is something almost unreal about Wooden, in his dedication to the team. If anything gets in the way, it is wrong, be it woman-chasing, or pot, or hair that may fly in a man's eyes and, for a split second, impair his vision. Or a goatee that in no way can affect a man's play, but may annoy the people who support the team — alumni, fans, press, people of influence.

Wooden is a perfectionist. Everything must be right, and in its right place. He even shows players how to put on

their socks, so that there are no wrinkles which might cause blisters. Players must nap or try to nap every afternoon before a game that night. The meal is served four hours before opening tip-off, because — says Wooden — it takes four hours for food to be digested. On a Thursday before a Friday night game at home (U.C.L.A. plays most of its games on Friday and Saturday nights), the entire squad goes to a nearby motel and beds down by 10:30, just so Wooden is sure his men have a proper sleep the night before a game. The team is released for classes on Friday, but it must report back to the motel by 3:30 P.M. for the pregame meal. Then the players bed down for the afternoon nap that must precede a night game. After the Friday game, the players return to the hotel. On Saturday, they are free until the inevitable afternoon meal and nap. After the Saturday night game, the players are free until Monday afternoon practice, at 3.

Wooden brooks little criticism. When Jack Hirsch, on a team back in the early nineteen-sixties, once said of the training-room food, "I can't eat this slop," Wooden told him to stay away until he could, which meant suspension from the team. Hirsch stayed away two weeks, and then came back and apologized, and was silent when he ate the slop, which usually is a juicy steak or prime ribs.

Wooden knows about these small rebellions. When he was in high school, playing under coach Glenn Curtis, Wooden took to baiting Curtis at times. "Once I grew some chin whiskers, just to see how far I could go." Curtis had him shave. Another time Wooden sounded off, and Curtis sat him on the bench for two games, even though Wooden was his prize player.

And Wooden can get emotional, even today. In last season's Notre Dame game, a revenge game because it had been the Irish who had last beaten U.C.L.A., Wooden became incensed when he thought Notre Dame's John Shumate was roughing up U.C.L.A.'s great center, Bill Walton. Wooden went over to the Notre Dame bench

where he allegedly told Irish coach Dick (Digger) Phelps, "If Shumate doesn't knock it off, I'll send Swen Nater in and you know what I'll have him do." Swen Nater, Walton's back-up man, stood 6-11 and weighed 238 pounds.

The implication was that Nater would do unto others what Shumate had done unto them. It was a rare outburst from Wooden. In this instance, the offending Shumate came over to the Bruin bench and apologized to Wooden, who felt so contrite he sat down a few days later and wrote a letter to the Notre Dame coach and Shumate, apologizing in turn for his behavior. "I acted hastily without thinking clearly and taking all things into consideration and, as usual, actions from emotions are seldom with reason," Wooden wrote in part.

Feelings must be kept in check, otherwise you do unreasonable things. Wooden tells of the time he was coaching in high school, and his team lost a game he felt it should have won. In the automobile on his way home with his wife, Nell, Wooden said, "Give me a cigarette. It doesn't pay a man to lead a decent life."

TODAY he says, "I'm better disciplined now. I wouldn't permit myself such feelings." The result is, when Wooden is upset during a game, a huge blood vessel forms on his forehead, and he has been known to bait referees mercilessly, if without profanity. Former U.C.L.A. guard Walt Hazzard says of Wooden: "He is one of the best bench jockeys in the world. He has an antiseptic needle — clean but biting."

The self-control for Wooden began in Indiana. He was born in 1910, the son of Joshua Hugh and Roxie Wooden. John's mother inherited a 60-acre farm near Centerville, Ind., a place with no electricity, no inside plumbing, and with water drawn from a hand pump. Life was tough. Once, one of John's brothers, Maurice, flung a pitchfork of manure in John's face. John cussed him out, and the two boys went at it with their fists. The elder Wooden

came into the barn and thrashed both boys, but it was John who got the worse licking because he had used foul language and had lost his temper.

The Wooden parents found an outlet for that temper. Joshua Wooden knocked out the bottom of a tomato basket and nailed it to a barn wall. Roxie Wooden made a ball of rags, sewed into cotton stockings. Johnny Wooden became hooked. He played ball when he wasn't picking tomatoes, milking cows or cranking the milk separator.

The family lost their farm in 1924. The family moved to Martinsville, Ind., where Joshua Wooden finally got a job, giving massages. John Wooden went to school, and played basketball, baseball and track. He was an All-American at Purdue (and is today the only man in Basketball's Hall of Fame in Springfield, Ill., as both player and coach). By early 1932, he and Nell Riley had saved $909.05, so they decided it was time to get married. The morning they were to marry, Wooden went to the bank to withdraw some money, only to find the bank had gone bust, and his money was lost.

After Purdue, where he received the highest grades of any basketball player in the Big 10, he got a coaching job at Dayton High in Kentucky for $1,800 a year. This was his only losing year in all the years he has coached. After his second season, he shifted to South Bend, Ind. He spent three years in the Navy in World War II, came out and stuck to coaching, putting in two years at Indiana State Teachers College. During his first season the team won the local conference, but when the National Association of Intercollegiate Athletics wouldn't let Wooden bring Clarence Walker, a black reserve, to the championship tournament in Kansas City, Wooden refused to let his team play.

In 1948, Wooden signed a three-year contract with U.C.L.A. That year, his team was expected to finish last in the Coast Conference. But Wooden's Bruins won 22 games that season and lost just seven; today Wooden calls it the most satisfying moment of his entire coaching career.

It took 16 years for U.C.L.A. to win its first national title; no U.C.L.A. team has lost a national title since 1967.

THE question remains: How important is any of this? To Wooden, of course, it's been a whole life in the making. So he is not the best judge, even though it is his judgment we seek. Is the winning streak harmful to the college game? Should basketball fans be shouting, "Break up the Bruins!" the way baseball fans shouted in the thirties, "Break up the Yankees!"?

"The winning streak is the best thing that can happen to the college game," says Wooden. "It gives incentive to other teams to beat us. And we need athletes as models of excellence—young people especially need models."

U.C.L.A.'s basketball teams —Wooden thinks—do a national service by their continued high level of skill. And Wooden expects the high level to continue. He never predicts national titles, but he said, sitting in his office, speaking quietly, "We're going to be one of the finest teams in the country this season. We're good enough to win it again. I'm not saying we will, but we're good enough."

JOHN WOODEN today has relaxed somewhat. He no longer conducts bed check on the road, to see if his players have met curfew. Today he will say, "How late do you want to stay out? Twelve, twelve-thirty?" And the players will say, "Twelve-thirty," and Wooden will nod. "I trust them. I rely on their integrity. I used to insist on a shirt, a tie and a jacket, on the road. Now they can wear what they want, provided they are neat."

His own dress took longer to change. In 1970, a writer described Wooden as having "all the sartorial splendor of an undertaker." It didn't bother Wooden, but it upset his wife. Nell insisted her husband change his way of dressing. "The next year," he says wildly, "I wore a blue shirt to the nationals."

Yet John Wooden has refused to permit his fundamental values to be changed. He tells his players, "You are here for an education. That comes first. Basketball comes second."

And he takes a refreshingly broad view of education. "A college education should prepare a person not only to make a living from a material point of view, but to enable him to be more understanding of the needs of society as a whole. Education is more than the means of acquiring possessions. It must help man live harmoniously with his fellow man."

Which may be another way of saying team play. ∎

December 2, 1973

Notre Dame Beats U.C.L.A. in Last 29 Seconds, Ending Streak at 88
Clay's Shot Wins, 71-70, as Irish Rally From 11-Point Deficit With 3:32 to Go

By GORDON S. WHITE Jr.
Special to The New York Times

SOUTH BEND, Ind., Jan. 19—U.C.L.A.'s record 88-game basketball winning streak came to an end today on the same court where the Bruins had last lost three years ago.

In a surprising and thrilling finish, unbeaten Notre Dame turned an 11-point deficit and apparent defeat in the last 3 minutes 32 seconds into a 71-70 victory.

Dwight Clay took a jump shot from the right corner and the ball went through for the winning points. With 29 seconds remaining, the Irish held on in a wild finale to beat the school that has been the National Collegiate champion for the last seven years and nine of the last 10.

The crowd of 11,343 fans in Notre Dame's Athletic and Convocation Center was almost stunned. It was a few seconds before belief registered, apparently, and then the fans swarmed on the court, smothering the Irish players and Coach Digger Phelps with wild undergraduate enthusiasm.

The Irish will obviously move up from No. 2 to No. 1 in the weekly polls, replacing U.C.L.A., which has been No. 1 since the semifinals of the 1968 National Collegiate Athletic Association championship tournament. The victory came 20 days after Notre Dame's football team became the No. 1 team by beating Alabama in an equally exciting Sugar Bowl game.

However, the basketball team will have to fight to retain its lofty spot because it meets U.C.L.A. in a return game a week from tonight at Pauley Pavilion in Los Angeles.

What made the victory more impressive was that the Irish beat the "Walton Gang," with Bill Walton playing the entire 40 minutes and playing very well. That U.C.L.A. could not get the ball to the big redhead at the end was a telling factor after Clay's shot.

Walton injured his back seriously in a fall during a game at Washington State last Monday, and had missed the last three U.C.L.A. victories. He played today with an elastic corset. He scored 24 points, had nine rebounds and intimidated Notre Dame throughout.

This was the first time Walton or any of the other Bruins had tasted defeat as varsity players. Walton, Tommy Curtis and Keith Wilkes are the outstanding seniors who went a long time before losing.

Phelps, in his third year as Notre Dame coach after leaving Fordham, said:

"This was great for college basketball. I'm sure everyone was rooting for us the way they used to root against the New York Yankees. The win was special for Notre Dame, for the kids, for my staff, for my mother and father [who were present] and for us all."

Describing the action of the final three minutes, Phelps said:

"We thought we had to to go to really pressing again, and so I put in Ray Martin [freshman from Long Island City, Queens] for Bill Paterno [freshman from Spring Lake, N. J.]. The kids never gave up and were incredible, just unbelievable."

The other Notre Dame players who went down the wire in the press when the Irish got their first and only lead of the game were Clay, John Shumate (defending against Walton), Adrian Dantley (a freshman from Washington) and Gary Brokaw, who led the game scoring with 25 points.

Big Leads Dwindle

U.C.L.A., which led by 17 points twice in the first half, and by 43-34 at the intermission, was in front, 70-59 with 3 minutes 32 seconds to go. Phelps ordered time-out 10 seconds later and set up a press, replacing Paterno with Martin.

Shumate connected on a hook shot over Walton with 3:07 remaining. But nobody could believe that this was the beginning of the end for the national champions.

Shumate, strong and quick at 6 feet 9 inches and 235 pounds, stole the ensuing U.C.L.A. inbounds pass right under the basket and easily scored again. Now the crowd sensed something and began hollering, "Shoo! Shoo!" for Shumate.

U.C.L.A. made the inbounds pass this time, but at mid-court Dantley, an amazing

freshman, stole the ball from Curtis and went in unchallenged for the basket that cut the margin to 70-65.

Another Turnover

U.C.L.A. tried something different, with Wilkes making a long, upcourt pass to Curtis. Curtis was behind Martin, who fell. But when Curtis got the ball, he ran with it and Notre Dame gained possession on the turnover.

The Irish worked for a good shot by Brokaw, the junior from New Brunswick, N. J., and the score was 70-67. Dave Meyers went in for a layup for U.C.L.A., but was charged with traveling. Again Notre Dame scored on the turnover as Brokaw hit a short jumper. The place went wild.

Now Wilkes tried to score on a drive, but he fouled Brokaw in the process for the fifth U.C.L.A. turnover in those final minutes.

The Irish wanted to work the ball to Shumate with less than 45 seconds remaining. But Shumate wasn't open, so Brokaw got the ball to the open man, Clay, who hit on the jump shot and fell into the crowd as he came down.

The Bruins, at a signal from Coach John Wooden, called time-out with 21 seconds to go, plenty of time for them to get the winning shot. But Curtis shot from 25 feet and missed, Meyers missed a tip-in of the rebound and Walton got his hands on the ball, but not enough to control it

for a good shot.

After a Notre Dame player knocked the ball out of bounds with 6 seconds to play, U.C.L.A. worked the ball to Walton, who was off on a 12-foot shot. Two Bruins missed follow-up shots as time ran out.

Thus U.C.L.A., which set the collegiate record with 61 victories in a row by winning here a year ago, was doomed to have its new record end here.

After the game Clay said: "It was one of the greatest feelings I've ever had. I looked out at Gary [Brokaw] with the ball when he was trying to get it into Shoo. Then I saw the defense shift in to Gary and I was alone, so I called to him for the ball."

Shumate, who played well against Walton despite the big man's excellent performance, said: "Walton's a devastating player. He's got everything." Then he raised his arm and pointed, "We're No. 1."

Phelps said: "When they shot 70 per cent in the first half, they were something. Whew! They're a great team, just great. Now we have to get ready for Kansas Tuesday night and then St. Francis Thursday night, and then we get ready for U.C.L.A. again.

"Sure it was a great victory, but what we want most of all is a bid to the N.C.A.A. championship, so each game means as much as each other game as they approach. Undefeated isn't so much as not

losing too many to lose that bid."

Then he added with a laugh: "I hope I get a call from President Nixon saying we shouldn't fly to Los Angeles because of the fuel shortage."

Notre Dame has a 10-0 record and U.C.L.A. is 13-1. This was only the sixth defeat for U.C.L.A. in the last eight seasons during which Wooden's Bruins have won 218 games.

Wooden said:

"Once we got the game to break the record, it was relatively meaningless. We knew it would end sometime. Now we have to win our conference to defend our national title."

Then the coach added, "The travel call against Curtis and the charge call on Wilkes were important."

Asked if he had objected to the officials' calls on those late key plays, Wooden replied, "They were close and could have gone the other way."

Wooden refused to permit reporters to talk to his players after the game. "Only winners talk," he said. However, he had repeatedly closed the dressing room to reporters after his teams had won N.C.A.A. championship games.

U.C.L.A. (70) Wilkes 6. 6-7, 18; Trgovich 3, 1-1, 7; Walton 12, 0-0, 24; Curtis 3, 3-4, 5; Meyers 5, 0-2, 10; Lee 0, 2-2, 2; Johnson 0, 0-0, 0. Totals—29, 12-16.
NOTRE DAME (71)—Brokaw 10, 5-7, 25; Clay 2, 3-4, 7; Shumate 11, 2-4, 24; Dantley 4, 1-1, 9; Novak 0, 0-0, 0, Paterno 2, 0-0, 4; Martin 1, 0-0, 2 Totals—30, 11-16.
Half-time score—U.C.L.A. 43, Notre Dame 34

Technical fouls Meyers, Brokaw.
Attendance—11,34.

January 20, 1974

Coaches: 12% Foul in Recruiting Fives

By GORDON S. WHITE Jr.
Special to The New York Times

GREENSBORO, N.C., March 24—More than one eighth of the 229 major colleges and universities that play basketball—about 29 or 30 institutions—are making illegal offers to athletes in order to recruit them, according to a year-long survey released today by the National Association of Basketball Coaches.

The study indicates that of the colleges trying to attract high school athletes with improper inducements, all are offering money, 80 per cent are offering automobiles and more than half are offering clothing.

The survey was conducted by 10 college head or assistant basketball coaches on a committee headed by Frank Arnold, an assistant to John Wooden at the University of California, Los Angeles. Arnold submitted the report to the N.A.B.C. at its annual convention here today.

Arnold said 12.8 per cent of the institutions in America were making illegal offers to youngsters.

"Forty per cent of the youngsters interviewed were offered illegal inducements," he added.

The New York Times recently published a series of articles that indicated widespread malpractice in recruiting that "our alums are the report does not touch on any other sports, such as major college football.

Arnold's committee interviewed 25 recently graduated college basketball players who were highly recruited when in high school, 25 current high school stars now being recruited, 25 sets of parents of such athletes and 25 athletic directors at major basketball colleges.

According to the N.A.B.C. study, some of the athletes who finished their college careers had accepted illegal offers when they went to

college. Arnold gave no indication of what colleges and players had been involved because all athletes, parents and athletic directors interviewed were promised that the information would be confidential.

However, all of the illegal recruiting was conducted by members of the National Collegiate Athletic Association, the study said.

Arnold's committee recommended that steps be taken to correct the problem, stating that "our alums are the biggest problem." He said that alumni and friends of universities were the ones most responsible for the illegal offers.

The committee suggested that an investigator be hired for each of the eight N.C.A.A. districts, to be financed by some private organization, such as the Ford Foundation. Arnold said he had not approached any group to fund this plan, but that he expected it would cost about $500,000 a year.

The N.A.B.C. is meeting in conjunction with the final of the N.C.A.A. basketball tournament, which will be played tomorrow night in the Greensboro Coliseum. North Carolina State will meet Marquette.

A year ago, N. C. State was unable to play in this tournament because it was serving one year's N.C.A.A. probation for illegal recruiting practices involving its best player, David Thompson. Now Thompson will play for the Wolfpack in the title game.

Florida State reached the N.C.A.A. basketball final two years ago after having served a probation for wrongly recruiting some of the players on that team. Florida State was criticized at the time.

Norm Sloan, N. C. State's coach, was asked today if he felt that his squad deserved criticism for the same reason. He replied, "I don't think any such criticism is justified, and that is all I'm going to say."

In other business, the United States Basketball Writers Association asked its members, most of whom serve The Associated Press weekly poll, not to name in their top 10 selections any college team that is under probation from the N.C.A.A.

This action is similar to a step taken by the American Football Coaches Association last January when it recommended that its members not name a probation team to the top 10 on the weekly United Press International poll. The actions are requests, not mandatory.

It is expected that the N.A.B.C. also will ask its members on the U.P.I. weekly basketball ranking committee to eliminate teams serving probations.

The A.P. electors are sports writers and broadcasters. The U.P.I. uses coaches for its polls.

March 25, 1974

N. C. State Takes Title, 76 to 64

Marquette Beaten in N.C.A.A. Final; U.C.L.A. Third

By GORDON S. WHITE Jr.
Special to The New York Times

GREENSBORO, N.C., March 25 — North Carolina State won the National Collegiate Athletic Association basketball championship for the first time tonight, a year after the only undefeated team in the school's history had been barred from the N.C.A.A. tournament.

The Wolfpack broke open a close battle late in the first half to beat Marquette, 76-64, in the title game before 15,742 persons in the Greensboro Coliseum and a national television audience.

Thus the Carolinians became the first team other than U.C.L.A. to win the crown since 1967. That was the year the University of California, Los Angeles, began a string of seven straight championships.

U.C.L.A. had to settle for third place as the Bruins rallied to beat Kansas, 76-61, in the consolation game. It marked the end of Bill Walton's brilliant college career. The big Bruin redhead played 20 minutes and led the rally early in the second half.

Last season N.C. State had to sit by and watch as U.C.L.A. moved to its seventh straight title. The school had been put on probation for a year by the N.C.A.A. for irregularities in recruiting David Thompson, an outstanding player from North Carolina.

Tonight Thompson was the individual star, as he had been all season for a team that lost only one game. He scored 21 points and did everything well.

However, the Wolfpack got a break when Al McGuire, the Warriors' coach, drew two quick technical fouls in

Associated Press

Monte Towe, right, of North Carolina State and Lloyd Walton of Marquette going after a loose ball during last night's N.C.A.A. final at Greensboro, N.C.

the first half, which, according to McGuire, "cost the game."

Marquette's young team (with only one starting senior) had fought from 8 points back to take the lead by a point when the officials called a foul against a Warrior in a scramble under the Marquette basket. The man fouled was Thompson. McGuire complained and drew his first technical.

Shortly afterward Bo Ellis, a big freshman, seemed to have blocked a driving layup by State's Phil Spence cleanly. But Ellis was called for goaltending, and McGuire ran onto the court in a rage. Again he was hit with a technical.

Each technical amounted to 5 points for the Wolfpack (the two foul shots off the referee's call, the technical and a subsequent basket on taking possession after the technical).

When McGuire and others had calmed down, the Wolfpack moved in two minutes from a 28-27 deficit to a 37-28 lead. It was never headed thereafter, and the title went to the State of North Carolina for the second time in the tournament's history. The University of North Carolina won it in 1957.

The officials, who will long be remembered for their calls in this game, were Jim Howell of the Southern Conference and Irv Brown of the Western Athletic Conference.

McGuire said: "North Carolina State is a better ball club than Marquette. Officials never win or lose a game.

"But I would say I gave two 5-point plays. I'd rather not discuss the calls 'cause I'm absolutely correct."

Until the technical, Marquette's slow, patient offense had managed to keep control of the situation before the highly partisan crowd. Using a "wheel" attack around Tommy Burleson, State's 7-foot-4-inch center, Marquette waited for the right chances to shoot.

The plan was paying off and, at the same time, causing State to miss the pace of its fast attack. Then came the break. State took over and ran a high-speed attack with a big lead in hand. Free to take chances, Thompson, Monte Towe and Mo Rivers made a bit of recklessness bring dividends.

Maurice Lucas of Marquette matched Thompson with 21 points and had 13 rebounds. Ellis had 11 rebounds and did well for a freshman, considering that much of his job was to hold off Burleson, who is 7 inches taller.

It was much a case of a young team primarily of freshmen, sophomores and juniors playing an experienced team with some individuals, such as Thompson and Burleson, who were about the best in their positions in college basketball. Towe, at 5-7, the shortest player in the tournament, is one of the most effective guards in the country.

State beat U.C.L.A. last Saturday in the semifinals and gained revenge for its only loss of the season on Dec. 15. It had to win two difficult tournaments in three weeks for the crown, first taking the Atlantic Coast Conference playoff March 9, after victories over North Carolina and Maryland.

Norm Sloan, State's coach, said:

"The last three weeks seemed like an eternity. We might have had more tough games to get here than any other team in N.C.A.A. tournament history."

CHAMPIONSHIP

NORTH CAROLINA STATE (76)

	fgm	fga	ftm	fta	reb	a	pf	pts
Stoddard	3	4	2	2	7	2	5	8
Thompson	7	12	7	8	7	2	3	21
Burleson	6	9	2	6	11	0	4	14
Rivers	4	9	6	7	3	5	2	14
Towe	5	10	6	7	3	2	1	16
Spence	1	2	1	3	2	0	3	3
Moeller	0	0	0	0	0	0	0	0
Total	26	46	24	34	33	14	17	76

MARQUETTE (64)

	fgm	fga	ftm	fta	reb	a	pf	pts
Ellis	5	16	0	0	11	1	5	12
Tatum	2	7	0	0	3	1	4	4
Lucas	7	13	7	9	13	0	4	21
Walton	4	10	0	0	2	2	3	8
Washington	3	13	5	8	4	0	3	11
Delsman	0	0	0	0	0	0	2	0
Daniels	1	3	1	2	0	2	3	3
Campbell	2	3	0	0	1	0	3	4
Homan	0	4	1	2	6	1	2	1
Brennan	0	0	0	0	0	0	0	0
Total	25	69	14	21	40	7	29	64

fgm—Field goals made. fga—Field goals attempted. ftm—Free throws mad. fta—Free throws attempted. reb—Rebounds. a—Assists. pf—Personal fouls. pts—Total points.
North Carolina State 39
Marquette 30
Referees—Jim Howll (S.C.) and Irv Brown (WAC).
Attendance—15,742.

March 26, 1974

The suspended players were Hairston, of Detroit; Wilson, of Dowagiac, Mich.; Peter Davis, Brooklyn; Bill Glover, Pontiac, Mich.; Benny White, Detroit; Bob Chapman, Saginaw, Mich.; Lovell Rivers, Detroit; Cedric Milton, Denver, and Terry Furlow and Tom McGill, both of Flint. Chapman and Wilson are sophomores, and Furlow, Milton and White are juniors. The rest are seniors.

Tropf, who is nearly 6 feet 7 inches tall, started at center and played well under the circumstances. He led all scorers with 21 points, although Indiana, one of the top-rated teams in the country, substituted players often after building a half-time lead of 53-22.

Several of the junior varsity players, four of whom are black, were home for the holidays and had to travel about 80 miles to play in the game. Ganakas had called them immediately after the morning walkout.

Tropf, one of two players on the varsity who are white (the other, Jim Dudley, is injured), said after the game that some of the suspended players had told him, "It isn't anything personal."

Terms of the suspension were not defined by Ganakas. One of the players said, "We won't have anything to say until we talk to Burt Smith," the Michigan State athletic director.

Smith, who is in San Francisco for National Collegiate football meetings, is not expected back on campus until Wednesday.

INDIANA (107)—Bay, 5 0-0 10; Green, 5 2-2 12; Benson, 6 1-2 13; Wilkerson, 4 0-0 8; Buckner, 1 2-2 4' Laskowski, 5 0-0 10; Abernathy, 1 0-0 2; Radford, 4 0-0 8; Ahlfeld, 2 0 10 4; Wisman, 4 0-0 8; Haymore, 6 0-0 12; Noort, 5 2-2 12; Allen, 2 0-0 4; Total 50 7-8 107.
MICHIGAN STATE (55)—Loft, 2 0-2 4; Bird, 2 0-0 4; Tropf, 8 5-7 21, Talaga, 3 2-2 8; Lockett, 2 0-1 4, Flowers, 2 0-0 4; McGray, 2 0-2 4, Vanden Bussche 3 0-2 6; Total 24 7-16 55.
Half-time score—Indiana 53, Michigan State 22. Fouled out—none, Total fouls—Indiana 15, Michigan State 11. Attendance—6,500.

January 5, 1975

---

10 Blacks at Michigan State Suspended in Rift With Coach

Special to The New York Times

EAST LANSING, Mich., Jan. 4—All 10 black players on the Michigan State basketball team were suspended today after they walked out of a team meeting before their Big Ten game against Indiana.

Coach Gus Ganakas, who issued the suspensions, was forced to play the game with members of the junior varsity and Jeff Tropf, a white and the only remaining member of the varsity. Indiana, the defending conference champion, ran away with a 107-55 victory, inflicting the worst defeat on Michigan State in the school's hisory.

The walkout which took place at a morning meeting, occurred when Ganakas announced that Tropf, a freshman who had seen only limited action in previous games, averaging 3.3 points a game, would start in place of Edgar Wilson, a sophomore forward.

"When they came to my name," Tropf said after the game, "the coaches said that I was supposed to guard [Steve] Green. Lindsay Hairston [Michigan State's star center and captain] said he didn't think I should start. He said they should start an older, more mature guy to guard Green.

"But coach didn't think so, and they walked out."

Although the incident appeared to have racial overtones, Ganakas said: "They are my players. I feel good compassion, good feeling between us. It might have been caused by a lot of things, not one thing. I don't know."

A mixed reaction of cheers and boos from many of the 6,500 fans greeted the announcement of the suspension 10 minutes before the start of the game. Marshall Dill, the school's star sprinter, and Charlie Baggett, quarterback of the football team, walked with the suspended players in front of the home stands shortly before the remaining squad came on the court.

Asked for an explanation, all 10 players replied, "No comment." Then they went into the stands to watch the game to the mixed cheers and boos of the fans.

Women's Basketball Draws 11,969

By LENA WILLIAMS

Two women's collegiate basketball teams, Queens and Immaculata, got their chance to play at Madison Square Garden yesterday, and they rebounded, set picks, went to the offensive boards and generally dazzled the 11,969 spectators.

Immaculata, the three-time national women's collegiate champion, defeated Queens, 65-61, but Coach Cathy Rush was as pleased by the size of the crowd as she was by the victory.

"We proved that people will pay to see women play basketball," said Coach Rush above the noise of her shouting, cheering players in the dressing room. "There were two of the best women's teams out there today and when you're good, people will come to see you play."

The game, the first of an afternoon double-header, was the first women's intercollegiate basketball contest ever held at the Garden. Fairfield defeated Massachusetts, 78-67, in the second game, a men's contest, but more than half the crowd had left before the finish. A Garden employe estimated the crowd had dwindled to about 4,000 by half-time of the men's game.

Immaculata, a women's Catholic college located near Philadelphia, improved its won-lost record to 14-2, and was led by Mary Schraff, a 5-foot-8-inch guard who had 12 points and nine rebounds.

"I remembered that they [Queens] had beaten us last year and stopped our 35- game winning streak. That really hurt," said iss Scharff, a sophomore. "I wasn't concerned about scoring as much as I was finding the open man or girl and getting to the boards. We were nervous at first, but by the second half we calmed down and started moving the ball better."

College women play men's rules with a 30-second clock.

There were banners, pom poms, a mascot, and a cheering section of at least 500 students who had come by bus to cheer for the Macs.

Two sophomores from Immaculata, who described themselves as avid basketball fans, said they had purchased their tickets more than a month ago, and were confident that the Macs were on their way to their fourth consecutive women's national title.

Lucille Kyvallos, the Queens coach, said after the game: "We played a good game, but I saw areas for improvement, especially on defense. At least we didn't play a sloppy game. Both teams looked extremely good and the crowd reaction was fantastic."

And while the crowd was predominantly female, Miguel Gaston, a City College male student who is enrolled in a basketball course, was "quite surprised" by the women's game.

"I thought they would play like girls, but they're really hustling out there," he said, pausing to watch Debbie (The Pearl) Mason of Queens go in for a lay-up. "She is simply fantastic. She has moves like Earl Monroe."

Ed Rush, coach Rush's husband and a referee for the American Basketball Association, was pleased that the girls got caught only once on the 30-second violation.

"We have the 30-second rule in the A.B.A. and it really helps the flow of the game," Rush explained. "I think the men's collegiate teams are going to have to institute the 30-second rule sooner or later to keep the flow of the game going."

According to both coaches, the institution of men's rules helped spark an interest in the women's game and led to the Garden invitation.

Although there is no written agreement with the Garden, Miss Kyvallos said she feels certain that Queens will be invited back.

Fairfield, which has now won seven of its last nine games, helped its chances for a National Invitation Tournament bid with its victory over Massachusetts.

Massachusetts, with a 14-7 record, entered the game with a four-game winning streak and hopes for a postseason tournament berth. Fairfield's record now stands at 11-11.

Fairfield's Ralph Rhen, a senior forward, led all scorers with 24 points. He gave the Stags their biggest lead, 13 points, midway in the first half.

Fairfield shot 57 per cent from the floor, while Massachusetts managed a 43.5 field goal percentage.

IMMACULATA (65) -- Muth, 2 5 6 9; Scharff, 6 0-0 12; Martin, 0 3-4 3; Canuso, 3 4-4 10; Crawford, 2 3-5 7; Gross 3 1-1 7; Gable, 5 1-3 11; Sims, 2 0-0 4; Van Buskirk, 0 2-4 2. Totals—23 19-29.
QUEENS (63)—Manning, 4 0-0 8; Marquis, 4 0-0 8; Weiss, 0 2-5 2; Chait, 6 2-2 14; Mason, 6 1-3 13; Gwyn, 2 0-0 4; Schneider, 5 0-0 10; Rullo, 0 2-2 2. Totals—27 7-12.
MASSACHUSETTS (67)—Murphy 5 6-6 16; Pyatt 10 0-0 20; Town 4 1-1 9, Burke 0 0-0 0; Estridge 2 3-5 7; Endicott 2 3-4 7; Duarte 4 0-0 8. Totals—27 13 14
FAIRFIELD (78)—Mahon 4 5-7 13; Penn 9 6-8 24; Balkun 3 0-1 6; Kelly 1 5-8 7; Odums 5 6-7 16; Nolan 3 0-0 6; Pietka 2 0-0 4; Finn 1 0-0 2 Totals—28 22-31
Half time score—Fairfield 39, Massachusetts 35. Attendance—11,969.

February 23, 1975

U.C.L.A. Five Beats Kentucky, 92-85

Using Only One Substitute, Wooden of Bruins Retires With 10th N.C.A.A. Title

By GORDON S. WHITE Jr.
Special to The New York Times

SAN DIEGO, March 31 — The University of California, Los Angeles won the National Collegiate basketball championship tonight for the 10th and last time under the direction of Coach John Wooden.

The Bruins, proving speed more valuable than muscle, raced up and down court from start to finish to beat a powerful University of Kentucky team, 92-85, in Wooden's final game before retirement.

When it was done, the crowd of 15,153 at the San Diego Arena remained to give Wooden, the Wizard of Westwood, a standing ovation for about four minutes.

In increasing their record of national basketball titles to 10 in the last 12 years and 8 in the last 9, the Bruins beat the school closest to them in national titles. The Wildcats have four.

Although he would not admit it, this victory in his final game of 27 seasons as the U.C.L.A. coach may have been Wooden's most satisfying. This was a team not as strong as many of his former national champions—one not rated certain of the crown when the season began.

Wooden said following the thrilling triumph, "To say I thought we would win [the title] back then would be stretching a point."

But Dave Meyers, the senior star of the team, said: "I wanted to do it for Coach all season. He's done a masterful job with the team that lost [Bill] Walton and [Keith] Wilkes," stars of the three preceding seasons.

Most unexpected of all, however, was the fact that U.C.L.A. beat Kentucky using only six players. This was the first time Wooden used only six players in a nation-

Associated Press

Dave Meyers of U.C.L.A. falling to the floor after diving for ball picked off by Rick Robey of Kentucky in National Collegiate championship game in San Diego.

al championship game. It paid off as the half - dozen slim, tall men kept up an unusually fast pace and achieved what U.C.L.A. teams in 1964 and 1965, and from 1967 through 1973, had achieved. And those teams had such star players as Walt Hazzard, Lew Alcindor, Sidney Wicks and Bill Walton.

Battle of Boards

The mighty six who won this year's crown were Meyers, Marques Johnson, Rich Washington, Pete Trgovich, Andre McCarter and Ralph Drollinger, the man who came off the bench and had the finest game of his career.

The running Bruins took off against the strong but slower Wildcats and managed to go through 40 minutes of hard physical action without losing one man through personal fouls. However Meyers, Washington, Trgovich and Drollinger finished with four fouls each—one short of banishment.

What they did was beat such big men as Bob Guyette, 6 feet, 9 inches and 240 pounds; Rick Robey, 6-10 and 240; Mike Phillips, 6-10 and 235 and Dan Hall, 6-10

and 235.

They beat them because Washington and Drollinger gained position under the boards. In perhaps the most important statistic U.C.L.A. outrebounded Kentucky, 55 to 49. Most of this season, the Southeastern Conference co-champions had been beating teams off the boards.

Other winning factors involved the way Trgovich, a 6-4 guard, defended against Jimmy Dan Conner, the pride of Kentucky's corps of strong, tall guards. Conner was held to 9 points. Trgovich, meanwhile, had an excellent night on defense and scored 16.

Trgovich, a senior, scored 10 of U.C.L.A.'s 12 points in a five-minute period late in the first half when the Bruins took the lead for keeps. The Wildcats however, moved within a point with 6½ minutes left in the game.

Washington, voted the outstanding player of the tournament, paced U.C.L.A.'s scoring with 28 points. Many of these came on rebounds and the 6-9 sophomore's short field goal from the baseline with 1 minute 23 seconds to go gave U.C.L.A. an 88-83 lead to virtually assure the victory.

Meyers had 24 points, Drollinger 10, McCarter 8 and Johnson 6. It just didn't matter that Kevin Grevey, Kentucky's leading scorer, had 34. He was scoring well off screens set up for him. But the only big man on Kentucky who managed to score well was Guyette, the senior, who had 16 points.

Robey had only 2 points before fouling out. Phillips had only 4 and Hall only 2. Kentucky needed more from its big men.

Drollinger, the 7-foot-1 junior who has been criticized because he was not an Alcindor or Walton, was unusually strong under the boards. The frail Drollinger stood in there for 16½ minutes and beat off the Kentucky rebounders Coach Joe Hall kept fresh by sending them into the game in relays.

The victory allowed the Bruins to forget some things, such as a 22-point loss to the University of Washington during the regular season that was the third worst defeat the 64-year-old Wooden suffered in his 40 years as a head coach in high school and college ranks. For his

last season Bruins won 28 and lost 3.

Indiana University was the favorite to win the tournament. It was the first time since 1966, when U.C.L.A. was not in the tourney, that the Bruins were not picked to take the title.

U.C.L.A. had difficulty getting to the title game, winning a first-round game with Michigan in overtime, another game over Montana by just 3 points and the semifinal thriller with Louisville, 75-74, in overtime when Washington sank the winning basket with four seconds remaining.

Louisville went to overtime again in the consolation game, beating Syracuse for third place, 96-88.

CHAMPIONSHIP GAME

U.C.L.A. (92)—Meyers 9 6-7 24, Johnson 3 0-1 6, Washington 12 4-5 28, Trgovich 7 2-4 16, McCarter 3 2-3 8, Drollinger 4 2-5 10. Totals—38 16-25.

KENTUCKY (85)—Grevey 13 8-10 34, Guyette 7 2-2 16, Robey 1 0-0 2, Conner 4 1-2 9, Flynn 3 4-5 10, Givens 3 2-3 8, Johnson 0 0-0 0, Phillips 1 2-3 4, Hall 1 0-0 2, Lee 0 0-0 0. Totals—33 19-25.

Half-time score—U.C.L.A. 43, Kentucky 40. Fouled out—Robey. Total fouls—U.C.L.A. 19, Kentucky 28. Technical—Meyers. Attendance—15,153.

April 1, 1975

The Girl on the Men's Team Casts an Eye Toward Fashion

By SHAWN G. KENNEDY

Cyndi Meserve did not go to Pratt Institute last fall to play basketball. She was more interested in fashion.

But before the term had ended Miss Meserve was known on campus and throughout the country as "the girl who plays basketball," when she became the first woman to play on a National Collegiate Athletic Association Men's varsity team. But next term may find her again playing with women.

"She got a lot of mail," said Tony Missere, Pratt's basketball coach, during an interview at the school's Brooklyn campus. "Letters from little girls who wanted instruction, from prisoners in Florida and even white orchids from Rome."

Miss Meserve nodded and smiled as the coach talked about the magazine, newspaper and television interviews, fan mail from around the world and the resolution in the Maine assembly honoring her for her "outstanding achievements and exceptional accomplishments."

"But sometimes I think too much attention was paid to the fact that I was a woman

basketball player and not enough to what I did on the court," she said. "People constantly harped on things like dressing facilities and my position on women's lib."

That she really didn't have a position, Miss Meserve said, riled a few people who

apparently expected more than just basketball from the first female in the game.

For Miss Meserve, an 18-year-old freshman who played on a girl's high school team in Livermore Falls, Me., the problems of adjusting to the demands of the men's game and keeping up with fellow players on the court soon gave way to those that come to a sports world anomaly.

"There were times early in the season when it seemed that more reporters, photographers and camera crews were at our practice sessions than players," Mr. Missere said with a laugh.

"I enjoyed playing with the men," Miss Meserve said. "I liked learning the different aspects of the men's game. It's faster than women's basketball and some of the rules are different."

But how did the men feel? Especially the player who threatened not to play if Miss Meserve was put on the team?

Miss Meserve said that her teammates were supportive throughout the season.

"They were great," she said. "Even during games like the one with Kings Point

where the crowd kept chanting 'We want Cyndi, we want Cyndi.'"

"I think that once the season began and the guys realized that Cyndi was serious about playing ball and that she was a valuable team member, the few who had objected in the beginning changed their minds," Mr. Missere added.

Steve Lightburn was one of them.

"I guess I rejected her in the beginning," he added. "But Cyndi did all right." Mr. Lightburn said that despite his change of heart he would like to see a stronger all-male team next year.

Belford Diggs, another Pratt player, was more generous.

"Cyndi scored and brought people out for the games," he said. "And she seemed to be able to outmove some of the guys. I think women might have a slight advantage, their reflexes are faster."

No Big Welcome

But none of the Pratt players said they welcomed women into the game or that they expected coed teams to invade intercollegiate basketball.

Thomas Flahivem, captain of the basketball team at St. Joseph's, another Brooklyn school, said he had watched Miss Meserve play when his team met Pratt last season, and although he said he thought she was a "pretty good athlete" he did not feel that women belonged on the men's team.

"I have reservations about women playing with the men," Richard Vogel, another St. Joseph's player, said. "Basketball is not supposed to be a contact sport, but it is. It can get very physical."

But Miss Meserve and other women who want to play with the men have at least one player in their corner. Luis Blas, a Baruch College senior who guarded Miss Meserve during a game, said:

"I wish more women would play. I think coed teams would be fun. I appreciated her position as the first woman to play, and I was thrilled to have played the year she played."

Basketball is her sport, but Miss Meserve hopes to make fashion a career. She turned down opportunities to go to schools that did have women's basketball in favor of Pratt, because of its fashion design program.

"I haven't made any solid career plans yet," she said the other day. "But this semester I took pattern making, fashion sketching, textiles and design, and right now I'm sort of leaning toward sportswear design."

That day Miss Meserve did not look like a basketball player. Dressed in a pale green two-piece dress with a long, full skirt, a roll-up sleeved big top, and a green and white scarf knotted around her neck, she looked as if foul line shots and field goals were the farthest fhings from her mind.

So what about next year? Will Miss Meserve play again as one of the eight returning lettermen (letterpeople?) or was one season of playing with the men enough?

"Every player must try out every year," Mr. Missere said. "So we don't know now who will be on next year's team. And we have a brand-new sports facility that we hope will attract potential players."

The coach went on to say that the new facility has increased the chances of a junior varsity team and a women's team as well.

"I'd rather play on a women's team," Miss Meserve said: "and I hope it becomes a reality next year."

May 23, 1975

Indiana Takes N.C.A.A. Title by 86-68

Michigan Is Defeated in Final— Rutgers Loses to U.C.L.A. for Third Place, 106-92

By GORDON S. WHITE Jr.
Special to The New York Times

PHILADELPHIA, March 29 —Indiana won a war.

The prize for victory in the last battle was the 38th National Collegiate Athletic Association basketball championship for the undefeated Hoosiers.

It was a battle from the start, a physical struggle of body contact and bruises with one hospitalized athlete, before Indiana managed to whip Michigan, 86-68, tonight in the title game at the Spectrum.

Bobby Wilkerson, a standout 6-foot-7-inch guard, suffered a mild concussion early in the game and was in Temple University Hospital by the time his teammates were leaping with joy and celebrating the third N.C.A.A. basketball title in Indiana University history.

Shortly before the start of one of the hardest-fought college basketball championship games, the University of California, Los Angeles, handed Rutgers its second loss of a big season by beating the Scarlet Knights, 106-92, in the third-place contest. Rutgers, which suffered its first loss after 31 victories in the semi-finals to Michigan Saturday, was not criticized by its coach, Tom Young, following a good but losing effort against U.C.L.A. He had leveled strong criticism against his team after the defeat by Michigan.

First Title Since 1953

Coach Bobby Knight, the 35-year-old disciplinarian who demands near perfection, got just about that from his players in the second half so that Indiana became only the seventh team in N.C.A.A. history to win the national title at the conclusion of a perfect season.

Knight was sweating, minus his coat and tie, and willing to talk for hours after the team won Indiana's third N.C.A.A. championship

Associated Press
Kent Benson of Indiana grabbing ball as Michigan's Tom Bergen defended

101

and first since 1953.

Johnny Orr, the usually humorous Michigan coach, declared Indiana "for sure the No. 1 team" after his team lost to the Hoosiers for the third time this season. Indiana beat the Wolverines twice during the Big Ten Conference season and beat them by the widest of the three margins in the first N.C.A.A. title game involving teams from the same conference.

The muscle needed in this test of strength and the scoring were provided down the stretch by Kent Benson, the strongest of the Hoosiers; Scott May, the big, husky forward, and Quinn Buckner, the one-time football player, who is a strong guard. These three scored 36 of Indiana's first 38 points in the second half when the Hoosiers rallied from a 35-29 halftime deficit to take the lead for good.

Benson, who commands respect with 245 pounds on a 6-11 frame, scored 25 points in all and the 6-7 May, who shoots out of a crowd as well as anyone, had the high for the game of 26 points. Buckner tallied 16.

This was the finale of the college careers for May, Buckner and Tom Abernethy, the three starting seniors who were around to celebrate at the end. Wilkerson is also a senior who started his final Indiana game. But he played only 2½ minutes before being knocked unconscious.

The crowd of 17,540 in the Spectrum and the national

television audience watched for nine minutes before the 6-7 guard was carried to a dressing room on a stretcher and action resumed. He regained consciousness there and was taken to the hospital.

Wilkerson was knocked out like a prize fighter when he ran up court in an unsuccessful attempt to prevent Michigan's Wayman Britt from scoring on a fast-break layup. Both players went up, the ball went through the net, and after the shot, Wayman's left elbow struck Wilkerson over the left temple. He was probably unconscious when he hit the floor. Attending physicians said he suffered a "mild concussion."

Buckner said after the game: "We knew then we just had to go at it a little tougher with Bobby out. And we did."

May said: "There was no panic after Bobby left. We've been behind before. We're used to it."

Benson, May and Buckner found ways to work in close for baskets in the second half and led the defense, the biggest factor in Indiana's success. The Hoosiers stuck with the faster and quick Michigan players until they had the Wolverines whipped.

Michigan's best big man, Phil Hubbard, couldn't make it all the way against Benson as he fouled out with 7½ minutes to go. The Hoosiers were in control then and it

was obvious Indiana was going to succeed U.C.L.A. as the champion.

For Knight the national title was the reward for being a tenacious, driving and hard taskmaster ever since he became a head basketball coach in 1965. After six seasons as the coach at Army, Knight moved to Indiana where he has built for this moment through five seasons of work and controversy.

The 6-5 former Ohio State player is noted for defense on the court, words with officials on and off the court and running battles with many of his critics. But he proved his method is successful tonight as big men, recruited for the job, won the title after he molded them to play his kind of basketball.

Green Paces Michigan

Rickey Green, one of the shortest and the quickest of the Wolverines, scored 18 points to be Michigan's high man. He established himself as the fast and quick man throughout the tournament.

After U.C.L.A. won the consolation game, the Rutgers coach, Young, said, "We certainly weren't embarrassed against U.C.L.A." Following Rutgers' loss to Michigan Saturday, Young had said his team was "embarrassed" and "stunk out the place."

Marques Johnson was the hero for the Bruins as he scored 30 points and got 18 rebounds in one of the best

games of his career. But a year ago he shared in the national title, the 10th in 12 years for U.C.L.A. This was the second time in the last 13 championship tournaments that U.C.L.A. finished third.

Gene Bartow, in his first year as head coach at U.C.L.A., fell short of the usual Bruins' goal, which is the national title. He succeeded John Wooden, who coached all 10 national champions at U.C.L.A. and retired after last year's championship.

Indiana is now moving along in the way U.C.L.A. did under Wooden as the Hoosiers have won all 32 games this season and 64 of their last 65 games. Indiana's last defeat was to Kentucky in the third round of the 1975 N.C.A.A. tournament.

CHAMPIONSHIP GAME

MICHIGAN (68)	G.	F.	P	INDIANA (86)	G.	F.	P
Britt	5	1-1	11	Abernathy	4	3-3	11
Robinson	4	0-1	8	May	10	6-6	26
Hubbard	4	2-2	10	Benson	11	3-5	25
Green	7	4-5	18	Wilkerson	0	0-0	0
Grote	4	4-6	12	Buckner	5	4-9	16
Bergen	0	0-0	0	Radford	0	0-0	0
Staton	2	3-4	7	Wisman	0	2-3	2
Baxter	0	0-0	0	Crews	0	2-2	2
Thompson	0	0-0	0	Valavicius	1	0-0	2
Hardy	1	0-0	2	Haymore	1	0-0	2
				Bender	0	0-0	0
Total	27	14-19	68	Total	32	22-38	86

Halftime—Michigan 35, Indiana 29.
Referees—Bob Wortman and Irv Brown.
Attendance—17,540.

U.C.L.A. (106)	G.	F.	P	RUTGERS (92)	G.	F.	P
Washington	5	1-2	11	Sellers	8	7-10	23
Greenwood	2	1-2	5	Copeland	9	0-2	18
Drollinger	6	0-0	12	Bailey	3	1-1	7
McCarter	11	4-4	26	Jordan	4	0-2	8
Johnson	11	8-12	30	Dabney	9	3-5	21
Townsend	3	2-2	8	Anderson	4	5-6	13
Vroman	0	0-0	0	Conlin	0	0-0	0
Smith	3	2-2	8	Hefele	1	0-0	2
Spillane	2	0-0	4				
Olinde	1	0-0	2				
Total	44	18-24	106	Total	38	16-27	92

Halftime score—U.C.L.A. 57, Rutgers 49.
Referees—Charles Fouty and Jim Bain.

March 30, 1976

Marquette Beats N. Carolina, Wins Title for McGuire, 67-59

By GORDON S. WHITE Jr.

By The Associated Press

ATLANTA, March 28—Al McGuire went out of basketball tonight as the champion.

Usually wise-cracking or yelling at something or someone, the coach of Marquette University had his head bowed and tears were rolling down his face when the buzzer sounded and his Marquette Warriors had beaten North Carolina, 67-59, in the title game of the National Collegiate Athletic Association tournament at the Omni.

The 48-year-old McGuire thus had the biggest prize of his life on the final day of 20 years as a head basketball coach. His streetwise players, the type he always recruited, had scratched and clawed and outsmarted North Carolina to conclude the 39th annual national tournament before 16,089 fans and a national television audience.

McGuire, who is leaving coaching to become a business executive in Milwaukee, the home city of Marquette,

had taken eight previous Marquette teams into the national tournament, only to fall short. His 1974 team got as far as the final game but lost to North Carolina State.

Tonight, McGuire's city slickers were not going to let this one go, even though it looked as if they would blow it all early in the second half. The result was the first national title for the university and for McGuire. Marquette will have many more chances. McGuire won't.

In what was a battle of basketball wizards, McGuire had the manpower to beat Coach Dean Smith's team. Smith had coached the United States to the Olympic gold medal in basketball last summer.

Before the title game, the University of Nevada, Las Vegas, defeated the University of North Carolina at Charlotte, 106-94, in the consolation game for third place.

McGuire admitted after the championship game that "I was emotional

for a while. I feel washed out. This time the numbers came up right."

McGuire has spent 13 years as head coach at Marquette, and seven before that at Belmont Abbey. He started his basketball on the playgrounds of Far Rockaway, Queens, and continued it as a player for St. John's Prep and St. John's University. He finished the top man because players like himself—"back-alley scrappers," he called them—won for him.

The outstanding player of the tournament was Butch Lee, a Puerto Rican-born guard who lives in the Bronx and grew up playing the street basketball McGuire always knew. Lee scored 19 points tonight. There was Bo Ellis, the big, lanky senior from Chicago, who had 14 points for Marquette. And there was another city-type player, Jim Boylan of Jersey City, who was the scrappiest of the bunch tonight and also made 14 points.

Jerome Whitehead, a Baptist minister's son from Waukegan, Ill., took 11 rebounds and had 8 points. Gary Rosen-

United Press International

North Carolina's John Kuester (15) taking tumble over Gary Rosenberger of Marquette at N.C.A.A. final in Atlanta

berger, a Milwaukee shooter, got a couple of important baskets from outside, and Bernard Toone of Yonkers was there when muscle counted. Bill Neary was the seventh and remaining player for the Warriors, who fit their name tonight.

Marquette, an independent team, and North Carolina, champion of the Atlantic Coast Conference, opened slowly. It was a process of feeling for weaknesses—and finding few. The early patient tactics put things right up McGuire's back alley.

McGuire said: "We played a chess game a while out there. Then it got tough."

Marquette moved to a 39-27 lead at halftime as Lee, Whitehead, Ellis and Toone kept sneaking in the baseline "back door" for points while the Tar Heels began missing. Each team was still taking its time shooting. There were few breakaways for quick points, and the Warriors controlled the boards at this time.

Rough on Inside

But when the second half started, North Carolina came out running in an attempt to catch up, and Marquette was missing, turning the ball over and slipping about in some confusion.

Finally, North Carolina caught the Warriors and even passed them at 45-43. The North Carolina fans went wild. The game seemed to turn, and it seemed that perhaps McGuire was never going to have his title.

But the coach called timeout, yelled a lot, stormed about and had no chance to hear his wife, Pat, who was seven rows back in the seats standing and screaming to Al, "Shut up." The Marquette players probably didn't hear

much from their coach in the noise of the Omni. But they came back settled down and ready to play their kind of game again.

They once more kept North Carolina from getting inside, as they had in the beginning. There was the key. And when North Carolina went into its famed four-corner offense for three minutes after that slim, 2-point lead, Marquette handled it just perfectly. Marquette was not enticed into making rash mistakes, and eventually Carolina failed as Bruce Buckley shot from the four-corners attack—and Ellis blocked it. Marquette had the inside under full control, and North Carolina never used the four-corners again.

Marquette got back in front, 47-45, when Ellis fed Boylan after a long spell of working the ball around for a shot. It was inside control for the Warriors that did it, but there was plenty of time left for Carolina—8½ minutes.

The teams were again both stalling, but it was a rougher game. Contact was constant, although points were rare. The two North Carolina freshmen —Mike O'Koren and Rich Yonakor— were doing the best they could to defend against Ellis and Whitehead. And Phil Ford, the fine Carolina guard, was working the ball and trying shots.

But Marquette held fast and North Carolina was fouling, in large part trying to gain control of the ball. The Warriors made 14 of their last 20 points on free throws, missing only one foul shot down the stretch, and became winners in fact at the foul line.

But Not Smith

In one incident, the officials took a long time to explain a foul situation

in which Marquette's Toone elbowed an opponent after the ball was blown dead by a Carolina foul. A technical against Toone for elbowing drew two shots that Walter Davis made, but it was too little too late. A jump ball followed because it was an "advantageous jump-ball situation" a foul after the ball was dead.

All this didn't deter the Warriors, who were about to be the champions. Ellis controlled the jump to prove this point.

Davis, who scored 20 points for North Carolina, got 10 of his team's last 12. No one else could do much in those late stages to upset the street gang

CHAMPIONSHIP GAME								
NORTH CAROLINA (59)								
	fgm	fga	ftm	fta	reb	pf	a	pts.
Davis	6	13	8	10	8	4	3	20
O'Koren	6	10	2	4	11	5	0	14
Yonakor	3	5	0	0	4	0	1	6
Ford	3	10	0	0	2	3	5	6
Kuester	2	6	1	2	8	5	6	5
Cretsion	1	1	0	0	0	0	0	2
Zaliagiris	2	3	0	0	0	3	0	4
Bradley	7	1	0	0	0	2	0	2
Buckley	0	1	0	0	3	0	0	0
Wolf	0	1	0	0	1	0	0	0
Colescott	0	0	0	0	0	0	0	0
Coley	0	0	0	0	0	0	0	0
Doughton	0	0	0	0	0	0	0	0
Virgil	0	0	0	0	0	1	0	0
Total	24	51	11	16	26	24	15	59

MARQUETTE (67)								
	fgm	fga	ftm	fta	reb	pf	a	pts.
Ellis	5	9	4	5	9	4	1	14
Neary	0	2	0	0	0	1	0	0
Whitehead	2	9	4	4	11	2	2	8
Lee	6	14	7	7	3	1	2	19
Boylan	5	7	4	4	4	3	0	14
Rosenberger	1	1	4	4	1	1	1	6
Toone	3	6	0	1	0	1	0	6
Total	22	47	23	25	28	13	8	67

North Carolina .... 27 32—59
Marquette .... 39 28—67
Referees—Paul Galvin and Reggie Copeland.
Attendance—16,086.

from Marquette. O'Koren, another Jersey City player, made 14 for North Carolina but had his hands full against the big men while playing defense.

Marquette became champion at its own game. The Warriors' style prevailed throughout this tournament, with the title game poducing the lowest point total since Loyola of Chicago defeated Cincinnati in overtime, 60-58, in the 1963 final. But then, McGuire has always claimed that "teams lose to us by only a few points and go away thinking they are still better than us."

The victory gave Marquette a 25-7

won-lost record for the season—hardly an impressive one compared with those undefeated teams from the University of California, Los Angeles, that won titles and with the Indiana team that won a year ago at the end of an undefeated season. But back when McGuire announced his retirement in midseason, the team lost two home games, a rare thing for Marquette. Then the Warriors lost three more home games and things looked hopeless. But Marquette finished by winning nine of its last 10 games, including five in this tourney. Those were as impressive as any undefeated season because the title came

at the end.

Despite the bruising struggle to the wire in the second half, the only injury of note seemed to be McGuire's left foot. He kicked the scorer's table in anger during the first three minutes of the game and came away limping for a few moments. That was the McGuire most fans know so well.

They did not know the McGuire with tears falling for a few seconds after the game. But basketball fans never saw McGuire win an N.C.A.A. title before.

March 29, 1977

Adolph Rupp, Basketball Coach Who Won 879 Games, Is Dead at 76

By SAM GOLDAPER

Adolph Frederick Rupp, the most successful coach in the history of college basketball during 42 years at the University of Kentucky, died last night in the University Medical Center at Lexington. He was 76 years old.

Mr. Rupp, who retired in 1972 after winning 879 games and four national titles, was suffering from cancer of the spine and diabetes. He disclosed his illness to a few close friends late last year and said then that his doctors considered his condition inoperable. He was admitted to tthe Medical Center Nov. 9.

In Kentucky, Mr. Rupp was not only the dean of basketball coaches, but also for more than 40 years he was the only "Baron" in a land of honorary colonels.

No more rabid enthusiast for the state of Kentucky existed than Mr. Rupp, a Kansas boy who traded a Midwestern twang for a soft-spoken drawl. He had a true Chamber of Commerce outlook on life in Kentucky and delighted in reciting the glories of the state.

A heavy-set man, and a pleasant one when he wasn't coaching, Mr. Rupp was dynamic, controversial and colorful. Because of his estate in the rolling farm country outside Lexington, where he tended to his prize Herefords and crops of burley tobacco, he was known to all as The Baron of Bluegrass Country.

Since his favorite coaching attire, out of superstition, was usually a double-breasted brown suit, he also picked up the nickname of the Man in the Brown Suit. At other times he was referred to as Mr. Basketball and Ol' Rupp and Ready.

Victory in First Game

In the first college basketball game he coached in 1930, his fast-breaking Wildcats raced to a 67-19 victory over Georgetown (Ky.) College. In the 41 seasons that followed, he took his teams into tiny, old gymnasiums, new field houses and big-city arenas, where he was often hooted and despised, but always respected.

Unlike some coaches, Mr. Rupp rarely played the role of a substitute father to his players. He was not the chummy sort. He had stern and demanding qualities, inherited from his German-imigrant father. He had reverence for order and precision and demanded it from his players. To some persons, he appeared to be a mean old man.

"A lot of people think we run a Marine Crops outfit," he once said. "Fine, if they think that, that's fine. I knew when I

came here that the only way I could be successful would be to go out and win these basketball games."

Joe Hall, the Kentucky coach who succeeded Mr. Rupp and for many years was his assistant and chief recruiter, once said:

"Coach operates from an extreme competitive desire and has a strong dread for losing."

Regardless of the reason, he always put forth this kind of effort. On his weekly tlevision shows he often said:

"We have to win, we just have to win. Goodness knows, no one wants to win any more than we do."

Winning with Mr. Rupp's passion. Someone once recited to him the famed Grantland Rice line," When the one Great Scorer comes to write against your name, he marks not that you won or lost, but how you played the game.

To this, Mr. Rupp answered:

"Well now, I just don't know about that. If winning isn't so important, why do you keep score?"

Mr. Rupp's achievements were endless. During his coaching tenure and his 879 victories more than any other basketball coach. Under his leadership, Kentucky won four National Collegiate Athletic Association championshps and was the runner-up twice. The Wildcats also won 27 Southeastern Conference titles. Mr. Rupp was honored for his achievements by election to the Helms Athletic Foundation Hall of Fame and the Basketball Hall of Fame in Springfield, Mass.

During his fight to remain as the Kentucky coach after he reached the mandatory retirement age of 70 in 1972, he said, "If they don't let me coach, they might as well take me to the Lexington cemetery."

Mr. Rupp remained in basketball until his death. After his retirement, he was president of the Memphis Tams of the now-defunct American Basketball Association and vice chairman of the board of the directors of the Kentucky Colonels.

Retirement Resisted

His 1948 championship team and the Phillips Oilers of the Amateur Athletic Union combined to represent the United States in the Olympic Games. Kentucky also won National Collegiate titles in 1949, 1951 and 1958.

During the 1969-70 season, Mr. Rupp started to show the effect of his age and poor health, but he refused to retire. That season, looking ghastly and with his voice raspy, he spent five weeks in bed, arising only to go to games, practice

sessions or to his doctor.

During Kentucky's first few games, he sat with his foot supported by a cushion on a chair. His foot ailment was complicated by his diabetic condition.

On Dec. 26, 1967, when Kentucky defeated Notre Dame, 81-73, the victory—No. 772—established Mr. Rupp as college basketball's leading winning coach. The honor previously belonged to Forrest (Phog) Allen of Kansas, who retired with 771 victories after 46 seasons of coaching.

During Mr. Rupp's winning habit, he became a victim of his success. He never heeded criticism, and his recruitment of players was said to have reached every hamlet in Kentucky and its adjoining states.

But with all his success, Mr. Rupp had trying moments, especially in October, 1951, when three of his former players admitted they had accepted $1,500 in bribes to lose deliberately a National Invitation Tournament game at Madison Square Garden on March 14, 1949.

The Kentucky players were involved in a national basketball scandal that touched many college players throughout the nation.

During the trial in New York, in which the thre eformer Kentucky players were placed on indefinite probation, Judge Saul S. Streit in General Sessions Court condemned the athletic practices of the University of Kentucky.

He described them as "the acme of commercialism and overemphasis."

In August, 1952, the Southeastern Conference suspended Kentucky from basketball competition. Three months later the N.C.A.A. penalized the university for rules violations and Kentucky canceled its 1952-53 basketball season.

The following season, Mr. Rupp and his team, the Wildcats, were back. They won all 25 games.

Mr. Rupp was born on Sept. 2, 1901, in Halstead, Kan., where his father homesteaded a 163-acre farm.

December 11, 1977

Women's Basketball: It's Improving With Age

By FRED FERRETTI

In 1899 they wore pantaloons and the nine players on each side of women's basketball teams were forced to root themselves in areas of the court from which they could either pass or shoot.

Today it is tee-shirts and sateen shorts, and women move freely and feint and guard with arms waving, they dribble unrestrainedly and they drive and lay up as aggressively as any men. Women's basketball has evolved.

It is no longer a polite, pallid imitation of men's basketball, in which femininity must be insured, but basketball, played by women. The Association for Intercollegiate Athletics for Women, wich governs women's sports, says that of its 822 member schools more than 650 compete in basketball.

Rising Interest Noted

According to the National Federation for State High Schools Association the 14,931 high schools which have women's sports report 388,000 participants in basketball programs. In 1971 the federation reported 294,000 women in sports programs of all kinds; today that figure stands at 1.6 million.

The numbers aside, there are other indicators of a rising interest and participation of women in basketball. Schools such as Penn State, North Carolina State, UCLA, LSU, the United States Military Academy, the Universities of Tennessee, Maryland and Rutgers have fielded teams to join the traditional women's basketball squads from places like Delta State, Montclair State, Wayland Baptist, Immaculata, Old Dominion and Queens College.

Most colleges actively recruit women basketball players, and according to the womenSports Scholarship Guide, most major colleges now have basketball scholarships for women as well as men.

Women's basketball also has aroused an interest. At last weekend's Women's Invitational Tournament at Madison Square Garden, Delta State, national champion for the last three years, beat Montclair State, 71-58, and almost 7,000 fans were there. And last March, when Delta State played No. 2-ranked Immaculata and Montclair State played Queens College, 12,336 people showed up. Louisiana State's coach Jinks Coleman says "We started out with 20 fans a game." Now his Lady Tigers play to 2,000 and "we're teaching the school about women's basketball."

"It used to be that half the crowd was men making fun of the women players," Stan Gorlick of Montclair State says. "Now it's everybody rooting for their teams." Gorlick pays tribute to Montclair State's 5-feet 10-inch forward Carol Blazejowski, who "is the equal of any man as a pure shooter,"

The New York Times/William E. Sauro

Montclair State's Carol Blazejowski (12) fighting for ball with Rutgers' player last Sunday at the Garden. Montclair won tournament game, 84-64.

and who scored 52 points in the Garden in March. "Perhaps they haven't the speed nor the physical size, but Carol can shoot the ball with anybody, and handle as well as anybody. Maybe she could play pretty well against a good male college guard too."

Demand for Tall Girls

Because of the increased popularity of women's basketball, recruiters now look for what they look for in men. The days of the 4-foot-11-inch guard are gone. Now colleges want women who are 6 feet or over. Delta State's fine player Lusia Harris was 6 feet 4 inches, and California Polytechnical from Pomona has a starting lineup of women who average 6 feet 2 inches. Says Delta State's coach Margaret

Wade, "Now there is a big demand for the taller girls—everyone will be fighting for them soon."

Nor are the women burly types, as the male-outlined stereotypes would have it. Most are muscular, though slim simply because they are athletes and some, such as Ramona Von Boekman of Delta State, are strikingly attractice. According to Karen Johnson, executive secretary for the Association for Intercollegiate Athletics for Women (A.I.A.W.), which is part of the National Association for Girls and Women in Sport (N.A.G.W.S.), "there was a time when the woman who went out for basketball was kind of a masculine type, but that's not the case any longer.

"I expect it has to do with acceptability of women in the sport. It is highly visible and popular."

Women's basketball is less defensive these days than in the past and this reflects an evolutionary change in the rules of the game.

The first official rules for women's basketball were formulated in 1899 among the Ivy-influenced women's schools such as Vassar and Radcliffe They called for nine women to a side, each confined to a particular space, and the game was restricted to passing the ball from space to space and and shooting it. It gradually became a six-woman team, with three guards who stayed at one end of the court and played only defense and three forwards who stayed at the other end and shot. There was no crossing the center line, thus making it essentially a three-on-three half-court game.

Initially, women could not dribble the ball, then gradually they were permitted to dribble the ball once, actually a bounce, before passing or shooting. In the 1950s women were allowed to dribble twice; by the 1960s it had increased to three times. Now there is no such restriction.

Gradually the three-three combination changed as well to four and two, and then about 10 years ago a five-woman team was adopted, identical to the men, and all court differences died. Today the differences are minimal.

Unlike college men's basketball, the women have a 30-second clock—they must shoot the ball within 30 seconds of possession—and they do not have a formal backcourt. The ball may be passed back and forth at will without backcourt violation. Quarters are 10 minutes long instead of 12, and they do not have a three-to-make-two points penalty shot procedure. They do receive a one-and-one, basket and penalty shot.

Long gone as well is a guarding re-striction called "boxing," which forbade two women to guard one opposing player.

With these alterations, women's basketball is essentially similar to regulation men's basketball. The gradual relaxation against so-called unfeminine movement came, Miss Johnson says, "because society simply said women can be more mobile, so sports relaxations followed naturally."

With relaxations of the rules the sport has boomed, particularly in the last half-dozen years, and national champions began being named in 1972, when Immaculata, of Philadelphia won the title. It repeated in 1973 and 1974. Delta State of Cleveland, Miss., won in 1975, 1976 and 1977.

Leagues abound and now there are state A.I.A.W.s and regional A.I.A.W.s. In March there will be a national A.I.A.W. tournament at U.C.L.A. and this weekend in Atlanta, representatives of women's basketball are meeting to arrange that tournament. Professional women's basketball is taking shape, and in international amateur competition, women's basketball is becoming a major sport.

According to Diana Smith of the Amateur Basketball Association of America, in Jacksonville, Illinois, which sanctions all international women's competitions, two of the best women's teams ever were fielded last summer.

At the Pan American Federation games in Squaw Valley, the United States won against teams from Canada, Mexico, Peru, Brazil and Puerto Rico. Then later in July in Mexico City another team of American women won another division of the Pan American Federation.

Although there has been women's basketball in Europe for at least two decades, only in the last 10 years has it acquired status. And only in the last Olympics, at Montreal in 1976, was there a women's basketball competition. The American women won a silver medal. An Italian journalist, Dario Colombo, who writes for the magazine Giganti del Basket, wrote after the Olympics, "The real women's basketball is played in the U.S.A. not in Europe. Not because the U.S.A. won the silver medal but because they had a style of play that was pleasing to the eyes as well as efficient: aggressive defense, speed, fast break and a frenetic rhythm for 40 minutes.

"With this system Ann Meyers (U.C.L.A.) and her companions broke the pattern of traditional East European women's basketball.

"You don't deal a 20-point drubbing to the Bulgarians and the Czechs without a valid organization. The U.S.A. women could win it all at Mocow."

According to C. Robert Paul Jr. of the U.S. Olympic Committee, several women's teams are in formation for the next Olympics. He says that "women's basketball is in as many countries as there are entries and I guess that's 140. How good are they? Well, the only good team in Montreal was the American women. I wouldn't bet against them."

Not if they're as good as Lusia Harris, a member of that silver-medal-winning team in Montreal, who was drafted by the New Orleans Jazz of the NBA. She declined and has since graduated. Nobody doubts, least of all the women players, that they'll soon be drafted. Anybody who can score 52 points in a game like Montclair State's Blazejowski simply has to be able to help somebody. Maybe the Nets?

January 8, 1978

Givens Scores 41, Kentucky Wins N.C.A.A. Title, 94-88

Wildcats Top Duke, Take 5th Basketball Crown

By GORDON S. WHITE Jr.
Special to The New York Times

ST. LOUIS, March 27—The University of Kentucky became the National Collegiate Athletic Association basketball champion for the fifth time tonight when Jack Givens, a senior from Lexington, Ky., scored 41 points to lead the Wildcats to a 94-88 victory over Duke University.

Givens, a 6-foot-4-inch forward who hit from all points of the perimeter, was even more effective against Duke's zone defense by working inside to the foul line, where he took passes for short jumpers.

His 41 points before a crowd of 18,721 in the Checkerdome and a national television audience were not only a career high for the senior but also were only 2 points short of the individual record in the 40 years of N.C.A.A. championship games.

Bill Walton of the University of California, Los Angeles, scored 44 points when U.C.L.A. beat Memphis State in the 1973 N.C.A.A. final, making 21 of 22 field-goal attempts. Walton achieved that total in the same arena, which was then called the St. Louis Arenathen.

Third-Best Scoring Effort

Givens, who made 18 of 27 field goals and 5 of 8 free throws, turned in the third best individual scoring effort in a championship game. Gail Goodrich, also of U.C.L.A., had 42 points when the Bruins beat Michigan in 1965.

Givens was scoring at a record pace in the first half when he had 23 points to help Kentucky gain a 7-point advantage. Running, stopping and leaping for line-drive jump shots from the outside and driving inside for close-range scores, Givens scored Kentucky's last 16 points in the first half, and he kept it up with 18 points in the second half.

The Kentucky fans, waving blue and white banners and screaming until the end, stormed the court after the victory as Givens was raised to the shoulders of his teammates and carried around the floor. It was a celebration Kentuckians have felt was long overdue.

Once the dominant university in college basketball, this was Kentucky's first national title in 20 years. It also was the first championship for Kentucky under Joe B. Hall, who has coached the Wildcats for six seasons after succeeding the late Adolph Rupp.

Mike Phillips of Kentucky blocking a shot by Mike Gminski of Duke as teammate Truman Claytor watches during the first half last night in St. Louis.

United Press International

N.C.A.A. Box Score

CHAMPIONSHIP

DUKE (88)

	min	fgm	fga	ftm	fta	reb	a	pf	pts
Banks	37	6	12	10	12	8	2	2	22
Total	200	29	59	30	34	35	14	22	88
Gminski	37	6	16	8	8	12	2	3	20
Harrell	24	2	2	0	0	0	1	3	4
Spanarkel	40	8	16	5	6	2	3	4	21
Suddath	9	1	3	2	3	2	0	1	4
Bender	16	1	2	5	5	1	4	3	7
Goetsch	6	0	1	0	0	1	0	1	0
Total		29	59	30	34	35	14	22	88

KENTUCKY (94)

	min	fgm	fga	ftm	fta	reb	a	pf	pts
Givens	37	18	27	5	8	8	3	4	41
Robey	32	8	11	4	6	11	0	2	20
Phillips	11	1	4	2	2	1	5	4	4
Macy	38	3	3	3	4	0	8	1	9
Clayton	24	3	5	2	4	0	3	2	8
Lee	20	4	8	0	0	4	2	4	8
Shidler	15	1	5	0	1	1	3	3	2
Aleksinas	1	0	0	0	0	0	0	1	0
Williams	11	1	3	0	0	4	0	2	2
Sowan	8	0	2	0	0	2	0	1	0
Stephens	1	0	0	0	0	0	0	0	0
Courts	1	0	0	0	0	0	0	0	0
Gettelfinger	1	0	0	0	0	0	0	0	0
Casey	0	0	0	0	0	0	0	0	0
Total	200	39	68	16	25	32	20	26	94

Halftime score—Kentucky 45, Duke 38.
Technical foul—Duke bench.
Attendance—18,721.

Rupp, who died last December, coached Kentucky to national titles in 1948, 1949, 1951 and 1958.

Duke's loss marked the second time it had reached the N.C.A.A. final to no avail. The Blue Devils were beaten by U.C.L.A. in the 1964 championship. Hall took Kentucky to the final in 1975 when Givens played as a freshman, but the Wildcats lost, also to U.C.L.A.

Kentucky became the first team to win the basketball championship while being on probation for what the N.C.A.A. said were violations of its rules. Kentucky is serving the second year of a two-year probation that carried no sanction against postseason play. The biggest penalty was to restrict Kentucky to recruiting only three basketball players last year and again this year. A team is normally allowed to recruit six basketball players a year.

Prior to the game there were two threats made on the life of Eugene Banks, the outstanding freshman starter for Duke. Banks was not told about the threats until after the game. Wayne Duke, chairman of the N.C.A.A. basketball committee, said: "A male caller telephoned the arena and said something like, 'If Banks plays this'll be the last game he plays.' There was another call to a St. Louis TV station later."

Duke said the police and Checkerdome authorities were notified and that Banks's coach, Bill Foster, was told just before the game. Plainclothes police sat near the Duke bench during the game, but there was no incident.

'Not Going to Worry About It'

When Banks was told about the threats after the game, he said: "I'm not going to run or hide or worry about it. If that's what someone wants to do, so be it. I believe in God, and as long as I have my faith, I won't worry about it."

Banks turned in an excellent offensive performance with 22 points, the most for the Duke squad. He hit eight of eight free throws in the first half when Duke almost stayed even with Kentucky and Givens through excellent free-throw shooting. During the first half Duke, the nation's leading foul-shooting team, hit 20 of 21 free throws.

But Duke could not handle Givens, who exploited Duke's zone defense that got spread a bit too thin. While attempting to prevent the Kentucky guards, Kyle Macy and Truman Claytor, from feeding 6-10 Rick Robey and 6-10 Mike Phillips inside, Duke sent its guards out to apply pressure. After the game Hall explained why that strategy backfired:

"Hank Iba [former Oklahoma State coach] once told me never to spread your defense from baseline to midcourt because you would leave a big gap in there around the foul line. Duke was coming out and attacking our guards and we flashed Jack [Givens] in on the post. We went to that almost exclusively."

Robey, another senior who was a starter in the 1975 championship game,

had 20 points tonight and 11 rebounds This was about a match with Mike Gminski, the 6-11 Duke sophomore who scored 20 points and took down 12 rebounds.

But no one could do anything to compare with Givens's performance. Possibly the most exciting part of Givens's play was the way he hit his line-drive shots from 20 to 30 feet. He jumped high to make sure the ball would get over the tall Duke defenders, and he never lofted the ball much. The ball would zip on a line to the back of the rim and plunk down through the net.

Givens finished his college career with 2,038 points and, along with the other seniors on the team, finished with a second major championship. Kentucky won the National Invitation Tournament in 1976.

Hall managed to get Kentucky into some trouble late in the game when, with an 11-point lead and less than 90 seconds remaining, he began taking his first-string players out. He took Givens out with 47 seconds to go and Duke trailing by 6 points.

But Duke suddenly got a couple of baskets, and Hall quickly put his starters back. With a 4-point lead in the last 10 seconds, Kentucky got the ball to James Lee, another senior, who ran in and stuffed the ball for the final basket of the game. That squelched the hopes of a Blue Devil team that was the youngest ever to play in an N.C.A.A. championship game. All of its starters will be back next year.

The victory gave Kentucky a final won-lost record of 30-2, and Duke ended at 27-7.

Arkansas Takes Third Place

In the third-place game preceding the final, Ron Brewer scored on a 22-foot jump shot at the final buzzer to give Arkansas a 71-69 victory over Notre Dame. Brewer had scored after two steals during the final 46 seconds of the first half to break a tie and give Arkansas a 4-point lead at halftime. The Razorbacks finished with a 32-4 mark and the Irish 23-8.

March 28, 1978

Michigan State Defeats Indiana State for N.C.A.A. Title

Johnson's Magic Leads 75-64 Victory — Bird Held to 19

By GORDON S. WHITE Jr.
Special to The New York Times

SALT LAKE CITY, March 26 — Michigan State grounded The Bird with a touch of Magic and a magnificent zone defense tonight to win its first National Collegiate basketball championship and end Indiana State's chance to achieve an unbeaten season.

Despite a heavy load of personal fouls that created serious problems down the stretch, the Spartans held fast to an early lead and beat the Sycamores, 75-64, in the final of the 41st National Collegiate Athletic Association tournament before 15,410 persons in the Special Events Center of the University of Utah. The loss was the only one for Indiana State in 34 games this season. Michigan State finished with a 26-6 record.

Earvin (Magic) Johnson, who played the entire second half with three personal fouls, was his usual spectacular self, scoring 24 points for the winners. Larry Bird, the big man for Indiana State with a three-year career average of more than 30 points a game, was kept to only 19 points, his lowest scoring game in five N.C.A.A. tournament contests.

As a result, Indiana State, the eighth undefeated team to reach the final, became only the second of them to lose in the championship game. Ohio State was the first when the Buckeyes were losers to Cincinnati in 1961.

Big Week for Big Ten

Michigan State had been to three previous N.C.A.A. tournaments and only one previous Final Four, a semifinal loss to North Carolina in 1957. With tonight's victory, the Spartans gave the Big Ten Conference a sweep of the two major post-season college tourneys. Indiana won the National Invitation Tournament last Wednesday.

Jud Heathcote, who concluded his third season as head coach of Michigan State, summed up the Spartans' achievments well after the title was his. "I feel a combination of relief and elation," he said. "The players have accomplished so much. And they saved their best play for the tournament."

Led by Johnson, Greg Kelser and Terry Donnelly, the Spartans swept through five tournament games after gaining a third of the Big Ten crown with Iowa and Purdue. On the road to the N.C.A.A. title, the Spartans beat Lamar by 31 points, Louisiana State by 16, Notre Dame by 12, Pennsylvania by 34 and then the No. 1 ranked team in the nation, Indiana State, by 11.

No Losses in Tourney

In winning the title, Michigan State became only the second team to do so with as many as six losses for the season. Kentucky did it with six losses in 1958 and Marquette with seven in 1977.

But there was no beating the Michigan State defense during this tournament and there was little any team could do to stop the fast offense triggered by the magic of Johnson's passing.

This defense stopped Bird after no other team could do so in this tourney. The 6-9 senior had scored 22, 29, 31 and 35 points in his four previous tourney games. What's more, Michigan State closed down the Indiana State passing lanes, and held Bird to only two assists.

"We defended him with an adjustment and a prayer", Heathcote said.

But while Heathcote was praying on the bench, Johnson, Kelser, Ron Charles and Jay Vincent shared the work of defending inside at the baseline. They crowded Bird like a flock of vultures every time he approached the baseline on offense. Bird's mates just could not get the ball to him very often and when they did, Bird would hesitate, something he rarely does.

Bird Only 7 for 21

A couple of times during the first half Bird got to the top of his jump and could not decide whether to shoot or pass off. This led to missed shots and missed passes as the Bird hit only seven of 21 field-goal attempts — 33 percent. He had hit 53 percent before tonight. The Sycamores' team percentage was 42.2, but their failure at the free-throw line, where they connected on only 10 of 22 attempts cost them.

Donnelly, the 6-2 junior guard for Michigan State, also contributed to the defense against Bird. His task was to play the Indiana State guard with the ball one-on-one in the zone and minimize his chance of passing the ball to Bird.

Donnelly also contributed 15 points, 13 in the second half.

But all of this hard defense led to trouble. Johnson and then Kelser were forced to the bench with three personal fouls before the first half ended. Vincent, who played with an injured foot

United Press International and Associated Press
Johnson driving toward basket for 2 points in game Spartans won, 75-64.

all through the tournament, drew four personal fouls in only 19 minutes of play. Charles eventually fouled out.

Kelser, a senior playing his final game for the Spartans, went through the final 12 minutes with four personal fouls. He scored 19 points.

Although it was the defense that turned the tables on Indiana State, Michigan State got off to another of its spectacular offensive shows early in the game. This enabled the Spartans to go in front by 16 points in the first two minutes of the second half.

Too Much to Catch Up

After leading by 37-28 at intermission, Michigan

State did not let foul problems bother it as Kelser hit on a six-foot jumper in the lane that sent the Spartans on a string of 7 straight points.

During its unbeaten streak, Indiana State had rallied to win a number of times but never had to fight back from more than an 11-point deficit. The 16-point edge Michigan State built was just too much.

From the start, Michigan State began running points at high speed and when Donnelly hit from the right corner at 4:26 of the first half, the Spartans were in front by 9-8. Never again were they behind. That long corner shot set the Big Ten team on a 9-point string. During this surge, Bird made one bad shot missing the rim and Johnson took a rebound and made an outlet pass to Mike Brkovich, the other Spartan guard, who took it all the way for a basket and a 3-point play.

De Paul Takes Consolation

Through it all, however, Heathcote was obviously concerned about Bird. "I thought every shot the Bird took would go in," the Michigan State coach said.

Indiana State's man-to-man defense didn't appear to bother Johnson. He made one of the game's most exciting moves when he drove the baseline around Alex Gilbert only to be facing Bird, standing his ground under the basket.

Kelser was coming down the lane to Johnson's left and the Michigan State sophomore faked a pass to Kelser. Bird took the fake and moved just a bit to defend Kelser coming into the basket. Johnson kept the ball and made an easy layup.

Such spectacular play may have been Johnson's last for Michigan State. It is expected that the Lansing, Mich., athlete who stayed home to play college ball will declare hardship and be drafted into the pros for next season.

De Paul, which lost to Indiana State in the semifinal round Saturday, saved third place, beating Penn, 96-93, in overtime of the consolation game. Mark Agguire scored 34 points for De-Paul and Tony Price had a career high of 31 points in his final game for the Quakers. Although they lost, the Quakers came out of the tournament with their heads high after having been embarrassed by Michigan State, 101-67, Saturday. Penn came from 23 points back to force the overtime.

March 27, 1979

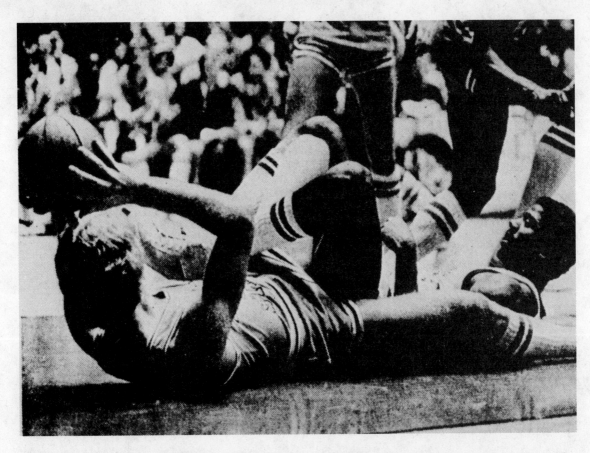

Indiana State's **Larry Bird**, foreground, looking for a teammate from lower angle than usual after colliding with Michigan State's **Earvin Johnson** during the first half of N.C.A.A. championship game last night at Salt Lake City.

CHAPTER 2

PRO BASKETBALL

Bill Russell (left) and Wilt Chamberlain battle for
the ball. Russell was the first black coach of a
major pro team. Many consider him to be the best
basketball player in the history of the game.

Professional Basket Ball League.

Professional league basketball will be tried in Brooklyn this Fall and Winter, with the formation of the Inter-State Basketball League, in which the Knights of St. Anthony A. C., an organization affiliated with the Amateur Athletic Union, holds one of the six franchises. Eugene Kinkead, Sheriff of Hudson County, New Jersey, is President of the new organization, which will succeed the inactive Hudson River and New York State Leagues. Other officers of the new league are John J. O'Brien of Brooklyn, Secretary, and W. J. Downey of Paterson, N. J., Treasurer. Up to date franchises have been granted to Brooklyn, Kingston, Stamford, Elizabeth, Paterson and Jersey City, and unless some other cities signify their intention of entering teams before Oct. 22 the above circuit will remain intact for the season. The teams entered have already signed the best of the professional players in the East. Brooklyn's season will open on Friday, Oct. 22, on the Knights of St. Anthony's Greenpoint court, with Kingston as the opposing team.

October 8, 1915

Basket Ball Players Under Ban.

CHICAGO, Jan. 8.—Eight members of the Hardin County basket ball team of Kenton, Ohio, have been declared professionals and suspended from the Central A. A. U., it became known today, because they are alleged to have accepted money for playing. Members of the team, it was alleged, divided $75 on Christmas Day at Fort Wayne, Ind. The Hardin County team was rated as one of the strongest in Ohio.

January 9, 1916

BASKET BALL FIVE RESIGNS.

Morningside Team's Action Makes Investigation Unnecessary.

Members of the Morningside A. C. who have been playing professional basket ball have severed their connection with the club, it became known yesterday. This will make unnecessary the proposed investigation of the Morningside A. C., which was to have been undertaken by the Metropolitan A. A. U. Registration Committee.

S. Belsky, Captain of the basket ball team, has sent in his registration card to the A. A. U., declaring his intention of playing as a professional. Belsky was a high jumper and held the position of Chairman of the Morningside A. C Athletic Committee. This office will in future be occupied by Fred A. Niles, Jr., Chairman of the Metropolitan A. A. U. Registration Committee.

January 19, 1919

SEVEN CITIES IN LEAGUE.

Professional Basket Ball Season Will Start This Week.

Professional basket ball will make another bid for popular favor this Winter under the auspices of the Inter-state League, recently organized in New York City, with Sergeant Arthur Guy Empey as Honorary President and John J. O'Brien Secretary and Treasurer. Seven cities have expressed their intention of joining the circuit. The reservation of players from all parts of the country by the various organizations, subject to modification and later change, was as follows:

NEW YORK—Clinton, Bockman, Leonard, Schmeelk, Fyfe, and Stapleton.

BROOKLYN—Sugarman, Cross, Grimstead, Suils, Muller, Griffen, Seaman, Harris, Barry, and Farrell.

PATERSON—A. Powers, C. Powers, A. Harvey, and Bruggey.

BRIDGEPORT—Dehnert, White, Ashmead, Reich, Malone, Stewart, and Shannon.

ANSONIA—Wassmer, Norman, S. Harvey, and Griebe.

PASSAIC—Sedran, Friedman, Tome, Kerr, Donahur, and Robinson.

JERSEY CITY—Dreyfus, Holman, Wright, Stannard, Bock, and Fowler.

Opening the season on Oct. 30, the league schedule will provide competition until the 1st of April, divided into two sections, the first half ending shortly after the New Year. The winners of both sections, if they should be different clubs, will then play a series of five games for the professional championship of the United States.

The opening week's schedule is as follows:

Oct. 30, Paterson at Passaic; Nov. 4, New York at Jersey City; Nov. 5, Brooklyn at New York; Nov. 6, Brooklyn at Bridgeport; Nov. 6, Jersey City at Ansonia; Nov. 8, Ansonia at Paterson; Nov. 9, Passaic at Brooklyn.

October 27, 1919

CELTICS WIN CHAMPIONSHIP

Take Eastern League Basketball Title by Defeating Trenton.

Special to The New York Times.

PHILADELPHIA, Pa., April 5.—A cyclonic rally in the final twenty minutes of play swept the New York Celtics into the Eastern League basketball championship tonight when they defeated the Trenton Potters in the third and deciding game for the title at the Camden Armory, a neutral floor, by the score of 27 to 22.

April 6, 1922

CELTICS NOSE OUT PALACE FIVE, 35-31

Rough Game Marred by Many Penalties at Garden—40 Points Made on Fouls.

CAPTAINS ARE SUMMONED

Beckman and Kennedy Receive Writs for Violating Sunday Law —St. Benedict's Wins.

Another sport made its debut in the new Madison Square Garden last night when the Original Celtics basketball team defeated the Palace Club five of Washington, D. C., 35 to 31. The game was one of the roughest ever witnessed on a local court and interest in the play was marred by the continual infliction of penalties.

The law again stepped in to interrupt the bow of basketball, just as it did last week at the start of the six-day bicycle race. Captain Johnny Beckman and Ray Kennedy of the Celtics and Palace five were served with summons for violating the Sabbath law. The play was not interfered with and few of the 10,000 fans who attended the game were aware that anything untoward had happened.

No less than 40 of the 66 points scored were made on free throws and there were twenty other attempts to score from the foul line that failed. It was a close game from start to the finish, with the Celtics holding a slight lead most of the way. The New York combination was clever in its passing and with its five-man defense guarded the opponents so closely that the latter were compelled to resort to long range shooting.

Rody Cooney of Brooklyn, left guard on the Palace five stood out with his sensational shooting. Four times in the first half he tossed the ball into the basket from the middle of the court. Chadwick, a new man in the Celtics' line-up from Wabash, stood out with his foul shooting in the first half, although most of the players on both sides excelled in this respect in the opening half of the game. In the second half the visitors lost their accuracy and made only two goals in thirteen shots from the foul line, which was largely responsible for their defeat.

In a preliminary game the St. Benedict's Prep School of Newark outclassed the St. John's Prep School five of Brooklyn, 53 to 14. The Jersey team was far more accurate in its shooting and St. John's was unable to cope with its passing.

The line-up:

CELTICS (35).		PALACE CLUB (31).
Borgeman	L.F.	Grody
Beckman	R.F.	Kennedy
Chadwick	C.	Haggerty
Holman	L.G.	Cooney
Dehnert	R.G.	Conaty

Goals from field—Dehnert 2, Beckman, Cooney 5, Conaty 2, Kennedy, Grody. Goals from foul—Chadwick 8, Borgeman 8, Beckman 5, Dehnert 5, Holman 3, Conaty 5, Cooney 4, Kennedy 2, Brody 2.

Substitutions—Palace Club: Conway for Haggerty, Haggerty for Conway, Conway for Haggerty.

Referee—Herman Baetzel. Time of halves—20 minutes.

December 7, 1925

CLEVELAND QUINTET CORRALS PRO TITLE

Defeats Brooklyn Arcadians, 23 to 22, Taking League Series With 3 Straight Triumphs.

GIRLS ALSO ARE VICTORS

They Conquer Edmonton Team, 15 to 10, and Take Lead in Race by Seven Points.

The Cleveland Rosenblums won the championship of the American Professional Basketball League by defeating the Brooklyn Arcadians, 23 to 22, in a close but slow game at the Seventy-first Regiment Armory last night. The contest was the final of the best three out of five games. Cleveland won three consecutive games, taking the first and second games, played last Wednesday and Thursday nights in Cleveland, by 36 to 33 and 37 to 21 scores respectively.

The Rosenblums came from behind in the first period of the men's game, and again in the second period, when the Brooklyn team rallied. The crowd of 2,000 spectators was roused to a high pitch of excitement in the final seconds of the game when Conaty, left guard for Brooklyn, had a chance to tie the score when he made a shot from the foul line. Conaty failed. Cooney, Brooklyn left forward had just scored a field goal that made the score 22 to 23.

Cleveland Nurses Lead.

Although Cleveland deceived the Brooklyn players by short, tricky passes at various stages of the game the main strategy of the invaders seemed to be to get a few points ahead and then play catch with the ball to prevent the Brooklyn players from getting a chance. In the final six minutes, when Cleveland's margin was never more than a point or two, the ball was "frozen" or passed from hand to hand for four minutes of the time.

A foul by Cooney opened the scoring and gave Brooklyn the lead. Kerr evened it for Cleveland, however, and then the visitors got a 4 to 1 lead. Brooklyn tied the score at 4 to 4 and later led at 9 to 4. Cleveland rallied and was ahead 11 to 10 at half time. The lead see-sawed in the second half for a time until Cleveland got a lead at 23 to 20 with six minutes to play.

Hickey Scores Eight Points.

It was then that the freezing tactics saved the game. Hickey was the high scorer of the game, making eight point for Cleveland. Husta of the Cleveland team and Ripley of the Brooklyn team made seven points each.

In a preliminary game the Newman Stern girls' basketball team, also of Cleveland, defeated the Edmonton girls' team of Alberta, Canada, 15 to 10 in the third game of the four-game championship series between the teams. The four-game series is being played on a total score basis, and the Cleveland girls now lead the Canadians by a seven-point margin. The final game will be played tonight at the Seventy-first Regiment Armory. The Newman-Stern girls now lead 59 points to 52 by virtue of a 23-to-16 victory in Cleveland last Wedesnday, 21 points gained last Thursday night when Edmonton won, 26 to 21, and 15 points earned last night.

The line-ups:

CLEVELAND (23).		BROOKLYN (22).
Husta	L.F.	Cooney
Hickey	R.F.	Schmeelk
Diegan	C.	Voss
Kerr	L.G.	Conaty
Russell	R.G.	Ripley

Goals from field—Russell 3, Husta 3, Hickey 2: Conaty 2, Ripley, Cooney, Schmeelk. Goals from foul—Hickey 4, Kerr 2, Husta; Ripley, Cooney 3, Conaty 2, Voss, Schmeelk.

Substitutions—Cleveland: None. Brooklyn: Bushman for Schmeelk.

Referee—Ward Brennan, Brooklyn. Umpire—A. Fitting, Erie. Time of halves—20 minutes.

NEWMAN S. (15).	POS.	EDMONTON (10).
Holmes	L.F.	Daisy Johnson
Kyr	R.F.	Dot Johnson
Wagemacher	C.	Smith
McAleer	L.G.	Bennie
Fisher	L.G.	McRae

Goals from field—Kyr 3, Wagemacher 2, Holmes, Daisy Johnson 3, Smith, Bennie. Goal from fouls—Kyr, Wagemacher, Kelly. Edmonton—None.

Substitutions—Newman Stern: Kelly for Fisher.

Referee—John O'Brien, St. Johns. Umpire—Frank Brennan, Brooklyn. Time of periods—Four of 8 minutes.

April 10, 1926

Pro Basketball for Garden; Rickard Takes Over Celtics

CHICAGO, May 11 (AP).—Tex Rickard and the Madison Square Garden Corporation of New York joined the American Basketball League today and took over the champion professional team of the country, the New York Celtics, giving the famous arena another sport. The Celtics will have a home schedule of twenty-six games. Joe Carr of Columbus, Ohio, President of the league, and Colonel John S. Hammond, Rickard's representative, began the negotiations at the league's schedule meeting here. Colonel Hammond, presented a letter from Rickard in which the promoter expressed the opinion that basketball will operate very successfully in the Garden and that the game has a big future.

May 12, 1927

'Oh, Pshaw,' Limit in Epithets For Pro Fives; $10 a Violation

CHICAGO, Dec. 30 (AP).—Henceforth professional basketball players of the American League may vent their ire only through the use of "Oh, pshaw," or some other harmless ejaculation. Profanity, when first used by a player, merits a warning from the referee. Second and subsequent offenses will call for a $10 fine each. Disputing a referee also becomes a costly affliction under new rulings. It will cost $5 or $10, depending upon the tone of the dispute.

December 31, 1927

CELTICS TURN BACK FORT WAYNE FIVE

Produce Smooth Floor Attack to Score 37-30 Victory Before 2,500 in Garden.

HOLMAN TALLIES 15 POINTS

Leads Local Five to 11th Straight League Triumph—Borgeman Stars for Hoosiers.

Meeting a desperately fighting quintet, which, although handicapped by a miserable start, continued to present a forceful front, the Original Celtics, representing New York in the American Basketball League, repulsed the Fort Wayne Hoosiers at Madison Square Garden last night, 37—30. A crowd of 2,500 fans turned out to witness the contest, and incidentally, the eleventh straight league victory for the local quintet.

Nat Holman, although playing a guard position and assigned to watch the scintillating Benny Borgeman, proved to be the big gun for the Celtics. He scored a total of 15 points and played a superb floor game. Shimek, left guard for the Hoosiers, was next high-scorer, with 6 baskets. Of these, five were scored in the first half.

The scoring started soon after the opening whistle, when Davey Banks dropped in a long shot. Holman added a foul and followed with a field goal. Joe Lapchick made it 7 points for the Celtics before the visitors got started. Shimek interrupted the locals' scoring tactics, making a goal from midfield.

Dehnert picked up for the Celtics with a score and he was followed by Lapchick and Banks, who rolled the New York score up to 13. Another interruption to the string was made by Shimek, who made his second goal. Banks sank two fouls to start the Celtics off once more.

The visitors perked up at this point and scored almost alternately with the locals, mainly on the efforts of Al Shimek, who tallied five times in the first half. The score at the end of the first session was 21-14 in favor of the Celtics.

Benny Borgeman added a point to the Hoosiers' total, scoring on a foul, to start the second half. Pete Barry more than nullified this contribution a moment later, however, when he scored a goal, his first of the game. Koehle scored after a fine bit of passing, and two successive goals by Borgeman brought the Fort Wayne total to 21 to 23 for New York.

Holman scored soon after, but the Hoosiers kept fighting, with Griebe making a goal. Dehnert again put a four-point margin between the teams when he made a goal. Holman and McElwain, who went in for Borgeman, alternated at scoring, each making a basket.

Then Holman electrified the crowd by making a goal of the longest shot attempted during the game. Shimek sank a long one, but Dehnert came back with one a moment later.

With the score 35—30 in their favor, the Celtics purposely kept the ball in midfield, passing it among themselves and refusing to make any efforts toward the basket. Holman snared an easy ne just before the game ended.

The St. Michael's High School team of Jersey City defeated the La Salle Academy quintet in the preliminary contest.

The line-up:

Celtics (37)	G.	F.	P.	Fort Wayne (30)	G.	F.	P.
Banks, lf	2	2	6	Borgeman, lf	3	2	8
Barry, rf	1	0	2	McElwain, rf	1	0	2
Lapchick, c	2	2	6	Griebe	1	1	
Holman, lg	6	3	15	Chadwick, c	1	0	2
Dehnert, rg	4	0	8	Shimek, lg	6	0	12
				Koehle, rg	1	1	
Total	15	7	37	Voss	0	0	0
				Total	13	4	30

Referee—Salador. Umpire—Mueller. Time of halves—20 minutes.

January 10, 1928

PRO QUINTETS MERGE INTO SINGLE LEAGUE

American and National Basketball Circuits Unite—Celtics Change Name to Hakoah.

A reorganized American basketball league will operate in professional basketball this season instead of the proposed Eastern and Western circuits, it was announced yesterday through The Associated Press.

After a joint conference between the holders of franchises in the old American League, which recently withdrew to the Middle West, and the National League, which was to takes its place in the East, it was decided to join the two into one organization. The combined circuit will retain the name of the American Basketball League.

The league will operate teams in Chicago, Cleveland, Fort Wayne, Ind., Rochester, N. Y., New York and Brooklyn, which were in the old circuit, while Trenton and Paterson, N. J., will be the newcomers. New York will be represented by a new team under the colors of the Hakoah Club instead of the Celtics.

John J. O'Brien, former head of the Metropolitan Basketball League, has been elected President of the new circuit.

November 10, 1928

PRO TITLE IS WON BY CLEVELAND FIVE

Captures World Series by Turning Back Rochester for the Fourth Time, 21 to 15.

TIED AT HALF-TIME, 7-7

Victors Pile Up Lead in Second Period—Play of Barry an Outstanding Feature.

CLEVELAND, March 24 (UP).—Cleveland won the American professional Basketball League world series tonight by defeating Rochester, 21 to 15. This was the fourth victory for Cleveland in the series to Rochester's one.

Cleveland started slowly in the game tonight but wound up like a whirlwind. After 18 minutes the score was 6 to 1 in favor of Rochester. The first basket was made by Pete Barry, whose play was outstanding. The half ended in a 7-to-7 tie.

In the second half Cleveland

rapidly piled up a lead, running away from its opponents.

Lapchick of Cleveland and Kintzing of Rochester were high point men, each with eight counters.

The line-up:

Cleveland (21)	G.	F.	P.	Rochester (15)	G.	F.	P.
Barry, lf	2	0	4	Chismadie, lf	0	3	3
Lapchick, rf	3	4	8	Allen, rf	1	3	3
Cunningham, c	1	0	2	Hearn, c	0	0	0
Husta, lg	3	0	6	Kintzing, lg	4	0	8
Dehnert, rg	0	1	1	Artus, rg	0	0	0
Total	9	5	21	Total	5	5	15

Referee—Salador. Umpire—Sinott.

March 25, 1930

PRO CIRCUIT DISBANDS.

American Basketball League Not to Operate This Season.

The American Professional Basketball League has definitely decided not to operate this season, President John J. O'Brien announced yesterday through the Associated Press.

O'Brien said a careful study of conditions in the various cities comprising the circuit had led directors of the league to decide against operating in the 1931-32 season. Granting an improvement in the business world, O'Brien said, the league planned to operate in 1932-33, possibly with an extended membership.

November 13, 1931

N. Y. 5 Named Knickerbockers

New York's entry in the newly formed Basketball Association of America will be known as the Knickerbockers and will wear this city's official colors of orange and

blue when play in the twelve-city professional circuit gets under way next winter. Neil Cohalan, former Manhattan coach, will direct the team, which is sponsored by Madison Square Garden.

July 24, 1946

BASKETBALL TIE-UP IS SET

National Association of Pro Leagues Organized

CHICAGO, Oct. 21 (UP)—The National Association of Professional Basketball Leagues, representing fifty-two teams, was organized today by a six-man executive board of the National and American Leagues and affiliated loops.

Ward (Piggy) Lambert, former dean of Western Conference basketball coaches, who resigned his Purdue post last winter and is now commissioner of the National Basketball League, announced the tie-up after a meeting today.

The National League membership includes Indianapolis, Chicago, Detroit, Oshkosh, Wis.; Sheboygan, Wis; Anderson, Ind.; Fort Wayne, Ind.; Rochester, N. Y.; Toledo, Youngstown, Ohio; Buffalo and Syracuse.

The American League, which has been in pro basketball longer than the National, which was organized in 1935, is made up of Philadelphia, Wilmington, Del.; Trenton, N. J.; Brooklyn, Paterson, N. J.; Newark, N. J.; Jersey City, Baltimore, Elizabeth, N. J., and Troy, N. Y.

October 22, 1946

17,205 See Chicago Five Beat Knickerbockers in Garden

NEW YORK QUINTET DEFEATED BY 78-68

Stags Down Knickerbockers in Overtime Period as Pro Basketball Returns

ROTTNER IS TOP SCORER

By LOUIS EFFRAT

Aside from the unexpected and —from a local viewpoint—unhappy outcome, the first major-league professional basketball game to be played at Madison Square Garden since 1929 couldn't have done more to pave the way for the success of the newly formed Basketball Association of America if the script had been prepared in advance.

Last night's only disappointment for the local fans was the fact that the New York Knickerbockers, 14 points in front at one stage in the first half, lost to the Chicago Stags, 78—68. Otherwise, it was a gala inaugural at the Eighth Avenue Arena, where for the past twelve years college court games have hogged the spotlight.

This being a play-for-pay circuit, it was most gratifying to those concerned that 17,205 spectators were on hand for the home debut of the Knickerbockers. Then there was a stirring regulation wind-up that saw Ossie Schechtman, former L. I. U. star, hit the target with a one-handed toss just thirty-five seconds before time ran out. This desperate shot brought about a 64-64 deadlock and, with the seconds ticking away, it necessitated, of course, a five-minute overtime period, the first in the league.

Original Celtics Perform

The crowd, which between halves, had been treated to a fur fashion show and an abbreviated basketball exhibition, in which the original Original Celtics—Nat Holman, Johnny Beckman, Dutch Dehnert, Joe Lapchick, Chris Leonard and Pete Barry—played a 1-1 tie with a team composed of New York Football Giants, was thrilled.

However, the extra session of the main attraction was anti-climax. The Stags, coached by Harold Olsen of Ohio State fame, now smoother and more forceful than the Knickerbockers, took complete command of the overtime period, counted five straight points that served as a cushion against any counter-rally that might develop, and won going away, the New Yorkers never getting closer than three points.

Off slowly, the Knickerbockers outsped the Stags to gain a 19-13 advantage at the end of the first quarter. By half-time it was 35—26, after the Knickerbockers had soared to a 31-17 bulge. So superior did Neil Cohalan's lads appear to be, that the coach, at that point, elected to substitute. Against the Knickerbocker Reserves, the visitors found new life but when Sonny Hertzberg, Ralph Kaplowitz and Schechtman were in action the Stags found the going much rougher.

Second Loss to Stags

Following the intermission, the second-stringers still were on the floor and when Hertzberg and Schechtman did return, the change in the New York attack was evident. However, Hertzberg and Schechtman, brilliantly though they did perform, were unable to supply the "lift" that was needed to bring the team back. As a result, the Knickerbockers, beaten by the Stags by a 16-point margin at Chicago recently, suffered their second defeat at the hands of the Windy City men, who gained undisputed possession of second place in the Western Division of the association.

Chicago was sparked by little Marvin Rottner, who used to play with Loyola of Chicago. Fast, shifty and accurate with his shots, Rottner inspired the Stags with an outburst of seven consecutive points in the second half, not to mention his expert feeding. He ended with twenty points and was the night's individual high. Hertzberg was the runner-up with nineteen points.

After Schechtman had tied the score on a neat pass from Nat Militzok of Hofstra and Cornell, and the teams had rested, the overtime began with Don Carlson setting a 2-pointer from fifteen feet out. Tall Chuck Halbert dropped in a foul and then converted a lead-pass from Jim Seminoff. That made it 69—64 and virtually clinched the decision.

Before the period ended, the Knickerbockers, with Militzok and Hertzberg doing the scoring, pulled up to within 3 points, 71—68, but Doyle Parrack hit for 4 quick points, Rottner followed with 3 and the debut of the Knickerbockers was ruined.

The line-up:

CHICAGO (78)	G.	F.	P.	NEW YORK (68)	G.	F.	P.
Jaros, lf	1	3	5	Hertzberg, lf	8	3	19
Parrack	5	3	13	Mullens	1	0	2
Carlson	3	0	6	Gottlieb, rf	5	0	10
Zaslofsky, rf	4	1	9	Murphy	2	1	5
Halbert, c	5	8	18	Stutz	1	2	4
Rottner, lg	9	2	20	Weber, c	0	0	0
Davis, rg	1	0	2	Rosenstein	2	4	8
Seminoff	2	1	5	Kaplowitz, lg	0	2	2
Kautz	0	0	0	Militzok	4	2	10
				Schechtman, rg	3	2	8
				Byrnes	0	0	0
Total	30	18	78				
				Total	26	16	68

Officials—Pat Kennedy and John Nucatola. Time of periods—4 of 12 minutes each. Overtime—5 minutes.

November 12, 1946

A SCRAMBLE UNDER BASKET IN GARDEN GAME

Hank Rosenstein (12) and Nat Militzok (wearing white shirt) of the Knickerbockers and Jim Seminoff of Chicago leaping for the ball after a New York shot bounded off the backboard.   The New York Times

The Original Celtics (New York, not Boston) dominated pro basketball in its infancy in the 1920's. Two of their stars, not in this photo, were Nat Holman and Joe Lupchick.

George Mikan (right), the first star of modern pro basketball, goes up over the Knicks' Nat Clifton in a 1953 game. At 6'10", Mikan was the dominating center of his time.

A Celtic Takes Over

By ARTHUR DALEY

IT'S a rather significant development that Joe Lapchick calmly turned his back on a life as coach at St. John's to accept a similar post with the professional New York Knickerbockers of the Basketball Association of America. "I'm just an old pro at heart," sheepishly admitted the one-time center of the immortal Original Celtics. But that's not the only reason. He had to have an abiding faith in the future of the play-for-pay phase of the dribble diversion to make the switch. That fat salary check he'll receive couldn't have swung the deal all by itself.

The first full season of the BAA, backed as it is by the solid financial support of arena owners in eleven key cities, has not been an unqualified success. There was too much spade work to be done for that. But the magnates are hardly despondent since they didn't expect to reap a golden harvest from the opening whistle. They set their sights in the future and that future still looks as though it's going to pay off.

The popularity of the sport never was higher than it is right now and pro basketball is bound to catch on eventually. After all, it took pro football more than a decade and a half to establish the fact that it's infinitely superior from a technical standpoint to the college game. The dribble artists should be able to convince the customers in less time than that.

There's a rather nostalgic touch to the fact that Lapchick has taken over the Knicks. He belonged to the glamour team of pro basketball in the old days and he neatly bridges the gap to the modern era. For one thing, he's been a tremen-

dously successful operative at St. John's from the very moment that he took over there, even though he accepted that assignment with qualms and misgivings.

The Persuasive Holman

Nat Holman was responsible for his taking the Redman post, of course, and, if Nat lived to regret it, he never made the admission. "Take the job, Joe," he urged, "I know that you can make good." So his former team-mate accepted the offer and then proceeded to whale the whey out of Nat's City College heroes more often than not. At any rate the Beaver mentor finally has gotten Lapchick out of his hair, not that their bristling court rivalry put the slightest dent in their personal relations.

The secret of the Lapchick success is not too carefully guarded a secret, though. It's the defensive alignments that he's always been able to set up. He has the uncanny knack of being able to watch an enemy team in action and instantly being able to detect flaws in the attack which can be exploited by adequate countermeasures. But that was an art he carried with him from his Celtic days. Like the old-time Yankees, their attack got the headlines but their defense won the ball games.

There probably never has been a team which could keep control of a fray the way the wearers of the Shamrock could. That's why they could afford to win a contest by a scant point or two, thus making the opposition look good and not damaging their own record. They'd take a slight

lead near the end and sit on it. When they'd stick Dutch Dehnert in the pivot, the ball would whip back and forth without the enemy even placing a finger on it.

Rarely did such strategy backfire. That's why the Celtics were able to compile one streak which saw them win 118 games while losing only 7. But when it did, their embarassment was monumental. One such occasion came when the Celtics played a pick-up five, headlined by Lou Gehrig. This quintet didn't belong on the same court with the slickest of all pro quintets.

Too Long a Delay

"Take it easy, fellows," implored the Iron Horse, "and let us look good for a while." The Gehrig team took the lead while the Shamrock wearers snickered politely. They could recapture that advantage whenever they wished. With amused restraint they trailed into the second half and into the closing minutes. But then their amusement ended. They just couldn't get unwound and thus were the mighty Celtics toppled by a hodge-podge, pick-up group which should have had to pay the full admission charge even to see them play.

That the old Celtic center would take over the Knickerbockers next year has been pretty much of an open secret all season long. Ned Irish wanted him from the start and had to prevail on his own personal friendship with Neil Cohalan to get the capable Neill to handle the Knicks on a temporary basis. The former Manhattan mentor

has done as good—or better—a job as could be expected.

The Madison Square Garden entry has been a long time in jelling. The Knicks felt morally obligated to load up with local talent to the exclusion of all others and few of them were able to make the grade. In fact, only five of the original twenty-two players in training camp have survived the campaign. With the mistakes of this season to serve as warnings and with the experience gained to serve as guide posts, the Knicks should be an infinitely superior aggregation in the years to come.

They've built up a small but solid clientele at their home court in the Sixty-ninth Regiment Armory and have done rather well in their few forays in the Garden with the 15,000 they drew last Sunday as the top mark in the league. They probably will do as well in their play-off battle with the Cleveland Rebels at the Garden again on Saturday.

In Cleveland, where the old Celtics once drew 15,000 for an afternoon game and as many more again at night, a record (?) of sorts was set recently when the Rebels played Boston while a blizzard raged outside. The total attendance that night was precisely 182.

Pro basketball will click in a big way sooner or later. In Lapchick the Knicks have corralled a coach who is very likely to make it sooner than later.

April 1, 1947

PHILADELPHIA FIVE WINS LEAGUE TITLE

Warriors Top Chicago, 83-80, to Take Association Final Play-Offs, 4 Games to 1

PHILADELPHIA, April 22 (AP)— The Philadelphia Warriors tonight won the Basketball Association of America's first championship, defeating the Chicago Stags, 83 to 80, to take the final play-off series, four games to one.

Howie Dallmar's field goal with less than a minute to play and Ralph Kaplowitz's free throw provided the winning margin before a crowd of 8,221 at the Arena. Joe Fulks made 34 points for Philadelphia to run his total for seventy games to 1,611, compared with the previous unofficial high pro mark of 1,404 set more than thirty years ago by Willie Kummer.

The Warriors received $14,000 to add to $10,000 they had picked up in the first two rounds. The Stags got $10,000 to add to $14,000 they had received for beating Washington in the play-offs between the two division winners. The Warriors finished second in the Eastern section.

The line-up:

PHILADELPHIA (83)				CHICAGO (80)			
	G.	F.	P.		G.	F.	P.
Musi, lf	6	1	13	Zaslofsky, lf	2	1	5
Fulks, rf	10	14	34	Carlson	4	3	11
Kaplowitz	1	6	8	Jaros, rf	4	0	21
Hillhouse, c.	3	3	9	Gilmer	3	0	6
Senesky, lg.	4	3	11	Halbert	1	0	2
Dallmar, rg.	2	3	7	Carlisle	1	3	5
Fleishman	0	1	1	Davis, lg	0	0	2
Rosenberg	0	0	0	Rottner	1	0	2
				Seminoff, rg	5	2	12
				Kautz	5	0	10
Total	26	31	83	Total	30	20	80

April 23, 1947

PRO COURT RULES REVISED

Association Raises Limit on Personal Fouls to Six

Six personal fouls will be allowed before a player will be ejected from Basketball Association of America games this season, it was announced yesterday by Maurice Podoloff, president of the professional circuit. This change takes cognizance of the fact that B.A.A. games last forty-eight minutes as against the forty minutes played in college basketball, where five personal fouls are the limit.

Another rule change from last year, brought out by Podoloff at a luncheon at Leone's Restaurant, is the limitation of squads to ten men, with the stipulation that at least nine must be in uniform for a game. In the B.A.A.'s inaugural 1946-47 season, teams were permitted to carry twelve players.

October 30, 1947

BASKETBALL LOOP QUITS

Sixteen Club Pro League Dies, After a Month—Loses $600,000

CHICAGO, Nov. 13 (AP)—The infant sixteen-club Professional Basketball League of America blew up today in a splash of red ink, dropping 160 players, plus managers and coaches, into the pro player market.

The league, stretching into thirteen Midwest and Southern states from St. Paul, Minn., to Houston, Tex., and Atlanta, Ga., lost a reported $600,000, including promotional expenses, in operating less than a month.

The suspension reduces the nation's field to two major professional circuits—the old established National League and the Basketball Association of America.

Maurice A. White, former Chicago industrialist, sponsored the Commercial Sports Advertisers, Inc., parent organization of the league.

The league was "financially unsuccessful," said James O. Brooks, attorney for the Commercial Sports Advertisers, Inc., in announcing the suspension.

Brooks said all players of the sixteen clubs had been declared free agents, which means they are permitted to negotiate with teams in the National League or the Basketball Association of America, provided they did not previously jump contracts with teams in these rival circuits.

This decision is particularly important to stars like George Mikan, 6 foot, 9-inch center, and Bobbie McDermott of the Chicago Gears. Mikan, an outstanding star in the nation, was playing for an annual salary of $12,000.

November 14, 1947

MIKAN MOST VALUABLE

National Court League Votes Honor to Scoring Leader

INDIANAPOLIS, April 3 (AP)— George Mikan, 6-foot, 10-inch center of the Minneapolis Lakers, has been voted the National Basketball League's most valuable player for the 1947-48 season.

Big George set six all-time league records — a 1,195 - point grand total, an average of 21.3 points in fifty-six games, 406 field

goals, a 17-goal total for one game, 383 free throws and a one-game total of 42 points.

Mikan broke the one-game record twice. He scored 41 points against Rochester midway in the season after committing four personal fouls in the first half. He later got 42 against Tri-Cities.

April 4, 1948

Title to Minneapolis Five

ROCHESTER, N. Y., April 17 (AP) — The Minneapolis Lakers defeated the Rochester Royals, 75—65, tonight to win the championship of the National Basketball League. The Lakers, winning the championship play-off series three games to one, went in front in the first ten seconds of play and were never headed.

April 18, 1948

BULLETS' FIVE WINS TITLE

Baltimore Downs Philadelphia, 88-73, to End Final Series

BALTIMORE, April 21 (AP)—The Baltimore Bullets ended the Basketball Association of America play-offs tonight by defeating the Philadelphia Warriors, 88—73.

The victory, fourth for Baltimore against two defeats in the finals, won the championship for the Bullets in their first season of B. A. A. play.

Baltimore went ahead to stay four minutes before the second quarter ended, and then outscored the visitors, 26 points to 17, in the third period to pile up a margin that was not overcome. Six ties marked the hectic second quarter. The half ended with Baltimore ahead, 37—31. The line-up:

BALTIMORE (88)				PHILADELPHIA (73)			
	G.	F.	P.		G.	F.	P.
Hoffman, lf	5	5	15	Fulks, lf	8	12	28
Schulz, rf	2	3	7	Musi, rf	1	6	8
Meinhold	1	0	2	Fleishman	0	2	2
Fuetsch	1	3	5	Kaplowitz	2	5	9
Simmons, c	4	4	12	O'Brien	1	1	3
Hermsen	4	4	12	Halbert, c	2	2	6
Lewis, lg	2	0	4	Beenders	0	2	2
Reiser, rg	5	6	16	Dallmar, lg	2	4	8
Jeannette	6	3	15	Senesky, rg	1	3	5
Klotz	0	0	0	Crossin	0	2	2
Total	30	28	88	Total	17	39	73

April 22, 1948

FOUR PRO QUINTETS JUMP TO NEW LOOP

National Loses Minneapolis, Indianapolis, Rochester and Fort Wayne to the B. A. A.

CHICAGO., May 10 (AP)—Four key clubs today quit the National Basketball League and simultaneously were accepted as new members by the rival Basketball Association of America.

The National League, left with eight franchise holders, immediately countered by severing a working agreement with the B.A.A. It declared that it would retain contracts of players on the four jumping teams—Minneapolis, Rochester, Indianapolis and Fort Wayne, Ind.

Asked whether this meant a court fight, a National loop spokesman said, "It's a scrap from here on and we know our rights."

The long-expected development came at a concurrent session of both leagues at the same hotel in what previously was scheduled as a joint player-draft meeting.

12 in Revised Line-Up

The new line-up gave the two-year-old B.A.A. twelve members. Holdovers are Chicago, St. Louis, Baltimore, New York, Providence, Philadelphia, Washington and Boston.

The B.A.A. corralled two of the N.B.L.'s best gate attractions in Minneapolis and Rochester, Western and Eastern division champions, respectively. Minneapolis' George Mikan broke every N.B.L. scoring record last season and was the league's biggest individual drawing card.

The National was left with Oshkosh and Sheboygan, Wis., Toledo, Ohio, Anderson, Ind., Tri-Cities (Moline, Ill.), Syracuse, N.Y., Flint, Mich., and a prospective Chicago entry. A Chicago franchise was granted to Edward J. McNulty, a steel tank company executive.

Leo Ferris, manager of Tri-Cities and National League vice-president, issued a "declaration of war" when the B.A.A. late this afternoon invited the N.B.L. to a joint draft session.

Open War on Players

"There will be no respect of player contracts and open war on signing players from now on," Ferris warned Maurice Podoloff, who today was re-elected B.A.A. president for two years.

Ferris said the Minneapolis, Rochester, Indianapolis and Fort Wayne players would be assigned among the remaining N.B.L. membership and possible new members. The N.B.L. claims membership applications from Des Moines, Denver, Dayton and St. Paul.

The four jumping clubs ascribed their switch to the fact that the B.A.A. was a "tougher league" and played before bigger crowds.

Indianapolis and Fort Wayne, members for eight and seven years, respectively, were first to bolt. Then Minneapolis, which started in the league last season, and Rochester, a member for three years, called it quits.

It also was disclosed that Oshkosh and Toledo had applied for B.A.A. membership, but their bids were tabled. Later Lon Darling, Oshkosh manager, declared his team would stick in the N.B.L., which he asserted "definitely won't fold."

Six in Each Division

Podoloff said the revised B.A.A. membership would be aligned as follows: Eastern Division — New York, Providence, Baltimore, Philadelphia, Washington and Boston. Western Division — Minneapolis, Rochester, Chicago, St. Louis, Fort Wayne and Indianapolis.

Paul Walk of the Indianapolis Kautskys resigned as National loop president and Tom Carneghie quit as publicity director during today's break-up.

Later in the day Ward (Piggy) Lambert resigned as commissioner of the National League. A league spokesman said the item of appointing a new commissioner would be taken up tomorrow.

Lambert, dean of Western Conference cage coaches before leaving Purdue, held the commissionership for one year at a salary of about $10,000. In submitting his resignation, Lambert said he planned to re-enter the coaching field.

May 11, 1948

Mikan Sets Garden Scoring Mark As Lakers Rout Knick Five, 101-74

Minneapolis Ace Sinks 48 Points, Highest B. A. A. Total Here, to Pace Mates to Record—Colone Stars for New York

MIKAN DROPS ONE IN FOR THE LAKERS

Minneapolis center scoring in the final quarter of the game with the Knickerbockers at the Garden yesterday afternoon.

The New York Times

By LOUIS EFFRAT

There was not enough room on the Madison Square Garden scoreboard to post the Minneapolis total, as the powerhouse Lakers routed the New York Knickerbockers, 101-74, in a Basketball Association of America matinee yesterday. Nor was there sufficient room on the floor for both the Knicks and George Mikan.

Although Big George was triple-teamed by the hapless and hitless home side most of the way, he managed to cage 48 points and sent the experts scurrying through the record books. There, it was ascertained, that Mikan's output was the greatest ever achieved in a B.A.A. game here and the Minneapolis aggregate of 101 was the greatest ever witnessed on the Garden hardwood.

The Line-Up

MINNEAPOLIS (101)				KNICKERBKERS (74)			
	G.	F.	P.		G.	F.	P.
Ferrin, lf	5	4	14	Colone, lf	8	5	21
Jaros, rf	5	3	13	Palmer	0	1	1
Gardner	0	0	0	McGaha, rf	1	2	4
Mikan, c	18	12	48	Ritter	2	2	6
Forman, lg	6	0	12	Rothenberg, c	1	0	2
Jorgensen	1	0	2	Knorek	4	4	12
Kachan	0	1	1	Gallatin	0	2	2
Dwan, rg	5	1	11	Lumpp, lg	3	4	10
				Van B. Kolff, rg	1	4	6
				James	2	2	6
				Noel	2	0	4
Total	40	21	101	Total	24	26	74

Officials—Nucatola and Boyle.

It was only because the Lakers were so intent on feeding Mikan that they did not crack all existing team totals in the league. Certainly, their 117 points against the Providence Steamrollers, the existing high, would have been surpassed otherwise. At that, only two seconds remained when Tony Jaros clicked with a 40-foot angle set that enabled his team to crack the century.

Aiming at Fulks' Marks

Mikan, who receives $17,500 per year from the Lakers and is the top-salaried performer in the B.A.A., was aiming at the 63-point record that is in the possession of Philadelphia's Joe Fulks. With better luck, he might have made it, because a dozen of his shots were close enough, but failed to drop through the net.

Slightly more than five minutes of the contest remained when Mikan fouled out and as he strode toward the bench he was accorded

the greatest ovation ever heard in the Garden. The 9,184 fans cheered for a full minute and Mikan had to rise and acknowledge the tribute.

The six-foot nine-inch, 24-year-old De Paul alumnus was a one-man gang in the strictest sense of the phrase. Hitting from all positions and with either hand, Big George, the loop's leading scorer, succeeded with eighteen of his thirty-seven floor shots and added twelve fouls. His 48 points tied his former B.A.A. high, which was made against Washington and Minneapolis and was the league standard until Fulks took over.

Nothing the Knicks attempted was able to stop Mikan. At half-

time he had 21 points, matching all the Knicks put together as the Lakers enjoyed a 53-21 advantage. At 4:05 the Knicks led, 7—5, but the visitors sprinted for 17 consecutive points, a 22-7 spread and thereafter no doubt remained about the outcome.

Braun Misses Contest

Joe Lapchick chose a sorry afternoon to return to active duty as coach of the Knicks. Without Carl Braun, suffering from a sore throat, and with other Knicks ailing, his team was no match at all for the Lakers. Incidentally, Jim Pollard, top-ranking forward, was not in uniform for the visitors.

Joe Colone, rookie Knickerbocker, was his team's high indi-

vidual with 21 points. There was, however, obviously no comparing him with the over-all brilliance of Mikan. As Lapchick put it, the Knicks were lucky to be breathing after Mikan did his job.

Mikan's 48 points represent the third highest total ever accomplished at the Eighth Avenue arena. Only Harry Boykoff's 54 against St. Francis and Mikan's 53 against Rhode Island State are ahead of yesterday's figures. The previous team high was 97, accounted for by three teams.

In two preliminary games, Abraham & Straus defeated Metropolitan Life, 55—41, and Regis conquered St. Ann's, 46—42.

February 23, 1949

Minneapolis Five Annexes Title By Defeating Capitols, 77 to 56

ST. PAUL, Minn., April 13 (AP) —Injured wrist and all, George Mikan pushed in 29 points tonight to spark the Minneapolis Lakers to a 77-56 victory over the Washington Capitols for the championship of the Basketball Association of America.

Mikan's total for the year is 2,001. In the sixth game of the best of seven series, the Lakers led all the way from the start before a crowd of more than 10,-000 in the St. Paul auditorium.

Mikan clearly dominated the game, both in points and on the backboards. His nine field goals and eleven free throws belied the fractured wrist he suffered in the fourth game of the series at Washington last Saturday night.

The injured limb was again encased in heavy tape, but he was able to move it at the elbow. His fingers also were loose enough for him to help the Lakers subdue Washington, four games to two.

A year ago, Mikan had carried the Lakers to the national basketball title.

Minneapolis went into an early

lead and it was 12—3 before the Caps even warmed up. It was 19—12 at the quarter and 40—24 at intermission. Later, the Lakers built up a lead of 24 points and then let it fall off to 19.

With Mikan collecting his 2,001 point midway in the fourth quarter, Minneapolis was able to breathe easily the rest of the way. It was the most convincing victory of the playoffs.

Kleggie Hermsen, who shared honors with Jack Nichols in trying to stop Mikan, led the Caps offensively with 12 points each.

The line-up:

MINNEAPOLIS (77)	G.	F.	P.	WASHINGTON (56)	G.	F.	P.
Pollard, lf	3	1	7	Nichols, lf	1	5	7
Carlson	0	2	2	McKinney, rf	1	3	5
Jorgensen	0	0	0	O'Keefe	4	2	10
Jaros, rf	3	4	10	Katkaveck	0	1	1
Mikan, c	9	11	29	Norlander	3	0	6
Ferrin, lg	5	1	11	Hermsen, c	3	6	12
Schaefer, rg	6	5	17	Scolari, lg	0	4	4
Forman	0	1	1	Hertzberg, rg	2	4	8
Gardner	0	0	0	Zinic	1	1	3
Dwan	0	0	0				
Kachan	0	0	0	Total	15	26	56
Total	26	25	77				

April 14, 1949

Rival Basketball Circuits Merge Into One Loop of Eighteen Clubs

Association and National League End Long Conflict, With Podoloff New President of Combined Two-Division Set-Up

By FRANK ELKINS

The long war between the Basketball Association of America and the National Basketball League ended yesterday.

With representatives of both major professional circuits present at the BAA office in the Empire State Building, negotiations for a merger were completed and the result was the inception of the National Basketball Association.

Starting this season, there will be one major pro basketball circuit of eighteen teams, ten from the BAA and the remainder from the NBI.

Duffey to Head Board

Maurice Podoloff of New Haven, Conn., who has headed the BAA since its inception three years ago, was elected president of the National Basketball Association and Ike W. Duffey of Anderson, Ind.,

president of the league, was named chairman of the board of governors. Another officer named at yesterday's harmonious session was Walter Kennedy, director of public relations for the BAA, who will hold that post with the new league.

Plans for the NBA are still unsettled. However, at a meeting scheduled for Chicago one week from today, when representatives from every member club will be on hand, much business is expected to be consummated.

Other officers are to be elected, their length of tenure decided upon, changes made in constitutional and court rules and a tentative schedule proposed.

The merger marks the end of open warfare among the pro circuits for "big-time" college players, who received contracts far out of proportion. This threatened the financial stability of many clubs.

The new league definitely will be divided into two divisions most likely on a geographical basis, with each team playing every other member of the league several times during the course of the season.

Lakers in Merger

The Minneapolis Lakers, last year's champions; St. Louis Bombers, Fort Wayne Pistons, Chicago Stags, Rochester Royals, Washington Capitols, Baltimore Bullets, Philadelphia Warriors, New York Knickerbockers and the Boston Celtics are the BAA members in the new group. Providence and Indianapolis were dropped.

For the National Basketball League, organized in 1937, the Syracuse Nationals, the Anderson Packers, Sheboygan Redskins, Tri-Cities Blackhawks, made up of players from Moline, Ill., Rock Island, Ill., and Davenport, Iowa; Denver Nuggets, Waterloo and Milwaukee, which has replaced the Oshkosh franchise, are part of the merger. Dayton and Hammond were dropped while the Indianapolis Olympians, consisting of last-year's Olympic-winning University of Kentucky quintet, were added.

August 4, 1949

MIKAN VOTED BEST OF STARS ON COURT

Minneapolis Player Gets 139 Votes and Luisetti 123 in Mid-Century Balloting

MINNEAPOLIS, Jan. 31 (AP)— Honored and appreciative. That was the reaction of George Mikan to word that he had been named as the greatest basketball player of the last fifty years.

Mikan was chosen in The Associated Press mid-century poll, in which sports writers and broadcasters all over the country participated. Mikan received 139 of the 380 votes cast. Hank Luisetti, Stanford star of thirteen years ago, was runner-up with 123.

Word of his selection came to the former DePaul University star at his home in Minneapolis' South Side. He was very much the young family man, taking time to discipline his 3-month-old boxer pup, answer the telephone, and paint his older son's cheek with antiseptic to avoid infection in a scratch the lad received playing with the pup.

He was keeping an eye on 21-month-old Terry because Mrs. Mikan and their 8½-month-old son were confined to bed with influenza.

The present-day Mikan, now the star of the Minneapolis Lakers of the National Basketball Association, presents a far different picture from the awkward youth of eight years ago. He carries his 240 pounds well distributed over his 6-foot 10-inch frame and moves with ease and grace. His heavy-rimmed glasses give him a studious air that is broken easily and often by an engaging grin and an occasional hearty laugh.

Mikan's ability to "get most of them" has brought him a 300-point leadership in the scoring records of the NBA. He has counted 1,307 points on 452 field goals and 403 fouls.

February 1, 1950

LAKER FIVE DOWNS SYRACUSE, 110-95

Wins N. B. A. Title Series, 4-2 —Mikan Registers 40 Points to Set Pace for Victors

MINNEAPOLIS, April 23 (AP)—Mr. Basketball—George Mikan of the Minneapolis Lakers — tonight paced his team to a 110-to-95 victory over Syracuse and the National Basketball Association championship. The Lakers took the best-of-seven series, 4—2.

Mikan registered 40 points in leading the Lakers, hitting on thirteen field goals and sinking fourteen fouls.

Three fights spiced the game which marked the third consecutive league championship for the Lakers. Police, in fact, had to interrupt a first-quarter set-to between Paul Seymour of Syracuse and Jim Pollard of Minneapolis.

Billy Gabor of Syracuse and Swede Carlson also tangled, and Gabor also took on Slater Martin of the Lakers in the wild second period. Player-coach Al Cervi was banished from the game midway in the third quarter when he complained too loudly at a foul.

Minneapolis lost four players on fouls after it had extended its margin to 81—56 at the three-quarter mark. The Lakers were able to score their 100th point with three minutes to go in the game, marking the eighth time of the year they had reached the century mark. A crowd of 9,812, largest ever to see a pro basketball game in Minneapolis saw the contest.

The line-up:

MINNEAPOLIS (110)	G.	F.	PF.	P.	SYRACUSE (95)	G.	F.	PF.	P.
Mikkelsen	3	6	5		Gabor, lf	4	6	6	14
Pollard, rf	5	6	6	16	Mack'ski, rf	6	5	5	17
Mikan, c	13	14	6	40	Hannum, c	4	1	4	9
Ferrin, lg	3	0	5	6	Schayes, lg	6	11	5	23
Martin	4	1	5	9	Seymour	2	3	5	7
Harrison, rg	2	1	6	5	Cervi, rg	1	1	0	3
Grant	3	0	4	6	Ratkovics	3	5	3	11
Schaefer	2	8	0	12	Levane	2	0	0	4
Carlson	3	4	2	10	Peterson	0	2	3	2
Hassett	0	1	2	1	Corley	0	0	4	0
Jaros	0	0	0	0	Chollet	1	1	0	3
Total	36	38	42	110	Total	31	43	35	95

Half-time Score—Minneapolis 51. Free Throws Missed—Syracuse: Macknowski 3 Hannum 3, Schayes 4, Seymour, Ratkovics 6, Peterson, Corley 3 Minneapolis: Pollard 3, Mikan 3, Ferrin 2, Carlson, Hassett.

April 24, 1950

Clifton, Negro Ace, Goes To Knickerbocker Five

The New York Knickerbockers made an expensive move toward strengthening their club yesterday by purchasing the contract of Nat (Sweetwater) Clifton, star center and leading scorer of the famed Harlem Globetrotters.

Clifton thus became the third Negro player to enter the ranks of the National Basketball Association. Washington recently signed two Negroes, Earl Lloyd of West Virginia State and Har-

old Hunter of North Carolina College. Boston has the draft rights to Charley Cooper, Duquesne ace, and is expected to sign him.

The purchase price for the 6-7, 225-pound Clifton was not disclosed. It would be no surprise if the Knicks paid more than $10,000 for him. Clifton reportedly received a $10,000 a year salary from the Globetrotters.

May 25, 1950

HARLEM FIVE A HIT ON EUROPEAN TOUR

Globetrotters Amaze Writers and Fans, Draw Record Crowds in England

LONDON, May 29 (AP)—Two American basketball teams—self-styled "missionaries spreading the gospel"—are wowing fans on an eighty-day European tour.

The barnstorming all-Negro Harlem Globetrotters and their American all-star opponents are displaying trick shots, dribbling, ball control and crazy court antics undreamed of here. Arenas are packed. Already plans are afoot for a 1951 return trip.

Pop-eyed British sportswriters say of the spectacular ball-juggling: "Amazing, uncanny, thrilling—like nothing we've ever seen!"

Similar reaction was reported from Portugal, where 5,000 fans watched a practice session; France, Belgium and Switzerland. Advance bookings for four other countries are heavy.

Owner-coach Abe Saperstein says in the first eighteen days he cleared the equivalent in European currency of $25,000 toward the $70,000 cost of the trip. The tour started May 5 in Lisbon.

The British Broadcasting Corporation televised the first London game and thousands of Englishmen who formerly sniffed at basketball as a girls' game, rushed for tickets.

"No, Aunt Agatha," wrote one sports scribe, "this isn't anything like the netball at your girls' school. In fact, it isn't like anything you've ever seen!"

"I thought we'd take a box-office whipping here," said Saperstein. "I expected 10,000 people but 50,-000 turned up." Biggest basketball crowd in London during the 1948 Olympics—when Britain's green entry was slaughtered—was about 4,000.

Many English customers confess they don't know a backboard from a basket—but love the Globetrotters' clowning.

At various times, Reece (Goose) Tatum, a lanky, loose-jointed hook-shot artist from Eldorado, Ark., had the ball under his shirt, between his legs and on top of his head. His "no-look" over-the-shoulder baskets astounded fans.

May 30, 1950

PISTONS TOP LAKERS, 19-18

Modern Low-Scoring Records for Pro Basketball Set

MINNEAPOLIS, Nov. 22 (AP)—In a record low-scoring National Basketball Association game, Rookie Larry Foust dropped a basket with six seconds to go that enabled the Fort Wayne Pistons to beat the Minneapolis Lakers tonight, 19—18.

The result cracked the Lakers home-court string of twenty-nine triumphs, which had extended since Nov. 27, 1949. It was Fort Wayne's first road victory of the season and put the Pistons into a tie with Tri-Cities for first place in the Western division, demoting Minneapolis to third.

Only eight field goals were scored, four by each club. That broke the previous modern professional basketball record of 13. The total of 37 points was another modern low, one under the previous mark.

George Mikan got 15 of the Lakers' points, including their four baskets.

November 23, 1950

ROYALS TOP KNICKS FOR CROWN, 79-75

Win Seventh Game of N. B. A. Finals in the Last Minute After New York Rally

By LOUIS EFFRAT
Special to THE NEW YORK TIMES.

ROCHESTER, N. Y., April 21—The 1950-51 basketball season ended tonight, with the Rochester Royals crowned National Association champions. They wrapped up the title with a dramatic finish that defeated the New York Knickerbockers, 79—75, in the seventh game of this best-of-seven series.

Against seemingly insurmountable handicaps, Joe Lapchick's New Yorkers gave their all, overcoming a second-period 14-point deficit and edging in front, 74—72, with two minutes left to play. As the seconds ticked away and the Royals surged back to a 75-74 lead, only to be deadlocked by Vince Boryla's foul, the 4,200 fans in the Edgerton Sports Arena watched in suspense.

This was it. This was an entire season dependent upon the movements of less than a minute, with the world professional basketball championship at stake. Fifty-nine seconds remained, when the Royals took time out to discuss their strategy. Most fans figured that the Rochester quintet would play for one shot, but with forty-four seconds to go Bob Davies made the winning, the championship move.

McGuire Fouls Davies

Having dribbled underneath, the former Seton Hall ace got into position for a short-range lay-up. However, Davies never was able to get off the shot because a desperate Dick McGuire fouled him. Awarded two shots, Davies sent both into the hoop and the Knicks were beaten.

Only two seconds were left when Jack Coleman, taking a bullet pass from Red Holzman, curled in a "gift" basket. This one did not matter. The pair of free throws by Davies was the crushing blow, and the Knicks, who had come so near to their first title, had to be satisfied with the runner-up position.

Off slowly, the Knicks were their own worst enemies at the start. Ten times during the opening twenty-four minutes the New Yorkers forfeited possession because of ragged passing. Time and again they missed comparatively easy scoring opportunities and when the half ended with Rochester on top, 40—34, it was the direct result of the Knicks' carelessness.

The Royals, with Davies and Arnie Risen their mainstays, did not play well either in the first half, but their mistakes were fewer and less costly than New York's. At three minutes and thirty seconds of the second period the Knicks had fallen behind by 32—18. However, the visitors improved and cut eight points from the Rochester lead at the intermission.

Hurt by some of the referee's decisions, the Knicks nevertheless continued to fight on, and the efforts of Max Zaslofsky, Harry Gallatin and Dick McGuire brought rewards. With five minutes left, New York got a bad break when Sweetwater Clifton fouled out. Then, with 1:53 left, Connie Simmons was charged with his sixth personal.

The enforced departure of New York's two big men gave the Royals a tremendous advantage. The taps and rebounds became almost exclusively Rochester property as Risen, Coleman and Arnie Johnson dominated possession. And yet, if the Knicks had been able to hold off the opposition forty-four seconds more, the outcome might have been different.

The Knicks' failure to produce a 20-point man was costly, too. Where Zaslofsky, who clicked with seven out of fourteen floor shots, and Boryla had each netted 16 points, the Royals pointed to Risen's 24 and Davies' 20. Thus, the court campaign was concluded, with Rochester succeeding Minneapolis as N. B. A. ruler.

The line-up:

ROCHESTER (79)	FG	ST	F	FT	Pts.	A.	PF
Coleman, lf	3	6	3	6	9	9	4
Johnson, rf	2	8	7	7	11	3	5
Saul	0	0	0	0	0	1	0
Risen, c	7	19	10	14	24	2	4
McNamee	0	1	0	0	0	0	0
Davies, lg	7	19	6	7	20	0	0
Calhoun	0	0	0	0	0	0	0
Wanzer, rg	5	11	3	3	13	3	1
Holzman	1	1	0	0	2	1	0
Total	25	65	29	37	79	19	18

KNICKERBOCKERS (75)	FG	ST	F	FT	Pts.	A.	PF
Boryla, lf	6	13	4	4	16	2	3
Gallatin, rf	5	8	2	3	12	1	2
Simmons	4	9	3	6	11	2	6
Clifton, c	4	11	3	6	11	2	6
Zaslofsky, lg	7	14	2	3	16	5	2
McGuire	1	8	2	2	4	5	2
Vandeweghe, rg	2	6	1	2	5	0	0
Lumpp	0	2	0	0	0	2	1
Total	29	70	17	25	75	19	32

Half-time score—Rochester 40, Knicks 34.
Officials—Lou Eisenstein and Stan Stutz.
KEY: FG, field goals; ST. shots taken; F. fouls; FT, free throws; Pts., points; A. assists; PF, personal fouls.

Pro Basketball Finals

(Best of 7 Games)

April 7—Rochester 92, Knickerbockers 65.

April 8—Rochester 99, Knickerbockers 84.

April 11—Rochester 78, Knickerbockers 71.

April 13—Knickerbockers 79, Rochester 73.

April 15—Knickerbockers 92, Rochester 89.

April 18—Knickerbockers 80, Rochester 73.

April 21—Rochester 79, Knickerbockers 75.

April 22, 1951

Mikan Sets Rebound Record

PHILADELPHIA, March 4 (AP)—George Mikan won his personal scoring duel with Paul Arizin tonight, tallying 41 points and setting a new National Basketball Association rebound record of thirty-six, but his Minneapolis Lakers dropped a final-second 83-81 decision to Arizin's Philadelphia Warriors. Arizin scored 27 points.

March 5, 1952

LAKERS WIN, 82-65, AND CAPTURE TITLE

Minneapolis Five Sets Back Knicks by 4 Games to 3—Play-Off Finale Is Wild

MINNEAPOLIS, April 25 (AP)—The Minneapolis Lakers closed out the long pro season tonight by taking the National Basketball Association crown, beating the New York Knickerbockers, 82 to 65. A $7,500 player jackpot went with the victory in the seventh game of the play-off series. It was the Lakers' fourth N. B. A. title in five years.

George Mikan, with 22 points, was the Lakers' scoring leader, but it was the injured Jim Pollard who provided the fourth-quarter spark that gave the winners their final 17-point margin for the championship by four games to three.

Defense Proves Strong

The Lakers' defense held the Knicks to ten field goals in the first three quarters. Only two Knicks—Max Zaslofsky and Connie Simmons—were able to attain double figures.

Zaslofsky matched Mikan's 22 and Simmons had 13. It was a wild game, enlivened by two technical fouls, one by Dick McGuire of the Knicks, the other by Mikan. There also was a double foul called against Vern Mikkelsen of the Lakers and the visitorss' Harry Gallatin.

Pollard missed the last two play-off games because of a back injury suffered a week ago tonight

in New York. Back in uniform tonight. He scored 10 points in the final frame on ofur field goals and a pair of gratis tosses.

Holds an Early Lead

The Lakers' dominance of the backboard was the key to their victory. New York's only lead was at 3—2 early in the contest. Minneapolis built its margin to 18—12 at the end of the first period and to 12 points, 34—22, before the Knicks surged back to within 7 at the half, which ended with the Lakers ahead, 36—29.

The crowd of 8,612 mobbed the Lakers after the finish of the contest and watched Mikan and his cohorts raise Coach Johnny Kundla to their shoulders.

The line-up:

MINNEAPOLIS (82)	G.	F.	PF.	P.	KNICKS (65)	G.	F.	PF.	P.
Mik'lsen, lf.	5	3	5	13	Simmons, lf.	4	5	1	13
Harrison ..	7	0	6	14	Kaftan, rf.	1	1	1	3
Pollard, rf.	4	2	2	10	Clifton, c..	1	6	4	8
Hitch	0	0	1	0	A. McGuire ..	0	5	4	3
Schultz ...	0	0	1	0	Gallatin ..	1	3	2	5
Mikan, c..	7	8	5	22	Lumpp	0	0	1	0
Saul, lg...	4	5	4	14	D. McGuire lg.	3	2	2	8
Martin, rg.	3	5	5	9	Vand'he. rg.	1	1	5	3
Hutton ...	0	0	1	0	Zaslofsky ..	7	8	4	22
Total	30	22	31	82	Total	18	29	24	65

Minneapolis ....18 18 13 33—82
Knicks ....12 17   8 28—65

Free throws missed — Simmons 2, Kaftan, Clifton, Zaslofsky 3, D. McGuire, Gallatin, Mikkelsen, Mikan 2, Hutton, Pollard 2.

April 26, 1952

Celtics Beat Nats In Fourth Overtime

Bob Cousy, record-breaker

By The Associated Press.

BOSTON, March 21—The Boston Celtics, led by the brilliant Bob Cousy, advanced to the second round of the National Basketball Association play-offs for the first time in their seven-year history today by defeating the Syracuse Nationals, 111—105, in four overtime periods at the Boston Garden. The victory was the Celtics' second straight in the best-of-three series.

Cousy set a new N. B. A. play-off record by scoring 50 points. He tossed in 10 field goals and connected on 30 of 32 throws

from the foul line.

The sensational former Holy Cross star tied the game at 99—99, with five seconds remaining in the third overtime session, with a long one-handed push shot.

In the fourth overtime period, the Nationals raced to a 104-99 lead but Cousy then sank a foul shot and two successive field goals. He connected with four more free throws as the Celtics pulled ahead to the victory.

The Celtics will meet the New York Knickerbockers in the first game of a best three-out-of-five series at New York Wednesday. The winner then will meet the survivor of the Western Division play-offs.

Cousy's performance topped the old N. B. A. play-off scoring mark of 47 set by George Mikan of Minneapolis last year.

A total of 107 fouls were called during the long game, 55 against Syracuse and 52 against the Celtics. In the end, the fouls caught up with the Nats as seven men had the limit of six, resulting in technicals every time they committed a foul.

Syracuse was handicapped further by the loss of Dolph Schayes, its top scorer, who was banished from the game with Boston's Bob Brannum for fighting at the four-minute mark of the second period.

A crowd of 11,058 watched the lead change hands often until the Celtics' final spurt in the fourth extra session.

Easy Ed McCauley scored 18 points for Boston, while teammate Bob Harris tossed in 14. Red Rocha was top man for Syracuse with 19 points, followed by George King with 16.

The line-up:

BOSTON (111)	G.	F.	PF.	P.	SYRACUSE (105)	G.	F.	PF.	P.
Donham, lf.	1	0	6	2	Schayes, lf.	2	4	2	8
Harris, rf..	4	6	6	14	Gabor, rf...	3	1	6	3
Cooper ..	2	5	7	9	Lochmueller	1	1	6	3
Brannum ..	3	0	1	6	Osterkorn ..	1	0	6	2
Mahnken ..	0	1	5	1	Lloyd, c....	4	5	5	13
Macauley, c..	4	10	6	18	Rocha	5	9	6	19
Mahoney ..	0	0	5	0	Jorgenson	2	4	6	8
Cousy, lg..	10	30	3	50	King, lg...	4	8	6	16
Sharman, rg.	3	3	6	9	Cervi, rg...	0	9	7	9
Rollins	0	2	5	2	Seymour ..	5	8	5	18
Total	27	57	52	111	Total	27	51	55	105

Boston ....21 19 22 15   9   4   9 12—111
Syracuse ......22 20 17 18   9   4   6—105

Free throws missed — Boston: Donham 3, Cousy 2, Mahoney, Cooper, Rollins; Syracuse: Rocha 3, Lochmueller 2, Lloyd 2, Gabor 2, Cervi 2, Jorgenson, King, Seymour.

March 22, 1953

LAKERS WIN, 91-84, TAKE PRO HONORS

Minneapolis Five Turns Back Knicks at Armory and Ends Series With 4-1 Edge

By MICHAEL STRAUSS

The Minneapolis Lakers continue to rule the National Basketball Association. They proved this conclusively last night when they defeated the Knickerbockers, 91—84, to end the play-off series for the loop crown after only five games. It was the second straight championship for the Westerners, who last year defeated the Knicks in a full seven-game set.

The Lakers were in command from the midway point in the second quarter to the finish and at half-time enjoyed a 44—35 lead. They increased this to a 20-point spread early in the third period, a margin that proved adequate despite a strong rally by the losers.

The Lakers, who now have won the league crown four times since the circuit was organized five years ago, carried off a purse of $16,500 for their work in the play-offs. The Knicks, losers in the series by four games to one, received $14,000 for their post-season championship play.

Last night's contest, played before a capacity crowd of 5,200 at the Sixty-ninth Regiment Armory, was one in which the trend changed drastically during the late stages of the third quarter and through the fourth. Although apparently hopelessly outdistanced, the Knicks rallied in the last twenty minutes and with forty seconds to go found themselves trailing by only 85—84.

Mikkelsen Sinks Foul

Vern Mikkelsen was fouled at this point and it proved to be the death knell to any hopes the New Yorkers may have harbored. The former Hamline star promptly converted his free throw and George Mikan followed with an easy bucket shot and another one-pointer. Five seconds remained to play as Mikan fed to Saul, who promptly laid up the game's final tally.

Mikan, who had sat out most of the last half because he had been charged with four personals, thus continued in the role as a Knick nemesis.

With Mikan on the sidelines for a good part of the contest—he also was benched for the last seven minutes of the second period—the task of carrying the visitors to victory fell on the shoulders of some of the other Minneapolis sharpshooters. Those who filled the breach most effectively included Jim Pollard, Slater Martin and Saul. Pollard scored 17 points while Martin and Saul each registered 13. Mikan, despite his comparatively short stay, was second high man for the invaders with 14.

As it developed, the call of Mikan to the bench in the second quarter proved the signal for some of the best work turned in by the winners. Tied nine times until that point, the visitors went to work in earnest and promptly broke into their first big lead, Jim Holstein and Mikkelsen setting the pace. The rally resulted in the Lakers' 9-point edge at halftime.

Lakers Continue Drive

The drive continued after the respite and the winners forged into a long lead that ended all doubt as to the outcome. They scored 11 points to open the third quarter before the losers could break into the scoring column. And when Jerry Fleishman, the former N. Y. U. star, came through with a hook shot, the cause seemed irretrievably lost. The score at that point was 55—37, after only four minutes twenty seconds.

But the home forces refused to quit. Digging in with an all-court press and harassing their foes at every turn, the Knicks closed the gap slowly but surely. Led by Connie Simmons, Ernie Vandeweghe and Vince Boryla, the losers brought the count to 69—60 as the third quarter ended. Simmons finishing the scoring for the session with an easy lay-up.

Bob Cousy (right) was the steady playmaker of the Boston Celtics throughout the 1950's.

Through the early phases of the final chapter, the Lapchick men were within striking distance of their rivals but just didn't seem to have enough to threaten. With Fleishman in the key role, the losers narrowed the score to 77—73 after 5:30. The Lakers, battling desperately, refused to give way and once again went into an 8-point lead after 7:55 as Carl Braun fouled out.

The removal of Braun was followed by some lightning-like maneuvers by the home team. Field goals by Clifton, two fouls by Harry Gallatin, another one-pointer by Dick McGuire and a set by Boryla brought the score to 84—82 at 10:15. Pollard tallied a foul but McGuire drove in with a lay-up to cut the margin to one point. It was as close as the losers could come to victory.

The contest was heightened by a brief display of fisticuffs between Boryla and Bob Harrison in the fourth period, but they were promptly separated. The officials, Ernie Heft and Sid Borgia, also came in for considerable abuse from the players during the latter portion of the fray, a situation highly appreciated by the crowd.

The line-up:

MINNEAPOLIS (91)				NEW YORK (84)			
	G.	F.	PF.	P.		G.	F.	PF.	P.
Mikkelsen, lf	4	3	4	11	Gallatin, lf	2	2	4	6
Pollard, rf	6	5	3	17	Boryla, rf	3	4	6	10
Holstein	5	0	2	10	Surhoff	0	0	0	0
Hitch	1	1	2	3	Clifton, c	3	1	6	7
Schmittker	0	1	2	1	Simmons	5	6	5	16
Mikan, c	4	6	5	14	V'deweghe, lg	5	4	5	14
Martin, lg	3	8	4	14	Braun, rg	5	9	6	19
Saul, rg	4	4	5	12	D. McGuire	1	1	1	3
Harrison	2	0	3	4	Fleishman	2	5	6	9
Skoog	2	1	3	5					
Total	31	29	33	91	Total	26	32	39	84

Minneapolis .... 19 25 25 22—91
New York .... 18 17 25 24—84
Free throws missed—Clifton, Braun 4, Boryla 2, Simmons 3, Fleishman 4, Martin 3, Saul 2, Mikan 3, Harrison 3, Holstein 2, Pollard, Hitch.

April 11, 1953

Indianapolis Out of Loop; N.B.A. Bars Bill Spivey

BOSTON, April 23 (UP)—The financially-ailing Indianapolis Olympians dropped out of the National Basketball Association tonight.

Maurice Podoloff, N. B. A. president, said, "as of this moment Indianapolis club ceases to function. It is not going to operate again. The N. B. A. is now a nine-team league."

Polotoff said the Olympians' president, Cliff Courtney, still might be able to sell the team.

Earlier today, the owners denied Bill Spivey, former Kentucky All-America player, entry to the pro loop. The board of governors decided unanimously to keep Spivey's name off the draft roster.

Spivey was recently tried on perjury charges in connection with the basketball "fix" scandal. The jury was unable to agree and it was indicated the case would be dropped.

April 24, 1953

Pro Basketball Drops Molinas, Ex-Columbia Star, for Wagering

By LOUIS EFFRAT

Jack Molinas, Columbia's 1953 basketball captain who joined the professional Fort Wayne (Ind.) Pistons, was suspended indefinitely yesterday because he had been betting on his team.

The suspension, tantamount to expulsion from his $9,600-a-year job, was announced at Fort Wayne by Fred Zollner, owner of the Pistons, and was immediately recognized here by Maurice Podoloff, the president of the National Basketball Association.

Mr. Podoloff, who led a four-week investigation, in which Indiana police and private operatives there and in this city participated, said he did not regard Mr. Molinas' action as a major or even a minor scandal.

"I call it a minor aberration that will not affect the league," he declared, adding that he was convinced this was "not a big operation, involving diabolical genius."

Mr. Molinas told The Associated Press at Fort Wayne: "It's true that I bet on some of our games—less than a dozen—but I always bet on us to win. I've never done anything dishonest in my life."

Rumors that Mr. Molinas, a forward, had been wagering on the outcome of Fort Wayne games reached Mr. Podoloff last month. The president started an investigation then, but it was not until 4:30 yesterday morning, following some eight hours of interrogation—Mr. Molinas and other Piston players were questioned—that Mr. Molinas wrote and signed the following statement:

"I have been a member of the Zollner Pistons basketball team since October, 1953. After being on the team for approximately a month, I called a man in New York. Knowing this man for a long period of time, I called him on the telephone and asked him if he could place a bet for me.

"He said that he could and would tell me the odds on the game either for or against the Pistons. After hearing the odds or points on the game, I either placed a bet on the Pistons or else told him that the odds were too great, and that I did not want to place a bet.

"Several times I talked to him over the phone and odds or points were not mentioned, and I told him that I thought on some occasions that we could win a particular game, and I placed a bet. I did this about ten times.

"At no time was there a payoff to throw any games made to me by the New York party. Nor was there any mention of the fact; however, the only reimbursements I received were for my phone calls which I made him. Also, I received approximately $400 for the total times I have been betting with him. This included the phone bill, also."

The name of the "New York man" was withheld by Mr. Podoloff. He said Indiana police were aware of his identity and that New York police were to be informed. At Fort Wayne, the police said "no criminal action whatsoever is planned against Molinas."

Deputy Chief Inspector Edward W. Byrnes, in charge of detectives in the Bronx, last night questioned Isidore Ratenski, about 54 years old, who operates a candy store at 154 East 188th Street, the Bronx. Inspector Byrnes said the questioning was "in connection with the Molinas basketball" case.

Mr. Zollner issued this statement:

"Molinas has been under investigation since the middle of December and, when confronted with the evidence, admitted in a signed statement that he had on numerous occasions called a connection in New York to obtain odds and points on games in which he was to play. He further admitted that he had on many of these occasions placed bets on these games.

"Maurice Podoloff, president of the N. B. A., reviewed the evidence in Fort Wayne last night and sanctioned the suspension because Molinas violated the N. B. A. rule, which prohibits any player from betting on a game in which he participates."

Mr. Podoloff, who credited Ike Gellis, sports editor of The New York Post, with having given the original tip on Mr. Molinas' action, said the 21-year-old athlete would be granted a hearing, if he decided to appeal. "However," the president asserted, "I do not think Molinas will request such a hearing. Even if he did, he would have to present a much stronger case for me to permit him to re-enter the league."

The National Basketball Association, now in its eighth season, has franchises in New York, Philadelphia, Baltimore, Syracuse, Boston, Rochester, Minneapolis, Milwaukee and Fort Wayne. The league had been free of scandals since its organization.

Not a Criminal Action

Unlike the shaving of points in college contests several years ago, when numerous players were arrested and convicted, the Molinas case is not a criminal action. It would have been if he had bet against his team. It is, though, a violation of the league's uniform player contract, which calls for expulsion of any player who "directly or indirectly bets money or anything of value on the outcome of any game played."

At Columbia, Mr. Molinas held virtually every basketball record. In his sophomore year, he was suspended for one semester because he had thrown a glass out the window, but he made up the lost time by attending summer classes.

The 6-foot 6¼-inch Molinas recently was named to the Western team that will oppose the East in the league's fourth annual All-Star game at Madison Square Garden on Jan. 21. Of course, he will be replaced.

Mr. Molinas was last seen in action here on Dec. 15, when Fort Wayne played the Boston Celtics at the Garden. That night, 13,837 fans saw the Celtics defeat the Pistons, 82-73, after Mr. Molinas had scored twenty points for the losers. According to rumors, the Boston club opened the favorite to win by the margin of 3½ points. The odds increased to 7½ points and subsequently, it was reported, the game was removed from the board.

Mr. Molinas did not go to the auditorium in Fort Wayne yesterday. Without him, the Pistons turned back the Milwaukee Hawks, 81-73.

January 11, 1954

LAKERS WIN, 87-80, TO RETAIN CROWN

Defeat Syracuse in Seventh Game of Pro Title Series —Pollard Sets Pace

MINNEAPOLIS, April 12 (AP) —The Minneapolis Lakers won their third straight National Basketball Association championship tonight with an 87-80 victory over Syracuse that crushed the Easterners' rags-to-riches playoff bid. The victory came in the seventh and last game of the series.

Jim Pollard, charter member of the Lakers in 1947, paced Minneapolis as it posted its sixth pro basketball championship in its seven-year existence. Pollard scored 21 points.

The Lakers started with a title in the old National League in 1947-48, added two more in the Basketball Association of America in 1948-49 and have since won three out of four in the N. B. A.

The Lakers started with a first-quarter burst that gave them a 17-14 advantage. The Nationals never came within 5 points thereafter.

Syracuse played without Billy Gabor, who was on the bench with a knee injury, and with three other stars in either bandages or casts.

The most bandaged of all, Dolph Schayes, scored 18 points to lead the Syracuse scoring.

Paul Seymour had 16 and three other National players were in double figures, but Syracuse couldn't match the fiery Minneapolis offense.

Along with Pollard, Dugie Martin and Clyde Lovellette tallied 12 points apiece and George Mikan hit 11. Lovellette was extremely effective in the second period, when he helped the Lakers to a 38-32 half-time margin.

The Lakers bagged 27 points in the third period, 21 more than they had scored yesterday in the third quarter of the series' sixth game.

Pollard, with 9 points, led the assault which gave the Lakers a lead of 16 points at 61—45 with three minutes to play in the period.

Syracuse fired back in the fourth period with Schayes leading the way. But Pollard and Lovellette help squelch the attempt.

Minneapolis shot at a 48 per cent clip, getting thirty baskets in sixty-four shots. The Laker defense held the Nats to sixty-two shots. Syracuse hit for twenty-eight field goals.

The line-up:

MINNEAPOLIS (87)	G.	F.	P.	P.		SYRACUSE (80)	G.	F.	P.	P.
Mik'lsen, lf.	3	1	5	7		Schayes, lf.	6	6	5	18
Pollard, rf.	8	5	2	21		Ost'korn, rf.	3	4	5	10
Holstein	1	2	2	4		Lavoy	4	2	5	10
Schnittker	3	1	5	7		Lloyd, c.	4	2	4	10
Mikan, c.	2	7	3	11		Neal	1	0	2	2
Lovellette	5	2	4	12		Seymour, lg.	6	4	8	16
Skoog, lg.	3	2	5	8		King	2	0	4	4
Martin, rg.	4	4	3	12		Kenville, rg.	3	0	4	6
Saul	1	3	5	5		Masino	1	2	3	4
Total	30	27	31	87		Total	26	24	38	80

Minneapolis ....17 21 27 22—87
Syracuse ....14 18 22 26—80

Free throws missed—Schayes 2, Osterkorn 4, Lloyd, King, Kenville 2, Lavoy, Neal 3, Pollard 2, Mikan 3, Skoog 2, Martin 3, Lovellette 4, Holstein 2, Saul.

April 13, 1954

BASKETBALL LOOP CHANGES 2 RULES

24-Second Time Limit Set on Possession Without a Toss in Move to Halt 'Stalling'

Emphasizing an effort to "speed up play," the directors of the National Basketball Association adopted two rule changes yesterday.

In their second session at the Roosevelt Hotel, beginning in the morning and continuing until late last night, they took steps to avoid "stalling." A seventy-two game schedule also was adopted for the 1954-55 season.

The directors decided to place a time limit of twenty-four seconds for a team to retain possession of the ball without taking a shot. A special clock will be used to check the elapsed time.

Applies at All Times

The time limit will be in effect, no matter where the team gains possession of the ball. After a successful goal, when the ball is taken out of bounds under the basket, the scored-on team will continue to have the usual ten seconds to get across the midcourt line plus fourteen seconds in which to get a shot away.

Should the team gain possession in the forecourt, as in the case of an offensive rebound, it will have twenty-four seconds to shoot.

The other major change puts a limit of six personal fouls upon each team per quarter of the regulation game. A penalty for excess fouling will be two free throws for every foul over six. In the event of a five-minute overtime period, each team will be permitted three fouls.

The present two-minute rule was eliminated. That rule, used in the last two minutes of regulation play, provided for a jump ball, between the fouling player and the player fouled, after each successful foul throw.

A move for stricter officiating also was approved.

Podoloff Elected Again

Maurice Podoloff was re-elected president of the association for a three-year term. He was granted wider powers to control players and officials. Podoloff received the authority to name a supervisor of officials if he so wishes. He plans to have a staff of ten full-time referees.

In line with efforts to supplement the referee's powers, it was voted that, with one exception, no player, coach or owner be permitted to speak to an official during a game from the floor or bench.

When the captain or coach of a team has called a time-out, the coach and captain can discuss with the referee any rule interpretation. They may not protest a decision. While the first violation of this rule calls for a technical foul charge against the offender, a second violation provides not only for the technical foul, a $25 fine, but automatic expulsion from the game of the guilty party.

April 24, 1954

BULLETS SUSPEND N.B.A. OPERATIONS

Baltimore Can Resume Play Next Season if Financial Problem Is Overcome

By WILLIAM J. FLYNN

The Baltimore Bullets received permission yesterday to suspend operations in the National Basketball Association for the remainder of the campaign. The Bullets can resume play next season if their financial difficulties are overcome.

The decision was made at a meeting of the board of governors at the Statler Hotel yesterday. The players on the Baltimore roster were distributed among the other clubs in the loop in a draft procedure based on present standings. They will be eligible to play tonight.

With the last-place club getting first choice, Frank Selvy, the association's leading scorer, went to Milwaukee. The players selected by the eight clubs continuing in the circuit will go back to Baltimore if the club operates next season.

The suspension and the option to return was requested by Frank Knox, executive vice president of the Baltimore club, which had won only three of fourteen games thus far.

Bullets Games to Count

The Bullets' games will count in the standing, but a revised schedule for the remainder of the season will be drawn.

Baltimore had joined the N. B. A. for the 1947-48 season after three successful years in the American League. The Bullets finished second in the Western division of the eight-team circuit the first year and won the championship play-off.

Since then, the team has slumped. Last spring it finished last in the Eastern division with a .222 percentage. The team lost the fans' support, and with debts accumulating, was unable to get the financial backing necessary to continue in operation.

The New York Knickerbockers, third to choose in the draft, obtained Paul Hoffman, a 6-foot 2-inch Purdue University graduate and Herman Hedderick of Canisius, now in the Army.

Milwaukee also got a serviceman, John Barber. The other players were selected as follows: Rochester, Don Henrikson; Boston, Bob Houbregs and Ed Miller (on suspended list); Syracuse, Connie Simmons; Fort Wayne, Al Roges; Minneapolis, Bob Leonard, now in the Army, and Philadelphia, Ken Murray.

Hans, Neal, King Not Picked

Three Baltimore players, Rollen Hans, Jim Neal and Dan King, were not picked by the other clubs. Al McGuire, who left the Bullets a week ago, was not listed among the players up for draft. The league rule limiting teams to ten players as of Dec. 1 was not changed.

Earlier in the day, the Knicks, who meet the Syracuse Nationals at Madison Square Garden tonight, added another new player to their roster, Bob Knight.

The 23-year-old back-court man, without prior high school or college experience, had played in the American League with the Hartford and Manchester (Conn.) clubs. He had scored 30 points against the Knicks in a pre-season exhibition a few years ago and was signed for a trial period yesterday after an impressive workout with the club at the Sixty-ninth Regiment Armory. The probable line-up:

KNICKS		SYRACUSE
(4) Braun	L.F.	Schayes (4)
(11) Gallatin	R.F.	Lloyd (11)
(19) Felix	C.	Rocha (16)
(15) McGuire	L.G.	Seymour (5)
(10) Baechtold	R.G.	King (3)

SUBSTITUTES
Knickerbockers—Knight (3), Cook (5), Hoffman (6), Clifton (8), Christ (9), Turner (16), Grigsby (17).
Syracuse—Gabor (7), Osterkorn (8), Kerr (10), Farley (12), Kenville (15).

November 27, 1954

Syracuse Five Defeats Pistons In N.B.A. Play-Off Final, 92-91

Nationals Gain Loop Title for First Time on King's Free Throw in Last Seconds

SYRACUSE, April 10 (UP)—The Syracuse Nationals, driving behind their six-year jinx over the Fort Wayne Pistons, won their first National Basketball Association play-off championship today. They defeated the Indiana team, 92—91, in a bitterly contested game.

Coach Charley Eckman's Pistons, the surprise team of the N. B. A. campaign, came here Saturday with a 3-2 edge in the four-out-of-seven series. But they never had won a game at Syracuse.

The Nationals pulled even yesterday by rallying for a 109-104 victory. Today, the Nationals, the Eastern Division champions, gained the play-off crown by running their home-court victory streak against the Pistons to 28—0.

George King was the hero of the hard-earned triumph. He broke a 91-91 tie and provided the victory margin by sinking a free throw with 12 seconds to go. Then he stole the ball to end Fort Wayne's last desperate rush. Both teams lost the ball for running as they scrambled through the final seconds.

Dolph Schayes had given Syracuse a 91-90 lead with 1:20 remaining by making good with two free throws. But George Yardley evened the score with a

The Line-Up

SYRACUSE (92)				FORT WAYNE (91)			
	G.	F.	PF.	P.		G.	F.	PF.	P.
Schayes, lf.	4	5	3	13	Hutchins, lf.	6	1	3	13
Rocha	1	9	3	11	Meineke	2	2	2	6
Ost'k'rn, rf.	0	3	1	3	Yardley, rf.	3	3	3	9
Lloyd, c.	4	4	4	12	Rosenthal	1	0	3	2
Kerr	4	5	5	13	Foust, c.	8	8	4	24
Seymour, lg.	4	3	2	11	Houbregs	2	1	3	5
King	6	3	3	15	Phillip, lg.	3	4	3	10
Farley, rg.	0	0	1	0	Zaslofsky	0	0	2	0
Kenville	3	9	5	15	Brian, rg.	8	3	4	19
					Walther	0	3	3	3
Total	26	40	27	92	Total	33	25	30	91

Syracuse .... 21 26 27 18—92
Fort Wayne .... 31 22 21 17—91
Free throws missed—Schayes, Rocha, Lloyd, Kerr, Seymour, Kenville 4, Hutchins 2, Yardley 2, Foust 3, Houbregs, Phillip.

free throw 20 seconds later. That set the stage for King's game-winning toss.

Fort Wayne led by 41-24 early in the second quarter. Billy Enville helped the Nationals cut the Piston margin. He entered the game at that point and scored 11 counters during the remainder of the second session to put Syracuse back in the running.

The Pistons held a 53-47 halftime lead, but it was 74—74 at the end of the third period. The score was tied at 87—87 with three minutes to go in the final quarter.

The winners had seven players who scored in double figures. Larry Foust of the losers was the game's high man with 24.

Each team won all the final play-off games on its home court. Syracuse took the first two games here, then lost three in the Midwest before returning home to capture the last two.

April 11, 1955

ST. LOUIS FIVE APPROVED

Pro Basketball League Accepts Shift From Milwaukee

The National Basketball Association's board of governors yesterday approved the transfer of the Milwaukee Hawks' franchise to St. Louis. In doing so, the N. B. A. ran into the threat of a suit for rejecting a franchise bid by a Washington group.

Morris Fox, leader of the Washington group, said he would accuse the N. B. A. of breach of contract. Fox said he had a letter from the N. B. A. promising a franchise.

If Fox carries out his threat, the N. B. A. will be faced with two suits. A Baltimore group has instituted court action charging the N. B. A. with violating the Anti-Trust Act.

St. Louis was a member of the N. B. A. but dropped out several years ago.

May 12, 1955

Basic Basketball Plays Are Diagramed for Fans

Lapchick Takes Time Out to Lift Screen on Techniques

By JOSEPH M. SHEEHAN

Basketball is here again and eyes that just were becoming used to split-T option plays and buck-lateral machinations out of single wing have to be refocussed.

To aid the readjustment, Joe Lapchick, the coach of the New York Knickerbockers of the National Basketball Association, obligingly diagramed a few basic basketball plays.

"They're very basic," Joe specified, smiling wryly, "I happen to have them right at hand because my team suddenly seems to have forgotten everything it knew and we're starting all over again from scratch."

If the coach hadn't been in so grim a mood, his attention might have been called to a favorite story revolving around a similar situation in football at Notre Dame.

The Irish had played one of their rare bad games and Frank Leahy, then their coach, was fit to be tied.

"Lads, there's only one thing to do," he said. "That's to begin at the very beginning. Now, this is a football. * * *"

No Time For Digression

Ciggy Czarobski, a whale of a tackle and also the squad wit, interrupted. "Wait a minute, coach," he said. "You're going too fast."

However, it was no time for such a digression. So Lapchick turned right to charting a few of the plays the Knicks and other teams use to get the baskets that pile up those three-digit scores.

"We'll limit this session to drawing a few pivot plays." said Joe. "The pivot play, invented by my old Original Celtic teammate, Dutch Dehnert, still is the bread-and-butter play of basketball."

Deploying his penciled pawns with three players in midcourt, one in the right-hand corner and one—the pivot man—in a "high post" position in the foullane keyhole just outside the fifteen-foot free-throw line, Lapchick set down three plays.

All start the same way, with a pass from the right-side midcourt player to the corner man. As the pass is made, the center midcourt player feints left and runs right into a position between the opponent guarding the right-side player and the basket.

This obstructive position is called a "screen" and can be taken legally if a halt is made before contact results.

Pivot Passes to Cutter

The right-side player feints right and cuts left, around the screen, on an arcing course toward the pivot man, who by this time has received a pass from the corner man.

The pivot man passes to the cutter as he goes whipping past and the cutter dribbles once, if necessary, and takes a driving shot from close range. This is the single-cut play diagrammed.

If the cutter has a lead over his guard when he takes the pass from the pivot man, the defender posted behind the pivot man should switch and cover the cutter.

The return pass play is designed to meet this situation. On this play, the pivot man, after dealing to the cutter, whirls in the opposite direction and receives a return pass en route to the basket.

Another familiar variation is

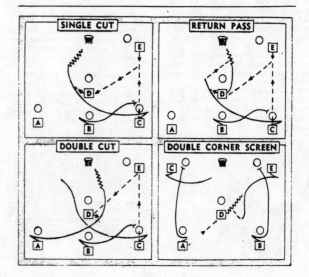

the "double-cut off a high post," if technical language must be used. As the diagram shows, everything proceeds the same except that the left-side midcourt man joins the fun, with a cut to the right of the pivot man.

The timing on the double-cut can be varied so that either cutter can race by the post first. As a rule, the second cutter will wind up with the ball, but it's not hard and fast. A smart pivot man will pass to the first man, if he is uncovered.

Or, as Ed Macauley of the Boston Celtics often does, the pivot man may fake to both cutters, keep the ball, turn and shoot. This is another counter to a switch by the guard assigned to the pivot man.

Double-Screen Described

The fourth play diagrammed here illustrates what Lapchick described as a "double corner screen." It evolves from a three-in, two-out alignment of players.

A pass from the left side midcourt player to the pivot man starts the play rolling. The two midcourt players break straight down court, after feints to the outside, and take screening positions on the guards covering the corner men.

The right-hand corner man (or it could be the left) will break around the screen toward the keyhole. Simultaneously, the pivot man dribbles on a slant toward the right-hand corner, thereby setting up another screen.

Behind this second screen, the corner man takes a short pass from the pivot man for one of the 15 to 17 foot one-handed shots that drop in so easily for the sharpshooting pros.

This double-screen play has an alternative end development. Timing his move to coincide with the delivery of the ball to the right-hand corner man, the left-hand corner man will cut around the screen there toward the basket.

If he is open, the right-hand corner man can pass to him for a lay-up shot rather than take the longer and consequently more risky one-handed toss.

"These are very fine plays," concluded Lapchick. "And they always work, on paper."

December 5, 1955

LAKERS SCORE, 135-133

Defeat Syracuse's Quintet in Record-Scoring Contest

SYRACUSE, Dec. 15 (UP) — The Minneapolis Lakers gained a thrilling 135-133 victory tonight over the Syracuse Nationals after three overtime periods. The game total of 268 points set a National Basketball Association record. The previous mark of 248 also was set at Syracuse, the home team defeating Anderson, 125 to 123, after five extra periods on Nov. 24, 1949.

In tonight's encounter the score was 105-all at the end of regulation play, 116—116 at the end of the first overtime session and 125—125 after the second extra period.

MINNEAPOLIS (135)	G.	F.	PF.	P.
Mik'lsen, lf.	9	7	6	25
Kalafat, rf.	1	3	2	5
Schnitker	.8	5	5	21
Garmaker	.1	1	0	3
Lovell'te, c.	13	4	6	30
Hitch	1	1	3	3
Skoog	3	6	1	12
Martin, lg.	6	8	2	20
Mencel, rg.	7	2	6	16
Total	**49**	**37**	**31**	**135**

SYRACUSE (133)	G.	F.	PF.	P.
Schayes, lf.	11	12	4	34
Rocha, rf.	1	3	2	5
Conlin	2	10	4	14
Tucker, c.	3	0	1	6
Kerr	13	3	3	29
Lloyd	1	1	3	3
King, lg.	7	1	5	15
Farley, rg.	9	3	6	21
Kenville	2	2	4	6
Total	**49**	**35**	**32**	**133**

Minneapolis	30	26	22	27	11	9	10—135
Syracuse	21	30	31	23	11	9	8—133

Free throws missed—Mikkelsen. Lovellette 2, Skoog, Martin, Schayes, Conlin 2, Kerr, King 3, Farley 4, Kenville.

December 15, 1955

Whistle Is Blown on Basketball Fans Who Find Too Much Tooting Foul

Frequent Blasts Keep Court Free From Chaos, Mayhem

By LOUIS EFFRAT

Basketball enthusiasts contend that theirs is the greatest of competitive sports. It's a game of continuous action. It's a game that calls for speed, stamina and shooting skill; for passing finesse, rebounding agility and ever-alert mental processes. It's a game that is played and watched by countless millions each season.

Since that day in 1891 when James Naismith suspended two peach baskets in the gymnasium at the Springfield (Mass.) Y. M. C. A., basketball has been part of the American sports scene. It is now a major sport at virtually every college and high school.

And for the post-graduates there is the National Basketball Association, the big league in which some of the professionals earn as much as $15,000 per season. There is no questioning the popularity of the sport. Nevertheless it has its detractors.

The late Jimmy Walker, New York's sports-loving mayor of the Roaring Twenties, apparently voiced the main objection. In a speech before the Metropolitan Basketball Writers' Association, Walker extolled the beauties of the game, its thrills and its tensions.

"Basketball is a wonderful sport," he said. "There is only one real drawback — too many blankety-blank whistles!"

Whistling in the Dark

The story is told about a midwestern referee, who repeatedly

Sweetwater Clifton demonstrates a block, or illegal screen, to permit Dick McGuire to shoot. Carl Braun is victim of the block on floor of the Sixty-ninth Regiment Armory.

blew his whistle, ruling that one player had committed four consecutive fouls. After each whistle the official attempted to explain the violation to the athlete. And after the fourth explanation the referee asked the young collegian:

"Do you understand me?"

"I'm sorry, sir," the polite youth replied. "I don't understand you, but I'm sure getting used to you."

If the whistle is an evil, it's a necessary one. Without one a game could not be played. Therefore, what some fans regard as basketball's weakness is actually its strength. Only the other day, Red Auerbach, the fiery coach of the Boston Celtics, weighed in with his defense of the whistle.

Said the man who probably has paid more fines for debating decisions than any other N. B. A. coach:

"If it were not for the whistle, basketball would be the roughest of all sports. The players move so fast and there is so much contact, even though this is supposed to be a non-contact game, the whistle helps to prevent injuries. Don't forget, our players wear no protection, like helmets for batters in baseball, masks for football players and pads for hockey players."

Clifton illegally blocks Braun again to keep path open for McGuire, shown dribbling

All Action Ceases

The whistle stops all movement on a basketball court. It is blown for any number of reasons—out-of-bounds, held ball, time out, discontinued dribble, injury—but it is blown mainly because someone has committed a foul.

A good guess is that a whistle is blown, for one reason or another, 150 times during a game. Statistics prove that at least one-third of the whistles are provoked by personal fouls.

There are various types of fouls. The most difficult one for the officials to call are charging and blocking. It is easy to spot pushing or holding. Hacking, which is a common "chop" across the arm, wrist or hand of an offensive player, gives little trouble to the referees.

However, the distinguishing line between a charge and a block often is thin, hardly discernible. It all depends on the official's position on the court at the instant of the violation. What may appear to the referee to be charging one time is interpreted as blocking another, and vice versa.

Except when a foul is committed during the act of shooting, the offended player receives one free throw. That is doubled when the player is "hit" while attempting to get off a shot. In college basketball five personal fouls eliminate a player from the game. The pros permit six before banishment.

Another difference is in the bonus shot. Among the collegians a second free throw is awarded if the first is successful. Among the pros all fouls become two-shotters when seven fouls have been charged in the same period.

Technical Foul Defined

Then there is the technical foul. That is invoked for noncontact reasons. Abusive language, unsportsmanlike conduct and persistent arguing with an official may bring about a technical foul. In addition to a free throw, the team that takes the penalty shot gets possession of the ball.

Too many blankety-blank whistles?

Perhaps, but they enable the referees to maintain control, without which there would be chaos and a certain amount of mayhem. The officials take no delight in blowing whistles. Their vigilance is a "must." Fearlessly and without prejudice they call 'em as they see 'em, unmindful of the score or of which team is in front. That's their job.

Many years ago a player blew his top after a referee had blown his whistle and called a third foul against the athlete. "If you call another foul against me, I'll kill you," he told the official.

Within a minute the referee spotted another infraction by the same burly fellow. Following a loud whistle, the arbiter turned, pointed to the offender and dramatically proclaimed:

"And before I die that's another foul against you."

Yes, what some fans regard as basketball's weakness is actually its strength—the whistle.

December 18, 1955

WARRIORS SUBDUE PISTONS FOR TITLE

They Triumph, 99-88, and Win Final Pro Basketball Series, 4 Games to 1

By The Associated Press.

PHILADELPHIA, April 7—The Philadelphia Warriors defeated the Fort Wayne Pistons, 99—88, tonight to win the National Basketball Association championship. The Warriors took the title play-off series, four games to one.

Joe Graboski, with 29 points, and Paul Arizin, with 26, led the Warriors, who broke open a tight game with a sensational rally in the waning seconds of the third period.

Just three years ago, the Warriors won twelve and lost fifty-

The New York Times (by Meyer Liebowitz)

Clifton, right, makes a foul by charging Harry Gallatin

seven games, finishing 34½ games out of first place, probably the worst mark in modern pro basketball. Two years ago, they were last, fifteen games off the pace. Last season they finished in the cellar, ten games behind the Syracuse Nats, the champions.

But tonight. the young talent, which kept Eddie Gottlieb, owner of the club, from throwing in the towel despite defeat and financial reverses, paid off handsomely. Arizin, Graboski, Neil Johnston, Tom Gola and company won Philadelphia's first pro basketball title since 1946-47 to wrap up the team's most successful year both on the court and in the box office.

The Warriors won this final best four-of-seven-games series, 4—1, losing only the second game in the set by a single point at Fort Wayne.

Coach George Senesky brought home a winner in his first year at the helm after succeeding owner Gottlieb, the only previous Warriors' mentor.

The Warriors broke the game wide open in the last three min-

utes of the third period. Ahead, 64—60. they thrilled the crowd of 11,194 by scoring 8 points while holding the Pistons to 3 to stretch their lead to 72—63 at the end of the period.

Gola Gets Vital Points

Gola, the first-year star, collected 4 of the vital 8. Arizin, whose 26 points made him the second highest scorer in play-off games—George Mikan is tops—and George Dempsey netted a basket apiece.

The Warriors peppered the basket in the final twelve minutes and Fort Wayne was unable to cut the margin to less than 7 points.

Graboski and Arizin each scored 6 of the Warriors' final 17 points. In the third quarter, Gola and Arizin, each with 10, accounted for 20 of the 28 scored by the Eastern Division champions.

The Warriors made 42 of 112 shots as against 30 of 92 for the Pistons.

However, Fort Wayne kept in the game with its excellent foul shooting. The Pistons, who bowed in the N. B. A. final for

The Line-Up

PHILADELPHIA (99)				FORT WAYNE (88)			
	G.	F.	PF.	P.		G.	F.	PF.	P.
Arizin. lf..10	6	1	26	Yardley. lf.11	8	2	30
Graboski.rf.14	1	5	29	Hutchins. rf.5	3	2	13
Beck 6	0	2	12	Cooper 0	0	0	0
Moore 0	0	2	0	Spears 2	0	3	4
Johnston. c..2	1	5	5	Foust. c ...4	10	6	18
Davis 1	0	2	2	Houbregs ...2	1	3	5
George. lg..3	0	6	6	Noble. lg ...1	3	1	5
Gola. rg ..5	6	5	16	Devlin. rg...4	0	2	8
Dempsey ..1	1	0	3	Phillip 0	1	1	1
				Brian 1	2	0	4
Total ...42 15 28 99				**Total ...30 28 20 88**			
Philadelphia 22	22	28	27—99				
Fort Wayne 24	19	20	25—88				

Free throws missed—Graboski 3. Johnston 2. Davis, George 3. Gola 3. Yardley 4. Hutchins 2. Spears. Houbregs 2. Devlin 3. Phillip.

April 8, 1956

the second straight year, converted 28 of 41 free throws. The Warriors netted 15 of 27 at the foul line.

George Yardley topped the losers in scoring with 30 points —high for the game—on eleven field goals and eight fouls.

Arizin's 26 points gave him a total of 289 for the ten play-off games—five against Syracuse in the semi-final and five against Fort Wayne. Only Mikan, who scored 303, 307 and 376 in play-off games for Minneapolis, tops Arizin's title-play output.

FT. WAYNE FIVE SHIFTED

Franchise Switch to Detroit Is Set Next Season

DETROIT, Feb. 14 (P)—The Fort Wayne Pistons today switched their franchise to Detroit.

Fred Zollner. club president, said that the Pistons, champions of the National Basketball Association's western division two years running, would begin a six-year contract at Olympia Stadium next October.

The team will be known as the Detroit Pistons. The Pistons will play most of their home games at the Olympia. which can accommodate 13.000 for basketball. Zollner said he hopes to play from five to seven games at his old Fort Wayne base.

In Fort Wayne Charley Eckman signed a new three-year contract to coach the Pistons.

February 15, 1957

Education of a Basketball Rookie

It's a big stride from college to pro basketball, even for a player like All-America Bill Russell. But the investment in him is paying off.

By ARTHUR DALEY

"MY favorite shot," said Bill Russell. "is to hold the ball ten inches above the basket and then drop it through the hoop."

He tried to keep a straight face but a grin broke through. So he added softly. "It's a shot I'm rarely privileged to make." Yet he actually has made it on occasion. Despite his joking, he really wasn't yearning for the impossible, only the infrequent.

The whimsical Mr. Russell is the latest sensation in professional basketball. At the age of 22 he no longer can be considered a growing boy. He now stands 6 feet 10. All future growth will be along educational lines because Big Bill signed for a post-graduate course in basketball when he joined the Boston Celtics just before Christmas. The amount he still has to learn appalls him.

It was only a year ago that Russell was starring for the University of San Francisco Dons, as unchallenged as the No. 1 college team in the country as Big Bill was as the No. 1 collegiate player. Whenever an All-America selector began to pick a team, he automatically filled in the name of Russell at the center spot and then said to himself, "Who else is there?"

ARTHUR DALEY, Times columnist and winner of the 1956 Pulitzer Prize for local reporting, played college basketball in the days when a 6-foot-2 player was a team's "big man."

ALL last season the professionals cast avid eyes in his direction but Wee William was in no hurry. Before he'd even think of cashing in on his talents, he wanted to represent the United States in the Olympic Games at Melbourne. Russell wound up as the big star of that show, too, and even provoked an "incident" of sorts. In a semi-final game against Bulgaria, he leaped high from under the basket as a teammate shot. A large Russell paw steered the ball through the hoop, scoring on one of those rare "dunk" shots.

"No goal," signaled a little referee from Singapore, who couldn't believe his eyes. It took fast talking by Gerald Tucker, the American Olympic coach, to convince Olympic authorities that Russell's sense of timing is so perfect that his dunk is a legal maneuver.

The professional season had been in progress for two months before Russell had completed his Olympic commitments and felt free to sign with the Celtics. In the brief time since, he has already achieved two things. He has given a hypo to the gate and he has made court fans conscious of a forgotten phase of the pro sport—defense.

It's certain that the increased receipts Big Bill brings to every box office will pay off the investment in him. By basketball standards the investment is huge; Russell is said to draw a salary of $24,000. Not even pro baseball has ever paid a salary of that size to a rookie, though it has not been so re-

strained in paying bonuses. The only man in the basketball league with a bigger paycheck is the utterly fantastic Bob Cousy, also of the Celtics. He gets—or so they say—$25,000.

IS Russell worth that much? The answer will have to be a hedging yes and no. Let's start with a few statistics by way of illustrating Wee William's tremendous drawing power through the turnstiles.

His debut was in the Boston Garden before 11,000, the largest crowd of the season, despite the fact that the game was televised and television strangles attendance. In his first appearance at Fort Wayne he almost tripled the average attendance; almost doubled it in Syracuse, despite a blizzard, and pulled in record crowds at Philadelphia and St. Louis. He drew more than 15,000 to Madison Square Garden in New York. He's been responsible for seasonal records virtually everywhere.

From that cash-in-the-till standpoint, then, Russell is manifestly worth his handsome salary. From an artistic standpoint he isn't entirely worth it—yet. But don't overlook that lonesome word "yet."

Professional basketball is as infinitely superior to college basketball as professional football is to college football or major league baseball is to college baseball. Even a unanimous All-America like Russell had to be taught this inescapable fact of life the hard way. The first shock he got was in the matter of size. Not being a dope, he naturally knew that the pro league was populated by big men. But it wasn't until he was on the court with them that he realized how big. In college, Russell rarely was matched against anyone as tall as he. Even rarer was the team with two giants. But in the pro league every team has at least one man and frequently two or three who don't have to yield to him in altitude. There are even three pro operatives who can look down on Russell.

Thus, Russell's normal height advantage is nullified to a considerable extent by the fact that the league quintets average approximately 6 feet 5. Also, most of the players seem to have had transfusions of kangaroo blood. They can jump unbelievably high. "They're bigger in two directions—up and out," Russell says with a sad shake of his head.

IN college, Russell never had any trouble in easing into the pivot position. With back to the basket he'd plant his feet firmly out beyond the foul zone and crouch over. If he pushed back to

crowd the defender, the defender gave ground. But in pro ball the defensive players are as immovable as brick walls. And if he leans into them under the basket for rebounds, there's no give as there was in college. The unyielding strength of these big pros both amazes and awes him.

"I could bluff 'em in college," says Russell with a wry smile. "I can't bluff 'em here."

The listener misinterpreted his remark to mean that feints don't work in pro ball. But Big Bill didn't mean that at all. He meant—and his embarrassment was obvious as he explained it—that his reputation was so monumental in college that he could rattle the opposition into committing errors or giving him openings. But to the pros he's just a rookie named Bill Russell. His new reputation has yet to be earned.

HOWEVER, his past reputation cannot be overlooked entirely. Although a prodigious scorer in college, at least half of the points Russell tallied came at point-blank range—from under the basket. There he's like a man on a pogo stick. Not only is he 6 feet 10, but he was an exceptionally good high-jumper who once cleared 6 feet 8. Hence he has a lot of bounce to the ounce, and is deadly on tipping in rebounds, on deflecting shots through the net and on being fed high passes underneath the hoop for what the trade calls "sucker shots." These methods of scoring are infinitely tougher in pro ranks than in college ranks.

A pro talent scout ordinarily would bypass a shot-maker of Russell's limited range. But Russell also is as tremendous

a defensive player as has been around in ages. Not only is he extraordinary in capturing enemy rebounds off the backboards, he's fast enough to race from one backboard to the other and is agile as a goal-tender.

Phil Woolpert, his coach at San Francisco, tells of the job he did against the University of California a few years back.

"Russell blocked twenty-five shots," he said. "I don't necessarily mean to imply that each would have dropped through the hoop, although that could have been the case. Actually, it's difficult to measure Bill's defensive value because much of it is psychological—a shooter hurrying a shot he shouldn't take in order to avoid him or not taking one he should take."

IT was this peculiar talent that Russell used as a pro in his first meeting with Neil Johnston of the Philadelphia Warriors, three times scoring leader of the pro league, who has averaged between 22 and 24 points per game for four seasons and has a one-game high of 50.

Above the crowd—Bill Russell, the Boston Celtics' prize rookie, outreaches an opponent.

Russell, whose long arms give him a wingspan of 7 feet 4 inches, blanked Johnston for thirty-eight minutes. The spectators gasped at such defensive wizardry. Basketball fans all over the country buzzed about it for days afterward. Everyone was impressed except Russell.

"Phooey," he commented disgustedly. "You call that defense? How many points did he make in the last ten minutes? I'll tell you. He made 20. When you stop a guy, he doesn't make 20 points on you."

Yet the psychological impact already has been heavy. Earl Lloyd of Syracuse, normally an under-the-basket shooter, stayed outside against Russell and fired from long range. He happened to be hot that night and pumped in 22 points, while Russell registered only seven and could snare only two rebounds in one half. But Lloyd's system wouldn't necessarily work another time.

Harry (The Horse) Gallatin of the New York Knickerbockers contributed heavily to the Russell education by using a whipsaw technique. He stayed outside and hammered accurately at long range. Big Bill came out to stop him and Harry the Horse drove past him for close ones and added up 26 points.

Nevertheless, these switches in offensive tactics indicate how Russell already has disrupted opponents' normal procedures. That's a high tribute, even if a left-handed one, to a rookie.

Meanwhile, Russell is making a heavy dent in public consciousness with his rebounding. Twice within a week he grabbed 30 opposition rebounds. How important that is defensively may be told by an axiom of basketball: never give a foe a second shot at the basket. Moreover, Russell's 30 rebounds are close enough to Johnston's league record of 39 to indicate that Russell some day will break that mark. It could even happen before this is in print.

Russell never doubted that he would be able to make a successful transition from the amateur to pro ranks. Furthermore, his new boss, Red Auerbach, agreed with him.

"The most comforting of my earlier discoveries," says Auerbach, "was the realization that Russell came to us with far better fundamental preparation than most rookies. He showed that he had been well coached by Woolpert in basic principles, especially in defense.

"My first concern, I guess, was whether or not he'd be

Bill Sharman (No. 21), a top Celtic scorer.   Bob Cousy, ace dribbler and playmaker.

accepted by the other players. The team was going well and leading the league—without a Russell. Nor could his reputation as a unanimous All-America impress anyone to the point of awe. The Celtics are loaded with All-America players—plus two super All-Americas in Bob Cousy and Bill Sharman.

"They only knew what they'd read about him in the papers. But Russell is an easy person to like and he has a wonderful dry wit. That wasn't enough, though, and one question was uppermost in everyone's mind: was he a good enough rebounder for pro ball? He has proved that.

"Then, we play a fast break and our center normally isn't much of a scorer because it isn't easy for him to break downcourt to be part of our attack. But Russell learned quickly and Cousy was the one who helped him adjust so rapidly. I also assigned Arnie

Risen, our center, to help Russell. Arnie is near the end of his career and he's doing all he can to make a star out of his successor.

"One thing I must say is that Russell learns fast because his biggest asset is his mental attitude. He has tremendous pride. He can be faked once but not twice."

Some critics claimed Russell was not a good enough long-range field-goal shooter to star in pro ball.

"Who the hell wants a guy 6 foot 10 to shoot from beyond the foul line?" exploded Auerbach. Then he calmed down and grinned.

"When Risen joined our club," he went on, "he couldn't shoot from beyond the foul line. But we taught him how. And he was willing to practice enough so that he's now a good shot from that far out. We can do the same with Russell. He's gonna be one of the great stars of pro ball."

Perhaps nothing accounts for the rapid advance of pro basketball more than the institution of the 24-second rule a few seasons back. This artful bit of legislation ordains that a team must take a shot at the basket within twenty-four seconds after it gets possession of the ball. Otherwise it forfeits control and the other side takes over. Two huge electric clocks at opposite ends of the court tick off the seconds.

Before the time limitations were ordered, the pros frequently stalled when they were ahead, especially during what should have been the dramatic closing minutes. Instead of shooting for points they didn't need, they kept possession, challenging the trailers to take away the ball. So many fouls resulted that the game degenerated into a foul-shooting contest. Most of the action came from the officials blowing their whistles on palpable infractions of the rules.

Attendance suffered, and the men who run the pro league were on the verge of despair. Then some genius thought of a time limitation. The arbitrary number of 24 seconds was picked. It was as perfect as Abner Doubleday hitting on 90 feet as the ideal distance between bases in baseball.

Once the 24-second rule went into effect stalling ceased. Now the game is played in the National Basketball Association at a breakneck pace, thus giving it an

BALL HAWK—A Russell defense specialty is interceptions.

instant and inherent crowd appeal that the collegiate brand lacks. The odd part about it is that the 24-second rule rarely has to be invoked. The pros instinctively sense when time is running out, almost as if they had clocks in their heads.

The pros also outlawed the yawn-producing zone defense. Hence they start out with a vast advantage over the amateurs: streamlined rules. Furthermore, nationally televised games spread their gospel all over the land. Whenever the University of North Carolina basketball team, ranked No. 1 in college ranks, is free to watch, Coach Frank McGuire assembles his squad in front of a television set. The purpose is not amusement but education of the collegians by the masters of the sport.

The pros have skimmed the cream off the college bottle. They have breath-taking shot-makers and play - makers. Some of the things they do strain credulity, such as Bob Cousy's dribbling down-court right-handed and then dribbling behind his back to break clear into a left-handed dribble.

How did the Celtics get Russell? When the 1955-56 season ended there was some

serious stock-taking by Walter Brown, owner of the Boston quintet, and by Auerbach. The Celtics had set a professional record for average point total per game during the season, a stunning 106. Yet they finished only second in the Eastern Division. Why? Because they also set a record for yielding the most enemy points per game—105.3. The average Celtic score therefore was 106 to 105.3. The Bostonians obviously couldn't win the championship on offensive strength alone. They'd have to bulwark their defense.

RUSSELL had been drafted by the St. Louis Hawks for one reason. The Hawks wanted to pry loose from the Celtics the high-scoring Easy Ed Macauley, an alumnus of St. Louis University, and the only way they could get Boston to yield him was to offer Russell. So the Celtics gave Macauley, a 20-point-per-game operative, for a defensive player.

Russell is no drag on the team offensively, however. He manages to hold his own and will have his hot nights when he'll score 25 points or so. Furthermore, his superior rebounding sets up the plays and

the points for Cousy, Sharman & Co.

"I'd seen some games on television," says Russell, "and I got the impression that there was no such thing as defense in the pro league. The shooters always seemed to be running wild. But now I know that the defense is excellent. It's the shooters who are ex-

traordinary because they score anyway."

The newest Celtic already has learned a lot.

February 24, 1957

Royals' Quintet Shifts Franchise to Cincinnati

ROCHESTER, April 3 (UP) —The Rochester Royals of the National Basketball Association became the Cincinnati Royals today in the league's second franchise shift for 1957.

In an earlier move carrying out the N. B. A. policy of going into major league baseball cities, the Fort Wayne club transferred to Detroit.

President Les Harrison of the Royals, blaming falling attendance for the move from Rochester, said a contract had been agreed upon to play in the 13,000-seat Cincinnati Gardens in the Ohio city. "We'll still be known as the Royals," said Harrison.

Rochester had major pro basketball for twelve years, but this year the club drew an average of only 2,500 fans per game. A 3,500 average was needed to meet expenses, Harrison said.

April 4, 1957

CELTICS WIN BASKETBALL TITLE IN DOUBLE OVERTIME

RAMSEY SETS PACE

His Overtime Play for Celtics Helps Beat Hawks, 125–123

By WILLIAM J. BRIORDY
Special to The New York Times.

BOSTON, April 13—The Boston Celtics captured their first National Basketball Association championship today by checking the St. Louis Hawks, 125 to 123, in two overtime periods at the Boston Garden. A capacity crowd of 13,909 saw the Celtics triumph to take the play-off series, four games to three.

This was one of the most thrilling finals seen in the his-,

Associated Press Wirephoto

BEDLAM IN BOSTON: Delighted fans hailing Tommy Heinsohn, center, yesterday after he starred for Boston Celtics in 125-123 victory over St. Louis Hawks in overtime game.

HIGH-FLYING HAWK: Charlie Share of St. Louis taking a rebound over the outstretched arm of Boston's Arnie Risen yesterday during the N.B.A. play-off at Boston.

Associated Press Wirephoto

tory of the league. The game produced splendid basketball by both teams. The action was so feverish that the fans were left limp when the last buzzer sounded.

The regulation contest ended in a 103-103 tie. The end of the first five-minute extra period found the teams still tied, 113 to 113. Then the Celtics, paced by Tommy Heinsohn, took command in the second five-minute overtime period to top Coach Alex Hannum's quintet.

Although the sharpshooting Heinsohn—he did not fare well from the foul line—showed the way for Boston with 37 points, it was the shooting of Frank Ramsey in the second overtime that guided the home team to triumph.

Heinsohn Out on Fouls

After Bill Russell hit on a lay-up and Heinsohn registered on a long jump toss at 2:44 of the second overtime, the Celtics

had a 121-to-120 lead. Then Heinsohn fouled out of the game at 2:50. He fouled Slater Martin and the doughty backcourt star of the Hawks made good on one of two free throws.

Then came Ramsey's all-important shots. He was fouled by Easy Ed Macauley and Frank converted at 3:25 to return the lead to Boston. Then Ramsey pegged a long one-hander at 3:45 and the Celtics had a three-point edge.

But the fighting Hawks refused to give up. Martin got a foul toss and Med Park made one of two conversions to put St. Louis one point behind with twenty-three seconds left. Then a foul for walking was called on Hannum and Boston took over with twelve seconds remaining.

Coleman Ties Score

After Hannum fouled Jim Loscutoff, the Boston player made the one-pointer with one second left to complete the scoring.

Time was still not up as Hannum unloosed a long desperation toss. The slick Bob Pettit—he topped the scorers with 39 points—then missed the rebound of Hannum's peg.

Heinsohn's lay-up with fifteen seconds remaining in the first overtime had the fans roaring. But Jack Coleman hit on a one-hander to make it 113-all. Bill Sharman of Boston then missed on a one-hander with four seconds left.

The first extra period saw both Ramsey and Coleman fail on two free throws after the score was knotted at 111-all. It was Pettit who sent the action-packed affair into overtime when he converted twice with six seconds remaining in the fourth quarter.

Russell, a bulwark on defense with thirty-two rebounds, kept Boston alive in the fourth quarter. After he hit on a pivot with twenty seconds left and Bob Cousy made one of two free throws, Russell blocked an almost certain field goal by Coleman. At that point Boston showed the way by 103-101. But then Russell fouled Pettit and the St. Louis star got his pair of one-pointers.

It appeared early in the fourth quarter that Boston was "going to town." When Cousy fed neatly to Phillips at 0:14 of the period, the Celtics had an 83-77 advantage. But the Hawks, led by the stylish Cliff Hagan, Pettit, Martin and Macauley, hit for nine points in a row to go ahead.

7 Free Throws Missed

Although he missed seven straight free throws during the game, Heinsohn was more than adequate from the field. He and Russell were the spearheads for Boston in the last period.

The Hawks turned in an excellent job. The work of Martin and Jack McMahon in the backcourt was superb, while Pettit and Hagan were tops up front.

Two tap-ins by Pettit in the last fifty-three seconds helped St. Louis to a 28-26 lead at the end of the first quarter. The Celtics, who dissipated the lead more than a few times in the first half, trailed by 53—51 at intermission. Martin and McMahon were so effective in the first two periods that Cousy and Sharman were held to 2 and 5 points, respectively, for the half.

Boston's attack clicked more smoothly in the third quarter. The score was tied seven times before Coach Red Auerbach's forces moved ahead. Cousy's pair of foul shots and Jack Nichols' lay-up after a pretty pass by Cousy gave Boston an 83-77 advantage at the close of the quarter.

Hagan had 24 points and Martin 23. Martin played the full fifty-eight minutes. A standout for Boston in the early going was the seasoned Arnie Risen. Arnie, "the old pro," was a welcome shotmaker for the champions while Cousy and Sharman were unable to find the mark. Risen collected 16 points. Russell had 19 while Ramsey made

16 markers. Cousy got 12 points, Sharman 9.

Pettit hit on fourteen of thirty-four shots from the floor and had nineteen rebounds. Heinsohn got seventeen of thirty-three attempts. Boston made forty-seven of 108 from the floor, while St. Louis had thirty-nine for 101. Incidentally, Hannum got into the game when Macauley fouled out at 3:25 of the second overtime.

Records Set by Series

The series between Boston and St. Louis proved the richest in the eleven-season history of the league. The seven games figure to gross about $160,000. The attendance of about 77,000 also constitutes a new high. The official figures will be announced by the league shortly. The Boston players will split up the winner's share of $18,500.

Auerbach shook hands with Ben Kerner, the Hawks' owner, before the game. Auerbach had punched Kerner in St. Louis last Saturday after they had engaged in a heated oral combat. . . . The fans mobbed the Boston players at the end of the game. . . . Among the onlookers were members of the Boston Red Sox. . . . There were thirty-eight changes of lead and twenty-eight ties in the game.

BOSTON (125)	G	F	P	P	ST. LOUIS (123)	G	F	P	P
H'nsohn, lf	17	3	6	37	Coleman, lf	4	2	6	10
Loscutoff,rf	3	0	5	5	Hagan	7	10	6	24
Ramsey	6	4	2	16	Share	0	5	4	5
Risen	6	4	6	16	Macauley, rf	2	5	6	9
Nichols	4	0	3	8	Hannum	0	0	1	0
Russell, c	7	5	5	19	Pettit, c	14	11	4	39
Sharman, lg	3	3	3	9	McM'on, lg	3	0	6	6
Cousy, rg	2	8	4	12	Martin, rg	6	11	3	23
Phillip	2	1	3	5	Park	3	1	1	7
Total	47	31	37	125	Total	39	45	37	123

Boston	26	25	32	20	10	12—125
t. Louis	28	25	24	26	10	10—123

Free throws missed—Heinsohn 7, Ramsey 1, Risen 3, Russell 5, Cousy 2, Phillip, Coleman 3, Hagan 4, Share 2, Macauley 3, Pettit 2, Martin, Park.

April 14, 1957

Russell Betters Mark As Celtics Win, 111-89

BOSTON, Nov. 16 (AP)— Bill Russell set a National Basketball Association rebound record with forty-nine and contributed 23 points tonight in leading Boston to its eleventh straight victory, a 111-89 triumph over the Philadelphia Warriors.

Russell, the 6-foot 10-inch former All-America and Olympic ace, bettered the N. B. A. single game rebound mark of thirty-nine held by Philadelphia's Neil Johnston.

In addition, Russell played a remarkable defensive game. Johnston tallied only one field goal, scoring when Russell was resting on the bench.

The Celtics captured 103 rebounds to break the previous team record of 93 set by the New York Knicks in 1953. They also topped the record of 102 for a game with one overtime period set by St. Louis in 1955.

November 17, 1957

Hawks Better N.B.A. Scoring Mark

PETTIT SETS PACE IN 146-136 GAME

Scores 51 Points for Hawks —Boston Quintet Crushes Minneapolis, 140-119

DETROIT, Dec. 21 (P)—Bob Pettit scored 51 points as the St. Louis Hawks set a league scoring record by defeating the Syracuse Nationals, 146—136, in a National Basketball Association game before 5,000 at Olympia Stadium tonight.

In the second game of the double-header, the Detroit Pistons marked the debut of their new coach, Red Rocha, by downing the Cincinnati Royals, 112—101.

Several league records were broken by the teams in the opener. They surpassed by 17 points the previous high for two teams in a single game, which was 265, set by St. Louis and New York in 1956. Their combined totals of 145 at the half

and 206 points at the third period also smashed league marks.

Syracuse Total A Record

Syracuse's losing total also was an N. B. A. record for the most points scored by a loser.

The game was marred by two technical fouls against the Syracuse player-coach, Paul Seymour. He eventually was chased from the bench by Referee Ernie Heft after threatening Dick Powers, the other official.

ST. LOUIS (146)					SYRACUSE (136)				
	G.	F.	PF.	P.		G.	F.	PF.	P.
Pettit, lf	18	15	3	51	Shayes, lf	22	11	5	55
Coleman	1	2	1	4	Palazzi	3	2	2	8
Hagan, rf	8	12	4	28	Conlin, rf	6	4	4	16
MacCauley	8	4	4	20	Kerr, c	15	3	4	33
Share, c	5	1	1	11	Lloyd	1	0	5	2
McMah'n, lg	4	5	4	13	Seymour, lg	0	0	0	0
Park	1	1	1	3	Costello	6	8	5	20
Martin, rg	3	5	4	11	Bianchi, rg	7	1	5	15
Wilfgong	2	1	1	5	Harrison	3	1	2	7
Total	50	46	23	146	Total	53	30	32	136

St. Louis Hawks ....33 40 29 44—146
Syracuse ....35 37 32 32—136
Free throws missed—Pettit 5, Hagan,
Park, MacCauley, McMahon 3, Martin,
Costello, Conlin, Kerr.

DETROIT (112)					CINCINNATI (101)				
	G.	F.	PF.	P.		G.	F.	PF.	P.
Noble, lf	2	1	0	5	Duckett, lf	0	1	2	1
Marshall	0	0	0	0	Paxson	4	7	3	15
Thieben, rf	3	0	2	4	Regan, rf	3	1	2	7
Gallatin	8	10	2	26	King	4	4	2	12
Yardley, c	11	9	5	31	Meineke, c	3	3	1	9
Jordon	1	0	0	2	Ricketts, lg	2	1	6	5
McGuire, lg	7	3	5	17	Pointek	2	0	2	4
Shue, rg	8	4	5	20	Twyman, rg	8	4	3	20
Dukes	2	0	5	4	Lov_ iette	13	2	2	28
Clifton	1	1	2	3	Lovellette	13	2	2	28
Total	42	28	26	112	Total	39	23	23	101

Detroit Pistons ....23 26 33 30—112
Cincinnati Royals ....23 27 28 23—101
Free throws missed—Thieben, Gallatin 2,
Yardley, Duckett, Paxon 4, Regan, King
3, Meineke, Ricketts, Pointek, Twyman.

December 22, 1957

SCHAYES BETTERS RECORD OF MIKAN

SYRACUSE, N. Y., Jan. 12 (UP)—Adolph Schayes today became the highest scoring player in professional basketball history. He surpassed George Mikan's previous record of 11,764 points as the Syracuse Nationals routed the Detroit Pistons, 135—109.

Schayes' 23 points gave him a total of 11,770. The 29-year-old ex-N. Y. U. star is now in his tenth season as a professional with the Nationals.

During his career with the Nats, Schayes has competed in 655 regular season games. His first year as a pro was in the National Basketball League, the other nine in the National Basketball Association.

The retired Mikan compiled his record over a nine-season stretch in the same two loops and played in 439 games. Neither player's total points include play-off contests.

Schayes cracked the mark with 5 minutes, 58 seconds remaining in the third period.

SYRACUSE (135)					DETROIT (109)				
	G.	F.	PF.	P.		G.	F.	PF.	P.
Shayes	6	11	2	23	Gallatin	5	5	4	15
Palazzi	6	8	3	20	Yardley	6	13	3	25
Conlin	7	6	5	20	Holup	6	1	3	13
Lloyd	1	2	4	4	Clifton	3	0	4	6
Kerr	2	1	4	5	Dukes	5	4	2	14
Hopkins	1	4	0	6	Jordan	2	1	3	5
Costello	8	10	3	26	Shue	6	6	3	16
Harrison	3	1	5	7	McGuire	2	2	6	6
Bianchi	8	4	4	20	Kenville	2	5	5	9
Seymour	2	0	1	4	Noble	0	0	1	0
Total	44	47	31	135	Total	36	37	30	109

Syracuse ....40 27 31 37—135
Detroit ....26 19 31 33—109

January 13, 1958

Celtics' Strong Finish Topples Knicks

RUSSELL SPARKS 113-111 TRIUMPH

Celtic Star Breaks Rebound Mark—Sears of Knicks Registers 38 Points

By WILLIAM J. BRIORDY

In one of the keenest National Basketball Association games seen at Madison Square Garden in many a season, the Boston Celtics outlasted the New York Knickerbockers for a 113-111 victory last night.

Records were established by the Celtics' 6-foot 10-inch center, Bill Russell, and the Knicks' 6-foot 9-inch forward, Ken Sears as the Knicks fell a game

behind the third-place Philadelphia Warriors in their bid for a play-off spot in the Eastern Division.

The Knicks, playing without one of their scoring aces, Willie Naulls, fought their hearts out to win this one. But they let the game get away from them in the last minute.

Russell came up with twenty-five rebounds for the division-leading Celtics to establish an N. B. A. season mark in that specialty. The big center, who batted away many a Knick shot, now has 1,280 rebounds in sixty games.

The old mark of 1,256 rebounds was set by Cincinnati's Maurice Stokes last season. Russell also contributed 16 points to Boston's cause as the slick Bob Cousy paced the visitors with 27.

A Record for Sears

For the Knicks, this was easily Sears's best game. He hit for 38 points and seized twenty-four rebounds. Playing forty-six minutes, he hung up a

Knick scoring high for a single season. Kenny has registered 1,124 points in sixty-one games. His total beats the old club record of 1,112 points by Carl Braun in 1955-56.

The most disappointed Knick was the fiery Richie Guerin. Guerin, who had tied the score at 105-all on a 3-point play in the fourth quarter, kept the locals alive when he drove in for a lay-up with 1:25 to put the Knicks ahead, 109—108.

But Cousy made two free tosses and Russell hooked one in at 11:15 for a 112-110 Celtic advantage. Then Guerin had his chance for another big moment and this time he failed.

Cousy fouled Richie and the Knicks stepped to the charity line with three chances to make two shots because the foul was Boston's seventh personal of the quarter. But Richie, who missed six of twelve free throws during the game, failed on all three tries and that finished the Knicks.

Sears rebounded for a goal

within fifteen seconds left to put the locals a point away. However, Guerin fouled Cousy and Bob made one of two free throws to complete the scoring.

Sears Breaks Loose

The crowd of 15,097 saw Boston, paced by Cousy, Russell and Frank Ramsey, build a 104-93 lead at 6:27 of the fourth quarter. Then the Knicks, on a 7-point spree by Sears, moved to within 104—100.

Ray Felix hit from underneath before Guerin made his 3-pointer for the 105-all tie. The Knicks also had the lead by 107—106 at 9:51 on a tap-in. While Sears was credited with the shot, it appeared that Felix had made the shot.

The Knicks, who led by 24—23 at the end of the first quarter and by 55—47 at half-time, trailed by 84—81 at the three-quarter mark. The locals enjoyed a 54-40 bulge late in the second period.

Naulls was ordered to bed a few hours before the start of

the game by Dr. Kazuo Yanagisawa, a Garden physician. Dr. Yanagisawa said Naulls was suffering from acute bronchitis. He may miss the Knicks' game at Syracuse tonight.

Boston's Jack Nichols suffered an injured left leg in the first half and sat out the second portion. Bill Sharman, who returned to action for the Celtics after being sidelined with a leg injury, got 11 points.

Howard Cann, New York University's coach for thirty-five years, was honored by the Grand Lodge of the Knights of Pythias before the game. Cann received the annual Pythian Award for long and meritorious service to sports.

Archbishop Molloy High of Jamaica, Queens, scored its twenty-sixth straight triumph over a two-year period by beating St. Helena's, 54—47, in the preliminary game. The victory was Molloy's twenty-second this season.

BOSTON (113)					NEW YORK (111)				
	G.	F.	PF.	P.		G.	F.	PF.	P.
Heins'n, lf	5	10	3	20	Sparrow, lf	3	5	6	11
Risen	4	3	6	11	Spoelstra	2	0	3	4
Tsi'ulos, rf	3	1	2	7	Sears, rf	15	8	5	38
Nichols	0	1	0	1	Felix, c	9	2	4	20
Russell, c	8	9	4	16	Tyra	1	0	1	2
Cousy, lg	9	9	2	27	Guerin, lg	4	6	5	14
Phillip	0	0	3	0	Sobie	2	3	1	7
Ramsey, rg	7	6	4	20	Braun, rg	5	5	2	15
Sharman	5	1	3	11	McCann	0	0	2	0
Total	41	31	27	113	Total	41	29	29	111

Boston 23   24   37   29—113
New York 24   31   26   30—111

Free throws missed—Heinsohn 4, Tsiompulos, Nichols, Russell, Cousy 2, Phillip, Ramsey 2, Sobie 3, Sears 3, Felix 2, Guerin 6, Sobie 3, Braun.
Officials—Sid Borgia and Willie Smith.

February 19, 1958

The New York Times (by Larry Morris)

FAST-BREAKING KNICK: Richie Guerin drives in to score while being guarded by Bob Cousy of the Celtics in the first period of the game at Madison Square Garden.

YARDLEY BREAKS MARKS

Piston Star Sets Total Point and Free Throw Records

MINNEAPOLIS, March 6 (UP) —George Yardley scored 49 points and broke two individual National Basketball Association records tonight as he paced the Detroit Pistons to a 132-116 victory over the Minneapolis Lakers.

Yardley shattered George Mikan's record for total points in a season. Yardley now has 1.953 points compared to Mikan's record of 1.932, established in the 1950-51 season.

He also broke the record for free throws, held by the Syracuse forward, Dolph Schayes. He made eleven free throws tonight to total 635, breaking Schayes' mark of 625 for a season. Yardley has two games remaining to hit the 2,000 mark in total points.

DETROIT (132)					MINNEAPOLIS (116)				
	G.	F.	PF.	P.		G.	F.	PF.	P.
Yardley	19	11	3	49	Mikkelsen	8	2	1	18
Dukes	6	4	4	16	Fleming	4	4	3	12
Holup	0	0	1	0	Ingram	3	1	6	7
Clifton	0	0	0	0	Erias	2	0	1	4
Jordon	3	3	5	9	Krebs	7	2	3	16
Gallatin	3	4	4	10	Foust	6	8	5	20
Shue	11	7	1	29	Garmaker	6	1	0	13
McGuire	4	4	3	12	Selvy	3	1	1	9
Noble	3	1	4	7	Leonard	3	5	2	11
					Hundley	1	0	3	2
Total	49	34	26	132	Devlin	1	2	0	4
					Total	44	28	26	116

Detroit 29   29   37   43—132
Minneapolis 17   26   37   36—116

Free throws missed—Yardley 4, Dukes, Jordon, McGuire, Fleming 3, Krebs 2, Foust 2, Leonard, Hundley.

March 7, 1958

Yardley Sinks No. 2,001 As Detroit Five Loses

SYRACUSE, March 9 (UP) —George Yardley, with 26 points today, became the first pro basketball player in history to score 2,000 or more points in a single season, but his Detroit Pistons lost to the Syracuse Nationals, 111—90.

Yardley made 13 points in the first period. Syracuse then switched defenses and used Earl Lloyd to check the Piston ace and he netted only one more point in the half.

Entering the final quarter of Detroit's season finale, Yardley still needed 9 points. Although his mates tried to feed him the ball, the defense handled him well.

With three minutes left, Yardley broke free on a pass interception and dunked the ball for his 2,000th point. He added a free throw to close out his scoring.

March 10, 1958

HAWKS NIP CELTICS FOR TITLE, 110-109

Pettit Registers 50 Points to Stifle Repeated Rallies by Boston in Last Period

By The Associated Press.

ST. LOUIS, April 12 — Bob Pettit's great 50-point game. including the winning goal with sixteen seconds left, paced the St. Louis Hawks to the world championship of pro basketball tonight with a 110—109 victory over the Boston Celtics.

The defending champion Celtics, with Bill Russell playing about twenty minutes with a heavily taped ankle, never gave up. They overcame a 10-point Hawk lead and went ahead early in the last quarter.

But Pettit's 19-point last quarter was decisive. The Hawks went in front to stay, 95—93, on Pettit's goal with 6:16 left. Three times after that the Celtics battled back to within a point. Each time the 6-foot 9-inch Pettit sank the goal that kept the Hawks in front. His last tally put his team in front, 110-107.

Sharman Paces Boston

Then Bill Sharman, who led Boston with 26 points. was allowed to score a lay-up unmolested with nine seconds left. The Hawks ran out the clock with little Slater Martin dribbling the ball.

A crowd of 10,218 gave the Hawks a standing ovation as the game ended and the St. Louis players lifted Pettit to their shoulders.

Martin held Bob Cousy, Boston's seven-time all-star, to 15 points.

Pettit's 50 points set a National Basketball Association record for a regulation-time play-off game. The old mark was 47 by George Mikan of the Minneapolis Lakers in 1947. Cousy also has scored 50 points in a play-off game, but that was a four-overtime contest

Big Bob Petit was a consistent and often spectacular scorer for the St. Louis Hawks in the late 1950's. He was a perennial all-star and often one of the N.B.A.'s most valuable players.

against Syracuse in 1953.

Pettit, a former Louisiana State All-America, made nineteen of thirty-four shots from the field and twelve of nineteen from the free-throw line.

The Hawks won the series, four games to two. St Louis took its games by a total of 8 points, while Boston posted two lopsided victories.

Pettit's spree gave him a 29.3 scoring average for the series. Frank Ramsey, who had a 22-point average going into the game, had only 8 points tonight.

St. Louis led at each quarter 22—18, 57—52, and 83—77. But Boston stayed close all the way and occassionally pushed in front.

ST. LOUIS (110)	G.F.PF.P	BOSTON (109)	G.F.PF.P
Pettit	19 12 1 50	Heinsohn	5 13 5 23
Hazan	5 5 6 15	Tsiropoulos	4 6 1 14
Macauley	0 2 5 2	Ramsey	3 2 6 8
Davis	2 1 2 5	Risen	4 3 12
Share	3 2 6 8	Nichols	0 0 0 0
Coleman	3 2 3 8	Russell	2 4 4 8
Martin	0 4 4 4	Cousy	4 7 3 13
Park	1 3 1 5	Sharman	10 6 4 26
McMahon	4 1 5 9	Jones	1 1 0 3
Wilfong	1 2 1 4	Phillip	0 0 4 0
Total	38 34 34 110	Total	33 43 30 109

St. Louis ....22 35 21 32—110
Boston ....18 34 25 32—109
Free throws missed—Pettit 3, Hazan, Davis, Martin 2, McMahon, Wilfong. Heinsohn 4, Risen, Russell, Cousy.

April 13, 1958

N. B. A. ACTS TO BAR RACIAL INCIDENTS

Sets Policy on Segregation Aimed to Protect Negroes From Embarrassment

By DAMON STETSON
Special to The New York Times.

DETROIT, Jan. 22—The board of governors of the National Basketball Association today announced a policy designed to protect Negro players against embarrassment stemming from segregated housing and dining facilities in some areas.

Maurice Podoloff, president of the N. B. A. said that each of the eight clubs in the association would insist, before making a commitment for a game in a neutral city, "on a clause which will adequately protect the club and player against any type of embarrassment."

The issue was raised at a meeting today as a result of a game in Charleston, W. Va., last Friday. On that occasion Elgin Baylor, rookie star with the Minneapolis Lakers, refused to play in an N. B. A. game at the West Virginia city in protest to the refusal of a hotel there to accommodate him with other members of the team.

Main Target of Action

The association's decision to insist on a protective clause in contracts for games in neutral courts was aimed particularly at discrimination against Negro players, Mr. Podoloff said.

He made it clear, however, that the association's intent was even broader and was aimed at

---

protecting players against any sort of discriminatory or embarrassing situations. He acknowledged, however, that there had been no actual vote by the board on the question but that it had informally agreed on the new policy.

The contest, at Charleston, was a home game for the Cincinnati Royals that had been switched to Charleston by mutual agreement of the two teams.

Robert E. Short, president of the Minneapolis Basketball Corporation, said that he had been given advance assurances that integrated hotel and dining facilities would be provided in Charleston.

Officials of the N. B. A. say there has not been any segregation problem during games played in the home cities of the eight teams in the professional league. But games have often been played in Southern cities where housing problems have arisen.

There are now Negroes on all of the eight teams in the association. Of the total of eighty players in the league roster, a spokesman said, twenty are Negroes.

After the Charleston game, H. Thomas Corrie, promoter for the American Business Club there, protested to Mr. Podoloff over the failure of Mr. Baylor to appear in the game.

Mr. Corrie urged that disciplinary action be taken against the Negro player and contended that the Minneapolis club had been advised on Dec. 29 that segregation was enforced in the city's hotels.

January 23, 1959

CELTICS TRIUMPH AS 7 MARKS FALL

Vanquish Lakers by 173-139 in Highest Scoring Game in Basketball History

BOSTON, Feb. 27 (UPI) — Seven National Basketball Association records fell today as the Boston Celtics crushed the Minneapolis Lakers, 173—139. It was the highest score ever recorded in basketball history.

The league president, Maurice Podoloff, was shocked when he heard the result. He said he would query officials of both teams tomorrow to determine whether defensive assignments were faithfully carried out or whether the teams "were goofing off."

"One hundred and seventy-three to 139!" asked Podoloff in disbelief. "That's unbelievable."

The Celtics set four N.B.A. marks—most points in a game by one team (173), most points in a half (90), most points in a quarter (52) and most field goals (72).

Losers Also Set Mark

The Lakers, who had won five of their last six games, helped break two more records — most points in a game (312) and most points by a losing team (139).

To complete the assault on records, Boston's Bob Cousy registered twenty-eight assists

---

to break the old mark of 21, set by Richie Guerin of the New York Knicks.

The Celtics' total points topped by 27 the old record of 146 set by the St. Louis Hawks last season against Syracuse. Their total also was 19 points above the college scoring mark set by Furman against The Citadel in 1955.

The two teams' 312 points eclipsed the record of 282, set when St. Louis downed the Nats, 146—136, in 1957.

The highest scoring game ever recorded by college teams was a 262-point affair in which the University of Baltimore defeated Catholic University, 146—121.

The now defunct Sheboygan (Wis.) team set the old N. B. A. field-goal record of 61, against Denver in 1950.

Crowd of 12,315 Attends

Today's contest, played before 12,315 fans, was scheduled for the afternoon because an ice show occupies the Boston Garden at night this week.

Tommy Heinsohn led all scorers with 43 points. Cousy had 31, Elgin Baylor, a rookie, paced Minneapolis with 23.

BOSTON (173)	G.F.PF.P	MINN'POLIS (139)	G.F.PF.P
Heinsohn	18 7 3 43	Baylor	7 14 4 26
Loscutoff	5 1 5 11	Mikkelsen	10 5 5 25
Conley	7 0 5 14	Krebs	2 1 5 5
Sharman	13 3 2 29	Garmaker	1 1 3 3
Cousy	10 11 3 31	Hundley	9 3 5 21
Swain	1 3 6 5	Foust	0 8 2 8
Ramsey	8 4 2 20	Leonard	5 6 4 16
S. Jones	4 0 1 8	Ellis	4 4 2 11
K. C. Jones	6 0 3 12	Fleming	5 3 2 13
		Hamilton	4 0 1 8
Total	72 29 30 173	Total	47 45 28 139

Boston ....40 43 38 52—173
Minneapolis ....30 34 31 44—139
Free throws missed—Heinsohn 4, Loscutoff, Ramsey, Garmaker, Hundley 2, Foust 3, Leonard, Ellis 2.

February 28, 1959

Celtics Trip Lakers and Sweep Basketball Title Series

SHARMAN BIG GUN IN 118-113 GAME

Sparks Celtics' Rally That Beats Lakers for Title— Baylor Gets 30 Points

MINNEAPOLIS, April 9 (AP) —Bill Sharman blunted the Minneapolis Lakers' last-gasp challenge tonight as the Boston Celtics won the National Basketball Association championship with a 118-113 victory. It was the first time a team had scored a clean sweep in the title play-offs.

Sharman's long one-handed

---

shots from the sides and from behind the foul circle bailed the Celtics out of trouble after Bob Leonard and Elgin Baylor had teamed to send the Lakers ahead.

The 32-year-old star finished with 29 points in one of the finest hours of his long pro career. However, he experienced the minor disappointment of seeing his record foul-shot streak snapped at fifty-six when he missed a free throw in the third period.

With the four-game sweep, Boston, most explosive team in league history, gained the distinction of being the first N. B. A. team to go through the title play-offs unbeaten. The Celtics captured the crown for the second time in three seasons.

Ramsey Also Stands Out

While Sharman's long-range blasting carried the Celtics in the fourth period, it was a lay-up by Frank Ramsey with a half-minute left that put the

---

final crusher on the Lakers' upset hopes.

Baylor led the Lakers with 30 points, and Leonard had 21. Tom Heinsohn, the tall, acrobatic Celtic frontliner, had 23 and Ramsey 24 in another superlative pinch-hitting role.

The victory stretched Boston's winning streak over the Lakers to twenty-two games, dating back to March 1, 1957, a dominance unequaled in the N. B. A.

The Lakers' scoring diversity offset the shooting of Boston's Ramsey, Heinsohn and Bill Russell in the first period, in which the score was tied twelve times.

It was 34—34 at the quarter, moved Boston into a 47-41 advantage early in the second period, but Vern Mikkelsen sparked a rally that sent them in front, 56—53, three minutes from half-time.

Heinsohn Takes Command

Here Heinsohn took up the offensive load for Boston and drilled three jump shots, plus a tap-in just before the buzzer, for a 64-62 Boston lead at the intermission.

With Ramsey and Sharman hitting consistently. Boston maintained a lead of from 2 to 8 points through most of the third period.

Baylor shoved the Lakers ahead, 95—93, early in the final period. But after Ramsey hit a 3-pointer to counter a field goal by Leonard. Sharman made two goals within 30 seconds to put Boston ahead to stay.

BOSTON (118)					MINNEAPOLIS (113)				
	G.	F.	PF.	P.		G.	F.	PF.	P.
Heinsohn	9	5	4	23	Baylor	12	6	4	30
Loscutoff	2	0	5	4	Mikkelsen	7	6	3	20
Ramsey	10	4	4	24	Ellis	1	0	1	2
Russell	5	5	1	15	Hamilton	0	2	1	2
Conley	3	4	5	10	Foust	2	0	4	4
Cousy	3	5	2	11	Krebs	6	1	5	13
Sharman	14	1	3	29	Garmaker	6	4	4	16
S. Jones	0	2	0	2	Leonard	9	5	2	23
K. C. Jones	0	0	0	0	Fleming	1	1	2	3
					Hundley	0	0	2	0
Total	46	26	24	118	Total	44	25	28	113

Boston ....34 30 24 30—118
Minneapolis ......34 28 25 26—113
Free throws missed—Heinsohn, Ramsey 2, Russell 3, Conley 2, Cousy 3, Sharman, Baylor 2, Mikkelsen 3, Leonard.

April 10, 1959

Celtics' Star Shares Gate in Record Pact

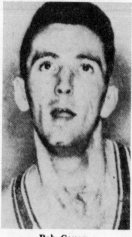

Bob Cousy

BOSTON, Sept. 14 (AP)— Bob Cousy, captain of the Boston Celtics and one of the smallest men in the National Basketball Association, today signed the biggest contract in the history of the league.

Cousy, 6 feet 1 inch, signed with the club president, Walter Brown, for a base salary and a percentage of the gate.

The exact amount of the contract was not announced, but Brown said, "If we do any business at all, no one who has ever played will be anywhere near him."

Wilt Chamberlain, towering star, recently signed with the Philadelphia Warriors for a reported $30,000. Brown said Cousy's contract would easily exceed that figure.

Cousy will be starting his tenth year in the league. He is 31 years old.

September 15, 1959

Chicago as Ninth Team in League
National Basketball Association Admits

COAST EXPANSION LOOMS IN 1961-62

Admission of Chicago Five Is First Step in N. B. A. Growth, Podoloff Says

Chicago received a franchise in the National Basketball Association yesterday, increasing the league to nine teams. The eight-member Board of Governors of the N. B. A. voted unanimously to accept the team, which is run by a group under the direction of Max Winter and Dave C. Trager. Winter was a former president of the Minneapolis Lakers in the N. B. A.

As yet unnamed, the Chicago team will begin league play at the start of the 1960-61 season. The team will compete in the Western Division of the N. B. A., along with St. Louis, Cincinnati, Minneapolis and Detroit.

The Western Division will be a five-team group. The Eastern Division will remain a four-team part of the N. B. A. The Eastern teams are New York, Boston, Syracuse and Philadelphia.

This marks the first time in the history of the N. B. A. that the league has expanded. Since its inception in 1949, when the Basketball Association of America and the National Basketball League combined, the N. B. A. has been cut in size from time to time.

Following yesterday's meeting at the Park Sheraton Hotel, Maurice Podoloff, the N. B. A. president, said, "We've got to expand. This is our first step."

Another official of the league said that the chances were good that Los Angeles and San Francisco would join the league some time before the 1961-62 season.

Scheduling problems must also be worked out in the next few months.

During the first season of the N. B. A. in 1949-50, there were seventeen teams divided into three divisions. The following season eleven teams played in two divisions and then, for two years, the league had ten teams in two divisions.

In the 1953-54 season there were nine teams in two divisions. From the 1954-55 season on, there have been the eight teams. The last city to drop out was Baltimore.

A Chicago group had a franchise in the league in 1949-50, playing as the Stags in the erstwhile Central Division of the N. B. A. That Chicago team had played the previous three seasons in the B. A. A.

September 17, 1959

Baylor Scores Record 64 Points As Lakers Halt Celtics, 136-115

MINNEAPOLIS, Nov. 8 (AP) —Elgin Baylor scored 64 points tonight, a National Basketball Association record, and led the Minneapolis Lakers to a 136-115 victory over the Boston Celtics.

Baylor's performance bettered the old record of 63 points set by Joe Fulks of Philadelphia in 1949.

The victory was the first for the Lakers over Boston in twenty-two regular-season games spanning three seasons.

Baylor, the league's rookie of the year last season, sank twenty-five of forty-seven field goal tries and fourteen of nineteen free throws.

With 1:24 left he hit one of three free throws to register his sixty-second point. Then, with thirty-one seconds remaining and with everyone in the Minneapolis Auditorium knowing he had the record within his grasp, Baylor hit a driving jump-shot from the side, ten feet out.

Baylor's previous high as a pro was 55 points last season. He registered 52 against Detroit in the first game of the current season. The 64 points eclipsed the individual Laker mark of 61 set by George Mikan in 1952.

M'NEAPOLIS (136)	G.	F.	PF.	P.	BOSTON (115)	G.	F.	PF.	P.
Baylor	25	14	4	64	Heinsohn	8	3	5	19
LaRusso	4	2	2	10	Russell	1	1	1	3
Foust	5	7	5	17	Cousy	4	5	0	13
Garmaker	0	0	0	0	Sharman	3	2	1	8
Hundley	6	4	3	16	Conley	3	1	4	7
Ellis	0	0	0	0	Richter	7	2	4	16
Hawkins	0	3	3	3	Ramsey	3	3	5	9
Krebs	0	0	3	0	S. Jones	6	10	2	22
Leonard	0	0	2	0	K.C. Jones	2	3	6	7
Fleming	7	3	3	17	Guarilia	3	3	3	9
Smith	4	0	4	8					
Hamilton	0	0	4	0					
Total	51	34	30	136	Total	40	35	31	115

Minneapolis ....33 34 33—136
Boston ....18 27 28 42—115
Free throws missed—Baylor 5, LaRusso, Foust, Hawkins, Fleming 4, Smith 2, Heinsohn, Russell, Cousy, Conley 2, Richter, Ramsey 2, S. Jones, K. C. Jones 2, Guarilia.

November 9, 1959

Schayes Passes 15,000 Points as Nats Subdue Celtics

Yardley Gets 47 Points

PHILADELPHIA, Jan. 12 (AP)—Dolph Schayes became the first pro basketball player to hit the 15,000-point mark tonight as the Syracuse Nationals defeated the Boston Celtics, 127—120, in a National Basketball Association contest.

In the second game of the double-header, the Philadelphia Warriors defeated the St. Louis Hawks, 126—108.

Schayes scored 34 points in the opener to bring his career total to 15,013. His team-mate, George Yardley, had 47 points.

Yardley's great shooting late in the first period and halfway through the second quarter sent Syracuse into the lead and the Nats relinquished it only once thereafter. In one stretch Yardley hit on twelve consecutive field goal tries.

Through the first half he made fourteen of seventeen attempts. His 30 points in that half broke a Convention Hall record, while his over-all total of twenty-one field goals broke the floor mark.

Schayes experienced difficulty at first but warmed up as the game progressed. With 2:48 to play in the third quarter, he sank a long set shot that put him on the 15,000-point mark. The game was stopped and the ball was presented to Schayes as the capacity crowd gave him a standing ovation. Schayes has been playing professional basketball for twelve years.

SYRACUSE (127)	G.	F.	PF.	P.	BOSTON (120)	G.	F.	PF.	P.
Schayes	8	18	4	34	Heinsohn	10	2	6	22
Yardley	21	5	4	47	Guarilia	3	0	2	6
Kerr	1	0	2	2	Russell	8	0	3	16
Greer	3	0	4	6	Cousy	3	4	3	10
Costello	7	5	4	19	Sharman	4	1	3	9
Barnett	1	1	0	3	K.C. Jones	2	3	2	7
Bianchi	0	0	2	0	Ramsey	9	4	6	22
Hopkins	0	2	0	2	Conley	3	0	6	6
Dierking	3	1	2	7	S. Jones	8	4	0	20
					Richter	1	0	0	2
Total	45	37	24	127	Total	51	18	31	120

SYRACUSE ....28 43 35 21—127
BOSTON ....31 27 28 34—120

Free throws missed—Schayes 2, Yardley 2, Greer 2, Barnett 2, Dierking 2, Heinsohn, Guarilia, Russell 2, Cousy, Sharman, K. C. Jones, Ramsey 2, S. Jones.

PHILA. (126)	G.	F.	PF.	P.	ST. LOUIS (108)	G.	F.	PF.	P.
Arizin	10	6	2	26	Pettit	2	6	3	10
Johnson	2	3	4	7	Hagan	9	8	6	26
Ch'mlain	13	11	3	37	Lovellette	12	1	3	25
Gola	6	2	4	14	McCarthy	3	2	3	8
Hatton	4	1	2	9	Martin	5	3	4	13
Sa'ldsberry	3	0	3	6	Share	3	0	3	6
Beck	8	0	1	16	Ferrari	6	1	0	13
Graboski	0	0	1	0	Gambee	2	0	2	4
Ruklick	2	0	1	4	Green	0	0	0	0
					Ferry	1	1	0	3
Total	51	24	22	126	Total	43	22	24	108

Philadelphia ....31 33 26 36—126
St. Louis ....27 20 30 31—108
Free throws missed—Arizin, Johnson, Chamberlain 7, Pettit 2, Hagan, Martin, Share, Gambee.

January 13, 1960

Pistons Win, 122-113

DETROIT, Feb. 9 (AP) — Wilt Chamberlain broke the National Basketball Association's single-season scoring record with a 41-point output tonight against the Detroit Pistons, but the Philadelphia Warriors lost the game, 122—113.

The rookie has scored 2,134 points, breaking the record of 2,105 established last season by Bob Pettit of the St. Louis Hawks.

Pettit set his record over a seventy-two-game span. This was Wilt's fifty-sixth game. He missed one of the Warriors' fifty-seven games because of influenza. The 7-foot 2-inch star has eighteen games in which to add to the record.

Chamberlain also set a league rebounding record for one season. His sixteen rebounds tonight ran his total to 1,613 for the year, one better than the mark set last season by Bill Russell of the Boston Celtics.

The Syracuse Nationals defeated the Cincinnati Royals, 117—111, in the opening game of the Olympia double-header witnessed by a crowd of 8,201.

DETROIT (122)	G.	F.	PF.	P.	PHILA. (113)	G.	F.	PF.	P.
Conlin	3	0	2	6	Arizin	9	5	5	23
Dees	4	0	1	8	Beck	0	0	3	0
Dukes	7	6	5	20	Ch'berlain	19	3	3	41
Howell	11	7	3	29	Gola	7	5	6	19
Lloyd	4	5	5	13	Graboski	1	2	1	4
McGuire	3	0	1	6	Johnson	0	0	0	0
McMillon	1	0	1	2	Rodzers	5	5	3	15
Noble	4	0	3	8	S'uldsberry	5	1	3	11
Shue	11	8	2	30					
Total	48	26	23	122	Total	46	21	24	113

SYRACUSE (117)	G.	F.	PF.	P.	CINCINNATI (111)	G.	F.	PF.	P.
Barnett	2	0	0	4	Bockhorn	3	1	1	7
Bianchi	3	1	4	7	Embrey	5	2	4	12
Cable	0	0	0	0	Gambe	5	1	0	11
Costello	7	4	3	18	Jordon	1	1	2	3
Dierking	3	0	3	6	Park	1	3	3	5
Greer	9	5	4	23	Reed	4	0	3	8
Hopkins	1	0	3	2	Rollins	6	5	4	17
Kerr	5	7	5	17	Twyman	15	7	5	37
Schayes	9	11	4	29	Wilfong	5	1	2	11
Yardley	3	5	4	11					
Total	42	33	30	117	Total	45	21	24	111

Syracuse ....33 31 27 26—117
Cincinnati ....28 26 23 34—111
Free throws missed—Bianchi, Kerr, Bockhorn 3, Embrey 6, Gambe, Park, Rollins, Twyman 3, Wilfong.

February 10, 1960

CELTICS CONQUER NATS, 124 TO 100

Russell Betters His League Rebound Mark With 51— Hawks Defeat Lakers

STANDING OF THE TEAMS

EASTERN DIV.	W.	L.	PC.	WESTERN DIV.	W.	L.	PC.
Boston	43	12	.782	St. Louis	32	21	.604
Phila.	38	16	.704	Detroit	23	32	.418
Syracuse	31	24	.564	Minn'polis	14	36	.280
New York	22	32	.407	Cincinnati	14	44	.241

February 6, 1960

BOSTON, Feb. 5 (UPI)—Big Bill Russell gathered fifty-one rebounds, bettering his own National Basketball Association record, and paced the Boston Celtics to a 124-100 triumph over the Syracuse Nationals at the Garden tonight.

Russell grabbed twenty-four rebounds in the first half and twenty-seven more in the final two quarters. His old mark was forty-nine, set Nov. 16, 1957.

The 6-foot 10-inch center, now in his fourth N. B. A. campaign, aided the Celtics offense with 23 points. That was 2 behind high-scoring team-mate Frank Ramsey. George Yardley and Dick Barnett shared scoring honors for the Nats with 19 each.

It was the Celtics' fifteenth straight victory at home.

BOSTON (124)	G.	F.	PF.	P.	SYRACUSE (100)	G.	F.	PF.	P.
Heinsohn	9	2	1	20	Schayes	5	3	4	13
Ramsey	8	9	3	25	Yardley	9	1	2	19
Russell	8	7	1	23	Kerr	3	1	0	7
Sharman	3	0	1	6	Bianchi	1	1	2	3
Cousy	7	3	0	17	Costello	0	0	2	0
Conley	7	2	3	16	Barnett	9	1	2	19
S. Jones	4	1	2	9	Dierking	1	0	4	2
K.C. Jones	0	0	1	0	Hopkins	6	4	2	16
Richter	1	0	0	2	Cable	2	1	2	5
Guarilia	0	0	0	0	Green	1	1	0	3
Total	50	24	12	124	Total	44	12	21	100

Boston ....29 35 36—124
Syracuse ....28 21 27 24—100
Free throws missed—Ramsey, Russell 3, Cousy, S. Jones, K. C. Jones, Cable.

February 6, 1960

The Cincinnati Royals' Jerry Lucas dares Elgin Baylor to go around him and score—and Baylor did just that. Baylor, who had an uncanny ability to manipulate and turn his body while already in the air, once scored 71 points in an N.B.A. game.

Wilt Chamberlain grabs a rebound against the Boston Celtics in 1962. Chamberlain set 10 scoring records that year, including 100 points in one game against the New York Knicks.

Chamberlain's 58 Points Set Garden Record in Warrior Victory Over Knicks

NEW YORK DROPS 129-122 CONTEST

Knicks, Now Mathematically Out of Play-Offs, Object to Wilt's Moves as 'Illegal'

By LOUIS EFFRAT

Wilt Chamberlain, the lanky lad who in less than one season has accounted for more "mosts" than most basketball players achieve in a career, fashioned another yesterday at Madison Square Garden.

In leading the Philadelphia Warriors to a 129-122 victory over the New York Knickerbockers, Wilt the Stilt—all 7 feet 1/16th inch of him—netted 58 points, the most ever scored by a player at the Garden.

This was the most notable of a flock of floor records set. Chamberlain drew cheers from most of the 8,140 fans and jeers from the Knicks in this exciting National Basketball Association encounter.

The spectators liked Chamberlain's point production, but the Knicks, and particularly the brass, did not like the way he went about it.

The Knicks also had another reason to fret. With this setback they were mathematically eliminated from the play-offs for the fourth time in the fourteen-year history of the N. B. A.

Guerin's Record Falls

Nor were the New Yorkers at all happy that the record Chamberlain surpassed had belonged to a Knick, the popular Richie Guerin. Guerin tallied 57 points against the Syracuse Nationals in a game here last December.

The Garden record for a college player is the 56 scored by Oscar Robertson of Cincinnati in a Holiday Festival game last year.

Mostly, the Knicks objected (although not officially) to what they called the "leaning tactics and other offensive fouls" committed by Chamberlain. Wilt the Stilt, whose twenty-six field goals set still another Garden record, enjoyed a field day despite the good defensive efforts of Charlie Tyra and Guerin. The pair double-teamed Chamberlain in the second half.

"Look at those elbows," was a shout the New York bench directed at the officials many times during the game.

The New York Times

58 FOR THE STILT: Wilt Chamberlain of Warriors surpassing Richie Guerin's Garden record of 57 points in game with the Knicks.

"He's leaning and backing up," was another.

Carl Braun, the coach of the Knicks, did not like what he saw, but his complaints were mild when compared with what Ned Irish, the Knick president, yelled.

Irish Yells 'Foul'

"When are the referees going to start calling offensive fouls against Chamberlain?" Irish demanded.

Overhearing Irish's complaint, Ed Gottlieb, the owner of the Warriors, asked: "What offen-

sive fouls? Chamberlain doesn't even make contact."

"I don't think Chamberlain makes one-third of his baskets legally," was Irish's final blast.

At any rate, Chamberlain's work in and around the keyhole was most effective. Seven times the former Kansas University ace "dunked" the ball through the hoop. At other times he hooked, jumped, rebounded and tapped superbly. He contributed 29 points to Philadelphia's 64-55 lead at the intermission.

Guerin, too, had an outstanding afternoon, caging 41 points. Johnny Green's rebounding and scoring might have helped win a game on any other occasion, but there was no offsetting Chamberlain's work.

Furthermore, the Knicks got little service out of Ken Sears, who was hampered by an injured leg, and none at all out of Willie Naulls, who was sidelined with laryngitis.

Knicks Lead Briefly

At one stage the Knicks trailed the Warriors by 17 points. Guerin, Green and Tyra then led a comeback that brought the New Yorkers a 114-113 edge halfway through the fourth quarter.

However, Chamberlain, Tom Gola and Paul Arizin put on the pressure and the visitors regained the upper hand. The score was tied thirteen times in the dramatic contest.

In earlier engagements in this, his freshman season among

the pros, Chamberlain had scored 58 points against the Detroit Pistons and 55 and 52 against the Cincinnati Royals.

Yesterday he became the first player in N. B. A. history to have topped 50 points in one game four times in one season. The one-game scoring record among the pros is 64, which Elgin Baylor amassed for the Minneapolis Lakers against the Boston Celtics this season.

Chamberlain, who disagreed with the critical remarks concerning his "offensive fouls," as did his coach, Neil Johnston, said he had no idea what the scoring ceiling might be. "Anyone score 100? Maybe so, but it won't be me," he said.

While 58 represents Chamberlain's high in the N. B. A., he once caged 90 points while playing twenty-six minutes in a high school game. Then there was the time, in an amateur league contest—Wilt did not remember the name of the league or the team — when he tallied 113 points.

PHILA. (129)					KNICKS (122)				
	G.	F.	P.F.	P.		G.	F.	P.F.	P.
Arizin, lf	9	2	4	20	Sears, lf	2	2	1	6
Hatton	2	0	1	4	Farmer	0	0	0	0
S'berry, rf	1	0	5	2	Green, rf	11	5	5	27
Graboski	2	1	2	5	Tyra, c	9	1	2	19
Ch'b'n, c	26	6	1	58	Palmer	5	5	1	15
Gola, lg	10	3	5	23	Guerin, lg	16	9	3	41
Johnson	2	1	4	5	Garmaker	4	4	2	12
Rodgers, rg	6	0	1	12	Bell, rg	1	0	2	2
					George	0	0	1	0
Total	58	13	23	129	Total	48	26	18	122

Philadelphia .... 32 32 35 30—129
Knicks .... 34 21 39 28—122

Free throws missed—Arizin 2, Chamberlain 3, Gola 2, Grabaski, Garmaker, George, Green 4, Guerin 2.

Officials—Sid Borgia and Earl Strom.

February 22, 1960

BOSTON QUINTET ON TOP, 148-128

9 Celtics Score in Double Figures — Naulls Tallies 29 Points for Knicks

STANDING OF THE TEAMS

EASTERN DIV.				WESTERN DIV.			
	W.	L.	PC.		W.	L.	PC.
Boston	59	16	.787	St. Louis	46	29	.613
Philad'phia	49	26	.653	Detroit	30	45	.400
Syracuse	45	30	.600	Min'apolis	24	50	.324
New York	27	47	.365	Cincinnati	19	56	.253

BOSTON, March 9 (UPI)—The Boston Celtics set a National Basketball Association record for games won in a season tonight while routing the New York Knickerbockers, 148-128, before 3,921 fans.

This was Boston's last game of the regular season and its

fifty-ninth victory against sixteen defeats. The old N.B.A. mark of fifty-two triumphs in one season was established by the Celtics a year ago.

All but one of the ten Celtics playing in the finale scored in double figures as the Eastern Division champions overcame a 2-point first period deficit with 38-point explosions in the second and third quarters and 39 in the fourth.

Bill Sharman led the Boston attack with 22 points. Tommy Heinsohn followed with 21. Willie Naulls led New York's scorers with 29 points.

BOSTON (148)					KNICKS (128)				
	G.	F.	P.F.	P.		G.	F.	P.F.	P.
Heinsohn	8	5	1	21	Naulls	11	7	3	29
Ramsey	6	0	1	12	Palmer	4	4	3	12
Russell	10	0	2	20	Tyra	4	0	4	8
Sharman	10	2	2	22	Guerin	7	0	2	14
Cousy	5	2	3	12	Bell	1	1	3	3
Richter	5	2	2	12	Garmaker	4	0	1	8
Conley	5	1	6	11	Green	10	0	3	20
S. Jones	4	4	0	12	Brown	4	0	2	8
K C Jones	4	3	1	11	George	5	1	1	11
Guarilia	7	1	0	15	Farmer	5	5	1	15
Total	64	20	17	148	Total	55	18	24	128

Boston .... 33 38 38 39—148
Knicks .... 35 34 33 26—128

Free throws missed—Heinsohn 2, Sharman, Conley, Guarilia, Palmer, Bell, Braun.

March 10, 1960

CELTICS DEFEAT HAWKS, 122-103, AND RETAIN TITLE

BOSTON FIVE WINS

Cousy, Russell Excel in 7th-Game Victory Over St. Louisans

By MICHAEL STRAUSS
Special to The New York Times.

BOSTON April 9—In a demonstration of New England hospitality calculated to make the St. Louis Hawks regret that they had ever left the banks of the Mississippi, the Boston Celtics won the National Basketball Association championship today.

The Celtics, playing at full speed all the way, roared to a 122-103 triumph before a crowd of 13,909 that packed the Garden to capacity. The victory, the fourth in the four-of-seven series, gave Boston the title for the second straight year.

A tumultous reception by the crowd followed the final buzzer. Rooters lifted Bob Cousy, known to many as Mr. Basketball, to their shoulders and carried him from the floor.

Other fans tried to follow suit with Bill Russell, the Beantowners' great backboard man. Russell, however, is a 6-foot 9-inch 215-pounder. After several attempts, his admirers had to give up. Instead, they pounded him on the back and head. The physical beating was almost as bad as the one he received during the game.

Hawks Are Outclassed

The Hawks made a valiant try, but they were outclassed in all departments. They were able to hold on for one quarter. Early in the second session, however, they slumped badly and the Celtics moved on to a going-away victory.

Cousy and Russell were the chief factors in the Celtics' glowing success. The shifty Cousy, as usual, excelled in playmaking and outside shooting. He had fourteen assists and 19 points. Russell emerged with the tremendous total of thirty-five rebounds, although he was double-teamed almost all the way.

Russell, who was cuffed about the head several times during the game—he was dazed once and had to ask for a time-out—had 22 points. He was outscored by only one team-mate, Frank

the team celebrates National Basketball Association championship victory over the St. Louis Hawks in Boston. Enjoying the cake is Bill Sharman, left. Bob Cousy is at right.

Ramsey, who was high for the game with 24.

The aggressive Tom Heinsohn had 22 points, as did Bob Pettit, who led the Hawk scorers.

Boston's superiority was nowhere clearer than in rebounds. The Celtics had eighty-three for the game to St. Louis' forty-seven. The victors sank fifty of 114 field-goal tries and St. Louis forty of eighty-seven.

Despite plenty of pre-game fuss by Ben Kerner, owner of the Hawks, about the presence of Jim Duffy as one of the two referees.. The contest was without officiating incidents. Duffy and Mendy Rudolph did a fine job in keeping the game, viewed

by a coast-to-coast television audience, moving at a fast pace.

This tempo proved to be ideal for the winners. They patterned their attack around the fast break, slowing up only when directed to by Cousy.

The Hawks, on the other hand, moved the ball more slowly downcourt and, for the first three quarters, stressed possession while awaiting opportunities to try for the basket.

In the fourth period the visitors finally speeded up their attack, but Cousy, Russell, Heinsohn and company were clicking with such efficiency that nothing the losers did helped. Halfway through the session the Hawks narrowed their deficit to 14 points at 108—94..

The effort marked their high-water mark for the quarter.

Only in the first session was the St. Louisans' play of championship caliber. Led by big Clyde Lovellette, Pettit and Si-hugo Green, they tied matters at 23—all after trailing from the game's start.

Cousy Sinks Long Set

Thanks to a 40-footer by Cliff Hagan, St. Louis even finished the period on the long end of a 30-29 count. When action was resumed, however, the Celtics lost little time in demonstrating who really was boss.

Cousy opened the scoring with a long set from the side and Ramsey drove in down the middle, Pettit interrupted the Beantowners momentarily with a one-hander, but Heinsohn connected with two quick hooks and the home team led, 37—32, after only 2:30.

Geography Argument Fails

Kerner began campaigning for a replacement for Duffy as a referee for the final game soon after the sixth game in St. Louis on Thursday night. Part of the plea was based on the fact that Duffy lives in Pawtucket, R. I., which the Hawks' owner maintained, "is practically in Boston." Kerner intimated that the arbiter might be swayed by home-town leanings.

Podoloff's answer Saturday was, "This game this afternoon will be Duffy's fourth in the series. He was living in Pawtucket when this play-off began. Why didn't Kerner beef about Jim then. To my knowledge, Jim hasn't moved his home in the last week."

The Celtics were the first team in the N. B. A.'s fourteen years to gain the pay-off play-offs for four consecutive years. No team had won the championship in successive years since 1954, when the Minneapolis Lakers, with George Mikan, Vern Mikkelsen and Jim Pollard at their peak, took their third straight crown.

BOSTON (122)					ST. LOUIS (103)				
	G.	F.	PF.	P.		G.	F.	PF.	P.
Heinsohn	10	2	5	22	Pettit	8	6	4	22
Ramsey	11	2	5	24	Hagan	7	5	4	19
Russell	7	8	2	22	Lovellette	8	2	4	18
Cousy	7	5	2	19	Green	7	3	4	17
Sharman	3	1	3	11	McCarthy	7	2	4	16
Conley	2	1	6	5	Piontek	3	5	2	11
S. Jones	8	2	1	18	Ferrari	0	0	0	0
K.C. Jones	0	1	0	1	Ferry	0	0	1	0
Richter	0	0	4	0					
					Total	40	23	23	103
Total	50	22	25	122					

Boston ....29 41 26 26—122
St. Louis ....30 23 25 25—103
Free throws missed—Ramsey. Russell 2. Cousy. Conley. K. C. Jones. Richter. Pettit 7. Lovellette. Green 3. McCarthy. Piontek.

April 10, 1960

Lakers Down Knicks as Baylor Sets League Record of 71 Points at Garden

COAST ACE EXCELS IN 123-108 GAME

Baylor, Lakers, Clips Own Mark Against Knicks— Pistons Win, 115-114

By ROBERT L. TEAGUE

Nobody wearing the livery of the New York Knickerbockers came close to keeping up with Elgin Baylor of the Los Angeles Lakers last night. The penalty was a record 71-point spree for the star forward and a 123-108 victory for the Coast quintet at Madison Square Garden.

A crowd of 10,132 gave him a standing ovation that lasted for nearly a minute when the 6-foot 5-inch athlete left the floor with his National Basketball Association mark.

His performance all but made the spectators forget the thrilling finish of the first game in the league doubleheader in which the Detroit Pistons erased a 20-point deficit and downed the Boston Celtics, 115-114, in overtime. The deciding basket came on a 20-foot jump shot by Gene Shue at the final buzzer.

Baylor was as unpredictable as he was unstoppable. He counted quite a few points on orthodox driving lay-ups and tap-ins, but a good number came from angles that seemed impossible. He frequently popped out of a concentration of milling players, twisted his body in mid-air and scored with a deft flick of the wrist that put a knowledgeable backspin on the ball.

Once Baylor had established the possibility of such maneuvers, the Knicks tried them. They had no success. To make matters worse, the home forces began finding it difficult to make even routine shots and fell farther and farther off the pace.

Baylor was greatly aided by the ball stealing and passing of Jerry West and by the threat that Rudy LaRusso posed with his jump shot from near the free-throw circle. Willie Naulls paced New York's attack with 35 points.

Knicks Gain Early Lead

Naulls and Ken Sears collected a total of 15 points in the first ten minutes, helping the Knicks assume a 17-10 lead. Tap-ins by Baylor and jump shots by West tied it at 21-21 out Naulls and Bob McNeill each turned in a 3-point play to stave off the threat for the time being.

High-flying rebounding by Johnny Green and his subsequent passes to Guerin and Naulls for lay-ups enabled the New Yorkers to retain a slim lead throughout most of the first half.

As half-time approached, however, LaRusso joined Baylor in the unstoppable class, connecting on one-handed jump shots while apparently off balance. a theft by West led to a lay-up by Frank Selvy, a former Knickerbocker. That tied the score at 55-all with 2:30 left in the second period.

Seconds later, West grabbed a rebound and passed to Baylor automatically. The Lakers went to the front for the first time, at 57-55, 1:35 before the intermission.

It was all Baylor and La-Russo in the closing minute of the half, which ended with Los Angeles ahead, 65-58. By connecting on fifteen of twenty shots in the first half, Baylor set a garden record of 34 points for one half. His fifteen field goals also established a one-half mark for the Eighth Avenue arena.

Naulls was the main reason why the Knicks were in close contention at this point, having tallied 20 points in the first two quarters.

Charlie Tyra and Naulls paced an uprising that caught the Lakers at 66—66 in the first two and a half minutes of the third quarter. Almost five minutes elapsed before Coach Carl Braun's quintet picked up another point, however. Meanwhile, Los Angeles ran 11 straight points—most of them by Baylor and West—making the count 77—66.

Elgin hitting on his driving lay-ups and tap-ins. His team enjoyed a 90-73

SETS LEAGUE MARK: Elgin Baylor of the Los Angeles Lakers, who scored 71 points against the Knickerbockers last night.

cushion when the third period ended. About the only question left in the time, it seemed, was whether the former Seattle star would also shatter the N.B.A.'s one-game record of 64 points which he set last season against the Celtics.

His team-mates fed him generously in the closing minutes and he got his record with 1:35 remaining.

LOS ANGELES (123)					KNICKS (108)				
	G.	F.	PF.	P.		G.	F.	PF.	P.
Baylor	28	15	5	71	Naulls,lf	14	7	4	35
LaRusso.rf	6	3	4	15	Budd	0	0	1	0
Felix	0	0	0	0	Sears.rf	0	5	1	5
Alcorn.c	1	0	5	2	Green	1	2	2	4
Hawkins	3	1	5	7	Tyra.c	3	3	1	9
Joliff	1	0	0	2	Imhoff	1	0	2	2
Selvy.lg	4	1	1	9	Palmer	4	2	1	10
West	2	3	2	10	Guerin.lg	7	1	5	15
Hundley.rg	3	1	2	7	George	0	0	1	0
Leonard	2	0	0	4	G'rm'k'r,rg	1	3	2	5
					McNeill	4	3	3	11
Total	50	23	25	123	Total	40	28	27	108

Los Angeles ....33 32 25 33—123
Knicks ....35 23 15 35—108
Free throws missed — Naulls. Budd 2. Guerin. Hawkins 4. Selvy 3. West 3. Hundley 2.
Officials — Mendy Rudolph and Dick Sheldon.

November 16, 1960

CELTICS VANQUISH WARRIORS, 132-129

PHILADELPHIA, Nov. 24 (UPI)—Boston strengthened its hold on first place in the National Basketball Association's Eastern Division tonight by defeating the Philadelphia Warriors, 132-129, before a capacity crowd of 11,003 at Convention Hall.

Wilt Chamberlain grabbed fifty-five rebounds to break the league mark of fifty-one set by Bill Russell against Syracuse last season.

Sam Jones' basket broke a 114-114 tie with 5:43 left. Two free throws by Gene Conley, two baskets by Sam Jones and a field goal by Conley was answered only by Andy Johnson's free throw as the Celtics led, 124—115, with 3:21 remaining.

Tom Heinsohn was the high scorer for the Celtics with 26 points. Sam Jones had 25 and Bob Cousy 23. Chamberlain was the game's high scorer with 34.

BOSTON (132)					PHILA. (129)				
	G.	F.	PF.	P.		G.	F.	PF.	P.
Heinsohn	10	6	4	26	Arizin	6	5	3	17
Luscutoff	3	0	5	6	Johnson	3	9	4	15
Russell	8	2	1	18	Chamb'ln	15	4	3	34
Cousy	9	5	2	23	Gola	7	0	6	14
Sharman	5	0	0	10	Rodgers	6	2	5	14
Conley	3	2	4	8	Graboski	4	1	3	9
Ramsey	4	2	6	10	Attles	10	2	5	22
K. C. Jones	2	2	1	6	Conlin	1	2	0	4
S. Jones	10	5	3	25					
Total	52	28	27	132	Total	52	25	29	129

Boston ......26 34 35 37—132
Philadelphia ......28 35 36 30—129
Free throws missed—Heinsohn 3. Luscutoff. Russell 2. Cousy 2. Conley. Ramsey. K. C. Jones 3. Johnson 4. Chamberlain 6. Rodgers 3. Attles 2. Conlin.

November 25, 1960

PISTONS REGISTER 120-103 TRIUMPH

Chamberlain Runs Season Point Total to 3,016 as Warriors Lose

FORT WAYNE, Ind., March 10 (AP)—Wilt Chamberlain of the Philadelphia Warriors tonight became the first National Basketball Association player to score more than 3,000 points in one season. But his 32-point performance failed to keep the Detroit Pistons from winning, 120—103. Chamberlain brought his year's total to 3,016.

The 7-foot-1-inch Chamberlain set the previous record of 2,707 points last year as a rookie.

He got the sixteenth point that gave him 3,000, thirty-eight seconds before the end of the first half.

Bailey Howell of Detroit outscored Chamberlain with 35 points. The Pistons had the better of it every quarter.

After trailing by 61—53 at the half, Philadelphia gained a 73-73 tie late in the third quarter on Joe Graboski's shot from the field. Gene Shue of the Pistons hit a field goal to break the tie and Howell made three straight baskets to spread the margin.

The victory enabled Detroit to break a third-place tie with the Cincinnati Royals in the Eastern Division. The Pistons have only one remaining game, however, at New York on Sunday. Cincinnati has two weekend games at Los Angeles.

DETROIT (120)				PHILA. (103)			
	G.	F.	PF.	P.		G.	F.	PF.	P.
Howell	14	7	4	35	Arizin	7	2	2	16
Lee	2	7	1	11	Graboski	6	2	2	14
McMillon	5	2	2	12	Johnson	1	1	4	3
Dukes	5	0	4	10	Conlin	2	1	1	5
Ferry	3	1	3	7	Ch'berlain	14	4	0	32
Shue	11	5	3	27	Gola	4	4	1	12
Jones	0	0	0	0	Rodgers	5	3	3	12
Noble	2	1	2	5	Attles	3	2	2	6
Ohl	6	1	2	13	Hattin	1	1	1	3
Total	48	24	21	120	Total	42	19	17	103

Detroit ....33 · 28 · 30 · 29—120
Philadelphia ......26 · 27 · 27 · 23—103
Free throws missed—Lee 3 McMillon, Ohl, Johnson, Chamberlain, Gola, Rodgers 2, Attles 3, Hattin.
Attendance—10,013.

March 11, 1961

New Pro Fives to Get 3 Points on Long Shots

CHICAGO, June 5 (AP)—A 3-point "long" field goal was adopted today by the new American Basketball League.

The A. B. L., which will open an eighty-game schedule Oct. 27, will score 3 points for a field goal made from behind a line twenty-two feet from the basket. All other field goals will count the regular 2 points.

The league, winding up a week-end business session, also voted to use the Olympic-size eighteen-foot free-throw lane in which the three-second rule applies.

The schedule will end around April 1. Play-offs of the East-West sections will be held in midseason as well as at the end.

June 6, 1961

---

78 POINTS SCORED BY CHAMBERLAIN

But Lakers Beat Warriors in 3 Overtimes, 151-147

PHILADELPHIA, Dec. 8 (AP)—Wilt Chamberlain of the Philadelphia Warriors scored 78 points tonight, breaking the National Basketball Association scoring record, but the Warriors were beaten by the Los Angeles Lakers, 151—147, in a triple-overtime contest before 4,022 at Convention Hall.

In the opener, the Detroit Pistons defeated the Chicago Packers, 133—107.

Chamberlain broke the mark of 71 points set by Elgin Baylor of Los Angeles in November, 1960, against the New York Knickerbockers. Baylor had 63 points in tonight's game. Baylor had set his record in regulation play, without any overtime periods.

Chamberlain had 53 points tonight when the regulation game ended in a 109-tie.

Over all, Wilt hit on thirty-one of sixty-two field goal attempts and sixteen of thirty-one foul tries for his 78 points. He also grabbed forty-three rebounds.

Immediately after the game, Chamberlain's record was pronounced official.

DETROIT (133)				CHICAGO (107)			
	G.	F.	PF.	P.		G.	F.	PF.	P.
Lee	5	4	2	14	Johnson	3	1	4	7
Howell	5	1	5	11	Walker	5	6	5	16
Dukes	9	3	4	21	Bellamy	11	1	3	23
Shue	5	5	3	15	Green	4	8	5	16
Ohl	5	4	1	14	Leonard	3	2	3	8
Ferry	6	1	0	13	Tyra	3	0	2	6
Scott	7	2	5	16	Davis	2	0	2	4
Jones	4	2	2	10	Graboski	3	1	2	7
Moreland	4	6	0	14	Piontek	1	2	1	4
Egan	2	1	0	5	Turner	4	0	1	8
Total	52	29	22	133	Total	43	21	28	107

| | | | | | | ETAO | SH | SHR |
Detroit ....36 · 33 · 31 · 33—133
Chicago ....24 · 23 · 23 · 37—107
Free throws missed—Osowick, Petro 4, Shue 2, Ohl, Bellamy 4, Green 5, Tyra, Piontek.

LOS ANGELES (151)				PHILADELPHIA (147)			
	G.	F.	PF.	P.		G.	F.	PF.	P.
Baylor	23	17	4	63	Arizin	6	7	6	19
Jolliff	1	1	4	3	McShery	4	2	5	10
Krebs	2	0	6	4	Chamb'rl'n	31	16	4	78
Hundley	0	0	2	0	Gola	2	2	6	6
West	10	12	3	32	Rodgers	6	1	6	13
Selvey	8	1	4	17	Attles	6	3	3	15
LaRusso	6	3	6	15	Conlin	2	2	5	6
Felix	5	0	6	10	Larese	0	0	0	0
Hawkins	3	2	3	7					
Sims	0	0	1	0	Total	57	33	35	147
Total	57	37	38	151					

Los Angeles 25 · 28 · 32 · 24 · 12 · 12 · 18—151
Phila. ....34 · 28 · 21 · 26 · 12 · 12 · 14—147
Free throws missed—Baylor 7, Polliff, Krebs, West 2, Selvey 2, LaRusso, Hawkins, Arizin 3, McShery, Chamberlain 15, Gola, Rodgers 2, Attles.
Attendance—4,022.

December 9, 1961

Schayes' Streak Ends At Record 764 Games

BOSTON, Dec. 27 (AP)—Dolph Schayes' iron-man performance ended tonight when the Syracuse Nationals met the Los Angeles Lakers in a National Basketball Association doubleheader at Philadelphia.

Schayes, his right cheekbone shattered, is in a hospital here. The 33-year-old highest scorer in league history was injured last night in a collision with Al Attles of the Warriors in the first game of a double-header here.

A spokesman at Massachusetts General Hospital said Schayes probably would be held another day or so, but doubted that he could play for several weeks.

Schayes had a consecutive-game streak of 764, including playoffs. He had been in every Nats' game since Feb. 17, 1952.

December 28, 1961

Chamberlain Sets Scoring Mark

135-117 GAME WON BY PHILADELPHIA

Chamberlain Gets Record 40 Points in 2d Half, Sets Regulation-Contest Mark

PHILADELPHIA, Jan. 13 (UPI)—Wilt (the Stilt) Chamberlain scored 73 points for a National Basketball Association record as he led the Philadelphia Warriors to a 135-117 victory over the Chicago Packers before 3,516 fans tonight.

Wilt's total exceeded the regulation-game mark of 71 set by Elgin Baylor of Los Angeles on Nov. 15, 1960, at New York. However, it was 5 points below Chamberlain's league mark of 78 set in a triple overtime game with the Lakers here last Dec. 8.

The 40 points posted by Wilt in the second half also was an N. B. A. mark, eclipsing the 39 Wilt had rolled up twice and Hal Greer of Syracuse reached once.

Chamberlain tallied 14 points in the first period, 19 in the second, 17 in the third and 23 in the final session. He surpassed Baylor's mark on two free throws with thirty seconds left to play.

The Warriors, who trailed only in the early moments of the contest, posted their sixth straight victory over the Packers.

PHILADELPHIA (135)				CHICAGO (117)			
	G.	F.	PF.	P.		G.	F.	PF.	P.
Arizin	8	10	1	26	Tyre	6	3	6	15
Meschery		3	4	11	Saulesberry	2	1	6	5
Chamberlain	29	15	2	73	Bellamy	17	1	6	35
Rodgers	3	1	5	7	Green	5	3	3	13
Conlin	2	0	4		Davis	1	2	5	1
Ruklick	0	0	4	0	Johnson	5		2	14
Attles	6	0	2	12	Piontek	2	2	3	6
Larese		0	2	2	Turner	0	0	0	0
Total	51	33	20	135	Total	49	19	27	117

Philadelphia ....34 · 30 · 38 · 33—135
Chicago ....29 · 29 · 32 ·—117
Free throws missed—Arizin 2, Chamberlain 10, Rodgers, Bellamy, Green 2, Johnson 3, Piontek 3.
Attendance—3,516.

January 14, 1962

Chamberlain Scores 100 Points

HERSHEY, Pa., March 2 (AP)—Wilt Chamberlain set a National Basketball Association scoring record of 100 points tonight as the Philadelphia Warriors defeated the New York Knickerbockers, 169—147. The combined score was an association record, too.

Chamberlain toppled many records with his awesome display. The 7-foot-1-inch Warrior center set a league record for field goals (36), free throws (28 of 32), most points for a quarter (31), and most points for a

Associated Press

Wilt Chamberlain

half (59).

The 316 points by the two teams surpassed the record of 312 made in Boston's victory over Minneapolis on Feb. 27, 1959, at Boston. The Celtics set a single-team record in that game, when they beat the Lakers, 173—139.

Crowd Roots for Wilt

The crowd of 4,124 shrieked, "Give it to Wilt, give it to Wilt," as the Philadelphian scored again and again on his fallaway shots.

The Warriors realized early that Chamberlain was hot. So they fed him the ball repeatedly. The Knicks tried to stall and then tried to mob Chamberlain with defense in an effort to slow his scoring.

In the final period Darrall Imhoff, who had been assigned to guard Chamberlain most of the night, fouled out.

When Wilt hit 100, a few seconds before the end, the fans swarmed onto the court. The game was held up until they were removed.

The Warriors seemed determined to run away with the game, scrambling to a 19-3 advantage. However, with Richie Guerin hitting, the Knicks drew closer and it was 79-68 at the half. But Guerin, with 39 points, Cleveland Buckner (33) and Willie Naulis (31) couldn't overcome the lift given the Warriors by Wilt. Chamberlaind had twenty-five rebounds.

Chamberlain's effort broke the league scoring record of 78 points, a mark he had set earlier this season.

The recognized collegiate scoring record also is 100, set by Frank Selvy for Furman against Newberry in 1954. Selvy now plays for the Los Angeles Lakers.

Two over-100 efforts — by Paul Arizin of Villanova and Bevo Francis of Rio Grande (Ohio) College—are not recognized by the National Collegiate Athletic Association because they were made against junior-college teams.

Among the records set tonight was one by the Knicker-

bockers. Their 147 points was the most ever scored by a losing team, topping the previous mark of 139 by Minneapolis against Boston in 1959.

Wilt said, "I wasn't even thinking of hitting 100, but after putting in nine straight free throws I was thinking about a foul-shooting record. It was my greatest game."

He credited his team-mates with helping him set the record. "It would have been impossible to score this many if they hadn't kept feeding me," he said.

PHILA. (169)				KNICKS (147)			
	G.	F.	PF.	P.		G.	F.	PF.	P.
Arizin	7	2	0	16	Naulls	9	13	5	31
Meschery	7	2	4	16	Green	3	0	5	6
Chamb'n	36	28	2	100	Imhoff	3	1	6	7
Rodgers		9	5	11	Guerin	13	13		39
Attles	8	1	4	17	Butler	4	0	1	8
Larese	4	1	5	9	Budd	6	1	1	13
Conlin	0	0	1	0	Butcher	3	4	5	10
Ruklick	0	0	2	0	Buckner	16	1	4	33
Luckenbill	0	0	2	0					
					Total	57	33	32	147
Total	63	43	25	169					

Philadelphia .... 42 37 46 44—169
Knicks .... 26 42 38 41—147
Free throws missed — Chamberlain 4, Rodgers 3, Ruklick 2, Naulls 2, Guerin 4, Butcher 2.
Attendance—4,124.

March 3, 1962

CELTICS' TRIUMPH SETS N.B.A. MARK

Boston Routs Nats, 142-110, for 60th Victory

BOSTON, March 13 (UPI)— The Boston Celtics broke the National Basketball Association record tonight for games won during the regular season. They scored their sixtieth victory by defeating the Syracuse National, 142—110.

The Celts wiped out the record they set during the 1959-1960 season. Syracuse, playing without the injured Dolph Schayes and Hal Greer, was outclassed in the second half of the game at the Boston Garden.

The game closed out the division champion Celtics' schedule.

BOSTON (142)				SYRACUSE (110)			
	G.	F.	PF.	P.		G.	F.	PF.	P.
Heinsohn	8	3	5	19	Gambee	7	2	3	16
Sanders	13	4	5	30	Shaffer	9	1	5	19
Russell	10	6	5	26	Kerr	8	8	0	24
S. Jones	4	4	1	12	Bianchi	3	1	3	7
Cousy	3	6	2	12	Costello	1	1	3	3
Ramsey	4	8	1	16	Roberts	7	2	5	16
K. C. Jones	2	1	3	5	Neumann	1	1	4	3
Phillips	0	2	2	2	Graboski	4	1	4	9
Guarilia	3	0	1	6					
Braun	7	0	0	14					
Total	54	34	25	142	Total	43	24	27	110

Boston .... 37 27 35 43—142
Syracuse .... 32 24 26 28—110
Free throws missed—Russell 2, S. Jones 2, K. C. Jones 3, Kerr, Roberts 2, Neumann.
Attendance—4,651.

March 14, 1962

TEN LEAGUE RECORDS SET BY CHAMBERLAIN

The National Basketball Association officially totaled Wilt Chamberlain's record point production of 4,029 yesterday and

credited the most prolific scorer in league history with nine other marks.

Winning the individual scoring title for the third straight year, the 7-foot-1-inch star of the Philadelphia Warriors became the first man in league history to enter the 4,000-point circle. He set a record with a scoring average of 50.4 points a game and established these other standards:

Most field goals attempted (3,159), most field goals made (1,597), most free throws attempted (1,363), most free throws made (835), most minutes played (3,882), most games scoring 50 or more points (44), most fouls missed in one season (528) and most points in one game (100).

Two other league records were established. Walt Bellamy, a Chicago Packers' rookie who wound up second in the scoring race with 2,495 points and a 31.6 average, eclipsed Chamberlain's field-goal percentage standard by hitting on .513 of his shots.

Oscar Robertson of the Cincinnati Royals, third in scoring with 2,432 points and a 30.8 average, surpassed his own assist record of 9.7 by averaging 11.2 a game. He also bettered the total-assist mark with 889, exceeding the 715 by Bob Cousy of the Boston Celtics.

The Celtics, who set a league record by winning sixty games, did not have a player among the ten leading scorers.

Chamberlain led the league in rebounds with 2,052 and an average of 25.6 and Dolph Schayes of the Syracuse Nationals was first in free-throw accuracy with a .896 percentage on 286 successful tosses in 319 chances.

THE LEADING SCORERS
(Total Games In Parentheses)

	G.	F.	P.	AV.
1—Chamberl'n, Phil. (80)	1,597	835	4,029	50.4
2—Bellamy, Chic. (79)	973	549	2,495	31.6
3—Robertson, Cin (79)	866	700	2,432	30.8
4—Pettit, St. Louis (78)	867	695	2,429	31.1
5—West, L. A. (75)	799	712	2,310	30.8
6—Guerin, Knicks (78)	839	625	2,303	29.5
7—Naulls, Knicks (75)	747	383	1,877	25.0
8—Baylor, L. A. (48)	680	476	1,836	38.2
9—Twyman, Cin. (80)	739	353	1,831	22.9
10—Hagan, St. Louis (77)	701	362	1,764	22.9

March 17, 1962

PIPERS SET BACK STEERS 106-102

Barnett Is Star as Victors Capture A. B. L. Crown

KANSAS CITY, April 9 (AP)—Dick Barnett scored 10 points in the final quarter as the Cleveland Pipers defeated the Kansas City Steers, 106—1022, for the American Basketball League championship tonight.

The victory was the third straight for the Pipers, who dropped the first two games in the three-of-five title series when it opened in Kansas City.

Cleveland, which failed to ap-

pear for the final game when it was originally scheduled for last night, came to play this one. The Pipers took an 8-point lead in the first quarter, but 13 points by Larry Staverman and a tip-in by Gene Tormohlen at the buzzer evened the count at 26-all.

Free throws were the difference as the Pipers left the court with a 49-46 half-time lead. Outscored, 13—16, from the field, Cleveland converted twenty-two of twenty-eight free throws by that point. Kansas City made fourteen of seventeen.

The Steers rallied in the third period and led, 76—72, before baskets by Barnett, Bob Keller and Connie Dierking pushed the Pipers in front, 79—77.

Bill Bridges, the game's leading scorer with 31 points, kept Kansas City in contention for the first four minutes of the final period, but a barrage of baskets by Barnett and Dierking vaulted Cleveland into a commanding lead.

CLEVELAND (106)				KANSAS CITY (102)			
	G.	F.	PF.	P.		G.	F.	PF.	P.
Darrow	1	7	3	9	Tormohlen	4	2	5	10
Barnett	10	6	3	26	King	2	0	3	4
Warley	2	1	0	5	Mantis	3	3	3	10
Cox	4	2	4	13	Bridges	13	5	5	31
Dierking	8	4	5	20	Staverman	10	6	5	26
Dees	3	6	1	12	Pruitt	0	0	0	0
Romanoff	0	0	2	0	Comley	2	0	4	4
Barnhill	5	3	2	14	Vann	1	0	1	2
Keller	3	1	2	7	Wilfong	3	4	1	10
					Patterson	2	1	3	5
Total	36	30	22	106	Total	40	21	29	102

Cleveland .... 26 23 30 27—106
Kansas City ..... 26 20 31 25—102
Three-point field goals—Cox 3, Barnhill, Mantis.
Free throws missed—Darrow, Barnett, Warley, Dierking, Dees, Keller 3, Tormohlen 3, Bridges, Vann.
Attendance—3,000.

April 10, 1962

Celtics Take Fourth Straight N.B.A. By Beating Lakers in Overtime

RUSSELL EXCELS IN 110-107 GAME

Celtic Equals Play-Off Mark With 44 Rebounds—Run of Crowns Is Record

BOSTON, April 18 (AP)—The Boston Celtics captured their fourth consecutive National Basketball Association championship tonight by vanquishing the Los Angeles Lakers, 110—107, in overtime on the heroics of Sam Jones and Bill Russell.

Boston led most of the way in the game, played before a capacity crowd of 13,909 fans in Boston Garden. But the Celtics had to beat down the tenacious Lakers in a five-minute extra session after Frank Selvy had brought Los Angeles even in the final forty seconds of regulation play.

The Celtics were in dire trouble because personal fouls late in the game had sent Tom Sanders, Jim Loscutoff and Tom Heinsohn to the bench. With seventy-four seconds remaining, Boston was leading, 100—96.

Selvy made it 100—98 with forty seconds to go and tied that score twenty seconds later. Then he barely missed on what would have been the winner with three seconds to go.

Baylor Gets 41 Points

The Celtics made it look easy in the overtime period. Sam Jones scored 5 of Boston's 10 points in the extra session and Russell added 4. Bob Cousy got the other point.

Elgin Baylor had put the Lakers in front, 102—100, with a pair of free throws at the outset of the overtime. But the visitors couldn't score from the floor until Tom Hawkins netted a pair of baskets in the final minute.

Baylor, who must report back to his Army duties at Fort Lewis, Wash., led all scorers with 41 points. Jerry West, who with Baylor sparked the Lakers' fourth-period comeback, had 35.

Probably the greatest single contribution in the game was made by the 6-foot 10-inch Russell, the league's most valuable players. He hauled in forty-four rebounds, tying a play-off record, and scored 30 points as the Celtics won the four-of-seven-game series, four games to three.

The Lakers won three straight N.B.A. crowns from 1952 to 1954 when the franchise was in Minneapolis. But never before had a team put four titles together.

A Defensive Battle

The Celtics did it despite a cluster of injuries and their second-half foul troubles. Los Angeles also suffered, losing the services of Rudy LaRusso, Baylor and Jim Krebs in the overtime period.

LaRusso went out after 1 minute 45 seconds. Baylor fouled out with two minutes left and Krebs followed a minute later with the score 110-103.

The game developed into a defensive battle after both teams got away to slow starts.

In the overtime period, Russell tied the score at 102-102 with a basket at the 1:10 mark. Sam Jones put the Celtics ahead when he tallied on a lay-up at 1:30. Fouled on the play, he also made good on the free throw for a 105-102 lead.

Russell converted on one of two free throws at 2:18 and sank another free throw at 3:10, increasing the lead to 107-102. After Selvy had hit on a free throw, Sam Jones sank a long jump shot with less than a minute to go.

After Hawkins' two late baskets, Cousy started dribbling the ball and ran out the remaining seconds.

BOSTON (110)	G.	F.	PF.	P.	LOS ANGELES (107)	G.	F.	PF.	P.
Heinsohn	3	2	6	8	Baylor	13	15	6	41
Ramsey	4	15	6	23	Hawkins	2	0	4	4
Sanders	3	0	6	6	LaRusso	3	1	6	7
Loscutoff	3	0	6	6	Jolliff	0	0	2	0
Russell	8	14	2	30	Krebs	4	0	6	8
Cousy	3	2	4	8	Felix	0	2	3	2
K. C. Jones	1	0	2	2	West	14	7	4	35
S. Jones	12	3	2	27	Hundley	0	0	1	0
Braun	0	0	1	0	Selvy	2	6	3	10
Guarilia	0	0	1	0					
Total	37	36	36	110	Total	38	31	35	107

Boston ...22 31 22 25 10—110
Los Angeles .22 25 28 25 7—107
Free throws missed—Heinsohn, Ramsey, Russell 3, Cousy 8, S. Jones, Baylor 6, La Russo 2, Felix 2, West 2, Selvy 2.
Attendance—13,909.

April 19, 1962

American Basketball League Failure Makes 100 Pro Players Free Agents

N.B.A. EYES STARS FROM RIVAL LOOP

But Kansas City Clubowner Considers Bid to Revive the American League

CHICAGO, Jan. 1 (AP) — With all clubs operating in the red, the American Basketball League has suspended operations and thrown some 100 players on the market as free agents.

"Not a single club was operating in the black," said Commissioner Abe Saperstein. He announced the decision to suspend yesterday after telephone conferences with club directors.

Several National Basketball Association Clubs reportedly are in touch with A.B.L. players to whom they have N.B.A. rights through draft and trade procedure.

St. Louis Hawks are said to be interested in Bill Bridges of Kansas City, the A.B.L. top scorer, and his six-foot-nine teammate, Gene Tormohlen.

King Drafted by Zephyrs

Larry Staverman and Morris King of Kansas City and Roger Kaiser of Pittsburgh are said to be on the shopping list of the Chicago Zephyrs. the Zephyrs drafted Kaiser and King and traded Dave Piontek to Cincinnati for the rights to Staverman.

Syracuse is said to be anxious to get Ben Worley of Long Beach, drafted last summer. San Francisco is interested in Wille Spraggins of Philadelphia, a Warrior draftee last year.

The prize catch may be the former Ohio State All-American Jerry Lucas. The rights are held by the Cleveland Pipers, who withdrew from the A.B.L. and sought an NBA franchise without avail.

Lucas has not played a pro game so far. He was a draft choice of the N.B.A.'s Cincinnati Royals.

Some reports place losses of the A.B.L. at $1,000,000 last year and $250,000 this season.

Ken Krueger, owner of the Kansas City Steers, said he would try to reorganize the A.B.L. A Pittsburgh Rens spokesman said that team would seek an N.B.A. franchise.

Krueger Gives Plans

Of reorganization plans, Krueger said in St. Louis:"Oakland and Long Beach want to continue and a Pittsburgh representative has indicated that club might want to stay in the new set-up. I have suggested that Johnny Dee. the Kansas City coach, be appointed commissioner under any such new realignment. We might be able to move the Philadelphia franchise to another city."

The six-team loop, founded by Saperstein two years ago, had games scheduled through March 17.

Saperstein declared the second-year champion to be Kansas City with a 22-9 record.

Long Beach finished 16-8, Pittsburgh 12-10, Oakland 11-4, Philadelphia 10-18. Chicago 8-20.

An A.B.L. innovation was the three-point field goal initiated for shots made 25 feet or more from the basket.

January 2, 1963

Celtics Down Lakers

COUSY STANDOUT IN 112-109 GAME

LOS ANGELES, April 24 (U P I) — Bob Cousy finished a 13-year pro basketball career tonight by leading the Boston celtics to a 112-109 victory over the Los Angeles Lakers and a record fifth straight National Basketball association title.

The 34-year-old Cousy injured his left ankle early in the fourth quarter when the Celtics had a 9-point lead at 92—83. While he was on the bench the Lakers almost closed the gap.

Cousy returned with the Celtics leading, 100—99, steadied the team and directed Boston to its clinching victory in the four-of-seven-game series. The Lakers had two triumphs.

Cousy got 18 points but was outscored by his teammate. Tom Heinsohn who had 22. Heinsohn played a big part in the closing minutes when he sank four free throws to put the Celtics in front, 112—107.

the Celtics in front, 112—107.

Elgin Baylor had a poor first half, scoring only 9 points as Tom Sanders stuck to him step for step. The Laker star managed to spring loose in the second half and scored a total of 28 points for the night. Jerry West of the Lakers topped all scorers with 32 points.

The game was played before a record Sports Arena crowd of 15,521.

This was the second straight Celtic victory over the Lakers in the N.B.A. final playoffs. Boston won last year in. an overtime period in the seventh game.

BOSTON (112)				LOS ANGELES (109)			
	G.	F.	P.		G.	F.	P.
Cousy	8	2	18	Selvy	1	1	3
Havlicek	8	2	18	Wiley	3	0	6
Heinsohn	8	6	22	Baylor	11	6	28
K. C. Jones	3	3	9	LaRusso	9	1	19
S. Jones	2	1	5	West	13	6	32
Ramsey	4	2	10	Ellis	3	3	9
Russell	5	2	12	Krebs	0	0	0
Sanders	9	0	18	Barnett	4	4	12
Total	47	18	112	Total	44	21	109

Boston .... 33 33 26 20—112
Los Angeles ... 35 17 28 29—109

Free throws missed—Boston: Havlicek, Heinsohn 3. K. C. Jones, S. Jones 2, Ramsey, Russell 3. Los Angeles: Selvy, Wiley, West 4.

Personal fouls—Boston: Cousy 4, Havlicek 2, Heinsohn 4. K. C. Jones 3, S. Jones 3, Ramsey . Russell 3, Sanders 5. Los Angeles: Selvy 3, Wiley 3, Baylor 3, La-Russo 4, Ellis, Krebs 3, Barnett 3.

Attendance—15,521.

April 25, 1963

N. B. A. APPROVES SYRACUSE SHIFT

Pro Basketball Will Return to Philadelphia This Year

By MICHAEL STRAUSS

The National Basketball Association's Board of Governors yesterday unanimously approved a shift of the Syracuse franchise to Philadelphia.

The stage for the change was set earlier this month when Darny Biasone, owner of the Nationals, sold his controlling stock to a Philadelphia group. Yesterday's ratification was necessary to make the move official.

"The cost of operation has risen too high to keep a major league club in Syracuse," said Biasone. "The area just does not have enough population to enable a major team to flourish."

Scheduled to take over as president of the new club — which still will be known as the Nationals — is Irv Kosloff, who represents the majority of the new stockholders. Other promi-

nent stockholders are Isaac Richman and D. Donald Jamieson, attorneys in Philadelphia, which long had been the home of major-league basketball.

Last season, Philadelphia, where the Sphas played in the American League three decades ago, was without representation in the N.B.A. The absence was caused by the sale of the Warriors, a charter member in the league, to a San Francisco group that moved the franchise to the coast.

Now Syracuse, a stronghold of professional basketball, is without major league representation. The city was a member of the old National Basketball League. It entered the N.B.A. when the National League and the Basketball Association of America merged in 1949.

Syracuse has been unable to make the Nationals a profitable investment, primarily because the Nats played at War Memorial Coliseum, the smallest home arena in the circuit.

Since their appearance in the N.B.A., the Nationals almost always have fared well in the records. Last season, they finished second in the Eastern Division, but lost in the first round of the playoffs to the Cincinnati Royals.

May 23, 1963

Walter Kennedy Is Selected to Succeed Podoloff as President of N. B. A.

PAY IS ESTIMATED AT OVER $25,000

Kennedy Term Undisclosed —Podoloff Steps Down After 17-Year Rule

By MICHAEL STRAUSS

In a move that had been predicted for weeks, the National Basketball Association named J. Walter Kennedy, 49-year-old Mayor of Stamford, Conn., as its new president yesterday.

Kennedy will succeed the 73-year-old Maurice Podoloff on Sept. 1, Podoloff, retiring with "a comfortable pension," has presided over the league since it was organized in 1946. Originally, the league was known as the Basketball Association of America.

Kennedy was named after a unanimous vote by the club owners. The election was held during the third session of their annual

NEW N.B.A. PRESIDENT: J. Walter Kennedy, left, Mayor of Stamford, Conn., who will resign in August for basketball post, shown with his predecessor, Maurice Podoloff.

meeting at the Hotel Roosevelt. No salary was announced but Kennedy revealed it was well over ¢225,000.

"My pay as Mayor of Stamford is ¢12,500," he said. "This represents only part of my income, since I also have been active as public relations consultant for years. I can't disclose my salary but I will say it is more than double my annual pay as Mayor."

Kennedy did not reveal the length of the term of office but indicated his contract was for longer than a year.

A Sport He Loves

"Personally, I am taking this job feeling I am going to hold it for a lifetime," he said. "I have harbored additional political ambi-

tions but I am passing them up in order to get back into a sport I love. I wouldn't be making a change if I didn't feel it was going to last."

Kennedy plans to resign as Stamford's Mayor in August. He explained that the Sept. 1 starting date was agreeable for all concerned since it would enable Podoloff to clear his desk of current business and would enable him to complete his duties as Mayor.

Kennedy said he planned to keep the league's offices in the Empire State Building in Manhattan. He said he would sit in on league business "from time to time" until he actually took over his new position. He emphasized he realized he was stepping in at a time when the N.B.A. had reached new heights in prosperity.

Praise for Podoloff

"If I could look forward to retiring in 17 years under the same circumstances as Podoloff," he said, "I'd be the happiest character in the world. He's done a great job through years that really represented problems."

The club owners named Podoloff honorary chairman of the Board of Governors. The retiring president said he was vague about what his duties would be in that capacity.

The meeting is expected to end today with discussion of the schedule for the 1963-64 campaign. Yesterday the officials raised the playoff pool from ¢125,000 to ¢150,000, confirmed Boston as the site for the league's all-star game in

January and decided not to consider applications for new franchises at this time.

May 2, 1963

Zephyrs Are Bullets Now
BALTIMORE, June 4 (AP)—Baltimore, the new entry in the National Basketball Association, will use the nickname of Bullets. The club, which came from Chicago, was called the Zephyrs last season.

June 5, 1963

Warriors Beat Knicks as Wilt Breaks Record

NEW YORK LOSES IN BOSTON, 118-89

Chamberlain Sinks 18 Field Goals in Row—Celtics Pin 114-78 Loss on Lakers

BOSTON, Nov. 27 (AP)—Wilt Chamberlain set a record for consecutive field goals tonight as the San Francisco Warriors crushed the New York Knicks, 118-89, in a National

Basketball Association game.

In the second game of the double-header, the Boston Celtics defeated the Los Angeles Lakers, 114—78.

Chamberlain scored 38 points and hit 18 shots in a row after missing on his first attempt. None of his shots traveled more than six feet during the record run, which was not broken because Wilt sat out the fourth period.

The previous mark of 13 was set by Larry Costello while playing for Syracuse in a game at Boston Dec. 8, 1961.

Chamberlain scored only 8 points in the first period, then got 24 in the second quarter as the Warriors piled up a 74-41 lead at halftime.

Guy Rodgers of the Warriors had 15 assists in the first half. Rodgers got only one more assist, leaving him far short of the N.B.A. record of 28 he holds jointly with Bob Cousy.

The Celtics' victory was their sixth in a row and 13th in 14 league games.

The Celtics were in command throughout as Sam Jones scored 14 points in the first period to spark a 28-17 lead.

The Lakers cut the deficit to 4 points in the second quarter, but the Celtics got 9 straight points.

Boston led by as much as 43 points early in the final period. Elgin Baylor of the Lakers, hobbled by a charley horse, was held to 13 points. Jerry West was high for the losers with 16 points.

Sam Jones led Boston's attack with 20 points. Boston now holds a 2-0 edge in season play with Los Angeles.

SAN FRANCISCO (118)				KNICKS (89)			
	G.	F.	P.		G.	F.	P.
Hightower	2	1-2	5	Green	3	1-4	7
Meschery	4	7-8	15	Chappell	7	0-3	14
Chambrln	18	2-3	38	McGill	10	2-2	22
Phillips	4	0-2	8	Heyman	5	0-1	10
Rodgers	5	1-1	11	Gola	0	2-4	16
Hill	6	1-2	13	Conley	0	5-6	5
Thurmond	5	2-4	12	Butcher	0	0-0	4
Sears	1	3-3	5	Rudometkin	2	0-1	4
Windsor	2	0-0	4	Hoover	2	1-1	5
Lee	4	1-1	7	Butler	2	0-0	4
				Duffy	1	0-0	2
Total	50	18-26	118	Total	39	11-22	89

San Francisco .... 28 46 25 19—118
Knicks .... 21 20 27 21— 89

BOSTON (114)				LOS ANGELES (78)			
	G.	F.	P.		G.	F.	P.
Heinsohn	6	3-4	15	Barnett	3	0-3	6
Sanders	6	4-7	16	West	5	6-7	16
Russell	6	2-5	14	Ellis	7	2-4	16
S. Jones	7	6-6	20	La Russo	0	6-7	6
K.C.Jones	2	1-1	5	Baylor	5	3-4	13
Naulls	2	2-3	6	Selvy	3	1-2	7
Ramsey	2	3-3	7	Nelson	1	3-4	5
Havlicek	6	4-4	16	Wiley	2	0-0	4
McCarthy	1	0-0	2	King	1	3-4	5
Lovelette	3	0-1	6	Krebs	0	0-0	0
Loscutoff	2	0-0	4	Reed	0	0-0	0
Seigfried	1	1-1	3				
Total	44	26-35	114	Total	27	24-35	78

Boston .... 28 22 30 34—114
Los Angeles ... 17 20 18 23— 78

Attendance—13,909.

November 28, 1963

Kerr Plays 707th Game to Set N.B.A. Mark

FORMER RECORD OWNED BY COACH

Schayes Sees His Mark Snapped — Celtics Beat Hawks, 107 to 100

PHILADELPHIA, Dec. 28 (AP)—Johnny Kerr of Phila-

delphia tonight played in his 707th consecutive game for a National Basketball Association record as the 76ers defeated the Los Angeles Lakers, 114-100.

Kerr, 31 years old, broke the mark of 706 set in 1961 by Dolph Schayes, now the coach of the 76ers.

Hal Grer led the 76ers with 24 points and Kerr made 23. Jerry West of Los Angeles was high for the game with 29.

Kerr hasn't missed a game since he started playing in the

league 10 years ago. Schayes set his record of 706 while with the Syracuse Nationals, now the 76ers, from Feb. 17, 1952, through Dec. 26, 1961.

Kerr and Schayes are the only players in the 18-year history of the league to surpass the 700-game figure in regular-season play.

The game was marked by several injuries, including a mild concussion suffered by Mendy Rudolph, the referee. He collided with Rudy LaRusso of Los Angeles and both fell to the floor. Rudolph was taken to the Philadelphia General Hospi-

tal and the other referee, John Vanak, finished the game alone. LaRusso was able to continue.

PHILADELPHIA (114)				LOS ANGELES (100)			
	G.	F.	P.		G.	F.	P.
Walker	5	5-7	15	Baylor	9	8-9	26
Worley	7	4-8	18	LaRusso	2	8-8	12
Kerr	9	5-6	23	Wiley	0	0-0	0
Costello	4	0-0	8	West	11	7-8	29
Greer	9	6-6	24	Barnett	5	6-8	16
Neumann	3	0-0	6	Nelson	1	2-5	4
Bianchi	3	1-1	7	Ellis	3	1-1	7
Greenspan	1	3-4	5	Selvy	1	1-3	3
Dierking	1	0-0	2	Reed	0	0-0	0
White		2-2	6	Krebs	0	0-0	0
				King	1	1-2	3
Total	44	26-34	114	Total	33	34-44	100

Philadelphia .... 29 28 26 31—114
Los Angeles ..... 25 29 25 21—100

Fouled out—Worley, Greer.
Attendance—3,162.

December 29, 1963

East All-Stars Protect Early Lead and Defeat West Five

ROBERTSON VOTED MOST VALUABLE

Game's Other Players Are Far Below Form Before 13,464 Fans at Boston

By LEONARD KOPPETT
Special to The New York Times

BOSTON, Jan. 14—The National Basketball Association's lifelong knack of finding some way to tarnish its best moments manifested itself again tonight as the East defeated the West, 111—107, in the 14th annual All-Star Game before 13,464 at the Boston Garden.

This time it was the players, not the owners, who spoiled the chance to have the N. B. A., still struggling after 18 years for a true major league image, put its best foot forward. By bringing to a head an old grievance about not having a pension plan, they came within minutes of a public relations disaster.

The largest collection ever of basketball stars had been assembled by Walter Brown, the president of the Boston Celtics and the host. The original Celtics of the 1920's, young old-timers from the 1940's and 1950's, and today's top 20 stars were on hand. Television cameras were bringing the story to viewers across the nation.

Until a few minutes before game time, however, it seemed a player strike was coming. The game did start late, and had it then lived up in quality to some of the brilliant All-Star performances of the past, some glamor might have been salvaged.

A Drab Game

Instead, the game was lackluster. No one can say whether fatigue from travel difficulties or absorption with pension problems was the cause; there have been drab All-Star Games

Associated Press Wirephoto

IN THE STRETCH: Bailey Howell (18) of the West and Oscar Robertson (14) of the East reach for a rebound in the first period of the pro all-star game at Boston Garden.

before. What can be said is that these players, who talk so often of the importance of "the right mental attitude" toward a game, spent the day negotiating instead of resting, thinking of retirement pay instead of basketball.

So the whole story of the game can be summed up simply: After an even 21 minutes, the East managed an 11-2 burst for a 59-49 half-time lead. This soared to 18 points soon after intermission, and the West could never quite catch up, although it closed to within 4 points in the third and fourth quarters and to 3 with 30 seconds to play.

Oscar Robertson, a star.

among stars no matter what else is happening, was awarded the most valuable player trophy. He scored 26 points, made eight assists and took down 14 rebounds. No one else scored more than 19 (Wilt Chamberlain and Bob Pettit), no one else got more than five assists, and only the giants outrebounded him — Russell with 21, Chamberlain with 20 and Pettit with 17.

This was Robertson's fourth All-Star Game, two for the West and two for the East, and he has never been on a loser. It's not a coincidence. The East now leads in the series, 9—5.

January 15, 1964

The Line-Ups

EAST (111)	G.	F.	P.	WEST (107)	G.	F.	P.
Heinsohn	5	0-0	10	Pettit	6	7-9	19
Lucas	3	5-6	11	Baylor	5	5-9	15
Russell	6	1-2	13	Bellamy	4	3-5	11
Robertson	10	6-10	26	Rodgers	3	0-0	6
Greer	5	3-4	13	West	8	1-1	17
Chappell	1	2-2	4	Chmberl'n	4	11-14	19
S. Jones	8	0-0	16	Wilkens	1	1-1	3
Embry	6	1-1	13	Howell	1	0-0	2
Walker	2	0-0	4	Ohl	3	2-2	8
Gola	0	1-2	1	Dischinger	2	3-3	7
Total	46	19-27	111	Total	37	33-44	107

East .... 25 .... 25—111
West .... 22 .... 27 .... 28 .... 30—107
Attendance—13,464.

N.B.A. Players Threaten Strike In Dispute Over Pension Plan

Special to The New York Times

BOSTON, Jan. 14—A long-smoldering dispute between National Basketball Association players and owners concerning the establishment of a pension plan erupted in an implicit strike threat that caused a delay in the start of tonight's East West all-star game.

The game went on only after a direct confrontation between the 20 all-stars and J. Walter Kennedy, the league president, in the East's dressing room less than 15 minutes before the scheduled starting time.

A crowd of 13,464 was in the Boston Garden and television cameras were ready for a nationwide network showing of the game.

Introductions had been scheduled for 9 P.M. It was 8:55 P.M. when Bob Pettit came out of the dressing room meeting, which Kennedy had left a few moments earlier, and notified the league president that the all-stars would play. They had never actually said they wouldn't, but that was the implication of their actions during the preceding hours.

Dispute Began in 1957

The history of the dispute is long and complicated. It began here in Boston, seven years ago, when the players openly threatened to strike on the afternoon of the 1957 game.

An immediate meeting with Maurice Podoloff, the league president then, established the effectiveness of the N.B.A. Player Association, of which Bob Cousy was a leader. Several improvements were obtained in contract and playing conditions and pension planning was begun. The game went on.

Since then, virtually no headway has been made in establishing any pension plan, and players have expressed bitterness at what they consider calculated delaying action by the owners.

The president of the players' group is Tom Heinsohn of Boston. Pettit is vice president. Each team has a player representative and there is a pension plan committee.

The owners have designated Fred Zollner, the owner of the Detroit Pistons, as their representative in whatever pension plan dealings there might be.

Today's events and their background, as described by Kennedy in a hastily called press conference while the game was beginning, went this way:

In September, when Kennedy succeeded Podoloff, Heinsohn and Lawrence Fleischer, a lawyer representing the player group, told Kennedy they wanted to discuss pensions when the owners met here in January.

Kennedy said he inherited correspondence that showed Podoloff had forwarded a specific pension plan to Heinsohn in 1961 or 1962, and that Hein-

sohn had neither accepted nor rejected it.

In November, Kennedy relayed Heinsohn's request for a January meeting to the owners. They turned it down, saying they wouldn't discuss the subject until Heinsohn accepted or rejected the plan that had been offered.

Then Kennedy set up a meeting involving himself, Zollner, Heinsohn and other player committee members, but with no lawyers on either side. This was held this morning, and with Heinsohn were John Kerr of Philadelphia, Tom Gola of New York and Guy Rodgers of San Francisco.

At this meeting, it developed that Heinsohn and Podoloff were involved in a misunderstanding. Heinsohn hadn't realized that the specific plan offered needed an answer. It was then agreed that, if the players would accept the offered plan, implementation of it would be taken up at the next meeting of the owners, possibly in February but certainly in May.

This agreement was put in writing, signed by Kennedy and Zollner, and apparently accepted by the four players.

During the afternoon, the owners met to discuss changes in the league constitution, a complex matter. Three times Kennedy was given a message to "call Fleischer." He continued to preside over his own meeting and did not answer.

Meeting Called Quickly

At about 5:40 P.M., Kennedy was in his hotel room. Heinsohn and Pettit joined him. They said he must meet with their lawyer at 6:30 P.M. Kennedy said he couldn't but that if it was imperative he would meet them in 10 minutes.

At 5:50 P.M. Kennedy, in his room, met with Fleischer, Heinsohn, Pettit, Bill Russell of Boston and Lenny Wilkens of St. Louis. The players demanded a meeting with all the owners before game time to put in writing a promise to put into effect now the pension plan discussed this morning.

Kennedy said this wasn't possible, but in the course of the next hour and a half he spoke to the representatives of all the clubs. They were unanimous in their refusal to meet, because of the assurance Zollner had given earlier. The players now said they weren't satisfied with these assurances.

At 8:25 P.M., Kennedy appeared in the dressing room. He repeated the refusal and made a brief speech about the background case. After 20 minutes or so, the players asked him to retire so that they could vote.

Just what messages were sent by various owners to their own players wasn't clear, but one report had Bob Short of the

Lakers threatening to fire his stars, Elgin Baylor and Jerry West, if they didn't come out.

At 8:55 P.M. Pettit told Kennedy they would play.

"They never actually said they wouldn't," Kennedy repeated.

"Did you surmise it?" he was asked.

"You surmise it," answered Kennedy. "I'm just describing what happened.".

This is the most serious breach the players and owners have had to date. It came at a time when little talk about it had been in the air. Evidently the fight is just beginning.

LEONARD KOPPETT
January 15, 1964

Pettit Takes Over As Highest Scorer With 19,215 Points

ST. LOUIS, Feb. 8 (UPI)— Bob Pettit got 18 points tonight and became the highest scorer in National Basketball Association history, but the St. Louis Hawks dropped a 103-97 game to the San Francisco Warriors.

The 31-year-old Pettit has 19,215 points and passed the Philadelphia 76er player-coach, Dolph Schayes, who scored 6 points against the Los Angeles Lakers for a total of 19,209.

Pettit was held to 3 points in the first period. Then after he

had made two baskets early in the second period, the game was stopped and the former St. Louis Cardial star, Stan Musial, presented him with a trophy and the game ball.

The Warriors took a 29-26 first-period lead and a 48-44 half-time advantage. They increased their margin to 66-53, but the Hawks rallied to take an 80-77, lead after three periods.

Richie Guerin of the Hawks fought with Gary Phillips in the third period. The officials permitted both to remain in the game, although Guerin grabbed Phillips around the waist and flung him to the floor.

Phillips tied the score at 84—84 in the fourth period, but Chico Vaughn put the Hawks ahead permanently.

Wilt Chamberlain, with 30 points, was high for the Warriors. Guy Rodgers added 25, and Tom Meschery and Wayne Hightower contributed 15 each. Zelmo Beaty was high for St. Louis with 22. He fouled out in the fourth period.

Pettit was off his usual marksmanship, connecting for seven of 14 field-goal attempts and four of 10 free throws. However, he made 18 rebounds against 17 for Chamberlain.

SAN FRAN. (103)	G.	F.	P.	ST. LOUIS (97)	G.	F.	P.
Champ'n	10	10-16	30	PeHit	7	4-10	18
Hightower	5	5-7	15	Hagan	4	5-5	13
Meschery	3	9-9	15	Beaty	10	2-4	22
Attle	1	1-2	3	Wilkens	1	1-2	3
Phillips	5	3-5	13	Guerin	6	2-2	14
Rodgers	11	3-6	25	Bridges	4	1-1	9
Thurmond	1	0-0	2	Barnhill	1	0-0	2
				Farmer	0	0-0	0
Total	36	31-45	103	Vaughn	5	6-9	16
				Total	38	21-33	97

San Francisco 29 29 19 26—103
St. Louis 26 26 28 17— 97
Failed out—Beaty.
Attendance—8,644.

February 9, 1964

Celtics Down Warriors, 105-99, and Gain Sixth Consecutive N.B.A. Title

BOSTON CAPTURES FINAL SERIES, 4-1

Celtics First Professional Team to Win Major Title Six Straight Years

By GORDON S. WHITE Jr.
Special to The New York Times

BOSTON, April 26—The Boston Celtics, long the power of the National Basketball Association, extended their domination to record proportions tonight. They gained their sixth consecutive championship with a 105-99 victory over the San Francisco Warriors in the fifth game of the final playoffs and took the series 4 games to 1.

No other major professional team had won its championship more than five times in a row. The Celtics had been tied with the Yankees and the Montreal Canadiens of the National Hockey League, who had won the World Series and the Stanley Cup, respectively, five straight times.

In a game with many moments of sloppy play, the Celtics had let a big lead slip away and then held on just long enough as time ran out on the Warriors. With 15 seconds to go, Bill Russell dunked a rebound with the strong pushing authority of a man trying to drive the ball through the floor. That made the score 103—99 for Boston and settled the issue. The crowd of 13,909 went wild with joy.

Not waiting for the game to finish, some fans charged to the side court, raised Coach Red Auerbach of the Celtics to their shoulders and tore his jacket off in the process. Order of sorts was restored for the last seconds and then Auerbach and the Celtic players rode the shoulders of happy fans after the final buzzer signaled the Celtics' seventh N. B. A. crown in the last eight years.

No Change in Fortunes

The noise in the Boston Garden lasted a long time, and happy followers tramped out with something to be proud about. The Celtics had not been expected to have it so easy according to the experts before the season began nearly seven months ago.

Bob Cousy, the man who had led the team to its six previous championship drives, was no longer with the Celtics. Boston's basketball fortunes were expected to drop.

But starting fast and moving on steadily, the Celtics easily

won their eighth straight Eastern Division crown. Then they eliminated Cincinnati in the Eastern playoffs before finishing off the Warriors.

Tonight's game, however, was not a typical example of the stuff of which the Celtics are made. They didn't have things at all their way on their friendly home court and had to rally from an early deficit to win.

Russell did his usual fine job defending against Wilt Chamberlain, giant of this sport of giants. Wilt didn't score for the first six minutes. Although he produced a 30-point effort, Wilt usually must do much better for San Francisco to win.

Sam Jones Sparks Surge

Tom Heinsohn was the scoring hero for the champions, making 19 points, but it was Sam Jones who got the Celtics off and winging to a big lead as the second half started.

Leading, 45—41, at intermission, Boston surged further ahead with Sam Jones sinking 6 of the club's first 10 points in the second half to help build

a lead of 56—47. Then Boston raised its margin to 11 points three times in the third period.

But Coach Alex Hannum's Warriors weren't giving up and the Celtics had some more moments of bad play left. San Francisco chipped away at the lead and eventually gained a 78-77 advantage at 1:31 of the fourth period when Chamberlain made one of his fine fall-away shots from a few feet away.

Willie Naulls, once a New York Knick, popped the ball in from 15 feet out to get the lead back for the Celtics at 79—78 10 seconds later.

From that point, Boston had the advantage but by no means full control of the situation. Trailing, 100—92, with a couple of minutes to go, San Francisco poured in 5 straight points to trim the lead to 3 points. Then it got only 2 points away before Russell slammed the ball through the hoop after Heinsohn had missed a lay-up.

Russell, Heinsohn, K. C. Jones, Frank Ramsey and Jim Loscutoff have been on all of the championship Boston teams. The road to great success began

in the spring of 1957 when Auerbach's forces won their first N.B.A. title. With the exception of 1958, Boston has won ever since.

By winning, the Celtics finished the season with an extra $51,500. Boston got $25,000 for taking the playoff finals and previously had earned the balance with the best won-lost percentage in the league, the Eastern Division championship and the Eastern Division playoff title.

The Warriors added $17,000 as their share of the playoff finals and wound up with a total of $41,500.

BATTLE OF BIG MEN: Wilt Chamberlain (13), of San Francisco and Tom Sanders of Celtics leaping for a rebound in title game in Boston. The Celtics won contest, 105-99.

United Press International Telephoto

BOSTON (105)	G.	F.	P.	SAN FRAN. (99)	G.	F.	P
Heinsohn	7	5-6	19	Meschery	3	3-6	9
Sanders	5	1-1	11	Thurmond	3	5-6	11
Russell	5	4-5	14	Ch'mlin	12	6-9	30
S. Jones	7	4-8	18	Attles	4	3-8	11
K. Jones	3	1-1	7	Rodgers	8	3-3	19
Naulls	2	0-0	4	High'wer	2	6-7	10
Clizak	6	2-3	14	Hill	0	0-0	0
Ramsey	7	4-4	18	Lee	3	3-3	9
Total	42	21-28	105	Total	35	29-42	99

Boston .... 22 23 29 31—105
San Francisco .... 24 17 30 28— 99

Fouled out—Sanders, Rodgers, Hightower.
Officials—Powers and Strom.
Attendance—13,909.

PETTIT BETTERS 20,000-POINT MARK

Scores 29, but Hawks Lose to Royals by 123-106

CINCINNATI, Nov. 13 (UPI)—The Cincinnati Royals beat the St. Louis Hawks, 123-106, tonight despite a 29-point effort by Bob Pettit, who became the first player in the National Basketball Association to score 20,000 points.

Pettit passed the mark when he dropped in a field goal early in the second quarter.

The Royals' victory was their second in a three-day span over the Hawks and gave them a 3-1 edge in their series.

Jerry Lucas tossed in a game high of 30 points and grabbed 19 rebounds for the Royals. Oscar Robertson, playing for the first time since injuring his right eye Nov. 1, scored 22 and Jack Twyman 25 for the victors.

Lucas scored 11 of his points during the first six minutes of the last quarter and departed from the game along with other regulars with the Royals leading by 22.

Pettit entered the game with 19,993 points for his 11-year career in the N.B.A. A 29-point effort increased his total to 20,022.

The game was interrupted and Pettit was presented with the game ball after the 20,000th point.

CINCINNATI	(123)				ST. LOUIS	(106)		
	G.	F.	T.			G.	F.	T.
Arnette	1	0-0	2	Barnhill	2	2-2	6
Backman	4	3-5	11	Bently	7	2-2	16
Embry	3	3-6	9	Bridges	3	1-1	7
Hairston	0	0-0	0	Farmer	3	0-0	6
Hawkins	2	1-2	5	Guerin	6	1-1	13
Lucas	12	6-6	30	Hagan	1	0-1	2
Olsen	4	2-2	10	McGill	4	0-0	8
Robertson	7	8-9	22	Mullins	2	5-5	9
Smith	1	5-5	7	Pettit	12	5-6	29
Thacker	1	0-0	2	Silas	1	1-4	3
Twyman	10	5-5	25	Vaughn	1	2-2	4
Wilson	0	0-0	0	Wilkens	3	3-5	9
Total	**45**	**33-40**	**123**	**Total**	**42**	**22-29**	**106**

Cincinnati ... 29 ... 29 ... 32 ... 33—123
St Louis ... 26 ... 28 ... 22 ... 30—106
Attendance—4,679.

November 14, 1964

76ers Buy Chamberlain for $300,000 and 3 Players

ST. LOUIS, Jan. 13 (UPI)—Wilt Chamberlain was sold by the San Francisco Warriors tonight to the Philadelphia 76ers for cash, two players and the rights to a third player.

The Warriors received Connie Dierking and Paul Neumann and the rights to Lee Shaffer, who has been working out in Durham, N. C., after refusing to sign his 76ers' contract.

Haskell Cohen, the National Basketball Association's publicity director, made the announcement. Cohen did not disclose the amount of money that changed hands, but it was estimated at $300,000.

Chamberlain will report immediately to the 76ers. The announcement of the big deal was made immediately after the East defeated the West, 124—123, in the N.B.A.'s 19th All-Star game.

A 7-foot-1-inch 275 pounder, Chamberlain is the greatest scoring star in the history of college or professional basketball. He is currently leading the N.B.A.'s scorers with 1,490 points and an average of 38.9 per game.

His Top Performance

On March 2, 1962, at Hershey, Pa., Chamberlain reached the height of his career when he became the first pro to score 100 points in a game. Chamberlain led the Warriors (then a Philadelphia franchise) to a 169-147 victory over the New York Knicks that night with 36 field goals and 28 free throws.

The N.B.A.'s scoring champion in every season he has played in the league, Chamberlain set a record by averaging 50.4 points a game during the 1961-62 season. He averaged 37.6 points a game as a rookie, 38.4 in 1960-61, 44.8 in 1962-63 and 36.9 in 1963-64.

Chamberlain shut off all telephone calls to his hotel room when he heard about the announcement and said that he would not speak to anyone until he gave personal instructions to let calls through.

A much-sought high school star who went to Kansas University, Chamberlain had his scoring exploits tempered by the fact that no team for which he had played had won a national championship. His nemesis among the pros has been Bill Russell of the Boston Celtics, who controlled his scoring and rebounding sufficiently to enable the Celtics to defeat Chamberlain-led teams with regularity.

Started With Globetrotters

Chamberlain was a basketball sensation at Overbrook High School in Philadelphia and received dozens of offers from colleges. He went to Kansas, but quit the university with a year of eligibility left and, in 1958, signed a $65,000 contract with the Harlem Globetrotters. That contract made him the highest-paid basketball player in history.

Chamberlain left the Globetrotters at the end of that season and signed with the (Philadelphia) Warriors, with whom he began his N.B.A. career in 1959.

Neither Dierking nor Neumann has shown impressive scoring ability in the N.B.A. But Shaffer was a standout performer. The 6-7 forward broke into the league with Syracuse in 1961-62, averaging 16.9 points per game. He upped this figure to 18.6 in 1962-63, but dropped to a 13.1 average when the Syracuse franchise was moved to Philadelphia last season.

Shaffer currently is on the suspended list. He had several clashes with the 76er coach, Dolph Schayes, last year, and this season was unable to come to a salary agreement with Philadelphia.

Dierking, 6—9, joined Syracuse from the University of Cincinnati in 1958-59, and after two seasons with the Nationals was dropped to minor-league competition. He returned to the 76ers last season and averaged 6.5 points in 76 games. His average for 38 games this season was 7.8.

Neumann, a 6-1 guard, enjoyed his best season last year, when he averaged 11.6 points for the 76ers. He broke into the N.B.A. with Syracuse in 1961. He's been the 76ers' second leading scorer this season with a 14.3 average in his first 39 games.

January 14, 1965

Celtics Close Season With Record 62d Victory

RUSSELL EXCELS WITH 36 REBOUNDS

BOSTON, March 21 (AP)—The Boston Celtics, relying on Bill Russell, Sam Jones and Tommy Heinsohn, closed their best season in the National Basketball Association with a record 62d victory today as they defeated the Cincinnati Royals, 116-99.

The Royals' star, Oscar Robertson, did not play because of an injury to his left instep. However, he is expected to be ready for the playoff opener with Philadelphia Wednesday.

The Celtics earlier had bettered the previous season mark of 60 victories, which they had set three years ago.

The Royals tried repeatedly to narrow the Celtics' margin, once getting to within 2 points at 37-35. But the Celtics, shooting poorly from the outside in the first half, did a fine job breaking men loose under the basket and gradually widened their lead.

Russell finished with 23 points and 36 rebounds. Heinsohn had 16 points and Sam Jones 19. Jerry Lucas with 26 and Adrian Smith with 23 led the Royals.

In addition to the winning mark, the Celtics, who will begin the playoffs against either the Royals or Philadelphia on April 4, finished the regular season $14,000 richer. They receive $12,000 for taking first place in the Eastern Division and $2,000 for the best won-lost record in the league.

BOSTON	(116)				CINCINNATI	(99)		
	G.	F.	P.			G.	F.	P.
Heinsohn	7	2-4	16	Twyman	3	3-3	9
Sanders	5	1-2	11	Lucas	11	4-8	26
Russell	10	3-3	23	Embry	4	0-2	8
S. Jones	6	7-1	19	Arnette	2	0-1	4
K. Jones	6	0-0	12	Smith	8	7-8	23
Naulls	4	2-2	4	Hairston	5	1-1	11
Havlicek	7	3-5	17	Olsen	5	1-1	11
Thompson	1	0-0	2	Ina	2	0-0	4
Siegfried	1	0-0	2	Hawkins	0	0-0	0
Counts	1	0-0	2	Wilson	0	1-3	1
Bonham	3	2-2	8				
				Totals	**41**	**17-27**	**99**
Totals	**48**	**20-25**	**116**				

Boston Celtics ... 27 ... 24 ... 29 ... 36—116
Cincinnati Royals ... 20 ... 22 ... 28 ... 29— 99
Attendance—9,154.

March 22, 1965

Celtics Beat 76ers in Series Finale

HAVLICEK STARS IN 110-109 GAME

Steal in Last Seconds Halts 76ers as Celtics Capture 9th Eastern Title in Row

By GORDON S. WHITE Jr.
Special to The New York Times

BOSTON, April 15 — The Boston Celtics, forced tonight to put on one of their strongest battles in years, just managed to beat the Philadelphia 76ers, 110-109, and win the Eastern Division championship of the National Basketball Association for the ninth straight season.

There was nothing easy to the triumph before the 13,909 fans who filled the Boston Garden for the seventh and deciding game of the playoff finals. Each team botched up a routine toss-in from out of bounds during the last five seconds of play.

The failure by the 76ers was the more costly of the bad plays. As a result, the Celtics will meet the Los Angeles Lakers, starting here Sunday in the N.B.A. final playoffs. Coach Red Auerbach's Celtics will be going after their seventh consecutive league title in that four-of-seven-game series.

It was a wild finish tonight. With the score at 110-107 and the Celtics apparently assured of victory—only five seconds remained - - Wilt Chamberlain easily made a layup as all the Celtics stepped out of his way to make sure they didn't foul the big man.

This made the count 110-109, Boston. Then Bill Russell tossed the ball inbounds over Chamberlain's outstretched hands.

But the ball hit the guidewire supporting the backboard and the 76ers were given the ball out of bounds. Now they had one last chance for a winning shot. Hal Greer stepped out of bounds and tossed in toward Chet Walker 30 feet away.

Havlicek Gets the Ball

John Havlicek of the Celtics rushed between Walker and the ball, slapped it down, took it over and the crowd went wild. Havlicek tossed the ball high in the air, and the Celtics were carried off along with Auerbach on the shoulders of happy fans storming the court. Boston had won the series, 4 games to 3.

It was a particularly sad moment for Chamberlain, the league's leading scorer, who has failed to pace a team to an N.B.A. title in six great years of professional basketball. He worked hard tonight, possibly harder than he did in any of the three victories the 76ers gained in this series.

Despite the fact that he and the 76ers battled from far back to take a lead, however, it was Boston that managed to grab the honors.

Sam Jones, the fancy shooter from outside, made 37 points. Havlicek, the Buckeye from Ohio State, got 26 and that important steal late in the game.

The Celtics were heavy favorites. Only the home team had won in the six previous games and only the home team had looked good in those games.

The Celtics took off as if this was all there was to it— being at home. They managed to build an 18-point lead in the first six minutes of play with a 30-12 margin. The crowd was wild, with expectations of a romp.

76ers Storm Back

But the 76ers of Coach Dolph Schayes weren't having any of it. They got the last 9 points of the first quarter, trailed at that point, 35-26, and came on to pass the Bostonians before the half had ended.

Then Boston had its turn at fighting from behind, its easy chore turned into a desperate drive by proud men. The Celtics were the kings of the league and they intended to remain so.

When Havlicek connected on a set shot at 2:40 of the third quarter, Boston passed Philadelphia at 67-66. The Celtics had been down by 5 points two minutes earlier, but that shot by Havlicek was the last time the lead shifted.

Yet the shot was far from a deciding one. It was work and more work for the Celtics to hold. And when the final seconds produced the joy, sudden disappointment and then joy again, all the work had been worth it. The Eastern playoff title was here again.

Chamberlain managed to get 32 rebounds to 29 for Russell tonight, but Russell was credited with a most unusual nine assists. Chamberlain made 30 points, Russell 15.

BOSTON (110)	G.	F	P	PHILA. (109)	G	F	P
Heinsohn	1	0-0	2	Walker	10	4-5	24
Sanders	8	2-2	18	Jackson	3	2-4	8
Russell	7	1-2	15	Chamberlain	12	6-13	30
S. Jones	15	7-9	37	Greer	5	2-2	12
K.C. Jones	2	2-3	6	Costello	1	1-1	3
Havlicek	10	6-7	26	Gambee	6	13-14	25
Siegfried	2	2-3	6	B'anchi	3	1-1	7
				Kerr	0	0-2	0
Totals	45	20-26	110	Totals	40	29-42	109

Boston .... 35 26 29 20—110
Philadelphia ..... 26 36 20 27—109
Fouled out—Gambee.
Attendance—13,909.

April 16, 1965

Celtics Beat Lakers, 129-96, and Take Record 7th Straight N.B.A. Title

42-POINT QUARTER COMPLETES ROUT

Celtics Hit 21 Field Goals, a Record, in Last Period— Russell Gets 30 Rebounds

By GORDON S. WHITE Jr.
Special to The New York Times

BOSTON, April 25 — Six months and nine days after the start of the National Basketball Association season, the campaign ended today just as everyone expected it would— with the Boston Celtics the league champions for the seventh straight year, a record.

Coach Red Auerbach's Celtics brought down the curtain by trouncing the Los Angeles Lakers, 129-96, and took the playoff title, four games to one,

United Press International Telephoto

ANOTHER SEASON, ANOTHER CHAMPIONSHIP: Boston fans swamp Celtics and Coach Red Auerbach, with cigar, after victory over Los Angeles. John Havlicek is at left.

DETERMINATION: Bill Russell of Celtics has eyes for the basket only as he drives for 2 points against Gene Wiley of Los Angeles in deciding game of N.B.A. playoffs.

United Press International Telephoto

scoring was far from enough to overcome the balanced Celtic attack.

The Lakers managed to stay within reach of the Celtics during the first 15 minutes of play, gaining a 36-all tie after three minutes of the second quarter. But the Celtics scored 8 straight points at that juncture and were never caught again.

During that streak Russell was hurt when West slapped at the ball and stuck a finger in Russell's right eye. When play resumed, Russell had some difficulty seeing where the rebounds were going.

The runaway gave the Celtics a record for 1964-65 of 37 victories in 40 games played at the Boston Garden, their home court. And home was a happy place for the Celtics today.

April 26, 1965

Celtics Reward Russell With Their Top Dollar

BOSTON, Aug. 25 (UPI)— Bill Russell of the Boston Celtics became the highest-paid player in pro basketball today when he signed a three-year contract with the National Basketball Association champions for a salary he said was "in excess of six figures for each season."

Russell, voted the most valuable player in the N.B.A. last season, was believed to have insisted on a yearly figure higher than that given Wilt Chamberlain by the Philadelphia 76ers. Chamberlain signed a three-year contract last week reported to call for $110,000 a season.

August 26, 1965

before a capacity crowd of 13,909 at Boston Garden. No other professional major sports team has been a champion seven consecutive seasons.

The Celtics pulled away from the Lakers as the fans screamed louder and louder on each shot late in the game. The Celtics ran up 20 straight points in the fourth period to virtually clinch the game and the championship.

Auerbach, professional basketball's most successful coach, lighted his victory cigar with eight minutes to go in the game, threw a handful of the cigars to the fans seated behind the bench and smiled during almost all the rest of the game.

Auerbach's complacency was well-founded. The Celtics completed the rout with 42 points in the final period, hitting on 21 field goals, an N.B.A. playoff record for one quarter.

The title was the eighth N.B.A. crown for the Celtics in the last nine seasons. Auerbach has coached the Bostonians to all of them.

Russell Hugs Auerbach

Once again it was a team effort that propelled the Celtics, with big Bill Russell leading the way by controlling the rebounding. His 30 rebounds kept the Celtics in command and enabled the Celtic regulars to get an early rest.

When Auerbach took Russell out of the game with six minutes to go, the crowd went wild. Russell, usually unsmiling,

BOSTON (129)				LOS ANGELES (96)			
	G.	F.	P		G.	F.	P
Heinsohn	2	2-4	6	LaRusso	3	8-10	14
Sanders	8	0-0	16	E s	6	3-5	15
Russell	6	10-11	22	Wiley	2	0-0	4
K. C. Jones	9	2-2	20	West	13	7-8	33
S. Jones	10	2-3	22	Barnett	0	0-0	0
Havlcek	8	2-2	18	Nelson	2	2-2	6
Nau s	5	0-0	10	Hazzard	4	7-9	15
Seafried	5	1-1	11	Imhoff	0	3-4	3
Counts	0	0-0	0	K ng	2	0-0	4
Thompson	2	0-0	4	McG l	1	0-0	2
Bonham	0	0-0	0				
Totals	55	19-23	129	Totals	33	30-38	96

Boston Celtics .... 33 24 30 42—129
Los Ang. Lakers .. 26 22 23 25— 96
Attendance—13,909.

walked over to Auerbach and, grinning widely, gave his coach a big hug.

Russell, Tom Heinsohn, K. C. Jones and Sam Jones have been on each of the seven straight championship teams. Russell and Heinsohn are the only members of the Celtic team that won the N.B.A. title for the first time in 1957.

With the teams apparently tense, the action was sloppy in the first half. Errors were more frequent than expected for a championship game.

Boston's string of seven straight titles started in 1959 when the Celtics beat the St. Louis Hawks. They also beat the Hawks in the playoffs in 1960 and 1961.

Russell and Sam Jones led the Boston scorers with 22 points each and K. C. Jones equaled his career high for a single game with 20 points.

The Lakers' top scorer, Jerry West, got 33 points, high for the game. But once again his

Chicago Five Assigned to West And Bullets Will Shift to East

CHICAGO Jan. 27 (AP) — The National Basketball Association officially awarded a franchise to the Chicago Bulls today for $1.6-million. The 10th league member was assigned to the Western Division, shifting the Baltimore Bullets from the Western to the Eastern Division.

The addition of the Bulls, the third Chicago team to attempt competition in the N.B.A., was announced after a meeting between Commissioner Walter Kennedy, two N.B.A. officials and Dick Klein, heading a five-man Chicago syndicate.

The Bulls, who will start N.B.A. play in the 1966-67 season, will be allowed to select 18 players from a pool screened from the other nine league members. The Bulls will be allowed to take two play s from each club after the freezing of seven men on the 12-man active roster of each club.

The pool will be established, Kennedy said at a news conference, about May 1, before the N.B.A.'s regular player draft.

In the player draft, the new Chicago entry will pick 19th in the first round, will get the third and fourth picks in the second round, and every 10th pick thereafter.

The surprising draft set for the new club precluded the chance of the Bulls getting college basketball's standout senior, all-America Cazzie Russell of Michigan, a resident of Chicago.

Klein a former Northwestern University star and player with the pro Chicago Gears basketball team in the nineteen-forties, said the Bulls would play most of their games in Chicago's International Amphitheatre. Klein said he would explore the possibility of doubleheader programs in the Chicago Stadium, where the first Chicago N.B.A. team, the Stags, played from 1946 to 1950.

Klein said a coach for the Bulls had not yet been selected.

Klein's associates in the franchise operation included E. J. Higgins, Harold Mayer, Elmer Rich Jr. and Newton P. Frye Jr.

Under the new N.B.A. alignment, Chicago will be in the Western Division with Los Angeles, St. Louis, San Francisco and Detroit. The Eastern Division will include Baltimore, Cincinnati, Boston, Philadelphia and New York.

The Bulls bring N.B.A. basketball back to Chicago after a lapse of more than two years. In 1963, the Chicago Zephyrs, who began operations in 1961, moved to Baltimore.

Meeting with Kennedy and Klein were Ben Kerner of the St. Louis Hawks and chairman of the N.B.A. expansion committee, and Franklin Meiuhi, of the San Francisco Warriors

January 28, 1966

Basketball Court(ship) Paid Off For Rick Barry

Hale of Miami Took Special Interest in Son-in-Law

By JERALD POSMAN

Rick Barry, a young man who married the boss's daughter and received expert training with his father-in-law's firm, now holds a position in a business that hires a limited number of young men each year and makes use of only a few of these.

From the depth on his underhand foul shot to the height on his looping jump shot, he has demonstrated all the qualities that have made him — in his first year — the newest star in the National Basketball Association.

The 22-year-old forward is averaging 25 points a game and almost single-handedly transformed the San Francisco Warriors — who finished last in the Western Division last year — into a contender for second place in their division. Most of Barry's success can be attributed to Bruce Hale, basketball coach at the University of Miami.

The coach would have small parties for his players at home and at one of these Barry met Pamela Hale. The coach, seeing in Barry possibly more than a suitor, attempted to insure not only happiness but success for a prospective son-in-law.

Hale, therefore, placed the 6-foot-7-inch Barry at a forward position instead of at center on the Miami team, knowing that he was not tall enough to play center in the pros.

"When I came to the Warriors I was used to the run-and-shoot style of professional basketball because of my training at college and therefore the transition became easy," Barry says.

The difference between college and professional basketball is immense. One player refers to the basketball played in the N.B.A. as "rugby basketball."

"I returned to scrimmage with my college team after my first year in the pros and found I was bouncing the kids around like tennis balls. I can just imagine the coaches wondering at what kind of monster they had produced," the player said.

Hale knew all about the elbow duels between pros jockeying for position on shots and rebounds, so he devised a special development program for Barry before the rookie left for training with the Warriors.

The coach would place one man on either side of Barry and one man behind him and have Barry shoot for the basket and retrieve the ball. Sometimes Barry would have three men between him and the basket and Hale would order him to get the rebound.

"There was one exercise where someone would throw a ball against the backboard, I would go for the rebound and two men — one on each side — would just slam into me," Barry says.

Barry, who doesn't carry too much weight on his 6-7 frame, gives the impression that he wouldn't have the strength and stamina needed to be a top pro. But he plays close to 48 minutes each game. Barry has trouble sleeping and — according to the Warrior coach, Alex Hannum — is extremely tense on the court. All these contribute to a loss of weight that constantly puts him at less than 200 pounds.

"We have him on a high protein, high calorie, high anything diet, but it doesn't seem

The New York Times (by Barton Silverman)

A high-strung youth, Rick Barry, spends a few minutes by himself before going into court

to work. He worries too much," Hannum says.

When Barry is not moving on the court the tension builds within him. He says he used to stay up until 4 A.M. after a game, trying to explain to himself what he did wrong, playing the game over move by move. Now he attempts to do this all before a game, because in the N.B.A. — where teams play from three to six games a week — practice sessions are part of competition.

"You begin to see the things that throw off your game. I won't take a shower the day before a game because the hot, then cold water saps my energy and makes me feel tired and sluggish," Barry says.

In his senior year at Miami, Barry was the top college scor-

er in the country, averaging 37.4 points a game. But many high-scoring college stars have failed in attempts to play in the N.B.A.

Attempting to avoid possible failure, he spent much time after his marriage last summer shooting baskets with his wife's help. They would play a game where Pam or Rick took a shot and the other would have to duplicate the play.

"We even played against each other. I would only shoot from 20 to 25 feet out and Pam would be able to take shots from close to the basket," he says.

"She beat me a few times— but that's not so strange. We both had the same coach."

February 13, 1966

Chamberlain Gets 20,884th Point for a Record

CHARLESTON, W. Va., Feb. 14 (AP) — Wilt Chamberlain broke the National Basketball Association career scoring record tonight as he led the Philadelphia 76ers to a 149-123 victory over the Detroit Pistons.

Chamberlain scored 41 points and raised his career scoring total to 20,884 points, 4 better than the mark set by Bob Pettit, now retired, of the St. Louis Hawks. Chamberlain is in his seventh season in the N.B.A. Pettit played for 11 seasons.

Throughout the first half, Chamberlain acted as a playmaker and scored but 10 points. But he stepped up his production after the intermission and in the last period he registered 19 points.

Wilt also became the No. 2 man in career rebounding, again surpassing Pettit. When he grabbed his fourth rebound early in the game, he sent his career mark to 12,852, second only to Bill Russell of the Boston Celtics.

PHILADELPHIA (149)				DETROIT (123)			
	G.	F.	P.		G.	F.	P.
Cham'lain	16	9-17	41	V. Arsdale	4	0-0	8
Greer	11	6-6	28	Tresvant	8	2-3	18
Jones	8	1-2	17	Scott	7	7-8	21
Walker	6	1-1	13	Kojais	4	0-2	8
Cunn'gham	6	6-7	18	Reed	3	3-4	9
Ward	2	1-1	5	Barnhill	6	1-3	13
Gambee	3	4-4	10	Miles	8	1-3	17
Jackson	3	5-6	11	Vaughn	5	5-6	15
Bianchi	3	0-0	6	DeBus'ere	4	2-2	10
				Strawder	2	0-0	4
Totals	58	33-44	149	Totals	51	21-32	123

Philadelphia 35   35   40   39—149
Detroit 26   25   27   45—123
Fouled out—Tresvant.
Attendance—4,100.

February 15, 1966

Auerbach Hopes Final Season Is Winning One

Celtics Pilot Seeks Record Eighth Title in Pro Basketball

By ARNOLD LUBASCH

In fiercely competitive professional basketball, known for such giants as Wilt Chamberlain and Bill Russell, perhaps the most effective performance over the years has been turned in by a short, stocky, baldish man with a fondness for lighting a big cigar before the game is even over.

Fans and foes of the Boston Celtics recognize him at once as Arnold (Red) Auerbach, the winningest coach in professional sports, now seeking his eighth consecutive championship of the National Basketball Association.

Auerbach, who has announced that he will retire at the end of this season, will make his last appearance in Madison Square Garden as a coach next Saturday, when the Celtics meet the New York Knickerbockers.

"I'm tired," he said in a recent interview, explaining why he was retiring as coach. "I'm so tired."

Machines Need Rest, Too

"I feel like a machine," he said. "You go at full speed for 20 years, you have to rest the machine. There's the mental thing, the fact that you're tired of the continuous pressure year after year, tired of the travel, tired of the referees, tired of the hostility from the crowds outside of Boston."

The colorful and controversial 48-year-old coach made it clear, however, that the weariness had not weakened his determination to retain the N.B.A. championship.

"We came to play and we came to win," he said firmly. "They'll have to take it away from us. We're not going to give it to anybody."

Although he will relinquish his coaching duties at the end of the season, Auerbach will remain with the Celtics as the club's executive vice president and general manager. He indicated that he would devote a lot of time to scouting.

His successor as coach has not yet been named. But it must be abundantly clear to all potential candidates that Auerbach will be an extremely tough act to follow. Besides his record for wining the most games, he holds the informal record for paying the most fines.

Auerbach's towering temperament has made him the scourge of referees from coast to coast. A referee's unfavorable decision sends him leaping from the bench, clenching a tightly rolled program in one fist and stamping his foot in fury as he directs a stream of well chosen invective at the offending official.

For the last decade, his Celtics have dominated the league,

with an explosive fast break, rugged defense and relentless determination to win. A hallmark of the well balanced Celtics is the ability of everyone to score in double figures while no one dominates the scoring.

Auerbach noted with undisguised displeasure that the success of Boston's fast break had been attributed for years to Bob Cousy, before the retirement of the great backcourt star.

"We did it before Cousy," Auerbach said, "and we did it after Cousy. Not that I want to take anything away from Cousy. He was the best one coming down the middle on a fast break."

Cousy Called 'Fancy Dan'

In 1953, after Cousy joined the Celtics, Auerbach berated him as a "Fancy Dan" and Cousy indicated a desire to be traded. Their initial conflict gave way to mutual respect over the years, however, and Auerbach came to call Cousy

The New York Times
Red Auerbach in characteristic posture on the sidelines

"the greatest player the sport has ever had."

Auerbach now says that "Bill Russell is the best all-round player" he has ever seen. He said his top all-star team would consist of Russell, Bob Pettit, Elgin Baylor, Oscar Robertson and Cousy.

Maintaining there is nothing unusual about his coaching style, Auerbach said, "We don't really do anything different; we just spend more time on it."

"I credit most of it," he said, "to Bill Reinhart. We use predominantly the fast break he taught me in college at George Washington. He was 20 to 30 years ahead of his time."

After college, Auerbach coached high school basketball in Washington and then entered the Navy. He was a native of the Williamsburg section of Brooklyn, where he played basketball for Eastern District High School before attending a local junior college and then going on to George Washington.

In 1946, fresh out of the Navy

at the age of 28, he talked his way into the job of coaching the Washington Capitols in the newly-formed professional basketball league.

Had One Losing Season

Auerbach has been a coach in the league since its inception. He led the Capitols for three seasons, the old Tri-City Blackhawks for one season and the Celtics for the last 16 seasons. His only losing year was with the Blackhawks.

Last Jan. 12, he reached the record milestone of 1,000 victories as a professional coach. All but 152 of the successes with the Celtics.

The league, which was professionally and financially shaky when it started, has improved dramatically, and Auerbach contributed considerably to its success.

"It's just a simple, natural change, the success of a major sport over 20 years," he said. "We've done a job starting something new and making it accepted. The major change is the increased ability of the players, the coaches and the referees."

His team has been a consistent winner ever since the arrival of Russell a decade ago. But the average age of his regulars is now over 30 and the Celtics appear hard-pressed.

In the closing minutes of a game, when Auerbach feels certain the Celtics will win, he lights a cigar. His victory cigar has become a ritual. And he notes that the cigar industry is supplying him with free cigars as well as paying him for his endorsement.

March 13, 1966

Bill Russell Named Boston Celtic Coach

By GORDON S. WHITE Jr.
Special to The New York Times

BOSTON, April 18—Bill Russell became the first Negro to direct a major professional sports team today when he was named to succeed Arnold (Red) Auerbach as coach of the Boston Celtics, eight-time champions of the National Basketball Association.

The 6-foot 10-inch, 32-year-old Russell will continue to play when he takes over the team next season as the highest-paid coach or manager in professional sports history.

No figures were given by the Celtics today, but it was estimated that Russell would receive an increase of $25,000 as coach, raising his income to $125,001 a year. He has two years to go on a three-year player contract that calls for $100,001 a year.

When the Philadelphia 76ers

signed Wilt Chamberlain to a $100,000 contract this season, the Celtics rewarded Russell with that sum plus a dollar to make him the highest-paid player in the game.

Auerbach, who has coached the Celtics for 16 years, is retiring from coaching to devote his time to being the Celtics' general manager. He has been coach and general manager for two years.

Russell has not signed a contract as coach, but Marvin Kratter, the owner and chairman of the board of the Celtics, said that "was nothing really."

"We have shaken hands on an agreement and that's all that counts now," he said.

Auerbach said the club and Russell agreed on the new post two days ago after Russell had considered the offer for a month.

The Celtics are in trouble in their chase for their ninth straight N.B.A. title, but the club officials were all smiles during a news conference at the Hotel Lenox today.

Fourth Coach of Celtics

Russell is the fourth coach of the Celtics. John (Honey) Russell was the first, serving from 1946 through 1948. He was followed by Alvin (Doggie) Julian, now the coach at Dartmouth. After two seasons, Julian was succeeded by Auerbach.

Russell was an all-America at the University of San Francisco, where his height made it simple for him to score. K. C. Jones was also on that San Francisco team, which won two National Collegiate basketball titles and 55 games in a row.

Russell was the star of the United States Olympic basketball team that won the gold medal in the games held in the fall of 1956 in Melbourne, Australia. Russell reported to the Celtics in December of that year.

The Celtics had traded Ed Macauley and Cliff Hagan to the St. Louis Hawks for the Hawks's second draft choice in the spring of 1956. Boston used that draft choice to pick Russell and another choice of its own to select K. C. Jones. Jones served in the Army and could

not report to the Celtics until the 1958-59 season.

Before Russell joined the Celtics, the team had failed to win either an Eastern Division or league championship. In his first season with the Celtics, they won the division and league titles and began their long string of successes.

Since then the Celtics have won all but one of the Eastern Division regular-season titles. The exception was this season, when Philadelphia beat them by a one-game margin.

The Boston club has been in every championship playoff from 1957 through 1966. They have been beaten in the playoffs only once, in 1958 when the Hawks beat them in seven games. In that playoff, Russell was injured, missed two games, and was ineffective in the final contest.

Russell has been regarded as the catalyst who made champions of the Celtics. Even Bob Cousy, the Celtics' great star from 1950 through 1962, could not get them into title contention until Russell came along.

Frank Ramsey, a former star of the Celtics, said today that "Russell is the team leader and has been all his time here. So it is only natural he becomes the coach."

Russell's forte as a Celtic has been his defensive work and control of the backboards. He is the leading rebounder in N.B.A. history. In 10 seasons he has taken 19,761 rebounds.

Basketball and wise investments have made Russell wealthy. He owns a 500-acre rubber plantation in Liberia and a restaurant in Boston, and has designed a basketball shoe that will be on the market next year.

Russell succeeds a successful, if not altogether popular, coach. A nervous man during a game, Auerbach jumps up and down, yells at officials and is frequently expelled from the court for such actions.

Asked if he expected to be that type of coach, Russell said, "As a player I am one of my best assets, so it wouldn't be very good to get kicked out of the game."

April 19, 1966

Celtics Defeat Lakers, 95-93, for Eighth Title in Row and 9th in 10 Years

RUSSELL PACES BOSTON'S ATTACK

Scores 25 Points, Gets 32 Rebounds—Baylor Held to One Basket in First Half

By GORDON S. WHITE Jr.
Special to The New York Times

BOSTON, April 28—The Boston Celtics won their eighth straight National Basketball Association title tonight by beating the Los Angeles Lakers, 95-93, and continued the longest championship reign in the history of major professional sports. This triumph in the seventh game of the final playoff gave the Celtics their ninth N.B.A. title in 10 years.

Thus they sent their retiring coach, Red Auerbach, out of the coaching business as a winner. The 48-year-old Auerbach lighted his last victory cigar—the sign that he is sure of winning a game—with 25 seconds to go after Sam Jones had sunk a 35-foot shot. And when he did, it sent the 13,909 fans filling Boston Garden into a screaming state of joy.

At the final buzzer, hundreds of fans stormed the court. With his shirt half torn off, Tom

Sanders finally gave up and took what was left of it off and tossed it to the crowd.

It was a typical Boston triumph, one engineered through muscular strength on defense and fast-breaking attacks that lasted the full 48 minutes. Never were the Celtics behind and, after they got the first 10 points, the Lakers never got as close as 2 points until the last four seconds.

Russell at His Best

Bill Russell, the giant of the Celtics who will be the player-coach of the Celtics next season, played at his best, scoring 25 points (tops for the Celtics) and getting 32 rebounds (high for both teams).

The Celtics became the first team in 14 years to finish as the runner-up in the regular-season Eastern Division race and go on to the title. In fact, never before had the Celtics, who finished second to Philadelphia in the East, played in the semi-finals before going on to the championship.

Tonight Boston showed no signs of the ragged play that cost so dearly when, after the Celtics had led in the playoff, 3 games to 1, they lost two straight to the Lakers. Those defeats were the result of sloppy play on Boston's part as much as improved action by the Lakers.

But this time the Celtics shaped up and defended so well that Elgin Baylor, one of the Lakers' two big scorers, made only 18 points, and only 2 in the first half. Jerry West scored

36 points, high in the game, but the other Lakers couldn't penetrate Boston's defense.

Baylor Given No Chance

Baylor hit on only one of nine shots in the first half. He was forcing shots and missing because he never really was given a good chance by the Celtics.

From the moment John Havlicek hit on a short pop shot three seconds after the game-opening tap, there was a distinct feeling that Boston had things under control.

The Celtics built their lead to 19 points at the 2:01 mark of the third quarter when Sam Jones hit with a rebound for a 59-40 margin. It wasn't really downhill from then on, it was just a cagey game by Boston in which the Celtics managed to sit on a good lead for a long time.

Sam Jones scored 22 points

and Havlicek made 16. Sanders and his replacement, Don Nelson, did most of the good defensive work on Baylor. Sanders, however, was forced to sit out a lot of the action. He drew three quick personal fouls and was up to five early in the third quarter.

Russell is the only member of the team who has played on all of the championship squads. Auerbach has been the coach of all of them.

BOSTON (95)				LOS ANGELES (93)			
	G.	F.	P.		G.	F.	P.
Havlicek	6	4-6	16	Goodrich	2	2-3	6
Sanders	3	1-1	7	King	1	0-1	2
Russell	10	5-5	25	Ellis	5	2-3	12
S. Jones	10	2-2	22	West	12	12-16	36
K. Jones	2	1-1	5	Baylor	6	6-6	18
Siegfried	4	4-5	12	Hazzard	5	2-5	12
Nelson	2	4-4	8	Larusso	2	3-4	7
Naulis	0	0-0	0	Imhoff	0	0-0	0
				Boozer	0	0-0	0
Totals	37	21-24	95	Totals	33	27-38	93

Boston 27   26   23   19—95
Los Angeles 20   18   22   33—93
Attendance—13,909.

April 29, 1966

Sports of The Times

By FRANK LITSKY

His Brother's Keeper

MONTICELLO, N. Y., Aug. 17—"Eight years ago," said Jack Twyman today, "Maurice Stokes was dead. Now he's going to get better because he has amazing desire. He doesn't feel sorry for himself. He feels that what happened happened. He's going to beat this thing. I really believe that."

"This thing" is traumatic encephalopathy, a brain injury. Eight years ago, it struck down Stokes, a magnificent 6-foot-6-inch physical specimen who was becoming one of the great players of professional basketball. His progress since then is a tribute to his raw courage. It also is a tribute to Twyman, a man of rare backbone who became his brother's keeper.

Jack Twyman is 32 years old and the son of a Pittsburgh steel company foreman. Maurice Stokes is 33 and the son of a retired Pittsburgh steel molder. They played against each other in high school and in summer playground leagues, but they were not especially good friends. They broke into professional basketball together with the Rochester (now Cincinnati) Royals, but they were still not close. They had different friends, different interests, different colors.

Brotherly Love

What they had in common, though they did not know it, was brotherly love. It came to the fore in 1958, the Royals' first year in Cincinnati. Stokes was knocked cold in the final game of the regular season, but he was revived three minutes later and seemed all right. The next day, in a plane flying from Detroit to Cincinnati, he became violently ill and lapsed into a coma. A day later, with

Associated Press

Jack Twyman
Thanks to his aid, another man has "returned to life."

Stokes in the hospital, the Royals were eliminated from the playoffs.

The players returned to their homes, confident that Stokes would be well in a week or two. Only Twyman, who had just opened an insurance business in Cincinnati, remained.

"After a week or two," said Twyman, "I saw how sick he was and how much money he would need. Certain things had to be done, and I was the only one there, so I had myself named his legal guardian. I'm sure others would have done the same."

Twyman raised money for medical bills that became overwhelming. Even now, the weekly tab for rehabilitation, nurses, hospital room and doctors runs close to $1,000 a week. So far, the cost has been almost half

a million dollars, and the end is not in sight. Though workmen's compensation pays 60 to 65 per cent of the bills, money must be found elsewhere.

The annual Maurice Stokes benefit basketball game, played here tonight at Kutsher's Country Club, raised more than $10,000. Donations come from people who never knew Stokes but are touched by his struggle. When more money is needed, Twyman goes out and gets it.

The bills are large because Stokes is so dependent on others. He has lived in hospitals in Cincinnati for eight years, either in bed or a wheelchair. He has left Cincinnati only twice in that time—this year and last to attend the benefit game here.

He spends his mornings in physical therapy, his afternoons in occupational therapy—writing letters on an electric typewriter or making professional-quality ceramics.

But he has a long way to go. Every move is labored and hard to come by. His speech is improving. His nervous system is intact, but he must retrain his extremities.

His mind is alert, and he stays abreast of politics, music and sports. He reads bestsellers and books on history. His sense of humor is keen. Yesterday, when he saw Dolph Schayes, a playing rival, he put his hand on his elbow and laughed. So did Schayes, who had one of the meanest elbows in the game.

When a friend recently was hospitalized for a week and was kept for a month, Stokes sympathized with him. "Damned if the same thing didn't happen to me," Stokes said.

"I get renewed from him," said Twyman. "When I need to be picked up, I go to see him. He does a lot for me. You know, that could be me lying there. I may have a sense of values ingrained, but you don't go around life with medals on your chest."

If your name is Jack Twyman, you should.

August 18, 1966

Seattle Is Awarded Franchise

TEAM WILL START IN 1967-68 SEASON

Move Is Part of Expansion Plan to Add Eight Clubs Over Next Four Years

CHICAGO, Dec. 20 (AP) — The National Basketball Association awarded a franchise today to Seattle to begin operations in the 1967-68 season.

President Walter Kennedy said that the N.B.A. owners at a meeting here unanimously named Seattle as the first city in an expansion program aimed at adding eight teams to the N.B.A. over a four-year period.

The N.B.A. is now composed of 10 teams.

The selection of another fran-

chise from among San Diego, Pittsburgh or Cleveland, will be made at a later date by the N.B.A. to join Seattle as a new member in 1967-68.

Three Groups Involved

Kennedy said the N.B.A. within the next two or three weeks, would select one of three bidding groups to operate the Seattle franchise.

"We are not at liberty to identify the groups involved," Kennedy said.

"The N.B.A. is pleased to establish the first major league sports team in the northwest area."

Kennedy said that the Seattle entry would play its home games in the Seattle Coliseum, which seats 14,000.

The President said the cost of the Seattle franchise and method of player stocking still were to be determined.

After 1967-68, the N.B.A. will add two new franchises each season for the following three years.

The Chicago Bulls started as

a 10th N.B.A. member this year, joining Baltimore, Cincinnati, Boston, New York, Philadelphia, Detroit, Los Angeles, St. Louis, and San Francisco.

December 21, 1966

San Diego Is Accepted As 12th Team in N.B.A.

SAN DIEGO, Jan. 11 (UPI) —San Diego has been awarded the 12th franchise in the National Basketball Association, Walter P. Kennedy, the N.B.A. president, said tonight.

The franchise, purchased for $1.75-million, will be operated by Robert Breitbard and Associates, the owners of the San Diego International Sports Arena and the San Diego Gulls of the Western Hockey League.

The $6-million arena was completed last year and seats about 13,000.

San Diego and Seattle, also chosen to join the N.B.A. next season, will choose 15 players each later this year from a draft involving players from other N.B.A. clubs.

San Diego and Seattle will begin competing in the league next season.

January 12, 1967

Mikan Is Hired as Commissioner by Newly Organized Pro Basketball League

NO RAIDS PLANNED ON N.B.A. PLAYERS

Zaslofsky Will Coach Local Entry in 10-Team League — Play Starts in Fall

By LEONARD KOPPETT

Brandishing something of an olive branch in one hand and the tallest commissioner in sports, the American Basketball Association formally set up shop as a second major league yesterday by hiring George Mikan as commissioner.

In his first official action, the 6-foot-10-inch Mikan, who was once designated as "the player of the first half of the twentieth century," declared a "no-war" policy with respect to the National Basketball Association, the first and so far only fully successful major professional basketball league, now in its 22d season.

Mikan, an all-America choice at De Paul in the early nineteen-forties, played center for the Minneapolis Lakers, who became perennial champions of the N.B.A. He teamed with Jim Pollard, Vern Mikkelsen, Slater Martin and Whitey Skoog to dominate the Western Division for many seasons.

"We do not intend to raid the N.B.A. for players," Mikan said. "I haven't read the current N.B.A. contract and I don't know what it says, but we feel we must honor contractual obligations. We hope, of course, that some big stars and others will be in a position to come to us; if they are free, we want to talk to them.

"But we have not talked to Wilt Chamberlain or Oscar Robertson or anyone like that. We are setting up shop and inviting all qualified players, anywhere in the world, to come talk to us. But we do not intend to get into any legal hassles."

This attempt to start the new league in a peaceful manner was significant, even though a spokesman for the Oakland franchise had declared that he was certain Chamberlain was going to the new league.

Competition for Players

Open warfare from the start by the A.B.A. would add immense financial burdens to an already expensive undertaking. Inevitably, competition will develop for stars coming out of college and for many average professional players, but there was no atmosphere of challenge among the owners of the teams

that gathered at the Hotel Carlyle yesterday.

"We simply believe there is room for two leagues, operating independently," was the refrain.

The new league will have 10 teams, and intends to begin play in the fall. New York, Pittsburgh, Indianapolis, Minneapolis and New Orleans form the Eastern Division; Dallas, Houston, Kansas City, Oakland and Anaheim (in the Los Angeles area) form the Western Division.

"We are aiming at a 70-game schedule," said Mikan. "Our playing rules will be a composite of N.B.A. and college rules. All these details have to be worked out—I just took the job this morning. But within two or three weeks we should have answers."

The New York franchise is owned primarily by Arthur J. Brown, of the A.B.C. Freight Forwarding Company. Max Zaslofsky, a former St. John's star who played 10 seasons in the N.B.A. with the Chicago Stags and New York Knickerbockers, will be general manager and the first coach of the New York entry. A part-owner is Mark Binstein, who brought the idea for joining the league to Brown.

Singer Bowl Sought

Where will the New York team play? Madison Square Garden is out of the question, since it owns the Knickerbockers of the N.B.A.

"We are already negotiating with the city for leasing Singer Bowl on the site of the World's Fair in Flushing," said Zaslofsky. "It can be covered over and converted into an indoor arena seating 14,000 people or so for between $1 and $2 million. We are interested in doing that at our expense."

Until that can be done, the

team will seek a temporary home in an armory or perhaps in the Coliseum at Columbus Circle, where up to 6,000 people could be accommodated for basketball.

The other owners are largely lawyers, engineers, real estate operators and other established businessmen in the cities involved. The president of the Oakland franchise is Pat Boone, the singer. The New Orleans group is headed by Sean Morton Downey Jr., who is in the music and concessions business.

Agreements for dates have been entered into with suitable arenas in all cities but New York—the Convention Center in Anaheim, the Civic Arena in Pittsburgh, the Sam Houston Coliseum in Houston, the Dallas Memorial Auditorium in Dallas, the Municipal Auditorium in Kansas City, the Oakland-Alameda County Coliseum in Oakland, the Loyola University Fieldhouse in New Orleans and the Metropolitan Sports Center in Minneapolis. These are buildings in the 8,000-15,000 capacity range.

Mikan has a three-year contract at an undisclosed salary, estimated in the $40,000 range. He will maintain his headquarters in Minneapolis, where he is an attorney, but the league will also maintain one office in New York and one in California.

The president of the league is Gary Davidson, one of the four owners of the Dallas team.

The new league plans to have a draft of college players "as soon as the college season is over," which would mean late March and a month earlier than the usual N.B.A. draft. Competition in bidding for drafted players is inevitable between the leagues, even if existing contracts are honored.

Stable financial backing was stressed by league spokesman. Each owner has agreed to put up enough money to operate for two years, which means about $500,000; the New York operation, with its special problems, is expected to cost about $700,-000 the first year.

Art Kim and James Ackerman, co-owners of the Anaheim franchise, owned a team in the American Basketball League, which lasted 2½ seasons between 1960 and 1962. They lost money then, but they are optimistic now.

"In the American League," said Kim, who is part-owner of the Harlem Globetrotters, "the owners had the necessary financial resources, but not the dedication to stick it out. This group does have the dedication. That's why we're back in business."

The principal owners, most of whom were present at the meetings here the last two days, are Gabe Rubin, Pittsburgh; William Witmere, Charles Frazier and Cloyce Box, Houston; Kim and Ackerman, Anaheim; August Speth, Davidson, John Klug and James M. Peters Jr., Dallas; Brown and Binstein, New York; James Trindle, Kansas City; Boone, Ken Davidson and Dennis A. Murphy, Oakland; Downey, L. Torrey Gomila, Ronnie Kole, James A. Ware, Lionel J. Cunningham and Charles G. Smither, New Orleans, and L. P. Shields and Fred Jefferson, Minneapolis.

The Indianapolis franchise was still being competed for by two groups. In addition, Donald Regan, an attorney from Newport Beach, Calif., headed a group that will get an additional franchise when more teams are added, possibly before the first season begins.

February 3, 1967

N.B.A. and Players Settle Dispute

Pros Claim Victory, but League Says It's Not Total

The National Basketball Association playoffs, which had been threatened by a player strike, will begin as scheduled on Tuesday, even though disagreement still exists about the exact nature of the agreements reached during all-night bargaining that had begun on Monday.

Yesterday afternoon the players announced that they had decided to "participate" in the

playoffs because "they got what they wanted." Oscar Robertson, the president of the Players Association, and Larry Fleisher, the attorney for the association, said this meant they had an agreement in writing that assured them the players' pension proposals would be met.

Walter Kennedy, the president of the N.B.A., then took exception to implications that the players had "won," or that the owners had "yielded," or that any specific feature of the pension plan had been guaranteed.

It was possible for both sides to claim victory. The owners had set a deadline of noon yesterday for "assurances" from the players that they would play. That deadline was met,

but only after the players received what they, at least, construed as approval of their basic request.

That request is for a pension plan that would provide about $600 a month for a 10-year man at the age of 65, and retroactivity to the beginning of the career of every player now active.

It seemed clear that the unanimity of the players, who reaffirmed their strike decision over the weekend, led to the 36 hours of negotiation that produced the settlement.

Kennedy said in a letter to Fleisher:

"I assure you that the board of governors of the N.B.A. is not in disagreement with the players on the principle of their requested pension coverage. The owners cannot, however, commit themselves at the present time to a specific plan, but have authorized a study of several alternative plans as well as the tax problems involved. I can assure you that a satisfactory plan will be adopted no later than June 8, 1967, the date of our annual meeting."

To the players, agreement in "principle" and "satisfactory plan" meant the $600 level and retroactivity. To Kennedy, the fact that no specific amount was mentioned was significant. In effect, what the players have is Kennedy's personal promise to lead the owners to full agreement.

Other points of agreement, reached in prior negotiations, include:

¶A medical and insurance program in accordance with player requests.

¶Elimination of games played immediately before and after the All-Star game.

¶Limitation of the regular schedule to 82 games (one more than this season).

¶Formation of a player committee to review the standard player contract before next season.

¶Further discussion of exhibition-game pay.

March 15, 1967

76ers Top Warriors, 125-122, and Capture N.B.A. Playoff Title on Coast

4TH-PERIOD RALLY LEADS TO VICTORY

76ers Overcome a 5-Point Deficit—Barry Scores 44 in Losing Effort

By BILL BECKER
Special to The New York Times

SAN FRANCISCO, April 24 —The Philadelphia 76ers made a magnificent fourth-period comeback tonight to defeat the San Francisco Warriors, 125-122, and win the National Basketball Association championship.

Philadelphia overcame a 5-point deficit starting the final quarter to pull out its fourth victory in six games of the grueling final playoff series.

A crowd of 15,612 watched the finale in the Cow Palace and 4,483 saw the exciting game over a closed-circuit television hookup in the Oakland Coliseum.

Billy Cunningham, a reserve forward, gave the 76ers the lift they needed as he scored 13 points in the final 12 minutes. But over all, it was the steady play of big Wilt Chamberlain and Wally Jones, a hot-handed guard, that spelled victory.

Chamberlain Is Leader

Jones led his team with 27 points, with Chamberlain next with 24. The 7-foot-1-inch Wilt also blocked six shots and pulled down 23 rebounds.

For the losers, Rick Barry again was high, with 44 points. He received yeoman aid from Jeff Mullins and Jim King, two guards who accounted for 23

Associated Press Wirephoto

WILT IS THWARTED: Paul Neumann of Warriors spoiled first-period shot by Wilt Chamberlain (13) of the 76ers in N.B.A. playoff last night in San Francisco.

and 19 points, respectively, mostly from far out.

Barry averaged 41 points a game for the six-game series.

The winning Philadelphians earned $87,500 for their victory. The Warriors will receive $72,-500 to split into shares for the individual players.

The 76ers actually won the game at the free-throw line, getting 64 free throws to the Warriors' 29. They made 41.

San Francisco led, 72-68, at half-time. Both teams went on a scoring spree in the first quarter to set a N.B.A. playoff record for a period.

N.B.A. Playoff
Philadelphia vs. San Francisco
April 14—Phila. 141, S. F. 135 (o't).
April 16—Phila. 126, San Fran. 95.
April 18—San Fran. 130, Phila. 124.
April 20—Phila. 122, San Fran. 108.
April 23—San Fran. 117, Phila. 109.
April 24—Phila. 125, San Fran. 122.
Philadelphia wins four-of-seven game series, 4-2.

With Chamberlain showing tremendous aggressiveness and Jones sinking 16 points, the Philadelphias edged the Warriors, 43-41, in the first period. The 84-point total eclipsed the previous playoff record for a quarter of 73 set in 1962 by Boston and Los Angeles.

Then, just as suddenly, the 76ers turned cold both on the floor and at the free-throw line. With Barry and Mullins setting the pace, the Warriors moved ahead. Mullins scored 7 consecutive points and later sank two long jump shots.

San Francisco seemed to be wearing the 76ers down with fast-breaking attack. Barry all scorers at half-time with 23 points, followed by Jones with 21. Chamberlain had 17, Mullins 15.

King, a long-shooting guard, hit for five baskets in the third quarter to keep the Warriors ahead. At one stage, midway in the period, the Warriors had a 12-point lead, 94-82.

Then Hal Greer hit on three 20-footers for Philadelphia and the 76ers were back in contention. San Francisco led, 102-97, as the final period began.

PHILADELPHIA (125)	G.	F.	P	SAN FRAN. (122)	G.	F.	P
Walker	8	4-5	20	Barry	16	12-13	44
Jackson	5	3-6	13	Hetzel	4	0-0	8
Chamb'rl'n	8	8-16	24	Thurmond	4	4-8	12
Greer	5	5-7	15	Neumann	1	0-0	2
Jones	8	11-15	27	Attles	3	0-0	6
Cunningm	4	9-13	17	King	9	1-1	19
Guokas	4	1-2	9	Lee	1	0-0	2
Gambee	0	0-0	0	Meschery	3	0-0	6
				Mullins	9	5-7	23
Totals	42	41-64	125				
				Totals	50	22-29	122

Philadelphia .... 43 25 28 29—125
San Francisco .... 41 31 30 20—122
Fouled out—Thurmond.
Attendance—15,612.

April 25, 1967

Barry Accepts $500,000 Contract

Rick Barry signing Oakland American Basketball Association contract at the home of Pat Boone, owner, Monday.

Associated Press Wirephoto

SAN FRANCISCO, June 20 (UPI)—Rick Barry, a star for the San Francisco Warriors of the National Basketball Association, announced today he had signed a three-year contract with the Oakland Americans of the American Basketball Association. Barry's defection gave the A.B.A. its first superstar and seventh N.B.A. player.

Barry would not disclose the exact terms of the pact signed last night with Pat Boone, the Oakland owner, but it is believed to be for about $500,000.

Franklin Mieuli, the Warriors owner, who called the defection a "move which could shatter the whole concept of professional sports in the United States," said a suit against Barry, the Americans and the A.B.A. would be filed immediately.

Barry, the N.B.A.'s top scorer last season with 2,775 points, said the contract he signed with Oakland was strictly a basketball one. Mieuli, who conferred with Rick for about an hour before the announcement, said he believed the pact included fringe benefits such as a stock option in the Americans and a

possible career in show business. Boone is a recording star and actor.

"The offer Oakland made me was one I simply couldn't turn down," Barry said. "I'm not at liberty to reveal its exact terms but I think it makes me one of the highest paid players in pro basketball."

Wilt Chamberlain of the Philadelphia 76ers and Bill Russell earn close to $125,000 a year, and Nate Thurmond, Barry's teammate with the Warriors, last week signed a three-year contract with San Francisco estimated at $100,000 a season.

"This is the saddest day of my life, also the most frustrating," Mieuli said. "I had and still have real affection for Barry, but there was nothing I could do to hold him. Money wasn't a factor in his defection, but the fringe benefits were.

The other N.B.A. players who have jumped to the A.B.A. are Wayne Hightower from Detroit to Denver, Bob Love from Cincinnati to New York, Jim Barnes from Los Angeles to Dallas, Clyde Lee from San Francisco to New Orleans, Joe Strawder from Detroit to Pittsburgh and Chico Vaughn from San Diego to Pittsburgh.

June 21, 1967

Milwaukee and Phoenix Obtain N.B.A. Franchises for Next Season

NEW CLUBS TO PAY $2-MILLION EACH

Fee to Include Selection of 18 Players From Rosters of Existing 12 Teams

Milwaukee and Phoenix, Ariz., were added to the National Basketball Association yesterday, giving the 22-year-old professional league 14 teams for next season.

Each of the new franchises will pay $2-million as an entry fee, which will include the selection of 18 players for each new team from the rosters of the existing teams. The league expects to have 18 teams by 1970.

Arrangements for the latest expansion were completed yesterday morning at a meeting of the Board of Governors in New York, and followed the pattern set last year, when Seattle and San Diego were added to the league. They paid $1,750,000 each for the rights to 15 players from the pro pool.

Milwaukee will be in the Eastern Division, Phoenix in the

Western, and a new schedule pattern will be worked out. At present, N.B.A. teams play an 82-game schedule, each team in their own division eight times and in the other division seven times. A comparable seven-and-six format for 14 teams would result in an 84-game schedule.

Four Seasons in Milwaukee

For Milwaukee, this will mark a return to N.B.A. competition. The Hawks, currently leading the Western Division, represented Milwaukee for four seasons before moving to St. Louis after the 1954-55 campaign. They had gone to Milwaukee from Tri-Cities (Moline, Ill.) in 1951.

For Phoenix, this will be its first participation on an accepted major league level in any sport.

To stock the new teams, the following procedure will be used:

Each of the 12 existing teams will list seven players to be retained. All the rest will go into the expansion pool. (Most teams carry 12 players.)

From the expansion pool, the new teams will choose alternately, the first choice to be determined by the toss of a coin.

However, as soon as one man is picked from any existing club, that club will be allowed to reserve one other player from the list it submitted.

Eventually, 36 players will be chosen, three from each of the 12 teams.

College Draft Procedure

In the draft of college players, the new teams will be given seventh and eighth places in the rotation, with the team that lost the toss for the pro pool taking precedence in the college draft. In other words, the teams that finish with the six poorest records this season will make their college draft selections; then the two new teams will choose; then the remaining six teams will pick. That sequence will be followed through all rounds of the draft.

Both new teams have multiple ownership. The owners in Phoenix are Carl Eller, a Phoenix businessman; Donald Pitt, a Tucson attorney, and Richard L. Bloch, an investment banker in Beverly Hills, Calif., but a recent Phoenix resident.

The Milwaukee group is much larger. The principal figure is Weley Pavalon. He, his brother, Morris, and Kenneth Parelskin are officers of Career Academy Inc., a system of special schools. William Liebman and Donald Chapman are members of an investment firm, Loewi & Company. Other co-owners are Marvin L. Fishman, a realtor; Gerald J. Kahn, an accountant, and Dr. James Schelble.

At 14 teams, the N.B.A. will have the second largest membership in its history. In 1949-

50, when the Basketball Association of America merged with the National League to form the N.B.A., it operated with 17 teams in three divisions.

By 1954, the league was down to eight teams. A ninth team was added in 1961 (Chicago, which subsequently moved to Baltimore). The present Chicago team made it a 10-team league in 1966.

Playoff Money Increased

An increase in the prize money for this season's playoffs and in the number of games to be played in the opening round was also announced by the N.B.A. The playoff pool will be $320,000, instead of the $280,000 last season, and all series will now be four-of-seven games, instead of three-of-five in the first round.

The prize money will be distributed as follows:

The team with the best winning percentage in the entire league will get $5,000.

The team finishing first in each division will get $17,500 apiece. Second place will be worth $10,000, third place $5,000.

All the teams participating in the first round of the playoffs will get $15,000 apiece. In the next round, the winning teams will get $20,000 and the losers $15,000. In the final, the champion will add $35,000 to his total, the runnerup $25,000.

January 23, 1968

Bullets Pick Unseld and Knicks Choose Hosket in Draft

N.B.A. DENOUNCED BY RIVAL LEAGUE

Mikan of A.B.A. Sees Early Draft Causing 'War'—He Charges Broken Pledge

By DEANE McGOWEN

Westley Unseld, a two-time all-American for the University of Louisville, was chosen by the Baltimore Bullets as the National Basketball Association completed a preliminary two-day telephone draft of college players yesterday.

The draft, limited to first choices, was unusual and was intended to beat the rival American Basketball Association in signing the leading college seniors.

It was reported in Louisville that the Kentucky Colonels of the A.B.A. had offered Unseld

$500,000 for a four-year contract.

Last week the San Diego Rockets, last-place finishers in the Western Division, signed Elvin Hayes of Houston, the 1968 college player of the year, to what was reported as a four-year contract for $440,000.

The N.B.A.'s regular draft will be held here May 8. Its preliminary action brought a sharp rebuke from George Mikan, commissioner of the year-old A.B.A.

Raises Olympics Query

From league headquarters in Minneapolis, Mikan said:

"This puts us in a terrible spot. I guess we will have to enter into the unholy war of going after these ballplayers."

Mikan continued:

"What about the N.B.A. pledge to allow these ballplayers to play in the Olympics? They are going out and signing all these fellows. Now we'll have to go ahead and try to sign them. What is their feeling on the Olympics?"

Mikan noted that the A.B.A. had held an "evaluation" draft

at Louisville March 9, then added:

"We're going ahead with our draft on April 27. Our teams still are in consultation with the players whose names they received at Louisville."

Meanwhile the New York Knickerbockers, picking 10th, chose Bill Hosket of Ohio State, a Big Ten first-team selection the last two years.

Hosket, 6 feet 7½ inches tall and weighing 228 pounds, is a cornerman and a rebounder. He averages 19.5 points and 12.3 rebounds a game in his three-year college career.

Bill Hewitt of Southern California was chosen by the Los Angeles Lakers, who immediately announced they had signed the 6-6 star to a three-year contract, but did not give the terms. Hewitt said he had been close to signing with Denver of the A.B.A.

The Boston Celtics selected Don Chaney of Houston. They picked 12the in the 14-team round.

Phoenix, one of the league's two expansion clubs that will start playing next season, went

for Gary Gregor of South Carolina, while the St. Louis Hawks named Skip Harlicka, also of South Carolina.

The Philadelphia 76ers, last year's champions, picked last and chose Shaler Halimon of Utah State. He was the nation's eighth leading scorer with a 26.8 average, and is regarded as a good rebounder.

Milwaukee, the other expansion team, selected Charles Paulk of Northeast Oklahoma. Both Milwaukee and Phoenix will be stocked by the 12 other clubs on May 6.

Bob Kauffman of Guilford College, Greensboro, N. C., signed with the Seattle Supersonics of the N.B.A. He was their first choice.

The other draftees:
Chicago—Tom Boerwinkle, Tennessee.
Cincinnati,—Don Smith, Iowa State.
Detroit—Otto Moore, Pan American.
San Francisco—Ron Williams, West Virginia.

April 4, 1968

Celtics Beat 76ers, 100-96, for 3d Straight and Take Eastern Title

BOSTON'S DEFENSE PACED BY RUSSELL

He Holds Chamberlain to 14 Points in 7th Game—Jones, Havlicek Lead Attack

By DAVE ANDERSON
Special to The New York Times

PHILADELPHIA, April 19 — Surrounded by bedsheet banners that insulted them as "old men," the Boston Celtics dethroned the Philadelphia 76ers as champions of the National Basketball Association tonight with a 100-96 victory in the seventh-game showdown of the Eastern Division final playoffs.

The Celtics, whose eight-year reign was ended a year ago by the 76ers, qualified to oppose the Western Division winner,

the Los Angeles Lakers, in the four-of-seven-game championship series, starting Sunday in Boston.

In the final minute three big plays by Bill Russell, the symbol of Celtic supremacy during their glory years and now the team's coach as well as its 34-year-old center, enabled Boston to add a footnote to N.B.A. history as the first team ever to win a four-of-seven-games series after trailing 3-1.

With the Celtics leading, 97-95, and 34 seconds remaining on the Spectrum clock, Russell missed his first foul shot, but connected on his second to provide a 3-point lead.

Jones Misses Jump Shot

Following a Philadelphia time-out with 32 seconds left, Wally Jones, who had scored 18 points while playing on a bandaged right knee, missed a jump shot. In the scramble for the rebound, Wilt Chamberlain battled with Don Nelson, forcing a jump ball at the foul line. Chamberlain tapped the ball to Chet Walker.

In driving for the basket, Walker penetrated too far too close to Russell, who blocked it. Hal Greer, who sparked the

76ers in the second half, tossed a jump shot. But the ball ricocheted off the rim and the 6-foot-10-inch Russell snatched it. Moments later, two foul shots by Sam Jones assured the triumph.

At the buzzer, Russell flung his fists high in the air, a rare emotional gesture for him.

"At this point," Russell acknowledged later, "this is the most satisfying victory of my career. But we haven't won anything yet. We've got to beat L.A. to be champions again."

Unexpectedly, the Celtics won three of four games at the Spectrum, while the 76ers won two of three in Boston.

Chamberlain Is Contained

Russell provided only 12 points, but he neutralized Chamberlain, his 7-foot rival, who scored only 14 points. Sam Jones, another 34-year-old relic of the Celtic reign, produced 22 points and John Havlicek contributed 21. But perhaps the difference was the 18 points accumulated by Larry Siegfried.

In addition to his scoring, Siegfried limited Greer to only 4 points in the first half as

the Celtics took a 46-40 lead.

In the third quarter, Wally Jones and Greer led the 76ers to brief leads of 51-50 and 56-55, but entering the final quarter, the Celtics had regained a 4-point edge at 73-69. Again the 76ers rallied, leading at 81-79 and later at 88-87, but Havlicek, Howell and Nelson regained a 95-90 lead.

Chamberlain, however, was unable to contribute to the 76er attack. Strangely, he took only two shots from the floor in the second half, and scored only 2 points, to the discomfort of the silenced sellout crowd of 15,202. The crowd had come to bury the Celtics' "old men," but departed praising them.

BOSTON (100)				PHILADELPHIA (96)			
	G.	F.	P.		G.	F.	P.
Embry	0	0-3	0	Chamber'n	4	6-15	14
Havlicek	7	7-7	21	Green	1	2-6	4
Howell	8	1-3	17	Greer	8	6-6	22
S. Jones	9	4-4	22	Guokas	2	0-0	4
Nelson	5	0-0	10	Jackson	7	1-1	15
Russell	4	4-10	12	W. Jones	8	2-2	18
Siegfried	7	4-4	18	Melchionni	0	0-0	0
Hhacker	0	0-0	0	Walker	8	3-6	19
Total	40	20-31	100	Total	38	20-36	96

Boston..................26 20 27 27—100
Philadelphia...........21 19 29 27— 96
Fouled out—W. Jones, Howell.
Attendance—15,202.

April 20, 1968

John Havlicek became the mainstay of the Boston Celtics with the retirement of Bill Russell. Havlicek's fierce competitiveness combined with great skills made him a superb team player.

Willis Reed (#19) was the heart of one of the most exciting teams in N.B.A. history: the 1969-70 New York Knicks.

Celtics Defeat Lakers, 124-109, and Capture N.B.A. Title, 4 to 2

St. Louis Hawks Sold To a Group in Atlanta

By BILL BECKER
Special to The New York Times

LOS ANGELES, May 2—The superb Boston Celtics won their ninth National Basketball Association championship in 10 years by trouncing the Los Angeles Lakers, 124-109, tonight in the sixth and final game of their hectic playoff. The Celtics won the series, four games to two.

The victory was a supreme team effort, as the coach and center, Bill Russell, turned over the heavy duty to his smooth-working colleagues. John Havlicek led the Celtic attack with 40 points.

Havlicek did everything, hitting on jumpers up to 20 feet from the corners, dribble-driving through to the basket, and

making 12 free throws in 12 tries.

Much to the dismay of most of the 17,392 spectators, Havlicek received strong support from Bailey Howell, his running mate, who scored 30 points. The Celtic pair completely overshadowed the Laker stars, Elgin Baylor and Jerry West.

Baylor was high scorer for the Lakers with 28 points, but West, apparently hampered by a twisted ankle, was far off form and wound up with only 22. The rest of the Lakers were ice cold and the Celtics had no trouble extending their lead to 21 points midway in the fourth quarter, 111-90.

Russell didn't have to turn on the defensive heat as Howell and Havlicek helped him hawk rebounds at both ends of the court. But in the final quarter

Russell blocked several shots to frustrate all Laker hopes of a comeback.

Russell had 19 rebounds, Howell 11, Havlicek 10. Mel Counts, 7-foot Laker center, grabbed 25 rebounds, but failed to turn any of them to any serious advantage.

BOSTON (124)				LOS ANGELES (109)			
	G.	F.	P.		G.	F.	P.
Havlicek	14	12-12	40	Baylor	13	2-4	28
Howell	13	4-5	30	Hawkins	6	0-2	12
Russell	5	2-2	12	Imhoff	1	0-0	2
Siegfried	7	8-9	22	Clark	7	3-6	17
S. Jones	6	0-0	12	West	8	6-7	22
Nelson	2	0-1	4	Counts	5	1-3	11
Thacker	0	0-0	0	Goodrich	5	1-2	11
Embry	0	0-0	0	Mueller	0	0-1	0
Graham	0	0-0	0	Crawford	3	0-1	6
J. Jones	1	0-0	2				
Sanders	0	0-0	0				
Weitzman	1	0-0	2				
Totals	49	26-29	124	Totals	48	13-26	109

Boston .... 35 35 24 30—124
Los Angeles ...... 28 22 28 31—109
Attendance—17,398.

May 3, 1968

ST. LOUIS, May 3 (UPI)—The St. Louis Hawks of the National Basketball Association have been sold to a group in Atlanta, it was announced tonight by Ben Kerner, the club's owner.

Kerner said the sale was subject to approval of the board of governors of the N.B.A., who will meet in New York City next Tuesday to vote on the transfer.

Kerner said it was expected the Hawks would play at the Alexander Memorial Coliseum on the campus of Georgia Tech. An Atlanta Coliseum with a seating capacity of 16.000 is in the planning stages.

May 4, 1968

76ers Trade Chamberlain to Lakers for 3 Men

PHILADELPHIA, July 5 (AP)—Wilt Chamberlain, the Philadelphia 76ers' record-cracking giant, has been traded to the Los Angeles Lakers for three players—Darrall Imhoff, Archie Clark and Jerry Chambers—and an undisclosed amount of cash, The Associated Press learned today.

It was also learned that the National Basketball Association 76ers have named Jack Ramsay, the general manager for three years, as their new coach. Ramsay succeeds Alex Hannum, who resigned one year after leading the 76ers to their only N.B.A. title, and now is

coach of the Oakland team in the rival American Basketball Association.

Ramsay, reached at his summer residence at Ocean City, N. J., had "no comment" on the trade.

He said, however, that it "appeared unlikely that we will sign him" for the 1968-69 N.B.A. season.

"If you're looking for odds, I'd have to say they were not in favor of us signing him," Ramsay said. "And if we didn't sign him we'd have to find another solution."

Asked if Chamberlain was traded and if Ramsay was named the new coach, the gen-

eral manager replied:

No Comment on Trade

"We have made no statement and we have no comment to make on that," he said.

The trade, however, has been confirmed for the Associated Press by a reliable source.

Chamberlain, 32 years old, considered basketball's greatest offensive player, will team with Los Angeles' great pair of Jerry West, a guard, and Elgin Baylor, a forward.

The 7-foot-1-inch Chamberlain, in nine years in the league, is the only player ever to score more than 25,000 points. He has been on nine all-star and all-league teams. The last two

years, N.B.A. players named him the league's most valuable player.

The 76ers traded Chamberlain after a contract impasse over his salary. Already reported to be the highest-salaried athlete in the world at $250,000-a-year plus, Chamberlain is said to have demanded a three-year, million-dollar pact from the 76ers. He also is believed to have demanded a say in the naming of the team's coach.

It was learned Irv Kosloff, 76ers' owner, refused to consider the Chamberlain money package, and said flatly he would not let Chamberlain dictate the coaching choice. Kosloff, reportedly felt his team would not win another title with Chamberlain and decided to trade the giant center while he still had value.

July 6, 1968

Celtics Conquer Lakers by 108 to 106 and Capture N.B.A. Crown

By LEONARD KOPPETT
Special to The New York Times

INGLEWOOD, Calif., May 5—In a game whose complexion shifted more wildly than a schizophrenic chameleon, the Boston Celtics added another championship to their collection by beating the Los Angeles Lakers tonight, 108-106, in the seventh and deciding contest of the National Basketball Association final playoffs.

It was Boston's 11th title

in the 13 years that Bill Russell has been its center, and its second in the last three seasons, during which Russell has also been the coach. In six of those finals the Celtics defeated a Laker team anchored by Jerry West and Elgin Baylor, but this time Los Angeles also had Wilt Chamberlain, who was supposed to make it invincible.

Instead the amazing Celtics, written off as "aging" by many experts and only fourth in the Eastern Division during the regular season, produced the

smart, opportunistic, team-minded basketball that has characterized them for years, and also had that little bit of good fortune that every champion needs.

Playoff Record for West

West, his movement hampered by a leg injury but his shooting touch unimpaired, scored 42 points. He set a playoff record by accumulating 556 in the 18 games the Lakers had gone through, surpassing the mark of 521 set by Rick Barry

for San Francisco two years before. West also won the automobile presented by Sport magazine to the outstanding player of the series.

But that symbolized, as clearly as anything, the difference between the teams. The Lakers had brilliant individuals, the Celtics played as a unit with five parts.

Boston started with hot outside shooting by Sam Jones, John Havlicek and Em Bryant, which created a 24-12 lead. When West started to find the range, the Lakers came back and were only 1 point behind in the final seconds of the half. But Jones made two free throws after the buzzer on a foul by Tom Hawkins near midcourt.

In the opening minutes of the second half the Lakers seemed to have the momentum, achieving a tie at 60-60. At that point, however, their offense died and they went without a point for more than five minutes.

Wilt Is Inhibited

During that stretch Chamberlain committed his fourth personal foul, and the pendulum swung far in Boston's favor as Wilt became inhibited on the defensive board, which he had controlled completely.

An 11-0 spell led to a Boston margin that soared to 91-74 just before the third period ended. Jones and Havlicek were now joined by Don Nelson in making tough baskets and through the first couple of minutes of the final quarter the Celtics traded baskets and seemed in command.

But then the Lakers started inching up again, while first Russell and then Havlicek committed their fifth personals. Wilt had committed his fifth late in the third period, and it now became a key issue as to which man would foul out first.

He Hurts His Knee

Instead, an injury intervened. Wilt hurt his right knee coming down with a rebound with 5:45 to go and Boston's lead at 103-94. He hobbled around the court for a couple of plays, but finally had to sit down at 5:19, with the margin down to 7 points.

Now, with Mel Counts playing center, the Lakers had motion that some critics (including, at times, Coach Bill van Breda Kolf) said Chamberlain's presence had prevented. The all-but-exhausted Celtics were on the defensive, West was hot and with 3:07 still to play it was anybody's game with Boston leading by only 103-102.

The capacity crowd of 17,568 was screaming endlessly as both sides missed a couple of scoring opportunities, but that bit of luck came Boston's way at 1:17.

Havlicek, caught on the right side with time for a shot running out, had the ball deflected out of his hands by Keith Erickson. But it went to Nelson, at the foul line, and his shot hit the rim, went straight up and fell through for 105-102.

With 24 seconds to go, two free throws by Larry Siegfried wrapped it up, 107-102, and the last 4 Laker points during the last seconds meant nothing.

BOSTON (108)	G.	F.	P.	LOS ANGELES (106)	G.	F.	P.
Howell	4	1-2	9	Baylor	8	4-5	20
Havlicek	11	4-7	26	Erickson	2	2-3	6
Russell	2	2-4	6	Chmberlain	7	4-13	18
Bryant	9	2-3	20	Egan	3	3-6	9
Jones	10	4-4	24	West	14	14-18	42
Nelson	6	4-7	16	Hawkins	1	0-0	2
Siegfried	2	3-4	7	Counts	4	1-2	9
Total	**44**	**20-31**	**108**	**Total**	**39**	**28-47**	**106**

Boston 28   31   32   17—108
Los Angeles ... 25   31   31   30—106
Fouled out—Jones, Erickson.
Attendance—17,568.

May 6, 1969

United Press International

DELICATE BALANCING ACT: Wilt Chamberlain sinking an off-balance shot in last night's playoff game. Bill Russell (6) and Sam Jones, partly hidden, watch the action.

Hawkins Quits A.B.A. to Join Suns

LOS ANGELES, June 20 (AP) —Connie Hawkins has jumped from the American Basketball Association and signed with the Phoenix Suns of the rival National Basketball Association, dropping in the process his $6-million lawsuit against the N.B.A.

The move was announced today, following a closed meeting of N.B.A. directors.

Walter Kennedy, commissioner of the N.B.A., said he had approved a contract under which the 6-foot-8-inch Hawkins will play for Phoenix beginning this fall. The 28-year-old Hawkins was considered one of the outstanding players in the young American Association.

Richard Bloch, owner of the Suns, said at his home in Beverly Hills, "It's official. Hawkins will play with the Suns next year."

Hawkins, who plays either as a center or forward, signed a contract reportedly in six figures on a multi-year basis.

The $6-million lawsuit against the N.B.A. dates back to his college career in 1961 with Iowa. He was barred by the league for allegedly introducing a gambler to a fellow player.

The loss of Hawkins was a blow to the A.B.A., already hurt when Lew Alcindor of University of Los Angeles, California, signed with Milwaukee of the N.B.A.

Hawkins played out his option with the Minnesota Pipers

United Press International
Connie Hawkins

last season. The Pipers also appear to be in trouble. Bill Erickson, club president, said the team had lost $300,000. A contemplated switch to Pittsburgh, their original home, might collapse with Hawkins unavailable.

Kennedy summoned the N.B.A. directors to meet in closed session yesterday at the Forum, home of the Los Angeles Lakers.

Kennedy's statement said:
"I am approving today a player contract under which Connie Hawkins will play for the Phoenix Suns beginning next season.

"It has always been the policy of the N.B.A. to make every effort, consistent with fairness to the player involved, to keep

itself free of any contact or even suspicion of contact, with anyone who has ever been associated with gambling or fixing.

"N.B.A. counsel now has advised me, on the basis of the evidence so developed, that the employment of Hawkins as a player by an N.B.A. team will not be inconsistent with that policy."

Hawkins played a year with the old Pittsburgh team and the last two with Minnesota.

Hawkins got a boost today from Alcindor. Speaking in Milwaukee, the three-time All-American said, "I've seen the best in the N.B.A., but I've never seen anyone better than Hawkins."

June 21, 1969

mittees discussing a possible merger.

The 6-foot-8-inch, 225-pound Haywood rushed into basketball prominence during the Olympic Games In Mexico City last October when he led the United States team to a gold medal.

When he returned to the University of Detroit, he was one of the hottest box-office draws in college basketball last season. On the Detroit campus the students made detours to get a glimpse of him at basketball practice. Advance ticket sales for the 9,000-seat Memorial Fieldhouse in Detroit more than doubled last season. Because of Haywood, Madison Square Garden set up a Feb. 7, 1970, date for the Titans to meet Fordham.

Haywood was the nation's leading rebounder with a 21.5 average and finished fourth in scoring with a 31.8-point average. At Denver, one of the four A.B.A. franchises which was reported to have made money last year, Haywood will play for John McLendon, who was an assistant coach to Hank Iba at the Olympic Games. McLendon is the only Negro coach in the A.B.A. and one of three in pro basketball. Bill Russell of the Celtics, who recently retired, and Len Wilkens, the new coach of Seattle, are the others.

"I consulted my high school coach, and legal guardian, Will Robinson, in Detroit before going to negotiate," said Haywood during a news conference. "We set a price which we both agreed on and we felt if Denver would meet our terms it would be okay to sign."

August 24, 1969

Haywood Quits College, Signs $250,000 Pact With Denver

Special to The New York Times

DENVER, Aug. 23—Spencer Haywood, the rugged, overpowering, University of Detroit all-American, in a surprise move today left school and signed a professional contract with the Denver Rockets of the American Basketball Association. The 20-year-old Haywood, who would have entered his junior year next month, was believed to have signed a long-term contract for more than

$250,000.

"I am very surprised at the signing," said J. Walter Kennedy, commissioner of the National Basketball Association, from his home in Stamford, Conn. "Our constitution does not allow an N.B.A. team to sign a player who has entered college until his class has graduated."

Donald Ringsby, president of the Rockets, said the club re-

ceived permission from the A.B.A. president, James Gardner, to sign Haywood under a league bylaw that states: "In cases of extreme hardship, a player may be signed before his class graduates."

Haywood, who is not married, supports his mother and nine brothers and sisters.

The signing of Haywood was the second major move by the A.B.A. in less than a week. Last Wednesday the A.B.A. moved its Oakland franchise to Washington, putting it in competition with the Baltimore Bullet franchise of the N.B.A. The moves can be considered unusual at a time when the N.B.A. and A.B.A. have com-

Knicks Down Royals, 106-105, in Last Two Seconds for Record 18th in Row

FRAZIER WINS IT ON 2 FOUL SHOTS

Knicks, in Final 16 Seconds, Erase 5-Point Royal Lead Engineered by Cousy

By THOMAS ROGERS
Special to The New York Times

CLEVELAND, Nov. 28—The New York Knickerbockers executed one of the most remarkable pressure rallies in the 24-year history of the National Basketball Association tonight to turn an almost certain defeat by the Cincinnati Royals into their 18th straight

victory, a league record.

Trailing by 105-100 with 16 seconds left, the Knicks jammed 6 points into the hoop in the remaining time to finish on top, 106-105.

A crowd of 10,438 filled Cleveland Arena with tumultous shouting through the final minutes when it seemed the Royals would end the New York victory streak just as they had snapped an attempt by the 1959 Boston Celtics to reach 18 straight.

When Oscar Robertson fouled out of the game (after having scored 33 points and made 10 assists), it seemed remarkably apt that he was replaced by Bob Cousy, the Cincinnati coach, who was a star on the Celtics for many years.

Cousy Sets Up Score

When Cousy entered the game, the Royals held a 101-98 lead with 1 minute 49 seconds

left. After a New York basket by Walter Frazier, Cousy passed to Norm Van Lier, who hit from the right side.

Cousy, after having been fouled by Bill Bradley, then drew an ovation by sinking two foul shots that ran Cincinnati's lead to 105-100.

"All I could think about then was that the streak was over and we'd have to start all over again on another one," said Frazier afterward.

Other Knicks and Coach Red Holzman also admitted they had thought they were finished at that point. But Willis Reed was fouled by Tom Van Arsdale and sank two foul shots with 16 seconds left, after which Cousy called time out.

Then came the play that put the Knicks back into contention.

On a midcourt out-of-bounds pass by Cousy, Dave DeBusschere swept in front of Van Arsdale, stole the ball and

The Line-Up

CINCINNATI (105)

	min.	fgm.	fga.	ftm.	fta.	reb.	A.	pf.	pts.
Cousy	2	0	0	2	2	0	0	1	2
Dierking	41	8	14	3	6	14	3	3	19
ʼr	12	0	3	0	0	0	2	0	0
Green	41	8	11	3	3	20	1	0	19
Rackley	7	0	1	0	0	1	0	1	0
Robertson	43	15	23	3	4	6	10	6	33
Smith	6	1	2	0	0	0	0	0	2
Turner	7	3	4	3	5	3	0	2	9
Vʼn Arsdʼle	36	6	14	2	2	3	1	5	14
Van Lier	45	3	14	1	2	5	5	7	7
Total	240	44	86	17	24	52	17	24	105

KNICKS (106)

	min.	fgm.	fga.	ftm.	fta.	reb.	A.	pf.	pts.
Barnett	33	2	8	1	2	4	1	3	5
Bowman	4	1	2	1	1	1	1	0	3
Bradley	32	6	12	1	2	2	1	4	13
DeBʼschʼre	33	2	8	2	2	9	1	4	6
Frazier	44	10	19	7	9	7	5	3	27
Reed	44	8	22	3	4	13	1	3	19
Riordan	19	5	7	0	2	2	1	1	10
Russell	16	8	10	2	2	7	0	1	18
Stallworth	15	2	3	1	1	3	0	1	5
Total	240	44	91	18	25	48	11	21	106

Min.—Minutes played. FGM—Field goals made. FGA—Field goals attempted. FTM—Free throws made. FTA—Free throws attempted. Reb—Rebounds. A—Assists. PF—Personal fouls. Pts—Total points.

Cincinnati	30	22	26	27—105
Knicks	23	32	22	29—106

Referees—Bob Rakel and Richie Powers.
Attendance—10,438.

drove to the hoop for a lay-up that made it 105-104 with 13 seconds remaining.

Knicks Force a Break

The Knicks needed one more break and they got it when Reed pressured Van Arsdale, who was bringing the ball up court, and tipped the ball to Frazier.

The speedy guard took off toward the basket and threw up a jumper that missed with two seconds to go. But Van Arsdale had fouled Frazier on the shot and Frazier went to the line for two shots.

"I knew I had to come through," he said later. "If I had missed those shots, I wouldn't have gone back to the dressing room."

Frazier calmly sank both to send New York ahead, 106-105.

"They never touched the net," he chuckled. "I've got ice water in my veins."

Reed sealed the victory by intercepting the Cincinnati inbounds pass and the Knicks went screaming into their dressing room to shout at one another about the impossibility of it all.

The Royals played excellent basketball as Robertson, Connie Dierking, Johnny Green and Van Lier dominated the flow of the game.

Only a strong second period of shooting by Cazzie Russell, Mike Riordan, Dave Stallworth and Nat Bowman—who hit on 12 of 16 shots—kept the Knicks in the game after the regulars had put in a flat first quarter.

The Royals rallied strongly after trailing at the half, 55-52, to take a 78-77 lead into the fourth quarter.

With Robertson and Green doing most of the scoring, the Cincinnati lead reached 101-96 before Frazier hit a jumper. Robertson then fouled out, Cousy went in and the last-minute dramatics began.

The victory was New York's 23d in 24 games and increased its Eastern Division lead over Baltimore to six games. The Knicks play the Detroit Pistons tomorrow night in New York.

November 29, 1969

East Wins N.B.A. All-Star Game, 142-135; Reed Is Named Most Valuable

VICTORS DISSIPATE BIG LEADS TWICE

Robertson, in 10th Game, Gets 21 Points for Record All-Star Total of 230

by LEONARD KOPPETT
Special to The New York Times

PHILADELPHIA, Jan. 20—Although they dissipated big leads twice, the East All-Stars defeated the West in the 20th annual National Basketball Association All-Star Game, 142–135, tonight before a crowd of 15,000 in the Spectrum and a national television audience.

Superior on paper, especially after Nate Thurmond was lost to the West by injury, the East seemed superior on the floor most of the time. It led by 18 points during the first half and by 24 early in the fourth quarter.

The West narrowed the margin rapidly in the closing minutes and excited those who had invested in the opinion that the final margin would be more or less than 9½ points, but it never got quite close enough to threaten to win.

14th Victory foe East

It was the 14th victory for the East and the seventh in the last eight years.

The margin did not go below 6 points until the last 20 secons, and reached 5 with only five seconds to play.

In the final analysis, Oscar Robertson and John Havlicek, plus Hal Greer, kept things in hand by destroying the pressing defense the West tried. The same group, with Dave DeBuschere and Willis Reed, broke the game open late in

Associated Press

HUSTLING UNDER THE BOARDS: West's Elvin Hayes gets rebound, assisted by Connie Hawkins, in All-Star game's first period. Willis Reed (19) and Billy Cunningham watch.

the third quarter with an 18–3 burst that turned an 88-82 lead into an apparent 106-85 rout.

It was Reed, however, who earned the most valuable player award, because his dominant play in the first quarter gave the East com-

mand of the game. He and Robertson wound up with 21 points each and Willis had 11 rebounds.

But Oscar earned a longer-lasting distinction. Playing in his 10th All-Star Game, he became the highest scoring player in the

history of this monument to basketball glamour. His career total now stands at 230 points, surpassing the total of 224 Bob Pettit amassed in 11 games. His average of 23, of course, is the highest—and he doesn't seem anywhere near the end of the line.

Robertson in Command

In a sense, he was the key man in this game, too. The East had taken a 24-13 lead through Reed's leadership in the first quarter, and when Lew Alcinder relieved him, the West simply couldn't handle Lew's size. With Greer hitting, an 11-0 spurt made it 35-16 at the quarter. It was 58-40 halfway through the second period, and the West's front-court had scored only three baskets.

But it got back into contention as Elvin Hayes, Bill Bridges and Elgin Baylor made the last eight baskets of the half and cut the margin to 5 points with a 10-1 explosion right after intermission.

At 88-82, however, Robertson took command, stealing the ball and setting up Havlicek, who scored 9 straight points. DeBusschere joined Robertson in sniping and Reed, DeBusschere and Havlicek hit both boards. When Alcindor replaced Reed halfway through the rally, the East just rolled on until St led, 120-94.

It was 125-104 with six minutes to play, and the East had a noticeable letdown. Hayes, Jerry West, Joe Caldwell and Lou Hudson started hitting for the West, and the margin sank slowly at first. But with about three minutes to go, the West started a 9-point run to 131-125 at the two-minute mark, and Oscar and Havlicek had to stabilize things again.

Hayes wound up high man in the game with 24 points, while West had 22.

January 21, 1970

N.B.A. Adds Cleveland, Houston, Buffalo, Portland, Ore.

NEW TEAMS TO PAY $3.7-MILLION EACH

Vote for Expansion Is 11-3 —Group Named to Reopen Merger Talks With A.B.A.

Special to The New York Times

INGLEWOOD, Calif., Feb 6— The National Basketball Association voted today to expand to 18 teams for next season with the addition of four new franchises.

New franchises, announced after a meeting of the league's Board of Governors, were granted to Portland, Ore., Houston, Cleveland and Buffalo. The price tag was fixed at $3.7-million for each new team.

In a second action, Walter Kennedy, the N.B.A. commissioner, appointed a committee to reopen talks on a possible merger with the rival American Basketball Association.

The action was taken on the suggestion of Judge Alfonso J. Zirpoli of the San Francisco District Federal Court and at the request of Jack Dolph, the A.B.A. commissioner.

Judge Urged Talks

The A.B.A. had filed a suit against the N.B.A. in San Francisco, which Judge Zirpoli had refused to dismiss and instead had asked both leagues to resume merger talks and work out their differences.

The committee formed to talk merger was also a victory for Ned Irish, the president of the New York Knickerbockers, who was known to be against expansion without merger.

Irish was appointed to the merger committee, along with Sam Schulman, owner of the Seattle SuperSonincs, and Abe Pollin, president of the Baltimore Bullets.

Schulman, who will chair the committee, and Irish were members of the merger group that negotiated with the A.B.A. last summer before the talks broke down.

Jack Kent Cooke, owner of the Los Angeles Lakers, disclosed that the vote in favor of expansion was 11-3 and that he opposed the move. Cooke said he voted against expansion because he felt the league should be "strengthened" before it was enlarged.

There were earlier reports and statements by the Portland and Cleveland groups that they had abandoned expansion negotiations because the price tag was too high.

Will Participate in Draft

They were enticed back with concessions that permitted them to participate in this year's first round of the college player draft and as equal partners in sharing the television revenue when the new contract is negotiated.

The new teams will pick seventh, eighth, ninth and 10th in the draft.

The expansion teams will be stocked by the present 14 teams. Each team will be permitted to protect seven of its players on the active list.

After the first player is selected by one of the expansion teams from the player pool to be created, that team will be permitted to pull back one more player. Each team will give up a total of three players.

The Portland franchise was granted to a syndicate headed by Harry Glickman. The Houston franchise went to a syndicate headed by Alan Rothenberg; the Cleveland franchise to a syndicate headed by Nicholas Mileti and the Buffalo franchise to a syndicate headed by Peter Crotty of Buffalo and Philip Ryan of New York.

February 7, 1970

Bucks Trounce 76ers, 156-120, on Record Playoff Score and Lead Series, 2-1

ALCINDOR TALLIES 33 POINTS IN ROUT

Bucks, Leading by 52 After 3 Periods, Also Set Field Goals and Assist Marks

By GEORGE VECSEY
Special to The New York Times

PHILADELPHIA, March 30— Lew Alcindor and the Milwaukee Bucks went on the road for a playoff game for the first time in their professional lives tonight and all they did was crush an experienced team and set a scoring record.

In what might be a preview of the next generation in the National Basketball Association, the 7-foot-1-inch rookie and his teammates murdered the hometown 76ers, 156-120, scoring the most points for one game in the history of the N.B.A. playoffs.

But the game wasn't as close as the final score might indicate. The Bucks led by 52 points after the third period and they played the last five men for the final period. Alcindor played 33 minutes and scored 33 points.

Home Away From Home

The victory was the second for the Bucks in three games in the opening round of the Eastern Division playoffs. The first team to win four games advances to the Eastern final.

The Bucks had split the first two games in Madison, Wis., which served as their home site because the court in Milwaukee was temporarily unavailable.

Before tonight, there was reason to speculate that road games in the playoffs might put far more pressure on a young team than regular-season games would. That speculation ended shortly after 8 P.M.

A 4-Minute Contest

The Milwaukee club was founded in the 1968-69 season and did not qualify for the playoffs. This year it finished second in the Eastern Division; it had something to do with their new center. But they are also well-coached by Larry Costello and, at least tonight, they seem willing to blend together with Alcindor's overwhelming presence.

Philadelphia struggled to stay close in the early minutes and trailed, 10-8, after 4 seconds. But then Jon McGlocklin, the four-year man from Indiana, paced a 10-point surge that opened up the game irrevocably.

Walt Frazier (left) guards Jerry West—two of the greatest guards to ever play the game.

This is known as intimidation. Kareem Abdul-Jabbar blocks a shot by the Kings' Don Kojis. Kojis may think twice before shooting again in this game.

Alcindor, leaning forward, hardly utilized his full height, never seemed to be looking for his own shot, yet he demolished Darrall Imhoff within 7½ minutes. Luke Jackson, almost one-legged since he snapped his Achilles tendon last year, and George Wilson later tried to hold Alcindor down. But the Bucks never tried to force the ball in to the giant. They had too many other assets.

Show of Cohesiveness

McGlocklin had 24 points and Flynn Robinson finally broke loose from Wally Jones's karate defense for 20 points. Bobby Dandridge, the fourth-round draft choice from Norfolk State, also had 18 points as did Fred Crawford, the former Knick.

But the best thing about the Bucks was their cohesiveness. Alcindor had a 10-foot jump shot at one point, but chose to pass to McGlocklin, a few feet closer. McGlocklin then slipped a pass to Dandridge for an easy layup. Any of the three shots would have been acceptable to the coach.

If the Bucks can be so polished in the first road playoff game in their history, what will they be like in the forthcoming rounds — or the forthcoming season?

The 79 points in the second half tied the playoff record . . . the 67 field goals set a record as did the 46 assists . . . the previous high point total for a playoff game was the 145 by St. Louis against Detroit on March 25, 1958. The Spectrum was sold out; with 15,244 fans, for the first time all . . . naturally, the Philly fans booed the late announcement of a door prize of two tickets to the next game, on Wendesday. . . . Alcindor had 17 rebounds to lead both teams.

PHILADELPHIA (120)				MILWAUKEE (156)			
	G.	F.	P.		G.	F.	P.
Clark	9	2-4	20	Alcindor	13	7-8	33
B. C'ngham	4	2-4	10	Chappell	6	0-0	12
Greer	6	0-0	12	Crawford	6	6-7	18
Guokas	5	1-1	11	D. C'ngham	4	0-0	8
Hetzel	6	5-6	17	Dandridge	8	2-2	18
Imhoff	0	0-0	4	Greacen	1	0-1	2
Jackson	4	0-2	8	M'G'cklin	10	4-5	24
Jones	6	2-2	14	Robinson	9	2-2	20
Ogden	5	2-4	12	Rodgers	0	0-0	0
Washington	4	2-7	10	D. Smith	5	1-2	11
Wilson	1	0-0	2	G. Smith	3	0-1	6
				Williams	2	0-0	4
Total	52	16-28	120	Total	67	22-28	156

Philadelphia ....14 27 31 48—120
Milwaukee ....40 37 47 32—156
Attendance—15,224. March 31, 1970

KNICKS SET BACK LAKERS, 111-108

Foul Shot by Reed Decides Overtime Victory on Coast

By LEONARD KOPPETT

Special to The New York Times

LOS ANGELES, April 29—The New York Knickerbockers, making up a 14-point deficit at half-time and deprived of victory in regulation time by Jerry West's 55-foot shot in the final second, went one up on the Los Angeles Lakers tonight by winning in overtime, 111-108, in the third game of the National Basketball Association's final-round playoffs.

Willis Reed, scoring 38 points, sank a free throw with 1:27 to play to break a 108-108 tie, and after West, who scored 34, missed a shot, the Knicks got the clinching goal from Dick Barnett with four seconds left. Barnett, who missed his first nine shots in the game and didn't get a basket until midway through the third quarter, also made a vital basket that gave New York a 100-99 lead 18 seconds before regulation time ran out.

Five seconds after that, Barnett fouled Wilt Chamberlain, who was having a great game in every respect and even sinking more than half his free throws. Wilt missed the first gut made the second, tying the score, and the Knicks worked for a final shot that would assure them of victory or, if they missed, a tie.

DeBusschere took it, a 17-foot jumper, with three seconds to go, and that seemed to settle matters, because Los Angeles had no timeouts left. But Chamberlain, flipping the ball in bounds, got it to West in time for Jerry to make a one-handed leave from about 12 feet behind the center line. It went in and the extra period became necessary.

By this time, the Knicks had an edge in freshness, since Chamberlain and West had played every minute, and in foul situation, since Elgin Baylor, Happy Hairston and Dick Garrett, had five apiece. Two goals by DeBusschere helped the Knicks open a 108-105 lead, but the Lakers tied it again on Garrett's jump shot and West's free throw. But Baylor fouled out as he hacked Reed on a rebound of a shot by Barnett, and Willis made the free throw.

Chamberlain finished with 21 points and 26 rebounds, while Reed had 17 rebounds, while Reed ahd 17 rebounds and DeBusschere 15, as well as 21 points. Barnett, making seven baskets in his last nine attempts, wound up with 18.

KNICKS (111)							
	Min	FG-A	FT-A	R	A	P	T
Barnett	46	7-18	4-5	2	4	5	18
Bowman	4	0-1	2-5	2	0	2	2
Bradley	37	3-13	1-1	3	8	4	7
DeBusschere	44	10-20	1-1	15	3	2	21
Frazier	49	8-17	3-4	11	7	2	19
Reed	49	17-30	4-8	17	3	2	38
Riordan	10	0-2	0-0	3	1	2	0
Russell	16	1-5	0-0	3	1	3	2
Stallworth	9	1-3	2-2	2	1	2	4
Warren	1	0-0	0-0	0	0	1	0
Total	265	47-109	17-23	68	24	23	111

LOS ANGELES LAKERS (108)							
Baylor	45	4-13	5-6	12	11	6	13
Chamberlain	53	7-10	7-13	26	4	4	21
Egan	5	1-1	0-0	1	0	0	2
Erickson	46	9-17	1-2	4	3	2	19
Garrett	44	6-14	1-1	4	3	5	13
Hairston	19	3-3	0-0	3	0	5	6
West	53	11-28	12-16	7	9	2	34
Total	265	41-86	26-38	57	28	24	108

Knicks ....20 22 22 34 9—111
Los Angeles ...26 31 26 24 9—108
Officials—Mendy Rudolph and Jack Madden.
Attendance—17,500. April 30, 1970

Knicks Take First Title, Beating Lakers, 113 to 99

Frazier Scores 36 Points, Reed Excels on Defense Despite Ailing Knee

By LEONARD KOPPETT

The New York Knickerbockers, displaying their finest qualities with the limited physical but important spiritual aid of a limping Willis Reed, won the championship of the National Basketball Association last night by routing the Los Angeles Lakers, 113-99, at Madison Square Garden.

Walt Frazier, with 36 points and 19 assists, was the most brilliant individual, but this, like most Knick successes, was basically a team enterprise.

Darlings of the basketball world and a subject of national sports interest since November, when they set a league record by winning 18 games in a row, the Knicks finally achieved the first title in their 24-year history by winning the seventh game of the final round of the playoffs. It was their 101st game this season.

By winning, the Knicks gave New York's happy sports fans their third professional world championship in 16 months. The football Jets won the Super Bowl game in January, 1969, and the baseball Mets took the World Series last fall.

For the 19,500 screaming spectators, the Knicks produced a staggeringly effective defense, their trademark throughout the season. In addition, their shooting was deadly in the first quarter as they built a 38-24 lead.

Soon they had a 51-31 margin and it didn't dip below 20 points until the closing minutes.

Reed, as always, was an indispensable element, but in an unusual fashion. He had injured a muscle in his right leg that runs from the pelvis to below the knee early in the fifth game of the series, when the series was tied in games, 2-2. His injury seemed to doom the Knicks to defeat, because it left them with no counterweapon to Wilt Chamberlain, the 7-foot-2-inch giant who is the Laker center and the greatest scorer in basketball history.

But the Knicks rallied to win that game, which meant they were still alive when Chamberlain and the Lakers crushed

The New York Times
Walt Frazier in the game

them in Los Angeles on Wednesday night, while Reed sat on the bench. If Reed had been unable to play last night, the Knicks would not have been expected to win.

Reed Gets First Basket

As it turned out, after a late-afternoon examination by Dr. James Parkes, some pain-killing injections, a few minutes of shooting practice and another injection just before the game began, Reed was able to start. He took the first shot at the basket, with the game 18 seconds old, and made it.

A minute later, he hit another, making the score 5-2, and the effect on his teammates was electric.

"He gave us a tremendous lift, just going out there," said Coach Red Holzman afterward. "He couldn't play his normal game, but he did a lot of things out there and he means a lot to the spirit of the other players."

What Reed did was occupy Chamberlain. He presented enough of a defensive problem to keep the big man within bounds—and the other four Knicks simply ran away from the other four Lakers.

The Knicks shot better, de-

TWO OF 36: Walt Frazier of the Knicks going around Jerry West of Lakers for 2 of his game-high 36 points.

The New York Times

COOL FINISH TO HOT CONTEST: Willis Reed pours the champagne—over his head—following Knicks' victory over Los Angeles Lakers, 113-99, at Madison Square Garden for the National Basketball Association championship.

fended better, hustled more, defended better, hustled more, ran faster, jumped higher, passed more accurately and stole the ball more often.

Reed Wins Award

When it was all over, Reed's line in the box score was unimpressive: just those two baskets in five shots, no free-throw attempts, three rebounds, four personal fouls. But his season-long contribution was tak into consideration and he was given the car that Sport magazine awards to the outstanding player of the final round of the playoffs.

As the game wore on, Reed felt more pain, and moved more slowly, even though he had another shot of pain-killer at half-time. But the early momentum he helped give the Knicks was enough.

Frazier in particular, and the team in general, showed a characteristic the Knicks had displayed before: the ability to fire their best effort in the most important situation. The three best performances they gave in six weeks of post-season competition were in the seventh game of the Baltimore series, which got them past that most serious hurdle; the fifth game against Milwaukee, which wrapped up the series

against Lew Alcindor's team, 4 games to 1, and this one.

Dave DeBusschere, the rugged forward whose arrival from Detroit more than a year ago transformed the Knicks into a great team (by allowing Reed to move to center as well as by DeBusschere's own contributions) had another superb game. He had to do the heavy rebounding, taking down 17, and scoring 18 points.

Dick Barnett, the oldest Knick, scored 21. As Frazier's partner in backcourt, he had provided the outside shooting the Knicks always needed. He was the only Knick who had played in a final round before, with the Lakers in 1962 when they lost to Boston in seven games. The victory was especially sweet to him.

Bradley Plays Well

Bill Bradley, not at his best in much of the series, was in top form this time, with 17 points and five assists. And the much-appreciated Knick bench —Nate Bowman as Reed's relief, Dave Stallworth, Cazzie Russell and Mike Riordan—did its share, although only Bow-

The Line-Up

KNICKS (113)

	min	fgm	fta	ftm	fta	reb	a	pf	pts
Barnett	42	9	20	3	3	0	2	4	21
Bowman	21	3	5	0	1	5	0	5	6
Bradley	42	8	18	1	1	4	5	3	17
DeB'schre	37	8	15	2	2	17	1	1	18
Frazier	44	12	17	12	12	7	19	3	36
Reed	27	2	5	0	0	3	1	4	4
Riordan	10	2	3	1	2	2	2	4	5
Russell	6	1	4	0	0	3	0	0	2
Stallworth	11	1	5	2	2	2	1	3	4
Total	240	46	92	21	23	43	30	25	113

LOS ANGELES LAKERS (99)

	min	fgm	fta	ftm	fta	reb	a	pf	pts
Baylor	35	9	17	1	2	5	1	2	19
Chamb'l'n	48	10	16	1	11	24	4	1	21
Egan	11	0	2	0	0	0	2	0	
Erickson	36	5	10	4	6	6	9	3	14
Garrett	34	3	10	2	2	4	1	4	8
Hairston	15	2	5	2	2	2	0	1	6
Tresvant	12	0	4	3	3	2	0	2	3
West	48	9	19	10	12	6	5	4	28
Total	240	38	83	23	38	49	17	19	99

Min.—Minutes played. FGM—Field goals made. FGA—Field goals attempted. FTM—Free throws made. FTA—Free throws attempted. Reb.—Rebounds. A—Assists. PF—Personal fouls. Pts.—Points scored.

| Knicks | 38 | 31 | 25 | 19—113 |
| Los Angeles | 24 | 18 | 27 | 30— 99 |

Referees—Mendy Rudolph and Richie Powers.

Attendance—19,500.

man played as much as usual (and more).

For Coach Red Holzman, who also took over as general manager last March, it was a complete triumph. He succeeded Dick McGuire as coach halfway through the 1967-68 season, and the Knicks have been winning regularly ever since. Eddie Donovan, who built the team as general manager before resigning to take over the new Buffalo club, was also present to enjoy the victory.

And probably no one enjoyed it more than Ned Irish, original and present president of the club, who saw the Knicks fail in the final round in 1951, 1952 and 1953 before going into a long decline that Donovan finally reversed.

For the Lakers, the result was

bitter disappointment. They have now reached the final round, and lost, seven times in the last nine years. All their previous defeats were at the hands of the Boston Celtics, led by Bill Russell. Now they had failed again, even though Reed —who is not, for all his virtues, the equal of Russell at his best —was hurt.

Elgin Baylor and Jerry West, who played on all those teams, must now carry the cruel "loser" label another year, along with Chamberlain, who has been on one title-winner in

his 11-year career.

Lakers Play Poorly

And the fact is, the Lakers played badly. They had one tiny chance to make a game of it, when the Knicks started missing their shots in the third quarter, but couldn't generate a sustained offense. They became progressively disorganized as the Knicks harried and outran them. They didn't make their own good shots, and they gave the Knicks too many good ones.

Chamberlain finished with 24 rebounds and 21 points, West

with 28 points, Baylor with 19; but these were just numbers. Joe Mullaney, their first-year coach, thought they tried too hard to catch up too quickly after New York's hot start.

"We fell into a faster tempo," he said, "instead of trying to get back 2 points at a time. We just can't play that kind of pace against a team like the Knicks."

To reach the final, the Lakers defeated Phoenix in seven games and Atlanta in four straight.

May 9, 1970

N.B.A. and A.B.A. Agree to Merge, Subject to Approval of Congress

PLAYERS TO FIGHT MOVE VIGOROUSLY

Cite Antitrust Violations —Congressional Action Is Unlikely This Year

By SAM GOLDAPER

The 24-year-old National Basketball Association and the three-year-old American Basketball Association agreed yesterday to merge, subject to the approval of Congress.

The N.B.A., meeting in Atlanta, voted 13-4 in favor of the merger, while the vote of the 11 teams in the A.B.A., meeting in Denver, was unanimous. The N. B. A. commissioner, Walter Kennedy, who would be the commissioner of the single league if the merger is approved, issued the joint statement for the leagues.

Sources in Washington indicated yesterday the chances of Congress acting on the merger this year were slim.

The leagues are legally barred from merging by a United States District Court injunction, but the court has allowed the leagues permission to seek Congressional approval. The court injunction was issued in May in a suit filed by the N.B.A. Players Association opposing any merger.

Congress approved a merger of the National and American Football Leagues in October of 1966 as a rider to an appropriation's bill but there was no opposition from the players of either league at the time. The pro football merger ended a costly bidding war for player talent and pro basketball is

seeking to do the same.

Players Play to Lobby

"I cannot believe that Congress would approve a merger which is so clearly anti-competitive and prejudicial to the players," said Ira Millstein, the attorney for the N.B.A. players. "If the merger was approved the players will clearly suffer because competition for their services will be eliminated. The only source of competition for the players is the existence of two leagues. I would expect the players will vigorously oppose any attempt to obtain such legislation."

Oscar Robertson of the Milwaukee Bucks, president of the N.B.A. Players Association, said by telephone from his home in Cincinnati, "We're going to fight a merger in every way we know how. We think it's a violation of the antitrust laws and

it clearly eliminates competition."

Robertson said he expected many of the players to make personal appearances in Washington to lobby against the approval of a merger.

The merger agreement provides for 28 franchises in 27 cities or areas, with New York holding two franchises — the Knicks and the Nets.

Areas of Agreement

In addition to the 28 teams the agreement calls for at least two new franchises to be established before the single league schedule goes into effect.

Each club in the A.B.A. would pay $1.25-million over a 10-year period to the N.B.A. with the exception of Washington. The Capitols were excused from the indemnity in lieu of moving their franchise out of Wash-

ington.

Also agreed on was a single league schedule as early as practicable but no later than the 1973-1974 season. Until then there would be a world championship playoff between the two league winners, interleague play and a common draft.

The A.B.A. also agreed to develop a pension plan comparable to the one in the N.B.A. and to introduce a minimum salary at the N.B.A. level. The present N.B.A. minmum salary is $13,500 a season, but plans call for it to be "significantly increased."

A statement on the merger, issued by the leagues, said: "Unless legislation permitting a single league is enacted, disintegration of the A.B.A. is only a matter of time."

June 19, 1970

Gentleman's Agreement

Economic Feasibility Deemed Reason Pros and Colleges Back 4-Year Rule

By LEONARD KOPPETT

The Spencer Haywood case has brought to the limelight the "four-year rule," which prevents professional basketball and football teams from signing a player until four years after he enters college.

Why is there such a rule at all? And why do college and professional administrators, whose interests differ in so many other ways, both staunchly support this system?

And how can they get away with a practice that, many lawyers feel, is an avowed conspiracy in restraint of trade?

The usual answers given to these questions bristle with idealism. "The boy" must not be "enticed" away from his invaluable college education by fabulous financial offers while he is still "immature," college coaches often say. The same argument has been used, or accepted, by legislators when

the antitrust question has been raised. And even the pros, who don't really have to, tend to discuss the rule as some sort of moral obligation.

Profits for All

The real answers, however, are entirely economic.

Stripped of solicitous justifications (however sincere in a particular case), the four-year rule thrives because it suits the common financial interest.

For colleges, it means protecting the supply of cheap labor.

For professionals, it makes possible the draft system, which reduces bidding for talent, and it helps maintain the free farm system the college teams constitute.

And it is significant that in baseball, a sport that does not have big-business status in college and does not use college competition as a major element in preparing big leaguers, a much looser set of restrictions exists.

A Plus for System

Even from this strictly commercial point of view, however, there is something to be said for the system in terms of the athlete. If it is true, as both colleges and pros believe, that this arrangement is essential to their economic health, it then makes possible the context in which the individual player can eventually prosper.

Nevertheless, in a particular case—like Haywood's—the questionable legality of these procedures is obvious. An Olympic star, a college all-America as a sophomore, Haywood decided he wanted his professional career to start immediately in 1969. By what right should 25 private businesses—the members of the National Basketball Association and the American Basketball Association—agree among themselves not to offer him employment? And by what right could the colleges, separately and through their national association, openly urge those businesses to do so, and even threaten reprisals if they didn't?

Actually, Denver of the A.B.A. did hire Haywood, and no issue was made of it for two reasons: the new league was happy to have a star, and the shaky legal ground was well understood by the pro establishment.

How Draft Works

Yet, when Haywood, already a pro, was signed by Seattle of the N.B.A., the four-year rule became a burning issue within that league, causing the most serious internal strife of its 25-year history.

The difference was a crucial one: Seattle was bypassing the draft process, and its fellow members couldn't take that.

And the draft process is the key.

In the draft, each pro club selects, in turn, the negotiation rights to a player coming out of college. When there are two rival leagues, as in basketball now and in football until recently, the player can make the two teams that drafted him bid against each other. When there is only one league, there is no bidding: the player can come to some sort of terms with the team that drafted him, or not play.

The order of selection is such that each year's weakest teams get first pick, so that over a period of time competitive balance is maintained and even improved. An especially rich club can't outbid a less affluent one for

new talent because it can only deal with its own drafted players.

But to make the draft effective there must be a common starting point. That's what the four-year rule provides. If it weren't there, all the pro clubs would have to compete with each other all through a college player's career. That would be expensive, and it would antagonize the free farm system.

The desire of college coaches and other officials to protect their charges from "seductive" pro offers would be more impressive if their own activities were less competitive.

Seduction by Colleges

Colleges seek out, pursue, offer inducements to and sign to "letters of intent" high school athletes, and they do it with more intensive scouting systems than the pros use to evaluate collegians. A significant percentage of bigtime college athletes do not make normal progress toward a degree, if they get one at all. By openly providing athletic scholarships and other benefits, and by collecting large sums in gate receipts, colleges create an employe-employer relationship in practice no matter how much they deny it in theory.

What college governing bodies call "regulations" limiting recruiting and financial aid are remarkably similar to "ceilings" placed on salaries and bonuses by professional groups from time to time.

It is certainly true that if all pro teams were free to pursue any promising player —a Wilt Chamberlain or a Lew Alcindor right after high school or freshman year, for instance—everyone's expenses would soar. Without the likelihood of profit, neither large-scale college nor well-paying pro teams would exist.

But the price of this practical arrangement is the individual's right to choose professionalism when he wants. Many a promising college sophomore or junior has had his earning power reduced or even wiped out by an injury as a senior.

Rules Vary With Sport

The actual rules differ in each sport.

In football, only college players are subject to draft, the year their entering class graduates. (A player who enters college in 1971, even if he drops out after one semester, cannot be drafted until the spring of 1975). But a high school graduate, if he does not enter college, can be signed without going through the draft.

In basketball, the four-year rule is the same, but a high school player cannot

be signed for one full year after graduation if he does not enter college.

In baseball, there is a "free-agent draft" which selects players as soon as they finish high school. However, if a player has not been signed by the time he attends his first college class, he cannot be signed until his entering class graduates—unless he reaches his 21st birthday before that, or becomes academically ineligible. In any case, he then goes through the draft again.

But the purpose of all these rules is the same: to control and diminish bidding for the services of talented athletes.

January 10, 1971

BUCKS TROUNCE 76ERS, 142 TO 118

Greer Gets 20,000th Point Before Spectrum Crowd

PHILADELPHIA, Jan. 29 (AP) —Hal Greer joined the National Basketball Association's 20,000-point career club tonight, but the Philadelphia 76ers lost to the Milwaukee Bucks, 142-118, before a sellout crowd of 15,246 at the Spectrum.

Greer brought his 13-year career total to 20,001 with a driving underhand shot at 4 minutes 7 seconds of the final period. The 34-year-old Greer collected 10 field goals and a free throw for 21 points.

Greer joined Wilt Chamberlain, Elgin Baylor and Jerry West of Los Angeles; Oscar Robertson of the Bucks and Bob Pettit, former St. Louis star, as the only players in the N.B.A. to reach the 20,000 mark.

MILWAUKEE (142)				PHILADELPHIA (118)			
	G.	F.	P.		G.	F.	P.
Dandroe	7	7-10	21	Washtn	3	2-2	8
Smith	5	2-3	12	B. Cunhm	7	4-6	18
McGlkin	9	5-6	23	Awtrey	2	3-4	7
Robrtsn	7	7-9	21	Greer	10	1-2	21
Alcindor	12	7-11	31	Clark	9	3-4	21
Zopf	0	0-0	0	Howell	6	5-10	17
Allen	6	3-3	15	Foster	3	0-0	6
Freeman	1	1-2	1	Ogden	1	0-0	2
D. Cunnhm	2	1-2	5	Jackson	4	0-0	8
Boozer	6	1-1	13	Crwford	3	4-4	10
Total	54	34-48	142	Total	48	22-32	118

Milwaukee 32   31   28   41—142
Philadelphia 28   32   23   35—118
Attendance—15,244.

January 30, 1971

OVERTIME DEFEAT ENDS BUCK STRING

Bulls Win, 110-103, to Halt Streak at 20 Games

CHICAGO, March 9 (UPI)—Bob Weiss scored 6 points, Chet Walker got 3 and Bob Love 2 in a five-minute overtime period tonight as the Chicago Bulls beat Milwaukee, 110-103, to end the Bucks' winning streak at 20 games. The regulation-time score was 99-99.

It was the first victory of the season for the Bulls over the Bucks after five defeats and the triumph enabled them to retain their 1½-game lead over the Phoenix Suns in the battle for second place in the National Basketball Association's Midwest Division.

MILWAUKEE (103)				CHICAGO (110)			
	G.	F.	P.		G.	F.	P.
Smith	4	0-0	8	Walker	8	4-5	20
Dandridge	2	1-4	5	Love	8	7-9	23
Alcindor	18	3-3	39	Boerwinkle	6	9-12	21
Robertson	8	4-5	20	Sloan	8	5-5	21
McGlocklin	9	2-3	20	Guokas	4	0-0	8
Webb	0	0-0	0	Weiss	4	4-5	12
Allen	3	0-0	6	Baum	1	0-0	2
Cunninghm	0	1-1	1	King	0	0-0	0
Boozer	1	2-2	4	Fox	1	1-3	3
Total	45	13-18	103	Total	40	30-39	110

Milwaukee 27   23   21   28   4—103
Chicago 22   19   36   22   11—110
Attendance—16,277.

March 10, 1971

Sonics Retain Haywood In Out-of-Court Compact

Seattle Submits to N.B.A. Fine of $200,000

By LEONARD KOPPETT

An out-of-court settlement of the Spencer Haywood case, leaving the basketball star the property of the Seattle Super-Sonics as far as the National Basketball Association is concerned, was announced yesterday by Walter Kennedy, N.B.A. commissioner.

The settlement ended an antitrust suit brought by the player and Seattle against the N.B.A. in Federal District Court in Los Angeles. It removed a major obstacle to completion of merger between the N.B.A. and the American Basketball Association.

The main remaining obstacle is the opposition of virtually all members of the N.B.A. Players Association. They got a court order last spring that prevented the leagues from merging, but did allow them to submit merger plans to Congress, which could pass legislation permitting an exception to the antitrust laws.

Another suit, in which Denver of the A.B.A. is suing Haywood for breach of contract, is not affected by the N.B.A. settlement. That trial is continuing before Judge Warren J. Ferguson, who heard the N.B.A. case.

N.B.A. Forbids Switch

Haywood played with Denver last year and led the A.B.A. in scoring. This year he jumped to Seattle, but the N.B.A. refused to grant him eligibility because he had not yet gone through an N.B.A. draft, which includes only players whose original college class is graduating.

That refusal brought about the antitrust suit and Haywood played in 33 games between Dec. 30 and the end of the season after Judge Ferguson had issued a temporary injunction preventing the N.B.A. from ruling him ineligible.

The agreement announced yesterday, but worked out last Tuesday at a league meeting, listed four main conditions:

1. All litigation will be dismissed "with prejudice," which means the case cannot be re-opened.

2. Seattle will pay the league a $200,000 fine for violating league regulations, but will keep the rights to Haywood, whose name will not be put through the 1971 draft.

3. Seattle will take its regular turn in the 1971 draft, scheduled for Monday.

4. All protests filed by other N.B.A. teams about games Haywood played against them have been dismissed.

However, one aspect of the case persists. Last Monday, Judge Ferguson ruled the so-called "four-year" rule violated antitrust laws. Since the case in which he made that ruling has been dropped, it cannot be appealed.

There is great confusion about what that ruling means. Can the N.B.A., as it has said it would, cling to that rule? The A.B.A. has already accepted the ruling at face value by signing Johnny Neumann, the Mississippi sophomore, to a Memphis contract this week.

Kennedy commented on this situation in a carefully worded prepared statement that began: "I don't think Judge Ferguson's decision can be simply summarized."

Careful restudy of the N.B.A. draft rules is needed in the light of that decision, Kennedy said, and can't be completed in time for this year's draft.

"But future drafts may need different rules," he said.

That means the N.B.A. intends to abide by the four-year rule in Monday's draft and that it continues to believe it is the right way to operate.

And since the merger must pass through Congress anyhow, this feature of basketball operation may be clarified in that process.

March 27, 1971

Bucks Sweep Bullets, Take Crown

By LEONARD KOPPETT
Special to The New York Times

BALTIMORE, April 30 — Led by Oscar Robertson, the one extra needed ingredient to make the presence of Lew Alcindor fully productive, the Milwaukee Bucks won the National Basketball Association championship tonight. They completed a four-game sweep of a final round only the second one in the 25-year history of the league.

The Bucks trounced a scrappy but overmatched Baltimore team, 118-106, holding the upper hand from the first quarter on. In the four games of the final round, the Bullets were beaten by margins of 10, 19, 8 and 12 points, but each game was really more one-sided than that.

When the Boston Celtics took four straight from the Minneapolis Lakers in the 1959 final, the margins were 3, 20, 3 and 5 points.

Robertson scored 30 points, hitting 11 of his 15 field goal attempts, and had nine assists. The man who has been called the most talented single basketball player yet produced has waited 11 years to get into the N.B.A. final, toiling 10 of them with Cincinnati teams that never had an overwhelming center. Now, at the age of 32, he shares in the treasured title in his 886th N.B.A. game.

However, as brilliant as Oscar was, Alcindor was of more fundamental importance—as Oscar's own career history proved. In his second pro season, Alcindor, who has just turned 24, added basketball's biggest prize to an almost unbroken succession of victories through his high school and college years. Even last year, as a rookie with no Oscar to quarterback the team, he led the Bucks to the second best record in the league.

In this game, Alcindor scored 27 points, exactly his average for the three preceding games. For 14 playoff games, he averaged 26.6, and during the regular season he won the scoring championship with a 31.7 average for 82 games.

He was the league's most valuable player during the regular season—and no one could quarrel with his designation as the outstanding player of the final, for which he earned the sports car given each year by Sports Magazine.

Other individuals have had their moments in the star-studded N.B.A., but these two —like Bill Russell of the champion Celtics and perhaps half a dozen others through the years—have the special quality of blending their play to make less talented teammates reach maximum effectiveness.

The Bullets have brilliant individuals, too, and the two hot ones tonight were Wes Unseld, who outrebounded Alcindor, 23-12, (but scored only 11 points) and Fred Carter, hitting from the corners again and scoring 28 points. Gus Johnson played, bad knees and all (he'll have an operation soon), and Earl Monroe had a good first quarter before his battered legs gave out altogether. But the Bullets just couldn't stay close.

They never gave up, however, when one might have expected them to. In fact, they had two brief fistic flurries in the first quarter — Monroe with Jon McGlocklin and Jack Marin with Bob Dandridge (who was carried bodily out of the conflict by Gus Johnson).

Baltimore's one surge produced a 15-10 lead, but the Bucks outscored the Bullets, 21-7, in the last six minutes of the first quarter. They ran the lead to 19 points before it shrank to 60-47 in the last two minutes of the first half.

The Bullets opened the second half with a challenge that made the score 60-53—only to be hit with a 10-0 burst. Trailing, 82-64, with four minutes to go in the third period, they might have called it a season, but they didn't: They plugged away and narrowed the margin to 12 points. They didn't let Milwaukee pull away conclusively until the middle of the final period.

Victory meant about $15,000 a man to the Bucks in total playoff winnings, while Baltimore came away with about $10,000 a man. By sweeping through the playoffs with a 12-2 record, the Bucks recorded the best post-season performance on record, surpassing the 10-2 posted by the Minneapolis Lakers, led by George Mikan, in 1950.

MILWAUKEE (118)

	min	fgm	fga	ftm	fta	reb	a	pf	pts
Alcindor	44	10	16	7	11	12	7	2	27
Allen	23	2	6	0	0	3	1	2	4
Boozer	11	2	3	1	2	4	0	5	5
Cunin'shm	4	0	1	0	0	1	0	0	0
Dandridge	41	9	16	3	5	12	6	2	21
Greacen	3	0	1	0	0	0	0	0	0
M'Glcklin	29	4	9	4	5	0	1	2	12
McLemore	11	2	5	1	2	1	1	0	5
Robertson	38	11	15	8	9	3	9	2	30
Smith	34	6	9	2	3	7	2	4	14
Webb	1	0	0	0	0	0	0	0	0
Winkier	1	0	1	0	0	0	0	0	0
Total	240	46	82	26	37	49	27	19	118

BALTIMORE (106)

	min	fgm	fga	ftm	fta	reb	a	pf	pts
Carter	44	14	24	0	0	2	3	3	28
Gu.Johnson	5	0	2	0	0	4	1	1	0
GeJohnson	27	4	12	3	3	7	2	0	11
Loughery	29	8	14	2	2	0	1	2	18
Marin	37	5	17	2	3	4	0	2	12
Monroe	22	6	14	0	0	1	2	4	12
Murry	2	0	0	0	0	0	0	0	0
Tresvant	28	4	10	0	2	5	0	5	8
Unseld	39	3	12	5	8	23	10	5	11
Zeller	7	2	7	2	2	2	0	1	6
Total	240	46	112	14	20	49	22	28	106

min–Minutes played. fgm–Field goals made. fga–Field goals attempted. ftm–Free throws made. fta–Free throws attempted. reb–Rebounds. a–Assists. pf–Personal fouls. pts–Total points.

Milwaukee	31	29	29	29	118
Baltimore	22	25	30	29	106

Attendance—11,842.

May 1, 1971

N. B. A. MODIFIES ELIGIBILITY RULE

Revises 4-Year Edict to Aid College 'Hardship' Cases

BOSTON, June 24 (AP)—The National Basketball Association, modified its so-called "four-year rule," today to permit hardship cases among collegians to join its pro ranks.

J. Walter Kennedy, the pres-ident of the N.B.A., announced the change in the rule after a long discussion by club owners at the league's annual meeting.

Under the revised rule, a player who has not completed his college educatio may request permission to join an N.B.A. club. The player must prove he is a hardship case based on what Kennedy called "financial condition, his family, his academic record, or lack of it, and his ability to obtain employment in another field."

Under the long - standing N.B.A. rule, a player could not be signed or drafted by a league club if he had college eligibility remaining. The new language is similar to that of the American Basketball Association, which has signed many players with eligibility remaining.

Kennedy declined to disclose who made the motion or what the vote was in the change of the rule, which is most likely to disturb the members of the National Collegiate Athletic Association.

Many colleges throughout the country have barred A.B.A. scouts because of that league's rule permitting hardship cases among collegians to join the pro ranks.

June 25, 1971

Lakers Run Streak to 27

United Press International

THE BIG MAN MISSES ONE: Wilt Chamberlain of the Lakers couldn't make it with this backhand shot during last night's game against the Bullets in Baltimore. At left is Baltimore's Wes Unseld. The Lakers won, 127 to 120.

Shatter Record, Beating Bullets by 127-120

BALTIMORE, Dec. 22 (UPI)—The Los Angeles Lakers set a major-league professional record of 27 consecutive victories by beating the Baltimore Bullets, 127-120, tonight.

Jerry West, who scored 37 points, clicked for 14 in the second quarter when the Lakers jumped from a 32-28 first-quarter deficit to a 62-50 lead at half-time. The Lakers went ahead by 25 points to 94-69 with five minutes remaining in the third quarter.

The Bullets cut the deficit to 118-110 with 3:20 left but Wilt Chamberlain sank a foul shot and West hit a jumper with 1:33 remaining that stopped the Baltimore rally.

The Lakers' victory eclipsed the previous major-league record of 26 straight triumphs set by the 1916 baseball New York Giants.

West has played in every game in the streak after shaking off an ankle sprain. West's three straight baskets sparked an 8-point string that put Los Angeles ahead for good, 52-43, midway in the second quarter.

Baltimore shot only 23 per cent in the second period and scored only 9 points in the final eight minutes of the first half.

The triumph put the Lakers' won-lost record to 33-3 while Baltimore dropped to 12-21 and suffered its third straight loss.

The Lakers' last loss was on Oct. 31 against the Golden State warriors.

The Lakers didn't do too much celebrating after setting the record.

"We don't want to sound blase," said Chamberlain, "but we did our celebrating when we won No. 21. That was the big one."

The 21st victory broke the National Basketball Associa-tion record.

"I don't want to take anything away from baseball," said Bill Sharman, the Laker coach, "but I think it's harder to win this many in basketball. We have tougher travel conditions, have to fight the home court advantage which doesn't mean as much as in baseball."

"I played with the Golbetrotters when they won 445 in a row," Chamberlain said. "And they were all on the road."

LOS ANGELES (127)				BALTIMORE (120)			
	G.	F.	P.		G.	F.	P.
Chamber'n	2	2-3	6	Chenier	6	1-1	13
Ellis	1	2-2	4	Clark	14	7-10	35
Goodrich	8	12-13	28	Driscoll	0	1-2	1
Hairston	6	6-6	18	Love	7	1-1	15
McMillan	12	1-2	25	Marin	10	1-1	21
Robinson	3	3-3	9	Riordan	1	0-0	2
West	17	3-3	37	Stallworth	6	3-3	15
				Unseld	9	0-0	18
Total	49	29-32	127	Total	53	14-18	120

Los Angeles ....28 34 40 25—127
Baltimore ....32 18 38 32—120
Attendance—6,453.

December 23, 1971

LAKERS WIN BY 44, THEIR 33D IN ROW

Hawks Walloped. 134-90—Los Angeles Shoots 62.5 Per Cent in First Half

ATLANTA, Jan. 7 (AP)—The Los Angeles Lakers extended their record-shattering winning streak to 33 games tonight by routing the Atlanta Hawks, 134-90, in the National Basketball Association.

Jim McMillian led the way early and Gail Goodrich late as the Lakers made the victory one of their easiest.

By shooting 62.5 per cent in the first half and holding the Hawks to 35.8 per cent, Los Angeles turned the game into an early runaway.

The Lakers have not lost since Oct. 31.

McMillian got 20 of his 26 points in the first half and Goodrich got 18 of his 23 in the second half. Wilt Chamberlain was the dominating factor under the boards.

Late in the third quarter, with the score, 92-61, the Atlanta coach, Richie Guerin, benched his starters for a rookie-studded line-up.

LOS ANGELES (134)				ATLANTA (90)			
	G.	F.	P.		G.	F.	P.
Chamber'n	5	4-4	14	Adams	3		7
Clea'mors	2	0-0	4	Bridges	7	3-5	17
Ellis	4	1-2	9	Christian	3	0-0	6
Goodrich	11	1-1	23	Guma	4	0-0	8
Hairston	1	3-4	5	Hud'burton	3	0-0	6
McMillian	12	2-2	26	Hudson	4	0-0	8
Riley	8	1-1	17	Maravich	6	5-6	17
Robinson	9	1-1	19	May	6	2-2	14
Trapp	2	1-1	5	Payne	1	0-1	2
West	4	4-5	12	Trapp	3	0-0	6
				Washington	3	3-3	9
Total	58	18-22	134	Total	38	14-20	90

Los Angeles .....30 32 32 40—134
Atlanta ....34 22 17 27—90
Attendance—7,192.

January 8, 1972

30,000TH POINT FOR CHAMBERLAIN

But Lakers Bow, 110-109, to Suns on His Misplay

PHOENIX, Ariz. (AP) — Wilt Chamberlain scored a career regular-season record 30,000 points tonight but a goaltending call on the Laker center with three seconds left in the final period gave the Phoenix Suns a 110-109 National Basketball Association victory over Los Angeles.

Chamberlain's record came with 2 minutes 9 seconds left in the third period when goaltending was called on the Suns center, Neal Walk.

Chamberlain, who finished the game with 19 points ironically was responsible for the Suns last and winning basket as he attempted to block a shot by Connie Hawkins.

Chamberlain, in addition to his 30,000 regular-season point total, has sored an additional 3,210 points in playoff competition.

LOS ANGELES (109)	G.	F.	P.	PHOENIX (110)	G.	F.	P.
Chamberl'n	6	7-12	19	Counts	0	0-0	0
Goodrich	7	5-5	19	Green	2	1-1	5
Hairston	7	3-3	17	Haskins	8	3-3	19
McMillin	12	2-4	26	Layton	3	1-1	7
Riev	0	2-2	2	Hawkins	7	1-1	15
Trapp	0	0-0	0	Moore	2	2-2	6
West	9	8-10	26	Silas	3	2-2	8
				VanArsdale	8	4-4	20
Total	41	27-36	109	Walk	12	6-7	30
				Total	45	20-21	110

Los Angeles ....20 28 29 32—108
Phoenix ....28 27 29 26—110
Attendance—12,534.

February 17, 1972

Dave Anderson

The Significance of Wayne Embry

As inconspicuously as possible for anyone 6 feet 8 inches and 255 pounds, **Wayne Embry** has eased into history as the first black general manager in major league sports. He has been entrusted with the "operation of the ball club," as he describes it, meaning the Milwaukee Bucks, the National Basketball Association champions. Incredibly, sports has survived the arrival of an Afrotopped brain in the front office. In two games since his appointment, the ball hasn't gone flat, the backboards haven't toppled, the polished floors haven't opened into a chasm. Equally important, Wayne Embry, who will be 35 years old in two weeks, has survived his new stature.

Sports of The Times

"I don't like to think there's any great significance to it for me," he was saying. "But it might be significant to humanity and society in general. If society chooses to look upon it as significant, maybe it is."

He was wearing a dark blue suit, a flowered blue and white shirt, a white tie and shiny size 17 black boots. His brown eyes peered through gold-rimmed glasses and he puffed on a cigar, befitting a man on an executive level with Red Auerbach of the Boston Celtics, one of his former bosses.

"If it wasn't for Red," he said in his firm voice, "I'd probably be in marketing for Pepsi-Cola now. Not that that would be bad, but I'm happier doing this."

The Attitude

Six years ago, after eight seasons as a bulky center with the Cincinnati Royals, he was discouraged. But he was talked out of retirement by Auerbach, who wanted him as a backup for Bill Russell, then the first black coach in major league sports.

"Red gave me my confidence back," Embry recalled. "I might get only a couple of rebounds, but after the game he'd mention it and slap me on the back. That was important. I was a man again."

Earlier the son of a body-and-fender worker had been discouraged as the first black student at Tecumseh High School in Springfield, Ohio, between Columbus and Dayton. The first day he got off the school bus, he noticed stares.

"I heard them saying nigger this, nigger that, I wanted to quit," he remembered. "But my parents told me that you have to believe in yourself as a man, that if you don't, nobody will. Ever since then, that's been my attitude in life."

His attitude was tested two years ago. After playing for the Bucks during their first season, he returned to Boston as a city director of recreation.

"We had a great thing going," he recalled. "We had 1,600 kids in the summer basketball league. But it was a civil service job. I'm too sincere and honest and sensitive to be involved with politics. The system was more important than what was being done for the kids."

When he resigned, 750 people attended a dinner in his honor, a tribute to his popularity.

Joining the Bucks' front-office staff, he hired a white

George Kalinsky

The Bucks' Wayne Embry has survived his new stature

Massachusetts high school coach, John Killilea, as an area scout. Auerbach has since hired Killilea as the Celtics' chief scout. Day by day, Wayne Embry became more important in the Bucks' organization. He was instrumental in the trade for Oscar Robertson, his Royal roommate for six seasons. And when Ray Patterson, the club president, resigned recently to take over the Houston Rockets next season, a new front-office leader was needed. The 11 directors on the Bucks' board voted unanimously for Wayne Embry.

"Wayne is qualified to be the general manager," Oscar Robertson says. "If a man is qualified, he should be doing the job. To hear some people talk, you'd think a black man had a third arm."

"It's time," says Dick Barnett, the New York Knicks' elder statesman, "that the owners deserted their game of musical chairs. They hire and fire the same guys. Give a black man a chance to get fired."

Or to get fined. Before the Bucks-Knicks game at Madison Square Garden the other night, Wayne Embry was moving through the crowd to his courtside seat when he heard the public-address announcement of the game officials—Jake O'Donnell and Manny Sokol.

"Manny Sokol," he moaned, shaking his head. "Manny Sokol."

He sounded just like any of the white general managers.

March 11, 1972

Kansas City to Get Cincinnati Royals

KANSAS CITY, March 14 (AP)—The Cincinnati Royals, plagued by poor home attendance, capped a three-month search for a new home base today by shifting their National Basketball Association franchise to Kansas City.

Only the official approval of other N.B.A. members stands in the way of the transfer to this city, which already has successful sports organizations in the Chiefs of the National Football League and the Royals of the American Baseball League. A National Hockey League franchise is also being sought.

Joe Axelson, the Royals executive vice president and general manager, who appeared here at a news conference, said it was clear by last December the team "was not going to make it in Cincinnati" and that he was able to convince Max Jacobs, chairman of the board, of the need for action.

"We had only two choices —either sell the team or move it," Axelson said.

Axelson, who said San Diego had been among the other leading contenders for the franchise, called Kansas City "a great basketball city. Cincinnati is not."

Axelson anticipated no difficulty in gaining N.B.A. approval for the transfer. The transfer will require approval by 13 of the 17 members on the board of governors.

A statement said the Royals hope to play "at least 21 games in Kansas City's Municipal Auditorium during the 1972-73 season, and approximately 10 each in Omaha and St. Louis, depending on building scheduling availabilities."

[This feature of the plan, however, generated opposition from the N.B.A. Players Association, whose members are against "regional" franchises because they mean no real home base for a player and his family. Larry Fleischer, counsel for the Association, dispatched a telegram to the league office to that effect.

["The question came up before, when the Warriors were going to play half in San Diego and half in Oakland," he said, "and we objected then. As it turned out, they play only a few games in San Diego, and lots of teams play a few home games elsewhere. But when it's a matter of 33 per cent or 50 per cent of the home

The New York Times/March 15, 1972

The Royals plan to move from Cincinnati to Kansas City and play their home games also in St. Louis and Omaha.

schedule, the players don't want it."]

Others in Kansas City representing the Royals included Coach Bob Cousy and Larry Staverman, assistant general manager in charge of promotions.

Cousy, sixth coach since the Royals transferred from Rochester, N. Y., in 1957, aroused the anger of Royals' fans by trading Jerry Lucas to San Francisco in October, 1969, and Oscar Robertson to Milwaukee in April, 1970.

Axelson said he hoped to keep the team's nickname even though Kansas City had

a baseball team with the same nickname.

Tom Van Arsdale, team captain, said the transfer was "a real shock."

"I don't want to go to Kansas City, that's for sure," he said. "Deep down I felt if we went anywhere it would be San Diego. They have more knowledge of professional basketball . . ."

Ambrose Lindhorst, Royals attorney, who made today's announcement in Cincinnati, said "no decision has been made about Cousy continuing as coach."

March 15, 1972

Foul!

*The Connie Hawkins Story.
By David Wolf.
400 pp. New York: Holt,
Rinehart & Winston. $7.95.*

By JONATHAN B. SEGAL

"I think back," says Paul Silas, a teammate of Connie Hawkins, "to when Connie and I played . . . right after high school. I try and conceive what it would have been like for me, at that age, to have my college years taken away, to be scorned as a crook, to be forced to go out and face life. I couldn't have. . . . But he did."

To fill in the details a bit, Hawkins, the subject of "Foul!," was a great black schoolyard basketball player from New York's Bedford-Stuyvesant section who became, in the jivin', hand-slapping, pressure-cooker world of ghetto ball, a revered figure for his spectacular and

flashy play. Although he was unprepared for college academically, emotionally and socially, Hawkins went to Iowa University on an athletic scholarship in 1961; he soon became involved in a gambling scandal. Called back to New York, he was pressured into making false admissions of guilt and was not only unfairly expelled from college, but in effect banned from the National Basketball Association, then the only major pro league.

All that without a conviction or even an indictment against him. After years of excelling in newly-created bush leagues and with the Harlem Globetrotters — for whom Hawkins has some unkind words — he was urged to sue and, in 1969, won the right to play in the N.B.A.

David Wolf was instrumental in clearing Hawkins's name. In a Life magazine article in May, 1969, he wrote: "Evidence recently uncovered indicates that Connie Hawkins never know-

ingly associated with gamblers, that he never introduced a player to a fixer, and that the only damaging statements about his involvement were made by Hawkins himself—as a terrified, semi-literate teen-ager who thought he'd go to jail unless he said what the D.A.'s detectives pressed him to say. Hawkins, in other words, did nothing that would have justified his being banned by the N.B.A."

After this excellent Life piece, Wolf broadened his perspective to write this much-too-long study of Hawkins. Unfortunately, in so doing he has lost some of his objectivity and focus. "Foul!" successfully shows how an underprivileged black man was victimized by a fat-cat, unfeeling Establishment, and basketball is its setting and vehicle. But to overburden the reader with locker-room vignettes and play-by-play action, which Wolf does, weakens the book's impact.

Part of the story is how Hawkins spent his wasted years and how successful he was after his belated entrance into the N.B.A., but it is not significant enough to warrant scores of pages of adulatory reports of box score achievements and character building performances. Especially since, no matter how good Hawkins might have been, deprived of proper coaching and competition in his formative years, he will never be a complete ballplayer. He is an excellent, exciting offensive performer, but even Wolf in a moment of candor says: "In truth, Connie would never become an accomplished defender." (Dick Barnett of the New York Knickerbockers, after being guarded by Hawkins in a game, called the match-up "an insult to my offensive ability.")

Connie Hawkins comes off here as a sympathetic figure not only because his great promise as a youngster makes the injustice he suffered seem especially repugnant. An insecure child ("until I got good at basketball, there was nothin' about me I liked"), he grew up in the ghetto, excelling in the playgrounds and forming vivid memories of police brutality. Wooed by hypocritical, meat-peddling college recruiters who turned his "pumpkin into a Cadillac Eldorado," he was then shattered by the scandal.

"If our methods got a kid to make a false confession, I'm sorry, but we had a job to do," said a detective involved in the case. The outcome: a teen-ager deprived of a chance to pursue his chosen career because of bad newspaper publicity and a narrow-minded, callous commissioner and his merry band of owners who blacklisted Hawkins before even investigating.

Wolf has left the ghetto slang of Hawkins and other principals intact, and it is an effective device, although I think Pete Axthelm describes the black schoolyard life in a more stylish manner in "The City Game." And Wolf can write with flashes of style, grace and insight, but he lost his way here. A reader doesn't need to be told how good a ballplayer is, he can judge that for himself. The reader, though, does need to be told—again, again and again—of injustice and hypocrisy. Wolf has taken what could have been a pungent social commentary and almost turned it into just another book about a ball-player. ■

March 26, 1972

LAKERS WIN 69TH FOR N.B.A. RECORD

Set Other Marks as They Rout Sonics, 124-98, to End Regular Season

By BILL BECKER
Special to The New York Times

LOS ANGELES, March 26—The Los Angeles Lakers set a National Basketball Association season record of 69 victories by defeating the Seattle Super-Sonics, 124-98, tonight in the final game of the regular season.

Using their entire team, the Lakers easily outclassed the crippled SuperSonics, who played without Spencer Haywood and two other injured regulars. Gail Goodrich led the Lakers with 24 points.

Los Angeles set another N.B.A. mark by going over 100 points in 81 of their 82 games. The Lakers wound up with 69 triumphs and 13 defeats for an .841 percentage or a half-game better than the 68-13 record (.840) established by the 1966-67 Philadelphia 76ers.

West Gets Assist Mark

Wilt Chamberlain, the Laker center who was the kingpin of that champion Philadelphia team, said: "I hope we can go all the way now." He declined to compare the two teams.

"Different teams, different eras," he observed.

Jerry West set a Laker record for assists and clinched the league assist title with a total

of 747, an average of 9.7. He had 11 tonight for the Pacific Division champions.

"I would trade all the records for the championship," said Coach Bill Sharman. "We have a tough job coming up with Chicago, the best defensive team and maybe the most physical on the boards in the league."

Los Angeles opens the four-of-seven-game playoff with the Bulls here Tuesday.

The one jarring note in the victory was Happy Hairston's ankle injury. The Laker forward was to undergo X-rays, al-

though the injury appeared to be only a sprain.

Hairston Is Needed

"Without Happy," said Sharman, "Wilt would be at a disadvantage against the Bulls' tough rebounders."

Sharman, in his first year as Laker coach, directed the team to a record-shattering 33 straight victories early in the season. The team won 36 home games and lost only five, another N.B.A. record.

Chamberlain had 23 rebounds to raise his season total to 1,549. Hairston had 1,045.

A crowd of 17,505 watched the finale in the Forum. The

game was halted with 2 minutes 45 seconds to play for presentation of the ball to Fred Schaus, the Laker general manager.

At that stage the Lakers were safely ahead by 24 points.

SEATTLE (98)				LOS ANGELES (124)			
	G.	F.	P.		G.	F.	P.
Heard	9	3-5	21	Hairston	6	6-6	18
Kojis	4	1-1	9	McMillian	4	2-2	10
McDaniels	6	4-4	16	Chamberlain	3	1-2	7
Winfield	2	6-7	10	West	4	6-6	14
Brown	5	1-2	11	Goodrich	11	2-4	24
Clemens	4	3-3	11	Riley	8	3-3	19
Cross	4	2-2	10	Trapp	7	0-0	14
Ford	5	0-0	10	Ellis	4	1-1	9
				Robinson	4	1-2	9
				Cleamons	0	0-0	0
Total	39	20-24	98	Total	51	22-26	124

Seattle .... 16 30 29 23— 98
Los Angeles .... 32 29 28 36—124
Attendance—17,505.

March 27, 1972

Lakers Capture First N.B.A. Crown

By LEONARD KOPPETT
Special to The New York Times

INGLEWOOD, Calif., May 7—The National Basketball Association title, sought so long by the Los Angeles Lakers and especially Jerry West, finally came their way tonight as they defeated the New York Knicks, 114-100, and won the final round of the playoffs, four games to one.

West scored 23 points and made his usual all-round contributions, but it was Wilt

Chamberlain, playing with a heavily taped sprained right wrist, who really dominated the game. He scored 24 points, grabbed 29 rebounds and played 46 minutes. And even before the game ended, it was

announced that he had won the sports car given by Sport Magazine to the most valuable player of the series.

The Knicks, who had won their only championship two years ago at the expense of the Lakers in seven dramatic games, put up a good fight for three quarters, and trailed by only 85-83 one minute into the final period. But the Lakers took complete command at that

LOOKING: Lakers' Wilt Chamberlain tries to pass between Knicks' Jerry Lucas, left, Dean Meminger

Associated Press

point, and ran out their victory while a capacity crowd of 17,505 whipped itself into a frenzy of "We're No. 1" shouts.

This was the eighth time in the last 11 years that the Lakers had reached the final round. Before they came here from Minneapolis 12 years ago (in West's rookie year) they had won five N.B.A. titles in the Georg. Mikan era. But here, they never had a dominant center until Chamberlain joined West (and the now retired Elgin Baylor) four years ago.

Best Season in N.B.A. History

In 1969 the Lakers went to seven games but lost by 2 points to the Boston Celtics in Bill Russell's last year. In 1970 they lost the final game to the Knicks. And West could remember way back in 1962, when the Lakers forced the Celtics into overtime of the seventh and final game before yielding.

But now they had it, at the end of the most successful season any team has ever had in the N.B.A.'s 26-year history. They won 69 regular-season games, including 33 straight, and 81 altogether—all records.

It was Chamberlain's second title. In 1967 he led the Philadelphia 76ers to a championship, and that team held the games-won record the Lakers broke this season.

For the other Laker regulars, it was the first real title opportunity. Jim McMillian, who scored 20 points, is a second-year player from Columbia. Gail Goodrich, who returned to the Lakers after two seasons in Phoenix, was only a reserve in his earlier Laker days. And Happy Hairston, the New York University alumnus who played for Detroit and Cincinnati, came to the Lakers only during the 1969-70 season.

Sharman's Notable Feat

In the final game, for the first time in the series, the true potential difference between the teams in rebounding showed up. Wilt's injury made an apparent difference. The Knicks were outrebounded, 31-16, in the first half, and completely demolished in the fourth quarter. In fact, the Lakers were at their best in the final stages of both the fourth and fifth games, when they could smell victory.

It was also a notable triumph for Bill Sharman, a Los Angeles native, in his first year as coach of the Lakers. Once a star at the University of Southern California, then a main element in the championship Celtic teams of the 1950's, then a successful coach who took the San Francisco Warriors to the final round in 1967 (where they were beaten by Chamberlain), Sharman won the American Basketball Association championship last year with the Utah Stars. Now he has won the biggest prize of all in his home town, and the scope of his coaching accomplishments is unusual.

The final tally in rebounding was 67-39. Chamberlain and Hairston, between them, outrebounded Dave DeBusschere and Jerry Lucas, 43-23.

For a while the Knicks kept pace by forcing more turnovers and shooting better outside, but in the last quarter the Lakers took charge in those departments, too. Walt Frazier scored 31 points and Earl Monroe 16 for the Knicks, but the usual Knick offense didn't function in the second half—and probably the fine Laker defense was the reason.

KNICKS (100)				LOS ANGELES (114)			
	G.	F.	P.		G.	F.	P.
Barnett	0	0-0	0	Chamb'rl'n	10	4-9	24
Bradley	4	4-4	12	Cleamons	1	0-0	2
Debusschere	6	1-3	13	Ellis	0	0-0	0
Frazier	14	3-6	31	Goodrich	6	13-14	25
Jackson	4	2-2	10	Hairston	4	5-5	13
Lucas	5	4-4	10	McMillian	8	4-5	20
Mast	0	0-0	0	Riley	2	3-4	7
Meminger	2	0-0	4	Robinson	0	0-0	0
Miles	0	0-0	0	Trapp	0	0-0	0
Monroe	4	8-8	16	West	10	3-5	23
Paulk	0	0-0	6				
Rackley	0	0-0	0				
Total	39	22-27	100	Total	41	32-42	114

Knicks .... 24 29 25 22 — 100
Los Angeles ..... 26 27 30 31 — 114
Fouled out—DeBusschere.
Attendance—17,505.

May 8, 1972

Mr. Electricity on Court
Julius Erving

Newspaper clippings about Julius Erving wallpaper the trophy case in the local high school in the village of Roosevelt, a predominantly black middle-class town on Long Island. His photograph is prominently displayed at the Theodore Roosevelt elementary school were he was the guest speaker at last June's graduation exercises. The sign on the gate at Roosevelt Park reads: "This is where Julius Erving learned

Man in the News

the game of basketball."

"Everybody in the entire community talks about him continuously," said Art Flechner, the Roosevelt district athletic director. "They live and breathe his every movement."

The 6-foot-6-inch Erving, who starred for the Virginia Squires of the American Basketball Association last season, signed to play for the Atlanta Hawks of the National Basketball Association. But the N.B.A. awarded the rights to him to the Milwaukee Bucks, setting off probably the most serious internal squabble in the history of the N.B.A.

Erving and the Hawks filed a $2-million antitrust suit yesterday against the N.B.A., charging the league with preventing him from playing with the Hawks.

The basketball uniform Erving wears has little bearing on his game or the excitement he offers the fans. They have learned to chant, "Dr. J, Dr. J" when he leaps high on the fast break and transfers the ball under his left leg before passing off or dunking the ball.

Praise From Meminger

"I played a lot of basketball against him this summer in the Rucker League [Harlem playground league]," said Dean Meminger of the Knicks, "and the excitement he generates is unbelievable. He is a gifted person and when spectators come to see Dr. J, they come to see a novelty. You never know what to expect from him. He is a master of all aspects of the game. It's just a matter of time before he perfects them."

Erving, who was born on Feb. 22, 1950, wears a size 15 sneaker, but it's his hands, his long arms and leaping ability that make him a star on the court.

"I really don't know how big my hands are," Erving once said. "I take a size 13½ ring and the biggest gloves made. If I get my fingers on the ball I can control it."

"Julius lived and breathed basketball when he was at Roosevelt," said Flechner. "He was just a great kid when he was here. His vast potential for basketball greatness definitely showed when he was a senior. He was all-County, all-Long Island and played in several state tournaments.

He Helps the Kids

"He graduated in 1968, but he always comes back to help the kids, talking to them and helping them in the playgrounds. He always emphasizes academics over sports to the kids. Even this summer, he was back in the playgrounds. He has never forgotten that's where he started."

Fans say they named Erving Dr. J because of his precise and delicate moves with a basketball, but Erving tells it differently.

"When I was in high school," he said, "a friend of mine kept telling me he was going to be a professor, so I told him I was going to be a doctor, and we started calling each other that, professor and doctor."

After his graduation from Roosevelt, where, according

Looked up to in his community.
(Erving at Hawks' training camp on Sept. 12.)

to Flechner, Erving's scholastic average was in the mid 80's, he went to the University of Massachusetts. In two seasons of varsity basketball, he led the nation in rebounding each season and set 15 school records as he scored 1,370 points.

"People only saw his scoring and rebounding," said Jack Leamon, the Massachusetts coach, "but he was a great passer, too. He could hit a man at three-quarter court during the fast break and he was a standout on defense."

After his junior season, Erving signed a four-year contract with the Squires for $500,000, which was to be paid over a seven-year period. During his rookie season in the A.B.A., where he averaged 27.2 points a game, he signed what was reported to be a $1-million-plus, five-year

Knicks Dethrone Lakers in Five Games, 102-93

contract with the Hawks.

"I was naive when I decided to turn pro," said Erving last February when he switched agents, and talks with other N.B.A. teams began. "I didn't know much about contract negotiations. The life of a pro athlete is a short one and after hearing about the money that is being tossed around, I don't think my contract is a fair one. I have proven myself and I don't think I'm being paid the market value for the type of player I think I am. I deserve considerably more money."

September 26, 1972

Archibald Sets Mark For Assists; Kings Win

KANSAS CITY, Nov. 21 (AP)—Nate Archibald set a National Basketball Association record for assists in consecutive games as the streaking Kansas City-Omaha Kings defeated the Phoenix Suns, 101-96, tonight for their fifth straight victory and ninth in 10 games.

Archibald, who led the Kings with 37 points, had 11 assists. It was the 10th consecutive game in which he had posted 10 or more assists. He was previously tied with Oscar Robertson, Guy Rodgers and Wilt Chamberlain.

November 22, 1972

N.B.A. and Players Sign a Basic Pact

A comprehensive bargaining agreement, first in the history of the National Basketball Association, has been signed by the Players Association and Commissioner Walter Kennedy on behalf of the league, the Commissioner's office announced yesterday.

The three-year contract covers minimum salaries, pensions, arbitration procedures, the playoff pool and other matters that had been agreed to separately in the past. Larry Fleisher represented the players in negotiations with a committee of club owners.

Under the agreement, the minimum salary will become $20,000 next season, the highest minimum in professional sports. The pension benefits of $720 a year for each year of service, payable for life, will now be available at age 50. Clubs must keep a minimum of 11 players on the active list.

March 6, 1973

KNICKS WIN TITLE; TOP LAKERS, 102-93

New York Triumphs in Five Games for 2d Crown in 3 Years—Reed Is Star

By LEONARD KOPPETT
Special to The New York Times

INGLEWOOD, Calif., May 10—The New York Knicks, who personify the ultimate basketball virtue of team play as few teams have in the history of the sport, won the 1973 National Basketball Association championship tonight by beating the Los Angeles Lakers, last year's champions, 102-93.

By winning four straight games after losing the opener here nine days ago, the Knicks reversed the pattern of last year's final, when the Lakers took four in a row after losing the first game. Then, the Knicks were handicapped by an injury to Dave DeBusschere, who also missed the last seven minutes tonight with a sprained right ankle. But this time the Lakers had a hobbled Jerry West and a virtually useless Happy Hairston, who was a regular last year but was just recovering from a knee operation now.

More Defense-Minded

It was the second championship in the 27-year history of the Knicks, one of only two teams still in action from the league's first season. In 1970, they beat the Lakers in a dramatic seven-game series, also exemplifying team balance over individual brilliance. But this year's group, more defense-minded than the 1970 team, won more decisively even though during the 82-game regular season it won fewer games than Boston, Los Angeles and Milwaukee.

Willis Reed, the unquestioned hero of 1970 but only one of many Knick assets this season after two injury-wracked years, once again was awarded the car Sport magazine gives to the outstanding player of the world championship competition. But those presenting the award made it clear that it was partly symbolic, to the captain of a team on which on one could truly be singled out.

Willis did produce his third straight strong game against Wilt Chamberlain, the central problem for any team playing the Lakers. He scored 18 points, got 12 rebounds and made seven assists, and over the last three games he made 28 shots in 53 attempts for .528. Chamberlain, more offense-oriented than in previous games, had 23 points, 21 rebounds and three assists.

Lakers Lead at Half

But the Knicks were more in command in this game than in the previous ones, although, consistent with the pattern of the entire series, disproportionate foul calls against the team in the lead helped cause late-game excitement.

The Knicks had a 23-16 lead at the quarter, but lost it during a second period in which the Lakers shot 13 free throws and the Knicks none. Trailing, 41-39, at half-time, the Knicks produced a 32-18 third quarter that sent them into the final 12 minutes with a 71-59 lead.

Within 3½ minutes, however, the Knicks found themselves in foul trouble, and a lead that was a big as 14 started to shrink. Shortly after DeBusschere's injury (with the score 79-69) the team foul count was 8-3 against the Knicks and it was 84-80. The inevitable Knick shooting slump had appeared by now, and a couple of turnovers, and there were still four minutes to play.

But a basket by Bill Bradley (who scored 20 points) off a feed from Reed provided breathing space. A jumper by Reed, a 3-pointer by Earl Monroe (who scored 23) and another jumper by Reed had the Knicks lead that was as big as 14 apparently secure at 93-82 with only 1:52 left.

But West hit, Chamberlain stole the pass in and scored a 3-pointer, McMillian hit and suddenly it was only 95-91 with 1:04 still to go.

Monroe made only the first of two free throws at 0:52, but five seconds later Reed swiped the ball as Goodrich tried to drive, and finally Monroe got a basket on a goaltending call against Wilt. Now it was 98-91 with about 23 seconds to go, and the title was secure.

Knicks' Box Score

NEW YORK (102)	min	fgm	fga	ftm	fta	reb	a	pf	pts
Bradley	43	10	22	0	0	7	5	5	20
DeB'schr	32	1	9	0	0	8	4	3	2
Frazier	48	8	16	2	6*	9	5	2	18
Jackson	18	2	7	2	2	7	2	4	6
Lucas	19	5	9	0	0	2	1	3	10
Meminger	15	2	2	1	1	1	2	2	5
Monroe	34	8	15	7	11	2	4	4	23
Reed	31	9	16	0	0	12	7	5	18
Total	240	45	96	12	20	48	30	28	102

LOS ANGELES (93)	min	fgm	fga	ftm	fta	reb	a	pf	pts
Bridges	40	2	7	5	7	12	0	6	9
Ch'berl'n	48	9	16	5	14	21	3	3	23
Counts	4	0	1	0	0	3	0	1	0
Erickson	25	1	4	0	0	5	0	4	2
Goodrich	40	11	23	6	6	5	1	4	28
Hairston	7	0	3	0	0	2	0	0	0
McMillian	41	8	17	3	5	6	3	3	19
Riley	7	0	0	0	0	0	0	1	0
West	33	5	17	2	3	5	4	1	12
Total	240	36	88	21	35	59	11	27	93

min-Minutes played. fgm-Field goals made. fga-Field goals attempted. ftm-Free throws made. fta-Free throws attempted. reb-Rebounds. a-Assists. pf-Personal fouls. pts-Points.

Knicks	23	16	32	31—102
Los Angeles	16	25	18	34— 93

Referees—Don Murphy and Darell Garretson.
Attendance—17,505.

It was the first championship for Monroe, who played most of his career in Baltimore, and for Jerry Lucas, whose long bombs reappeared in the second half and helped. Reed, Bradley, DeBusschere, Frazier and Dick Barnett (who didn't play) were members of the 1970 team. For the Lakers, it was their seventh final-round defeat in eight tries during the last 12 seasons.

May 11, 1973

Pacers Take Title, Downing Colonels

By The Associated Press

LOUISVILLE, Ky., May 12—Indiana won its third American Basketball Association title today with an 88-81 victory over the Kentucky Colonels in their seventh and deciding game.

The Pacers used a tight defense to subdue the Colonels, who fell victim to the so-called home-court advantage in this four-of-seven-game series.

The Colonels, outplayed through most of the game, were helpless in the third period when they scored 11 points, lowest figure in a playoff series.

Coach Joe Mullaney, in his second season with the Colonels, made repeated changes in his line-up in an attempt to stall the Pacers' drive, but nothing worked.

In the closing minutes of the nationally televised game a fan raced out onto the floor and was hauled away by the police. Seconds later another fan was ejected from Freedom Hall.

As the fourth period opened, Walt Simon hit a turn-around jump shot to cut the Indiana margin to 66-54. Artis Gilmore connected on a long shot from outside the circle to make it 66-56, but Gus Johnson hit from the side, and Indiana was never threatened thereafter.

George McGinnis of the Pacers scored 27 points, high for the game. He was selected

the most valuable player of the playoffs, and won a new automobile.

Gilmore led Kentucky with 19 points and Rick Mount, who dropped in three 3-point field goals in the closing seconds, had 16. Donnie Freeman had 15 points for Indiana.

The triumph was Indiana's third at Louisville in the series.

Kentucky shot a cold 38 per cent from the field, managing to sink only 30 of 79 shots. Indiana hit on 41.6 per cent (32 of 77) of its field-goal attempts.

The Pacers won the rebounding battle, 55-47, with Darnell Hillman topping the winners with 13. Gilmore had a game-high 17 rebounds.

Indiana jumped out to a quick 7-0 lead and maintained that margin much of the first half with their largest lead being 9 points.

Kentucky took a brief 1-point lead late in the half but Indiana took a 42-41 lead at half-time on a layup by Roger Brown. The lead changed hands six times at the start of the

second half before Indiana went on a 17-4 spree.

INDIANA (88)				KENTUCKY (81)			
	G.	F.	P		G.	F	P
Hillman	3	1-2	7	Simon	4	3-3	11
McGinnis	11	5-6	27	Issel	5	2-2	12
Daniels	2	5-5	9	Gilmore	8	3-5	19
Freeman	6	3-4	15	Dampier	4	2-5	10
Lewis	3	5-5	11	Mount	5	3-4	16
Keller	1	4-4	6	Ladner	3	0-0	7
Johnson	1	1-2	3	Thomas	0	2-3	2
Brown	5	0-0	10	O'Brien	0	2-2	2
				Russell	1	0-2	2
Total	32	24-28	88	Gale	0	0-1	0
				Total	30	17-27	81

Kentucky 18   23   11   29—81
Indiana 24   18   24   22—88
Fouled out—Ladner.
Three-point goals—Mount 3, Ladner 1.
Attendance—16,597.

May 13, 1973

Pros Dazzle to Make the Point: 'Stay in School'

By PAUL L. MONTGOMERY

Julius Erving, known to every kid in Harlem as Dr. J, swooped toward the ceiling of the City College gymnasium, came down flying with the ball and loped down court toward the basket. In the crowd, a rising cheer began, like a wave gathering to break on a rocky shore.

"The operating table is ready, and the Doctor's got his scalpel out," said the public address announcer.

In six strides, Dr. J was across the foul line and into the air again, hovering like a helicopter as he faked left, flicked the ball to his right hand and held it aloft. Artis Gilmore, the 7-foot 4-inch center of the Kentucky Colonels, made a desperate block but the ball was already past him, stuffed through the hoop. The backboard trembled with the recoil, and the crowd exploded in a prolonged "Aaaaaah."

Celebration of Art Form

"That was the Doctor," said the announcer. "Everytime he operates, the patient dies."

All this weekend, devotees of the sport have been gathering in C.C.N.Y.'s Mahoney Gym at 138th Street and Convent Avenue for an end-of-summer display of pure playground basketball. It is called the Mobil Harlem national professional summer basketball championship, but less than a tournament, it is a celebration of an art form.

The six competing squads were pick-up teams of professional players from the National and American Basketball Associations, plus lesser-known stars from the minor leagues. Though the New York and New Jersey teams were the winners, the several thousand spectators gloried more in individual performances than cumulative scores.

The New York Times/Larry Morris
Julius Erving performing his version of the layup shot in C.C.N.Y. gym Thursday. Tom Bush plays for Chicago.

Melvin Respress: "You got to keep your mind on what you're doing, or you'll never improve."

This has been Dr. J's summer in Harlem. The 23-year-old, 6-foot 6-inch forward, traded to the New York Nets earlier this month from Virginia in a $4-million transaction, is emulated on every crowded asphalt court from Mt. Morris to High Bridge.

Aspiring stars who have mastered Walt Frazier's behind-the-back dribble and Earl Monroe's between-the-legs pass now practice the Doctor's layup, a swooping drive in which the ball is crooked between the hand and forearm and lashed rather than pushed toward the basket.

Wherever the game is played, it is played with fierce concentration. "You got to keep your mind on what you're doing or you'll never improve," said Melvin Respress at a clinic conducted by some of the players in the gymnasium on Saturday. "Somebody's always wanting to take the ball away from you."

The 12-year-old youth, wearing overalls and a turned-around golf hat, was the smallest player on the court, but he moved among the forest of legs with confidence, swearing softly to himself when the ball escaped him. Only when he launched a rocket from the foul circle that went in did he allow himself a smile.

Fred Crawford, who played for four N.B.A. teams and now owns the Appletown sporting goods store on 145th Street, said that the clinics gave the players an opportunity to get close to the youngsters.

Eddie Younger, who played on the great Harlem Renaissance teams of the nineteen-thirties, said basketball had always been something special in the neighborhood.

The players on the local teams were drawn from the summer league run by Harlem Professionals, Inc., a multi-layered nonprofit organization that has tournaments for youngsters, operates clinics staffed by players like Dean Meminger of the Knicks, Nate Archibald of Omaha and Billy Paultz of the Nets, and contributes to charities like Harlem Prep.

The slogan of the organization, growing out of the program founded by the late Holcombe Rucker, is "Each One, Teach One." Robert McCullough, the commissioner, said he had found that the athletes command respect in their youth work.

"The kids really listen to them," he said. "Our whole message is 'Stay in school, basketball is just a vehicle for getting an education.'"

The players—representing teams from Chicago, Washington, Louisville, Buffalo, New Jersey and New York—donated their services. One concession to the high-priced talent—Dr. J, for example, is paid $350,000 a year—was to move the tournament indoors from the uneven surface and limited facilities of its traditional site, the Rucker Playground at 155th Street and Eighth Avenue. The organization is trying to get the city to resurface the playground and add stands so that the game outdoors can be resumed.

In the final yesterday, it was New York, with Dr. J, Archibald, Paultz and Hawthorne Wingo of the Knicks, against New Jersey, with John Baum and Larry Kenon of the Nets. Walt Szczerbiak, who will play in Europe, and Sonny Dove, at present unattached. New York won, 134-128.

Beyond the scores, though, the most-ringing cheers were for the stylish elaboration of spins, shots and stuffs that mark uptown basketball. "You always see the players trying something new," said Fred Crawford. "I've been out of the pros for two years, and I'm still learning new things."

August 27, 1973

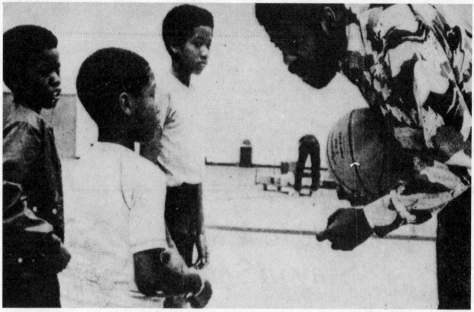

Fred Crawford coaching the youngest group of boys in the weekend clinic at C.C.N.Y.

Celtics Bow As Havlicek Hits 20,000

BOSTON, Jan. 11 (UPI)—Connie Hawkins scored 14 of his 22 points in the third period tonight as the Los Angeles Lakers rallied from a 7-point half-time deficit to top the Boston Celtics, 111-103, in a National Basketball Association game.

John Havlicek of Boston scored 26 points, bringing his career total to 20,003—making him the eighth player in N.B.A. history to reach that plateau.

The 6-foot-5-inch former Ohio State star, the Celtics' No. 1 draft choice in 1962 and now the team's captain, joins a select group.

The seven who made it before were Wilt Chamberlain, now coach of San Diego in the American Basketball Association; Oscar Robertson of Milwaukee; Elgin Baylor, a former Laker; Jerry West of Los Angeles; Hal Greer, a former Philadelphia 76er; Bob Pettit, a former St. Louis Hawk, and Walt Bellamy of Atlanta.

LOS ANGELES (111)—Hawkins 9 4-8 22; Hairston 6 3-4 15; Smith 6 0-1 12; Price 9 3-4 21; Goodrich 7 8-8 22; Riley 3 4-4 10; Bridges 2 1-2 5; Washington 0 0-0 0; Counts 0 0-0 0; Hawthorne 0 0-0 0; Love 1 2-2 4. Totals—43 25-33.
BOSTON (103)—Havlicek 10 6-9 26; Nelson 1 2-2 4; Cowens 5 5-5 15; Chaney 5 0-0 10; White 8 0-0 16; Westphal 3 0-0 6; Silas 7 1-1 15; Kuberski 1 1-2 3; Finkel 0 0-0 0; Williams 0 0-0 0; Downing 2 0-0 4; Hankinson 2 0-0 4. Totals—44 15-19.
Los Angeles   23 16 35 37—111
Boston   26 20 22 35—103
Total fouls—Los Angeles 18, Boston 26.
A—15,320.

January 12, 1974

Pro Basketball: Diploma vs. Dollar

By SAM GOLDAPER

At a time when schoolboy athletes are being heavily recruited and virtually assured of a diploma, only 62 per cent of the nation's basketball professionals have their college degrees.

Of the 200 players on the 17 National Basketball Association teams, 129 graduated and 71 did not. In the 10-team American Basketball Association, 62 players have their diplomas and 42 don't, a survey by The New York Times disclosed.

Only two players on the 12-man Kansas City-Omaha Kings roster earned their degrees, the lowest figure among N.B.A. teams. By contrast, nine of the 10 Virginia Squires of the A.B.A. have graduated.

A Farm System

The figures are hardly surprising. They point up that college basketball, in a gradual shift to big business, has become a farm system for the pros.

In recent years, with the emergence of the A.B.A. to challenge the N.B.A. for player talent, the lure of big-money contracts has turned player heads from the classrooms to a greater concentration on impressing pro scouts.

"After my junior year," said John Gianelli, an engineering student at the University of the Pacific before coming to the New York Knicks, "I lost interest in school. I thought I had a future in pro ball. I hoped to sign a good contract. A good

three-year contract in pro basketball is better than the money you can earn in 10 to 15 years at a steady job."

Bill Bradley, the Princeton graduate who became a Rhodes Scholar and then a New York Knick, is an outspoken critic of college recruiting practices.

"College basketball and football should exist on a semipro level," said Bradley. "Athletes should be paid to play for a university in exchange for either money or their education. The choice should belong to the athlete."

Bradley feels recruiting exploits youngsters, and leads to a misplaced sense of values in the athlete and the administration of the college.

"Actually," he said "the

recruiting by college basketball and football is all part of a minor league system, and should be considered that way. The pros should finance them."

Rick Barry, the Golden State Warriors' leading scorer, stressed the value of a college degree.

"There are no guarantees to making the pros or staying there," said Barry, a graduate of the University of Miami. "The degree is something to fall back on. College is a place for an education, not a training ground for the pros. If it's a minor league for the pros, let's specify it and pay athletes and give out certificates that they attended basketball practice."

A Traveling Man

College athletes, primarily basketball players, complain that practice session and travel take away from their studies. Barry admits that in

his last semester, because of travel and postseason tournament play, he attended only 28 days of classes.

Henry Bibby of the Knicks, who has degrees in sociology and physical education from the University of California, Los Angeles, agreed with Barry.

"I don't buy this garbage that you can't study in season. U.C.L.A. provided plenty of tutors and people always wanted to help the athletes. That's what school is all about. You go for an education. How many guys make it to the pros? I went to college with the idea of making a living with my degrees. Pro basketball was the bonus."

Recruited at 14

Dean Meminger of the Knicks went back to Marquette for his diploma in sociology and philosophy.

"A college degree doesn't

really prepare you for anything," said Meminger, "but it was important for me to become the only child in my family to get one. All black parents want an education for their kids. They feel an education is instrumental in helping solve some of the pursuits of black people, which is equality.

"But college basketball in reality is pro basketball disguised as amateurism. I was a pro when I was 14 years old and Rice High School recruited me. They gave me tuition, room and board."

The Box Score
N.B.A.

	Degrees	
	Yes	No
Atlanta Hawks	8	4
Boston Celtics	9	3
Buffalo Braves	10	2
Capital Bullets	8	4
Chicago Bulls	8	3
Cleveland Cavaliers	8	4
Detroit Piston	8	4

Golden State Warriors	8	3
Houston Rockets	7	4
Kansas City-Omaha Kings	2	10
Los Angeles Lakers	10	2
Milwaukee Bucks	5	6
New York Knicks	8	5
Philadelphia 76ers	8	3
Phoenix Suns	9	3
Portland Trail Blazers	9	3
Seattle SuperSonics	4	8
Totals	**129**	**71**

A.B.A.

	Degrees	
	Yes	No
Carolina Cougars	9	2
Denver Rockets	6	4
Indiana Pacers	5	6
Kentucky Colonels	7	4
Memphis Tams	5	5
New York Nets	4	7
San Antonio Spurs	4	7
San Diego Conquistadors	6	3
Utah Stars	7	3
Virginia Squires	9	1
Totals	**62**	**42**

March 13, 1974

Celtics Win Title in 7th Game

Bucks Lose for Third Time at Home, 102-87

By THOMAS ROGERS
Special to The New York Times

MILWAUKEE, May 12—The Boston Celtics finally got their champagne shower today and soaked in it gleefully after winning the National Basketball Association championship with a 102-87 triumph over the Milwaukee Bucks. It was their 12th title in 18 years, but their first since 1969.

In winning the final series, 4 games to 3, the Celtics topped the Bucks for the third time in four games at the Milwaukee Arena. The Bucks took two of three decisions in Boston Garden. Thus, the series saw five triumphs by the visiting team in a sport where the home team generally has a pronounced advantage.

As always, the Boston victory was a team effort full of defensive all-court pressure, a greyhound offense and tons of hustle. Standing out, though, was Dave Cowens, the 6-foot-9-inch center, who led both teams with 28 points and 14 rebounds and survived the test of the fourth quarter with five personal fouls.

Today he was more than the equal of Kareem Abdul-

United Press International

Celtics' John Havlicek and Tom Heinsohn, coach, enjoying the glow of victory yesterday. At the left is Jo Jo White, also of Boston.

Jabbar, who — although ignored by his teammates on offense for a long period— still tallied 26 points and grabbed 13 rebounds.

After scoring 14 points in

the first quarter, the 7-2 offensive star did not pick up another point for 18 minutes, midway in the third quarter. In that span he took only three shots.

"The other guys never got the ball to him—except for one play," said Coach Larry Costello of the Bucks, puzzled and disappointed at his team's failure to use its chief weapon. "The Celtics were fronting him and double-teaming him with a sag."

"We played Kareem differently today," admitted Coach Tom Heinsohn. "We tried to stop him from getting the ball. He's a great, great player. There's never been anyone of his caliber. You have to change everything just to play against him."

With Abdul-Jabbar out of the offensive picture, the Celtics used the opportunity to speed from a 22-20 lead after one quarter to a 53-40 advantage at the half and a 65-50 margin midway through the third quarter before Abdul-Jabbar finally began to get the ball again.

He and Mickey Davis then led a charge that cut Boston's edge to 71-68 in the first minute of the fourth quarter. Things looked fine for the Bucks then because

Cowens had just drawn his fifth personal and seemed on the verge of fouling out.

"It was the end of the season," said Heinsohn, hungry for his first coaching title. "I never thought of taking him out. We were going to win or lose with Dave."

They won with him.

Cowens started a Boston countersurge with a running hook from the left of the lane that began a key 8-point spurt for the Celtics. Jo Jo White, Paul Westphal and Paul Silas followed with driving layups as Milwaukee went three minutes without a point.

The Bucks then struggled to an 87-79 deficit with 4 minutes 35 seconds to play. They had a vague chance, but the Celtics doused it for good with 11 straight points —6 by John Havlicek, 4 by Cowens and 1 by Westphal, who played 31 fine minutes

because Don Chaney was in foul trouble.

Meanwhile, the Bucks were on another offensive vacation. They shot wildly and were beaten off the boards, going scoreless this time for 3:13. When Jon McGlocklin finally ended the drought with a jump shot, the score was 98-81 with 1:20 to go, and the crowd was streaming for the exits.

"Boston's defense beat us," said Costello. "Their team concept of pressure was more than we could handle. With all the adjustments we tried, we just couldn't cope with it. Boston is a great team with no weaknesses. At least I haven't been able to find any."

The championship was Boston's first since Bill Russell retired five years ago, ending the Celtics' dynasty of the late 1950's and the 1960's. The team was almost entirely rebuilt by Red Auerbach, the

general manager, and by Heinsohn, a former Celtics' scoring star.

BOSTON (102)	min	fgm	fga	ftm	fta	reb	a	pf	pts
Havlicek	46	6	20	4	4	9	6	3	16
Nelson	17	2	4	2	2	5	3	1	6
Cowens	47	13	25	2	2	14	4	5	28
Chaney	23	3	8	0	0	3	1	5	6
White	43	6	15	4	4	3	6	4	16
Westphal	31	4	11	4	7	3	6	5	12
Silas	29	5	11	4	4	9	1	2	14
Finkel	1	0	0	0	0	1	0	0	0
Hankinson	1	1	1	0	0	0	0	0	2
Kuberwski	1	0	1	0	0	0	0	0	0
A. Williams	1	0	0	2	2	0	1	1	2
Total	240	40	96	22	25	47	27	26	102

MILWAUKEE (87)	min	fgm	fga	ftm	fta	reb	a	pf	pts
Dandridge	45	6	12	2	4	3	0	6	14
Warner	29	0	3	1	2	9	3	5	1
Abdul-Jab'r	46	10	21	6	11	13	4	1	26
Davis	33	6	9	3	3	5	2	31	15
Robertson	44	2	13	2	2	3	11	4	6
Perry	12	3	7	0	0	4	0	3	6
McGlin	21	6	8	1	2	0	2	2	31
R. Williams	2	2	3	0	0	0	0	0	4
Lee	2	0	1	0	2	1	0	3	0
Driscoll	2	1	3	0	0	4	1	1	2
Garrett	2	0	0	0	0	0	0	0	0
Total	240	36	81	15	26	42	23	25	87

min—Minutes played. fgm—Field goals made. fga—Field goals attempted. ftm—Free throws made. fta—Free throws attempted. reb—Rebounds. a—Assists. pf—Personal fouls. pts—Total points.

Boston	22	31	18	31—102	
Milwaukee	20	20	26	21— 87	

Referees—Mendy Rudolph and Richie Powers. Attendance—10,938.

May 13, 1974

Schoolboy Accepts $3-Million Pro Offer

By GERALD ESKENAZI

Moses Malone became the highest salaried teen-age athlete in the United States yesterday by choosing a seven-year professional basketball deal, with a potential value of $3 million, instead of playing for the University of Maryland.

The 19-year-old from Petersburg, Va., 6 feet 11 inches tall, was acclaimed as the country's top high school basketball star last season. Although he posted only a C average throughout high school, more than 300 colleges offered him scholarships—about a quarter of all the colleges in the United States that field basketball teams.

In becoming the first player to go directly from high school to pro basketball, Malone was also offered a $120,000 scholarship fund by the Utah Stars of the American Basketball Association. He will get $30,000 as a bonus for every year of college he completes if he decides to attend any college of his choice in the off season.

It was a banner day for the A.B.A. In addition to obtaining Moses, the league kept, at least temporarily, one of its stars from jumping to the National Association. He is George McGinnis, who signed

The New York Times/William E. Sauro
Moses Malone with James A. Collier, Utah Stars' owner

a two-year contract to remain with the Indiana Pacers. However, the New York Knicks, who offered him a $2.4-million six-year deal to jump, may still get him next year.

Young Malone's mother works as a $100-a-week packer in a supermarket. She said, "I put the price on the meat."

The price of basketball talent was the main theme yesterday during the Malone news conference, held at the Royal Box at the Americana Hotel. His mother, Mary, sat quietly next to her 210-pound only child.

All questions of money were dismissed as "personal" by his lawyer, Lee Fentress of Washington, and by Jim Collier, the Stars' president.

Driesell Mission Fails

They had been with Malone day and night for the previous four days, interrupted occasionally by Coach Lefty Driesell, who left the Maryland campus to try to persuade Malone to keep his commitment to the school. Malone had agreed to go to Maryland, where classes began this week. Driesell is considered one of the country's most persuasive recruiters.

However, the Stars drafted Malone last spring, which meant they had the right to negotiate with him. Many observers believed they had selected him as a publicity stunt, since no player ever had been asked to make the move directly to the pro ranks.

Malone's salary will be between $150,000 to $200,000 a year. The rest of his money would be in bonuses—if he becomes rookie of the year, if he makes the All-Star team, if he is among the top 10 scorers in the league. These are standard clauses in basketball contracts.

At times, Malone and his mother showed the wearying effects of the intense pressure of the last week.

When asked his date of birth he snapped, "See my lawyer." His lawyer said it was March 23, 1955.

When asked his middle name, he said, "They call me Sweet Moses." His middle

name is Eugene.

And when Mrs. Malone was asked what role she had played, she replied tiredly, "It's his life. He has to make his own decision."

When he wasn't meeting with lawyers and owners, said Moses, "I walked around town and talked to people." One of those he talked with was 17-year-old Leroy Cole, a neighbor.

"We brought it down both ways," said Cole. "We talked about the advantages of college and the advantages of the pros. Basically, it came down to the fact that this was his dream, and his dream

became a reality."

Collier, the club owner, conceded he might face situations a pro club never had to contend with before because of Malone's age. "We've got a teen-ager on our hands," he said. "We'll have to place him with the right people on the club."

Meanwhile, the 23-year-old McGinnis, a college dropout, has a year to ponder whether to shift to New York.

He didn't actually spurn the Knicks' offer. The Knicks had been under the impression he would be a free agent

for the 1974-75 season. But the Pacers had an option that gave them McGinnis's service for the campaign.

Under his new deal with the Pacers, though, he can leave the club after 1974-75 by buying out his option for $84,000 for the 1975-76 season.

The 6-8 McGinnis is considered the A.B.A.'s second-most-valuable property behind Julius Erving of the New York Nets. McGinnis was second in scoring and rebounding last season.

August 30, 1974

Russell Shuns Hall of Fame Bid

SEATTLE, Feb. 9 (UPI) — Seattle SuperSonics' coach Bill Russell, the former Boston Celtics' star who was elected to the National Basketball Hall of Fame yesterday, said today he would refuse induction.

The decision brought a startled reaction from Lee Williams, executive director of the Hall of Fame in Springfield, Mass.

Williams said today that he had received no formal refusal by Russell and that he was shocked to hear of Russell's decision.

Russell would not explain his decision except to say, "For my own personal reasons, which I don't want to discuss, I don't want to be a part of it. I'm not going. They know that. I've felt this way for many years."

"I haven't talked to him," said Williams. "The last time I spoke with him was in Phoenix at the All-Star game. I told him of the arrange-

ments being made and he didn't indicate that he would refuse."

The Boston Celtics' general manager, Arnold (Red) Auerbach, who coached Russell when he was the Celtics star center, expressed disappointment in Russell's move.

"Yes, I'm a little disappointed," he said. "It's the biggest honor you can get in the National Basketball Association, and besides, how many other people have been nominated for the Hall of Fame in their first year of eligibility?"

However, Auerbach said he couldn't speak for Russell, adding, "he's his own man. Let him do what he wants."

There was some opinion that Russell's decision had racial undertones since there are no other black players from the N.B.A. in the Hall of Fame.

"If that's so, then he [Russell] is wrong," said Williams. "We have the original

Rens in our honors court. They were elected in 1961 and consist of seven black players. Also, Robert O. Douglas, owner and manager of the Rens, is in the Hall of Fame."

Auerbach would not comment on Russell's well-known dislike for individual awards, saying "I have enough problems of my own without worrying about that."

Celtics' coach Tom Heinsohn, a former Russell teammate, said he wasn't surprised by the move because "nothing he does surprises me. Nobody deserves the Hall of Fame more than Bill Russell and I can't imagine why he's doing this."

"It's interesting that Russell would come out with a statement like this without calling anybody here," said Williams.

February 10, 1975

United Press International
Lawrence F. O'Brien

N.B.A. Picks O'Brien As New Commissioner

By SAM GOLDAPER

Lawrence F. O'Brien, former Postmaster General and chairman of the Democratic National Committee, will be the new commissioner of the perience, were voted on by ciation. The 18 N.B.A. owners ended a long search for a successor to Walter Kennedy Friday in Chicago by electing O'Brien unanimously.

The official announcement will be made tomorrow at a

news conference.

Kennedy, who has been the N.B.A. commissioner for 12 years, is retiring June 1. Kennedy was in Springfield, Mass., yesterday where he was elected president of the Basketball Hall of Fame.

The N.B.A. owners had made many attempts to pick a commissioner since Kennedy announced in July, 1973, his intention to retire when his contract ended. Eleven months later, Henry Steinman and Alan Rothenberg, both

lawyers with basketball ex-National Basketball Association owners. Steinman garnered 13 votes, one short of the necessary 14, and Rothenberg received the other five.

Since then the N.B.A. owners have held numerous special meetings but failed to find a candidate who could attract sufficient votes.

O'Brien's name was first suggested at a meeting in New York on March 3, but no vote was taken then.

The selection of O'Brien

comes as a major surprise because he has no basketball background. It was thought Simon Gourdine, whom the owners had elected deputy commissioner earlier this year, would assume the office without actually being given the title.

Gourdine, the highest black executive in sports, is expected to remain as O'Brien's chief adviser, especially since the league's contract with the National Basketball Players' Association ends June 1.

Last week, Sam Schulman, the owner of the Seattle SuperSonics said, "Sports has reached the stage where Congress has to step in."

Schulman's comment may have been a tipoff as to why the owners finally decided on O'Brien, an important political figure in Washington. The N.B.A. faces an antitrust lawsuit by the American Basketball Association and the N.B.A. Players Association has a suit against the owners challenging the reserve clause.

O'Brien could be the intermediary the league needs to effect some kind of accommodation with the A.B.A. and as the N.B.A. spokesman before Congress.

O'Brien first came into political prominence as the director of the late John F. Kennedy's Senatorial campaigns in Massachusetts in 1952 and 1958. He was director of organization for Kennedy's Presidential campaign in 1960 and manager of the late President Lyndon B. Johnson's national campaign in 1964. Four years later he was the manager of the Presidential campaign for Senator Hubert H. Humphrey.

The 57-year-old O'Brien served as national chairman of the Democratic party from March, 1970, until he resigned after the Democratic National Convention in July, 1972. He was appointed to his cabinet post by President Johnson in August, 1965.

It is believed O'Brien will receive a three-year contract at an annual salary of $150,000.

O'Brien, a native of Springfield, Mass., will be the third commissioner since the league's inception in 1946. The first commissioner was Maurice Podoloff, and upon his retirement, he was replaced by Kennedy.

Under Kennedy the N.B.A. doubled in size from nine to 18 teams and obtained lucrative television contracts.

In Springfield, meanwhile, three old-timers were enshrined in the Basketball Hall of Fame and Bill Russell, who was elected to membership but refused induction, was installed in absentia.

Enshrined were the late Emil Liston, founder of what evolved into the national Association of Intercollegiate Athletics; Robert (Fuzzy) Vandiver, outstanding high school and college player in Indiana, and Joseph Brennan, a pro player from 1919 to 1936 and later coach at Manhattan and St. Francis Colleges.

Russell, the former Boston Celtic star, refused induction "for personal reasons," but the Hall of Fame director, Lee Williams, said Russell was installed because "it would be like going to the Baseball Hall of Fame and not finding Babe Ruth's plaque."

Hayes Celtics' Problem

Tom Heinsohn spent most of yesterday watching films. The Boston Celtics' coach tried to figure out why his team broke down in the second half Sunday against the

Washington Bullets and what to do about Elvin Hayes in the second game of the Eastern Conference playoffs tomorrow night at Landover, Md. Heinsohn also looked to the future and watched films of college players in preparation for next month's draft.

The most pressing problem was dealing with Hayes, the Bullets' 6-foot-9½-inch forward. Hayes likes to set up low on the right of the baseline and go up for a turnaround jump shot. Most of Hayes's 14 baskets that led the Bullets to a 1-0 lead in the four-of-seven-game series came on that kind of shot.

The Celtics' immediate concern is whom to match Hayes against Dave Cowens, the redhaired Celtic center, normally is paired with Hayes. Cowens started off guarding Hayes Sunday but picked up two quick fouls, and Heinsohn switched to Paul Silas. Hayes was too quick for Silas and too big for Cowens. Boston's alternatives are to try and keep the ball away from Hayes by fronting him. The Buffalo Braves double-teamed Hayes, but it didn't help much. The Celtics can also hope that Cowens can rough up Hayes without fouling him.

Phil Smith, the Golden State backcourt rookie, will not play tommorow night in

the second game of the Western Conference final playoffs against the Bulls in Chicago. Smith suffered a scratched cornea of the left eye Sunday night in the Warriors' 107-89 triumph. Because of the unavailability of the Oakland Coliseum, the third game will also be played in Chicago on Sunday.

Rick Barry and Keith Wilkes, the Warrior forwards, battered the Bulls for 64 points.

Dick Motta, the Bulls' coach, said: "If we play like that again, we'll lose in four games."

April 29, 1975

Colonels Win Title In A.B.A.

By SAM GOLDAPER
Special to The New York Times

LOUISVILLE, Ky., May 22 —Jim Bradley, a reserve, stood on a locker smoking a big cigar. Artis Gilmore's Afro hairdo was filled with confetti and his body was covered with champagne that his Kentucky Colonel teammates had poured over his huge 7-foot-2-inch frame.

The wild scene was in the Colonels' locker room tonight after Kentucky defeated the Indiana Pacers, 110-105 before 16,622 fans at Freedom Hall and won the American Basketball Association championship for the first time.

The title came in the fifth game of the four-of-seven-game series and ended seven long years of frustration for the Colonels. It came in the 751st game in Colonels' history, with their eighth coach, and third in three seasons, and after several changes in ownership.

"The big fellow was responsible," yelled Wilbert Jones, pointing to Gilmore. "We won because of him. He did it. He did it. His rebounding was unbelievable."

Everybody agreed. Gilmore, who pulled down an A.B.A. playoff record of 31 rebounds, 23 off the defensive boards, and scored 28 points, was voted the most valuable player in the playoff series. He will receive an automobile from Sport magazine.

"You could have cut the car up seven different ways," said Hubie Brown, the Colo-

nel's coach.

But there was something for everybody. Mrs. Elly Y. Brown, chairman of the board and president of the Kentucky franchise, and her husband, John Y. Brown, who works behind the scenes, announced that the entire team would receive a paid vacation to Las Vegas.

While Dave DeBusschere, the new commissioner of the A.B.A., was presenting the championship trophy to the Colonels and the Browns, an electrical storm blacked out the huge arena several times, interrupting the ceremony.

Gilmore was especially overpowering in the second half when the Colonels needed him most to offset a Pacers' charge that was led by Billy Knight, the rookie from the University of Pittsburgh, and George McGinnis, the A.B.A.'s leading scorer. They collected 71 points between them, 45 in the second half. Knight scored 40 points, hitting on 18 of his 29 shots from the floor.

That the Pacers tried to win mostly with Knight and McGinnis was part of their big problem.

"We proved to them that basketball is a five-man game, not two," said Jones, who at times was matched against both Knight and McGinnis.

McGinnis, slowed by a sore left ankle that was injured in the third game of the series, had a poor shooting performance in the first half. He also committed six turnovers, more than any other Pacer. Five of those errors came in the first two periods when both teams started off playing run-and-shoot basketball, and defense, at times, was almost forgotten.

It was only after the Colonels went to their pattern offense that they cut down on their turnovers. They had 10 at half-time and committed only two in the second

half.

There was more to the Colonels' 22d victory in the last 25 games than the intimidation by Gilmore. There was help from everywhere.

Ted McClain, whom the Colonels added to their roster when the Carolina Cougar franchise went out of business, scored 19 points, some at key moments in the game. He also came up with six steals to give him 15 for the playoffs, a league record.

McClain's record was one of three set. Gilmore's 31 rebounds was a playoff mark, and McGinnis, in his 18th playoff game, surpassed the 554 points that Rick Barry scored in 1972, playing for the New York Nets. McGinnis finished with 581 points.

The Colonels also got a big lift from Lou Dampier, who moved the club well with 12 assists and from Marv Roberts, a reserve who scored 14 points, hitting on 7 of 11 from the floor. Roberts, playing for his third A.B.A. team, grew up in Brooklyn and attended Wingate High School.

"Big difference from last year," said Brown, who won the title in his first season as the Colonels' coach. Last year about this time he sat in a dejected Milwaukee dressing room after the Boston Celtics had beaten the Bucks for the National Basketball Association championship. Brown was the Bucks' assistant coach for two seasons before moving to Kentucky.

This year, Brown's Colonels first defeated the Nets in a special playoff game for the regular-season Eastern Division title, then beat the Memphis Sounds in the first round of the playoffs and the Spirits of St. Louis, 4-1, in the Eastern final. Indiana eliminated the San Antonio Spurs and the Denver Nuggets, Western Division champions, to reach the final.

KENTUCKY (110)	min	fgm	fga	ftm	fta	reb	a	pf	pts
Jones	24	4	16	2	2	6	3	3	10
Issel	44	7	15	2	2	12	2	4	16
Gilmore	47	11	20	6	8	31	5	1	28
Dampier	40	6	9	0	0	1	13	4	12
McGinn	39	8	21	3	3	6	7	5	19
Averitt	17	5	12	1	2	3	2	2	11
Roberts	24	7	11	0	2	2	0	0	14
Thomas	5	0	1	0	0	0	0	2	0
Total	240	48	105	14	19	61	31	25	110

INDIANA (105)	min	fgm	fga	ftm	fta	reb	a	pf	pts
Hillman	33	0	4	2	3	10	1	2	2
McGinnis	43	10	20	8	11	11	9	5	31
Elmore	44	4	13	2	3	11	1	5	10
Knight	47	18	29	4	5	8	4	1	40
Joyce	39	7	14	1	2	0	2	2	16
Brown	6	1	1	0	0	0	0	1	2
Buse	9	0	0	0	0	3	0	0	0
Keller	17	0	6	4	4	1	2	2	4
Edge	2	0	0	0	0	0	0	0	0
Total	240	40	87	21	28	44	19	19	105

Three-point goals—McGinnis 3, Joyce 1.
min—Minutes played. fgm—Field goals made. fga—Field goals attempted. ftm—Free throws made. fta—Free throws attempted. reb—Rebounds. a—Assists. pf—Personal fouls. Pts—Points scored.

Indiana	29	19	28	29—105
Kentucky	29	25	26	30—110

Referees—Jack Madden and John Vanak.
Attendance—16,622.

May 23, 1975

United Press International

Al Attles, Warriors' coach, and Bullets players during a fracas on the court in Washington in the first period yesterday. From the left—Elvin Hayes, Mike Riordan, Wes Unseld and Phil Chenier.

Warriors Capture Title on 4-0 Sweep

By LEONARD KOPPETT
Special to The New York Times

LANDOVER, Md., May 25—Displaying the same poise and team balance that had carried them into the title playoffs, the Golden State Warriors won the 29th National Basketball Association championship today by completing a four-game sweep of the Washington Bullets with an almost unnecessarily dramatic 96-95 victory.

The exciting circumstances, ignited in the opening minutes of the game when Coach Al Attles was ejected for rushing to the defense of his star, Rick Barry, obscured the essential simplicity of what had been happening since this series began here exactly a week ago.

The Warriors, with no players of great reputation aside from Barry, simply played sounder basketball, especially on defense, than the Bullets, who had enjoyed a more impressive season. In all the pressure situations, the Warriors proved more controlled and more effective and became only the third N.B.A. team to win the title in four games. The other two were the 1959 Boston Celtics and the 1971 Milwaukee Bucks.

And they did all these things again, with Joe Roberts, the assistant coach, in charge on the bench while Attles was back in the dressing room with a little television set. The Warriors wiped out a 14-point deficit, and when they fell behind again by 8 points in the last five minutes, they wiped that out, too.

As in the second game, which they won at home by a point, the Warriors had half a dozen chances to win and lose in the closing seconds, and all the final scoring plays fell on the shoulders of Butch Beard, the 28-year-old guard from Louisville who has played five N.B.A. seasons.

With 1:45 left, Beard's driving layup gave the Warriors the lead, 94-93. The Bullets lost possession on a bad pass, and neither side was able to score through a series of tension-building turnovers until Beard was finally fouled with 19 seconds to go. He made the first free throw but missed the second, so that the Bullets still had a chance to tie. But with 9 seconds left, a shot by Phil Chenier was rebounded by Beard, who was fouled by Elvin Hayes in backcourt.

That meant Beard had three chances to make 2 points, which would wrap up the game. He missed the first two, but sank the third for a 2-point margin that withstood a final tip-in basket by Wes Unseld.

In a sense, however, the details were false drama because of the 3-0 lead the Warriors had in games. No team has ever overcome such a deficit in any N.B.A. playoff series, so that even if this game had turned out the other way, the Warriors would have still held a commanding advantage at 3-1.

Yet, the fact that they never stopped driving, especially after such an upsetting beginning, was typical of the way the Warriors had played the last two games of the semifinal round from Chicago, after trailing 3-2, and the four in the final. They trailed by at least 13 points at some stage in five of the six games, and three of those five were on the road.

"They simply played sounder, better basketball than we did," said Unseld, his disappointment showing but his sense of honest evaluation unimpaired.

"We tried, but they played better," said K. C. Jones, the Washington coach. Pressed for a more technical description, he added: "They took the middle away from our offense and we didn't adjust to that fully enough or soon enough."

"We never panicked, we just kept on doing what we knew we had to do," said Barry, whose 20-point total in this game in no way reflected the all-around importance of his 43 minutes played. "Even when we fell 8 behind at the end we just knew we were going to come on and win. We could see they were tired. Our whole bench was saying, 'we're going to win this'—8 down, in a road game. You figure it out. In the showdown we just never panicked and they did."

Barry had scored 38 points in the third game and, regardless of anything else, was Washington's central problem.

Mike Riordan, the former New York Knick who had to play him, started challenging him physically right from the start today and was charged with three fouls in the first 3½ minutes, but there was lots of other contact that wasn't called.

The third foul found Riordan with a wrestling hold on Barry, and Attles came racing from the bench into the scuffle. Referee Richie Powers ejected him for that reason.

As things turned out, Barry didn't get to the free-throw line even once in the entire game. As expected, he was rated the most valuable player in the series.

GOLDEN STATE (96)	min	fgm	fga	ftm	fta	reb	a	pf	pts
Barry	43	10	24	0	0	3	5	4	20
Wilkes	32	5	13	2	3	8	0	3	12
Ray	26	6	8	0	2	11	2	1	12
Beard	25	6	12	4	7	5	2	4	16
C. Johnson	23	2	5	0	0	4	2	2	4
Smith	21	2	6	2	4	3	1	1	6
Mullins	21	4	7	0	2	4	3	3	8
Dickey	13	4	7	0	0	2	1	2	8
G Johnson	22	4	6	0	0	11	2	3	8
Dudley	6	0	1	0	0	2	1	0	0
Bridges	3	1	1	0	1	0	1	2	2
Total	240	44	90	8	18	52	20	25	96

WASHINGTON (95)	min	fgm	fga	ftm	fta	reb	a	pf	pts
Hayes	41	7	13	1	2	8	1	6	15
Riordan	21	3	11	2	2	1	3	3	8
Unseld	44	9	14	1	1	16	1	4	19
Chenier	44	8	17	10	10	5	11	3	26
Porter	48	9	16	1	6	1	8	5	19
Robinson	10	0	2	0	0	1	3	2	0
Weatherspn	5	1	5	2	2	4	0	1	4
Kozelko	9	2	2	0	0	0	0	1	4
Haskins	2	0	0	0	0	0	0	0	0
G bbs	4	0	3	0	0	1	0	0	0
Total	240	39	83	17	23	37	28	24	95

min—Minutes played. fgm—Field goals made. fga—Field goals attempted. ftm—Free throws made. fta—Free throws attempted. reb—Rebounds. a—Assists. pf—Personal fouls. pts—Points scored.

Golden State	20	28	22	26—96
Washington	30	22	21	22—95

Referees—Richie Powers and Manny Sokol.
Technical fouls—Golden State coach Attles 2.
Attendance—19,035.

May 26, 1975

Blacks in Pro Basketball: The White Stars Benefit

By STAN LOVE

I was sitting on the bench a few minutes before a game, watching the Golden State Warriors warm up, when all of a sudden it hit me. For a minute the situation reminded me of one of those questions on the intelligence tests they used to give us in high school—the kind that went, "Pick out the word on the following list that doesn't belong with all the others."

Here's the list: Al Attles, Joe Roberts, Rick Barry, Keith Wilkes, Clifford Ray, Butch Beard, Charlie Johnson, Steve Bracey, Derrek Dickey, Charles Dudley, George Johnson, Phil Smith. That's the entire coaching staff and playing roster of the Golden State Warriors as of early in the 1974-1975 basketball season. (Jeff Mullins was out with a broken bone in his hand.) The one name that doesn't belong? Rick Barry, of course. He's the only man on the team whose skin is white.

It's amazing when you think about it. In a year when professional baseball was overcome with self-congratulation because it finally had a black manager; in a year when professional football fans in two major cities were seriously debating whether a black man had enough guts to be a starting quarterback; in that same year a profession-

al basketball team, almost without notice, took the floor with both coaches and nine-tenths of its team black.

Black Is Dominant

The National Basketball Association has come a long way from the days when it finally integrated a few token blacks. Now it has reached the point where the only *white* player on a team leading its division is a superstar forward who routinely scores 30 or more points a game. I wonder if any of the Warriors ever kid Barry by telling him everybody knows white players have to be much better than black ones, because if management has a choice between two players of equal ability it will go for the soul brother every time.

The Warriors are hardly unique, of course. A lot of teams have only a couple of white players, and there were black coaches at Detroit, Seattle, Portland and Washington that season as well as Attles at Golden State. There were two black general managers in the league, and a black lawyer, Simon Gourdine, was named deputy commissioner of the N.B.A. Over all, professional basketball must be 75 to 80 percent black.

Financially, this puts the white players in a strong position. We probably **get** better contracts than we might other-

wise because management feels it really needs us. The best recent example of this is Bill Walton. He's a fine player, of course, but when Portland refers to him as a franchise maker, it isn't only his ability the club is talking about.

It's strictly a business consideration. The white fans still make up the biggest part of the crowds because they have the most money. And just as black fans probably got tired of seeing five white guys running around the floor for so many years, so a lot of white fans must get tired of watching all-black teams. Everybody needs somebody he can identify with, especially since the black isn't the invisible man any more because of the way race consciousness has come to the front in the last 10 or 15 years.

A Financial Pinch

There are people who think the increasing number of black players in the sport is the single biggest financial problem facing basketball because of white-fan reaction. Even Bill Russell, a black, has expressed this viewpoint.

If the league starts to stagger under the weight of what we're being paid and the corresponding rise in ticket prices, then the fact that the people with the most money (whites) won't want to pay to see the people with the most basketball ability (blacks) may make the problem worse. Recently, I saw the results of a study that showed attendance at baseball games tends to drop off when a black pitcher is scheduled to start. It's all part of the same thing.

When you get away from thinking about race in financial terms, there are other kinds of considerations. Sure, there is animosity between blacks and whites, and race is often a part of it, but mostly it's just the normal antagonisms that come up between teammates no matter what their color. In other words, it's trouble between players who happen to be black and those who happen to be white.

November 23, 1975

Stan Love played four years in the National Basketball Association. In October, on the day he signed with the Baltimore Claws of the American Basketball Association, the team went out of business. This article is excerpted from the new book "Love in the NBA: A Player's Uninhibited Diary," by Stan Love and Ron Rapoport, by permission of the publisher, Saturday Review Press/E.P. Dutton & Co., Inc. © 1975 by Stan Love and Ron Rapoport.

Top N.B.A. Stars Were Subsidized

By PAUL L. MONTGOMERY

For at least five seasons beginning in 1968, each team in the National Basketball Association was paying part of the salary of such superstars as Rick Barry, Kareem Abdul-Jabbar and Elvin Hayes, according to documents on file in Federal District Court here.

The pool arrangement, totaling at least $1.5 million, was initiated at the height of the N.B.A.'s struggle with the American Basketball Association over players and franchises. It was apparently designed to enable the N.B.A. teams to outbid the A.B.A.

In 1968, for example, the 14 N.B.A. teams contributed a total of $547,100—payable over three years at $13,026.20

a year—toward the salaries of the league's first-round draft choices, who included Wes Unseld, Don Chaney and Hayes. The contributing teams apparently made the payments directly to the teams employing the players.

There was a similar arrangement for the 1969 draft, where the top choices included Abdul-Jabbar, Neal Walk and Lucius Allen. In Abdul-Jabbar's case, the Milwaukee Bucks paid the first $500,000 of his five-year contract, the pool paid the next $300,000 and the Bucks paid the balance, which was not disclosed.

There was also a cooperative agreement in 1969 to enable the San Francisco team to hire back

Barry from the A.B.A. The pool agreed to pay all of Barry's salary above $100,-000. In a typical year, 1973, each N.B.A. team contributed $6,985.30 toward Barry's $218,750 salary at San Francisco.

It is understood that the pool arrangements for the 1968 and 1969 drafts expired with the players' initial contracts. It is possible, however, that Barry's salary continues to be shared among the N.B.A. teams.

What's more, Barry's salary was found to be only the fourth highest among N.B.A. forwards. Bill Bradley of the Knicks, at $325,000 for this season, makes nearly $90,-000 more.

Rick Barry
$237,500 a year

Simon P. Gourdine, the N.B.A. deputy commissioner, declined to comment on any aspect of the case or to ac-

Spencer Haywood
$302,000 a year

John Havlicek
$250,000 a year

Elvin Hayes
$202,000 a year

Jim McMillian
$200,000 a year

Who Gets How Much

In March, 1975, apparently as an aid in salary negotiations, the National Basketball Association office issued a confidential memorandum giving the salaries of the forwards it judged to be the best in the league. Following are the contract terms of each of the players listed after Bill Bradley:

Spencer Haywood, Seattle. Five years beginning in 1973-74 for a total of $1,510,000, payable at $152,000 a season for the first four, $302,000 in the fifth year and deferred compensation of $100,000 a year from Jan. 1, 1979 to Jan. 1, 1984. (Haywood continues to be paid under this contract with the Knickerbockers.)

John Havlicek, Boston. Four years beginning 1972-73 for a total of $1 million, payable at $250,000 a year. There was also a $75,000 interest-free loan with repayment to begin in 1975.

Rick Barry, Golden State. Four years beginning 1974-75 for a total of $950,000, payable at $237,500 a year.

Elvin Hayes, Washington. Five years beginning 1972-73 for a total of $1,010,000, payable at $100,000 a year and deferred compensation of $100,000 a year from October, 1977, through October, 1981. There was a $10,000 bonus at signing.

Jim McMillian, Buffalo. Five years beginning 1973-74 for a total of $1 million, payable at $150,000 in 1973-74, $165,000 in 1974-75, $180,000 in 1975-76, $195,000 in 1976-77, $210,000 in 1977-78 and deferred compensation of $10,000 a year for 10 years beginning in January, 1988.

Rudy Tomjanovich, Houston. Six years beginning 1973-74 for a total of $1 million, payable at $100,000 a season and deferred compensation of $100,000 a year from 1979-80 through 1982-83.

Bob Dandridge, Milwaukee. Four years beginning 1973-74 for a total of $600,000, payable at $80,000 in $150,000 in 1976-77 and deferred compensation of 1973-74, $110,000 in 1974-75, $135,000 in 1975-76, $45,000 in 1978, $30,000 in 1979, $25,000 in 1980 and $25,000 in 1981. In addition, there was a $100,000 loan to be repaid in eight annual installments beginning in October, 1974.

Bob Love, Chicago. Five years beginning 1972-73 for a total of $706,000, payable at $70,000 in 1972-73, $75,000 the next four seasons, and deferred payments of $24,000 a year from 1979 through 1992.

Steve Mix, Philadelphia. Three years beginning 1973-74 for a total of $140,000, payable at $30,000 in 1973-74, $45,000 in 1974-75 and $60,000 in 1975-76. (Mix's contract was the only one that did not have a no-cut provision.)

knowledge that a pool arrangement was in existence. The court documents, however, which include memorandums from the former N.B.A. commissioner, Walter Kennedy, to team owners and pages from the N.B.A. ledgers, establish the fact.

There is no direct evidence in the papers that the A.B.A. teams had such an arrangement, though there were reports to that effect after the league's founding in 1967. The league, through its counsel, Michael H. Goldberg, declined to comment on the matter, pointing out that it was a subject of pending litigation.

The documents on file do make clear that some A.B.A. teams got reductions in their league assessments for signing such stars as Julius Erving and David Thompson, and that all of the A.B.A. teams guaranteed the first $700,000 of Thompson's contract in the event his employer, the Denver Nuggets, went into default.

The documents revealing the pool are part of a 15-foot stack of papers filed in the Federal suit known as the Oscar Robertson case. In addition to the public record, there are more than 31,000 N.B.A. documents and depositions that are sealed.

The suit began in 1970 as an action by Robertson and 13 other players against the N.B.A. seeking an end to the reserve clause and other contractual provisions. Later, the A.B.A. filed suit against the N.B.A., charging that the senior league engaged in monopolistic practices designed to drive competitors out of business. The suits were then combined in one complex case.

The players' action is being settled out of court. The A.B.A.'s antitrust action still stands, however, and is scheduled for trial before Judge Robert L. Carter on June 1.

The court record contains many of the closely held financial secrets of professional basketball. Among other revelations in the papers, all based on documents or sworn statements, are the following:

¶A confidential memo from Gourdine dated March 12, 1975, listing the salaries of the "ten best" forwards in the N.B.A. indicates that Bradley, a nine-year man, is the highest paid at that position. Bradley, whose 1975-76 salary is $325,000, makes more than Spencer Haywood ($302,000), John Havlicek ($250,000), Rick Barry ($237,500), Elvin Hayes ($202,000), Jim McMillian ($200,000), Rudy Tomjanovich ($166,666), Bob

Dandridge ($150,000), Bob Love ($141,200) or Steve Mix ($45,000).

¶For the 1974-75 season, when they were the A.B.A. defending champion, the New York Nets claimed a loss of $1,497,840 on their Federal tax return. The team's gross revenue was $2,326,925, including $2,083,000 in gate receipts. The season's payroll was $1,350,000 for players and $85,000 for coaches.

¶When Wilt Chamberlain was the coach of the San Diego Conquistadors in the 1973-74 A.B.A. season, the team paid him $510,000 while the salaries of his 11 players totaled $469,000. In that season, the Conquistadors had gate receipts of $241,551.50. Needless to say, the team is now defunct.

¶Though the Nets did not announce it when they traded Larry Kenon to San Antonio last summer, they remain obligated to pay $325,000 toward the forward's salary

and deferred payments, extending through 1983.

The N.B.A. pool arrangements for the 1968 and 1969 drafts were complex. The 1968 draft choices covered were Hayes, Unseld, Bob Kauffman, Tom Boerwinkle, Don Smith (later Zaid Abdul-Aziz), Otto Moore, Charlie Paulk, Gary Gregor, Ron Williams, Bill Hosket, Don Chaney and Shaler Halimon.

The players were signed to three-year contracts at totals ranging from $313,000 for Unseld and $308,000 for Hayes to $77,000 for Williams. The individual clubs paid most of the cost—$200,000 for Hayes, $156,000 for Unseld, $75,000 for the rest —and the pool paid the balance, coming to $39,078.60 for each team.

The next year, the pool paid $300,000 toward the contract of the first draft choice (Abdul-Jabbar), $150,000 for the second (Walk), $100,000 for the third (Allen) and so forth.

According to a person familiar with league operations at that time, the pool for the 1968 and 1969 drafts was arrived at by a "gentlemen's agreement" among the owners without participation of the league office. The decision to supplement Barry's salary was taken at a league meeting, the source said.

Among the documents in the file is a letter from Wayne Embry, general manager of the Milwaukee Bucks, to the league office complaining that several teams were in arrears on their payments toward Abdul-Jabbar's contract.

A letter from Paul L. Snyder, owner of the Buffalo franchise, to Commissioner Kennedy in January, 1973, makes a plea for sharing of salary information so that owners have a standard of comparison. He states that his expansion team could have saved "hundreds of thousands of dollars" on salaries if he had known what players on other teams were getting.

Kennedy replied that salaries of other players were available on request by telephone at the league office, but could not be put in writing. In his 1975 memo, Gourdine did give salaries of the forwards the league office considered the best, apparently as a guide for salary negotiations.

Sworn statements by players who were a party to the suit show the huge advances in salary made after the founding of the A.B.A. Robertson's first contract

with Cincinnati in 1960, for example, was for $33,333 a year for three years plus an unstated percentage of gate receipts. His last contract, at Milwaukee in 1974-75, was for $250,000 plus $20,000 from the playoffs.

Havlicek's contracts with Boston also show modest raises until 1969, when he negotiated but did not sign with the Carolina Cougars of the A.B.A. The threat of those negotiations apparently produced a big increase in his next contract.

In his statement, Havlicek listed his salary as follows: 1962-63, $15,000; 1963-64, $18,000; 1964-65, $21,000; 1965-66, $25,000; 1966-67, $32,000; 1967-68, $50,000; 1968-69, $55,000; 1969-70, $140,000; 1970-71, $140,000; 1971-72, $140,000; 1972-73, $250,000; 1973-74, $250,000; 1974-75, $250,000; 1975-76, $250,000. Havlicek also listed his income from summer camps, endorsements and personal appearances. The largest total for any one year was $14,800 in 1973.

Archie Clark stated that he signed for $11,000 in 1966-67; his last contract, for three years beginning in 1972, was for a total of $650,000. Jeff Mullins got $12,000 in 1964-65, and is getting $160,000 this season. Chet Walker got $12,000 in 1962-63, and $180,000 in 1974-75.

Financial statements filed by the A.B.A. teams as part of their damage suit against the N.B.A. also provide a look at a professional sports team's financial dealings.

Roy L. M. Boe, the principal owner of the Nets, filed the statement for his team. He said that he and undisclosed partners bought the franchise for $1,000,000 from the ABC Freight Forwarding Corp. in May, 1969, paying $250,000 on the date of purchase, $50,000 in May, 1971, and $100,000 in each year thereafter.

The new corporation, called Long Island Sports Enterprises Inc. until it became a limited partnership last October, issued 13,441 shares at $1 par value when it was founded. Another $1,500,000 was raised from shareholders as promissory notes or convertible debentures.

In the last three seasons, the Nets have reported a loss on their tax return — $284,-146 in 1972-73, $735,600 in 1973-74, and $1,497,840 in 1974-75. Gross revenues in those years were $2,425,514, $2,731,891 and $2,326,925, respectively.

For 1974-75, the Nets listed revenue from sale of tickets at $2,083,000 (on attendance of 415,312), revenue from programs and souvenirs at $49,000, and an undisclosed amount from television, for the total of $2,326,925.

Expenses listed by the team for 1974-75 included the following: rent, $206,300; advertising, $25,000; equipment, $16,000; salaries and fringe benefits for players, $1,350,000; salaries and fringe benefits for coaches, $35,-000; transportation, $145,000; game, team, arena and league assessments, $830,000; sell-

ing and promotion, $205,000; general and administration, $500,000; interest, $235,000.

On its 1974-75 balance sheet, the Nets put their assets at $4,913,336 and their liabilities at $10,841,103 (including $2,716,000 for capitalization of long-term, no-cut player contracts).

March 21, 1976

Havlicek Breaks Point Record

PHILADELPHIA, March 20 (UPI)—John Havlicek set a National Basketball Association record by scoring over 1,000 points for the 14th consecutive season but it was a jump shot by Jo Jo White with 49 seconds left in overtime tonight that sparked the Boston Celtics to a 103-96 triumph over the Philadelphia 76ers.

The game was viewed by 18,516 fans, the largest crowd to ever see the 76ers.

Havlicek achieved his mark late in the first period when he made a free throw for his third point. He surpassed the 13 consecutive 1,000-point seasons, of Oscar Robertson, Jerry West and Bob Cousy. Wilt Chamberlain also had 13 1,000-point seasons, but not consecutively.

The game went into overtime at 90-90 after Fred Carter scored two free throws with 37 seconds remaining in the fourth period.

March 21, 1976

Nets Win Second Title in 3 Seasons

Nuggets, Up by 22 Points, Lose, 112-106, in Sixth Game

By PAUL L. MONTGOMERY
Special to The New York Times

UNIONDALE, L.I., May 13 —In an astonishing comeback from a 22-point deficit with 17 minutes left in the game, the New York Nets defeated the Denver Nuggets, 112-106, tonight and won the championship of the American Basketball Association for the second time in three seasons.

The sixth game of what may have been the league's last championship series appeared to belong to Denver midway through the third quarter. But the Nets put on a slashing, clawing, full-court press and, point by point, scrambled their way back.

Denver, losing more of its

composure with each reduction of the lead, went five minutes without scoring during one stretch and looked like a defeated team long before the end. In the fourth quarter, the Nuggets committed an encyclopedia full of dribbling, passing and shooting errors and were outscored, 34-14.

"My guys showed tonight that they're not only great players but good people," said Kevin Loughery, the victorious coach. "We put it all together when we had to, and that's what it's all about."

It was the second championship for the Nets, who began life as the New Jersey

Americans when the A.B.A. was founded in 1967. They won in 1973-74, Loughery's rookie season as coach, and tonight's title was the first won by a New York team in a major sport since then.

It was a team effort. Julius Erving, who was brilliant throughout the series and was the unanimous choice for most valuable player, scored 31 points and had five steals during the Nets' surge. John Williamson got 24 of his 28 points in the second half and was a scoring demon, seemingly putting in a basket every time his team needed one. Brian Taylor had 24 points and broke up Denver's defense with his drives down the middle. Jim Eakins, a backup center acquired in midseason, played 34 minutes in place of the injured Kim Hughes and had a 3-point

play near the end that was pure determination.

Buzzer Never Sounds

Even Rich Jones, a seven-year A.B.A. veteran, survived an awful shooting night (1 for 12) and contributed four steals and nine rebounds to the comeback.

"This is my first championship, man, and it's so beautiful I don't know what to say," Jones said. "I don't know what the future is going to bring for this league, but I want to enjoy this night."

There was an ecstatic capacity crowd of 15,934 at the Nassau Coliseum for the game that began cheering during the singing of the National Anthem, quieted when the Nets fell far behind, then erupted with prolonged roars during the Nets' surge.

By the time Rich Jones put in a layup with three seconds left to close out the scoring, the Coliseum was a bedlam of noise. Fans raced down the aisles and scampered on the court, canceling the last futile seconds of play.

Denver started the game in its sticky, overplaying defense and it was as effective as Coach Larry Brown could wish. There were no easy shots for New York, and by the half the Nets were down, 58-45, on 37 percent shooting.

Through the early part of the third quarter, the disciplined Nuggets' offense kept building on the lead. David Thompson, the league's rookie of the year, was scoring at will and finished the game with 42 points.

With five minutes left in the quarter, the score was 80-58 and it looked as if the Nets would have to return to Denver for the seventh and deciding game of the series on Sunday.

At that point, Loughery put in the defense he denotes by the code name "Yellow" —a scrambling, full-court press in which three defenders swarm round the ball while two frontcourt players patrol beyond the halfcourt line to prevent breakaways.

Mining the Nuggets

Point by point, steal by steal, the Denver lead was chipped away. By the end of the quarter, the Denver lead was reduced to 92-78, and thereafter the Nuggets could do nothing right when they had the ball, giving it up almost as soon as they touched

The Nugget cause was not helped by fouls called on Bobby Jones and Dan Issel, both of whom had to leave the game with six fouls be-

fore it was over.

"Their press was great," said Brown. "We just lost our poise. The game got very physical and when it gets physical it gets tough for us."

The Nets took their first lead since early in the first quarter with 2:19 to play when Williamson lofted in a jump shot from the corner to make the score 106-104. Denver had one more chance with the score at 108-106 and with 1:29 left. Marvin Webster got hold of the ball after Williamson dribbled it off his foot.

Eakins got his sixth foul stopping Webster, but the rookie center missed both free throws. A moment later, Webster was called for goaltending on a Taylor layup and the outcome was sealed. Oddly, Erving did not score a basket in the fourth quarter.

Afterward, the Net dressing room was awash with champagne, smiling players and backslapping visitors.

"Lotta guts, lotta guts," said Roy Boe, the team's owner, greeting each player in turn.

DENVER (106)	min	fgm	fga	ftm	fta	reb	a	pf	pts
Jones	33	2	5	0	0	9	5	6	4
Thompson	36	16	23	10	12	7	0	2	42
Issel	34	14	25	2	2	20	3	6	30
Williams	35	5	9	4	4	1	3	2	14
Simpson	35	1	9	2	2	2	3	1	4
Webster	18	1	3	0	2	6	0	2	2
Towe	16	2	3	2	2	0	5	5	6
Gerard	13	1	5	0	0	3	1	3	2
Beck	20	0	4	2	2	2	1	2	2
Total	240	42	86	22	26	50	21	29	106

NETS (112)	min	fgm	fga	ftm	fta	reb	a	pf	pt
Erving	45	10	19	11	16	19	5	2	31
Jones	29	1	12	0	2	9	2	4	2
Eakins	34	6	10	3	3	3	1	6	15
Taylor	43	9	24	4	4	1	3	2	24
Wil'mson	36	12	20	4	4	7	2	3	28
Bassett	23	2	5	0	0	3	1	6	4
McClain	9	0	5	1	2	0	1	1	1
Melch'ni	4	2	3	0	0	1	0	1	4
Skinner	17	0	1	3	5	7	1	3	3
Total	240	42	99	26	39	55	16	28	112

Denver 26 30 34 14 106
Nets .... 23 22 33 34—112
Three-point goals—Taylor 2.
Referees—Norm Drucker and John Vanac.
Attendance—15,434.,

May 14, 1976

Celtics Outlast Suns; Fan Attacks Referee

By PARTON KEESE
Special to The New York Times

BOSTON, June 4—Surviving three overtimes, thousands of rioting fans and two endings, the Boston Celtics defeated the Phoenix Suns, 128-126 tonight. The victory was marred, however, by an attack by a Boston Garden fan on one of the referees, Richie Powers. The nearly miraculous, emotion-packed victory gave the Celtics a three-game-to-two lead in the four-of-seven National Basketball Association championship.

With two seconds remaining in the second five-minute overtime and Phoenix leading by a point, John Havlicek of Boston sent a running jump shot through the hoop. Thinking their team had rescued victory from certain defeat, the fans poured onto the court, both to celebrate their hero and to bereate the referees for what they considered earlier injustices.

With hundreds of exuberant and beer-drinking fans pummeling players, themselves and the officials, it wasn't long before fights began. Powers was grabbed by a fan and had to force his way free. A number of Suns' players, towering above the crowd, had to push and shove their way to the sidelines.

While the police dragged Powers's assailant away, the referee held up two fingers to indicate that the game wasn't over. He was hardly noticed as the fighting and

the celebrating continued on the court.

After 10 minutes, the fans were finally moved to the perimeter while Phoenix plotted its last shot. Coach John MacLeod had called an illegal time-out, knowing he had no more left but he risked a technical foul just to be able to throw the ball in at midcourt, which the rules would not allow otherwise.

Jo Jo White sank the foul to put Boston ahead by 2,

but Gar Heard of Phoenix threw in a long jumper at the buzzer to tie the score at 112-112 and send the game into a third overtime.

Again the fans, now surrounding the court like overgrown hedges, began getting ugly with the Phoenix players and several times the police had to break up near altercations. Fans in the upper balconies were throwing cups, waste paper and rubber balls among the debris, slow-

Richie Powers, referee, restraining the Celtics' Dave Cowens, who tried to go after Curtis Perry of the Suns in the first quarter at Boston last night.

ing the game to a walk.

Unlike the regulation contest, which had ended sensationally at 95-95, and the first overtime, which also tied, 101-101, with a late basket, the third overtime saw the Celtics run up a 6-point lead with 36 seconds to go.

With the fans still running on the court and trying to touch the players on the bench, the Suns nearly came back again, scoring two baskets with 12 seconds left. But White dribbled the time away to sew up the triumph, and the selout crowd of 15,-320 was finally allowed to go where it wanted.

"That was the most exciting, draining and most dangerous game I've ever been associated with," said a subdued but still angry MacLeod. "Something's wrong when you can't even coach in a huddle without fans fighting with your players the whole time. I'm surprised nobody was seriously hurt."

The real surprise was that the game was even close after Boston had nearly blitzed the Suns in the first quarter by taking a 36-18 lead. At one point the Celtics led by 22, their largest margin of the night as Havlicek, White and Dave Cowens were controlling the

boards and helping the Celts shoot for a .607 percentage.

"They came out all jazzed up," noted MacLeod, "and I give them credit for that. But it's an unnatural way to play, so unrestrained as that. You have to pay for it later, and that's just what Boston did."

Phoenix came within 7 points in the third period, as Alvan Adams, the N.B.A. rookie of the year, began excelling on his turnaround shooting and passing. By scoring 11 consecutive points, and with Ricky Sobers leading the comeback, the Suns tied the game at 68-all.

BOSTON (128)									
	min	fgm	fga	ftm	fta	reb	a	pf	pts
Havilcek	58	8	19	6	7	9	8	2	22
Silas	44	8	11	1	1	14	4	6	17
Conena	55	9	23	8	11	19	4	6	26
White	60	15	29	3	3	6	9	2	33
Scott	33	3	14	0	0	4	3	5	6
McDnld	13	3	5	2	2	1	3	2	8
Ard	16	3	6	2	2	2	1	1	8
Kuberski	13	2	5	0	0	3	0	1	4
Stacom	3	0	0	0	0	0	0	0	0
Nelson	20	1	4	2	2	4	1	1	4
Total	315	52	116	24	29	62	33	26	128

PHOENIX (126)									
	min	fgm	fga	ftm	fta	reb	a	pf	pts
Perry	52	10	20	3	4	15	6	5	23
Adams	37	9	16	2	2	9	5	6	20
Westphal	42	11	20	3	3	2	2	4	25
V. Ardnle	35	1	5	3	4	4	1	1	5
Erickson	4	0	2	0	0	0	1	0	0
Avtrex	23	2	3	3	3	4	0	6	7
Lumpkin	12	0	2	0	0	1	4	0	0
Newthorne	8	1	3	2	2	4	0	3	4
Total	315	53	112	20	24	53	29	28	126

June 5, 1976

Celtics Win, 87-80, and Take 13th Title
Suns Foiled in Six Games

Special to The New York Times

PHOENIX, Ariz., June 6—The Boston Celtics, pro basketball's dominant team over the last two decades, wrapped up another National Basketball Association title today with an 87-80 victory over the Phoenix Suns.

For the Celtics, who captured all three of their play-off series by 4-games-to-2 margins, the championship was the 13th in 20 years. For Phoenix, an eight-year-old franchise that finished the regular season with a 42-40 won-lost record, the defeat ended an astonishing bid by one of the longest shots in the 10-team playoff field.

A sellout crowd of 13,304 in Memorial Coliseum and a national television audience watched an incident-free defensive struggle between two teams still weary from Friday night's triple-overtime, Celtic victory in Boston.

Jo Jo White, who carried much of the Boston offensive load throughout the series, was voted the most valuable player in the final round. But today, Charlie Scott, Dave Cowens and John Havlicek were just as instrumental for Boston.

Scott, who had fouled out of the previous five games and was bogged down in an 11-for-44 shooting slump, led all scorers with 25 points. He added 11 rebounds and three assists, and was the catalyst in the fourth-period spurt that blew the game open.

Cowens, playing the last 10 minutes with five fouls, and Havlicek, playing the whole series with a muscle tear in his left foot, combined for 11 fourth-period points that turned a 66-66 tie

The Celtics' Jo Jo White preparing to shoot as Paul Westphal of the Suns flies by

Associated Press

into a 77-71 Boston lead.

Scott scored 9 points and made three of his five steals in the final period. He also contributed two key rebounds as the Celtics closed out their third straight series this year on the loser's court, having previously disposed of the Braves in Buf-

falo and the Cavaliers in Cleveland. Oddly, the last four Boston titles have been won on the road.

With Cowens and Paul Silas showing the way, the Celtics continued their rebounding reign in the series, winning the overall battle, 53-39, today, with a 25-15

second-half edge.

Alvan Adams led Phoenix with 20 points, 11 in the third period, when the Suns erased an 11-point deficit and tied things at 54-54.

The teams lurched through the early minutes of the final period never more than 4 points apart.

"When the game was up for grabs, it was a question of pure guts."
—Tom Heinsohn, Celtics' coach.

The Celtics' Charlie Scott, who had fouled out of the five previous final-round games, keeping his eye on the referee as he defended against the Suns' Paul Westphal. No foul was called on the play. Celtics won, 87-80.

Associated Press

20 points, and Westphal had 6. A jumper by Keith Erickson represented the only scoring by a Phoenix forward in the period. Scott led the Celtic "attack" with 6 points.

The pace slackened in the second period, with neither team geting a point until Garfield Heard hit a 12-footer at 9:35.

The Celtics' 5-point halftime lead was achieved largely by their 12-for-12 foul shooting. Their shooting from the field was .302 but the Suns were only a little better at .378.

Phoenix's Keith Erickson, who had sprained his right ankle in the fifth game, re-injured the ankle in the first minute of the second period, was helped off the court and never returned.

Not Enough Shooting

Coach John MacLeod of Phoenix said afterward: "We did too much dribbling and running for the ball, which means nobody was going to the basket.

"Our players felt they would win today, but Boston drove us out of our patterns. But certainly nobody has to be embarrassed about being associated with the Phoenix Suns any more."

In their surprising climb to the final round, the Suns eliminated the Seattle Super Sonics and the Golden State Warriors, last year's N.B.A. champions.

For winning the title, the Celtics received a total of $250,500 from the playoff pool. Phoenix collected $185,500.

BOSTON (87)

	min	fgm	fga	ftm	fta	reb	a	pf	pts
Havlicek	42	4	15	2	2	4	3	4	10
Silas	44	3	7	4	13	3	4	10
Cowens	44	10	16	1	1	17	0	5	21
Scott	42	9	24	7	9	11	3	5	25
White	45	5	15	5	8	5	6	3	15
Kuberski	10	0	3	4	4	2	0	1	4
McDonald	5	1	3	0	0	1	0	3	2
Ard	4	0	0	0	0	0	0	2	0
Nelson	4	0	0	0	0	0	0	2	0
Total	240	32	83	23	28	53	15	29	87

PHOENIX (80)

	min	fgm	fga	ftm	fta	reb	a	pf	pts
Heard	42	4	11	3	4	10	1	4	11
Perry	35	4	7	0	0	7	2	3	8
Adams	42	7	16	6	8	9	6	5	20
Sobers	41	7	20	5	6	6	2	2	19
Westphal	33	6	11	2	2	3	1	2	14
Vn Arsd'le	23	2	6	0	0	1	1	4	4
Erickson	2	1	2	0	0	0	0	0	2
Awtrey	6	1	1	0	1	1	0	0	2
Hawthrne	11	0	3	0	0	2	0	3	0
Total	240	32	77	16	24	39	13	33	80

Boston ....20 16 19 30—87
Phoenix ....20 13 23 24—80
Referees—Darrell Garretson and Jake O'Donnell.
Attendance—13,306.

June 7, 1976

But after Ricky Sobers' free throw put the Suns ahead, 67-66, with 7 minutes 25 seconds to play, Havlicek and Cowens went to work.

Hondo gave the Celtics the lead for good with a pair of free throws, and Cowens stole the ball, dribbled the length of the court and cashed in a 3-pointer.

On the next Boston series, Cowens converted a pass from Scott, Havlicek hit a long jumper, and Cowens put in a whirling jumper.

The best the Suns could manage during this spree were a pair of free throws by Adams and another pair by Paul Westphal. They never got over that Celtic burst. The loss was their second in the last 21 games at home.

Havlicek, who was only one for eight from the field in the first half, moved past Wilt Chamberlain into third place on the career playoff scoring list with the first of two free throws that sparked the clinching spurt. Havlicek has 3,605 playoff points and trails only Jerry West and Elgin Baylor.

"You get yourself so worked up psychologically and physically," said Havlicek, "that you wonder sometimes if it's really worth it. But after it's over, it feels like 15,000 years lifted off your shoulders."

"We had to gut it out all the way," said Coach Tom Heinsohn. "Phoenix has a fine team with a great shooter. When the game was up for grabs, it was a question of pure guts. Everyone was tired, but our guys have been there before and did it."

White, who had only 15 points today but led Boston with 130 in the six games, said:

"Our offense really wasn't that great, but defense will do it for you every time, and and our defense did it." That was especially true in the first half.

Boston came out of it with a 38-33 lead, believed to be one of the lowest halftime point productions by each team and by both teams combined in the championship series since the introduction of the 24-second clock more than 20 years ago.

The teams were never more than 4 points apart and the score was tied eight times in a first period that featured 16 turnovers, nine by the Suns.

With both teams effectively shutting off the passing lanes, the guards accounted for most of what scoring there was.

Sobers had half of Phoenix's

Pro Basketball Leagues Merge; New York to Retain Two Teams

By SAM GOLDAPER

Special to The New York Times

HYANNIS, Mass., June 17—The National Basketball Association and the American Basketball Association finally merged today into a 22-team league.

Four of the A.B.A.'s six teams —the New York Nets, the Indiana Pacers, the Denver Nuggets and the San Antonio Spurs —have been absorbed into the N.B.A. and will play in the 1976-77 season.

Each of these franchises will pay $3.2 million in cash to the N.B.A., with the first payment of $1 million due on July 15 and the remainder on Sept. 15. The Nets also must indemnify the Knicks for moving into their New York territory. The Nets play their games at Nassau Coliseum in Uniondale, L.I.

Mike Burke, president of the Knicks, said the indemnification would be "roughly in the same ball park" as the Islanders paid the Rangers when the Long Is-

land team joined the National Hockey League in 1972. The Islanders' owners, some of whom also have a share of the Nets, are paying Madison Square Garden $4 million over a 20-year period. The Garden owns the Rangers.

More negotiations between the Knicks and Nets will be held and they could result in trades that could possibly lower the Nets' indemnification payments.

Since the A.B.A. began as an 11-team league for the 1967-68 season, it had 22 different franchises, seven commissioners and had been involved in countless lawsuits. The league contends it has lost $40 million.

The A.B.A. started the 1975-76 season as a 10-team league, but in rapid succession the Baltimore Claws folded on Oct. 20 and the San Diego Sails dropped out Nov. 10, followed by the Utah

Stars on Dec. 3 and the Virginia Squires May 10.

The Kentucky Colonels and Utah Rockies, who were to take over the Spirits of St. Louis franchise next season, were left out of the consolidation and they will be paid about $3 million each by the four teams accepted into the N.B.A.

The Kentucky and Utah players will be dispersed in a special draft in which the 18 N.B.A. teams, plus the four newcomers, will participate. The Chicago Bulls will have the first pick because they had the worst record in the league. They are expected to select Artis Gilmore, the 7-foot-2-inch Kentucky Colonel center. Several other outstanding players will be available, among them Moses Malone, Maurice Lucas and Marvin Barnes.

There could be a lot of trading or selling of draft picks. The Knicks are almost certain to bid for at least one of those stars to fill their need for an overpowering big man. The Knicks are scheduled to pick sixth in the dispersal draft.

The New Orleans Jazz had drafted Moses Malone, who played for St. Louis, and the Los Angeles Lakers had taken Mark Olberding of the San Antonio Spurs in lieu of their first-round selections in the 1977 college draft. Today those teams were given back their top picks after dropping their rights to those players.

Joe Caldwell, the overpowering center of the Philadelphia 76ers had signed for delivery next season; Don Chaney, the former Boston Celtic backcourt man, and Lonnie Shelton were placed in the "further negotiations" category. Shelton, who contends he was coerced into signing with St. Louis, has since been drafted by the Knicks.

Intensive merger negotiations between Larry O'Brien, the N.B.A. commissioner, and Dave DeBusschere, his A.B.A. counterpart, began at the suggestion of Federal Judge Robert L. Carter of the Southern New York District Court. He asked both sides to attempt an out-of-court settlement of the A.B.A. antitrust suit against the N.B.A.

Lawyers for both sides are scheduled to appear before Judge Carter tomorrow to tell him what progress has been made. But he already has been informed of today's agreement.

David Stern and Michael Cardozo, the N.B.A. lawyers who worked until 6:30 this morning to hammer out the agreement with Bob Carlson, the A.B.A. lawyer, figured it would take 60 to 90 days before all deals were completed.

Although many problems may still develop in future negotiations, nothing is expected to hinder the ultimate agreement. Especially since

each N.B.A. owner will receive almost $700,000 and there is an almost additional $5 million awaiting them in the third year of their television contract with CBS. The television network had promised the extra money if the N.B.A. would accept at least four teams into the league.

The vote for the consolidation was 17-1, with the unexpected dissenting vote cast by Sam Schulman, the owner of the Seattle SuperSonics. Schulman had been a leading proponent for the merger for almost eight years.

"It was a protest vote," said Schulman. "There were some little things they did that upset me, like taking away some of the draft rights certain teams had held."

Would Schulman have voted against the merger if his was the deciding vote? He smiled and offered a "no comment."

O'Brien, who spent most of his first year in office determined to take pro basketball out of the courts, has now succeeded in effecting two major settlements of problems that had cost the league more than $1.5 million in legal and court costs this year. During the N.B.A. All-Star break a settlement of the so-called Oscar Robertson antitrust suit was made with the N.B.A. Players Association.

The N.B.A. advisory committee, consisting of Abe Pollin of the Washington Bullets, Burke, William Wirtz of the Chicago Bulls and William Alverson of the Milwaukee Bucks, plus O'Brien and Simon Gourdine, the deputy commissioner, came to the league's annual meeting with merger plans involving four, five and six A.B.A. teams.

The owners favored the four-team plan while Ozzie Silma, the owner of the Spirits of St. Louis, sat around for four days hoping that plan would fail and the N.B.A. owners would eventually admit his team.

When the $3.2 million cash settlement was finally substituted yesterday for the original $4.5 million five-year payout plan, Prentice Yancey, the general counsel of the A.B.A. Players Association, was summoned from Atlanta. During the all-night nego-

tiations, Yancey entered into an accord that included the honoring of all present A.B.A. contracts, including those of players who may not make it to the N.B.A. A pool was also set up that would pay off the contracts of those players whose teams had folded.

Yancey said the A.B.A. player representatives would have to approve the deal.

As for the new N.B.A. teams, their rosters were frozen as of May 1. They will not share in any television monies for the next four years and, should the league decide to share gate receipts in the future, they would be excluded from the vote. In the N.B.A. the home team weeps all the receipts. The new teas will have no say in their elegiment in the league's from divisions.

Larry Fleisher, the general counsel of the N.B.A. Players Association, sail, "It's better to have two teams disbanded rather than six. I don't think the A.B.A. would have been able to survive another year."

June 18, 1976

Erving Trade Is Official; Nets' Fans Complaining

By SAM GOLDAPER

After 19 hours of continuous negotiations that ended at 3 P.M. yesterday, the trade of Julius Erving by the New York Nets to the Philadelphia 76ers became official. The immediate reverberations were:

• More than 100 ticket-holders lodged complaints at the Net offices in Carle Place, L.I., and the nearby Nassau Coliseum. One season ticket-holder took court action, seeking the return of his money.

• Coach Kevin Loughery and his players, in Oakland, Calif., for their opening game tonight, were shaken. Some used harsh words in criticizing Roy Boe, the club president, for having sold Dr. J, pro basketball's most exciting player.

• Mike Burke, president of the Knicks, said Boe had refused his initial offer of $2.5 million, plus players, for Erving.

• Long lines formed early in Philadelphia to buy tickets for 76er games. The 76ers open the season tonight at home against the San Antonio Spurs.

As a tired-looking Pat Williams, 76er general manager, emerged from the negotiations at the offices of Bob Carlson, the Nets' lawyer and one of Boe's many partners, he said, "Dr. J. is a 76er."

The sale of the 26-year-old star was made after he had refused to report to the Net training camp until Boe renegotiated the four remaining years of his $1.9 million, seven-year contract. Erving charged that Boe had reneged on several promises regarding bonuses and the renegotiation of the contract. Erving

came to New York for the 1973–74 season from the Virginia Squires of the now-defunct American Basketball Association.

How much did F. Eugene Dixon, the wealthy 76er owner, pay the financially troubled Boe for Erving? The guessing started at $3 million, the price Boe had placed on Dr. J. Dixon said only that the figure was high.

Team With a Big Payroll

Erving, who participated in the negotiations until 3:30 A.M., signed a six-year contract with Philadelphia for $3.5 million. That was in addition to what Dixon had paid Boe. After a few hours rest, Erving went to Lenox Hill Hospital for a physical examination, which the 76ers had requested. Dr. Jeffrey Minkoff, the Knicks' doctor, did the examination and gave him a clean bill of health.

Asked why so much money was being invested in Erving, Williams said:

"His availability got the juices flowing. He is a great attraction and we're trying to sell out a building of almost 18,000 seats."

It has been estimated that a sellout crowd at thS Spectrum in Philadelphia is worth $108,000. If all the games were sold out, it would hardly be enough to meet the 76er payroll, which included huge salaries for George McGinnis, Doug Collins, Fred Carter, Caldwell Jones and Daryl Dawkins.

"There is a lot more to income than ticket sales," said Williams. "If we're successful and get deep into the play

George McGinnis, playing for the Indiana Pacers, scored 39 points in this game. McGinnis, a big man who can score, has been much sought after by several teams in the N.B.A.

Julius ("Dr. J.") Erving is the shiftiest operator in short pants. His repertoire of shots and moves is virtually endless. He is shown here playing for the New York Nets.

offs, there are revenues from local television, cable television, radio, ads for programs, the sale of novelties and other merchandising. We're looking to Erving as a long-range thing, playing out his career here. All we have to do is win and we'll do all right.

"I saw an example of his drawing power when we sold more than 250 tickets in the first few hours of the morning. Also, I tried to call my office for more than two hours and couldn't get through, and we had just installed 12 new phone lines."

No Action by O'Brien Seen

Most of those who called the Net office and the Coliseum were critical of the sale. Some expressed hope that Larry O'Brien, commissioner of the National Basketball Association, would void the trade, as Commissioner Bowie Kuhn did when he refused to let the Oakland A's sell Vida Blue to the Yankees.

But there was no chance of that happening. A spokesman for the N.B.A.A. said: "The 76ers have submitted the contract. It will be expeditiously reviewed in the same manner as all player contracts. Assuming that it is in full compliance with the constitution, bylaws and procedures of the N.B.A., it will, of course, be approved."

The Nets told callers there would be no ticket refunds because, they said, the club had promised to provide basketball, not any particular players. But Herb Krohn, a lawyer of Merrick, L.I., said angrily that he would file suit today in Nassau County District Court for $714, the price of two season tickets.

"I was induced to buy tickets on the basis that Dr. J would play in the Nassau Coliseum," said Krohn. "I could assume that if he became injured or ill, it was out of the Nets' control, but be selling him they did something within their control. I'm not a rabid fan,

Associated Press

Roy Boe
Owner of the Nets

it's not earthshaking, but I feel I've been taken."

The sale also set off a controversy between Boe and Burke.

"Five teams—the Knicks, Buffalo, Los Angeles, Milwaukee, and Philadelphia—had contacted the Nets about Erving," said Boe. "Contrary to reports that the Knicks were the first team to contact us, and because of their assistance in putting the merger agreement together, they were given certain considerations in the negotiations. We establish certain parameted and, as it turned out, their offer was least competitive of all."

Burke, in revealing the Knicks' initial offer for Erving, said:

"When we first contacted Boe, they

did establish certain parameters, and that was that it would cost the Knicks $1 million more than any other team to acquire Erving. Our proposal compared favorably with the $3 million which Philadelphia is reported to have paid. Subsequent to our first offer, the Knicks were excluded from competitive bidding.

"We are very disappointed that we were not allowed to get into the competitive bidding after that initial proposal. He's a severe loss to the New York area."

On the eve of the opening game against the Golden State Warriors, Coach Loughery said: "The players to replace Erving at this moment are not available. It's tough to play Abraham Lincoln and George Washington in the frontcourt." He alluded to the financial transactions.

Erving will be in uniform tonight wearing No. 6 at the Spectrum.

"He's a 42 long, 34-inch waist and 15½ sneaker size," said Williams. "We have everything in readiness. He originally asked for No. 32, the uniform he wore with the Nets, but I told him that was Billy Cunningham's old number and that we planned to retire it. He told me he admired Cunningham and there would be no problem. He chose No. 6."

Dixon's involvement with the 76ers represents a switch in interest for him from horse racing to basketball. The 54-year-old owner has been active in thoroughbred racing for three decades as owner, breeder and administrator. According to racing sources, he decided to dispose of all his thoroughbred holdings because his wife an children were more interested in basketball than racing.

Dixon inherited much of his wealth from his uncle, the late George D. Widener, who was chairman of the Jockey Club from 1950 to 1964.

October 22, 1976

Blazers Win Title, Beating 76ers by 109-107

Fourth Victory in a Row After 2 Losses
—Walton Voted Top Player in Series

By LEONARD KOPPETT
Special to The New York Times

PORTLAND, Ore., June 5—The Philadelphia 76ers finally came out of their trance today, but the Portland Trail Blazers rose to the challenge and held them off in a 109-107 victory that gave them the National Basketball Association championship.

Ahead by 12 points with six minutes to play, the Blazers saw their lead dwindle to 4 points in less than two minutes, and down to 3 with 51 seconds left—an eternity in pro basketball.

But Maurice Lucas, who had a generally poor game, sank one of two free throws with 27 seconds to play and a basket by George McGinnis—who snapped his series-long slump and had a 28-point game—made it 109-107 with 18 seconds to go. And after forcing

a jump ball and getting possession, the 76ers got three good shots at the tying basket, jumpers by Julius Erving, Lloyd Free and finally McGinnis again. But all three missed.

So the Blazers, in the seventh year of their existence, became the first team in the 31-year history of the league to win four straight games in the final round after losing the first two. They had lost two in Philadelphia but had won the next two here by huge margins, and had held off a last-quarter Philadelphia rally at the Spectrum there Friday night.

From their point of view, it was the triumph of teamwork and good planning, built around a supercenter like Bill Walton, whose superb play throughout the series also brought him the car that constitutes the Outstanding Player Award sponsored by Sport

Magazine. His contributions in this final game were decisive: 23 rebounds, 8 blocked shots and 7 assists, along with 20 points.

"This is the finest team and the finest people I've ever coached," declared Coach Jack Ramsay, accepting the Podoloff Trophy and almost breaking into an all-court smile (but not quite). "This is what I've aimed for since becoming a professional coach—but I would feel the same way and say the same thing about these players even if we hadn't won."

For Philadelphia, however, the result was one shot short of what had been building up since October, when their new owner, F. Eugene Dixon, made a $6 million deal to add Erving to McGinnis and Doug Collins and other players of highly regarded individual talent. Tabbed as league-champions-to-be, the

Associated Press

Philadelphia's Julius Erving going up for basket as Portland's Bill Walton defends. Portland gained fourth victory for N.B.A. title, 109-107.

Blazers' Box Score

PHILADELPHIA (107)

	min	fgm	fga	ftm	fta	reb	a	pf	pts
Erving	43	17	29	6	7	6	8	2	40
McGinnis	41	12	23	4	7	16	2	5	28
C. Jones	27	5	8	0	0	4	2	6	10
Bibby	37	3	6	0	0	2	5	3	6
Collins	39	3	9	0	0	5	2	3	6
Mix	8	1	3	0	0	0	1	0	2
Dawkins	11	2	3	0	1	1	0	1	4
Free	19	0	6	9	12	3	2	3	9
Catchings	2	0	0	0	0	1	1	1	0
Bryant	12	1	4	0	0	3	2	3	2
Dunleavy	1	0	0	0	0	0	0	1	0
Total	240	44	91	19	27	41	25	28	107

PORTLAND (109)

	min	fgm	fga	ftm	fta	reb	a	pf	pts
Gross	40	12	16	0	0	5	3	2	24
Lucas	39	3	12	9	12	10	5	5	15
Walton	42	8	15	4	5	23	7	4	20
Davis	39	4	8	5	6	3	3	2	13
Hollins	43	10	22	0	1	8	3	1	20
Calhoun	8	3	3	0	0	0	0	2	6
Neal	13	2	4	0	0	2	2	3	4
Twardzik	14	2	5	3	6	1	0	4	7
R. Jones	2	0	1	0	0	0	0	0	0
Total	240	44	86	21	30	55	23	23	109

Philadelphia	27	28	27	25—107
Portland	27	40	24	18—109

Referees—Richie Powers and Jake O'Donnell.
Attendance—12,951.

Jones and the revived McGinnis, and playing much more agressively than they had in the three preceding games, the 76ers took a 22-18 lead and seemed headed for more before Jones picked up his third personal foul in the eighth minute of the game. With Daryl Dawkins in his place, and Free replacing Collins at times, the 76ers had the wrong combination, and were outscored, 39-20, over the next 13 minutes of play. That made it 57-42, and it was 67-55 at the half.

From then on Philadelphia actually played better, but the hole was too deep to climb out of. Bob Gross, who scored 24 points and made 12 of his 16 shots, turned out to be the offensive saver for the Blazers. Two particularly acrobatic shots, one off a rebound and one off a drive, went in to make it 99-90 when the 76ers were generating strong momentum early in the fourth quarter.

And rebounding was another key. The Blazers had a 14-5 edge in that category in the second quarter in building their lead and a 55-41 edge for the game. They made nine baskets on offensive rebounds.

So Portland, having reached the playoffs for the first time, went all the way, beating Chicago, Denver and Los Angeles en route to the final. The only other instance of a team winning the final round after losing the first two games was in 1969, when Bill Russell's last Boston Celtic team defeated Los Angeles in seven games.

June 6, 1977

76ers left here today believing that they still would have made it if a tying basket would have given them a chance in overtime, and then in a seventh game at Philadelphia Wednesday.

And when it was over, Erving and McGinnis made emotional speeches to their teammates in a closed dressing room, before Coach Gene Shue and all the 76ers trooped into the Portland dressing room to congratulate their conquerors. Erving spoke of not downgrading what they had achieved by reaching the final, and spoke of what had been learned for next year. McGinnis told the other players how sorry he was that he hadn't been able to contribute as much as expected during his sub-par performance in almost all the playoff games.

In this one, however, McGinnis was in regular-season form from the start. He hit his first three shots, and that made the 76ers competitive again. Erving, as brilliant as always, produced 40 points and almost single-handedly pulled the 76ers back into the game when they were trailing in the second half.

Actually, however, the game turned on two other factors. One was the foul trouble that forced Caldwell Jones, the Philadelphia center, to the bench in the second quarter. With Jones in the game, then and later, the 76ers were getting a fair matchup with Walton; without him, their middle was wide open on defense, and McGinnis had to wind up playing Walton, springing leaks elsewhere.

The other was the fact that the Portland guards were simply too fast and too good for the 76ers guards. Collins didn't shoot much because McGinnis had revived, but even so, the three Portland backcourt regulars outscored Philadelphia's three, 30-4, in the first half.

With a starting line-up including

Lakers' Kermit Washington Fined $10,000

After viewing the videotape, above, in his office, Commissioner Larry O'Brien handed out the stiffest penalty in National Basketball Association history to Lakers' Kermit Washington, right, for fight with Rudy Tomjanovich of the Houston Rockets.

By SAM GOLDAPER

Disturbed by excessive violence in the National Basketball Association, Commissioner Larry O'Brien yesterday handed out the largest fine in sports history. He penalized Kermit Washington, a Los Angeles Lakers' forward, $10,000 and suspended him for at least 60 days and possibly for the rest of the season.

The fine was levied after the 6-foot-8-inch, 230-pound Washington struck Kevin Kunnert, the Houston Rockets' 7-foot center, and Rudy Tomjanovich, a Rockets' forward, Friday night in Los

Angeles. The 6-foot-8-inch Tomjanovich is in Centinela Hospital Medical Center in Inglewood, Calif., with a double fracture of the jaw, a broken nose and a concussion.

Operation Required

A hospital spokesman said yesterday that Tomjanovich would require an operation. "They have to treat the swelling first," the spokesman said, "then wire his jaw. Rudy may go back to Texas for the operation."

There was no estimate of how long Tomjanovich, the Rockets' best player and the league's 15th leading scorer,

would be sidelined. At present, he is in the hospital's intensive-care unit.

Washington, the Lakers' first-round draft choice in 1973, may apply to O'Brien for reinstatement after 60 days. The Lakers have 26 games scheduled during that period. Since suspended players are not paid and are not permitted to take part in team activities, it was estimated that a 60-day suspension would cost Washington a total of $50,000.

"The stringent penalty reflects the severity of Washington's action on the court," O'Brien said. "A careful review of two videotapes of the game, reports from officials and statements from witnesses persuaded me to take this action."

The incident took place early in the third quarter when Washington grabbed Kunnert, who had pulled down a rebound and had thrown an outlet pass. After Kunnert tried to pull himself free and swung an elbow in the process, Washington began a series of punches from in close. Kareem Abdul-Jabbar, the Lakers' center, tried to break up the fight. He grabbed Kunnert and also grabbed Washington's arm.

Kunnert Floored

Washington then unleashed a right-hand punch that floored Kunnert, who was momentarily stunned but uninjured. Bob Rakel, one of the two officials, immediately ejected Washington.

Meanwhile, Tomjanovich, who was about 30 feet away from the incident, led a group of players to his fallen teammate.

It was then that Washington spun around and smashed Tomjanovich. The Rockets' forward fell backward, landed on his head and lay motionless for several minutes. Tomjanovich, who was bleeding from the nose and lip, was helped off the court and taken to the hospital.

After Washington punched Tomjanovich, an angered Tom Nissalke, the Houston coach, said, "It was the most malicious thing I've ever seen in basketball. It was a sucker punch."

Unfortunate Mistake

After the game, Washington said "I saw him coming and I just swung. I had no idea who it was. Now that I've talked to other people, I understand Rudy wasn't going to fight. He's never even been in a fight. It was an honest, unfortunate mistake."

After O'Brien's penalty was announced, Washington and the Lakers withheld comment.

Later last night, the president and the general manager of the Rockets said the club would sue Washington. Ray Patterson, the Houston executive, said the suit would claim that the incident jeopardized the stability of the franchise.

O'Brien has been concerned with the growth of violence in the last two seasons. Last season he asked for and received powers from the owners to levy suspensions and fines of up to $10,000.

During last season's championship series between Philadelphia and Portland, O'Brien fined Maurice Lucas of the Trail Blazers and Darryl Dawkins of the 76ers $2,500 each for their parts in a brawl.

This season, Abdul-Jabbar broke his right hand while blind-siding Kent Benson of the Milwaukee Bucks. The Lakers' center was fined $5,000 for the incident. Adrian Dantley of the Indiana Pacers was suspended for three days after pursuing Dave Meyers of the Bucks in the locker-room area after a game.

O'Brien recently formed a committee to explore ways of avoiding violence. That committee included Simon Gourdine, the deputy commissioner; John Joyce, the league's director of security; Larry Fleischer, general counsel of the National Basketball Players' Association; Norm Drucker, supervisor of officials; Jack Ramsay, the Trail Blazers' coach; Joe Axelson, president of the Kansas City Kings; Bob Lanier of the Detroit Pistons, and Earl Monroe of the Knicks.

That committee held its first meet-ing last Monday, yet, violence continues and everyone is asking why.

Said Monroe: "We talked about it a lot last week, but nothing has come of it. I don't think we can put our finger on it because we don't understand emotions. Maybe three referees are the answer. I know officiating has to have something to do with it. The players are getting bigger, better and stronger, and if that's happening, then the officiating has to be upgraded. They, by their actions, set the example for the tempo of the game."

Drucker said: "Although the basketball court is 90 by 50 [feet], most of the time you have 10 players congregating in an area of 20 by 16. Basketball is a game of driving, setting picks, going for offensive and defensive rebounds and players running into the blind side. It causes problems."

Lanier said: "If there were three officials on the floor, and the third had more responsibility than just watching the lines, it would keep guys from unnecessarily abusing each other. The game has gotten too fast for two men to handle. Flagrant things don't just happen, they build up. It's only when things get out of hand that people explode like that."

The use of three officials has been discussed for several years, but the owners have always vetoed the idea because of the additional cost involved.

O'Brien's action yesterday ranks among harshest penalties in sports history.

In 1947 Leo Durocher, then manager of the Brooklyn Dodgers, was suspended for a year for conduct detrimental to baseball because of his association with a known gambler.

Denny McLain, who won 31 games while pitching for Detroit in 1968, was suspended by Commissioner Bowie Kuhn, because of McLain's involvement with gamblers, for one year in February 1970. The suspension was lifted six months later in August 1970.

In 1963, Paul Hornung of the Green Bay Packers and Alex Karras of the Detroit Lions, were suspended for a year for betting on National Football League games involving their teams.

In 1974, Harland Svare, the general manager of the San Diego Chargers, and several players on the N.F.L. team were fined a total of $40,000 in a drug-related case.

The late Jack Molinas was banned from pro basketball for life for wagering on games. For an act of violence, Abdul-Jabbar's $5,000 fine was the largest before Washington's penalty was levied.

Randy Smith is in his seventh season with the Buffalo Braves and during that stretch, he has had 61 different teammates, no counting rookies in training camp. Player No. 61 arrived last week when Scott Lloyd, who was released by the Milwaukee Bucks, signed a two-year contract. . . . Maurice Lucas, the Portland Trail Blazers' power forward, speaks of Walter Davis, the Phoenix Suns' rookie: "He's a good player and he is handling the pressure well. Not many rookies can take the pressure the way he does."

December 13, 1977

Why N.B.A. Teams Succeed at Home

By MEL WATKINS

In the National Basketball Association, one theme—apart from an outbreak of violence — has insistently played itself out from court to court and city to city. No coach has missed it, no player or fan; it is the inescapable fact that the team playing at home wins more often than the team on the road.

Now a computer study by The New York Times has codified the phenomenon for the first time. And the study makes clear that, among other things, the natural culprits, the referees, are far from wholly to blame.

The computer analysis shows that there is a 4.4-point advantage for the home team in N.B.A. games. The study, based on games through Dec. 31, 1977, shows that teams score 4.4 more points than their team average when at home and 4.4 fewer when playing on an away court.

The study further shows that the officiating—at least with regard to the number of free throws attempted—is not a significant factor in the 67.4 percent winning record for home teams. In games played through Dec. 31, home teams have had only a marginal advantage of two free throws a game.

Still, the home advantage as a factor in won-lost records has been increasing gradually since the 1971-72 season, when it was 58.2 percent. Last season's total home-court record was 618 victories, 284 losses, or a 68.5 percent advantage for the home team.

This figure represents the sixth-highest percentage in the league's 30-year history. Moreover, except for the 1965-66 season, in which home teams won 68.9 percent of their games, the 1976-77 percentage was the highest in 20 years.

Last season, no N.B.A. team had a winning road record—not even the powerful squads like Portland, Philadelphia and Los Angeles. And only the Atlanta Hawks (19-22) and the struggling New York Nets (10-31) had losing home records.

Teams such as Buffalo (7-34 on the road) and Milwaukee (6-35), which lost more than 82 percent of their road games, still managed to win nearly 60 percent of the time at home. And none of the four teams (Los Angeles, Denver, Portland and Houston) that won more than 85 percent of their home games could win even 40 percent on the road.

Through the end of last month, with nearly half the schedule completed, Portland (9-5) was better than .500 on the road. There were five other teams

Computer Study of N.B.A. Teams

The table at the right introduces a computerized team-power rating system developed by The New York Times to evaluate the relative strengths of squads involved in round-robin league play. In this case, the system has been used to evaluate the 22 teams in the National Basketball Association through games of Dec. 31.

The team-power rating is designed to measure a club's relative proficiency. The highest-ranked team is assigned a rating of 1.000 by the computer, and the other teams are rated in descending order in relation to this maximum.

To determine a team's proficiency, the computer evaluates its margins of victory or defeat for each game, modifying these results by weighing three factors: the caliber of the opponent, whether the game was played at home or away, and the time of the season when it took place.

For example, a team-power rating is improved more by a 2-point victory over the Portland Trail Blazers, a strong team, than by a 5-point victory over the New Jersey Nets, a weaker one. Because of a team's home-court advantage (4.4 points on the average), a 3-point triumph by the New York Knicks over the Nuggets in Denver is more significant than a 3-point Knick victory over Denver in New York.

Further, in terms of current team strength, a four-game winning streak in December means more than an earlier such streak —in October, say.

Because of these factors, a power rating does not necessarily reflect a team's position in the league standings. Nor, because of chance, scheduling and the many other variables entailed in specific team matchups, will TPR necessarily predict the outcome of a game.

In effect, a power rating is derived by examining how a team could be expected to perform against a hypothetical average opponent on a neutral court.

After a number of games have been played, the computer establishes the average score per game for the hypothetical team. It rates each team's proficiency in relation to the proficiency of this average team. The rating for the hypothetical team in the table's TPR listing would be the median—.8855—which lies between the ratings for the 11th and 12th ranked teams.

The table provides rankings for games played by a team at home and away, as well as for overall performance. The last three columns give the average margin of victory or defeat for all games and for home and away games.

To illustrate: Until Jan. 1, Portland had outscored its opponents by an average of 9.8 points in all games. It had outscored its opponents by an average of 13.3 points at home and 5.4 points away. The New York Knicks' average margin of victory was 0.4 for all games with the at-home victory average of 4.1 points offset by a 4.3-point losing margin on the road.

Team Power Rating By Computer				Average Margin of Victory or Defeat Per Game		
	Ranking Overall	Home	Away	Team Power Rating	All Games	Home Average= +4.5	Away Average= –4.5
Portland	1	1	1	1.000	+ 9.8	+13.3	+ 5.4
Phoenix	2	5	3	.936	+ 3.5	+10.5	– 2.5
Philadelphia	3	3	5	.923	+ 4.8	+ 8.9	0.0
Chicago	4	4	11	.918	+ 2.6	+ 6.4	– 1.1
Denver	5	2	12	.916	+ 1.6	+11.5	– 7.1
Washington	6	6	6	.916	+ 2.2	+ 6.6	– 1.8
Seattle	7	11	7	.897	– 0.3	+ 4.7	– 5.6
Los Angeles	8	10	8	.892	+ 0.5	+ 2.1	– 1.5
San Antonio	9	8	14	.891	+ 0.6	+ 4.6	– 3.1
New York	10	9	13	.887	+ 0.4	+ 4.1	– 4.3
Cleveland	11	13	9	.886	– 0.3	+ 3.2	– 4.1
Milwaukee	12	19	2	.885	+ 0.1	+ 4.1	– 4.0
Detroit	13	21	4	.882	– 1.1	+ 4.0	– 8.2
Atlanta	14	17	10	.877	– 2.1	– 1.1	– 3.1
Indiana	15	15	15	.875	+ 0.6	+ 3.6	– 2.5
Houston	16	14	17	.864	– 1.9	+ 2.2	– 5.9
Golden St.	17	7	19	.861	– 1.3	+ 5.4	– 6.3
Kansas City	18	18	18	.857	– 1.6	+ 2.6	– 5.8
Buffalo	19	20	16	.854	– 2.6	+ 0.5	– 5.7
New Orleans	20	16	20	.852	– 2.6	+ 4.3	– 8.8
Boston	21	12	21	.840	– 4.4	– 0.1	– 7.8
New Jersey	22	22	22	.805	– 7.7	– 2.0	–12.7

whose winning percentages hovered near .500. Still, the anomalies were no less evident than they were last season:

¶Boston, a team with the second-worst record in the N.B.A., was winning 59.9 percent of its home games.

¶Denver had a near-perfect record at home (15-1) but had won only six of 13 games on the road.

¶Golden State, winning 80 percent of its home games, had won only 15 percent away.

Statistics can be as malleable as Silly Putty, but no matter how you mold them these figures seem irregular.

The home-team advantage exists to some extent in every sport. In professional football it is estimated that the home field is usually worth 3 points, and home teams win four of seven games. In professional hockey the home team is only a 7-6 favorite.

The most basic question with regard to the N.B.A. seems to be whether there is some intrinsic peculiarity in professional basketball that causes turnabouts so extreme, whether the home-away seesaw is being tilted by some force beyond the players' abilities and control.

The rigor of traveling is the explanation given most often: a Tuesday night game at Boston, a Wednesday flight to New Orleans and a game on Thursday, followed by a late-night flight to Newark and a game Friday evening at Piscataway, N.J.

"Players are simply tired," suggests Coach Kevin Loughery of the Nets, "and it shows more at the end of a road trip than at the beginning."

Red Auerbach, Boston Celtics president and general manager, puts it succinctly. "The players

The New York Times/Keith Meyers

A psychological boost from the crowd.

are bored on the road," he says. "They wander around the hotel, hang out in the lobby. There's nothing to do—they're bored."

cinctly. "The players are bored on the road," he says. "They wander around the hotel, hang out in the lobby. There's nothing to do—they're bored."

At any rate, it appears that the pace the one-night stands followed by late trips to another city and a game the same day or the next, has its effects. Norm Drucker, N.B.A. supervisor of officials, says: "The home-team players have the advantage because they have a normal social existence. They get up and relax during the day. Emotionally and psychologically they are more at ease. They're ready for the game."

And George McGinnis, Philadelphia 76er forward, says: "Playing at home is like sleeping in your own bed. You're used to it; you're comfortable."

"Most fans think every basketball court is alike," says McGinnis. "You know they're all the same size, and the baskets are the same height. But, really, every court is different.

"I'm familiar with the Spectrum, and I know the backboards, the rims. But in another arena it's different; you have to adjust. Every bucket is different.

"In New Orleans's Superdome, the feeling is entirely different. You look up through the glass, and all you see is space—that big dome. It's like playing on a football field. I guess it's the feeling of emptiness. You're used to the crowd behind the boards, and it's tough to play there."

●

Another disadvantage to the visiting team, usually, is the effect of the crowd. This can never be measured

precisely, but the roar certainly affects individual players.

Anyone who has played before a large crowd, or sat in Boston Garden during the Celtics' heyday or in Madison Square Garden during the chant of "Defense! Defense!" knows something of the psychological boost that spectators can generate for their team.

N.B.A. referees have received an inordinate amount of criticism this season. Coach Willis Reed of the New York Knicks has been outspoken, but so have Chicago's Ed Badger and Milwaukee's Don Nelson. The implication has been that, as one player put it, referees "tend to lean toward the home team" on close calls. Despite the complaints, no clear-cut pattern emerges with regard to more fouls against visiting teams, as the study by The Times shows.

But clearly referees can influence the outcomes.

Earlier this season in Boston, a Knicks-Celtics game was decided by a backcourt foul that appeared to be no more than the usual hand-checking that had occurred throughout the game; this time Jo Jo White was awarded two free throws with less than 10 seconds left, and Boston won the game, 121-119.

On the other hand, in a recent game in Milwaukee, Earl Strom and Mel Whitworth, the referees, called six technical fouls on Coach Nelson, his assistant coach and a Bucks player. Atlanta outscored Milwaukee by 29-13 from the foul line on the way to a 109-96 victory.

So the so-called "homer" seems to be a thing of the past, a remnant from the N.B.A.'s early days, when there

were fewer teams situated in small cities.

●

Still, Larry O'Brien, N.B.A. commissioner, says, "Basketball is a highly emotional game, and with fans' close proximity it's not humanly possible for officials to maintain total balance." And though O'Brien insists that "there is no evidence that officials don't call them as they see them," it does seem apparent that referees get caught up in the excitment, the flow, the emotional pitch of a game.

It appears that whatever effect officials have on the home-court advantage derives not so much from how many fouls are called against the home or visiting team, but when these fouls are called, how the timing affects a team's momentum. The outcome of a game can even hinge on the fouls that are not called, as happened in a recent Philadelphia-Phoenix game at th Spectrum.

The 76ers overcame a 14-point deficit during an eight-minute span of helter-skelter basketball filled with physical contact. During this rally, the referees were quiet, while the Spectrum fans created an atmosphere of virtual hysteria.

No one pretends that there is a simple reason for the lopsided home-away records. And, as the home-team advantage approaches 70 percent, there is some concern at the commissioner's office.

"I have no ready answer," said O'Brien, "But there is talk of mroe discussions about scheduling changes to ease the travel burden, and about a third referee.

January 9, 1978

Issue and Debate

Should N.B.A. Legalize the Zone?

By LEONARD KOPPETT

The zone defense has been forbidden in the National Basketball Association since the league began in 1946. For many years, there has been disagreement within the league about the necessity or wisdom of that ban, but in practice, some elements of a zone defense have been used widely by many teams. This season the issue has been raised more dramatically than ever before by the actions of Richie Powers, one of the N.B.A.'s oldest and most respected referees.

In a game in Atlanta, Powers imposed the rule-book penalty for using a zone—a technical foul—on the Hawks, a call that is rarely made. Afterwards, Powers stated he felt strongly that the zone should be allowed and that although the Hawk defense had violated the letter of the rules, it was an "admirable" and effective defense that should be permitted.

A couple of weeks later, before a game between the Hawks and the New Jersey Nets Powers went further: He notified both teams that he would not penalize them for using the zone openly, and the game was played that way. As a result, Powers was heavily fined and suspended for a few games by Commissioner Larry O'Brien for having taken the law into his own hands, but the long-standing argument had been

given wide publicity: should the zone be banned or shouldn't it?

The Background

Theoretically, in a zone defense, each defensive player guards an assigned area of the floor, picking up whatever offensive player comes through and letting him go when he leaves; in a man-to-man defense, each defender covers a specific offensive player wherever he goes. Since the crucial area in basketball is the small one near the basket, a zone defense can make it easier to deny that area to the offense without committing fouls.

But pure zone or pure man-to-man is rarely the issue. Most modern teams play some kind of combination defense that employs both principles. Even in the most orthodox man-to-man, when two defenders suddenly trade assignments by calling "switch," or when they drop back to give a poor shooter room so that they can "help out" against a strong center, they are getting into zone activities. The N.B.A. has changed the wording of its no-zone rule several times in an attempt to refine exactly what is permissible, but given the fluid nature and high speed of basketball play, it is almost impossible to make precise rulings.

Originally, however, the no-zone rule had a very specific universally accept-

ed purpose. A zone defense, by making penetration difficult, encourages the team that's ahead or weak in outside shooting to stall; it promotes holding the ball out by the offense until the defense (if it is trailing) abandons the zone. And such a style of play would have been suicidal to a new league trying to sell a new product (pro basketball) to the public after World War II.

Even so, stalling and strategic fouling proved to be serious problems, and in 1954 the league adopted the 24-second clock. A team must try a shot within 24 seconds of gaining possession, or it loses the ball. This has completely eliminated the kind of stalling tactics provoked by a zone, so the original rationale has not applied for more than 20 years. Nevertheless, a strong segment of opinion thinks the zone should be outlawed for other reasons, and that's the substance of the present dispute.

For Zone Defense

Those who want the zone make the following points:

¶ Since the stalling problem has been eliminated by the time limit on shooting, that danger cannot be generated by use of the zone.

¶ Without that game-spoiling danger, the zone is a legitimate, honorable and

Associated Press

Richie Powers

interesting defensive tactic.

¶ Attempts to forbid the zone do more harm than good by building in a constant irritant. Since the zone defense is so hard to define, so easy to disguise and so seldom called by the referees, teams complain when it isn't called and on the rare occasions when it is called. The game is hard enough to officiate without this extra problem.

¶ In a sport where the average team score is 100 points per game, giving an added weapon to the defense can't do any harm.

¶ A pure zone shouldn't bother professional teams much, since the general shooting ability is so great. The fact is, against star centers like Kareem Abdul-Jabbar it is often harder to score from under the basket than from medium range outside.

¶ A defense that isn't pure zone, but definitely has some zone features, is what many teams use now anyhow.

¶ If the traditionally accepted consequences of zone defenses are true—less likelihood of defensive fouls, more board control for the defense, more emphasis on good outside shooting—they should be welcomed rather than shunned.

Against Zone Defense

Those who believe the zone should not be allowed make the following points:

¶ A zone increases the advantage already enjoyed by the few teams with super centers or greater overall size because it decreases the chance of getting them into foul trouble, and helps their rebounding position.

¶ Many games among the 892 that now constitute the regular season become one-sided because one team is having a poor shooting night. A zone in such situations would make those games worse, and increase the number that might become one-sided.

¶ The 24-second clock makes the zone defense too effective since the offense can't move the ball long enough to create a crack in it.

¶ So long as the zone is forbidden, the disguised, partial or hybrid zones do no real harm. But if there were no prohibition, coaches would use such tight zones that games might be re-

duced to an outside-shooting contest, without the speed and action that make basketball popular. The prohibition acts as a limitation within reason, even if it isn't enforced as an out-and-out ban.

Prospects

Since the N.B.A. started, drastic changes have been made in rules concerning fouls, free throws, the width of the foul lane and other important items. It is almost certain that attempts will be made to redefine the no-zone rule by next year, and quite likely that eliminating the ban altogether will get consideration within a few more years. An obvious possible compromise would be an increase in

the time limit on shooting to 30 seconds.

The game being played today is so different, physically, from the game of the 1940's that it is unlikely so old a rule will be kept indefinitely. The overriding fact is that in the 1940's, with no time limit on shooting and a foul lane only six feet wide, only 28 percent of the field-goal attempts were successful; currently, with the time limit, a 16-foot lane, taller defenders and much greater sophistication on defense, shooting accuracy runs about 47 percent. That increase in shooting skill may eventually allay fears that the zone would be a "deadening" influence.

April 4, 1978

Thompson Gets 73, Gervin Gets Title

By SAM GOLDAPER

David Thompson of the Denver Nuggets thought he had won the National Basketball Association scoring title with a 73-point performance against the Detroit Pistons yesterday afternoon, but George Gervin of the San Antonio Spurs took it from him about seven hours later.

Gervin, whose San Antonio Spurs were at the Superdome in New Orleans to play the Jazz last night, responded with 63 points. He played 33 minutes and scored on 23 of 49 shots from the field and 17 of 20 from the free-throw line. He thus finished the 82-game regular reason with an average of 27.22, to Thompson's 27.15. The per-game average determines the scoring championship.

Obviously helped by his teammates in an effort to get the scoring title during Denver's 139-137 loss to the Detroit Pistons, Thompson went on a rampage. His total of 73 points was the third highest for a single game in the 32-year history of the N.B.A. It was also believed to be the closest scoring race in league history, coming down to the final day of the regular season.

Wilt Chamberlain, playing for the Philadelphia Warriors, scored 100 points against the Knicks on March 2, 1962 in Hershey, Pa. and 78 against the Los Angeles Lakers in 1961. He also had two 73-point games.

Surpasses Baylor

Before Thompson's feat yesterday, Elgin Baylor, now the coach of the New Orleans Jazz, was the player with the second highest scoring output. Baylor, then with the Lakers, got 71 against the Knicks in 1960.

Thompson scored 32 points in the first period on 13 baskets and six free throws. That set N.B.A. marks for points and field goals in a period.

But Gervin broke that record when he scored 33 points in the second quarter enroute to a 53-point halftime performance.

Thompson took 23 shots and made 20 in his first-half, 53-point total (the

The Box Scores

NUGGETS VS. PISTONS

DENVER (137)

	min	fgm	fga	ftm	fta	reb	a	pf	pts
Jones	15	2	2	0	0	3	2	0	4
Wilkerson	32	1	8	0	0	5	3	5	2
Issel	32	6	9	2	2	9	10	2	14
Thompson	43	28	38	17	20	7	2	2	73
Roberts	34	5	8	2	2	5	1	5	12
Ellis	23	2	4	1	1	4	6	2	5
LaGarde	14	2	5	3	4	4	2	3	7
Simpson	24	4	9	1	0	3	1	1	9
Cook	4	1	1	0	0	3	1	1	2
Calvin	9	3	4	1	2	0	0	1	7
Smith	10	1	2	0	0	1	1	1	2
Total	240	55	90	27	32	44	30	24	137

DETROIT (139)

	min	fgm	fga	ftm	fta	reb	a	pf	pts
Carr	39	10	18	5	6	9	1	2	25
Shumate	41	8	11	4	4	9	1	4	20
Poquette	27	5	7	1	2	5	0	1	11
Money	33	11	24	1	1	2	4	3	23
Ford	35	8	14	3	4	4	9	3	19
Bostic	15	4	8	2	5	4	0	0	10
Skinner	30	6	8	11	11	5	3	4	23
Price	24	2	2	0	0	2	5	4	4
Total	240	54	102	27	33	40	23	21	139

DENVER .... 42 41 23 31—137
DETROIT .... 36 33 35 35—139

Referees—Jake O'Donnell and Hugh Hollins.
Attendance—3,482.

SPURS VS. JAZZ

SAN ANTONIO (132)

	min	fgm	fga	ftm	fta	reb	a	pf	pts
Dietrick	31	2	3	2	2	3	2	5	6
Kenon	23	6	8	1	2	5	1	2	13
Paultz	28	3	6	0	0	6	2	2	6
Gale	13	2	3	0	0	2	0	1	4
Gervin	33	23	49	17	20	2	1	3	63
Dampier	12	2	4	0	0	0	1	1	4
Green	16	0	2	0	0	3	1	2	0
Olberding	23	3	4	2	4	4	0	2	8
Bristow	20	3	5	0	0	4	4	2	6
Silas	20	4	6	2	2	0	3	0	10
Layton	21	5	8	2	2	0	8	1	12
Total	240	53	94	26	30	29	23	22	132

NEW ORLEANS (153)

	min	fgm	fga	ftm	fta	reb	a	pf	pts
Robinson	44	11	22	2	2	20	3	2	24
James	36	12	23	6	7	4	4	5	30
Kelley	28	9	14	3	5	16	6	3	21
Goodrich	38	13	24	0	0	2	9	1	26
Bailey	33	8	12	4	5	6	7	5	20
Sanders	11	1	3	0	0	2	2	4	2
Boyd	13	3	4	0	0	2	4	0	6
Griffin	17	5	7	1	2	4	3	1	11
Merriweather	20	6	9	1	3	7	5	1	13
Total	240	68	119	17	24	63	49	22	153

San Antonio .... 34 40 20 38—132
New Orleans .... 44 34 32 43—153

Referees—Joe Cushue and Mike Mathis.
Attendance—8,336.

other points were on foul shots). Gervin equaled Thompson's 53-point first half, making 19 of 34 field-goal attempts.

Before the big shootout, the N.B.A. mark for points in one quarter was held by Chamberlain, with 31, during his 100-point game.

Thompson's mark for the most field goals in a quarter bettered the record held jointly by Chamberlain and Cliff Hagen, formerly of the St. Louis Hawks. They had each made 12 in one period.

In 43 minutes of playing time he made 28 of 38 shots from the field and 17 of 20 from the free-throw line. He also had seven rebounds and two assists.

"They got me the ball and I was hitting," said Thompson. "Everything was going in for me in the first half. I couldn't keep up with the pace in the second half, though, I got a little tired."

Larry Brown, the Nuggets' coach, said: "David said he felt bad because we lost. He thanked the team for helping him."

The Spurs moved the ball to Gervin every chance they got in the second half. But once his total had reached 59, one more than he needed for the title, Coach Doug Moe took him out to a standing ovation. Gervin left with 10½ minutes remaining in the third period and sat out the next 8 minutes.

"That was a phenomenal performance," said the Spurs' coach. "We were going to George exclusively and the Jazz were trying to stop him exclusively and it was something to watch."

Gervin said the Jazz didn't want him to win the title against them.

"All the Jazz defenders were tough and they kept a hand in my face all night," he said. "I was pressing early and I didn't have my rhythm, but I got it after seven or eight minutes. After I got the points I needed I asked to come out because I was a little tired and wanted to catch my breath."

Gervin closed out the season with 2,232 points on 864 baskets in 1,611 attempts. Thompson finished with 2,172 on 798 field goals in 1,546 attempts.

April 10, 1978

David Thompson in action: He's now basketball's highest-paid player.

The New York Times/Larry Morris

Thompson: 5-Year Pact At $750,000

The Knicks will not get David Thompson. The high-scoring 6-foot-4-inch Denver star has decided to remain with the Nuggets and will become the highest-paid player in National Basketball Association history.

The 24-year-old Thompson signed a five-year contract, agreed upon late Monday night, for $750,000 a year. Kareem Abdul-Jabbar, the Los Angeles Lakers' center, had been the highest-paid player at $650,000. Pete Maravich of the New Orleans Jazz was next at $600,000.

"I don't know whether or not we would have tried to get Thompson," the Knicks' president, Mike Burke, said yesterday. "Eddie Donovan was going to sit down and play a theoretical chess game when the season was all over: If we get Thompson then can we get 'X' or 'Y?'"

Donovan is the Knicks' general manager. According to Burke, "there was no foregone conclusion that Donovan would have picked him. Of course, we had to be interested."

"David felt strongly about staying in Denver," said Larry Fleisher, his lawyer, "and the money he received, in his mind, is close to what he felt he would make in the free-agent market."

The Nuggets' agreement with Thompson came several hours before they learned yesterday that Peter Seitz, the arbitrator, had ruled Brian Taylor a "free agent by mutual consent of both parties at the completion of the season." Taylor, the Nuggets' playmaking guard, walked out on the team last Jan. 16. He claimed his contract had been breached and he declared himself a free agent. Denver claimed his contract had not been breached.

The walkout had angered Carl Scheer, the Denver president and general manager, and Larry Brown, the coach. They had said they did not want him back. Thus, they considered Seitz's ruling a victory.

The Nuggets celebrated Thompson's signing by presenting him with an automobile last night before the start of their Western Conference semifinal playoff series against the Milwaukee Bucks. The car was for Thompson's 73-point performance on the final day of the regular season against the Detroit Pistons.

Thompson could have become a free agent at the end of the season, and would have created the biggest bidding war in sports history. When he signed in 1975 with the Nuggets, then an American Basketball Association team, it was for $500,000 a year for five years. However Thompson retained the option to become a free agent after three years. That contract is now void, superseded by the new one.

The possibility of Thompson going on the open market caused Larry O'Brien, the N.B.A. commissioner to warn teams last month that he would fine anyone caught tampering with him $250,000.

April 19, 1978

Bullets Defeat Sonics by 105-99 for N.B.A. Title

First-Time Victors Turn Back Rally by Seattle in Final Period

By LEONARD KOPPETT
Special to The New York Times

SEATTLE, June 7—Experience, poise, strength and the timely bounce tilted the final decision to the Washington Bullets tonight as they won the National Basketball Association championship series by beating the Seattle SuperSonics, 105-99. The seventh-game triumph ended the longest season of the league's 32-year history.

The Bullets held the lead from late in the first quarter of an extremely rough game, and had to play the last eight minutes without Elvin Hayes,

their star forward, who had fouled out. But Wes Unseld, the Bullet captain and often underappreciated center; Charley Johnson, an emergency acquisition in midseason, and Mitch Kupchak, the young giant who eventually will inherit Unseld's job, made the key plays down the stretch.

The Sonics, finishing a season that started with a 5-17 won-lost record under Coach Bob Hopkins and turned enormously successful when Lenny Wilkens took over, never gave up and made a final run in the fourth period.

Seattle, down by 13 points going into the last quarter, got within 6, fell back to 10 with three minutes to play, and came on again.

Decisive 3-Point Play

They were behind by 98-94 with 90 seconds left—plenty of time by N.B.A. standards—when the Bullets missed a shot and three Sonics scrambled after the rebound. As the ball skidded along the floor off arms and bodies, it went through Marvin Webster's legs to Kupchak, who scooped it up, scored and

Bob Dandridge of the Bullets trying to get around Seattle's Gus Williams, left, and John Johnson last night

Associated Press

added a free throw after being fouled on the play.

The 7-point margin proved decisive, although the excitement did not end there Seattle cut the deficit to 101-97 when Jack Sikma fouled Unseld with 26 seconds left, and Unseld missed both free throws.

With 18 seconds to play, Paul Silas scored for Seattle by rebounding a miss by Fred Brown, and the score was 101-99. Six seconds later, with little choice, Silas fouled Unseld in backcourt as the Sonics took a chance that he would miss again.

He did, but it was only the first shot of a three-for-two penalty, and Unseld sank the next two for a 103-99 lead with 12 seconds left. Seattle got one more shot, missed and Bob Dandridge put in the final basket on a breakaway.

Balanced Offense

The victory, as well as being a marvelous team effort—Dandridge and Johnson scored 19 points each; Unseld and Tom Henderson 15 each; Kupchak 13, and Hayes 12—also represented a series of immense personal triumphs.

For Unseld, who was named the most valuable player of the series, it was the culmination of a 10-year career that changed the fate of the Bullet franchise, in a season he almost decided not to play because of chronic knee trouble. The Bullets are the only team in the league that has made the playoffs in each of the last 10 seasons, a period that coincides with Unseld's presence.

For Dick Motta, the Bullet coach, who was always acknowledged as a defensive whiz but was often seen as an overintense taskmaster in his eight seasons with the Chicago Bulls, it was "what I've been waiting for all my life." In two seasons with the Bullets, he has emerged as a calm, controlled, witty and philosphical person, and has not lost any enthusiasm. The tone he set undoubtedly helped the Bullets fight back from a 3-2 deficit in games.

For Abe Pollin, the principal owner who bought the team in Baltimore, built an arena in Landover, Md., and moved to the national capital, it was the end of a 15-year struggle. The Bullets had experienced a number of play-off disappointments, including 4-0 final-round shutouts in 1971 and 1975.

For Hayes, as often criticized as admired despite his performance in nine N.B.A. seasons, it was a sort of vindication, even though he was on the bench at the end. Just before he fouled out he scored two baskets that checked an early Seattle rally, and he was glowing afterward.

"Nobody can take it away from us now," he said.

Young Sonic Team

As for the Sonics, four of their five starters had fewer than three seasons of pro experience, and the fifth, John Johnson, was discarded by Houston and Boston at the start of this season. Jack Sikma was a rookie, Webster, playing in good health for the first time, and Dennis Johnson were in their second seasons, and Gus Williams was a third-year player.

None were starting when Wilkens took charge, and Brown and Silas, who were, became team leaders and invaluable players while coming off the bench. Under Wilkens the Sonics won two-thirds of their games, posting a 54-27 record, including the playoffs.

They lost the last two, however, for the simplest of reasons—they could not sink their shots with their normal accuracy. Washington's tight inside defense has something to do with the Seattle problems, but the Sonics missed normal shots, too, and a bushel of close-in follows. In getting beaten by 35 points in the sixth game, they shot only 34 percent from the field. Tonight they shot 39 percent, but all season, and in all the playoffs until this game, they shot 45 percent. The difference was enough to lose.

Sonics' Box Score

WASHINGTON (105)

	min	fgm	fga	ftm	fta	reb	a	pf	pts
Dandridge	42	7	18	5	7	9	2	4	19
Hayes	38	5	10	2	5	11	1	6	12
Unseld	43	4	7	7	12	9	6	4	15
Grevey	16	2	7	0	0	2	1	2	4
Henderson	41	6	9	3	4	2	7	2	15
C. Johnson	30	9	21	1	2	4	3	4	19
Ballard	16	2	9	0	0	2	1	1	4
Wright	1	0	0	0	0	0	0	0	0
Kupchak	26	6	8	1	1	8	1	4	13
Total	**240**	**41**	**89**	**23**	**38**	**47**	**21**	**31**	**105**

SEATTLE (99)

	min	fgm	fga	ftm	fta	reb	a	pf	pts
J. Johnson	25	5	11	0	0	4	4	3	10
Sikma	38	7	14	7	10	9	5	5	21
Webster	43	9	12	11	16	10	3	5	27
D. Johnson	33	6	14	4	5	2	4	6	16
Williams	27	4	17	4	5	3	5	1	12
Brown	31	9	18	1	3	5	5	2	19
Silas	26	2	5	0	0	10	0	1	4
Seals	4	0	3	0	0	1	0	0	0
Total	**240**	**35**	**91**	**29**	**43**	**53**	**13**	**23**	**99**

Washington .... 21 22 24—105
Seattle .... 28 17 21 33—99
Referees—Jack Madden and Earl Strom.
Attendance—14,098.

June 8, 1978

Stylish Backcourtmen Put Sonics on the Road to N.B.A. Glory

By SAM GOLDAPER

GUS WILLIAMS is flashy on the court and quiet off the court. Dennis Johnson is more subdued on the court, but his off-court ways are those of a young man in a hurry. Together, Williams and Johnson formed the delicate backcourt blend that brought the Seattle SuperSonics their first National Basketball Association championship Friday night.

Williams and Johnson accounted for 44 points as the Sonics dethroned the Washington Bullets, 97-93. The Sonics won four straight games after losing the opener of the four-of-seven-game series.

When Williams was not scoring layups off the fast break or popping tough jump shots from long range, Johnson, who was named the most valuable player in the championship series, was faking one way and bursting loose for layups the other way or scoring on short turnaround jump shots.

The two guards had a combined average of better than 51 points a game, more than half of the Sonics' average output per game. Williams had 28.6 points per game; Johnson had 22.6.

Can't Stop Both of Them

"There are times they will stop Gus," said the 24-year-old Johnson, who is called D.J., "and sometimes they will stop me, but there are not too many times me and Gus will both have bad games."

The playing styles of Williams and Johnson are different. Williams is swift and creative and Coach Lenny Wilkens has helped make him a more explosive scorer by allowing him to free lance. Johnson is less explosive, but he is a complete player and defensively he is able to do things that Williams cannot.

"Talentwise, Gus and D.J. are perhaps the best backcourt that has ever played together in the N.B.A." said Paul Silas, the Sonics' forward who completed his 15th pro season. "I was sitting around the other day trying to think if there was ever a better backcourt pair, and all I could come up with was the Knicks' Earl Monroe and Walt Frazier. But I don't think they were any better.

"D.J. is great inside. He jumps so well, probably better than any guard in the N.B.A. and plays terrific defense. Gus penetrates very well and is an outstanding outside shooter. Together they don't create things for other people as much as they do for themselves. But they are so talented, it makes your job so much easier. Your eyes are usually totally on them."

The 6-foot-2-inch Williams, who averaged 19 points a game during the regular season and Johnson, who averaged almost 16, took divergent routes to Seattle.

The 25-year-old Williams was an all-American at Mount Vernon (N.Y.) High School and became one of the nation's outstanding guards at Southern California, where he arrived with an irregular, unorthodox and clumsy shooting style that bothered Bob Boyd, his coach.

Those Barefoot Days

"That's the way I learned to play," said Williams. "I used to lace on my sneakers and hitch a ride into the city, looking for a game. They were just pickup games, usually outdoors. The asphalt wasn't real smooth and there was broken glass around. The baskets didn't have nets and sometimes the hoops were bent and the backboards were dead."

But by the time Williams was ready to leave U.S.C., Boyd said: "He picks people's pockets. He plays with smoothness that's deceiving. He has amazing quickness that doesn't project itself in his outward appearance."

The Golden State Warriors made Williams their second-round choice, the 20th player selected in the 1975 draft.

"Right from his rookie season," said Rick Barry, who was his Warrior teammate and served as a television color announcer during the playoffs, "he had great anticipation. It was uncanny, really, when you think about it, the way he became a take-charge guy. He had all the tools, it was just a matter of his being able to put them together in the right situation.''

Overshadowed by Smith

Williams, whose brother Ray plays in the Knick backcourt, averaged 11.7 and 8.3 points a game in his two seasons with the Warriors where his play was often erratic and was overshadowed by Phil Smith, his backcourt mate.

After his two-year contract expired, he signed with the Sonics as a free agent. He averaged 18.1 points in the 1977-78 season, but it was his scoring during this year's playoffs that has made him the most recognizable Sonic. Williams scored 32,

Bullets' Elvin Hayes grabbing a rebound

21, 31, 36 and 23 points in the five games against the Bullets. With his scoring has come recognition. People are starting to take note of the baldish spot in the middle of his head, his high-top shoes, laced around his ankles and tied in the back, the words ''MAGIC'' written on his shoes and the socks with the No.1 painted on them.

Williams is not known for having a nickname, and someone asked in the Sonic dressing room recently again about the ''Magic,'' a nickname that Earvin Johnson is noted for, Williams said,''In here, I'm Magic. People don't know it, because no one writes about it.''

''When Gus is going well,'' said Dennis Johnson, ''he opens up a lot things for the rest of the guys. He passes off well.''

Williams had 17 assists in the series against the Bullets and Johnson had 30.

Unlike Williams, the 6-4 Johnson did not attraction until last season's Bullet-Sonic championship series when he blocked seven shots in the third game.,

Johnson was only 5-8 and the 11th man on his high school team. He played two seasons at Harbor Junior College and one at Pepperdine College and began to add height. He dropped out of school for a year and worked as a fork-lift operator in a warehouse.

The Sonics, who were looking for big guards, drafted Johnson on the second round in the 1976 draft. He was signed to a four-year contract at a salary that began at $45,000 and will reach $95,000 next season, although contract negotiations have begun and Johnson's asking price is reportedly $500,000 a year.

When he expressed dissatisfaction at his contract earlier in the season and indicated that he might leave Seattle, signs began to appear in the Kingdome urging Sam Schulman, the team owner, not to lose him the way he lost Marvin Webster to the Knicks. The signs read: ''D.J. Please Don't Go,'' and ''Let's Keep D.J.''

Johnson emerged as the league's biggest bargain after Wilkens replaced Bob Hopkins as the Sonics coach during the 1977-78 season with Seattle in last place in the Pacific Division with a 5-17 won-lost record. After Johnson was drafted, the Los Angeles Lakers filed a complaint questioning the legality of the draft. The Lakers said they didn't think he was eligible for the draft. By the time the N.B.A. completed its investigation and admitted that the Lakers had a valid argument, Johnson was already in a Sonic uniform.

One of Wilkens's first acts as coach was to put Johnson into the starting backcourt alongside Williams. The Sonics began to rise steadily, finishing second in the Pacific Division and advancing to the championship round where they were beaten by the Bullets in seven games.

Les Habegger, the assistant coach, refuses to get in the middle of Johnson's money squabble, but he said, ''I'm not saying D.J. is underpaid or overpaid, but Dennis is a bargain at whatever price. He has a great deal of ability and a great deal of pride. Combine those assets and you've got a pretty good player.''

Wilkens, second to Robertson on the N.B.A. career assist list, appreciates Williams's shooting, even though some of his shots are from reckless long range.

''He's just improving by leaps and bounds,'' said Wilkens. ''Everyone was surprised when he played so well last season, well he's playing even better this season, and he's going to keep improving.''

Dick Motta, the Bullets' coach, who watched films and tried to find ways of slowing down Williams, said, ''Gus is one of the premier guards in the league. He's definitely one of the quickest with the ball. He goes full speed all the time. He loves to run and you have to make sure that you've got somebody back on defense all the time.''

Bullets Box Score

FRIDAY NIGHT

SEATTLE (97)

	min	fgm	fga	ftm	fta	reb	a	pf	pts
J. Johnson	44	5	11	1	2	5	6	2	11
Shelton	37	7	16	0	0	8	2	5	14
Sikma	40	5	12	2	3	17	1	4	12
D. Johnson	48	9	22	3	3	4	5	4	21
Williams	29	8	18	7	9	2	3	1	23
Silas	21	1	2	0	0	6	1	5	2
Brown	19	7	10	0	1	3	3	2	14
Awtrey	2	0	0	0	0	1	0	0	0
Total	240	42	91	13	18	46	21	23	97

WASHINGTON (93)

	min	fgm	fga	ftm	fta	reb	a	pf	pts
Dandridge	4½	8	14	4	4	9	7	6	20
Hayes	48	12	25	5	8	14	0	5	29
Unseld	44	3	6	0	0	3	3	3	6
Grevey	3	1	3	0	1	0	0	0	2
Henderson	18	0	0	0	0	0	6	3	0
C. Johnson	20	4	8	0	0	1	0	3	8
Ballard	21	4	8	3	4	4	0	1	11
Wright	24	6	11	2	4	3	4	4	14
Chenier	20	1	7	1	2	3	3	2	3
Corzine	1	0	1	0	0	1	0	0	0
Total	240	39	83	15	23	38	23	27	93

Seattle	19	24	23	31—	97
Washington	30	21	18	24—	93

Referees—Jake O'Donnell, Joe Gushoe, Phil Minreak.
Techical foul—D. Johnson.
Attendance—19,035.

June 3, 1979

BASKETBALL, bas´kit-bôl, is the most widely played and watched team game in the world. It is also the newest of the major team games. Unlike games that evolved slowly through various forms before they acquired accepted playing rules, basketball was invented for a specific purpose at a specific time and place. In December 1891, in Springfield, Mass., the two-team court game was created by James Naismith, a 30-year-old instructor in physical education at the International Young Men's Christian Association Training School, now Springfield College.

Naismith's original assignment from Luther H. Gulick, his superior at Springfield, was to develop some form of athletic activity that could be used indoors during winter months in a northern climate. Baseball, football (both soccer and the American variety then developing), and many other outdoor games were well established and popular with participants and spectators. But between the end of the football season in autumn and the beginning of baseball the next spring, calisthenics and gynmastics were the only activities that indoor facilities permitted, especially in New England. These activities offered nothing as attractive as the exertion, competitive fire, scoring, and strategy of the outdoor team games.

Naismith, therefore, simply took a standard soccer ball, hung a peach basket at either end of his small gymnasium, divided his 18-man class into two nine-man teams, and made the object of the game an elementary one: to throw the ball into one basket while preventing the other side from throwing it into the other basket. Running with the ball was forbidden. In the 1897–1898 season, five-man teams became standard.

Essentially basketball is the same game today as it was in the beginning. It is now played in every section of the world, both by women and by men, in schools, colleges, and clubs, and at national and international levels. It has also become a major professional sport in the United States. No accurate statistics on players and spectators are available, but attendance at formally organized games in the United States alone exceeds 100 million each year. The Olympic Games program has included basketball since 1936. In addition, all the countries of Europe and the Americas and many nations in both Asia and Africa take part in various other international competitions.

HOW BASKETBALL IS PLAYED

The nature of basketball is the key to its popularity. The game requires equipment that is relatively simple and usually available: a flat rectangular playing surface (indoors or outdoors), two baskets, one ball, a timing device, and suitable shoes for the players. It calls for five-man teams, a manageable number, but it can be played happily for practice or recreation with any number down to "one-on-one." It can be as rough, physically, as the participants want to make it, although in theory basketball is not a contact game. It calls into play standard athletic skills—speed afoot, alert reflexes, quick thinking, marksmanship, and strength. Yet basketball does not demand extremely specialized functions by certain members of the team at the expense of other functions (as does the function of a pitcher in baseball, a goalie in hockey, or a quarterback in football). And its continuous action, with frequent scoring, appeals to both player and spectator. Regardless of the score, every player is constantly engaged, and except in time-outs, spectators always have something to watch.

The rules of basketball are not completely standardized. U.S. college teams, international amateur groups (including the Olympic Committee), and U.S. professionals differ. Rule changes are made almost every year. For example, in 1971, the rules for women's basketball were changed to make them similar to those for men.

The fundamental rules, however, are universal. Almost all variations deal with two basic problems: determining the proper degree of penalty for a foul, and finding some means of counteracting the advantage held by an exceptionally tall player.

Scoring. A *basket* or *field goal* counts two points. A *free throw* or *foul shot* is worth one point. Both are made by throwing the ball into the hoop from above: for a basket, from any point on the floor against the efforts of defenders; for a foul shot, from the free throw line without interference.

The ball. A basketball is spherical, 30 inches in circumference, and weighs from 20 to 22 ounces. Its cover may be of leather or of comparable synthetic material, usually orange or brown in color. It is inflated to a degree that enables it to bounce back about 50 inches when dropped onto a solid wooden floor from a height of 72 inches.

The Court. The recommended dimensions of the playing site (known as a *court*) are 94 feet long and 50 feet wide. However, courts down to two thirds of each of these dimensions have been accepted and used successfully. At the midpoint of each end of the court, a *basket* is suspended so that its rim is 10 feet above floor level and about 4 feet in from a point above the end line of the court called the *base line* or *end line*.

The basket itself is a metal ring, commonly called the *hoop*, 18 inches in diameter, with its plane parallel to the floor. It is attached to a *backboard*, a surface of glass or wood hung perpendicular to the floor. The backboard is usually rectangular, 6 feet wide and 4 feet high, but a smaller fan-shaped board also is used. The basket ring is attached to the backboard so that the back of the hoop is 6 inches from the surface of the board and about 12 inches above the lower edge of the board. Suspended from the hoop is a funnel-shaped net of cord. The net slows down the ball as it passes through the basket, making its passage more visible.

The playing area is divided in half by a center line midway between the baskets. At the middle of this line are two concentric circles, 2 feet and 6 feet in diameter. This is where the *center jump* takes place at the start of the game and at certain other times.

The most important floor markings are in front of each basket. Parallel to the backboard, and 15 feet from it, is the *free throw line*, also called the *foul line*, from which a player makes his free throws after he has been fouled. This line lies within a circle 12 feet in diameter, which is used as a restraining line when *jump balls* (similar to the center jump) must be held in that half of the court.

From the ends of the foul line to the base line run two lines that form the *free throw lane*, or *foul lane*. In U.S. college and amateur games, this lane is 12 feet wide, so that the pattern, when viewed from above, resembles an archway. (Formerly, when the lane was only 6 feet wide, the foul circle at its top make the figure look like a *keyhole*.) The professionals use a lane 18 feet wide, forming a rectangular restricted area wider than the actual free throw line. In international play the foul lane is 17 feet wide at the base line, and therefore its lines slant outward from the 12-foot-wide free throw line.

The inside of this foul lane area, whatever its size, is a restrictged zone. No offensive player may remain in it for longer than three seconds at a time. The purpose of this *three-second rule* is to prevent the tallest player, or best jumper, from taking up a dominating position close to the basket. In practice, the three-second restriction simply means that players must keep moving through this zone, and must make their *shots* (at the basket) and *passes* (to teammates) while on the run.

The entire back half of the court—that is, the half farther from the basket under attack—becomes a restricted area 10 seconds after a team gains possession of the ball. This rule prevents the offensive team from stalling or eluding the defense by withholding the ball from the offensive area.

Time. The team that scores more points in a stipulated time wins the game. American high schools and women play a 32-minute game divided into 8-minute quarters. Men's college teams play two 20-minute halves. Professionals use a 48-minute game, divided into 12-minute quarters. If the score is tied when the regulation time ends, *overtime periods*, usually of five minutes' duration, are played until a decision is reached. As many as six extra periods have been required to determine the winner in major professional and college competition.

Officials. Two officials, equipped with whistles, control play. One is the *referee*, who has superior authority in case of dispute. The other is the *umpire*. In practice their duties are indistinguishable. Both move all around the court, calling infractions, putting the ball in play, ruling on the legality of scoring and substitutions, and enforcing discipline. Usually, one official works from a position under the basket being attacked, while the other is at mid-court; when the action shifts to the other end, they switch assignments.

An *official scorekeeper* and a *timer* sit at a table alongside the court. The timer operates the clock according to the rules governing when time in "in" (ball in play) and when it is not.

The Teams. A basketball team is composed of five players. The *center, left forward,* and *right forward* are referred to as front court players, and the *left guard* and *right guard* as back court players. Their functions are much less differentiated than the functions of players in other popular team sports. All five have equal rights and restrictions under the rules, and they may range all over the floor, taking part in all offensive and defensive maneuvers. There are, of course, tactical specializations; but because the necessary teamwork requires very close cooperation, duties are remarkably interchangeable.

Each team has a *coach,* who sits on the bench with the substitutes and directs play. He chooses the starting lineup, makes substitutions, gives all basic strategic orders, and trains the players between games.

Substitution of players is allowed whenever play comes to a halt. There is no restriction as to the number of times a player may leave and reenter the game (unless he has fouled out).

Restrictions. Essentially, the only purpose of the game is to put the ball through the basket. All the restrictive rules are aimed at coping with the physical difficulties arising when players move at high speed in a relatively small enclosed space.

One set of restrictions deals with the mobility of player and ball. The player may not run with the ball in his possession. He may pass the ball to a teammate, shoot it at the basket, or move it around the court himself by using the *dribble*. A dribble consists of bouncing the ball continuously with one hand, while running, walking, or standing. Once a player stops dribbling, he may not start again; he must pass the ball or shoot it. If he breaks this rule, he is called for a *traveling* violation. Infractions that do not involve physical contact, such as traveling or remaining too long in the three-second zone, are called *violations,* and are punished by awarding possession of the ball to the other team.

A second set of restrictions deals with physical contact. Infractions that involve physical contact are termed *personal fouls,* or simply *fouls,* or sometimes *personals*. Since the basket is 10 feet above the floor and the playing area is confined, interference with the offensive players has to be restricted, or it would keep them indefinitely from scoring. Therefore, in general, no physical contact is allowed as a deliberate means of defense. the defender may not push, pull, trip, tackle, or in any other physical manner interfere with his opponent; in return, offensive players may not use body blocks or similar maneuvers to aid their teammates.

A player who is fouled is awarded one or more free throws. The player who committed the infraction is charged with a personal foul. When a player has been charged with the maximum number of personals allowed (five in high school, college, and amateur play, six among professionals), he must leave the game permanently. This disqualification of players is the most effective deterrent to fouling.

Other Rules. When the ball goes out of bounds, possession of it is considered lost by the team that last touched it in bounds, and the ball is awarded to the other team. When a ball rolls or bounces free within bounds, it is a free ball, and body contact is allowed between playes in the act of pursuing it.

When there is a *held ball* (that is, when players from opposing teams ae each firmly holding it) or some other indeterminate situation (such as an out-of-bounds play where both teams touched the ball simultaneously as it left the court), a *jump ball* is required. The referee tosses the ball straight up between the two opposing players, who try to tap it to a teammate and are forbidden to catch it or to interfere with each other.

When a score is made, the team scored upon puts the ball in play from out-of-bounds under the basket in which the points were scored. This applies to a free throw as well as a basket, provided the free throw is the last of any series of free throws awarded on one play. When a shot at the basket fails to go in, the *rebound* is in play and may be recovered by either team.

The above rules, with only minor variations, apply to all levels of basketball. In the treatment of free throws, however, there are important differences, and it is here that rule makers in all organizations have tinkered endlessly with the rules, changing the pattern from year to year.

Closely related, and even more important, is the time limit for shooting. Here, too, no uniformity has been achieved. In U.S. professioal play a *24-second rule* decrees that a team must make a try for a basket (defined as a shot that touches rim or backboard) within 24 seconds after gaining possession of the ball. If it does not, a violation is called, and the other team gains possession. In international amateur play a similar limitation applies, but for a period of 30 seconds. U.S. colleges and high schools, however, have resisted this attempt to prevent *freezing the ball* and have no such time limit on shooting. The freezing tactic is most often used by a team having a narrow lead with only a few minutes left in the game.

Generally, the penalty for fouling a man in the act of shooting is two free throws, and for any other foul one free throw. There are a number of variations, however, as follows:

In professional and international play, a personal foul by an offensive player is penalized by loss of possession but no free throw, although the foul does count toward disqualification for the man who committed it. In college games, an offense foul is punished by a free throw.

In international play, if a man is fouled while shooting and makes the basket anyway, the basket counts; the defender is charged with a foul, but there is no free throw. If the fouled player's basket attempt misses, he gets two free throws. In professional and college basketball, however, the older method is in force: a basket made while the shooter is being fouled counts, and the shooter gets one free throw in addition, making possible a *three-point play*.

In one way or another, all current styles penalize a team for excessive fouling in any half (or quarter)), regardless of how many fouls any one player may have committed. In professional basketball, the extra penalty is that the other team gets an additional chance to make the ordinary number of free throws: that is, two chances to make one, or three chances to make two. The penalty is imposed after a team makes six fouls in one quarter. In college, after six fouls in a half, a team enters a "one-and-one" situation. If the penalized team commits another foul that normally calls for one free throw, the offended player gets an extra shot, for an extra point, if he makes the first one.

The Sequence of Play. The game begins with a *center jump*—a jump ball held in the center circle, with the referee tossing up the ball. The team that gains possession works for a basket until it either makes one, is fouled, or loses the ball out of bounds or on a violation. Then the other team follows the same procedure. Time is "out" during all free throws, or when there is any abnormal delay caused, for example, by an injury or by retrieving a ball from far out of bounds. Teams may call a limited number of *time-outs* during a game for strategic reasons or to rest.

Techniques. The essence of basketball, an offense-oriented game, is shooting skill. Until recent years, the basic styles of shooting were a *lay-up* and a *set-shot*. In the lay-up, which is still basic, the player gets the ball near the basket and, while he is still on the run, curls it up and in, using the backboard as a carom surface. In a set shot, the shooter may use one or two hands, and he faces the basket with his feet firmly planted.

Centers have developed a *pivot* shot, which begins while the player has his back to the basket. This shot may be a sweeping one-handed *hook*, effective because the shooter's body keeps the defender away from the ball, or a little *spin*, gotten off while the player is in mid-air.

By far the most common shots in the modern game, however, are *jump shots* and *running one-handers*. The jump shot is exactly that: the shooter jumps straight up and releases the ball with one or two hands at the instant that he is at the top of his jump—out of reach of the defender, who can seldom make his counterjump soon enough. The running one-handers are less planned and fit well into a wide-open, fast-break offense. Equally important, but not equally enjoyable for most players, are the *ball-handling* skills—the arts of dribbling, passing, and other play involved in delivering the ball to an unguarded teammate. In an era of great shooting prowess, these skills have been relatively neglected in the United States, especially by exceptionally tall players. But teams in other countries, where tallness is not so common and where experience is more limited, stress these fundamentals to a greater degree.

Defense may consist of individual guarding or team patterns. Individual *man-to-man defense* is both a basic style of play and the name of a team strategy in which each player is assigned to cover one opponent wherever he goes on the floor. This is the prevailing form of team defense. Also extensively is some form of the *zone defense,* in which a player is given a specific area of the floor to guard and picks up any opposing player coming through it.

Offensive styles fall into two basic types. A *running game* (or *fast break*) depends primarily on getting a rebound at the defensive basket and swiftly moving the ball to the offensive basket before the opposition can recover its own proper defensive positions. In contrast, a *set pattern* develops at a fairly deliberate pace, and players move through one or a combination of prearranged patterns to create an opening for the shooter.

For the individual player, either quickness or size is essential. All the basic offensive maneuvers involve the ability to *fake*—that is, by some gesture, to fool the defender into committing himself in one direction while the offensive player moves in another and thus gains the one-step advantage that makes him free to shoot, pass, or receive a pass. The defender, in turn, must have the reflexes to recover from such fakes without losing his man. In both instances, the essentials are quickness of foot, hand, eye, and thought—agility as distinct from mere running speed.

Physical height, which involves also *effective height,* is of basic importance. The ability to jump can make a six-footer's effective height equal to that of a man a few inches taller who cannot jump as high or time his leap as well. Over an extended period, height determines the number of times a team will have possession of the ball, because capturing rebounds of missed shots is the primary method of getting possession. Offensively, a taller player is closer to the basket and has an easier shot. Defensively, he can block more shots near the basket (although interfering with the ball above the rim, known as *goaltending,* is forbidden) and can force the shooter to use an unnatural trajectory.

In theory, any position on the floor belongs to the man who occupies it first, and he must be given a reasonable amount of room in which to move. The responsibility for causing illegal body contact lies with the man who moves into a rival's clearly established path or position. After physical contact occurs, the referee must decide the *blocking*-or-*charging* issue: Did the offensive man *charge* into the defensive man, or did the defensive man *block* the offensive man's legitimate path of advance? It is strictly the referee's judgment that determines who fouled whom; a play may look different from a different angle, and the spectators are rarely impartial. For these reasons, there is more criticism of refereeing in basketball than in other mass spectator sports.

Ultimately, there is only one way to guard against a good shooter: to stay close, harry him, and prevent him from getting set for the kind of shot he likes at the spot he likes to take it. On the offensive, the best help a player can give a teammate is to *set a pick*—that is, get a position on the floor that will block off a defensive man without committing a foul.

SOME COMMON BASKETBALL TERMS

Assist. A pass or hand-off directly resulting in a basket by a teammate.

Backboard. The surface of wood or glass to which the basket is affixed, used to carom shots into the basket.

Back Court. The half of the court away from the basket under attack; the two guards are called *back court men*.

Basket. (1) The iron hoop through which goals are scored; (2) a field goal, worth two points.

Blocking. A foul by a defensive player who blocks the legal path of an offensive player; the opposite of *Charging*.

Center Jump. The method of putting the ball into play at the beginning of each period by having the referee toss up the ball between the rival centers.

Charging. A foul by an offensive player who charges into a defensive player who has legal position; the opposite of *Blocking*.

Dribble. Continuous bouncing of the ball, the only legal means of moving with the ball.

Fast Break. A style of offense in which a team attempts to race to the offensive basket before the defense can get set.

Field Goal. A basket scored from the floor; it counts two points.

Free Throw. An unobstructed shot from the foul line, worth one point, awarded as a penalty for a foul by the opposing team.

Free Throw Lane. The area on the floor bounded by the free throw line, the end line under the basket, and two connecting lines forming a 12-foot lane; also called *foul lane*.

Free Throw Line. A line, 15 feet from the basket, behind which the shooter must stand in attempting a free throw; also called *foul line*.

Front Court. The half of the court in which a basket is under attack.

Goal-Tending. Illegal interference with a shot above the rim of the basket.

Hand-off. Handing the ball to a teammate (instead of passing it).

Hook Shot. A sweeping, one-handed field goal attempt, with the shooter's back at least partially to the basket.

Hoop. (1) the rim of the basket; (2) synonym for basket in the sense of a score.

Jump Ball. A means of putting the ball into play by having an official toss it upward between two players.

Jump Shot. A field goal attempt in which the ball is released at the top of a vertical jump.

Lay-up. A shot from alongside the basket, using the backboard as a guide.

Man-to-Man Defense. A style of team defense in which each player is assigned one specific opponent to guard anywhere on the court.

Offensive Foul. A personal foul committed by a member of the offensive team, usually not involving a free throw as part of the penalty.

Palming. An illegal means of carrying the ball along while dribbling.

Personal Foul. Any of a variety of body-contact fouls; five (or, in professional ball, six) personals disqualify the player who commits them.

Pick. A legal method of providing shooting room for a teammate, by taking a position that "picks off" or blocks a defensive man.

Pivot. A position taken by a player with his back to the basket, at the head of or alongside the free throw lane, from which he can spin and shoot or hand off to teammates moving past him toward the basket; also, the floor area where pivot play is feasible.

Post. A synonym for pivot. "High post" means farther from the basket, "low post" closer.

Press. A style of defense in which offensive players are closely guarded and harried. (A "full-court press" is applied all over the floor; a "half-court press" only after the ball is brought across the mid-court line.)

Rebound. A shot that caroms off the basket or backboard and remains in play, to be recovered by either team.

Set Shot. A field goal attempt, with one or both hands, from a stationary position, usually relatively far from the basket.

Slough. A style of team defense in which players guarding men on the perimeter of the attacking formation "slough off" to help guard the pivot area or other special threat.

Switch. A defensive technique in which players who have man-to-man assignments switch responsibilities with each other as their offensive men cross paths.

Technical Foul. A foul imposed for misbehavior or for some technical rule infraction. The penalty is a free throw plus possession of the ball for the offended team.

Ten-Second Rule. The requirement that a team bring the ball across the mid-court line within 10 seconds after gaining possession.

Three-Pointer. A field goal made by a man who is fouled in the act of shooting, plus the free throw that he makes. But in the professional ABA, a field goal from beyond 25 feet counts three points.

Three-Second Rule. The restriction against offensive players taking up set positions within the free throw lane for more than 3 seconds.

Traveling. Illegally moving the ball by violating the dribbling rules.

Twenty-Four-Second Rule. In the professional NBA, the requirement that a team make a field goal attempt within 24 seconds after gaining possession of the ball; in international amateur competition, the limit is 30 seconds.

Violation. Any infraction not classified as a foul. The penalty is loss of possession of the ball.

Zone. A style of team defense in which each player is assigned to guard a designated floor area, rather than a specific opponent.

Bibliography

Auerbach, Arnold, *Basketball* (New York 1961).

Bee, Clair F., and Norton, Ken, *Basketball Fundamentals and Techniques* (New York, 1959).

Bell, Mary M., *Women's Basketball* (Dubuque, Iowa, 1964).

Bunn, John W., *Basketball Techniques and Team Play* (Englewood Cliffs, N.J., 1964).

Naismith, James, *Basketball, Its Origin and Development* (New York 1941).

Newell, Pete, and Bennington, John, *Basketball Methods* (New York 1962).

Wooden, John R., *Practical Modern Basketball* (New York 1966).

NBA Scoring Leaders

Year	Scoring champion	Pts	Avg
1947	Joe Fulks, Philadelphia	1,389	23.2
1948	Max Zaslofsky, Chicago	1,007	21.0
1949	George Mikan, Minneapolis	1,698	28.3
1950	George Mikan, Minneapolis	1,865	27.4
1951	George Mikan, Minneapolis	1,932	28.4
1952	Paul Arizin, Philadelphia	1,674	25.4
1953	Neil Johnston, Philadelphia	1,564	22.3
1954	Neil Johnston, Philadelphia	1,759	24.4
1955	Neil Johnston, Philadelphia	1,631	22.7
1956	Bob Pettit, St. Louis	1,849	25.7
1957	Paul Arizin, Philadelphia	1,817	25.6
1958	George Yardley, Detroit	2,001	27.8
1959	Bob Pettit, St. Louis	2,105	29.2
1960	Wilt Chamberlain, Philadelphia	2,707	37.9
1961	Wilt Chamberlain, Philadelphia	3,033	38.4
1962	Wilt Chamberlain, Philadelphia	4,029	50.4
1963	Wilt Chamberlain, San Francisco	3,586	44.8
1964	Wilt Chamberlain, San Francisco	2,948	36.5
1965	Wilt Chamberlain, San Fran., Phila.	2,534	34.7
1966	Wilt Chamberlain, Philadelphia	2,649	33.5
1967	Rick Barry, San Francisco	2,775	35.6
1968	Dave Bing, Detroit	2,142	27.1
1969	Elvin Hayes, San Diego	2,327	28.4
1970	Jerry West, Los Angeles	2,309	31.2
1971	Lew Alcindor, Milwaukee	2,596	31.7
1972	Kareem Abdul-Jabar (Alcindor), Milwaukee	2,822	34.8
1973	Nate Archibald, Kansas City-Omaha	2,719	34.0
1974	Bob McAdoo, Buffalo	2,261	30.6
1975	Bob McAdoo, Buffalo	2,831	34.5
1976	Bob McAdoo, Buffalo	2,427	31.1
1977	Pete Maravich, New Orleans	2,273	31.1
1978	George Gervin, San Antonio	2,232	27.2

NATIONAL BASKETBALL ASSOCIATION PLAY-OFF CHAMPIONS

Year	Champion	Year	Champion
1947	Philadelphia	1963	Boston
1948	Baltimore	1964	Boston
1949	Minneapolis	1965	Boston
1950	Minneapolis	1966	Boston
1951	Rochester	1967	Philadelphia
1952	Minneapolis	1968	Boston
1953	Minneapolis	1969	Boston
1954	Minneapolis	1970	New York
1955	Syracuse	1971	Milwaukee
1956	Philadelphia	1972	Los Angeles
1957	Boston	1973	New York
1958	St. Louis	1974	Boston
1959	Boston	1975	Golden State
1960	Boston	1976	Boston
1961	Boston	1977	Portland
1962	Boston	1978	Washington

AMERICAN BASKETBALL ASSOCIATIN PLAY-OFF CHAMPIONS

Year	Champion	Year	Champion
1968	Pittsburgh	1972	Indiana
1969	Oakland	1973	Indiana
1970	Indiana	1974	New York
1971	Utah	1975	Kentucky
		1976	New York

COLLEGE BASKETBALL

NCAA Champions

Year	Champion
1939	Oregon
1940	Indiana
1941	Wisconsin
1942	Stanford
1943	Wyoming
1944	Utah
1945	Oklahoma A&M
1946	Oklahoma A&M
1947	Holy Cross
1948	Kentucky
1949	Kentucky
1950	CCNY
1951	Kentucky
1952	Kansas
1953	Indiana
1954	La Salle
1955	San Francisco
1956	San Francisco
1957	North Carolina
1958	Kentucky
1959	California
1960	Ohio State
1961	Cincinnati
1962	Cincinnati
1963	Loyola (Chi.)
1964	UCLA
1965	UCLA
1966	Texas Western
1967	UCLA
1968	UCLA
1969	UCLA
1970	UCLA
1971	UCLA
1972	UCLA
1973	UCLA
1974	No. Carolina State
1975	UCLA
1976	Indiana
1977	Marquette
1978	Kentucky
1979	Michigan State

National Invitation Tournament Champions

Year	Champion
1938	Temple
1939	Long Island Univ.
1940	Colorado
1941	Long Island Univ.
1942	West Virginia
1943	St. John's
1944	St. John's
1945	De Paul
1946	Kentucky
1947	Utah
1948	St. Louis
1949	San Francisco
1950	CCNY
1951	Brigham Young
1952	La Salle
1953	Seton Hall
1954	Holy Cross
1955	Duquesne
1956	Louisville
1957	Bradley
1958	Xavier (Ohio)
1959	St. John's
1960	Bradley
1961	Providence
1962	Dayton
1963	Providence
1964	Bradley
1965	St. John's
1966	Brigham Young
1967	Southern Illinois
1968	Dayton
1969	Temple
1970	Marquette
1971	North Carolina
1972	Maryland
1973	Virginia Tech
1974	Purdue
1975	Princeton
1976	Kentucky
1977	St. Bonaventure
1978	Texas
1979	Indiana

INDEX